"The story of the peopling of America has not been written. We do not understand ourselves." So Frederick Jackson Turner challenged his fellow historians. It is true that there are gaps in the story of American immigration; the Middle Atlantic states have been referred to as "the forgotten region."

This is the first comprehensive history of the German immigration to a state of the Middle Atlantic region which shows the typical American juxtaposition of Anglo-Saxon and Continental European immigrants. The book opens with the beginnings of German immigration to the Calvert Colony around 1650 and traces the events to the present time, when the "last German-American generation" is being integrated into the American population.

Here are the pious Amish and the nineteenth century agnostic, the radical city laborer and the conservative Western Maryland farmer, the wealthy Bremen merchant and the poor steerage-class immigrant. They formed two chief settlements: the rural groups in the Western counties where they became acclimated before the middle of the nineteenth century, and the urban groups in and around the city of Baltimore, where for many decades they retired into a "Little Germany" isolation. The main interest of the author centers around the problem of their Americanization: when, how, and under what circumstances did the Maryland Germans throw off their past, and how fast and how thoroughly did they become Americans?

A "case history" of American immigration, the story of a special group under special circumstances, *The Maryland Germans* has broad conclusions and implications for immigration history in general.

THE MARYLAND GERMANS

A HISTORY

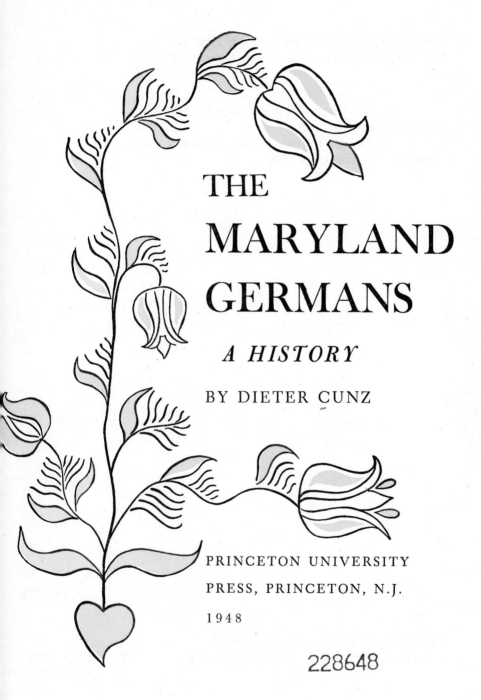

THE
MARYLAND
GERMANS

A HISTORY

BY DIETER CUNZ

PRINCETON UNIVERSITY
PRESS, PRINCETON, N.J.
1948

THE PUBLICATION OF THIS BOOK HAS BEEN MADE POSSIBLE
THROUGH THE AID OF
THE SOCIETY FOR THE HISTORY OF THE GERMANS IN MARYLAND,
FOUNDED IN BALTIMORE IN 1886

Printed in the United States of America by
Princeton University Press at Princeton, New Jersey

TO MY FRIEND AND COLLEAGUE

A. E. ZUCKER

ACKNOWLEDGMENTS

DURING seven years of research so many people in one way or another gave help and assistance to me that now when it comes to writing a page of acknowledgments I begin to realize that I shall never be able to enumerate their names and to give due credit to them. If asked, however, for the name of the person who more than anyone else deserves my thanks and my gratitude in this connection, I would not have to hesitate for a moment: Professor A. E. Zucker of the University of Maryland, who conceived the idea of this project, brought the author to the topic and the topic to the author and did everything possible to lead this undertaking to a satisfactory conclusion. Gaining his friendship in these years of collaboration is for me the most gratifying by-product of this book.

I am greatly indebted to the Society for the History of the Germans in Maryland, which with the funds of the late Ferdinand A. J. Meyer inaugurated this project. The officers of the society deserve my thanks for their understanding and cooperativeness: Professor William Kurrelmeyer, Professor A. E. Zucker, Mr. Lewis Kurtz, Mr. Charles F. Stein, Mr. Carl L. Nitze, Dr. Ernest J. Becker, the Reverend Fritz O. Evers, Mr. Walter E. Beuchelt and Colonel Robert Lee Slingluff. I regret that two of the officers who were always very interested in my work did not live to see the publication of the book—the late Mr. Karl A. M. Scholtz and the late Father John G. Hacker, S.J. Thanks are also due to the Carl Schurz Memorial Foundation for an initial grant to promote the project.

I received the friendliest assistance in all the Maryland libraries where I worked, especially in the Enoch Pratt Library and the Library of the Maryland Historical Society in Baltimore, in the University of Maryland Library in College Park and in the Hall of Records in Annapolis. I want to take this opportunity to thank in particular Miss Elizabeth C. Litsinger of the Enoch Pratt Library; Dr. Morris L. Radoff, State Archivist in Annapolis; Mr. James W. Foster, Dr. William D. Hoyt, and Miss Florence J. Kennedy of the Maryland Historical Society. I also appreciate the help given me by the Historical Society of Frederick County and the Washington County Historical Society. I am further indebted to the late Professor Veit Valentin of the Library of Congress, to Dr. Felix Reichmann of the Library of Cornell University, to Professor Lynwood G. Downs of the University of Minnesota, to Miss May Olson of

ACKNOWLEDGMENTS

Louisiana State University, and to Miss Miriam Brokaw of Princeton University Press for the great care in preparing the manuscript for the printer.

Dr. Ernest J. Becker, Mr. Frank G. Banta and especially Mrs. Alice H. Finckh deserve my thanks for their help in the final preparation of the text. I need not point out to the reader how much Mrs. Hilde Foss's illustrations enhance the value of this book. In the final stage of the project the suggestions of Mr. H. L. Mencken were most valuable; my thanks go to him for all he did. A word of appreciation is due to my colleagues Professor Arthur C. Parsons and Professor Augustus J. Prahl for their unfailing willingness to help whenever and wherever help was needed.

To the editors of various periodicals I owe thanks for their kind permission to reprint material already published in some of these journals: *Common Ground, Maryland Historical Magazine, William and Mary Quarterly, American German Review, Tyler's Quarterly Historical and Genealogical Magazine.*

When I conclude these bows of acknowledgment with a thankful nod towards Oskar Seidlin, I am reminded of the German saying *Eulen nach Athen tragen.* He knows, or ought to know, how much I owe him, and I mean it very literally when I say that without his constant encouragement I might never have finished this book. From the beginning to the end, from the stage of first orientation to the final proofs, his help and advice have been of inestimable value to me, more than I can ever express in the few insufficient words of a conventional acknowledgment.

DIETER CUNZ

University of Maryland
College Park, Md.
May 30, 1948.

CONTENTS

ILLUSTRATIONS

PLATES

These drawings are by Mrs. Hilde Foss

TEXT FIGURES

THE MARYLAND GERMANS

A HISTORY

Man hat gesagt und wiederholt: "Wo mir's wohlgeht, ist mein Vaterland!" Doch wäre dieser tröstliche Spruch noch besser ausgedrückt, wenn es hiesse: "Wo ich nütze, ist mein Vaterland!" Zu Hause kann einer unnütz sein, ohne dass es eben sogleich bemerkt wird; aussen in der Welt ist der Unnütze gar bald offenbar. Wenn ich nun sage: "Trachte jeder, überall sich und andern zu nutzen," so ist dies nicht etwa Lehre noch Rat, sondern Ausspruch des Lebens selbst.

. . . . .

It has often been said: "Where I am well, there is my homeland!" Yet, this comforting maxim were better worded: "Where I am useful, there is my homeland!" At home someone may be useless, and the fact will not be noticed at once. Abroad in the world the useless person will soon be spotted. So, if I say: "Try to be useful everywhere, to yourself and to others," then this is neither doctrine nor counsel, but the dictum of life itself.

GOETHE, *Wilhelm Meisters Wanderjahre*

INTRODUCTION

"THE story of the peopling of America has not been written. We do not understand ourselves." More than half a century ago, Frederick Jackson Turner put this challenge before his American fellow historians in his essay on "The Significance of History."[1] Fifty years of historical writings have tried to fill the gap at which Turner pointed. Yet, the more the historians do, the more they become aware of how much is still undone. Some scholars who undertook to write general comprehensive immigration histories have admitted that they could only scratch the surface. Too much of the necessary spadework is still lacking. To be sure, there are monographs on the Swedes, the Germans, the Irish and the Czechs in the United States. There are some even more detailed studies on the Poles and the Germans in Texas, the Irish in Nebraska, the Hollanders in Iowa, the Italians in New York, the French in Louisiana. These are the foundations on which the final historiographical monument to American immigration will be built. Here are for American historians the "wide open spaces" waiting for settlement and cultivation. Books must be written on the Germans in Missouri, the Scandinavians in Washington, the Russians in New Jersey, the Portuguese in California, the Swiss in Wisconsin, the Canadians in Massachusetts, to mention only a few, before something like a definitive history of American immigration can be recorded. The need for additional studies in the field of immigration history has often been acknowledged; however, the number of those who delve into this fruitful sector of American history is still comparatively small. It is most encouraging that in recent years two such eminent American scholars as Marcus Lee Hansen and Carl Wittke blocked out the lines for a systematic study of the history of American immigration. The present author is deeply indebted to the writings of these two historians, especially to such books as *The Atlantic Migration, The Immigrant in American History* and *We Who Built America*. Likewise, a collection of essays, *Foreign Influences in American Life*, approaching the problem from the sociological, cultural, historical, ethnical and economic point of view, has given help and guidance in the general orientation.[2]

[1] *The Early Writings of Frederick Jackson Turner* (University of Wisconsin Press, Madison, Wis., 1938), 64.

[2] *Foreign Influences in American Life*, edited by David F. Bowers (Princeton University Press, Princeton, N. J., 1944). This book offers also the most up-to-date and best critical bibliography on immigration history. Cf. also

With his fine scent for a promising track of scholarly pursuit, Frederick Jackson Turner had pointed to one particular section on the map of the United States which to him seemed especially suited for historical exploration. To quote from his essay on "Problems in American History": "One of these Atlantic sections has never been studied with the care due to its importance. The Middle region, entered by New York harbor, was an open door to all Europe. The South represented typical England, modified by a warm clime and servile labor; New England stood for a special English movement— Puritanism; the Middle region was less English than the other sections. It had a wide mixture of nationalities, a varied society, the mixed town and county system of local government, a varied economic life, many religions. In short, it was a region mediate between New England and the South, and the East and the West. It represents that composite nationality which the contemporary United States exhibits, that juxtaposition of non-English groups, occupying a valley or a little settlement and presenting reflections of the map of Europe in their variety. It was democratic and nonsectional, if not national; 'easy, tolerant and contented'; rooted strongly in material prosperity. It was typical of the modern United States. Now this section has been less studied than any of the others; it offers no such peculiarities as New England; it had not the slave to create an interest in it, as had the South; it was not productive of historians. It is to be hoped that before long this section will be given the study which its importance demands."[3]

This was written in 1892. As late as 1943 a contemporary scholar called the Middle Atlantic the "forgotten region," conspicuous for its lack of sectional tradition.[4] To American historians the region between the Hudson and the Potomac seemed less attractive than most other parts of the country. Yet it is here that one reaches quickest the core of the problem of immigration history on account of "that juxtaposition of non-English groups." From these premises, we justify our undertaking of writing a history of the Germans in Maryland.

George M. Stephenson, A History of American Immigration, 1820-1924 (Boston, 1926).

[3] Early Writings, 78 f.

[4] Richard H. Shryock in Pennsylvania Magazine of History and Biography, LXVII (1943), 115 ff. Cf. also Eric F. Goldman, "Middle States Regionalism and American Historiography," in Historiography and Urbanization, edited by E. F. Goldman (Baltimore, 1941), 211-20.

The articles, monographs, dissertations and biographies on the Pennsylvania Germans, if all put together, would fill hundreds of volumes. A recent bibliography covering only the colonial period lists more than 7000 items.[5] Yet, a comprehensive history of the German element in Pennsylvania has not been written. A history of the Germans in the State of New York was begun by a friend and contemporary of George Bancroft and remained fragmentary. The history of German immigration and German settlements in New Jersey and Delaware has never been touched, although a vast amount of material could easily be brought to light.

The history of the old Calvert Colony on the Chesapeake Bay should prove to be of particular value for everybody interested in German immigration. In no other Middle Atlantic state save Pennsylvania did the Germans play a more important part than in Maryland. The Maryland Germans themselves were well aware of that fact when in 1886 they founded a "Society for the History of the Germans in Maryland." It was a society of educated laymen; none of them was a trained historian. However, they did very well in preserving, collecting and even publishing material in their field. They paved the way for a more comprehensive and professional investigation.

In these organizations of dilettantes the detailed genealogical interest very often overshadowed the concern with general historical evaluation. Not infrequently the writers slipped into the old mistake of pointing out trees instead of describing a forest. To be sure, a study like this should preserve some genealogical and biographical data which otherwise might be lost. In order not to overburden the text, we have relegated material of this kind to the footnotes. Thus, the footnotes are occasionally rather long. We never considered it our task to give complete lists of German settlers, German-American businessmen or similar groups. We expect numerous protests from people who will tell us that "a history of the Germans in Maryland is incomplete which does not mention my distinguished ancestor, the Hon. ...." It was not our intention to glorify individuals, families, clans, groups or the Maryland Germans as a whole. The older school of German-American historians who outdid each other in

---

[5] Emil Meynen, *Bibliographie des Deutschtums der kolonialzeitlichen Einwanderung in Nordamerika, insbesondere der Pennsylvanien-Deutschen und ihrer Nachkommen 1683-1933* (Leipzig, 1937).

{ 5 }

overpraising and exaggerating sinned more than enough in this respect. We wanted to write a history, nothing else.

We were concerned with immigration, settlements, some outstanding individuals, and especially with the problem of Americanization. We need not point out that the history of a racial group in America must be more than just the story of the immigrant generation. We considered the second and third generation within the field of our investigation. After the third generation, the biological substance generally becomes too compound and the race consciousness too thin to justify further inclusion. Geographically speaking, we did not stop at the boundaries of the German Reich, whatever they may have been in the last centuries. We included in our study all German-speaking immigrants from Central Europe, i.e., Germany, Austria and the German-speaking part of Switzerland. Eighteenth-century immigration from Western Germany and Switzerland cannot be separated. The Palatinates and German Swiss came over together, settled, lived, worked and worshiped together and had generally the feeling that they belonged to each other. The sensitiveness of the Swiss in not wishing to be mistaken for Germans is of more recent vintage and largely produced by the political events in Germany after 1933.

One reason why the history of the various racial groups in the United States has been somewhat neglected by American historians is the language barrier. Of course, no scholar concerned with immigration history in general can possibly be familiar with the thirty-eight foreign languages that are used by the various newspapers of the country. However, for a historian who wants to write the history of one special national group, knowledge of this particular language is a prerequisite. Indeed, it should be one of his principal tasks to make accessible the source material to his fellow historians in the vernacular. The most important source material of this kind are the volumes of the foreign-language press. In our particular case we were very fortunate in having at our disposal newspaper files of Maryland-German papers covering more than a century. We drew extensively upon this almost inexhaustible source, which had hardly been tapped before. We made it our policy never to quote in German. From the point of view of literary values, this is no loss, since, for understandable reasons, most German-American journalists wrote a very inelegant, if not atrocious, German. From the historical point of view, this practice means a gain, since the material is thus integrated into

American historiography and afterwards can be used by scholars unable to read German. We believe that this is the only method by which scholars, working in the various departments of immigration history, can meet on a common platform. Thus, they can make their findings available to each other and finally coordinate and integrate them into an organic entity.

The history of America is the story of the "tired, poor, homeless, tempest-tossed, huddled masses," their children and grandchildren. They all, crossing the Atlantic on the long voyage to a new, unknown home, came from different backgrounds, with different abilities, with different hopes. Each state in the American Union offered different chances and opportunities. We shall try to show why so many Germans came to Maryland, how they settled and how they took root, why they needed the country and why the country needed them, how their individual and collective existence was blended into the history of America. It is a "case history" of American immigration, the story of a special group under special circumstances. Yet we may not be unjustified in hoping that from this special case some broader conclusions may be drawn for immigration history in general.

Frederick Jackson Turner made the statement: "We shall not understand the contemporary United States without studying immigration historically." If this book contributes one brick to the great structure of American immigration history, it will have served its purpose.

PART ONE

THE COLONIAL PERIOD

1640-1790

I. FORERUNNERS IN THE
TIDEWATER SECTION

N OCTOBER 6, 1683, a sturdy ship sailed into the port of Philadelphia. It was a good solid vessel, but not too fast. It had been on the Atlantic seventy-five days, which even at that time was above the average crossing time. The ship's name was the *Concord*. It had on board thirteen families, the first organized group of German immigrants to come to America. The description of the ship, the *Mayflower* of German pioneers, forecasts in a way the general tenor of German immigration as a whole: sturdy, solid and not too fast.

These German sectarians under their leader Franz Daniel Pastorius having the "desire . . . to lead a quiet, godly and honest life" had been attracted by William Penn. They were to become harbingers of the great stream of German immigrants "seeking land or religious liberty or both" who in the next century arrived year by year, month by month, often day by day. They pushed forward into the backwoods, penetrated into the hinterland, as they called it in their language. Boundaries did not mean very much to them. Soon the overflow drifted into the nearest province south of Pennsylvania, into the colony of the Calverts: Maryland.

The Province of Maryland, the land between the south bank of the Potomac and the fortieth parallel, was granted to the Calvert family by a royal patent of 1632. One year later, the *Ark* and the *Dove* took the first settlers to the shores of the new colony on the Chesapeake Bay. A provincial government was proclaimed, introducing a novelty which later became an essential part in the constitution of the country: separation of church and state. This was the first attempt at establishing religious freedom in the New World. Lord Baltimore welcomed without distinction every immigrant who cared to participate in his colonizing enterprise.

It can no longer be determined in just what year the first German settlers immigrated into the Province of Maryland. That there were Germans on the *Ark* and the *Dove* seems improbable.[1] Not until

---

[1] Heinrich Zschokke, a Swiss-German writer of the first half of the nineteenth century, reports in his historical novel, *Die Gründung von Maryland*, that in 1634 Lord Calvert allowed a few German settlers to come from Virginia, but this is an invention of the romantic poet. Cf. Erich Albrecht, "Heinrich Zschokke's Version of the Founding of Maryland," in *American*

the middle of the seventeenth century do we hear of a few German settlers in the colony of the Calverts. These early forerunners of German immigration were not very important. Only one of them rises above the anonymous mass and takes his place in the bright light of history—Augustin Herrman.[2]

Herrman's identity is historically verified many times, for he belonged to the prominent upper class. He corresponded and had personal contact with people like Peter Stuyvesant of New Netherland, Roger Williams of Rhode Island, John Winthrop of Connecticut, William Penn and Caecilius Calvert. He carried on vigorous political activities, which explains the fact that his name is to be found repeatedly in historical documents of the middle of the seventeenth century. We have historical data concerning only the forty years of his life in America. The story of his birth, childhood and youth in Europe is uncertain.

One of the facts that cannot be doubted is that Herrman's family originated in Bohemia. He himself confirmed this several times, and until the end of his life he preserved a deep affection for his Bohemian fatherland. Different nationalities, however, have made their home in Bohemia for many centuries. We can know that he came from Bohemia, and yet know nothing about his nationality. Germans and Czechs have claimed him as their own.[3] Arguments and demonstrations on both sides were not always fair. Both sides often exaggerated their claims, pushing each other to extremes. This quarrel between German and Czech historians was as senseless as it was unfruitful. Everyone who knows the scant historical material knows also that neither side is able to prove indubitably that the other is wrong. Moreover, the mistake was made of approaching the seventeenth century with categories of our own time, a basically unhistorical procedure.[4]

Although the time and place of Herrman's birth are disputed,[5]

German Review, VIII, vi (1942), 15 ff. A very uncritical discussion of Zschokke's novel is to be found in Paul C. Weber, America in Imaginative German Literature in the First Half of the Nineteenth Century (New York, 1926), 77, 111.

[2] Dictionary of American Biography, VIII, 592. Earl L. W. Heck, Augustine Herrman (Englewood, Ohio, 1941).

[3] Albert B. Faust, The German Element in the United States (New York, 1927), I, 161 ff. Thomas Capek, The Czechs in America (Boston, 1920), 9 ff.

[4] See Appendix I.

[5] Dieter Cunz, "Augustin Herrman, Origin and Early Events," Tyler's Quarterly Historical and Genealogical Magazine, XXIV (1942), 5 ff.

various indirect proofs give great probability to the version that he was "born in Prag in 1621." Our knowledge of the first decades of his life is equally vague. Apparently he went from Bohemia through Germany to Holland, where he must have lived for a few years, and thence to America. The statements that in Europe he served in the army of King Gustav Adolf of Sweden, and that in America he worked first as a surveyor in Virginia, are mere conjectures that can be neither proved nor refuted.[6] The first trustworthy word that we have of him is that in 1644 he was the New Amsterdam agent for a big Dutch merchant house, Gabry & Sons.[7]

From now on we meet him again and again. During the next fifteen years he was one of the men who shaped the political and commercial life of New Amsterdam. His relationship to Governor Stuyvesant was vacillating and ran through all the stages between enthusiastic friendship and fiercest enmity. His residence and his storehouse in Manhattan were on Pearl and Pine Streets, the business establishment adjacent to the warehouse of the West India Company. He dealt in everything that was needed in the colonies, particularly in furs, tobacco, wine, groceries, dry goods, and probably even Negro slaves. We find him as attorney and as executor, as co-owner of a ship *La Garce* and as proprietor of farms and great lots on both sides of the Hudson. It is said that he was the first man in the colonies to grow indigo.[8]

In the year 1647 Herrman began to take part in politics. In this year the people of New Amsterdam selected the Council of Nine Men, a group of prominent citizens who were to assist the governor in the administration of the colony.[9] Herrman entered the council as representative of the merchants. He belonged to the liberal party, the so-called "Country Party," which was opposed to Stuyvesant's

[6] Rudolf Cronau, *Drei Jahrhunderte deutschen Lebens in Amerika* (Berlin, 1909), 42. Thomas Capek, *Augustine Herrman of Bohemia Manor* (Prag, 1930), 13.

[7] *Calendar of Historical Manuscripts in the Office of the Secretary of State, Albany, N.Y.*, edited by E. B. O'Callaghan. Dutch Manuscripts 1630-1664 (Albany, 1865), I, 28.

[8] *Ibid.*, 46, 52, 95, 105, 110, 168, 239, 375. Together with his friend Adrian van der Donck, he owned the land where the city of Yonkers now stands.

New York Genealogical and Biographical Record, XI (1878), 58: "Made an experiment in planting indigo seed near New Amsterdam which grew well and yielded much, samples of which sent to the Netherlands were found to be better than common."

[9] J. R. Brodhead, *History of the State of New York* (New York, 1853), 475.

dictatorial form of government. It was during Herrman's term that the Council of Nine Men sent a delegation to Holland with complaints about Stuyvesant, the "Vertoogh": "to represent the poor condition of this country and to pray for redress." This letter, which is still in the Dutch Royal Archives in The Hague, is in Herrman's hand, and his name is the first among the signatures.[10]

The following years represent the low point in his life. We do not know many details. It is very likely that his business was ruined by the English Acts of Navigation. Within a short time he lost his entire fortune and contracted great debts. Stuyvesant, who hated Herrman for his antidictatorial policy, did everything he could to make his situation as difficult as possible. Finally he was put into jail for being unable to pay his debts. Not until 1653 do we find a document "granting Augustyn Heerman liberty and freedom, . . . he having settled with his creditors."[11]

Shortly thereafter, his rise started again. In spite of personal aversions, Stuyvesant esteemed Herrman's gifts and seemed especially to have respected his diplomatic talents. In the following years we find Herrman in Stuyvesant's service on several diplomatic missions in all parts of the New World—in Rhode Island, Massachusetts, Virginia, Maryland and Curaçao.[12]

Of all these journeys, the trip to Maryland was the most important for Herrman personally, since it became a turning point in his life. The mission was caused by boundary troubles between the Dutch and English living in the Delaware district. In 1655 Stuyvesant had taken over the Swedish colony on the Delaware. Up to that time the Swedish-Dutch settlers on the Delaware and the English on Chesapeake Bay had hardly come into contact with one another. A settlement claimed by the Dutch as well as by the English now began to develop and flourish on the borderline between these two spheres of interest—New Amstel, known today as New Castle. The settlers were Swedish and Dutch; but the land, according to the English, belonged to Maryland. For a while both sides rattled their swords menacingly but unsuccessfully, and then resorted to negotiation. In September 1659 Stuyvesant sent two of his best diplomats to Mary-

[10] Documents Relative to the Colonial History of New York (Albany, 1856), I, 258. Capek, A. Herrman, 13. Brodhead, 505.

[11] Hist. Manuscr., 132. In quotations from old documents the original orthography is preserved throughout.

[12] Ibid., 204, 278, 331. Brodhead, 554, 666-69.

land to straighten out the affair, Augustin Herrman and Resolved Waldron.[13]

We are well informed about this trip, for the two diplomats kept a journal which gives us a detailed report of their doings.[14] After an arduous trip by land and by water, they finally met with the governor and the Council of Maryland in Patuxent, where they delivered their credentials and a message from Governor Stuyvesant.[15] The conferences lasted several days. The Dutch diplomats were shown a copy of the charter of Lord Baltimore, according to which the disputed land belonged to Maryland. Herrman, however, pointed out that according to his patent Lord Baltimore was entitled to claim only those districts which had never before been settled by Europeans. Actually, the Charter did permit such an interpretation. Herrman's diplomatic talents are revealed in that from the first moment he recognized this Achilles' heel in Maryland's case. This principle, which Augustin Herrman was first to apply, was used again and again in later years. "To the arguments then used, and employed eighty years later in the interest of William Penn, the existence of the present State of Delaware, as independent from Maryland, is mainly to be attributed."[16] The Maryland authorities were naturally not too happy with the course of the negotiations, and suggested consulting first the authorities in the European mother countries. Waldron returned to New Amsterdam to report to Stuyvesant, while Herrman continued his trip to Virginia.[17]

Once more we find Augustin Herrman's name in the history of New Netherland. In the following year Stuyvesant sent two emissaries, Newton and Varleth, to Virginia with the suggestion that

[13] Christian Strack, "Die ersten Deutschen im nachmaligen Distrikt Columbia," *Berichte der deutschen Historischen Gesellschaft für den Distrikt Columbia* (Washington, 1905), I, 27. Hist. Manuscr., 339. Brodhead, I, 666. Capek, 15. Cronau, 42 ff.

[14] *Narratives of Early Maryland* (edited by C. C. Hall, N.Y., 1910), 309-32. The Journal is dated St. Mary's, Maryland, October 21, 1659.

Documents Relative, II, 88-98, 99-100.

Hist. Manuscr., 341.

J. Thomas Scharf, History of Maryland (Baltimore, 1879), I, 244 ff.

Percy G. Skirven, "Seven Pioneers of the Colonial Eastern Shore," Maryland Historical Magazine, xv (1920), 395 ff.

[15] *Maryland Archives*, III, 366. The message was in Dutch and was "Englished" by Mr. Simon Oversee.

[16] James Grant Wilson, "Augustine Herrman," Proceedings of the New Jersey Historical Society. Second Series, XI, ii (1890), 28.

[17] Brodhead, 669.

they should make use "of the aid and tongue of Augustin Herrman," who was at that time still in Virginia.[18] Lord Baltimore, however, had also discovered Herrman's talents and tried to assure himself of his services. From then on Augustin Herrman's life was separated from the history of the Dutch colony on the Hudson and indissolubly connected with the rise of the Calvert Colony on the Chesapeake Bay.

Apparently Augustin Herrman had enough of New Amsterdam, perhaps because of memories of his unhappy experiences there, perhaps because of his dislike for Stuyvesant's moody and dictatorial manner. At any rate, he had liked the land about Chesapeake Bay so much that in 1660 he made the suggestion to Lord Calvert that he would draw a map of the entire province, if in return he would receive a piece of property for his own. At the same time he presented a rough sketch of the projected map. No offer could have been more opportune for Lord Calvert. The Province of Maryland had boundary disputes with her neighbors to the north and the south, and those quarrels could be settled only with the help of a good map. In a letter of September 10, 1660, his lordship announced in the following words that he accepted the offer: "Having made Proffer to Caecilius the first absolute Lord proprietary of the Province of Maryland to make an Exact Mapp of the country if his Lordship would Please to grant unto his the aboves, Lands for Inheritance to his Posterity and the Priviledges of a Manor."[19] The governor, the Hon. Philip Calvert, was charged to turn over to Augustin Herrman one 4000-acre and one 1000-acre grant of "good plantable land."

In the next year, 1661, Herrman brought his family and servants

[18] *New York Genealogical Record*, 59. Brodhead, 683.

[19] Herrman kept a diary, in which he recorded the details of the founding of Bohemia Manor. This diary, which begins with June 13, 1681, was apparently intended as a sort of memorandum for the governor and the Council of Maryland. One copy lies in the State Archives in Annapolis; a second (supposedly prepared by a relative about 100 years later) is in the possession of the Maryland Historical Society. The diary was published as the Appendix to the *Fund Publications*, xxx, 29 ff. (Baltimore, 1899), "Memorandum or Journall of the first foundation and seeting of Bohemia Manor and Bohemia River Middleneck Adjacent Appendant," Herrman Manuscripts 7 (Maryland Historical Society).

Herbert H. Beck, "Augustine Herrman, Lancaster County's First Map Maker," *Papers of the Lancaster County Historical Society*, xxxv, xi, 261 (Lancaster, Pa., 1931).

H. Arthur Stump, *Augustine Herrman* (Baltimore, 1929), 13.

to Maryland. In 1651 he had married Jannetje Varleth, a Dutch girl from a very rich and respected family in New Amsterdam.[20] She bore him five children, Ephraim, Caspar, Anna Margerita, Judith and Francina.

The land that Augustin Herrman received lay at the northern tip of Chesapeake Bay. In memory of his homeland he gave the name Bohemia Manor to the first tract, granted in the year 1660. In the course of time still other pieces were added by purchase and by gift (Little Bohemia, Three Bohemian Sisters, St. Augustine's), so that the total estate finally contained 25,000 acres.[21] Since he wanted the undisputed ownership of the land, he immediately made terms with the Susquehanna Indians living round about. With the governor's permission he met them on Spesutie Island, about ten miles south of what is now Havre de Grace, and paid them a compensatory sum for their territory.

The history of the development of Bohemia Manor must be understood in connection with the current plan of the Calverts to elevate a new aristocracy in Maryland. The Lord Proprietor had the right to establish such manors and to detail personal jurisdiction to the manorial lords. By this provision the attempt was made to transplant old English institutions of self-government to the soil of the colony.[22] Seventy-four such manors were granted by the Calverts during the seventeenth century, but it is doubtful whether personal jurisdiction and the whole feudal system ever really began to function. The manorial system, which was beginning to die out even in England, was a complete anachronism in America. "In Maryland it was retained as a form of land tenure, long after the manor itself had ceased to have any social, political or judicial significance."[23] It

[20] Samuel S. Purple, *Records of the Reformed Dutch Church in New Amsterdam and New York: Marriages* (New York, 1890), 16. "Janneken Verlet, j.d. Von Uytrecht," is the name according to this source. It appears variously as Verlet or Varleth. Through the Varleths Herrman was related to Stuyvesant; Nicholas Varleth, his wife's brother, had married Anna Stuyvesant, the governor's sister. (*New York Genealogical Record,* XI, 56; XXII, 1. See also Wilson, 29.)

[21] Capek, 19-21. Between 1662 and 1685 the name of Augustin Herrman appears no less than nine times in the Records of the Land Commissioner in Annapolis. According to these records, his property increased to 25,039 acres.

[22] John H. Johnson, *Old Maryland Manors* (Johns Hopkins University Studies, Baltimore, 1883).

[23] J. Hall Pleasants, "Maryland Manorial Courts," *Maryland Archives,* LIII, 57. (*Maryland Archives* from now on is abbreviated as MA.)

is improbable that Augustin Herrman ever exercised his judicial power.

Augustin Herrman's plans were not limited to the founding of a private estate. In 1661 he obtained from Lord Baltimore a charter for the founding of a city. The lord in England promised "all reasonable privilegs" to Augustin Herrman, who was ready "to have the town called Ceciltown and the county Cecil County."[24] This is the first real mention of Cecil County in the early acts of the province. To the very end of his life Herrman hoped to attract settlers and to found a city on his territory. "I am now engaged in encouraging settlers to unite together in a village," he wrote to a friend in 1661.[25] These plans were never realized, but the place where he intended to erect Ceciltown is still called Town Point.

A step taken by Augustin Herrman at the very beginning of his life in Maryland should be particularly emphasized. He is distinguished by an action not unique but nevertheless one of the first of its kind in the history of the state. He was one of the first naturalized citizens of Maryland.

As early as 1660, Herrman's first year in Maryland, and shortly after he had outlined for Lord Calvert the plan for the map, occurred the so-called "denization."[26] "Augustine Herman . . . haueing of long tyme used the trade of this our Province . . . to be a free Denizen of this our Province of Maryland." Denization meant simply that the "free Denizen" had the right to gain, to possess or to sell land in the province. Augustin Herrman, however, put out more and more roots in the colony on the Chesapeake; and so, under date of September 17, 1663, we read in the *Proceedings of the Assembly of Maryland* "that an Acte of Naturalizacion be prepared for Augustine Herman, and his Children and his brother in Law George Hack and his wife and Children." The matter was allowed to slide for a time, and only taken up again when the old Lord Proprietary, Caecilius Calvert, vigorously urged Herrman's naturalization in a letter of 1665 from London to his "most deare sonne Charles Calvert

---

[24] George Johnston, *History of Cecil County* (Elkton, Md., 1881), 40.
[25] *Hist. Manuscr.*, 342.
Samuel Hazard, *Annals of Pennsylvania* (1850), 321.
Herrman Manuscr., 7.
In a petition in 1681 he speaks of founding a city, when he is having a tract of land endorsed to himself "for the good of a towne which we shall endeavor to propagate. . . ." *MA*, xvii, 84.
[26] *MA*, iii, 398. *Maryland Historical Magazine*, iii (1908), 170.

Esqr our Leivetenant and Cheif Governor of our Province of Maryland."[27] "Whereas Mr. Augustine Herrman," he wrote, ". . . hath . . . taken great paines and Care in order to the Draweing and Composeing of a certaine Mapp or Card of our said Province . . . you recommend the said Herman heartily and Effectually in our name to the Generall Assembly . . . in order to the Receiving some Reward . . . and that we will give Directions . . . for his immediate naturalisation." This set the bureaucratic machinery in motion, and the application for naturalization was approved by the next Assembly (May 1666). It was agreed that "the said Augustine Herman . . . borne at Prague in Bohemia and . . . [some other names] shall from henceforth be adjudged reputed & taken as Nrall borne people of this Province of Maryland. . . ."[28] Although the general naturalization statute apparently planned by the Lord Proprietary was wrecked on the disunity between upper and lower houses, later convenings of the Assembly repeatedly carried motions for naturalization. The case of Augustin Herrman is the first individual naturalization in Maryland, and indeed one of the first in the American colonies.[29] It is one of the first examples of the liberal American practice of naturalization, which has been so immensely important throughout American history.

If one leafs through the *Maryland Archives*, one finds the name of Augustin Herrman recorded again and again in the sixties and seventies of the seventeenth century. He soon took his place in public life in Maryland, just as he had previously done in New Netherland. His name occurs repeatedly in the Chancery Court Proceedings and in the Provincial Court Proceedings.[30] We find him in

[27] MA, I, 462; xv, 18.   [28] MA, II, 144.

[29] Edward B. Mathews, *The Maps and Map-Makers of Maryland* (Maryland Geological Survey, Baltimore, 1898), I, 302. By way of qualification, it must be added here that Augustin Herrman was not the only applicant. Several other immigrants became citizens at the same time.

[30] MA, LI, 117, 132, 133, 180, 288, 480; XLI, 353, 389, 403, 405, 406, 440, 461, 484, 496, 509, 512, 516, 574, 579, 580; XLIX, 61, 62, 63, 160, 163, 192, 201, 210, 253, 263, 265, 299, 341. A lawsuit with one of his neighbors, John Browning, may be cited as an item of interest. Browning had settled on a piece of land that Herrman claimed as his own. He sued Browning, but on the day of appearance he was so ill that he could not undertake the long journey to court. He drew up a detailed complaint against his neighbor which he entrusted to his contestant, John Browning, to be taken to court. Browning in turn faithfully delivered the complaint at court and had it read. Browning was ordered to vacate the disputed piece of land, whereupon he left the colony for good. Cf. J. A. Weishaar, "The German Element in Maryland up

public offices as Gent Justice, as Burgess, or as Justice of Peace of Baltimore County.[31] The people of Cecil County rightfully looked upon him as their first citizen, for again and again he acted as their spokesman. When the boundary disputes between Pennsylvania and Maryland repeatedly caused inconveniences to the settlers in northwestern Maryland, it was Augustin Herrman who sent the Council a petition for redress (1681). When the inhabitants of Baltimore and Cecil County were grievously troubled through continuous attacks by the Delaware Indians, it was Augustin Herrman whom the Council in St. Mary's charged with negotiating and making peace with them.[32] In the beginnings of the boundary dispute between Pennsylvania and Maryland, Augustin Herrman's name was mentioned again and again. His property was located in the disputed territory, and his house was often used as a meeting place for discussions.[33] William Penn was fully aware of the weight of Augustin Herrman's influence. He was one of the six prominent settlers to whom William Penn addressed his famous letter on September 16, 1681, choosing them on the ground of their "being Represented men of Substance and Reputation in your part of the Bay." He pointedly sent his missive to them "at their plantations in Pennsylvania," and demanded that they pay no more taxes to Maryland which they owed to Pennsylvania. The letter must understandably have caused the people of Cecil County considerable alarm, and for the time being they cautiously paid no taxes at all. Actually, Penn's message had no direct consequences, since Herrman and the five other prominent planters "gave little credit to it."[34]

Another public matter in which Augustin Herrman's name was often mentioned was the problem of runaway servants. There were numerous cases where servants ran away from their masters and disappeared into neighboring states. In 1669 the General Assembly took steps against this practice and ordered that "there be a Logg

---

to the Year 1700," Society for the History of the Germans in Maryland, Reports xv (1901), 30.

(The Reports of the Society for the History of the Germans in Maryland will be abbreviated from now on as SHGM.)

[31] MA, I, 505; II, 232; VII, 442; XVII, 43; XV, 38, 41, 69, 70, 77, 326. Maryland Historical Magazine, I (1906), 45.

[32] MA, XVIII, 135; XV, 175.   [33] MA, v, 369, 434; XVII, 105.

[34] MA, v, 285, 375.

Mathews, I, 312: "The letter ends any previous feeling of confidence in the good faith of Penn."

house Prison twenty ffoot Square built at Augustine Harmans in Batlemore County . . . ffit for the Surety and Safe Keeping of Runnawayes & ffugetives."[35] Apparently it was a thankless service that Herrman took over, for two years later he sent the Assembly a remonstrance in which he declared that he was losing money in this task and requested a new subvention.[36] The Assembly rejected his protest, and left him to settle his difficulties and the deficit caused by the Log house Prison with the authorities of Baltimore County.

Herrman's name does not always appear as that of a plaintiff. We find him also as a defendant. In 1676 he was brought to justice by his neighbor, Mr. Frisbe; and the Lower House gave the decision, immediately confirmed by the Upper House, that Augustin Herrman was "guilty of a Ryott in cutting Mr. Frisbe's Timber off his Land by force and under Collour of authority."[37]

Still more embarrassing was another transgression of the law. In the December session of 1646 the state attorney placed before the tribunal an accusation against six prominent Marylanders, among them Herrman, who had financial obligations for "goods unlawfully by the Burgomasters of Amsterdam imported into this Province contrary to the Act for encouragement of trade."[38] The question was whether these offenses were punishable under the Navigation Act of 1651, which excluded non-English ships from commerce with the English colonies. We do not learn how the case evolved. Possibly this affair was one reason why Herrman's naturalization dragged out so long, although there is no evidence that the whole matter bore any serious consequences for the accused.

Augustin Herrman knew that he could always count on the Calverts for protection if he got into difficulties, for in the eyes of Lord Baltimore all these greater or smaller offenses apparently mattered little in comparison with Herrman's great service to the colony—his map of Maryland. It had cost him trouble and money and ten years of labor, but it had paid many times over. It was the basis of his fortune and his unshakeable and influential position in Maryland.

Already in New Amsterdam Herrman had come in contact with

[35] MA, II, 193, 224.   [36] MA, II, 258, 261.   [37] MA, II, 480.
[38] MA, II, 299, 341, 342. P. xxii: "The transaction related to the smuggling of tobacco over the Elk River route to Delaware when that territory was still in the possession of the Dutch, and before it had been taken over by the English. Alexander d'Hinoyossa, the late Dutch governor of the Delaware River settlements at this time living in Maryland, though he soon after returned to Holland, figures prominently in the case."

cartographers, and about the middle of the century he had prepared a pictorial map of New Amsterdam. This little sketch appeared in a book by Arnoldus Montanus, *De Nieuve en Oubekende Weereld: of Beschrijving van America* (Amsterdam, 1671), on page 124.[39] Thus it was Herrman who drew the first view of the village that was destined to develop into the greatest city of America.

Herrman knew that boundary disputes could be settled, if at all, only with the aid of maps. When the boundary disputes between New Netherland and Maryland began, he had already called Stuyvesant's attention to the advantage of having a cartographic picture of the disputed territory. Since Stuyvesant had not responded to the suggestion, Herrman had brought his idea to Lord Calvert and found him more receptive.

Augustin Herrman's map, which was completed in 1670, is not the first map of Maryland. The territory that subsequently became the Calvert Colony was included in the drawing that John Smith made of the Chesapeake Bay country in 1608. The maps of Maryland drawn in the next sixty years, the Lord Baltimore map of 1635, the Farrer map of 1651 and the Alsop map of 1666, are all more or less copies of this first map by John Smith, and in many cases they are even inferior to this map. Augustin Herrman's map marks the first real progress.[40]

[39] In the older literature it is stated again and again that Augustin Herrman's drawing of Manhattan appeared as a vignette on a map in a book by Van der Donck, *Beschryvinge van Nieuw-Nederlant* (Amsterdam, 1655). This story goes back to E. B. O'Callaghan, *History of New Netherlands* (New York, 1855), II, 540 n. and 312-13. That this is an error is thoroughly proved in the authoritative work in this field, I. N. P. Stokes, *Iconography of Manhattan Island* (New York, 1915), I, 142, 154, 155. From a letter which Stuyvesant directed to the Dutch West India Company on October 6, 1660, it is evident that Herrman had sketched a picture of the settlement. Stuyvesant sends the directors a map of Manhattan and then continues: "In case you should be inclined to have it engraved and publish it, we thought it advisable to send you a small sketch of the city, drawn in perspectives by Sieur Augustine Haarmans three or four years ago, or perhaps you will hang it up in some place or the other there." (*New York Colonial Documents*, XIV, 486.) The sketch referred to is, however, apparently the one that appears in the book by Montanus, and not in that by Van der Donck.

[40] Mathews, II, 347 ff.

P. Lee Phillips, *The Rare Map of Virginia and Maryland by Augustine Herrman* (Washington, D.C., 1911); and Louis D. Scisco, "Notes on Augustine Herrman's Map," *Maryland Hist. Mag.*, XXXIII (1938), 343. These two essays contain detailed scientific and bibliographic descriptions of Herrman's map. An excellent transposition of the Herrman map into a modern map is to

The map consisted of four separate sheets, each measuring about 15½ by 19 inches. Placed together, the map came to about 37¼ inches in width and 31¼ inches in height. At the lower left two Indians are represented, and between them a tablet inscribed with the title of the map. At the lower right is a picture of Augustin Herrman. In the upper half are the coats of arms of the King of England and of Lord Baltimore. The coastal regions are drawn in considerable detail, whereas many white patches are left in the interior. Herrman followed the general practice of map makers of his day: lack of reliable information about the unexplored interior was compensated for by inserting brief descriptions. Thus we read in one place, for example: "The Land between James River and Roanoke River is for the most parts Low Suncken Swampy Land not well passable but with great difficulties And there in harbours Tygers Bears and other Devouringe Creatures."

Lord Baltimore's complete satisfaction with the map does not need to be reemphasized; the great grants of land to Herrman leave no doubt of the matter. In a letter addressed to Herrman from London we read: ". . . that His Lordship has received no small Satisfaction by the variety of that mapp, and that the Kings Majesty, His Royal Highness, and all others commended the exactness of the

---

be found in the article by J. Louis Kuethe, "A Gazetteer of Maryland A.D. 1673," *Maryland Hist. Mag.*, xxx (1935), 310 ff. Cf. also Harry F. Covington, "The Discovery of Maryland," *Maryland Hist. Mag.*, x (1915), 208; and Edward D. Neill, *Terra Mariae* (Philadelphia, 1867), 164. The map was engraved in London in 1673 by the famous engraver, William Faithorne. Although Faithorne was looked upon as one of the most important engravers of his time, Herrman was not satisfied with the work: ". . . slobbered over by the engraver faithorn defiling the prints with many Errours." (Phillips, 13.) From an advertisement in *The London Gazette*, 1674 (No. 873), we learn that the map was published and retailed by John Seller, one of the most famous hydrographers of England. The full title of the map was: "Virginia and Maryland As it is Planted and Inhabited this present Year 1670 Surveyed and Exactly Drawne by the Only Labour and Endeavour of Augustin Herrman Bohemiensis. Published by Authority of His Maties Royall Licence and particular Priviledge to Aug. Herman and Thomas Withingbrooke his Assignee for fourteen years from the year of our Lord 1673." Herrman kept exclusive rights of publication for fourteen years. In *Great Britain Calendar of State Papers, Colonial America and West Indies, 1669-1674*, 551, we read the license: ". . . whereas the copying or counterfeiting of said map would be very much to said Herman's prejudice and discouragement, all his Majesty's Subjects are hereby strictly forbidden to copy, epitomize, or reprint, in whole or in part, any part of said map, within the term of fourteen years."

work, applauding it for the best mapp that ever was drawn of any country."[41]

We do not know how many copies of the map were printed at that time. The larger a map is, the more perishable it is. Herrman's compendious map has been destroyed by time and decay; only two copies are extant today, one in Europe, in the British Museum in London, the other in America, in the John Carter Brown Library in Providence, R.I.[42]

The map had a great influence on the history of Maryland. The maps of Maryland and Virginia up to 1751 are almost literal copies of the Herrman map.[43] "It was admirably planned and equally well executed," George Washington said of it.[44] Its force may be felt into the nineteenth century, to the year 1833, when the first official topographical engineer was appointed in Maryland. Its greatest historical importance lies in the role it has played in the boundary dispute between Maryland and Virginia; we find a copy of the map as late as 1873 in the "Report of the Commissioners on the boundary line between Virginia and Maryland."[45]

The exact date of Herrman's death cannot be established, but the year 1686 is commonly accepted; in this year his will, which he had composed in 1684, was entered into the acts.[46] He designated that his estate should be inherited in the male line, or, if necessary, in the female, so that the eldest son should always receive it in entirety,

[41] Phillips, 12.
Wilson, *Fund Publications*, No. 30 (Baltimore, 1890), Appendix, 32.
[42] In the older literature (Neill, Mathews, Phillips, etc.) only the one copy in the British Museum is mentioned. The second copy that we know today was lost for a long time; only in 1930 did it come into the possession of the John Carter Brown Library. Reproductions of the Herrman map are to be found in the above-mentioned book by E. B. Mathews; in Clayton C. Hall, *The Lords of Baltimore and the Maryland Palatinate* (Baltimore, 1902); and in the *Fund Publications*, No. 34 (Baltimore, 1894).
[43] P. Lee Phillips, *Virginia Cartography* (Smithsonian Miscellaneous Collections 1039, Washington, 1896), 35 ff.
[44] Wilson, *Fund Publications*, No. 30, p. 13 (Baltimore, 1890).
[45] Mathews, 1, 369. Phillips, *The Rare Map*, etc., 3.
[46] The will is recorded in part in the Land Office at Annapolis. Herrman's original will is in the possession of the Historical Society of Pennsylvania in Philadelphia, a parchment with his signature and a wax seal. Cf. "Copy of the Will of Augustine Herrman, of Bohemia Manor," *Pennsylvania Magazine of History and Biography*, xv (1891), 321. Cf. also Townsend Ward, "Augustine Herman and John Thompson," *ibid.*, vii (1883), 88 ff. Concerning the later theft of the will and the suit by Herrman's son-in-law, Matthias Vanderheyden, see MA, viii, 323; xiii, 418.

indivisible and unalienable. If the family should completely die out, the estate should be turned over to the General Assembly of Maryland "for the Use and propagation and propriety of a ffree Donative Scoole and Colledge, with Divine protestant Ministery, hospitells and reliefs of poore and distressed people and travellers. . . ."

It is striking that Herrman's wife is mentioned only in passing in the will. His first wife, the Dutch woman Janneken, must have died in the early sixties, for her name is not mentioned in the document of naturalization along with those of all the children and the other relatives. A second marriage, into which Herrman entered in 1666 with Catherine Ward of Cecil County, seems to have turned out very unhappily.[47] In the words of the Labadist Jasper Danckaerts, who paid a visit to Bohemia Manor in 1679: "His plantation was going much into decay, as well as his body, for want of attention. There was not a Christian man, as they term it, to serve him; nobody but negroes. All this was increased by a miserable, double miserable wife; but so miserable that I will not relate it here."[48] A little later the pious traveler cannot refrain from speaking his mind about Catherine Ward again: "She is the most artful and despicable creature that can be found. By her wickedness she has compelled all the children to leave their father's house and live elsewhere."[49]

Thus, the life of the "First Lord of Bohemia Manor" seems to have ended by no means so gloriously as he had planned in his ambitious dreams. If one were to characterize Augustin Herrman, his ambition, normal but strongly developed, would certainly be the first trait with which one would have to begin. His driving motive was the wish to reach a respected position in civil life, and, more than that, to lead the life of a great gentleman, of an aristocrat. We read of fox hunts and audacious equestrian feats, and it was certainly not against his will that numerous tales and anecdotes grew up about him and his wild rides on his famous horse Gustavus.[50] Such exploits belonged to the life of a great gentleman, a rich landowner and a merchant prince, the founder of the entail Bohemia Manor. In the early history of Maryland the figure of Augustin Herrman stands as that of a great and bold aristocrat. He did not belong to that class of

[47] George A. Hanson, *Old Kent* (Baltimore, 1876), 80.
[48] *Journal of Jasper Danckaerts*, 1679-1680, edited by B. B. James and J. F. Jameson (New York, 1913), 115 and 131.
[49] *Ibid.*, 145.
[50] Charles P. Mallery, *Ancient Families of Bohemia Manor* (Wilmington, Del.), 15 f. Wilson, 30. Johnston, 37.

adventurers who squandered their energy and vitality in purposeless vagabondage. Rather, he knew how to apply his powers where they were most needed, how to make his talents useful in the ordered channels of constructive civil activity. "A man of Substance and Reputation," William Penn said of him, and with these words he characterized the essence of Herrman's nature.

"Augustine Herman, Bohemian, The First Founder & Seatter of Bohemia Manor, Anno 1661." At Herrman's own direction this was the inscription that adorned the gravestone of the founder of Cecil County.[51] The words held the concept of the beginning and the hope for a long-lasting, flourishing family. This was obviously one of Augustin Herrman's favorite ideas, but as if by a tragic whim of fate, that very desire was to be unfulfilled. The name and the family tradition of his house was destined to die out no more than half a century after the death of its "first Founder."

Ephraim, his oldest son, was born in New Amsterdam in 1652. For a time he was clerk in the Office of the Secretary of the State of New York,[52] then clerk of the Courts of Upland and New Castle, and from 1680 on, surveyor for the counties of St. James and New Castle. Even in New York he had entered into friendly relations with the Labadists, and he was later instrumental in getting them to settle in Cecil County. It was due to this relationship that his contacts with his father became cooler and cooler. At the end, Augustin Herrman mistrusted his oldest son to such an extent that, for fear that Ephraim might turn the family estate over to the Labadists, he added a codicil to his will.[53] In this codicil he named three of his friends and neighbors as "overseers and trustees," who should watch over the proper execution of his will. After the father's death the title of "Second Lord of Bohemia Manor" fell to Ephraim, but the latter died in the year 1689. It is said that he passed his last years in illness and mental derangement.

After Ephraim's death the title went to his brother Caspar Herrman.[54] The Third Lord of Bohemia Manor apparently possessed more of the father's vitality than did Ephraim. He represented New Castle County in the Pennsylvania General Assembly, 1683-1685;

[51] Mallery, 17. The gravestone is still to be seen today.
[52] Brodhead, 17.
[53] Johnston, 107. The codicil, written or dictated by Herrman himself, is in the possession of the Maryland Historical Society (Herrman Manuscripts).
[54] Wilson, 32. Mallery, 20. Johnston, 77, 170, 206.

and in 1694 he was elected member of the Maryland Legislature, where he represented Cecil County.

Caspar died in 1704 and passed the title on to his son, Ephraim Augustine Herrman, who had been born in 1683 at St. Augustine's Manor. He too filled several offices. He was colonel of the militia and member of the Maryland Legislature, where he represented Cecil County in 1715, 1716, 1728 and 1731.[55] Against the desires of its founder, the original family estate was gradually sold or farmed out. By 1733 seventy-five plantations had been disposed of by the Herrmans, most of them by the founder's grandson, Ephraim Augustine. On the other hand he purchased new property, for, like most important people of the times, he possessed a veritable mania for acquiring as much land as possible.

The fourth and last Lord of Bohemia Manor died in 1735. His only son, Augustine, who was still a minor at the time of the father's death, survived him by only four years. The last Herrman died in 1739.[56]

There are, on the other hand, numerous descendants in the various female lines. Children and grandchildren of the family have fought for decades in the courts of justice for their rights to Bohemia Manor. The "legal existence" of Bohemia Manor ceased at the time of the Revolution, after a life span of 128 years.[57] Collateral descendants of Augustin Herrman are still living in Maryland, Delaware and Pennsylvania. The Oldhams, Bouchells, Ensors, Thompsons and Bayards count him among their ancestors.[58] The land on which Bohemia Manor stood is at present in the possession of one of these descendants, the former Senator from Delaware, Thomas F. Bayard. The name of Bohemia Manor is still familiar in the region, but the name of the founder lives on only in the name of a sleepy little town near by, Port Herrman. Posthumously, fate granted this unsuccessful founder of cities the honor of having his name linked with the founding of a city.

A little remains to be said about the Labadists, who were already mentioned in connection with the dissension between Ephraim and Augustin Herrman. The Labadists were a sect founded in the middle of the seventeenth century by the Frenchman, Jean de Labadie.[59]

---

[55] Johnston, 173. [56] Mallery, 22.
[57] For details of the complex history of Bohemia Manor after the extinction of the male line, see Johnston, 175-85.
[58] Mallery, 25 ff. Vincent, 460.
[59] Jean de Labadie was born in 1619 near Bordeaux. He was at first a Jesuit,

The many persecutions that the Labadists suffered in Europe were doubtless the cause of their emigrating to the New World. Two of their members were sent to America in 1679 and 1680 to look about for a suitable location. The two agents, Jasper Danckaerts and Peter Sluyter, kept a faithful diary that affords us a detailed picture of the trip.[60] Danckaerts was Dutch, Sluyter German. The two Labadists stayed at first for a while in New York, then moved on through New Jersey and Delaware to Maryland. Practical and personal reasons attracted them there. The tolerant practice in religious questions invited them to the Calvert Colony. Moreover, they had met and won over Ephraim Herrman in New York. He had asked them to come to Maryland with a view to giving them a piece of his father's land to settle on.

In December 1679, therefore, the two arrived in Maryland. "Maryland is considered the most fertile portion of North America," the diary reports.[61] Through Ephraim they became acquainted with Augustin Herrman, who was at first so favorably impressed that he promised them a large tract of land for their prospective colony. The two travelers remained in Maryland for several weeks. They made various trips to the Eastern Shore, but the land promised by Augustin Herrman seems to have pleased them best of all they saw. The

---

but later he turned away from this order and embraced the teachings of Calvin. Cf. Schaff-Herzog, *Religious Encyclopedia* (New York, 1910), VI, 390. Theologically, the Labadists were related to the Dutch Reformed Church, but they placed more emphasis upon mystical, Adventist doctrines than did the other reformed groups. Not unlike the early Quakers in many respects, they put much weight on the "inward light" and on strict and Spartan rules of conduct in everyday life. Their teachings spread particularly in France, Switzerland, the Netherlands and western Germany. Labadie himself founded a strong, well-disciplined community in Holland, first at Utrecht and then at Amsterdam. In answer to an invitation from Princess Elisabeth of the Palatinate, he moved with most of his followers to Herford in Westphalia. Various difficulties started the Labadists on further wanderings. They paused in Bremen, then in Altona, and finally took up their abode in Wieuwerd in Friesland, a Dutch province near the German border. During these pilgrimages through western and northern Germany they had been joined by numerous Germans, of whom several took part in the founding of the sister colony in America.

[60] This diary chanced to be discovered in 1864 by Henry C. Murphy, who translated it into English and published it in the *Memoirs of the Long Island Historical Society*, 1 (Brooklyn, N.Y., 1867). A new edition appeared in New York in 1913, *Journal of Jaspar Danckaerts, 1679-1680*, edited by B. B. James and J. F. Jameson.

[61] *Journal*, 115.

diary tells in detail of the life of the early colonists, and particularly of the Herrman family. Herrman's children are all spoken well of, but of Augustin Herrman himself Danckaerts says, "He is a very godless person."[62] This remark must be considered in relation to its source, for, in the words of an earlier historian, the Labadists were "a sour sect."

The Labadists' bad report of Augustin Herrman was not to go unavenged. The two agents returned to Friesland in 1680, to come back three years later with the first group of Labadist settlers.[63] When they reached Maryland and prepared to take over their prospective land, it turned out that Augustin Herrman had changed his mind. He refused to have anything more to do with the Labadists or to give them any territory. This reversal is certainly not difficult to explain. When Augustin Herrman promised the land, he still had the founding of a city in mind and attracting colonists for it was a necessity. In the interval before the Labadists returned he had apparently obtained thoroughgoing information about them, and had learned that they were a stern sect living their Spartan life in seclusion and scarcely suited to become the basis of a thriving settlement. He felt, moreover, that they had influenced the judgment of his son Ephraim. There was danger that Ephraim would turn over to them great sections of the family estate that his father had so laboriously accumulated. Under the influence of the Labadists, Ephraim was more and more losing his sense of proportion. Finally, because the "inward light" so desired it, he even left his wife, in order to devote himself completely to the Labadistic way of life. This certainly did not improve the attitude of Augustin Herrman, the self-confident, ambitious progenitor of an old, aristocratic family. A violent quarrel arose, and the Labadists finally had to resort to law to force Augustin Herrman to fulfill his promise. In the end they received only the territory that has since been known as the "Labadie Tract." The transfer, dated August 11, 1684, was made out to Peter Sluyter (alias Vorstman), Jasper Danckaerts (alias Schilders), Petrus Bayard, John Moll and Arnold de la Grange. It amounted to 3750 acres.

[62] *Ibid.*, 145.
[63] Bartlett B. James, *The Labadist Colony in Maryland* (Johns Hopkins University Studies, Series xvii, No. 6, Baltimore, 1899), 38.
J. Th. Scharf, *History of Maryland*, i, 430.
Geo. Armistead Leaking, "The Labadists of Bohemia Manor," *Maryland Hist. Mag.*, i (1906), 337 ff.
G. A. Leaking, "A Visit to Bohemia Manor," *ibid.*, ii (1907), 143 ff.

The colony was established under the leadership of Peter Sluyter, who named himself bishop.[64] The group was officially subject to the mother church in Wieuwerd, but actually it was completely independent. During the half century of its existence it included about one hundred persons, a number that remained almost stationary. In spite of the fact that the first two apostles had on their trip of 1679-1680 expressed utter horror of slave labor and the growing of tobacco, the Labadists became acclimatized so quickly that they were soon industriously managing tobacco plantations worked by slaves.[65] Original plans for missions among the Indians were gradually forgotten. The sect did not cause a great sensation in Maryland. Peter Sluyter must have been a hard and stern "bishop," doing everything to make life as unenjoyable as possible for his little flock. When he died in 1722 the group had dwindled to a tiny number; five years later none was left.

It can no longer be determined how many Germans belonged to this sect, the first communistic settlement in the New World. Unquestionably there were Germans among them; Peter Sluyter from Wesel may serve as a proof. The sect did not exercise any great influence. It has been described here only because it is to a certain extent a vanguard of a type of German immigrants: those who sought asylum in the New World from the religious intolerance of the old home.

At the same time when Augustin Herrman was working on his map of the Province of Maryland and preparing a graphic portrayal of all that was then known, another German, John Lederer, was striving to penetrate into new and unfamiliar territory in the neighboring state of Virginia.[66] Although his activities belong principally to the history of that state, he deserves some mention here. He spent part of his life in Maryland, and we owe it to a high provincial official of Maryland that Lederer's only book, with its information on the astonishing accomplishments of this man, has been preserved.

He must have come to Jamestown, Virginia, about 1668—not

[64] In 1693 Sluyter, as pastor of the Labadists, received permission from the governor to contract marriages; MA, II, 398 f. For Sluyter's naturalization, see MA, XIII, 27, 42, 88, 126.

[65] Dittelbach, a dissenting member of the sect, expressed great anger over this fall from grace in his book *Verval en Val der Labadisten* (Amsterdam, 1692), (Journal, 134 n.).

[66] *Dictionary of American Biography*, IX, 91. (From this point on, this reference is abbreviated *DAB*.)

much earlier, for at the time of his first expedition (1669) he still spoke rather broken English. Since we know that besides his mother tongue, German, he spoke very good French and Italian and even wrote Latin, his defective English must be explained not from an ineptitude for languages but from the fact that he started his first expedition very soon after his arrival in America. His German origin has been repeatedly stated and never disputed.[67]

The development of the fur trade was at this time one of the most important economic problems of the young American colonies. The whites along the coast could not accomplish this end by sitting down and waiting for the Indians to bring them pelts. The colonists had to take the initiative themselves, to approach the indolent natives and bring the furs out from the interior. The interior, however, was still a white space on the map, separated from the coastal region by the insurmountable barrier of the Alleghenies. In 1669 the Hudson Bay Company was founded and began to carry on a vigorous trade in furs. One of its most active agents was the governor of Virginia, Sir William Berkeley, who would himself have liked to go into the unknown interior but was restrained by the Company, which considered his service along the coastal region more important. Again and again Governor Berkeley did all in his power to encourage others to explore the wilderness. It was just at this time that John Lederer came to Jamestown. We do not know whether he had expedition plans of his own or whether he started out at the instigation of the governor. At all events, he was the first to go under the governor's commission. In the years 1669-1670 he undertook three expeditions into the unknown mountain country of Virginia in order to find a passage to the West, to the fur region and to the Indian Ocean. To be sure, he did not find what he was seeking; but he was the first white man to travel through the west and southwest of Virginia, to draw a map of the territory, even though an imperfect one, and so to contribute his share in the opening of this part of the colony.

The first expedition, lasting from March 9 to 24, 1669, took him and three Indians up the Pamunkey River to the summit of the Blue Ridge. For the better part of a week Lederer wandered through the mountain forests without finding a passage to the other side of the Blue Ridge. Bad weather finally forced him to return.

[67] MA, II, 282; v, 84. William Talbot's foreword to Lederer's *Discoveries*, "To the Reader," 4. All citations from the *Discoveries* are made according to the new edition by George P. Humphry (Rochester, N.Y., 1902).

Far more successful was the second expedition, which Lederer began on May 20, 1670, from about the point where present-day Richmond lies. This expedition was apparently better prepared than the first. Lederer was accompanied by five Indians and twenty whites under the leadership of a certain Major Harris. On his first journey Lederer had obviously obtained the impression that the Alleghenies were impassable at the point where he had approached them and also for a considerable distance to the south. Therefore, on his second journey he turned more to the southwest "to avoid the mountains." He probably supposed that the westernmost of the principal ranges of the mountains could be crossed in Carolina. It must have been in the region where Sherwood is situated now that the expedition came upon a northward-flowing river which Lederer correctly recognized as the southern fork of the James River. Major Harris, in the mistaken assumption that the river was a southern arm of the great "Lake of Canada," declared that it was useless to go on. They should raise a stone monument to commemorate their discovery, and then turn back. Lederer insisted that they go on, and showed Major Harris a commission given him by Governor Berkeley and securing him the right to continue even without his English companions. After a few days his companions did turn back, while Lederer and one lone Indian crossed the James River and reached the source of the Roanoke River. He traversed the mountain ridge which forms the watershed between the Roanoke and the New River (approximately the boundary between Carroll and Grayson Counties today), and continued over a difficult route to the northwestern parts of North Carolina. In the region of present-day Burke County he was halted, for his way was blocked by a large lake which he named Uschery Lake. Moreover, he heard from the Indians that people whom he reasonably took for Spaniards lived a two and a half days' journey to the southwest. Since he did not want to come into contact with them, he turned back on June 28. The way home probably led through the northern part of North Carolina. On July 17, in the place that is now Petersburg on the Appomattox, he finally came to a settlement where he "was not a little overjoyed to see Christian faces again."[68]

There is much disagreement about the history of Lederer's second expedition and the descriptions given by the different writers are so

[68] *Discoveries*, 23.

contradictory that it is difficult to arrive at the truth of the matter.[69] The mysterious Lake Uschery, the end-point of the second expedition, has repeatedly proved baffling. Some historians have even gone so far as to place the lake in Florida. Others believe that Lederer turned back in the region of Augusta, Georgia; others, in South Carolina; still others, in North Carolina. This last view is certainly the most probable. The mysterious Lake Uschery was either the Catawba River, swollen by heavy rains, or James Lake in Burke's County, North Carolina. Lederer did not go farther south.

This second expedition was doubtlessly much more fruitful than the first. Nevertheless, what Lederer was actually seeking, what all

[69] E. A. Duykinck, *Cyclopedia of American Literature.*

Francis L. Hawks, *History of North Carolina* (1858), II, 43 ff.

H. A. Rattermann, "Der erste Erforscher des Alleghany-Gebirges," *Der Deutsche Pionier*, VIII, 399 (Cincinnati, Ohio, 1877).

Ralph M. Brown, "A Sketch of the Early History of South-Western Virginia," *William and Mary Historical Magazine*, 2nd S., XVII (1937), 502.

A. B. Faust, I, 27-28.

Christian Strack, "John Lederer," *Berichte der deutschen Historischen Gesellschaft für den Distrikt Columbia*, Washington, D.C., II (1906), 33 ff.

L. P. Hennighausen, "John Lederer's Book of Travels," *SHGM*, III (1889), 21.

Herrmann Schuricht, *A History of the German Element in Virginia* (Baltimore, 1898), I, 40.

John W. Wayland, *The German Element in the Shenandoah Valley of Virginia* (Charlottesville, Va., 1907), 11 ff.

"Fauquier's Aborigines," *Bulletin Fauquier Historical Society*, I (August, 1921), 3.

Edward D. Neill, *Virginia Carolorum* (Albany, N.Y., 1886), 326.

W. W. Scott, *History of Orange County, Virginia* (Richmond, 1907), 102.

Clarence W. Alvord and Lee Bidgood, *The First Explorations of the Trans-Allegheny Region by the Virginians 1650-1674* (Cleveland, 1912), 62 ff. and 131 ff. Alvord and Bidgood are the two historians who have exercised the most uncritical judgment concerning Lederer and have relegated the greater part of his report to the realm of fable. As we know today, this is an injustice. The best research into the problem of Lederer's second expedition is to be found in the excellent article by Lyman Carrier, "The Veracity of John Lederer," *William and Mary Historical Magazine*, 2nd S., XIX (1939), 435 ff. Carrier made the happy experiment of reconstructing Lederer's route and transferring it to a modern map of Virginia through comparison with two later expeditions, the Batts-Wood expedition of 1671 and the Needham-Arthur expedition of 1673. To him belongs also the honor of having investigated and refuted the senseless attacks of Alvord-Bidgood: "they fell into the common error in assuming that everything which they did not readily understand was not based on facts" (Carrier, 437). Carrier's article unquestionably takes the proper middle course between the excesses and deficiencies in the judgments of other historians, and certainly gives the most credible picture of the explorer.

explorers and voyagers of these times were seeking—a passage to the West and to the Pacific—had not been found. The Sara Indians had told Lederer that there were two passes through the range, one in the south (the one that he had avoided for fear of the Spaniards) and a second farther to the north "at a place called Zynodoa."[70] What the Indians had in mind was probably the pass on the upper Potomac. This, Lederer did not understand; he believed he could find a pass if he penetrated on into the west from the northernmost English settlement in Virginia, Talifer's House on the Rappahannock. A few weeks after the end of the second journey, therefore, he set out, August 20, 1670, on the third and last expedition. He started in the region of present-day Fredericksburg, Virginia, accompanied by a Colonel Catlet, nine English troopers and five Indians. Again he came to the crest of the Blue Ridge, but when he saw that more and higher mountains lay on the other side he decided to return.[71]

Little is known of what occurred after Lederer's return from the last expedition. It is certain only that he became unpopular in Virginia, and "that he was look'd on as so great insolence, that our traveller at his return, instead of welcome and applause, met nothing but affronts and reproaches."[72] Major Harris and his companions, who had deserted Lederer on the second expedition, tried to justify themselves by discrediting Lederer, using the rumor that he had wasted the tax returns of an entire year in his roving about. If one may believe Lederer's own words, the scorn at his expenditures was the reason for the general displeasure with him in Virginia. Another supposition is that his connection with his powerful patron, Governor Berkeley, did him more harm than good among the colonists.[73] Sir William Berkeley's stern rule was not very popular in Virginia. A few years later there was even a revolt against him, and it is not impossible that many people transferred their hatred of the governor to his protégé. Similarly confusing is another affair, in which the name of Lederer is mentioned for the last time in Virginia history. From an order book from Surry County, Virginia, under date of

[70] Discoveries, 27. There is no doubt that we have here one of the first, if not the first, references to the word "Shenandoah."

[71] The assumption of Virgil A. Lewis in History and Government of West Virginia (1906), 35, that Lederer crossed the Blue Ridge at Harpers Ferry, is certainly wrong. None of the expeditions passed so far north. The last journey ran approximately along the geographic latitude of Fredericksburg.

[72] Sir William Talbot on Lederer, Discoveries, 4.

[73] Carrier, 444.

November 20, 1673, we learn that he was in monetary difficulties and indebted to various persons.[74] This is only a very short and uncertain statement, and nothing final may be said about his indebtedness as long as no more fruitful sources are found.

Whatever may have been the reason for Lederer's general unpopularity in Virginia, it is definite that he soon began to feel his life in danger and fled to Maryland toward the end of 1670 or the beginning of 1671. Here he must soon have come in contact with a nephew of Cecil, Lord Baltimore, namely Sir William Talbot, the secretary of the Province of Maryland.[75] In the foreword to Lederer's book Talbot speaks of the beginning of their acquaintance: "Forced . . . into Maryland, he became known to me, though then ill-affected to the man, by the stories that went about him: Nevertheless finding him contrary to my expectation, a modest ingenious person, and a pretty scholar, I thought it common justice to give him an occasion of vindicating himself from what I had heard of him, which truly he did with so convincing reason and circumstance, as quite abolished those former impressions in me, and made me desire this account of his travels, which here you have faithfully rendred out of Latine from his own writings and discourse, with an entire map of the territory he traversed, copied from his own hand."[76]

The Latin manuscript of Lederer's report has been lost. Talbot's English translation appeared in London in 1672 under the title, *The Discoveries of John Lederer in three several Marches from Virginia to the West of Carolina and other parts of the Continent.* If one may believe Talbot and Lederer, the diary was originally "never designed for the press." Some doubt arises, however, for here and there the writing certainly has the nature of an apology. Lederer pointed out in several places that he would have accomplished more with a few active companions. It is not known whether the report was composed during the expedition, or later in Virginia or in Maryland. The *Discoveries* is the only source which tells us in detail of the course of Lederer's expeditions. Aside from that, the book offers valuable information on geographical, geological and ethnological matters, whose worth has often been recognized by scholars in the most

[74] *Virginia Magazine of History and Biography*, VIII, 324. This story of indebtedness looks rather inconvincing, since in 1673 Lederer had probably already left the state.

[75] Matthew P. Andrews, *Tercentenary History of Maryland* (Chicago and Baltimore, 1925), I, 324.

[76] *Discoveries*, 4.

varied fields—even by Alvord and Bidgood.[77] It is the first scientific report on men, vegetation and animals in the Virginia Valley. It is to the credit of the just and well-educated Sir William Talbot that he recognized the worth of Lederer's manuscript, translated it and thus preserved it for posterity.

In other ways, too, Lederer was better off in Maryland than in Virginia. He was by no means a jejune and impractical scholar. As is shown by the extremely precise and practical final chapter of his book, "Touching Trade with Indians," he never ignored commercial possibilities on his journeys.[78] His business sense was so strongly developed that after his arrival in Maryland he began to turn to practical advantage what he had learned. In March 1671 he obtained a trade charter from Charles Calvert, Lieutenant-General of the Province of Maryland.[79] The license gave him the right to trade in beaver and other pelts with Indians living in southwestern Maryland more than two hundred miles from the state border.[80] He might take from the province whatever articles of barter he needed. This was done with the knowledge and permission and under the protection of the Lord-Proprietor, Cecilius Calvert.

A point of interest in this charter is that it is the only document giving indisputable proof of Lederer's origin. Only here it is stated that he was from Hamburg. "To all Persons to whom these presents

[77] Cf. Hu Maxwell, "The Use and Abuse of Forests by the Virginia Indians," *William and Mary Historical Magazine*, 1st S., xix, 82; A. J. Morrison, "The Virginia Indian Trade to 1673," *ibid.*, 2nd S., i, 234; Charles E. Kemper, "The Settlement of the Valley," *Virginia Mag.*, xxx, 170; H. C. Grooms, "The Finding of Fauquier," *Tyler's Quarterly Magazine*, ii, 316; John W. Wayland, *History of Rockingham County, Virginia* (1912), 33; Alvord-Bidgood, 69.

[78] *Discoveries*, 29 ff.

[79] MA, v, 84. In the sentence where the name first occurs, it reads "Loderer" instead of "Lederer," but in the balance of the charter it is always correctly spelled. The Index of Vol. v of the *Maryland Archives*, however, cites only Loderer. This may be the reason why the document has previously been missed by historical investigation. The official date of the document is March 4, 1670. Actually this is March 4, 1671, since the time for the beginning of the new year was not changed from Annunciation Day to Circumcision Day in Maryland until 1752. Therefore, any date from January 1 to March 25 must usually be advanced in new style to the following year. It is quite clear that the trade charter was granted after the end of the expeditions, i.e., after August 1670, since it names a number of the Indian tribes with whom Lederer did not become acquainted until his second journey, in July 1670.

[80] This restrictive clause is to be explained by the Calverts' desire to bind the more remote sections into a stronger economic union with Maryland. Lederer was to concentrate on the more distant tribes.

shall come Greeting in our Lord God everlasting know ye that whereas Iohn Loderer a Hamburgher born but now Resident in Calvert County in the said Province of Maryland having formerly discovered several Nations of Indians. . . ." Previously only indemonstrable hypotheses were offered concerning Lederer's origin. The assumption that he was a "son of the Alps," an Austrian, has maintained itself most stubbornly, although with the least reason of all.[81] If we consider that Lederer was not merely a Mr. X for the Maryland provincial officials, but rather a man who stood out through his accomplishments from the mass of average applicants, we may suppose that the information about Lederer's origin as given in this document is authentic. An error through carelessness or negligence seems out of the question.

The last certain and unquestionable report on Lederer's sojourn in Maryland is furnished by the petition for naturalization in the Calvert Colony, which he and several other applicants made in April 1671.[82] The document says that he had lived "under the Dominion of the Emperor of Germany." The applicants request that "every of them shall from henceforth be adjudged Reputed and taken as

[81] This version is given by Rattermann in the above-mentioned article in *Der Deutsche Pionier*, and has been accepted uncritically by many historians. Cf. J. G. Rosengarten, "German Influence in America," *Lippincott's Magazine*, LXIX (1902), 501. Rattermann connects Lederer with a certain Lederer who published a geographic description of the Alps in 1691 (*Descriptio Geographicae et Geologicae de Montis Alpium, etc.*), or with an Austrian Franciscan monk of the same name who published a theological paper in Augsburg in 1661 (*Dissertatio apologetica qua cultus S.S. angelorum etc. in monte Gargona apparitio vindicatur*). There is no foundation for these combinations. The name Lederer occurs very frequently in Germany, and is still more common in Austria, where it is the word for tanner. (Cf. *Virginia Magazine of History and Biography*, L [1942], 131-33.)

The assumption that Lederer was a physician was previously based on a contemporary source of 1676, in which it was said "that about five year since there was a German Chirurgeon who obtained a commission from Sir Will Bartlet to travel to the South-West of Virginia and to make discovery of those parts. . . ." (Thomas Glover, *An Account of Virginia* reprinted from the *Philosophical Transactions of the Royal Society*, June 20, 1676, Oxford; reprinted in 1904.) Cf. Fairfax Harrison, *Landmarks of Old Prince Williams* (Richmond, 1924), 25 and 34; H. C. Groome, *Fauquier During the Proprietorship* (Richmond, 1927), 18. The thesis that Lederer was a doctor has meanwhile been definitely proved through the investigations of Professor Harold S. Jantz. See n. 83.

[82] MA, II, 282-83. The exact date of the application is not given. It was made during the session of the Assembly that met on March 27, 1671. Probably the document may be assigned to the first of April.

Naturell borne people within this Province of Maryland." We learn nothing more about the success of the petition, but we may assume that the naturalization was granted.

To be sure, Lederer remained in Maryland only two or three years. The end of his life is as obscure as its beginning; no more than four or five years lie before us in the clear light of history. Only recently have we learned that he appeared in 1674 in Connecticut and practiced medicine there with great success. Early in 1675 he left America, but we do not know whether permanently or only temporarily.[83]

His most noteworthy accomplishments are his map of Virginia and his book. It goes without saying that his map is very imperfect, but a more exact one could not be prepared in those times and under those circumstances. In many details it is even better and more comprehensive than Augustin Herrman's famous map.[84] The *Dis-*

[83] We owe this information to Professor Harold S. Jantz (Northwestern University) who discovered hitherto unknown material on John Lederer in the Winthrop Papers of the Massachusetts Historical Society. Several letters to and from Lederer indicate clearly that he lived in and near Hartford, Connecticut, in the summer of 1674. We have some very favorable testimonials about his medical skill. Israel Chauncy, a well-known scholar and respected physician, wrote to John Winthrop under date of September 28, 1674: ". . . his name begins to be much spoken of amongst us and much resort there hath bin to him for his counsel in other difficult cases . . . such as his Learning and Experience, that I do not know that I ever met with the like in one of his years; and therefore should account it a great favour if he might be prevaild with to abide in these parts. . . ." In a letter of November 19, 1674, he writes again: "I fear he will hardly have time to accomplish the cure before going out of the country: which all friends that have had experience of so great good by his endeavours, do much bewail, fearing that a man of so great skill, is too great a blessing for us. I doe understand by some lines lately received from a friend at Stamford that he is unwearyed in endeavours to do good; seldom being at liberty from patients night or day." In a letter from John Bishop to John Winthrop (December 9, 1674) we read: "Mr. Lederer . . . seems to be a man of singular & rich endowments, A general scholler & great Phisician as doubtles yorself do better understand then others can tell you, as having more acquaintance with him. . . . It is a great pitty he should leave the country. . . ." In December 1674 Lederer went to New York to secure passage for Germany. Since he could not make satisfactory arrangements, however, he returned to Connecticut, continued to practice medicine and finally took passage with Captain Jonathan Selleck from Fairfield for Barbados on January 16, 1675. He hoped to secure passage for home from there. His intentions on leaving were to go home only for a visit and then to return to Connecticut. On April 14, 1675, he wrote to John Winthrop from Barbados. While there he lived with the well-known Judge Sharpe. Apparently he soon left for Germany. Nothing is known about the end of his life.

[84] Carrier, 438.

J. W. Wayland, "The Pennsylvania-German in the Valley of Virginia,"

coveries was long completely forgotten. Not until the middle of the last century did interest in it reawaken, to be kept active by the occasional appearance of new editions.[85] This work, of such unusual cultural and historical interest, unveils for us the best portrait of its author. He was a thorough scholar and a brave explorer, not a romantic dreamer, but a man of sobriety and realism.[86] To be sure, he shared many of the incorrect contemporary concepts about the unknown American continent; but he must be credited with never having fallen prey to the illusion of so many of the men of his time, that it must be possible to see the Indian Ocean from the peaks of the Alleghenies.[87] Sir William Talbot's characterization of John Lederer is certainly not wrong when he calls him "a modest ingenious person and a pretty scholar."

Let us recapitulate what we have learned about the Germans in Maryland up to the end of the seventeenth century: there is Augustin Herrman, a merchant; the Labadists, a religious sect; John Lederer, a scholar. But where are the pioneers?

In the first settling of the land around Chesapeake Bay, the Germans played only a very minor role. The colony of Maryland was the private property of a Catholic lord, whereas the majority of German immigrants consisted of suppressed Protestants. They knew nothing

---

The Pennsylvania German, x (1909), 3. "The Map is remarkably correct, considering the hasty journey through the wilderness."

[85] Complete figures concerning the extant copies of the first edition of *Discoveries* (1672) are inexact, including those of the Union Catalog. First editions are to be found at least in the following libraries: (1) Library of Congress. (2) New York Public Library. (3) New York State Library. (4) New York Historical Society. (5) Cornell University, Ithaca, N.Y. (6) Newberry Library, Chicago. (7) John Carter Brown Library, Providence, R.I. (8) Williams College, Williamstown, Mass. (9) William L. Clements Library, Ann Arbor, Mich. (10) Indiana University, Bloomington. (11) University of Pittsburgh, Pittsburgh, Pa. (12) University of Pennsylvania, Philadelphia, Pa. (13) University of Virginia, Charlottesville, Va. (14) Harvard University, Cambridge, Mass. The British Museum in London has six copies, but two are incomplete.

[86] Dieter Cunz, "John Lederer, Significance and Evaluation," *William and Mary Historical Magazine*, 2nd S., xxii (1942), 175-85.

[87] *Discoveries*, 26. "They are certainly in a great error, who imagine that the continent of North-America is but eight or ten days journey over from the Atlantick to the Indian ocean." Lederer doubted, however, that there were any large navigable rivers on the other side of the Alleghenies. He believed that the North American continent was constructed like the South American: a range of mountains that sloped gently to the east and fell off steeply to the west. He had no notion of the Mississippi and the Rockies.

of the sympathetic tolerance of the Calverts' religious laws; or, if they knew of them, they distrusted them after their unhappy experiences under the ruling Catholic princes of Germany. Thus, at the turn of the seventeenth century, the Germans preferred other colonies—New York, Pennsylvania, Virginia. As private property rather than a crown colony, Maryland profited little from the organized mass shipments of German settlers arranged by the English government at the beginning of the eighteenth century. In spite of all this, a few isolated German settlers were to be found in Maryland toward the end of the seventeenth century. For the very fact that they are only a few lone cases, we may be justified in treating of them here in a little more detail.

The best known of them all is George Hack. We have already met him; he and his family were named as future citizens in the document of 1663 that spoke of Augustin Herrman's approaching naturalization. George Hack was born in Cologne, Germany, in about 1623. He studied medicine at Cologne University, received his doctor's degree and then emigrated to New Amsterdam. Here he gave up his medical practice in favor of commercial activities. Together with Augustin Herrman he opened a tobacco house, which soon began to flourish.[88] By 1651 the firm of Hack and Herrman was one of the largest and most successful tobacco houses in America. On the tobacco markets of Maryland and Virginia it developed into a sharp competitor of the Dutch West India Company. The Navigation Act of 1651, which excluded all non-English ships from trade with the colonies, put an abrupt end to the business, forced Herrman for a time into debtor's prison and caused Hack to leave New Amsterdam. He settled in Northampton County, Virginia, and returned to his original profession, medicine. In the beginning of the sixties he must have moved to Baltimore County, Maryland, where we find his name in 1663 in the Acts of the General Assembly.[89] He died, probably in 1665, before he achieved naturalization. Two sons were

[88] DAB, VIII, 70. Virginia Magazine of History and Biography, v, 256. William and Mary Historical Magazine, VIII, 237. George Hack was related to Augustin Herrman. Hack's wife was Anna Varleth, the sister of Herrman's wife, Janneken. Anna Varleth was active in the tobacco business, and later even carried it on alone under her own name. She is said to have equaled the most skilled merchant in energy and keenness.

[89] In the Maryland Archives his name often occurs. In 1662, for example, we read of a "Lycense to Dr. George Hack to transporte 20 barrels of Corne out of this Province" (MA, III, 459).

born to him, George Nicholas, who became the father of the Virginia branch of the family; and Peter, who founded the Maryland line of Hacks. As early as 1647 a John Hack is named in connection with a Court and Testamentary Business. A certain Sepherin Hack was killed by Indians in Maryland in 1661.[90] We do not know whether John and Sepherin were members of George Hack's family, but it is possible. In later times the name often appears as Heck. The original form lives on today in Hack's Neck, Virginia, and in Hack's Point, Cecil County, Maryland.

It is endlessly difficult to establish the nationality of settlers in these early times. The names help very little and are even often misleading. We read of a Christian Geist of Annapolis; from his name he might well be considered German, but we learn from his naturalization papers that he "was born under the King of Sweden."[91] Settlers with English-sounding names, such as Greening or Rayman, on the other hand, turn out to be Germans. Edward Beckler could have been a German by his name; if so, he was the first German in Maryland, for his name appears in a document of 1637.[92] We certainly will not err in claiming as Germans James and William Leisler, who appeared as witnesses in a court process in 1664, although we do not know whether they were relatives of the famous Jakob Leisler of New Amsterdam.[93] By the orthography of his name, a certain Peter Meyer may have been German; but we may dismiss him briefly, for we know of him only that in 1663 Governor Philip Calvert gave him a "Passe to depart this Province."[94] A certain Hans Dering, who is mentioned in a document of 1663, was certainly German; and in the case of John Sicks (1663) the note "Subject of the Royall Empire of Jermany" leaves no doubt about his origin.[95] John Stump, a Prussian, came to America about 1700 and bought a piece of land in Cecil County, near present-day Perryville, Maryland.[96] That a certain

---

[90] O. A. Keach, "The Hack Family," *Tyler's Quarterly Magazine*, VII, 253 ff. MA, IV, 332; III, 414, 432.

[91] MA, XXXIV, 146, 265; XXXVIII, 288. It would naturally still be possible for Christian Geist to have come originally from Germany. After the peace of Westphalia (1648) great parts of northern Germany (Vorpommern, Bremen, Verden, Wismar) were under the rule of the Swedish king.

[92] MA, I, 22.   [93] MA, IL, 269.   [94] MA, IL, 18.

[95] MA, I, 471; III, 489.

[96] *Biographical Cyclopedia of Representative Men of Maryland* (Baltimore, 1879); Stump was a cousin of the Prussian Baron Friedrich von Trenck, who played a part in the family history of Frederick the Great. The name seems originally to have been Stumpf.

Michael(a) Hacker, who is mentioned in connection with the case of a runaway slave and is identified simply as "spinster," was a German is a possibility, but it cannot be proved.[97] We read (1683) of a Simon Stein, "A servant,"[98] and (1718) of a Philip Eilbeck of Kent County—both indubitably German names. Philip Eilbeck was in a pitiable situation. We find his petition "That he has Been a Prisoner for Debt in Kent County almost Two years and haveing nothing whereby he Can discharge His body from Prison nor any likelyhood of Being Discharged—prays that an Act may Pass in his favor."[99] In spite of the unhappy state of the "Languishing Prisoner," the General Assembly moved with no particular speed. His name occurs again and again in the Acts, and we never learn what was finally done for the unfortunate man.[100] The servant Stein and the prisoner Eilbeck were undoubtedly not unusual cases among the few Germans in the colony at this time. Certainly there were many Germans among the poor people, but only by exception do their names appear in historical documents. In the upper classes German names are as good as nonexistent. Only once we read of a William Blankenstein, who with a few other prominent fellow citizens sent a letter of congratulations to the new King William III in London in 1689.[101]

Naturalization documents are the only safe sources, for there we do not have to depend upon the German sound of the names. Before 1730 we have about a dozen naturalizations where it is expressly stated that the new citizen was "a Native of Germany," "born in Germany," or born "under the Dominions of the Emperor of Germany." After the aforementioned naturalizations of Augustin Herrman, George Hack and John Lederer, in the next few decades followed those of Lawrence Christian and Martin Mugenbrough (1674), "borne in Germany";[102] Albert Greening and John Oeth (1721), "born under the Dominion of the Emperor of Germany and their Children now Residents in Ann arundel County"; [103] Joseph Lazear of Prince George's County with his children Joseph, Thomas, John, Elisabeth, Mary, and Deborah (also 1721);[104] a

---

[97] MA, IV, 165. Weishaar (p. 14) takes for granted that the Hacker spinster was German, but the name alone is not sufficient proof.

[98] MA, VII, 456.   [99] MA, XXX, 131.

[100] MA, XXX, 157, 158, 196, 211, 230, 234, 241, 283.

[101] MA, VIII, 147. Blankenstein's naturalization is mentioned in VII, 343, 345, 362, 400, 405, 406, 420, 444.

[102] MA, II, 400.

[103] MA, XXXVIII, 297; XXXIV, 280, 287, 291, 303, 312, 316, 329, 330.

[104] MA, XXXVIII, 288; XXXIV, 146, 147, 156, 160, 189, 207, 227, 265.

surgeon, Francis Ludolph Bodien of Kent County (1727);[105] John Woolf, an Annapolis cobbler with wife and child;[106] John Samuel Mynskie with wife and daughter "born in the Province of Brandenburgh in the Kingdom of Prussia" and now a blacksmith in Annapolis;[107] the already mentioned William Rayman of Annapolis, "borne in Germany under the Dominion of the Prince Palatine of Rhyne" (1728);[108] and finally Christian Peters from Cecil County, "a Native of Germany" (1729).[109]

When the first two Labadists, Danckaerts and Sluyter, came through Maryland on their initial trip in 1679, they met, probably in Kent County, on a farm "a person who spoke high Dutch"— which in all likelihood means German. The two travelers speak of him again a little later on: "We also found here the person who spoke high Dutch, and of whom we have before said a word. We were able to converse with him, but my companion could do so best. He resided on this plantation, and was a kind of proctor or advocate in the courts."[110] Danckaerts is the author of the diary; "my companion" means Sluyter, who came from Wesel in the Rhineland and was therefore able to talk more easily with the man "who spoke high Dutch." We learn, however, nothing about this German, neither his name nor from what part of Germany he originated.

In the older literature about Maryland and Delaware we read here and there of a German, or more exactly, of an Austrian, who settled on the Eastern Shore about 1680, one Cornelius Commegys.[111] Commegys possessed vast property in Maryland as well as in Delaware, and played a not unimportant role in the history of the seventeenth century. "Commegys from Vienna," as he is always called, was, however, not a German. He was a Dutchman who came from the little town of Vianen in South Holland. The similarity between the words "Vianen" and "Vienna" no doubt caused the confusion of

[105] MA, xxxviii, 403; xxxvi, 14, 15, 17, 55, 63, 64, 65, 66.

[106] MA, xxxviii, 406; xxxvi, 24, 25, 38, 55, 63, 69, 75.

[107] MA, xxxviii, 407; xxxvi, 24, 25, 38, 55, 63, 69, 75.

[108] MA, xxxviii, 422; xxxvi, 130, 133, 140, 212, 223, 224, 225, 233, 234, 263. The German spelling of the name was probably Reimann.

[109] MA, xxxviii, 424; xxxvi, 314, 316, 322, 387, 396, 398, 401, 404, 446.

[110] Danckaerts Journal, 118, 122.

[111] Francis Vincent, History of Delaware (Wilmington, 1870), 465. Vincent tells (p. 464) that, when the English took over Delaware, many Dutch and German families moved to Maryland. "They were, no doubt, brought there by the influence of Augustin Herrman." That is quite possible. Unfortunately, Vincent gives us no proof.

the local historians. The Commegys family were discussed in detail in Danckaerts' diary, which identifies them as natives of Holland.[112]

We may make particular mention of two outstanding Germans who lived in Maryland at the beginning of the eighteenth century, even if only for a few years: Justus Engelhardt Kühn and John Peter Zenger. The name of Justus Engelhardt Kühn occurs in the Maryland Acts for the first time in the year 1708.[113] We do not know anything of Kühn's youth, nor from what part of Germany he came, nor when he emigrated to America. Indeed, we know little of his life, and the little that we do know is restricted to his last nine years. His naturalization papers make it clear that he was a German and a Protestant. Apparently he came to Annapolis in 1707 or 1708. Shortly after he settled there he married, and in 1714 the Acts record the birth of "Thomas, Son of Jost. Englt. Kiihn and Elisabeth his wife." In April 1717 he became church warden of St. Ann in Annapolis. Not much later he abjured the Stuarts and declared his loyalty to the new English royal house of Hanover. He must have died a few months later. The administrator of his estate was none less than Charles Carroll, "The Settler" (1660-1720). Happily, some of Kühn's pictures have been preserved. They not only give evidence of his artistic ability, but show that he was the favorite portrait-painter of the highest social stratum of the province. All the paintings that we possess from his hand are portraits of members of the Digges, Darnall and Carroll families, the best names of the time in Maryland.[114]

John Peter Zenger was born in Germany in 1697 and came to New

[112] *Danckaerts Journal*, 121. "Commegys was from Vianen, and had a Dutch woman for a wife, who taught her children to speak the Dutch language; they therefore had a kind disposition towards Hollanders."

[113] For all that we know of J. E. Kühn we are indebted to the excellent study of J. Hall Pleasants, "Justus Engelhardt Kühn, an Early Eighteenth Century Portrait Painter," *Proceedings of the American Antiquarian Society*, XLVI (1936), Pt. II, 243-80. It is the only essay that we have on him. The name Kühn is often garbled in the Acts, appearing as Kiihn, Kyhn, Kitchin, Ketclin; but the two first names Justus Engelhardt identify him wherever he is mentioned.

MA, XXXVII, 235, 261, 283, 288, 289, 292, 321, 327, 369, 370.

[114] We have ten of Kühn's pictures, three portraits of children and seven portraits of adults. J. Hall Pleasants has pointed out that Kühn was the first painter in America who introduced a Negro slave into a portrait (Portrait of Henry Darnall III). All pictures are reproduced in the essay by Pleasants, who also gives exact information concerning the history of the pictures and the genealogy of the subjects.

York as a boy of thirteen. He was one of a group of emigrants from the Palatinate supported by Queen Ann.[115] Since the father had died en route and the mother was destitute, the children had to pay off the costs of their voyage by several years of service. Subsequently, John Peter Zenger settled in Chestertown, Kent County, Maryland. In October of 1720 the Assembly granted naturalization to J. P. Zenger "being an alien Borne in the uper Palatinate on the Rhine."[116] His name appears frequently in the archives of the year 1720-1721, for early in 1720 he had applied as a trained printer for the job of printing the laws of the Province of Maryland. In April 1720 we read: "Petitioner has the Liberty of printing the Bodys of Laws of each Sessions for the sev.ll Countys as also one for the Prov.ll Court One for the Upper House and one for the Lower House of Assembly And that he Bind the same with Leather And be Allowed for Each Body Seven hundred pounds of Tob.c. . . ."[117] Unfortunately, none of these printed volumes of laws is extant. We may be sure, however, that Zenger continued to print the Maryland laws for some time, for in August 1721 the General Assembly decreed that John Peter Zenger should print the laws of this session "as usual."[118] In spite of this auspicious start in Maryland, Zenger returned to New York in 1722. As is well known, his real activities began there. As editor of the *New York Weekly Journal* he became famous as one of the first American protagonists of freedom of the press.[119] This account, however, does not belong in a history of Maryland.

Without question, others of the group from the Palatinate settled in the colony of Maryland, but we have no definite information about them. Only once in the *Archives* of Maryland is explicit reference made to this group. On October 27, 1710, the House of Delegates passed the following decree: "This House being informed several Palatines were come to Settle in this Province and being

[115] DAB, xx, 648.

[116] MA, xxxviii, 277; xxxiv, 19, 20, 21, 31, 56, 79, 81, 83, 93, 110, 112.

[117] MA, xxxiii, 501, 557, 588, 639.

[118] MA, xxxiv, 255. Cf. Lawrence C. Wroth, *History of Printing in Colonial Maryland* (Baltimore, 1922), 50 ff.

Charles A. Barker, in his book *The Background of the Revolution in Maryland* (New Haven, 1940), 167, has pointed out this act as an early omen of the Revolution. In contrast to the custom of the secrecy-shrouded Parliament in the English motherland, the doings of the Assembly were here for the first time published and so exposed to general criticism.

[119] Cf. Livingstone Rutherfurd, *John Peter Zenger, His Press, His Trial and a Bibliography of Zenger Imprints* (New York, 1904).

willing & desirous to Encourage those poor People in their Industry have resolved that those Palatines with their Servants Shall be free this present year from paying any publick or County charge of Levy and to which they pray the Concurrence of the Honble Council."[120] The Council agreed without hesitation, "being likewise desirous to Encourage the said Palatines and make them as easy as possible." Where these Palatines settled and how many they were is not stated. Both pronouncements of the Acts make it clear, however, that the Assembly was glad to see the Palatinate immigrants come and eager to give them a good start in the new land.

[120] MA, xxvii, 496. The term "Palatine" became so much a part of the language of the time that it was later frequently applied to all German-Protestant immigrants, no matter from what part of Germany they came. Many of the so-called "Palatines" originated in Silesia or Holstein.

II. SETTLING THE BACKWOODS

VERY immigrant looks upon the sea as the last connection with his old homeland, and some particular drive is needed before he can force himself to turn his back to it. It is not necessary to add that in the America of the eighteenth century these psychological factors were strengthened by material difficulties that caused the immigrant to hesitate before entering the struggle with the uninhabited wilderness far from the protection of helpful neighbors.

In the 1730's a new chapter began in the history of immigration in Maryland. Although the colony was now a hundred years old, settlements were still restricted to the coastal region along the Chesapeake. This tendency toward coastal settlements is, as we have said, a common weakness among early immigrants; but in Maryland there was a yet more specific reason. Up to the middle of the eighteenth century the entire economic system of the state was built upon tobacco raising. Tobacco was the most common medium of trade and commerce. Tobacco as currency temporarily took the place of money.[1] But tobacco had to be shipped, and if possible without having first to be transported a long distance overland. Thus it was that everything in Maryland stood or fell with tobacco, and everybody concerned with it needed the water, the Bay. The unnatural overproduction of tobacco finally threw the economic system of the colony into such confusion that in 1748 tobacco cultivation was strictly limited by law. The planting of grain crops was recommended in its place—all the more so because the soil was being exhausted through the exclusive cultivation of the one crop.[2]

Development was possible for the colony only if the cultivation of grain was increased sufficiently to counterbalance that of tobacco, and if the colonists abandoned the principle of coastal settlements to utilize the untouched hinterland. As early as the seventeenth cen-

[1] In a report on the people of Maryland written toward the beginning of the eighteenth century, we read: "Tobacco is their Meat, Drink, Clothing and Money." Cf. Clarence P. Gould, *Money and Transportation in Maryland, 1720-1765* (Baltimore, 1915), and Vertrees J. Wyckhoff, *Tobacco Regulations in Colonial Maryland* (Baltimore, 1936).

[2] For this reason Governor Sharpe even planned to limit the raising of tobacco by law. The colony needed grain farmers. In 1737 a law was published "To Prohibit the Exportation of Grain, Bread and Flour."

tury, therefore, attempts were made in Maryland to influence immigrants to settle in the western sections. This was particularly difficult because of the fact that this region belonged in part to the disputed territory between Pennsylvania and Maryland.

It was in this very disputed territory that the government of Maryland first came into contact with considerable groups of German settlers. It was the fault of neither one that this first meeting, taking place under unfavorable circumstances in the explosive atmosphere of a boundary dispute, did not turn out to be entirely happy. We shall deal only briefly with the story, for the German settlers in the northern part of Maryland eventually fell to Pennsylvania when the boundary was fixed. Since none of the proprietors of Maryland and Pennsylvania was well acquainted with the conditions governing boundaries in America, bitter quarrels were waged for decades over the lines between their possessions, and the legal status of the settlers was very uncertain. The general movement of the Pennsylvania settlers was in a southwestern, that of the Maryland settlers in a northern, direction. Friction resulted when the two movements converged, and was followed later by open deeds of violence.[3]

Peace was maintained as long as the broad Susquehanna separated the two parties. In 1728 John Hendrick came from Pennsylvania to settle on the western side of the river, i.e., on the side away from Pennsylvania, at the mouth of Kreutz Creek.[4] The Pennsylvania authorities had long avoided encouraging settlers to cross the Susquehanna, since white relations with the Indians were vague in this territory and the Pennsylvanians did not allocate land that had not been previously purchased from the natives.[5] When, however, the Pennsylvania authorities began to fear that Maryland settlers from the south would penetrate the region west of the Susquehanna, in spite of the risk of contention with the Indians, they began to issue temporary licenses for settlement of the western side of the river. John Hendrick made the beginning. In the next few years numerous

[3] The best account of these boundary fights between the settlers of Maryland and Pennsylvania is found in Abdel R. Wentz, *The Beginnings of the German Element in York County, Pennsylvania* (Lancaster, Pa., 1916), a source used liberally in this section.

[4] It is not entirely certain whether Hendrick was a German or an Englishman. The name "Hendrick" occurs frequently in the lists of German immigrants to Pennsylvania, but no John Hendrick is found among them.

[5] This restriction caused Pennsylvania a certain disadvantage as compared with the government of Maryland, which gave out land without scruples concerning the rights of the Indians.

others, who had lived on the east bank of the river, followed and set up their habitations to the west and south of John Hendrick's farm. Whether John Hendrick was German or not is an open question, but those whom he drew after him were in all events almost exclusively Germans. Tobias Frey, Caspar Spangler, Henry Hendricks, Peter Gardener, Valentine Heyer, Martin Schultz—these are the names of a few of those who began to settle the Kreutz Creek Valley from 1730 on.[6]

At the same time, Maryland settlers pushed their way northward into this region, led by one of the most stubborn defenders of the Calvert land claims, Thomas Cresap.[7] Both sides now determined that the moment had come to confirm the legality of their claims through speedy occupation of the land. Thus it was that the government in Annapolis as well as that in Philadelphia began to encourage settlers to move into the disputed land. Each settler sent by one side was considered a living proof that the other side was wrong. A conflict soon became unavoidable.

One of the German pioneers in Kreutz Creek Valley was Michael Tanner. He was a Mennonite from Mannheim, Germany, who had been in America since 1727 and in the territory west of the Susquehanna, which was claimed by Maryland, since 1734. In 1736 he was attacked by a group of Marylanders (probably some of Thomas Cresap's following), taken to Annapolis and held there in prison for a while. Nor was his case unique. Another German, Balthasar Spangler from the Palatinate, who had settled in the disputed territory in 1733, was forced off his farm by Cresap in order to make room for one of the latter's own protégés. The same fate met Frederick Ebert, who had cleared and broken a piece of land. He was driven from it one year later by Cresap. Ffelty Shults, likewise a German, took it over. Another German had settled here and had had no dealings with the Pennsylvanians at all; on Cresap's urging he immediately took out a land grant from Maryland.

Events gradually became too exciting and adventurous to suit the

[6] Between 1733 and 1736 fifty-two licenses were issued for the west bank of the Susquehanna, almost all to Germans. They were, to be sure, only the above-mentioned temporary or so-called "Bluntston licences," which still lacked official confirmation. Wentz, York, 62.

[7] Matthew P. Andrews, *Tercentenary History of Maryland*, 1, 430 ff. Lawrence C. Wroth, "The Story of Thomas Cresap, A Maryland Pioneer," *Maryland Hist. Mag.*, IX (1914), 1-37. Kenneth P. Bailey, *Thomas Cresap, Maryland Frontiersman* (Boston, 1944).

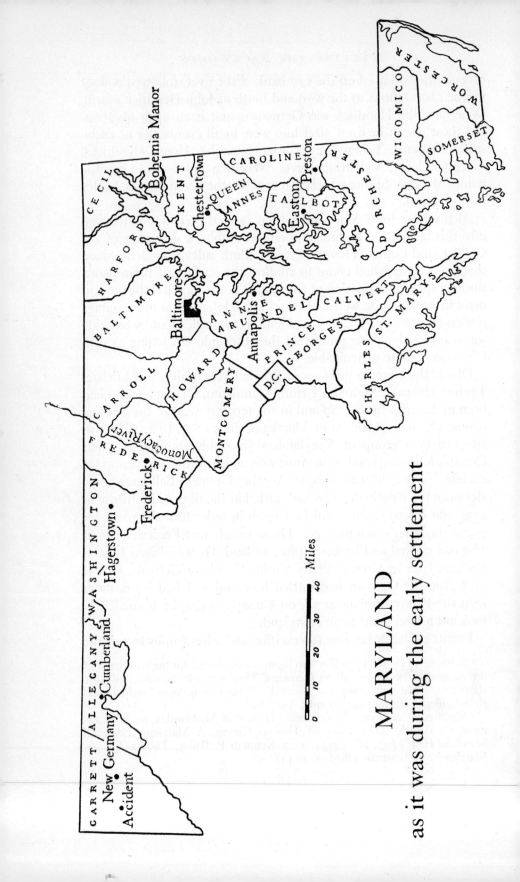

MARYLAND

as it was during the early settlement

taste of the German settlers. They were solid, peaceful farmers who desired well-defined and orderly conditions rather than this eternal quarreling and bickering over latitude and boundaries. Thomas Cresap, who loved the thrill and danger of his business and who appeared "with three hundred men in Arms . . . with Drums and Trumpets . . . to Strike Terror into the Inhabitants,"[8] was not the man to win the Germans for Maryland. The gentle Quaker spirit of the people in Philadelphia offered more hope of peace and order. The settlers came together, therefore, in August 1736 to write a letter to the governor of Maryland. "The Oppression and ill Usage We have met with from the Government of Maryland, or at least from such Persons who have been empovered thereby . . ." is the reason why "We therefore the Subscribers with many Others Our Neighbours being become at last truly sensible of the Wrong we have done the Proprietors of Pensilvania in settling on their Lands without paying Obedience to their Government do resolve to return to Our Duty and live under the Laws and Government of Pensilvania, in which Province we believe Ourselves seated."[9] Two days later they sent a similar petition to Philadelphia, where they were accepted in good standing by the Council and encouraged in their loyalty to Pennsylvania.

Thus began what has come in the history of Maryland to be called "The Revolt of the Germans."[10] Maryland authorities naturally refused to be cast aside by this letter, and charged the sheriff of Baltimore County to exact the taxes due or to arrest the rebellious citizens.[11] The fifty-six settlers involved in the uprising were mentioned by name in an order of arrest, which the Council of Maryland issued in October 1736, "for contriving signing and publishing a

[8] *MA*, xxxx, 128.

[9] *MA*, xxviii, 100. This letter makes it possible for us to reckon the number of German settlers in the disputed territory. The document published in the *Maryland Archives* bears only twenty-two signatures—certainly only a part of the settlers. In the unpublished Calvert Papers (No. 17), however, is a copy of the letter bearing fifty-six signatures. These fifty-six names are published in the Appendix of Wentz, *York*, 203. The original was sent to London and added to the evidence concerning the boundary dispute. There it was lost.

[10] Louis P. Hennighausen, "Die Revolte der Deutschen gegen die Regierung von Maryland," *SHGM*, iii (1889), 45 ff.

[11] *MA*, xxviii, 102 and 106. Rewards were even offered for the arrest. This measure had the desired result, for shortly thereafter a certain sum was paid out to Charles Higginbotham and several other men who had seized twenty-two of the settlers named on the warrant. *Ibid.*, 122.

seditious Paper and Writing against his Lordship and this Government."[12]

In this entire affair the problem revolved not so much about the German settlers as about the claims against Pennsylvania. Annapolis therefore followed the policy of placing the guilt, not on the German settlers, but rather on the government of Pennsylvania and on its agents. This is clear from a report which the governor of Maryland sent to the King of England in the year 1737: "That several Germans and Palatines being arrived some time ago in these Parts of your Majestys Dominions in America made their Applications and requests to this Government for the Liberty of Seating and Settling with their Families on Lands within this Provs which desires this Government not only thought reasonable but the People so deserving Encouragment that several Considerable Quantities of Land lying on the Borders of this Province adjoyning to the Province of Pennsylvania were allotted and Assigned them for their Residence and Support under the Authority of this Government & accordingly not less then fifty or sixty families of that nation immediatly took Possession of these Lands and paid their Proportion of the Taxes and demeaned themselves in every other Respect as Peacable subjects to your Majesty and unquestionable Inhabitants and Tenants of this Province until very Lately when through Unwariness and too much Credulity they suffered themselves to be prevailed on by the Emmissarys of Pennsylvania under Pretence of more than ordinary advantages to renounce openly their Submission to this Government & to declare their Resolution to transfer their Obedience to the Government of Pennsylvania. . . ."[13]

Although the displeasure of the government in Annapolis was directed more toward the Pennsylvania authorities than against the German settlers, it was naturally the latter who suffered directly in this conflict. It was impossible to remain neutral, and thus impossible to avoid running afoul the one side or the other. John Hendricks, for example, had for a short time lodged on his farm these Marylanders who were moving against the Kreutz Creek settlement; scarcely had they left when he was seized by the Pennsylvanians and thrown into the Lancaster County jail. The same fate overtook several other Germans, whom a fellow countryman, John Lochman, tried to free from the Lancaster jail. Four Germans who had sided with Pennsylvania—Michael Tanner, Conrad Strickler,

[12] MA, xxviii, 107.   [13] MA, xxxx, 113.

Henry Bacon and Jacob Welshover—were arrested by men from Maryland and imprisoned in Annapolis. Armed bands terrorized the region; many families had to abandon their homes temporarily; men were sitting for weeks in a Pennsylvania or a Maryland prison, some even lost their lives in the attacks.[14]

The quarrel came to a temporary end when on August 18, 1737, the King commanded the governments of Pennsylvania and of Maryland to allocate no more land in the disputed territory, and to wait until a final boundary ruling had been made.[15]

Incidents similar to those on Kreutz Creek occurred at the same time somewhat farther west, on the disputed boundary in the region that now forms the southwestern tip of York County, Pennsylvania.[16] This land too was settled by Germans, as is still evidenced today by names such as Manheim, Heidelberg, Marburg, Sinsheim. In contrast to the Kreutz Creek settlement, however, these communities were under the protection of Maryland from the very first. John Digges, a wealthy Irishman from Prince George's County, Maryland, had obtained an extensive tract of land here, entered in the *Acts* under the title, "Digges' Choice in the Back Woods." Digges then went over to the other side of the Susquehanna, praised his land loudly, much to the annoyance of the Pennsylvania authorities, and actually persuaded quite a number of the settlers to return with him back across the river and settle there.

The earliest purchase of land on "Digges' Choice" was made in 1731, according to the *Acts*, by Adam Forney, from the Palatinate. He bought the ground where the business section of Hanover, Penn-

[14] Wentz, *York*, 66 ff.

[15] As early as 1732 the two Proprietors had agreed to have the boundary surveyed again. A boundary line was then drawn, and mutually accepted, fifteen miles south of the southernmost tip of Philadelphia. Lord Baltimore, however, soon broke this treaty, whereupon he was sued by the Penns. In 1750 the suit was decided in favor of the Penns, and Baltimore was ordered to abide by his agreement. Since the tormented settlers on both sides of the boundary had meanwhile been sending out steady cries for help, the King had ordered the establishment of the "temporary line of 1739." It ran fourteen and one-fourth miles south of Philadelphia to the east bank of the Susquehanna, and fourteen and three-fourths miles south of Philadelphia to the west bank of the Susquehanna. Only gradually was an agreement reached in London concerning the execution of the new arrangement. In 1763 two experienced surveyors were finally sent to America—Charles Mason and Jeremiah Dixon. The result of their labors was the line drawn in 1767 and still maintained today—the Mason-Dixon Line.

[16] Wentz, *York*, 69 ff.

sylvania, now stands.[17] Andrew Schreiber settled four miles away in 1734. He too was under Maryland jurisdiction, for he bought the land, 100 acres for 100 pairs of Negro shoes, from the Marylander John Digges.[18] Other Germans from Pennsylvania soon followed suit and took over land on "Digges' Choice in the Back Woods"— David Jung, John Lemmon, Michael Will, Ludwig Schreiber, Peter Zarich, Martin Kitzmiller, Peter Jungblut, Matthias Merker, Peter Welby, William Oler, Jacob Banker, Peter Reisher, George Evenaar, Herman Updegraf, Peter Schultz, Matthias Ulrich, Peter Ensminger, Martin Brin, Martin Ungefare, to mention some of the German settlers who by the end of the thirties had moved onto this land claimed by Maryland.

They had all left their old country because they wanted to till their farms in peace and quiet. It was their misfortune, however, to choose the "disputed land," and thus to find themselves caught in the hot rivalry of the Calvert and Penn claims.

John Digges was a man of somewhat doubtful honor. His titles to the land that he had sold to the Germans were vague and not entirely unobjectionable, as his buyers soon realized. They wanted unequivocal terms, and repeatedly asked Digges to have the limits of his land officially surveyed and marked. The more stubbornly Digges refused, the more suspicious the settlers became. In 1743 they sent one of their own number, Martin Updegraf, to Annapolis to get a certified copy of Digges' charter.[19] It immediately became evident that Digges had sold far more land than he rightfully possessed. Digges hastened to obtain a tardy title to the land that he had already sold, but that was not so simple. The royal edict, which had caused the temporary line of 1739 to be drawn, specified that, although the land in the disputed territory which was already under ownership should remain under ownership, no more might be sold. After Digges had vainly sought to find a *modus vivendi* with the authorities in Philadelphia, he nevertheless succeeded in persuading

[17] Adam Forney was a tailor from Wachenheim in der Haardt. It is possible that his ancestors were French Huguenots who had fled to Germany after the lifting of the Edict of Nantes. His German Certificate of Dismissal is reproduced in English translation in *The Forney Family, 1690-1893*, 2 ff. He arrived in Pennsylvania with his wife and four children in 1721.

[18] Andrew Schreiber was also from the Palatinate, born in 1712 in Alstenborn. He is an ancestor of Admiral Winfield Scott Schley. See *The Shriver Family, 1684-1888*, by Samuel S. Shriver.

[19] Wentz, *York*, 79 ff.

the Land Office in Annapolis to grant him enough new land (3679 acres) to round out his previous holdings. This warrant of 1745 was contrary to the royal edict, but Digges interpreted the whole action as merely a resurvey and reorganization of his old and original possessions. The situation was further complicated by the fact that John Digges' new grant included the plantations of fourteen Germans who had settled under warrants from Pennsylvania and outside Digges' original land. Material for a conflict was at hand.

From Philadelphia and from Annapolis alike, attempts were made to intimidate the settlers. Thomas Cookson, the surveyor from Lancaster County, Pennsylvania, appeared and warned against violation of the royal command. Scarcely was he out of sight when Thomas Norris, deputy sheriff of Baltimore County, came to arrest two of the German settlers on the disputed land, Matthias Ulrich and Nicholas Forney, because they had not fulfilled their agreements with John Digges. On the way back the sheriff stopped at the house of Adam Forney, Nicholas' father. The elder Forney interfered and advised Matthias Ulrich and his son they should go to their homes and tell the sheriff to go to the devil, since they had bought their land from Pennsylvania and not from Maryland. A minor battle developed, with the result that the sheriff and his two assistants leaped onto their horses and made haste for Maryland. A few weeks later, however, another sheriff came with six armed men, who took the elder Forney to Baltimore and threw him in prison on the charge of resisting the officers of the law. Although he was treated rather roughly in prison, the sentence cannot have been too harsh, for not much later we find Adam Forney back home again.[20]

The German settlers in the "disputed land" left nothing untried. In 1747 they sent a petition to the surveyor of Lancaster County, and in 1749 another to the governor of Pennsylvania, in which they most urgently asked for speedy protection and help. Affairs nevertheless remained unsettled for the next few years, and the deeds of violence did not decrease. Not until after a tragic incident in 1752 did the hot tempers on both sides begin to cool off a little. When John Digges was trying to enforce his claims against one of the farmers, Martin Kitzmiller, the dispute again led to blows and finally to the death of Dudley Digges, son of the elder Digges. Pennsylvania decided that the land on which the struggle had occurred had belonged to Pennsylvania at the time of the royal decree (1739), and that, therefore,

[20] *Ibid.*, 83.

the Kitzmillers would have to be tried for the shooting in York. Naturally the trial evolved much more favorably for the Kitzmillers in York than would have been the case in Annapolis. Digges' claims on the land were doubtful, and the shot that had cost Dudley Digges' life was apparently an accident and not premeditated murder; the Kitzmillers were freed by the court in York. The only positive result of this occurrence was that from now on both sides acted with more caution and less violence. At the same time it was finally agreed that all land north of the temporary line of 1739 should belong to Pennsylvania, even if it lay within that part of Digges' holdings supplemented by the "resurvey."

This decision contributed greatly to the creation of clarity and peace. Quarrels occasionally occurred, but they were of a minor nature. A quietus came only when the two Proprietors in England united in friendship in 1763, and when the Mason-Dixon Line drew an unequivocal demarcation in 1767. Only then did the settlements, both those on Kreutz Creek and those on Digges' Choice, begin to flourish vigorously. Before that time they had been an eternal apple of contention between the Penns and the Calverts. The German settlers on Kreutz Creek and on Digges' Choice had found themselves just at the most hotly contested point, where they had had to endure more than their share of the wearisome boundary dispute. Both sides had looked upon them as a sort of buffer against an unfriendly neighbor, and probably no one greeted the Penn-Calvert peace as joyfully as the German settlers. Since all official connections between the Germans and Maryland were severed in 1767, and since we, too, intend to respect the Mason-Dixon Line, we leave them here and turn back to the real and uncontested territory of Maryland.[21]

In a valley some fifty miles southwest of Digges' Choice, on land belonging beyond any doubt to Maryland, we find the first mass settlements of Germans in the state. Their history, which we shall now record, ran from the very first a peaceful and happy course.

In spite of the fact that settlers who were willing to make their homes in the hinterland of the Calvert Colony obtained land under much more favorable conditions than the settlers along the coast, the western part of Maryland remained completely unopened during

[21] Reference is again made to Wentz's book for further information concerning the development of the settlements.

the first century of the colony's existence.[22] The history of Western Maryland begins with the year 1732.

In the neighboring state of Virginia similar problems existed with regard to the settlement of the inland regions. Here, too, attempts were made to lure settlers to the west. In 1714 twelve German and Swiss-German families, forced by adverse circumstances to leave North Carolina, had settled on the Rappahannock River in Virginia. A few years later they were augmented by twenty more German families, who had come directly from Germany. Germanna was the name of the colony, located where Spottsylvania County lies today. Since they failed in their efforts to make a thriving business of the newly founded iron industry, the settlers scattered over the surrounding territory and soon settled on the eastern slopes of the Blue Ridge. Toward the end of the twenties a German moved down from Pennsylvania into the Shenandoah Valley, and succeeded in drawing a few of his former friends and neighbors after him. Soon there was quite a group of German- and Pennsylvania-Dutch settlers in the northwestern corner of Virginia.

The settling was accelerated when various land speculators became interested in the region. In 1730 two Hollanders, John and Isaac Van Meter, obtained land grants in the Shenandoah to the extent of 40,000 acres. With the land they accepted the obligation of persuading forty families to move onto it within two years. As soon as they had signed the contract, they went to Pennsylvania to find settlers.[23]

In Colebrook Valley in eastern Pennsylvania lived a German named Jost Hite (probably originally Heyd or Heydt). He lived close to the unprotected boundary and was exposed to continual attacks by the Indians. In 1728 he and seventy-five other German settlers in the valley had turned to the government of Pennsylvania for protection against the Indians. The Quakers, however, preferred

[22] Clarence P. Gould, *The Land System in Maryland, 1720-1765* (Baltimore, 1913), 12. "Now that we are about Lycening our People, to make Remote Settlemts, we must likewise use the Proper Measures to protect them," writes Philemon Lloyd, judge of the Land Office, in 1722 (Calvert Papers, No. 2, 57). He alludes here to the uncertain state of affairs between the government of Maryland and the Indians concerning the legal title to the hinterland.

[23] For the immigration of Germans into Virginia, cf. the excellent book by John Walter Wayland, *The German Element of the Shenandoah Valley of Virginia* (Charlottesville, Va., 1907) 33 ff., and Herrmann Schuricht, *History of the German Element in Virginia* (Baltimore, 1900), I, 84 ff.

to suffer an injustice rather than to oppose force with force. Since his petition had remained unanswered, Jost Hite decided to take his numerous family and move on. In 1731 he bought a large piece of land that the Van Meter brothers had offered him in the Shenandoah Valley.

The settling of Pennsylvania had proceeded in a southwesterly direction, and had reached the Susquehanna by 1720. Here it had halted for a time, before it began hesitantly to cross the broad river. Only step by step had the settlers penetrated into the wilderness of Western Maryland. Now, with Jost Hite as the first man to accept the Meters' offer and strike out for Virginia, the movement became more pronounced. The Maryland wilderness lost some of its terror as it came to be viewed only as land to pass through on the way to the Virginia valley that was described in such glowing colors by the Meter brothers. Jost Hite did not have to strike out alone. The families of his three sons-in-law moved with him in 1732, along with twelve other families. He did not stop here. Following the example of the resourceful Meter brothers he obtained, together with a Scottish friend, no less than 100,000 acres of land. Then he went back north and persuaded some of the German settlers in Pennsylvania and New Jersey to move on to Virginia and acquire farms there. In 1733 the Meter brothers had obtained their necessary forty families. They drew others after them, and now began an unending stream of settlers, mostly Germans, flowing in a southwestern direction. All passed over an old Indian trail, the Monocacy Road, which led from Pennsylvania through Western Maryland to Virginia.

The government of Maryland followed the migration into the back country with great interest and no little envy. These land-hungry Germans moving over the Monocacy Road to the south were just the sort of people who were needed for Maryland. What if they could be induced to stay in Maryland, rather than to move on to Virginia?

Thus it was that, in March 1732, Lord Baltimore issued a proclamation that was, to be sure, valid for all newcomers in the province, but was unquestionably drawn up with an eye on the German migration between Pennsylvania and Virginia. "Wee being Desirous to Increase the Number of Honest people within our Province of Maryland and willing to give Suitable Encouragement to such to come and Reside therein Do offer the following Terms," so the document begins.[24] In brief, Lord Baltimore's suggestion was as follows. Any family that would arrive within the next three years and promise to settle in Maryland "on any of the back Lands on the Northern or Western Boundarys of our said province" should receive two hundred acres of land of their own choosing, completely free for three years; from the fourth year on they should pay a rent of one cent per acre per year. Moreover, "We doe Assure all such that they shall be as well Secured in their Liberty & property in Maryland as any of his Majesty's Subjects in any part of the British Plantations in America." This last statement had the purpose of assuring the people, together with the liberal offer of land, of at least as great advantages, if not greater, in Maryland than they could hope to find in Pennsylvania and Virginia. The proclamation was disseminated as rapidly as possible among the German settlers in Pennsylvania, and among those who were already on the move.

Lord Baltimore's offer had the desired result. Things could scarcely be better in the Shenandoah Valley, decided the Pennsylvania Dutch who were traveling over the Monocacy Road. They looked about them. The land appeared good, with its hills, streams and woods. It almost reminded them of their German homeland in the Palatinate, left so many years ago. They decided to accept Lord Baltimore's offer. They unpacked their wagons and forgot to move on to Virginia. In the first year, 1732, there were certainly no more than a half dozen families, but in the next and the following years came others. Each new family brought two or three more.

About this time, interest in the back country along the Monocacy River was increasing more and more in Maryland. The land speculators in particular scented the dawn of a new day. Within a short time they had obtained great stretches of land in Western Maryland; indeed, the authorities had to intervene to prevent the worst abuses. At the beginning of the thirties repeated complaints arose that land speculators were retarding the development of the back country. These men took out thousands of acres, not because they wished to cultivate them, but rather because they wished to hold them until they could sell under the most favorable conditions. They were in no hurry to survey the land that they possessed on paper; on the contrary, they insisted that no land should be surveyed in the districts in question until they had made their choice. This uncertainty concerning boundaries and ownership, along with the

[24] MA, xxviii, 25-26.

increase in the price of land through speculation, made Maryland most unpopular as a place for settling until about 1730.[25] "The said Practises have had this further Mischievous Effects," ran the report in 1732 of a committee in the Land Office which had investigated the situation on the Monocacy, "that several People who would have come from other parts and taken up some of the said back Lands and Settled on them, have rather Chosen and Settled in Virginia and Other places, than Involve themselves in Disputes, of which they could not have Easily to see an End."[26] This report clearly refers to the Pennsylvania Dutch migrating southward.

When the first two Labadists came to Maryland in 1679, they wrote in their diary: "The lives of the planters in Maryland and Virginia are very godless and profane. They listen neither to God nor his commandments."[27] We shall not try to decide whether or not the gloomy and morose Labadists saw things a little blacker than they were. Be that as it may, they would probably not have received so unfavorable an impression of the Pennsylvania Dutch in Western Maryland. The settlers who were driving their plowshares into the land along the Monocacy Road were a pious people. It makes no difference whether they had left their homes for religious or for other reasons: the Christian motive is the most important element of their character. The property that they carried with them was limited to absolute necessities; and yet—for these they considered absolute necessities—they had brought with them from Germany to Pennsylvania and from Pennsylvania to Maryland their great heavy Bibles, their song books and their prayer books. Each family possessed a copy of Johann Arndt's *Wahres Christentum* ("True Christianity") and a copy of the catechism, either the Lutheran or the Heidelberg edition according to whether they were Lutheran or Reformed. As soon as they were past the most difficult beginnings, they erected a school to educate their children in the Christian belief. A little later they built a church and commenced to look about for someone who could preach to them the word of God. The days of these early settlers were filled with the struggle against a wilderness of virgin forest, but the little free time that remained was devoted to the church and the community. If we read the church

[25] Gould, *Land System*, 63. Speaking of the time before 1730, Gould says: "No one seems to have appreciated the value of the labor of hard-working German farmers as contrasted with the more easy-going Marylanders" (p. 55).
[26] *MA*, xxxvii, 505.   [27] *Danckaerts Journal*, 135.

histories of these early colonies, we have an almost complete picture of their entire lives. The church records of the Germans in Western Maryland, therefore, furnish our principal source of information for the early period.

An estimated two-thirds of the Pennsylvania-Dutch settlers were Lutheran and one-third was Reformed. This fact immediately caused a certain difficulty. Maryland was a British colony and had a state church legally established and subsidized by the government, the Anglican or Episcopal Church. Each inhabitant of the province, whether a member of the official Church or not, had been forced since 1692 to pay a yearly tax of forty pounds of tobacco as a contribution toward the support of the Episcopal Church. The Anglicans represented a religious minority in the state, and this law was naturally very unpopular among the other denominations. The ruling should have applied automatically to the newly immigrated members of the German Lutheran and Reformed Churches; but the provincial government was so eager to make things as easy as possible for the settlers in Western Maryland that they did not enforce the law in this territory for many years. The German settlers were in this respect in a far better situation than their countrymen in the Shenandoah Valley in Virginia.

Troubles did not arise from the attitude of the colonial government, but they did develop from the disorganized state of the Lutheran and Reformed Churches in America. Once the settlers had built a simple church with great sacrifice and effort, their real problem began: where to find a pastor. The often vain and fruitless efforts of the congregations to find a regular pastor lasted for decades, but no failure seemed to discourage them.

Most active were the Lutherans, to which group most of the newcomers belonged.[28] At first they had taken turns in having members of the church read aloud to the best of their ability from the great German Bible. As early as the second year, however, the first Lutheran minister came to the Monocacy settlement: John Caspar Stoever. He was descended from a family of theologians in the Pa-

---

[28] We cite here the book, *The Lutheran Church of Frederick, Maryland, 1738-1938* (Lancaster, Pa., 1939), by Abdel Ross Wentz, who has studied the old church records with extreme care. It is one of the most dependable volumes on the history of Western Maryland. In discussing the Lutherans in Frederick we have followed Wentz's book extensively, even though specific indication is not always given in footnotes.

latinate, and had reached America in 1728 at the age of twenty-one.[29]
At first he had worked in Philadelphia, but gradually he extended his
sphere of activity to minister to scattered Lutherans living in Montgomery and Lancaster counties and even in a few localities in New
Jersey. When he took a trip in 1734 to visit his father, who was
preaching the word of God to German Lutherans in Virginia, he
passed through the Monocacy settlement in Virginia. On the journey
down he paused only briefly, but on the way back he stopped somewhat longer. It chanced to be a Sunday. Since it was commonly
known that he would be present, the settlers had gathered together
almost to a man on this twenty-third of June 1734, when young John
Caspar Stoever held the first German-Lutheran services on the banks
of the Monocacy. There was no church; the services and communion
apparently took place in a hayloft. On the same day Stoever performed the first Lutheran baptism in the settlement. The name of
the first child taken into the Christian Church in Maryland in a
German ceremony was Anna Margaretha Matthias. The father, John
Jacob Matthias,[30] had come with his wife from the Palatinate to Philadelphia in 1733, and had immediately migrated on to the Monocacy
settlement. His name occurs several times in the history of the
Lutheran community on the Monocacy.

From that time on Pastor Stoever came down every year from his
home in Earltown, Pennsylvania, to preach and to baptize among
the people on the Monocacy. In November 1738 he undertook a
second trip, in addition to his regular spring visit. The second trip
was especially significant, because on this occasion Stoever formed
the Lutherans on the Monocacy into a real congregation.[31] He was
not an organizer by nature, else he would probably not have waited
so long to take this step. However, he had seen on his journey that
the Moravians and other sects were living all about, and he wished to
forestall their influence. Thus he remained somewhat longer than
usual this time, preaching, marrying, baptizing, visiting the scattered
homes of the people. Finally, on Sunday, November 26, 1738, he

[29] R. B. Strassburger and W. J. Hinke, *Pennsylvania German Pioneers,*
Lists of Arrivals (Norristown, Pa., 1934), I, 22. Roy L. Winters, "John Caspar
Stoever, Lutheran Pioneer," *Lutheran Church Quarterly,* XVIII (1945),
285-96.

[30] The name appears in various forms: Matthews, Mathisis, Mathes, Mat-
theis, Mateas.

[31] The question of the exact historical beginning of the congregation has
been thoroughly investigated by A. R. Wentz, 46 ff.

held communion in a hayloft on the west bank of the Monocacy River, and subsequently conducted the election of several of the best-fitted members as deacons. The deacons were to mold the people together into a simple organization and to insure the smooth progress of a community life undisturbed by sectarianism.

Five years after the formal founding of the congregation, a second decisive event occurred. The exact date is clearly determined by an entry in the oldest book of church records.[32] In April 1743 Pastor Stoever was replaced by Reverend David Candler. Candler worked in the community for only one year, but it was undoubtedly due to his energy that the building of the church was undertaken. The oldest church on the Monocacy was a simple log building. We have no picture of it, but doubtless it was constructed like all other log churches on the American frontier: a severe, square-cornered building, without a tower or bells or ornament of any kind, inside a plain room with benches and a pulpit. This "wooden church," as the patriarch Muehlenberg called it when he preached here a few years later, was raised by the members of the community within a few weeks.

Like his predecessor, Stoever, Pastor Candler lived in Pennsylvania and came down to the Monocacy only from time to time. When he died, toward the end of 1744, there happened here what had happened in many places, and what Stoever had intended to prevent through organizing the congregation: the Moravians appeared and brought dissension. A Swedish preacher, Lars Nyberg, whom the simplehearted farmers had accepted in good faith as the savior of their souls, was shortly unmasked as a disciple of Zinzendorf's. The community was divided. Although the larger half held fast to Lutheranism, a not inconsiderable part went over to Moravianism and founded a community of its own.

The old Lutheran parish grew restless. The deacons, unlettered laymen and naïve farmers, felt unequal to the mellifluent Moravian ministers and turned for help to what they considered the center of Lutheranism in America, The United Lutheran Ministers of Pennsylvania in Philadelphia. It was just at the time when the great organizer, Henry Melchior Muehlenberg, was beginning his work. He knew how to help the hard-pressed community on the Monocacy, and sent them the Reverend Gabriel Naesman, a Lutheran pastor

[32] Christian Henry Rauch, a Moravian preacher who visited the settlement in March 1746, speaks of having held services in the church on the Monocacy. *Virginia Magazine of History and Biography*, XI, 372 ff.

from Sweden who could preach also in German. Naesman's extended visit in October 1746 contributed greatly to strengthen the shaken congregation and to restore normal and peaceful conditions.

Naesman's visit has an especial significance for historians, for he initiated the first church book of the parish. The first entry was made on October 31, 1746. Beyond doubt this day, which commemorates the beginning of the Lutheran reformation, was purposely chosen. From then on the church records give us a running account of what happened in the settlement on the Monocacy. The records are written in German, as are all Lutheran and Reformed Church records in Western Maryland in the eighteenth century. On the back of the thick, leather-bound volume are inscribed the words GEMEINE MANNACKES ("Congregation of Monocacy"). At the beginning we find the names of the members who contributed to the cost of the book.[33]

The very first sentence in the church book reads: "On October 31st, 1746, I, Gabriel Naesman, pastor at Wicaco in Philadelphia, preached in this new town situated in Manachasi." What does "new town" mean?

Up to this point we have purposely made no mention of a town or village of Monocacy. There was no village by this name, only individual dwellings scattered along the Monacacy River. The Germans spread year by year southward, almost to the Potomac. From the south, from Annapolis and Baltimore, English and Irish pioneers moved into the valley and helped to settle its lower reaches.[34] Here, on Carroll Creek, three miles west of Monocacy, the first town was laid out in 1745 and named, after the son of Lord Baltimore, Frederick.[35] Many of the old German settlers were among the people who

[33] This brief list doubtless presents a sort of social register of the more prosperous settlers. For that reason the names are mentioned here: Henry Sinn, Adam Stoll, Matthew Roessler, Adam Spuch, Hans George Schweinhardt, Peter Apfel, Philip Kuntz, Dieter Lehnich, Balthasar Fauth, John Verdriess, Valentine Verdriess, Hans George Hutzel, Jacob Mateus, John George Goetz, Jacob Bene, Conrad Kuntz, Jost Schmidt, John Peter Apfel, John Taffelmeyer, George Honig, John George Gung, Jacob Fauth, Henry Verdriess.

[34] Our theme limits us to the German sector of the population. The impression must not be gained, however, that Western Maryland was settled solely by Germans. Let it be clearly stated that pioneers of Anglo-Saxon parentage contributed to the settling of the back countries, even though their function was less important here than in other parts of Maryland.

[35] The source of the name "Frederick" is contested. Apparently the name was chosen in honor of the proprietor's son Frederick, then a boy of twelve and later the last Lord Baltimore. Another possibility, that it was named for Frederick Lewis, son of King George II and then Prince of Wales, is not very

bought the first lots in the new town.[36] It was a German, Thomas Schley, who built the first stone house in Frederick.

At first the German Lutherans in the lower part of the valley went to the old log church, built in 1743; but the church was ten miles away, and regular attendance was difficult. Thus, the members of the parish in the southern part of the valley (around the new city of Frederick), built their own little log church in the city. They stayed in the old parish, and their records continued to be set down in the old church book; however, they were no longer forced to go ten miles through wind and weather for their Sunday devotions. The parish life was divided for a while between "the church in the hills" and the "church in the town."[37]

From this time on there were two communities and two churches, but still no resident pastor. It is not surprising that the naïve congregations fell prey more than once to vagabonds and swindlers who took advantage of their pious desire for spiritual guidance. There appeared one day, for example, a man who called himself simply Carl Rudolf, but who let it be understood that he was really the Prince of Wuerttemberg. He carried impressive documents with heavy seals, which proclaimed that he was a Lutheran minister; for a certain honorarium he would be in a position to lead the congregation and provide its members with spiritual bread. The good-natured people let him have his way for a time, but eventually it turned out that the "Prince of Wuerttemberg" was a thief and a drunkard. He had already inflicted himself on most of the German settlements between South Carolina and New Jersey, and a few

---

convincing. Even more improbable is the hypothesis that anyone intended thus to pay reverence to the Prussian King Frederick the Great. The Monocacy settlers were from the Palatinate, not from Prussia. Frederick the Great was, moreover, at that time no more popular than any other German prince. The use of Frederick, as the name for the new county to be founded, appears for the first time as early as 1742 (MA, xxxxii, 292). That was only two years after the Prussian king's accession to the throne, and the inhabitants of the virgin forest along the Monocacy had probably never heard of him. There is no need to be disquieted by the headlines in a Washington paper (*Times-Herald*, November 11, 1939): "Prussian King Gave Name to Frederick."

[36] The town of Frederick was laid out on a piece of land known as "Tasker's Chance." It had been taken out in 1727 by Benjamin Tasker, who sold it to Daniel Dulaney in 1744.

[37] *Die Kirche am Gebürge und die Kirche in der neuen Stadt Friedrichstawn.* Up to 1784 this distinction was maintained. After the names of the councilmen always appeared the designation *aus dem Gebüsch—aus der Stadt* ("from the woods or from the town"). Cf. Wentz, *Frederick*, 77.

years later he landed in jail—where he belonged. Shortly thereafter came another of these "ecclesiastical tramps," as Wentz aptly calls them, who introduced himself under the name of Schmid. He offered his services not only as a Lutheran minister, but also as a dentist and bloodletter. This versatility aroused the suspicion of the farmers, still smarting from their experience with Carl Rudolf, and they soon sent Schmid (also called Empiricus Schmid) hastily on his way. Help finally reached them from the place whence they most earnestly desired it—the United Ministers in Philadelphia. In the summer of 1747 Henry Melchior Muehlenberg,[38] the great organizer of Lutheranism in America, came down over the Monocacy Road to stop for a few days and bring comfort to the troubled parish.

Muehlenberg has left us a detailed account of this trip to Frederick, which took place under the most adverse physical conditions, and of his sojourn on the Monocacy.[39] Baptizing and preaching were not his most important activities. Far more significant was his giving the congregation its first constitution. He wrote it into the church records and had it signed by some of the members "in the woods." Then he carried the book ten miles upstream to have the constitution signed also "in the town."[40] There were now at last definite rules

[38] DAB, XIII, 310 ff. H. M. Muehlenberg (1711-1781) came from Hannover, Germany. He had studied theology and had been a teacher in H. A. Francke's orphans' home in Halle before he accepted a call from the Lutheran United Congregation in 1741. In 1742 he came to Philadelphia. Immediately, with uncommon skill and indefatigable zeal, he began to organize Lutheranism in Pennsylvania and the surrounding states. After various trips to eastern Pennsylvania, New Jersey and Maryland, he was able to hold the first convention of the Evangelical Lutheran Ministry in Philadelphia in 1748. The reports on his activities, which he sent to Halle, are a priceless source of information on the early history of the Germans in the Middle Atlantic States. Muehlenberg and his descendants later appear repeatedly in public affairs in the United States. In 1779 one of his sons, Frederick, was Speaker of the First Congress of the United States.

[39] Nachrichten von Vereinigten Deutschen Evangelisch-Lutherischen Gemeinen in Nord America, absonderlich in Pennsylvania, 2 vols. (Halle, 1787), reprinted by Mann and Schmucker (Allentown, Pa., 1886, and Philadelphia, 1895), I, 352 ff. (cited from now on simply as Hallesche Nachrichten). An English translation of Muehlenberg's report on his journey to Maryland is to be found in Wentz, Frederick, 82 ff. The report vividly portrays the difficulties of such a missionary trip. The great distances and the primitive conditions of the country made the most rigorous demands upon the pastor. Johann Mittelberger, who in the middle of the eighteenth century published a book about his trip to Pennsylvania, says that the land was a paradise for farmers and laborers but a hell for horses and preachers! (Mittelberger, 11 and 50.)

[40] The constitution is quoted verbatim, with all signatures, in Wentz, Frederick, 90 ff.

for the eventual installation of pastors. If the constitution were followed, affairs such as those involving the pastors Nyberg, Rudolf and Schmid would henceforth be impossible.

The most notable point about this constitution is that it was written in English. Everything else in these first church records was in German. The choice shows Muehlenberg's keen foresight; he seemed to sense that English would soon be the official language of the new land. Even at the moment, however, the English constitution was advantageous for the German settlers. Most of them did not yet know enough English to deal with the authorities except through translators. If trouble were to arise for the German community on the Monocacy, they had only to show the Annapolis authorities their English constitution in order to clarify the situation.

At the end of the first paragraph we read: ". . . and the reformed Congregation shall have liberty for their lawfull minister." We are here reminded that we must not forget the other Germans for the sake of the Lutherans. The German population on the Monocacy at the time of Muehlenberg's visit (1747) is estimated at around a thousand.[41] The majority was undoubtedly Lutheran. Except for the Moravians, who did not really become numerous here until the second half of the century, we hear almost nothing of the various sects that sprang into such luxuriant growth among the Germans in Pennsylvania. Most of the non-Lutherans on the Monocacy may be reckoned as members of the Reformed Church.

In the same year when Henry Melchior Muehlenberg was helping the Lutherans to forge their congregation more solidly together, Michael Schlatter, the famous organizer of the Reformed Church of America, came to Frederick.[42] "In the 6th of May 1747, I journeyed to Monocacy, where, on the following day, I held preparatory service

[41] T. J. C. Williams, *History of Frederick County, Maryland* (Frederick, Md., 1910), I, 5.

[42] *DAB*, XVI, 435. Michael Schlatter was a German Swiss, born in St. Gallen in 1716. He placed himself at the disposal of the Reformed Synod of Holland for the work in Pennsylvania, and was sent to America in 1746. Here he started out on a vigorous and many-faceted career. First he organized the existing churches of Pennsylvania into a synod under the supervision of the Reformed Church of Holland. This Pennsylvania Synod, the "Coetus" of the Reformed Congregation of Pennsylvania, consisted of four ministers and twenty-eight elders. Next Schlatter began to weld together the widely scattered Reformed congregations, and undertook long journeys to the more distant sections of Pennsylvania, Maryland, Virginia and New Jersey. The forty-six communities that he found in these districts were formed into sixteen pastoral charges. Lack of ministers was the greatest problem to be faced.

to the Holy Communion and baptized twenty-six children, and, on the 8th, administered the most excellent Supper of the Lord, with peculiar interest and much edification, to eighty-six members. After divine service was ended, I read my instructions to the people. The congregation, anxious after spiritual food, listened with tears of joy and with gratitude to God, and forty-nine heads of families at once offered to raise for the support of a minister, in money and grain, the amount of forty pounds."[43] This is the first extant statement that we have on the members of the Reformed Church in Western Maryland.

The members of the Reformed Church were not so numerous as their Lutheran countrymen, and their church developed correspondingly more slowly. We know nothing of ministers or services before Schlatter's visit of 1747. Probably the congregation was permitted to share the first Lutheran log church. Perhaps they also held their meetings in some large barn, where someone read a selection from the Bible or from the Heidelberg Catechism. We may suppose that this office usually devolved upon the schoolmaster, Thomas Schley,[44] one of the most active and outstanding men of the settlement, of whom Michael Schlatter wrote: "It is a great advantage to this congregation that they have the best schoolmaster that I have met in America. He spares neither labor nor pains in instructing the young and edifying the congregation according to his ability, by means of singing, and reading the word of God and printed sermons in every Lord's day."[45]

Thomas Schley had landed in America in 1735 with about one

[43] Henry Harbaugh, *Life of Michael Schlatter* (Philadelphia, 1857), 154 ff. Schlatter's diary was first published in Dutch (Amsterdam, 1751), then in German (Frankfurt, 1752). Henry Harbaugh included an English translation into his Schlatter biography; however, his translation deviates very often from the original text. A more conscientious translation was prepared and edited by William J. Hinke in the *Journal of the Presbyterian Historical Society* (Philadelphia, 1905), III, iii, 105 ff. This, however, is only the beginning of Schlatter's diary; the publication of this translation was never completed.

[44] Thomas Schley is the eponymous ancestor of the large and well-known Schley family of Maryland and Georgia. One of his descendants was Admiral Winfield Scott Schley, 1839-1909. (DAB, XVI, 437.)

[45] Harbaugh, *Schlatter*, 177. The first regular minister of the Reformed Church, Th. Frankenfeld, also praised Thomas Schley's activity. (*Minutes and Lettres of the Coetus of the German Reformed Congregation in Pennsylvania, 1742-1792.* Philadelphia, 1903, p. 74. Cited henceforth simply as *Minutes and Lettres*).

hundred Palatinate families. Since his name appears in none of the Pennsylvania ship rosters, he may be presumed to have been one of the first to land in Annapolis or Alexandria, rather than to have come over the previously customary route across Pennsylvania. It was probably due to his good religious discipline that the Reformed congregation, although without a minister, passed intact through the early decades of its existence. On his first visit, Michael Schlatter paid it unlimited praise: "I must say of this congregation that it appears to me one of the purest in the whole country, and one in which I found the most traces of the true fear of God; one that is free from the sects of which in other places the country is filled."[46]

Besides Thomas Schley, Jacob Steiner may be mentioned as one of the first Reformed Germans on the Monocacy. His descendants were to play an important role in the later history of Maryland.[47]

We know nothing of itinerate Reformed ministers in the Monocacy settlement up to 1747. It is quite possible that the Lutheran ministers who served the Lutheran Monocacy community at first took the members of the Reformed Church also under their wing. The Reformed and the Lutheran congregations lived side by side in peace and tranquillity—a rare state in this century of orthodoxy and sectarianism. Disputes over dogma, elsewhere so hotly contested, seemed insignificant in this hard frontier life. The first child born in Frederick, after the city had been laid out in 1745, was Maria Barbara Schley, daughter of the schoolmaster who was the leader of the Reformed Church. He had no objection to having his child baptized by the Lutheran minister Naesman, who chanced to be present at the time.[48] A Reformed minister was not available, so what difference did it make? The child had to be taken into the Christian Church. Was one to be captious over petty points of dogma? When Muehlenberg came back to Frederick in 1758, while the Lutheran Church was still under construction, the Reformed congregation

[46] Harbaugh, Schlatter, 154.

[47] Jacob Steiner had immigrated to Philadelphia in 1731. He settled in Frederick County before 1736. Cf. Lewis H. Steiner and Bernard C. Steiner, The Genealogy of the Steiner Family (Baltimore, 1896).

[48] Wentz, Frederick, 66. Subsequently the baptism, which took place May 27, 1746, was entered also on the Reformed Church records. It is our first written monument of the community life of the German Reformed Church in Frederick. The first notices of baptism entered in the first church records are not in chronological order, for the first church record begins with the baptism of Elisabeth Stoll on February 6, 1747.

unhesitantly invited him to preach in their church, and he as un-hesitantly accepted.[49]

Michael Schlatter's visit gave new impetus to the Reformed Church. In 1748 the members built a log church on a piece of land given by Daniel Dulaney, the all-powerful landowner of Western Maryland.[50] Schlatter visited Frederick a second time (May 1748), while the church was still under construction. "On the 15th I preached in Fredericktown, in a new church, which is not yet fin-ished, standing behind a table upon which had been placed the holy covenant seals of Baptism and the Lord's Supper. After the sermon, I administered the Holy Supper to ninety-seven members, baptized several aged persons and children, married three betrothed couples and installed new elders and deacons."[51] Shortly after the building was completed, the first church book was procured. On its first page we read the inscription, *Johann Jacob Bruner kaufte dieses Schreib-buch für 50 Tr. in Frankfurt am Meyn, Anno 1749 d. 16 Aprile.* ("Johann Jacob Bruner bought this record book for 50 Tr. in Frank-furt a/M. on April 16, 1749.") No entries were made, however, until the first resident pastor was installed in 1753.

Three years after the founding of Frederick, the region along the Monocacy was divided from Prince George's and organized as a separate county. This indicates how astonishingly fast the settlement had developed. We have already mentioned the real-estate specula-tors who had secured great stretches of land in Western Maryland. Their greatest difficulty had originally been to find tenants for their properties. All had changed suddenly when the Germans began to flow into Western Maryland in the decades after 1730. They were the best customers the real-estate dealers could imagine—practiced farmers, hungry for land and ignorant of the English language and of the local laws. If they had had more money, they could have pur-chased their own land. Their financial straits forced them to settle first as renters, and thus to enter into a certain relation of depend-ency upon their landlords.

When Daniel Dulaney, one of the richest landowners in Western Maryland, initiated the venture of taking out considerable areas of land along the Monocacy, it was widely prophesied that his move

[49] *Ibid.*, 111. The great esteem paid to Muehlenberg is further attested by his having been invited to preach also in the Episcopal church in Frederick.

[50] The county court was for several years held in this building. Edward T. Schultz, *First Settlements of Germans in Maryland* (Frederick, Md., 1896), 8.

[51] Harbaugh, *Schlatter*, 176. Williams, *Frederick*, 6.

spelled financial ruin.[52] Only a few years later there was scarcely a rich man in Maryland who did not possess land in the west. Naturally, every effort was expended to attract new settlers. Charles Carroll, another landowner, once wrote: "Consider that I have paid Severall Sums out of my Pocket to persons who procured Tenants in particular to Mr. (Benjamin) Franklin I think about £7. Consider the many letters I have wrote on the occasion not only to people in this Province, but to Ireland and Germany with conditions on which I would Rent Lands."[53] Daniel Dulaney sent the Proprietor the copy of a letter which the Germans in Frederick—probably on Dulaney's instigation—had sent to their countrymen in the Palatinate, painting for them the glories of Maryland and urging them also to immigrate.[54]

Dulaney's relation to the Germans was at first simply that of landlord to renter, but gradually he began to take on the role of a patriarch. Financially he came to have a more and more personal interest in the German farmers in Frederick County, and we have various evidences that he more than once stood by them with generous assistance.

We have already mentioned that he gave the Reformed Church in Frederick the land on which it built its house of worship in 1748. Four years later the Lutherans also received a lot from him, with the stipulation that they raise a church on it within the next five years. It was again due to Daniel Dulaney that the Lutheran parish in Frederick finally, in 1752, obtained a permanent pastor.

Ever since Muehlenberg had given the parish its constitution, the Lutherans in Frederick had been visited by pastors only at irregular intervals. For a time the Reverend John Helfrich Schaum came down from York, Pennsylvania, a Hessian who had been raised in the orphans' asylum in Halle. Two itinerant preachers, Valentine Kraft and Christian Streiter, brought more unrest and confusion than spiritual leadership. In 1752 the first Lutheran resident pastor, the Reverend Bernhard Michael Hausihl, settled in the city.[55]

Hausihl came from Heilbronn, Germany. He had studied theology in Strassburg, and had been ordained in Holland. After marrying Sybilla Mayer, the daughter of a prominent citizen of Ulm, he emigrated with his father-in-law's family to America, landing in

---

[52] William Eddis, *Lettres from America* (London, 1792), 98 ff.
[53] Carroll Papers in the Maryland Historical Society (Box 38).
[54] MA, xxxiv, 697.   [55] Later the name is usually written "Houseal."

Annapolis in 1752. The father-in-law, Christopher Bartholomew Mayer, arrived with imposing letters of recommendation. No less than His Lordship "The Honble. Caecilius Calvert Esqr." had given him a letter from London addressed to Benjamin Tasker, President of the Maryland Council, reading as follows: "The bearer, Mr. Christopher Bartholomew Mayer, a gentleman from Germany inclining to visit the Province of Maryland, I am desired to give him a line on his arrival. Please therefore show him all civilitys and make the province agreeable to him during his stay."[56] Daniel Dulaney lived in Annapolis, where the Mayers landed. He persuaded the newcomers to settle in Frederick, and thus the Reverend Mr. Hausihl made his home there too.[57]

An indication of the degree to which the Lutheran parish in Frederick had become consolidated may be found in their building of a new church. The first log church had been built in 1743 on the Monocacy River. The second log church, which was raised by the Lutherans in Frederick in 1746, speedily became too small. When new life came into the community with the arrival of its first resident pastor, a decision was made to erect a larger and more enduring edifice of stone. As a matter of fact, this was not accomplished as easily as expected. The French and Indian War broke out, and Frederick became an important base of operations. Here George Washington met with Benjamin Franklin, General Braddock and Governor Sharpe. Fugitives appeared from the west, bringing disquiet and excitement. Not until 1759 could the building be continued. In 1762 the church was solemnly dedicated.[58] We have

---

[56] Williams, *Frederick*, I, 7.

[57] Christopher Bartholomew Mayer was born in 1702 in Durlach, Baden, but subsequently lived in Ulm. When he and his family left Ulm, he really intended to emigrate to Georgia. They were, however, detained for a year in Rotterdam, where his daughter married Hausihl. Since there were better prospects for a young Lutheran minister in Western Maryland than in Georgia, the Mayers changed their plans. Christopher Bartholomew Mayer, father of the Pennsylvania line of Mayers, died only six months after their arrival. Cf. Brantz Mayer, *Genealogy and Memoir of the Mayer Family* (Baltimore, 1878), 65 ff.; and F. B. Mayer, "Memoranda in Reference to Early German Immigrants to Maryland," *SHGM*, v, 15 ff.

[58] The names of those citizens who contributed to the building fund were inscribed in the church records. Here we find all the names of the most important German Lutheran families: Unselt, Haffner, Ringel, Kammerer, Specht, Kern, Hinkel, Sachs, Schmitt, Koenig, Bach, Buntsel, Jesserant, Kuntz, Appel, Lay, Kintzel, Grosch, Roemer, Burkhardt, Mayer, Lutz, Dannwolff, Müller, Spengler, Schreyack, Kruis, Böhm, Haas, Ankelberger, Witt-

precise information concerning the dedication ceremonies, since they were described in detail in the church records—not by Hausihl, who had accepted a call to Reading after seven years of service in Frederick, but by his successor, John Christopher Hartwick.[59] The communion celebrated on this occasion was partaken of by one hundred and seventy-five communicants, an unusually high number under the circumstances. The Lutheran parish was the largest of all the denominations in Frederick County.

The new church made it clear that the Lutheran congregation now gravitated about Frederick. The part of the congregation on the Monocacy "in the hills" became less and less significant and yearly smaller, until its remnants were finally absorbed by nearby Creagerstown. No building remains to remind us of the original parish; even the site of the first log church is no longer certain.

Difficulties with the ministers continued. The Reverend Mr. Hartwick, who had dedicated the church, had a wanderlust that never allowed him to be bound long to one place. He could have had more than one good position if he had been able to settle down. In Frederick, however, as elsewhere, he was not to be long retained. For a few years, the Reverend John Samuel Schwerdtfeger was invested with the Lutheran ministry, but he never succeeded in sustaining amicable relations with the synod in Pennsylvania. His activity in Frederick ended in 1768 "on account of various troubles."[60] Not until 1771, when the Reverend John Andrew Krug accepted the invitation of the congregation as presented through Muehlenberg, was the problem of a pastor solved for any length of time.

For the Reformed congregation, too, the advent of the first resident pastor was an occurrence of incisive importance. It was due to Michael Schlatter that a regular minister was obtained in 1753. He had gone back to Europe and told his fellow worshipers in Holland, Western Germany and Switzerland about the lack of

mann, Michael, Haucks, Gernhard, Sinn, Usselmann, Gertenhauer, Philipps, Hoff, Kinkele, Walter, Hoffmann, Spahn, Weichsel, Keller, Beder, Fleck, Weber, Rühl, Schott, Kreiger, Schaaf, Seidemann, Back, Zimmermann, Deter.

[59] Wentz, *Frederick*, 116 ff.

[60] Schwerdtfeger had emigrated from Germany without a penny to his name. When he arrived in Annapolis he was put up for sale by the ship owner for his fare. The Lutheran parish in York, Pennsylvania, had bought him on the auction block, obtaining his freedom by paying his passage.

ministers in America. His moving appeal, published in German and Dutch, was not without success; in 1752 he returned to America with six young Reformed ministers. One of them was Theodore Frankenfeld, who had been born in Western Germany and ordained in the Hague, and who was now sent to Frederick as pastor.[61] On May 4, 1753, he arrived, accompanied by Schlatter, and immediately took over the pulpit.[62] It is striking that in the church records he always entered only the day of baptism, never that of the birth of a child. Obviously he considered the spiritual birth far more important than the physical.

From this time on the Reformed parish was under the guidance of a regular resident pastor. We know comparatively little of Frankenfeld's activities; only once in the official minutes is an item entered concerning him, and that more of human than of religious interest. "Do. Frankenfeld is no less addicted to excessive drinking, so that we are afraid he will labor among his congregation with but little blessing if he does not change. We hope, and pray to God, he may change."[63] After 1755 his name no longer appears in the minutes, and in 1756 his entries in the church records cease. Apparently he died in that year; whether as a result of his "excessive drinking" or from other causes, we do not know.

His successor was John Conrad Steiner, a Swiss from Winterthur in Canton Zurich.[64] He had been in America since 1749, and had already gained some experience as a preacher in Lancaster, Germantown and Philadelphia before coming to Frederick. He stayed only three years, but they were strenuous years for him; aside from Frederick itself, he ministered to widely scattered Reformed settlements in Maryland, Pennsylvania and Virginia. The number of the communicants shows how quickly the parish grew: ninety-seven partook of the Lord's Supper administered by Michael Schlatter in 1748; when the Reverend Mr. Steiner conducted the Lord's Supper for his last time, eleven years later, there were one hundred and ninety-six. Steiner did not leave behind the most fortunate memories

[61] Henry Harbaugh, *Fathers of the German Reformed Church in Europe and America* (Lancaster, Pa., 1872), II, 93 ff.

[62] An original letter, which is pasted to the inside cover of the first church book, reports on Frankenfeld's arrival and the circle of his activities in his new post. The letter was published in *SHGM*, XXVI, 49.

[63] *Minutes and Lettres*, 102.

[64] Harbaugh, *Fathers*, 29 ff. Steiner was born in 1707 of a highly respected, influential family.

along the Monocacy, for the minutes cannot refrain from stating that, "Do. Steiner left Frederick with a heavy debt, altogether unseemly, and truly to the greatest offense of all since more favors were shown to him there, as all can testify, than he deserved."[65]

Steiner's successor was Philip William Otterbein.[66] He was born in 1726 in the little German town of Dillenburg in Nassau, and was one of those six young pastors who came to America with Schlatter in 1752. From Pennsylvania he went to Frederick, where he conducted the parish with much skill and energy from 1760 to 1765. In his first year in the pulpit work was begun, after the example of the Lutherans, on the construction of a more solid and spacious church. Again it was Daniel Dulaney who gave the land for the church and cemetery. The lumber from the old church was sold to Thomas Schley for ten pounds. For the new structure, each person gave his share in money or in labor.[67] The building was completed in 1764. In the official minutes of the Reformed Coetus the Reverend Mr. Otterbein received full recognition for his efforts: "In Frederick Do. Otterbein, in the last three years, has almost worked himself to death."[68] Shortly after the dedication of the church he left the parish, but we shall have cause to mention him again in our discussion of Baltimore.

About his successor, Carl Lange, who was in Frederick from 1766 to 1768, we know but little.[69] In the Reformed church books of Frederick we find as the most important fruits of these years a church constitution, recorded in 1767. We do not know whether its formulation was the consequence of a general reorganization after the completion of the new church building, or whether it originated from the personal efforts of the Reverend Mr. Lange. The Reformed constitution treats of approximately the same points as the Muehlenberg constitution of the Lutherans, but it is written in German. It is interesting to observe that the rationalistic, empirical spirit of the Age of Enlightenment had made itself felt even in the back-

[65] *Minutes*, 217. In Steiner's defense it must be said that the ministerial salary was so pitifully small that it must have driven anyone to contracting debts. For the rest, complaints against the not entirely irreproachable conduct of religious leaders in eighteenth-century Maryland were quite the order of the day. Conditions must have been worse among the official Anglican clergy.

[66] Harbaugh, *Fathers*, 53 ff.

[67] E. R. Eschbach, *Historic Sketch of the Evangelical Reformed Church of Frederick, Maryland* (Frederick, 1894), 17 ff.

[68] *Minutes*, 217.   [69] Harbaugh, *Fathers*, 151 ff.

woods of Western Maryland, as shown in the first sentence of the constitution: "When sound reasoning alone suffices to teach us, the word of God bears witness unto us, and experience of all times past ascertains for us, that order is the best of all things and that no kingdom, no house, no community of mankind may well and happily endure without proper order. . . ." The constitution was signed by all members of the community; the church book must have been carried around for many miles to reach the most distant parishioners for this purpose. There were in all the names of eighty-nine *patres familias* who lent their support to the constitution of the "Reformed Congregation in Friedrichstown in Manakese."[70]

Aside from this single positive accomplishment, Lange's pastorate is scarcely to be counted among the most fortunate periods in the life of the community. There was an endless series of petty jealousies and gossip, and of bickering with Otterbein, who still made occasional visits to Frederick.[71] We read in the *Minutes* of 1768: "A delegated elder of Frederick complained that the congregation there, during the pastorate and through the fault of Do. Lange had been brought into great confusion, and by his departure had become vacant, and that for this reason an unanimous desire was prevalent among the members for a prudent and faithful pastor."[72] Since out of the last four ministers the first had been a drunkard, the second had incurred debts, and the last had brought quarrels and strife into the parish, the common desire for a "prudent and faithful pastor" is entirely understandable. The wish was to be fulfilled. Toward the end of the sixties "a competent pastor," the Reverend Frederick L. Henop, took over the pulpit and continued in his office until well after the Revolution.[73]

About these two axes, the Lutheran and the Reformed Church, revolved the life of the Germans in Frederick in the first decades

[70] Here again some of the most important family names may be mentioned from the circle of the German Reformed brethren: Götzendanner, Deiwelbiss, Lingenheldter, Remsperger, Stöbhardt, Wollenschleger, Windroth, Schrupp, Rapp, Traut, Haugg, Bell, Mertz, Bentz, Stoll, Menn, Krebs, Schwartz, Holtz, Hoffmann, Schneider, Lehman, Meyer, Zimmermann, Müller, Hiltebrant, Kessler, Eberhart, Keller, Brengel, Michel, Brunner, Häfner, Huber, Adam, Wiedrich, Anders, Bohrer. Particular attention is called to the great percentage of Swiss-German names.

[71] For more detailed information, see the *Minutes*, 252-55, 275.

[72] *Minutes*, 261.

[73] When Henop took up his duties in Frederick, the congregation had 120 members (*Minutes*, 320).

after the founding of the settlement. There were few sects; Frederick did not welcome them. We have already mentioned that the Lutheran congregation summoned Lars Nyberg to be its pastor in the middle forties, and that he subsequently turned out to be a Moravian. In 1746 he converted a few members of the Lutheran congregation, founded a separate community with them and called for them a pastor from Bethlehem, George Ninke.[74] These Moravians at first had to hold their services in private homes. Usually they took place in the home of Jacob Weller, a Pennsylvania Dutchman.[75] When the people observed that the local attitude was and continued to be hostile, they moved away and founded a separate settlement, Graceham, four miles from the old Monocacy log church. Here they put up their own first log church, indeed the first Moravian church in Maryland.[76] They obtained their land from Daniel Dulaney; therefore the entire tract was called "Dulaney's Gift." The Moravian cemetery in Frederick, with its peculiar arrangement of graves, was still considered an especial point of interest in Maryland up to the end of the nineteenth century. The names of the founders of Graceham are almost entirely German: Moser, Harbaugh, Protzmann, Krieger, Reineke, Lydrick, Seiss, Schmidt, Herzer, Rosen, Richter, Schaaf, Zahn, etc.[77] The first of the Graceham settlers were from the Monocacy Valley, but there soon came an influx of Pennsylvania Dutch. From 1757 on the Moravian congregation had a resident pastor; the first baptism took place in 1759. In 1758 a parochial school was opened; at the start it was under the guidance of the pastor, but soon a regular teacher was engaged. This school existed for eighty years, up to the time when the public school took over its functions.[78]

Graceham and Frederick were not the only German settlements. In rapid succession new communities sprang up all about: Middle-

[74] Wentz, Frederick, 62. Williams, Frederick, 1, 6.

[75] The two Moravian itinerate preachers, Schnell and Brandmüller, mention Weller in their diary: "Towards evening we came to George Gumpf, with whom also Jacob Weller, and his wife, and Adam Gamb were staying." This was on the occasion of their visit to Frederick in 1749. Virginia Magazine of History and Biography, XI, 116.

[76] In Williams (Frederick County, 1, 6) is found a complete list of the pastors of the Graceham church. The names remain German until well after the Civil War.

[77] Schultz, First Settlements, 16.

[78] A. L. Oerter, The History of Graceham (Bethlehem, Pa., 1913), 24.

town (1740), Lewistown (1745), Myersville (1745), Mechanicstown (1751), Hauvers (1758), Leitersburg (1762).[79] Between 1760 and 1770 John Creager, from the Palatinate, settled on the Monocacy not far from the first log church and founded Creagerstown.[80] In 1768 a church was built on Rocky Hill, near Woodsboro, which was later used in common by Lutheran, Reformed and Presbyterian congregations. The former two denominations continued to hold their services in German here until 1830. German Reformed and Lutheran congregations built "Apple's church" in Mechanicstown in 1765.[81] About this time several Swiss Germans came to settle Harbaugh's Valley, which was named after its first settler, George Harbaugh.[82] A remark in the Minutes of the Reformed Coetus tells us the number of Reformed communities: "If Frederick, where Do. Otterbein is located becomes vacant, then certainly two preachers would be required in Maryland, for in the region of Maryland are nine strong churches."[83] Some Germans left the Reformed or Lutheran churches of their fathers and followed the call of Robert Strawbridge, the great Methodist preacher from Ireland. He came to America in 1760, settled at Sam's Creek in Frederick County and established the first Methodist church in America.[84]

About ten miles west of the Monocacy rise the gentle slopes of the Blue Ridge. They could not long halt the pioneers in their

[79] Jean R. Moser, "Settlement of Western Maryland, 1748 to 1776" (A Columbia University Master Thesis, 1940), 32. Daniel W. Nead, *The Pennsylvania German in the Settlement of Maryland* (Lancaster, Pa., 1914), 104. The Lutherans built a church in Middletown in 1755. When the Reformed minister Charles Lange came to Middletown in 1767, he held communion for thirty-eight people. (Harbaugh, *Fathers*, II, 153.) Mechanicstown, whose first settler was Jacob Weller, later changed its name to Thurmont. Leitersburg was named for Jacob Leiter, a German immigrant who purchased land here in 1762 and whose grandson, Andrew Leiter, laid out the town site in 1815. (*Maryland*, WPA Guide, 1940, 505, 515.)

[80] Williams, *Frederick*, I, 4. Schultz, 23. The name "Creager" seems to have been originally "Krüger" or "Krieger," a very common name in Southern Germany.

[81] Neal, 104. The Lutherans of Apple's church gave up their share about a hundred years later and built a church of their own in the nearby city of Thurmont. Cf. A. R. Wentz, *History of the Evangelical Lutheran Synod of Maryland* (Harrisburg, Pa., 1920), 397.

[82] Williams, *Frederick*, I, 8. Harbaugh, too, was Swiss. There were many Moravians among the settlers in Harbaugh's Valley.

[83] *Minutes*, 217. (Referring to the year 1763.)

[84] Williams, *Frederick*, I, 11.

forward march. The boldest moved some forty miles to the west. There, in the region between the present-day cities of Williamsport and Clearspring, stood for a long time the westernmost settlement, the most remote stronghold of civilization in the primeval forest, Conococheague. At first the people dared only hesitantly to advance so far. The French and Indian War interrupted the settling completely for a few years, but afterwards more and more settlers came. As early as 1780 the lots in Conococheague were apparently all distributed, for we hear that in that year Jacob Friend took out a plot of scarcely three acres and, to suit the circumstances, named it "None Left."[85]

The sale of land was authorized in the Conococheague territory in the late thirties. The Lord Proprietor had himself reserved a sector of 11,000 acres, Conococheague Manor. The first settlers came from the east and southeast; they were English or Irish, and belonged to the official Episcopalian Church. Only a few years later they were in the minority, however, for as soon as the territory was opened the Germans streamed in.[86] Some of them had broken away from the Monocacy and moved on west, but the majority came directly from Pennsylvania. They crossed the Susquehanna at Harris Ferry (now Harrisburg), proceeded to the Conococheague River and then followed its course.

The majority of these Germans, like those on the Monocacy, belonged to the Lutheran or the Reformed faith. It cannot be determined when a regular parish was formed. The first mention of the Germans on the Conococheague is an observation by Michael Schlatter on his visit to the Reformed church in Frederick in 1747: "If this congregation were united with the one called Conococheague, lying thirty miles distant, the two would be able to sustain a minister."[87] But neither the Lutheran nor the Reformed believers on the Conococheague were ever to have a pastor of their own. They were first served by the minister in Frederick, later by the one in Hagerstown. When Theodore Frankenfeld became pastor of the Reformed church in Frederick, he reported that he was to serve also the parishes of Conewago and "Conogogick," and this arrangement continued for the next decade. In 1764 there were some thirty

[85] T. J. C. Williams, *History of Washington County, Maryland* (Hagerstown, 1906), I, 22.

[86] Moser, 29. Wentz, Synod, 23.   [87] Harbaugh, *Schlatter*, 154.

families on the Conococheague who belonged to the Reformed Church.[88] The *Minutes* state in 1766 that: "The congregation at Canagetschick . . . humbly requests through us, that the Reverend Fathers would call a faithful candidate for them and send him over, Hasselbach by name, residing in or near Siegen. They are still living in poverty and in the wilderniss and they greatly need support."[89]

The Lutherans were in a similar situation. At first they stood under the Reverend Charles Frederick Wildbahn, who had his residence in McAllistertown, Pennsylvania (now Hanover), and served a rather wide circle of parishes.[90] Later the Reverend John Nicholas Kurtz occasionally came west from York, Pennsylvania. In 1772 the Lutherans on the Conococheague attempted to obtain a resident pastor of their own, and turned for this purpose to the Lutheran Ministerium in Lancaster. Muehlenberg mentions this request as follows: "A delegate appeared from vacant congregations in a region situated between the boundaries of Pennsylvania and Virginia in Maryland, and called by the Indian name Cannegotschick. . . . This district is said to be very populous and to abound in various sorts of sectarian agitators. The delegate presented a petition for an able teacher and pastor."[91] For unknown reasons, however, the petition was not granted.

Even if no minister was to be had, the people could still build a church. About 1750 they erected on a small hill, called Cedar Ridge, a log church which was later to be replaced by a stone building (1795).[92] Apparently the church was used by Lutheran and Reformed congregations in common.

The Conococheague settlement developed very slowly. The greatest trouble was the French and Indian War. Conococheague was the westernmost settlement and suffered most severely from the war. From the very beginning these frontier posts had been in contact with the Indians. Schlatter wrote of Conococheague in 1749 that the Indians in this region were "well disposed and very obliging and not disinclined toward the Christians," but their originally friendly relationship did not long endure. When the quarrels increased through the intrigues of the French colonial officials and

[88] *Minutes*, 227.   [89] *Ibid*., 243.
[90] Wentz, *Synod*, 24.   [91] *Ibid*., 25.
[92] A few names of the first German settlers on the Conococheague are: Barkmann, Brewer, Burkhardt, Startzman, Stull, Hauser, Shryock, Elwick, Wolgamuth, Snevely (Anglicized form of Swiss Schneebeli).

broke into open warfare, and the attacks of the Indians grew more and more frequent after 1756, further settling came to a complete halt for a few years. After Braddock's defeat in 1755 a regular panic broke out among the settlers. A single example will illustrate the situation. In the *Maryland Gazette* of March 11, 1756, we read in a report from Conococheague the following: "On our march to Toonaloways, about five miles this side Stoddert's Fort, we found John Meyer's house in flames, and nine or ten head of large cattle killed. About three miles and a half farther up the road we found a man killed and scalped, with one arm cut off and several arrows sticking in him; we could not bury him, having no tools with us for that purpose."

By summer 1756 most of the settlers had left their farms, built up with so much labor, and had fled to the east. In August of the same year George Washington wrote: "The whole settlement of Conocochieg is fled and there now remain only two families from thence to Fredericktown. . . . That the Maryland settlements are all abandoned is certainly a fact as I have had the account transmitted to me by several hands and confirmed yesterday by Henry Brinker, who left Monocacy the day before, and who also affirms that three hundred and fifty wagons had passed that place to avoid the enemy, within the space of three days."[93] "The fine Settlement on Conocochiegh is quite deserted," Governor Sharpe wrote in September 1756.[94] And in a report from Frederick published in the *Maryland Gazette* of July 19, 1763, we read: "Every day, for some time past, has offered the melancholic scene of poor distressed families driving downwards through this town with their effects who have deserted their plantations for fear of falling into the cruel hands of our savage enemies, now daily seen in the woods."

Not until the end of the war did the process of settling the west recommence. Even then, however, the original settlement on the Conococheague never came into full bloom; for in the meantime another town had been founded in the immediate neighborhood, Hagerstown, which soon became the business and social center of the region and later of the county.

Toward the end of the thirties there came into the territory along the Conococheague a young man who had recently emi-

[93] *The Writings of George Washington*, edited by John Fitzpatrick (Washington, 1931), I, 447; cf. also I, 463 ff.
[94] MA, VI, 484.

grated from Germany—Jonathan Hager.[95] Of his birthplace we know only that he came from Westphalia.[96] In 1739 he took out two hundred acres of land in the middle of the forest, thirty miles west of the nearest human habitation on the Monocacy. This first grant was called "Hager's Choice" or "Hager's Fancy." In 1753 he received a second grant, "Hager's Delight," comprising 1780 acres. From then on his property grew rapidly; by the middle sixties he possessed about 2500 acres.[97]

Of all the early German pioneers of Western Maryland, Jonathan Hager is the only one who is truly egregious. The Monocacy settlers clung together; and, if one of them dared to advance beyond the other homesteads, he was still careful to maintain easy contact with his neighbors. In the veins of Jonathan Hager flowed the blood of an adventurer. Fearlessly he gave up the safety of the towns and pressed forward into the new and unknown wilderness. He was more like Augustin Herrman than like the Palatinate peasants; and he was fated to reach with little effort the goal toward which Herrmann had vainly struggled for the whole of his lifetime—that of founding a city.

In 1762, then, Jonathan Hager began to lay out a city on his land and to sell individual lots.[98] In the last years more and more settlers had come in from Conococheague, the Monocacy, Pennsylvania, and the tidewater section of Maryland. Ten years after the city was laid out on paper, more than a hundred dwellings had been erected and an independent and vigorous community life had begun to develop. In a contemporary source of 1772 we read: "About thirty miles west of Fredericktown, I passed through a Settlement which is making quick advance to perfection. A German adventurer, whose name is Hagar, purchased a Considerable tract

[95] Faust, I, 173.

[96] It is assumed that he came from the principality of Wittgenstein in Westphalia. Mary Vernon Mish, Jonathan Hager, Founder (Hagerstown, 1937), 14 ff. The Pennsylvania Archives, Second Series, XVII, 122, and Rupp, Thirty Thousand Names, 101, give 1736 as the year of his arrival. According to these sources, he arrived in Philadelphia on the ship Harle. The epitaph on his gravestone in Hagerstown gives the dates: born 1719, died 1775.

[97] Williams, Washington, I, 23.

[98] Ibid., 60. The original plan included 520 lots, each having an 80-foot frontage and running back 240 feet. The lots were rapidly sold, or rather leased, for five pounds and an annual and perpetual ground rent of seven shillings and sixpence. A public square was reserved which still, in its original compass, forms the center of the city.

of land in this neighbourhood, and with much discernment and foresight, determined to give encouragement to traders, and to erect proper habitations for the storage of goods, for the supply of the adjacent country. His plan succeeded; he has lived to behold a multitude of inhabitants on lands, which he remembered unoccupied; and he has seen erected in places, appropriated by him for that purpose, more than an hundred comfortable edifices, to which the name of Hagar's Town is given, in honor of the intelligent founder."[99]

The name of the city has its history. Jonathan Hager had intended that it be called Elisabeth, in honor of his wife.[100] The name "Elisabeth" or "Elisabethtown," however, never achieved acceptance. "Hagerstown" was used from the very first, and finally completely supplanted the original name.[101]

Jonathan Hager played the role of the patriarch in his settlement just as Daniel Dulaney had done in Frederick. He took the lead on all public occasions, and the people went to him in any difficulty. When the church was to be built, he gave the land for it. When in 1762 George Washington presented his plan for making the Potomac navigable, Jonathan Hager and Thomas Cresap were elected as the Maryland representatives on the board of directors for the project.[102] Hager was the first German from Western Maryland to take an active part in the politics of the colony; in 1771 he was elected to the General Assembly as representative from Frederick County. As a matter of fact, difficulties immediately arose, which characterize the uncertain position of the immigrants. The majority of the Assembly declared that as a naturalized citizen he could not

[99] Eddis, 133.

[100] Jonathan Hager had married Elisabeth Kershner in 1740. Occasionally the name appears as Grischner.

[101] As we have seen, William Eddis speaks of "Hagar's Town" as early as 1772. In official rulings it is called "Elisabethtown" up until the beginning of the nineteenth century. In *The Washington Spy* of January 1, 1790, we read, "Elisabeth (Hager's) Town." The same form appears in other papers up until the turn of the century. *The Maryland Herald* (1812) found the compromise "Elisabeth Hager's Town." The name "Hager's Town" first appears in an official ruling in 1804. A bank founded shortly thereafter cleverly avoided the issue by calling itself "The Hager's Town Bank at Elisabeth-Town." Between 1808 and 1813 the two names are used interchangeably in laws, but in 1813 the name was legally made "Hager's Town." The modern form "Hagerstown" did not exist before 1829. Cf. Basil Soller's "Jonathan Hager—The Founder of Hagerstown," SHGM, II, 29.

[102] Williams, *Washington*, I, 61. Gould, *Land System*, 88.

hold a seat,[103] and actually the English law was against Hager. Within a week, however, the Lower House in Annapolis passed a law that gave full political rights to Jonathan Hager, and with him to all "foreign Protestants who have already settled in this province." Accordingly, Hager took his seat, and held it to the end of the session. Two years later (1773) he was again elected, and again the Committee on Elections raised difficulties.[104] Once more, however, they were removed by majority vote of the Assembly, so that Hager was able to complete his second term of office uncontested.

Like Daniel Dulaney in Frederick, Jonathan Hager in Hagerstown took an outstanding part in the development of religious organizations. At first he seems to have been in sympathy with the Moravians. In the diaries of the itinerate Moravian preachers his name appears again and again. "On March 11 (1748), I traveled to Jonathan Hager's to preach there. . . ." "On March 13 (1748), I preached in German in the fornoon and afternoon at Jonathan Hager's. So many people were present that the room was not large enough for them. . . . After the service . . . I took leave of my host Jonathan Haeger, who wept and was very sorry that I had to leave." "In Kanigelship Md. . . . Jonathan Haeger is our dear host." "On July 12th, they passed over South Mountain and came to Canigolschik. . . . Then they came to Jonathan Haeger, a friend of the brethren. . . . Haeger expressed his intentions of visiting before long the Congregation at Bethlehem."[105] Other quotations referring to Hager can easily be found in the Moravian diaries.[106] When a preacher appeared in these remote regions, everyone, no matter to what church he belonged, came to hear him. Thus, when we hear that the house was crowded for the sermon, this by no means indicates that the entire audience was Moravian. The interest of Jonathan

[103] The legal side of this question has been investigated in detail in the above-mentioned article by Basil Sollers, 22 ff. Among the representatives who voted for Hager's eligibility were Thomas Johnson and William Smallwood, the first and the fourth governors of Maryland. Among those who voted against Hager was Samuel Chase, later judge of the Supreme Court.

[104] They were based on a technical point. The law that had established Hager's eligibility bore the date of October 2, 1771; but Frederick, the last Lord Baltimore, had died on September 14 of the same year. For this reason the validity of the law was questioned.

[105] Mish, 19 ff.

[106] "Moravian Diaries of Travels," edited by W. J. Hinke and C. E. Kemper, Virginia Magazine of History and Biography (1903), XI, 116, 131, 236.

Hager himself, however, seems to have been deep-rooted at this time. Undoubtedly the Moravian brethren looked upon him as a firm support in this region, and Hager's plan to travel to Bethlehem speaks likewise for his very lively sympathy with the affairs of the sect.

That was toward the end of the forties. When Hager grew older he disassociated himself from the Moravians, joined the Reformed Church and took an important part in its activities. The lot on which the first Reformed church in Hagerstown was erected—and where the Reformed church still stands today—was given to the community by Hager. And it was in the preparations for the building of this church, in 1775, that Hager was accidentally killed.[107]

A brief word may be said about the two great churches in Hagerstown, the Reformed and the Lutheran. The Reformed congregation must have been formed shortly after the founding of the city. In the *Kirchenbuch vor die Reformierte Gemeinde in HagersStadt oder ElisabethStadt in Canageschik, Friedrich County in der Province Merelend* we find the first baptism entered in 1766; the name of the child was George Snyder. Until 1770 the pulpit was filled only by itinerate preachers. In that year, in answer to insistent pleas, the Coetus in Philadelphia sent the first resident pastor, Jacob Weymer, who remained with the congregation until 1790.[108] As soon as the people had a pastor of their own, they set about building a church. In 1771 a lottery was held for the new church—a custom quite common in those times. In 1774 the actual construction was commenced. A document which was placed in the cornerstone, and

[107] Concerning Hager's family and descendants, cf. Mish, *Jonathan Hager.* There were in all five men with the name Jonathan Hager: the son and the grandson of the founder of Hagerstown, and two others, who were not related to him at all, Jonathan Hager, the tavern keeper, and Jonathan Hager, the miller. Mish has carefully clarified the somewhat tangled threads of local history, and collected material about Hager's descendants. Hager's daughter Rosina was married to General Daniel Heister, also a German.

[108] Harbaugh, *Fathers,* II, 193. The *Minutes* (p. 269) characterize him: "He has led a quiet and godly life, having labored unweariedly for seventeen years in this province with catechizing, teaching school, and reading sermons to the edification of the people living on the borders, who are shepherdless, destitute, and impoverished by the Indian War. By means of these useful labors and through the special help of God, he has gained such a knowledge, that he is able to expound the word of God through his own meditation, according to the analogy of faith, and to apply it to the edification of souls; a man who has from all good people the testimony of an unfeigned simplicity and godliness." Cf. also *Minutes,* 305, 318.

a copy of which was entered in the church records, gives us the most important names of the first German families in Hagerstown.[109]

At about this same time the Lutheran parish began to develop. Its first official acts, conducted by itinerate preachers, were recorded as early as 1759.[110] In the same year as the Reformed congregation, the Lutherans received their first resident pastor, one Charles Frederick Wildbahn, and their first church constitution also dates from that year. When in 1772 Wildbahn turned the pulpit over to his successor, John George Young, the parish already numbered 271 communicant members. From 1772 on the Lutheran parish on the Conococheague was united with the larger and rapidly expanding Hagerstown parish.[111]

By the time of the Revolution the backland of Frederick County had developed so rapidly that in 1776 it was divided off into a separate unit, Washington County. Two towns vied to be the county seat, Hagerstown and Jerusalem. Jerusalem had been founded a few miles west of Hagerstown by Jacob Funk, also a German. Jonathan Hager's son-in-law, General Heister, who carried considerable weight in the political circles of Annapolis, used his influence in favor of the town founded by his father-in-law, and thus Hagerstown won the race.[112] Jacob Funk had to console himself with the subsequent change of the name of his town to Funkstown, as it is known today. Funkstown-Jerusalem possessed a church from 1771 on, where both Reformed and Lutheran services were held. The pulpit was filled by preachers from Hagerstown.[113]

Other settlements, founded by Germans or developed with their help, sprang up around Hagerstown. The spot where Sharpsburg now stands was first settled about the middle of the eighteenth

[109] Heyser, Wagner, Oster, Hauser, Bley, Becker, Weigand, Everhart, Gratig, Haushalter, Greenig, Seylar, Greilich, Herdli, Linck, Clampert, Jung, Schorfer, Conrath, Grepf, Detweller, Fischer, Blecher, Dieffenbach, Steinseyfer, Sestli, Ditz, Ditter, Frey, Kline, Kremer, Eichelberger.

[110] Wentz, Synod, 457.

[111] *Hallesche Nachrichten*, II, 733. Wentz, Synod, 25. A few names of the early members of the Lutheran parish in Hagerstown are: Steidinger, Veitnauer, Burghardt, Horn, Heimel, Wohlfahrt, Fruth, Stoltz, Huber, Trapp, Blum, Alter, Sautter, Reinhard, Edelmann, Hoss, Devildbiess, Beltzhuber, Hauschkel, Haushalter, Heidenauer, Giebler, Vogler, Nef, Freund, etc.

[112] Williams, *Washington*, I, 86.

[113] Wentz, Synod, 451. From a letter from the Lutheran pastor, Young, we learn that the Lutheran congregation in Funkstown numbered sixteen families in 1773, but by 1786 had grown to fifty families.

century. The town itself was not founded by a German, but after it was laid out so many Germans moved there that a Lutheran church had to be built for them.[114]

Four miles beyond Hagerstown, on Antietam Creek, a Lutheran church had been built in 1756 for the German families of the neighborhood. "About thirteen families of our church united, purchased ten acres of land, and built a sort of church as their circumstances allowed."[115] Ten years after the outbreak of the Revolution the congregation already consisted of sixty families.

Besides the two large religious groups, the Lutheran and the Reformed, there were naturally members of the various sects. There are, indeed, some indications that sectarianism flourished here in the western lands along the Conococheague much more than on the Monocacy. The Moravian itinerate preachers report that on their travels they frequently came upon German or Swiss followers of Count Zinzendorf. Near Hagerstown, they wrote, "We passed the night with a Swiss, Peter Rensch, who received us well." A smith named Hackemeyer helped them to cross the Conococheague. The next night they spent "uncomfortably—it is a poor family" at the house of Henry Wehr, "a countryman of Brother Gottschalk." Isaac Gerison received particular praise because he served the two apostles a roast squirrel. On the Monocacy, not far from Frederick, they came to a house whose owner received them somewhat ungraciously: "the host was a Mennonite and his name is Abraham Müller." These are only a few examples.[116] Undoubtedly there were other sectarians about the countryside than are here mentioned.

Catholics played only a very minor role among the early German

[114] Nead, 100. Williams, Washington, I, 464. Among the early families here were the Rohrbacks, Gardenours, Shulers, Neads and Harmanns. The Sharpsburg church later gained fame through the role that it played in the Battle of Antietam in the Civil War.

[115] Nead, 106. Before there was a resident pastor in Hagerstown, the Antietam Creek church belonged to the pastorate of the Lutheran minister in Frederick. Pastor Hausihl was the first one who had to make the long journey.

[116] Virginia Magazine of History and Biography, XI (1903), 113 ff., 372 ff. The Lutheran and Reformed Churches naturally did their utmost to suppress the activities of the Moravian ministers. When one of them asked a German settler, George Daelinger, if he might preach again in his house as he had done two years before, the farmer replied, "Not for fifty pounds," and told how his neighbors and his minister had censured him severely for having placed his house at the disposal of the Moravians on that previous occasion.

settlers. In the first place, the percentage of Catholics was relatively small among the immigrants. In the second, a sort of phobia developed against them in Maryland toward the middle of the eighteenth century, which grew to the pitch of hysteria during the French and Indian War when they were accused of secret conspiracies with the French. Particularly the Lower House of the Assembly was overly zealous in pointing out the "many and dangerous Innovations, against Law, made by the Popish Interest within this Province, and the great Growth of Popery and extensive Acquisitions of Popish Priests and Jesuits."[117] Again and again the Catholic bogy-man troubled the Acts of the Assembly in the fifties, sometimes even designated by name as a German Jesuit called Wappeler. In 1755 the Lower House formulated a law "for preventing the Importation of German and French Papists."[118] The preamble refers to the fact that in recent years numerous German, Irish and French Catholics, particularly Jesuits, had crossed into Maryland from Pennsylvania and Delaware and had procured land. It was feared not only that they would unite with the enemy, but also that they would lure "the good Protestant people" to Catholicism. The new law was to limit the influx of Catholics by a tax of five pounds for every German or Irish Catholic, and of two hundred pounds for every priest or Jesuit, who wished to immigrate to Maryland.

The first reference to German Catholics in Maryland dates from the year 1741, when a Jesuit just sent over from England, Father Henry Neale, requested German-speaking priests from his superiors in Europe. "The German gentlemen (two priests) have not yet arrived. Their presence is very much wanted. My heart has yearned when I've met with some poor Germans desirous of performing their duties, but whom I have not been able to assist for want of language."[119] The two "German gentlemen," Father Theodor Schneider and Father Wilhelm Wappeler,[120] arrived that same year and began their missionary activities among the Germans in Maryland and Pennsylvania. About ten years later another German

[117] MA, L, 51 ff.   [118] MA, LII, 89 ff.

[119] Paul G. Gleis, "German Catholic Missionaries in Maryland During the Eighteenth Century," SHGM, xxvi, 33-36. Lambert Schrott, Pioneer German Catholics in the American Colonies, 1734-1784 (New York, 1933), 35 ff.

[120] Theodor Schneider was born in Speyer in 1703. He was a professor from 1738 to 1739, and president of Heidelberg University. Wilhelm Wappeler (1711-1781) came from Westphalia. Illness forced him to return to Europe in 1748.

priest, Father Mathias Sittensberger, began to minister to the German Catholics in Maryland.[121] At the same time appeared a fourth, Father Ferdinand Steinmeyer.[122] The most successful of these German Catholics was Father Jacob Frambach, who came to America in 1738 and to Frederick, Maryland, in 1773.[123] He pursued an enthusiastic career all over Western Maryland, penetrated as far as the site of present-day Cumberland and obtained a small piece of land from Jonathan Hager's son in Hagerstown in 1786, on which he built a small Catholic chapel.

In passing we may mention also the names of a few of the German-Catholic priests who worked for a longer or shorter period in Maryland between 1760 and 1780: Jakob Pellentz, Lukas Geissler, Frederick Leonard, J. B. Diederick.[124] Generally speaking, however, the percentage of German Catholics in the settlements of Western Maryland remained insignificant throughout the eighteenth century. There were no separate parishes for them. Even where there were German Catholics present, therefore, they usually had to join churches whose priests were Irish and those whose language was English.

The law mentioned above, restricting Catholic immigration, was directed against Catholics generally and not by any means against Germans. Nothing would have been farther from the mind of the Assembly than retarding German immigration. On the contrary,

[121] Mathias Sittensberger (whose name often appeared in America in the Anglicized form "Mr. Manners") was born in 1719 in Landsberg in Bavaria. He arrived in America in 1752 and set up his headquarters first in Conewago, whence he regularly came into Western Maryland. From 1764 on he served in Bohemia Manor in Cecil County, Maryland, where he died in 1775.

[122] Ferdinand Steinmeyer was born in 1720 in Wuerttemberg. For a time he was professor at the University of Freiburg, and was apparently an important physician and natural scientist. In 1768 he became a member of the American Philosophical Society, and in 1779 a member of the Board of Trustees of the University of Pennsylvania. He died in Philadelphia in 1786. Occasionally his name appears in the Anglicized form "Mr. Farmer."

[123] John G. Shea, *The Catholic Church in Colonial Days* (New York, 1886), II, 66 and 287. Lambert Schrott, *op.cit.*, 74. Jacob Frambach was born in 1723 in the Rheinland. He worked in Frederick as pastor of "St. Stanislaus," a Catholic chapel which was built by an Italian Jesuit, Father Williams, between 1763 and 1765. Frambach took a most active part in the important Catholic Church politics. He attended the famous White Marsh Conference of 1784, and the first Catholic National Synod. After 1790 he served as the Vicar General of Bishop Carroll. He died in 1795.

[124] For further details, cf. the above-mentioned article by P. G. Gleis.

everything was done to encourage and to further it. In 1754 the Assembly passed a law "that no Germans . . . coming into this Province . . . shall be held or deemed liable to pay the Duty or Duties hereby imposed on Servants."[125] It was well understood how important the Germans had been and would continue to be in opening up the frontier. The astonishingly rapid development of Frederick County, a region settled principally by German farmers, spoke for itself. In 1730 the land on the Monocacy was still a wilderness; in 1748 it had to be formed into a separate county which by 1755 was the second county of the Province in population.[126] In 1739 the General Assembly decreed that a road should be built from Annapolis to the Monocacy to facilitate communication with this flourishing section of the Province.[127] "A lucrative trade is supported with the back country," wrote Eddis in 1771, ". . . and thus, by imperceptible degrees, from an humble beginning, has Frederick Town arisen to its present flourishing state."[128]

This road, which was built between Annapolis and the back counties, played a considerable role in the French and Indian War. Many of the settlers whom the Indians drove out of the Conococheague region fled northeast to Pennsylvania; but many others turned southeast, into the southern, protected part of Frederick County, and this latter group traveled over the newly built road. Many of them moved back after the end of the war; many probably also remained in the southern part of the country, along the Potomac. It is therefore probable that at this time the first Germans appeared in that part of Maryland which was later to form the District of Columbia.[129]

It is impossible to give exact or even approximate statistics on the pre-Revolutionary German immigration to Western Maryland. Ship lists like those in Philadelphia were not kept in Annapolis. There are no data on the great number of Pennsylvania Dutch who crossed the Susquehanna and settled in Maryland. Governor Sharpe,

[125] MA, L, 563.

[126] The census of 1755 gave Baltimore County a population of 17,238 and Frederick County 13,970. (Hills Papers Misc. in Maryland Hist. Soc.) Gould, Land System, 86.

[127] MA, xxxx, 220, 307 ff.   [128] Eddis, 101 ff.

[129] This question is discussed in detail by Christian Strack in "The First Germans in the Subsequent District of Columbia," Berichte der Deutschen Historischen Gesellschaft für den Distrikt Columbia, 1, 2, 25 ff. (Washington, D.C., 1905).

in answer to a questionnaire sent him from London in 1755, wrote that over 2000 Germans and about 5000 English had come into the Province between 1748 and 1755; but this is only an estimate and covers only seven years.[130] One point in particular should be made: the share of the Pennsylvania Dutch in the settlement of Western Maryland has long been overestimated. The first settlers on the Monocacy, in the early thirties, came exclusively from Pennsylvania, and the influx of Pennsylvania Dutch was continuous during the following decades. Very soon, however, German migration began to come in directly through Annapolis and Alexandria. It has been mentioned that Thomas Schley had landed with a hundred Palatinate families in Annapolis in 1735. Since that time German immigrants had surely entered year after year along this same route. For the years 1752, 1753 and 1755 we have partial figures on Germans landing in Annapolis, which give us a total of 1060 for these three years.[131]

Apparently there were not only redemptioners, but also free passengers among those immigrants, for on one occasion, in 1752, we read that a number of Palatinates, who had come from England on the ship *Patience*, carried a letter of recommendation from Lord Baltimore to Benjamin Tasker, President of the Council, which read in part: "I therefore desire you will give such necessary assistance to these people on their arrival, to forward them to Manockesy which I understand is in Frederick County or where else they shall want to go to settle within the province, as in your power, and that they may be accomodated in a proper manner. But the charges attending any such service to them must be done in the most moderate manner in respect to the Proprietor and to answer their requisites

[130] Strack, I, i, 44.
[131] F. B. Mayer, "Memoranda in Reference to Early German Emigration to Maryland," SHGM, v, 18.
September 18, 1752, Ship *Integrity*, Jo. Coward, Master, 150 tons, 6 guns and 14 men, baggage of 150 Palatine passengers from Cowes.
September 19, 1753, Ship *Barclay*, J. Brown, Master, 120 tons, 12 men, baggage of 160 Palatines.
November 8, 1753, Ship *Friendship*, baggage of 300 Palatine Passengers.
January 16, 1755, Ship *Friendship*, baggage of 450 Palatine Passengers.
These figures can lead to deceptive conclusions, for unscrupulous captains frequently loaded passengers and baggage on different ships. It is peculiar that record was always made of baggage, and not of passengers. Nevertheless, this figure (averaging 300 a year) agrees with that given by Governor Sharpe.

necessary to their services. The increase of people being always welcome. . . ."[132]

Maryland did not extend far to the west. It was nevertheless able to submit the small share that it could contribute toward the "Winning of the West" because the right settlers appeared at the right moment in the person of the Germans. From 1730 on, the type of the population of Maryland began to change. With the exception of Baltimore, the tidewater section was and continued to be predominately Anglo-Saxon. In the western part of the province something new arose, something typically American: the intermarrying of Anglo-Saxon and continental European immigrants, in this case the Germans. This difference between the coastal and the inland counties began to take shape in the very beginning, the difference between the Anglo-Saxon population on the Bay and the mixed and intermingled, characteristically "American" population of the back country.

Germans in America have often complained that their part in building the United States has not received sufficient recognition. This is certainly not true in the case of Western Maryland. Since the middle of the eighteenth century, reference has repeatedly been made to the services of the Germans in opening up the inland reaches of Maryland. A few statements of this sort may bring the chapter to a close. As early as 1745 Daniel Dulaney wrote in a letter to Governor Ogle: "You would be surprised to see how much the country is improved beyond the mountains, especially by the Germans, who are the best people that can be to settle the wilderness; and the fertility of the soil makes them ample amends for their industry."[133] William Eddis, an Englishman who had traveled about a great deal in the province, wrote in 1771 on returning from Western Maryland: "The richness of the soil, and the salubrity of the air operated, however, very powerfully to promote population; but what chiefly tended to the advancement of settlements in this remote district, was the arrival of many emigrants from the Palatinate, and other Germanic States. These people who, from earliest days, had been disciplined in habits of industry, sobriety, frugality and patience, were particularly fitted for the laborious occupations of felling timber, clearing land, and forming the first improvements;

[132] Williams, Frederick, I, 7.
[133] Richard H. Spencer, "Hon. Daniel Dulaney," Maryland Hist. Mag., XIII (1918), 24.

and the success which attended their efforts, induced multitudes of their enterprising countrymen to abandon their native homes, to enjoy the plenteous harvest which appeared to await their labours in the wild, uncultivated wastes of America."[134] And shortly before the outbreak of the Revolution, in 1773, Governor Robert Eden wrote to Lord Dartmouth and mentioned the Germans who had settled in Western Maryland with the following praise: "They are generally industrious laborious people. Many of them have acquired a considerable share of property. Their improvement of a Wilderness into well-stocked plantations, the example and beneficient Effects of their extraordinary industry have raised in no small degree a spirit of emulation among the other inhabitants. That they are a most useful people and merit the public regard is acknowledged by all who are acquainted with them."[135]

The German settlers on the Monocacy and the Conococheague could scarcely have asked for more favorable testimonials.

[134] Eddis, 99. William Eddis was Surveyor of the Customs in Annapolis.
[135] "Correspondence of Governor Eden," *Maryland Hist. Mag.*, ii (1907), 301 ff.

III. BUILDING A TOWN

IN WESTERN MARYLAND the Germans had been the first settlers. Later on, Irish, Scotch and English immigrants had joined them and lent their aid in the development of the back counties. Quite different was the development of the second great German settlement area, the city of Baltimore.

In the founding of Baltimore the Germans had no part. The city was not laid out until a full century (1729) after the founding of the Maryland Colony, and its development was at first slow and in competition with the old county seat, Joppa. Baltimore was founded by immigrants from the British Isles. By the time the Germans began to play a significant part in its development, the struggle for supremacy between Baltimore and Joppa had already been decided in favor of the former. By the middle of the eighteenth century the German element assumed an increasingly important role in Baltimore's development.

From the very beginning the German element in Baltimore took on a more urban character than its counterpart in Western Maryland. There on the banks of the Monocacy the Germans were at first exclusively farmers. Only gradually did a few of them, responding to community needs, turn to various trades. In Baltimore, on the other hand, no mention whatever of farmers can be found. There the callings peculiar to city life characterize German activity to the almost complete exclusion of all others. On the Monocacy the settlements were widely scattered to allow the farmers room for expansion: at first there were no corporate communities whatever. In Baltimore, on the contrary, activity soon became centered about a small urban core. In Western Maryland the problem was to wrest new arable acreage from the primeval forest; in Baltimore it was to create an urban commercial center within the old settlement of the tidewater section.

When it was that the first German appeared in the new city at the mouth of the Patapsco we do not know. There is a report that the house of the German, Andrew Steiger, the city's first butcher, bore the date 1741.[1] That is the earliest mention that we

[1] Thomas W. Griffith, *Annals of Baltimore* (Baltimore, 1824), 34. In 1759 Steiger bought a piece of land for a pasture for his cattle, long known as "Steiger's Meadow."

have of a German in Baltimore. Quite reliable, too, is an entry which reports that Thomas Sligh (Schley) owned a strip of land between Baltimore Town and Jones Town, that is, in the heart of present-day Baltimore.[2]

Three sources contributed to German immigration to Baltimore in the eighteenth century. First, the Pennsylvania Germans, although their contribution was smaller there than in the west. Second, the Germans who came directly from Europe and usually landed in Annapolis. And third, the Germans from Western Maryland. Many Frederick county settlers, attracted by the promising prospects of the flourishing city, migrated back east after a few years spent on the banks of the Monocacy.

In the 1740's reports begin to drift in of the arrival of individual Germans in Baltimore. Puritans no doubt would condemn them, but epicures would value them highly; for, following butcher Steiger, two Germans, Leonard and Daniel Barnetz, came to Baltimore from York, Pennsylvania, in 1748, and established the city's first brewery.[3] Valentine Loerch (occasionally appearing as Loersh or Larsh) erected an inn in 1753;[4] and the business proved so prosperous that another German, Jacob Meyer, a few years later felt encouraged to open a second (1758).[5] Presently there were others: Vitus Hartweg, a harness maker; George N. Meyers, a Pennsylvania German who came to Baltimore in 1753; John Schley, of the Frederick Schleys, who settled in Baltimore in 1754 and built a house on Gay Street; and the brothers Frederick and Peter Meyers, who probably also arrived in the early 1750's.[6]

A primitive and very incomplete directory of the year 1752 mentions among thirty names three which are undoubtedly German: George Strebeck, with the note "only wagoner, drove a single team"; Philip Littig, "whose wife was accoucheuse among the

---

[2] *First Records of Baltimore Town* (Baltimore, 1905), 22.

[3] "These gentlemen"—so say the *Annals of Baltimore*—"if not the first were among the first of the Germans, or the descendants of Germans, whose successive emigration from the province, with capital and industry employed here, contributed so essentially to aid the original settlers" (p. 29). See also: J. Thomas Scharf, *Chronicles of Baltimore* (Baltimore, 1874), 37. *First Records of Baltimore Town and Jones Town, 1727-1797* (Baltimore, 1905), 27.

[4] Griffith, 34.

[5] Griffith, 37. Loersh's inn was on the southwest corner of Baltimore and Gay Streets; Meyer's directly opposite on the southeast corner.

[6] Griffith, 34, 35, 37. Scharf, *Chronicles*, 49, 51.

German population"; and Jake Keeport, whose name may originally have been Kiepert or Kühbord.[7]

In 1761 a Pennsylvania German, Melchior Keener, came to Baltimore, built a tavern—although there were several of them already established—and in addition built a wharf and warehouse on Hanover Street.[8] Another German, George Lindenberger, was one of the five men who in 1769 founded the first fire-prevention service in Baltimore, the "Mechanical Company," which acquired an engine for that purpose.[9] A survey of the names of persons who came to Baltimore in 1771, or were established in business there, reveals, in addition to those already mentioned, the names of Barnett Eichelberger, Englehard Yeiser and Henry Schaeffe.[10] When the county court was moved from Joppa to Baltimore, Leonard Harbaugh, of an old Pennsylvania-German family, was active in an effort to preserve the old courthouse.[11]

One of the earliest Baltimore silversmiths was a German, William Hackle. Between the years 1763-1772 his name appears in land records, in the history of the old German-Lutheran church, and in the records of the Mechanical Company.[12]

[7] *First Records,* 48, 51. J. T. Scharf, *History of Baltimore City and County* (Philadelphia, 1881), I, 58. Griffith (p. 38) considers Keeport "German or Dutch." That Keeport was German appears certain from an official petition of several German citizens in 1767 (MA, xxxii, 195). Moreover, the name "Keeport" is also found in the Proceedings of the German Reformed Church (SHGM, xxiii, 31 ff.).

[8] Griffith, 39. Scharf, *Chronicles,* 53.

[9] Griffith, 45. Scharf, *Chronicles,* 64. George W. McCreary, *The Ancient and Honorable Mechanical Company of Baltimore* (Baltimore, 1901).

[10] Griffith, 49.

[11] Scharf, *Chronicles,* 62 f. "In the grading of Calvert street the bluff overhanging the Falls on which the courthouse stood was to be cut away, but it was very much desired to save the courthouse. Mr. Leonard Harbaugh, a zealous craftsman of Baltimore, pondered over the matter, and finally persuaded himself, and afterwards the Town Council, that he would preserve the favorite building by leaving it twenty feet in the air, after all the adjacent earth was taken away. Our town people thought this an incredible exploit, the dream of a bold projector; but Mr. Harbaugh knew what he was about, and successfully accomplished, in the face of that incredulous world which dwelt upon the banks of the Patapsco, this daring achievement."

[12] J. Hall Pleasants and Howard Sill: *Maryland Silversmiths 1750-1830* (Baltimore, 1930), 128. Contains also pictures of three still extant specimens of Hackle's work (Plate xxvi). In the erection of the Lutheran church building, and in the framing of the church constitution, Hackle took an active part. His work with the Mechanical Company seems to have had less

In 1754 Governor Sharpe wrote as follows to Lord Baltimore: "I have taken an Opportunity since my arrival of visiting Baltimore which indeed has the appearance of the most increasing Town in the Province, tho it scarcely answered the Opinion I had conceived of it: hardly as yet rivaling Annapolis in number of Buildings or Inhabitants; its Situation as to Pleasantness Air and Prospect is inferior to that of Annapolis, but if one considers it with respect to Trade, the extensive Country beyond it leaves no room for Comparison; were a few Gentlemen of fortune to settle there and encourage the Trade it might soon become a florishing place but while few besides the Germans (who are in general Masters of small Fortunes) build and inhabit there I apprehend it cannot make any considerable Figure."[13] This hardly prophetic opinion of the governor's indicates that he had little confidence in unaided German ability. That need not surprise us, for we find in the history of Western Maryland similar remarks about the Germans. However, the letter indicates that in the middle of the eighteenth century the Germans obviously supplied by far the largest number of immigrants, and that many of them had already achieved a moderate degree of prosperity. "The German settlers of Maryland and Pennsylvania were among the first to see the advantages of Baltimore Town as a place of commerce and trade."[14]

The Germans in Baltimore were no less religious and church-minded than their compatriots in Western Maryland. Here, as there, the group organization was founded on the basis of the church. While in Western Maryland the Lutherans were always a few steps ahead of the Reformed, in Baltimore the situation was just the reverse, for in the city there were many more in the Reformed congregation than in the Lutheran. The beginnings of religious organization may probably be placed in the early fifties. Both congregations, however, were too small and financially too weak to stand on their own feet. "Up to the year 1758," states the earliest church record of the Lutheran congregation, "both Lutherans and German Reformed worshipped together, and great friendship and harmony prevailed." The combined congregations

---

interest for him, as we hear of several fines that were imposed on him for "being absent" or for having "Bage and Bucket out of place."

[13] MA, vi, 57.

[14] Lawrence C. Wroth (ed.): *Baltimore—Its History and Its People* (New York, 1912), 682.

held their services in one of the English churches or in private residences, and relied on itinerant preachers—although they knew that these were "often of bad reputation and conduct." In 1756 they felt strong enough to consider the erection of a church under joint auspices.[15] In an old manuscript discovered after the Civil War in the archives of the German-Reformed church in Baltimore we read: "In the year 1756 or 1757, the congregation purchased a lot on which to erect a church . . . and appointed a committee to superintend the building of a church, which consisted of Andrew Steiger, Valentine Loersh, Frederick Meyer, Jacob Kühboard, John Soller and Conrad Smith. These men made preparation to build, and with the means they had they built the best church they could. We then called the Rev. John Christian Faber to become our pastor, and we are all in peace and love."[16]

Another report bearing upon the beginnings of church life is contained in the archives of the Lutheran Zion church, probably written by one of the most prominent members of that congregation, Charles Frederick Wiesenthal.[17] From it we learn that the "first regularly officiating pastor" was the Reverend Georg Bager.[18] A native of Simmern in the Hunsrück, Germany, he had come to America in 1752, and had held the laborious office of preacher for all the far-flung Lutherans in the Pennsylvania counties of York, Adams, Cumberland and Franklin. The Lutherans of Baltimore pleaded with him to include them in his circuit, and in 1755 he finally yielded to their request. That is why 1755 has been generally accepted as the birth year of the Lutheran Zion church; and until 1823, when the First English Lutheran church was founded, this remained the only Lutheran congregation in Baltimore.

Conditions at the outset were far from ideal. There was no church, and a preacher came only every other month or so. "For three consecutive years Rev. Bager came down from Pennsylvania six times a year, administering the spiritual functions in preaching

[15] J. T. Scharf, *History of Baltimore City*, II, 568 ff.

[16] Scharf, *Chronicles*, 40. The lot which was acquired for the first German church was at Charles and Saratoga Streets.

[17] "Early Accounts of the History of the Congregation," published in the *History of Zion Church of the City of Baltimore* by Julius Hofmann (Baltimore, 1905), 9 ff. See also Henry Scheib, "The Zion Church of the City of Baltimore," *SHGM*, II, 59 ff.

[18] His descendants have held high offices in the Lutheran community of Pennsylvania, under the name "Baugher."

and sacraments, and enjoying from this not more than five pounds a year. This was next to nothing indeed, as a reward, however, consisting only of eleven persons and the majority of them having no superfluous means, the good man was satisfied with it until the journey of over sixty miles became too arduous for him and he accepted another call."[19]

According to the Lutheran account, the erection of the church did not proceed with the "peace and love" which the document of the Reformed would have us believe. That there was a plan to build a church through the joint efforts of the two congregations there is no doubt. Two representatives of each congregation were to confer with a certain Mr. Lawson about a site. Obstacles soon arose when one of the Reformed members, Conrad Schmidt, stated that Mr. Lawson was unwilling to sell to the Lutherans—an objection which very naturally surprised them: "for we could not see why Herr Lawson should not take Lutheran money just as well as that of the Reformed; as the land was in reality in the market." As the Reformed members began to question whether a union of the two congregations was feasible anyway, the Lutherans sensed that a new turn of affairs was in the making and began "to fear a Jesuit trick" as the manuscript expresses it. Soon the matter was cleared up: "It happened that the Reformed preacher Herr Löshie asked Herr Richard Croxal for a lot on the hill to build there a German church. The latter at once was so generous as to give one without pay for that purpose. Now the murder was out, for the Reformed gentlemen all of a sudden declared openly that this land was given to them alone, they having asked for it, and that they did not care for the union any longer. Thus we poor, credulous Lutherans had, as in other cases, to go away with a flea in the ear."

But the Lutherans did not accept this decision without protest. "This could not happen without some of our hotheads flaring up; Mr. Jacob Rach especially was much stirred up. He took his yardstick and walked out to the iron foundry where Herr Croxal lived, two miles from here. He asked him whether it was to the Reformed alone that he had given the land, and informed him of the state of affairs, which excluded the Lutherans entirely." Whether Jacob Rach's threateningly wielded yardstick influenced Mr. Croxal's answer is a moot question. In any case, he stated emphatically that

[19] *Early Accounts*, 9 f.

"he had given the land to the German inhabitants in general, having supposed that they were all of one religion." Jacob Rach should have been content with that; "his great and laudable service" was generally recognized. Unfortunately, however, his Lutheran zeal was not altogether free from a spirit of intrigue, and so he asked Mr. Croxal, a Catholic, whether or not he was aware "that the Reformed, in the Heidelberg catechism, called the Catholics idolators, which also meant him, Croxal. The intention of Mr. Rach was doubtless to prejudice Herr Croxal against the Reformed"—so states the manuscript with keen insight. However, Mr. Croxal was a reasonable man, and considered that no expressions of the Heidelberg catechism, however aggressive they might appear, were directed against him personally—"which clearly proves that not all Catholics are as bad as they are often depicted." "We could not in all things approve of the zeal of our brother, Mr. Rach," says the manuscript with gentle reproach, but "we have to overlook these hot expressions, caused by the intrigues and double-dealing of the Reformed."

The subsequent course of events in this connection can best be learned from the old manuscript itself. "As soon as the Reformed had the piece of land and we had entered upon negotiations about it, they were beating about the bush, proposing to us that we should buy a lot abutting on theirs, thus being in a way still united. Yet we were to fence off our lot from theirs. This proposition seemed to us too subtle, nor could we in our innocence understand how this would look like a union, and why we might not as well be a hundred miles away from them. Thus the whole scheme of a union came to an end. One scabbed sheep will often mar the whole flock.

"Now we decided to test our own strength, and notwithstanding the fact that we were much weaker than the Reformed, we agreed to buy a piece of ground for a church and grave yard. It was resolved to ask Herr Lawson for the same property which had been proposed when the plan of amalgamation was in its first stages. This time, however, we did not care to make use of a Reformed agent, but deputed Herr Moritz Wörschler, schoolmaster; Mr. William Hackel, silversmith; Mr. Caspar Grassmuck, Mr. Michael Tieffenbach, and Carl Fried. Wiesenthal, medicinae practicus. These were requested to make a contract with Herr Lawson.

"It was necessary, however, to ask this man first whether he would

CARL FREDERICK WIESENTHAL (1726-1789)
Eminent physician, one of the first great names in the history of
the medical profession in Baltimore

JOHN STRICKER (1759-1825)
General, who gained fame in the defense of Baltimore in the
War of 1812

DAVID HOFFMAN (1784-1854)
Professor of law, internationally known authority, author of several fundamental studies for the legal profession

sell this property to the Lutherans. As he answered at once in the affirmative, the committee took the liberty to inform him that the Reformed gentlemen had assured us that previously he had not wanted us to have any part of the land, not even in common with the Reformed, as described in detail above. All this Herr Lawson, much surprised, fully denied; and thus the hidden intrigue of some of the Reformed members was revealed. We saw with regret that there were people who could even begin divine service with envy and hatred, and that the old saying came again to pass: Where a church for worship is built, there the devil builds a chapel."

As a result of these deviltries it came about that two "churches for worship" were built instead of one. The Reformed were again ahead, and in 1758 erected their first church in Baltimore.[20] We owe a brief description of this church to one of the members of the congregation: "Our first church was located up North Charles Street, and was approached with difficulty, especially by the aged and infirm, on account of the steep hill of sand they were obliged to climb every Sabbath in order to reach their humble place of worship. At that time we had no cushioned seats, no carpeted aisles, no sweet toned organ to aid in the musical exercises—no, not even a stove to warm the body. The cold northwest wind would pierce through the tender weather-boarding, and almost blow the light fabric off."[21]

Several years passed before the church acquired a regular pastor. At first the Reformed congregation, as was the custom in many localities, was supplied by itinerant preachers, of whom we know only one by name, the Reverend Mr. Lachey (Löshie). In 1768 they were fortunate enough to engage a resident pastor. About that we have the following report in the church records: "Baltimore, January 25, 1769. The first minister of this congregation was John Christian Faber, born in Mosback on the Neckar, in the Pfaltz, in Europe. His father was a preacher at Gimmeldingen on the river Haardt. May the blessing of God attend this enterprise, and may the church increase and flourish." Further information about Faber is supplied by the minutes of the Reformed Coetus: "A strong Reformed Congregation in Baltimore sent a call to Mr. Christian Faber. . . . According to an undoubtedly genuine certificate he had

[20] The church stood on the corner of Charles and Saratoga Streets.
[21] Scharf, Chronicles, 41.

been examined by the Reverend Consistory at Heidelberg, and had been ordained to the holy ministry" (1768).[22]

In the following year it is stated that "Do. Faber, who last year accepted a call to Baltimore with our consent and recommendation, and there ministers to two congregations, one in Baltimore and one on the Pipe Creek sent to the Reverend Coetus two written certificates from each of these congregations, stating that Do. Faber not only lived properly but also taught properly, inasmuch as he taught the clear Word of God of the Old and New Testament faithfully and diligently, so that these congregations are well satisfied with him."[23]

Actually, however, all was not sweetness and light. Apparently in premonition of the coming storm, Reverend Mr. Faber had provided himself in advance with a set of testimonials. Just what lay behind the opposition which soon arose against him in the Reformed congregation in Baltimore cannot be clearly established. The ever-recurring reproach against him was "that he was lifeless and unedifying," "not earnest enough in his conduct, and not energetic and active enough in his ministry."[24] That may have been true; but it is also possible that some part of the congregation had been stirred up against him by one of the many itinerant preachers, Benedict Schwope, "first mentioned in the Coetus Minutes of 1770 as preaching in the neighborhood of Baltimore—as not being a member of the Coetus—as having been charged with creating strife in the congregation of Mr. Faber."[25] The morals of the preachers were not always above suspicion; and when it became a question of forcing another out of his position and getting it for himself, all means were considered justifiable. It is no longer possible to decide whether or not the charges against Faber were justified; but it is clear that the Faber-Schwope controversy kept the Germans in Baltimore, and the Reformed Coetus in Pennsylvania very busy. In 1771 the minutes reveal that the situation in Baltimore was "not yet harmonious,"[26] that the congregation was split into two parties, and that all efforts at conciliation on the part of the Coetal delegates were rejected by the Schwope retainers, with the eternal objection that Faber was "not zealous and energetic enough." They

---

[22] Minutes and Lettres, 267. Harbaugh, Fathers, II, 400.
[23] Minutes, 287.
[24] Ibid., 310.
[25] Harbaugh, Fathers, II, 390.
[26] Minutes, 310.

themselves, on the other hand, were not lacking in zeal and energy; and in the mid-seventies built a church of their own, thus giving external expression to the schism.

The Reformed Coetus sent several delegates to Baltimore in a renewed effort at appeasement. It appeared that Mr. Schwope was really not as bad as had at first been assumed, "that he appears . . . in many respects worthy of recommendation, that he manifests eminent qualifications and . . . seems innocent of the misconduct charged against him, namely injustice and dishonesty."[27] Nevertheless, the delegates arrived at the wise conclusion that peace could not be restored until both parsons left the field, and a neutral shepherd of the flock, unburdened by strife, be installed in their places.[28] With this suggestion both parties were in accord—a settlement which touched Reverend Mr. Faber all the more lightly as he had a new position in prospect in Taneytown, Maryland. He therefore accepted the decision. Schwope, on the other hand, continued to preach with the excuse "that he personally did not insist, but his party desired that he should preach for them."[29] The old congregation however, was left completely without spiritual guidance. In the winter of 1771-1772 a newcomer, the Reverend George Wallauer, fresh from Germany, appeared on the scene, and at the solicitation of the Reformed church in Baltimore assumed the office of pastor. The only difficulty was that the Reverend Mr. Wallauer came "without any recommendation from the Fathers," i.e., from the mother church in Europe, "in consequence of which the Coetus did not receive him," and he therefore lacked official recognition.[30] The Reformed constituency in Baltimore, however, who were justifiably of the opinion that the situation was complicated enough as it was, promptly disregarded the Coetal quibble and placed themselves under the guidance of the Reverend Mr. Wallauer.[31] A suggestion of the Coetus, quite lacking in psychological insight, that perhaps the Reverend Mr. Schwope might be given a trial as joint pastor for the two congregations, was rejected with indignation by the Reformed congregation: "Their plain answer was: No!"

The prospect for unity grew ever dimmer as the separatist congregation acquired a new pastor in 1774. From this point on, history

[27] Ibid., 305. [28] Ibid., 311. [29] Ibid., 330.
[30] Harbaugh, Fathers, 399. [31] Minutes, 329.

makes no further mention of the Reverend Mr. Schwope, except that he disappeared "by death or removal." His successor was William Otterbein, whom we have already met as preacher for the Reformed congregation in Frederick.[32] In the interim he had held various posts in Pennsylvania, had spent a year in Europe and now assumed the post vacated by Schwope. Otterbein had a strong, attractive personality, active and energetic; therefore, his arrival in Baltimore was unwelcome to the older Reformed members, and with reason, "because they regard Do. Otterbein as a hindrance to the union that might ever be hoped for."[33] The Coetus realized this too, and suggested to the separatist congregation in Baltimore the name of a less positive man upon whom the two congregations might eventually agree. But Otterbein declined to yield: "according to his conscience, when if not to the many, yet to a few, it may be regarded as a means of edification." The Coetus had to accept the decision, and perforce recognized Otterbein's position. Thus in the mid-seventies the German Reformed in Baltimore were split into two groups: the old, original congregation, numerically the stronger, but whose pastor was not fully recognized by the supreme church council; and the separatist congregation, small but active, under an energetic and recognized pastor, now at the start of what was to become a forty-year pastorate, "laboring with a blessing in his new field," as he himself states. We shall have occasion to refer to him again in the post-revolutionary period.

Shortly after the Reformed congregation had built their first church, the Lutherans also began building theirs. This was in 1762, under the second pastor of the congregation. The first, Pastor Bager, had retired in 1758, after three years of service. His successor, John Kaspar Kirchner, had also been ordained in Germany. He had lived in York County, Pennsylvania, where he had served several congregations, and he now promised to come to Baltimore every six weeks to preach and administer the sacraments.[34]

The first church which the Lutherans built in the early sixties was a very modest affair. "As we were small in number and of but average means no large building could arise. Wisely we had to cut our coat according to our cloth, and erected only a wooden building which we would consider a schoolhouse until our revenues would

---

[32] Harbaugh, *Fathers*, ii, 59. Griffith, 63.
[33] *Minutes*, 345.   [34] Wentz, *Synod*, 29.

allow us to build the church proper. . . . The lot on which this church building is built, is upon a hill rising very steeply and is somewhat inconvenient for old people. If, however, a church with a steeple should be built upon it, it cannot help being seen from afar and will make a fine appearance." The anonymous author of the manuscript modestly avoids a comparison with Solomon's temple, even though the "ardent zeal" with which the little church was erected matched Solomon's. So "we had a church of our own without being exposed to further vexatious tricks which always would have molested us"—so states the manuscript, with an unmistakable oblique reference to the Reformed Church.[35]

Unfortunately, in 1763 Pastor Kirchner was transferred to the northern part of Pennsylvania so that he could no longer include Baltimore in his travel schedule. Nothing remained but to request old Pastor Bager, feeble as he was, to resume preaching in Baltimore from time to time; and in a spirit of Christian humility he consented to do so. Occasionally there were also visits from preachers who happened to be passing through. We have already met the restless, much traveled John Christopher Hartwick in Frederick. He was without doubt a man "of very good attainments and of exemplary conduct"—he just had too much wanderlust in him. In the war he had served as chaplain under General Amherst, and now found it hard to get used to a quiet, civilian course of life. He rushed through the country like a comet, now in Maine, then in Virginia, today in New York and tomorrow in Pennsylvania, preaching gladly wherever he was needed as long as nobody tied him down to one place.[36]

There were others besides Hartwick. Of one of them, Nikolas Hornell, a Swede who had served the German church in York for a while, we have a bit of information. As he spoke German rather

[35] *Early Accounts*, 14 f.
[36] A contemporary sketch has this to say about Hartwick: "He did not pass his days in listless inactivity, for we hear of him everywhere, wandering hither and thither, with characteristic restlessness, and with no certain dwelling place. . . . It is impossible to trace him in all his wanderings. Suffice it to say, that while he was a good and conscientious man, and faithful to his convictions of duty, his unfortunate peculiarities interfered with his usefulness, and prevented his remaining for any considerable period a pastor anywhere; and besides, it seemed as if the spirit of the wandering Jew had taken full possession of him, for in no case did obligations, however strong, bind him to the same people longer than six months, or at most a year." (See Julius Hofmann, *History of Zion Church*, 54.)

badly, his sermons were often quite unintelligible to his hearers. And since a congregation naturally wishes to understand the sermons of a pastor who is paid to deliver them, and since Hornell was furthermore "a hard Lutheran as to every paragraph of the Augsburg Confession," he was soon allowed to go his way. Again the Reverend Mr. Hartwick rushed through the city on one of his many excursions, and was even persuaded (perhaps because it was winter) to stay put for half a year. Sometimes, so it is reported, he preached in English. "He also had many English hearers. But one could see at once that he was German. However well he intended to do things, yet the Shibboleth was there."[37] Hartwick was well liked wherever he chose to stay for any length of time. His friendships not only covered a wide area geographically, but also widely separated social classes. He was genial and friendly with peasants and artisans, and at the other end of the social ladder was "well esteemed by Lord Fairfax in Virginia."

A happy solution of the pastor difficulty was found when in 1765 Parson Kirchner returned from Pennsylvania and settled on a farm which he had bought "in the Barrens" not far from Baltimore. He had won his way into the hearts of the congregation during his earlier service, and was therefore urged to fill the present vacancy. He accepted, and thereafter preached every Sunday in the little frame church of the Lutheran congregation. "He received fifty pounds per year, a sum, to be sure, small enough for a spiritual guide. He could hardly eat his fill. Yea, we have at times found him eating his bread with tears. He was poor which made him shy and despondent. But he was thoroughly honest and attended to his sacridotal office with dignity and without hypocricy as befits a minister. And though he was poor, he strictly observed his duties, punishing fearlessly the vices which came to his knowledge."[38]

In order better to regulate the affairs of the church, the Reverend Mr. Kirchner undertook the framing of a church constitution. The constitution of 1769, inscribed by the pastor in clear, legible script in the church register, and signed by thirty-five members of the congregation, henceforth became the foundation for the church life.[39]

[37] *Early Accounts*, 15.   [38] *Ibid.*, 16.
[39] The names: Wiesenthal, Lindenberger, Diel, Heckel, Löble, Schrimm, Litig, Röchting, Blechroth, Hahn, Kohl, Eltrerbach, Schrand, Rauch, Strieh-

The old frame church was not very solid, and after less than a decade of use had become so ramshackle that the decision was reached to build a new and stronger one. Since the financial resources of the congregation were still meager, it was thought wise to organize a lottery to supply the necessary funds. Its creation was entrusted to a schoolteacher named Wörschler, but the outcome of the undertaking was tragic. The schoolmaster, disregarding the former unhappy experience in joint efforts with the Reformed, told them of the lottery plan, and they persuaded him that it would be a good thing to run the lottery jointly. The details of the resultant effort are lacking. But if we may believe the report of the Lutherans, they—the Lutherans—had all the work and trouble connected with the lottery, while the Reformed garnered all the pecuniary benefits. "All we had to do was to look on with dry mouth and forget our grief," states the manuscript in its picturesque language.[40] However, the report should be taken with a grain of salt; for it is hardly credible that the Reformed were such rascals, and the Lutherans such fools.

So they proceeded to build the church without benefit of lottery. The old frame building was torn down, the lumber sold and a plain brick building erected which was for the time being to serve as a church, and later, when funds should become available for a larger church building, to be used as a schoolhouse.[41]

Shortly after the completion of the new building old Pastor Kirchner died (1773). His successor was Johann Siegfried Gerock, a scion of the famous Wuerttemberg family of theologians. He had been ordained in Darmstadt, and had migrated to America in 1753. He had served as pastor in Lancaster, Pennsylvania, and in New York City. When he came to Baltimore he already belonged to the narrowest circle of the followers of the patriarch Muehlenberg. The congregation had chosen wisely, for in human and spiritual qualities Gerock surpassed all his predecessors. His first achievement was a new church constitution. It was framed in 1773 and

---

bod, Küss, Brown, Dank, Kemmer, Miller, Breitenbach, Yeiser, Trombohr, Fass, Heyner, Brechtle, Herrmann, Schwarz, Rock, Werdenberger, Wörschler, Messersmith, Fürst.

[40] *Early Accounts,* 17.

[41] Griffith, *Annals,* 56. Scharf, *Chronicles,* 45. The church was situated on Saratoga Street, near the present location of Zion church.

signed by 147 members—an indication of how greatly the congregation had increased in recent years.[42]

On several occasions in the history of the Lutheran Church we have met the name "Wiesenthal." Dr. Charles Frederick Wiesenthal was not only a guiding spirit in his congregation, but also the first truly significant German in Baltimore. He is thus deserving of somewhat more detailed study.[43]

Of Wiesenthal's life before he came to America we know little. It is certain that he was born somewhere in Prussia in 1726. Family tradition reports "that he was physician to Frederick the Great." Details about that are lacking. His familiarity with the organization of the medical department of the Prussian army was shown during the Revolutionary War in his letters to the Maryland authorities, a fact which seems to lend to the tradition a somewhat stronger plausibility. It may be assumed without question that he belonged to the higher social class, and that he had received an excellent education. Whether or not he held an official medical degree we do not know; he himself makes no mention of one.[44]

In 1755 he came to Baltimore and remained there for the rest of his life. Why he settled in Baltimore Town, at that time a rather poor village with a few hundred inhabitants, we do not know. The route to Western Maryland was shut off just at that time—1755 was the year of Braddock's defeat—and settlers were returning

[42] The constitution, together with the names of the signatories, is published in Julius Hofmann, *Zion Church*, 20-24.

[43] The best presentation of his lifework is found in an article by Eugene F. Cordell, "Charles Frederick Wiesenthal, Medicinae Practicus, the Father of the Medical Profession in Baltimore" (*Johns Hopkins Hospital Bulletin*, nos. 112/113, 170-74, Baltimore, 1900). Cordell published numerous letters from Wiesenthal to his son Andrew. Cf. further: Griffith, *Annals of Baltimore*, 59. John R. Quinan, *Medical Annals of Baltimore* (Baltimore, 1884), 12 ff. E. F. Cordell, *Medical Annals of Maryland* (Baltimore, 1903), 13-18, 652, 656, 658-60, 662-65. F. R. Packard, *History of Medicine in the United States* (New York, 1931), I, 301 f. E. F. Cordell, *History of the University of Maryland* (New York, 1907), I, 6. A. B. Faust, *The German Element in the United States*, II, 399 f. Dieter Cunz, "Wiesenthal's Pioneer Medical Work," *American German Review*, IX, i (1942), 13 ff.

[44] One of his students, Dr. Ezekiel John Dornsey, who dedicated his thesis to Dr. Wiesenthal at Edinburgh in 1776, added an M.D. to his name. Another student, Dr. George Buchanan, who wrote a similar thesis in Philadelphia in 1789, gives the name without the title. Wiesenthal himself did not use the title of Doctor; in the acts of Zion church the name is given as Karl Fried. Wiesenthal, Medicinae Practicus.

from the war-threatened western part of the province. That may have been Wiesenthal's reason for not going to Frederick. Less easily understood is why he did not settle in the far more lively town of Annapolis. Perhaps he came to Baltimore in the company of others who made their home here; or perhaps he had a premonition that Baltimore held far greater promise for future development than Annapolis. We have no way of telling.

He at once took an active part in the organization of the Lutheran congregation; he married and became the father of four children. He took a lively interest in the public affairs of the city, and was naturalized in 1771. We shall have more to say later about his activities during the Revolution; in the present connection a brief account of his professional activity as physician must suffice. That activity won for him the title of "Father of the Medical Profession in Baltimore."

Wiesenthal's main interest was directed to one objective: to bring about the abolition of the quackery which was rampant everywhere, and to clear the way for the responsible professional practice of medicine. In 1786 Wiesenthal brought his views to the attention of the general public, and provided a basis for open discussion in newspaper articles and letters. His plan for a "medical establishment" was the following: to have the legislature create a board of three physicians, paid by the state treasury, whose business it would be to examine and approve applicants for the practice of medicine. The resultant fees were to be used for the purpose of creating and maintaining a medical library. It was further proposed that later a college be established, with the members of the board on the teaching staff. "To rescue the Dignity of Physic from that horrid State into which it is plunged within these few years and most especially since my Sickness will require a Herculean labor," wrote Wiesenthal in 1788 to his son Andrew, "and it will fall in some measure to your Lot to undertake the laborious Task." After the matter had been publicly discussed for a time, Wiesenthal on the 15th of December 1788 summoned all physicians in Maryland to a convention in Baltimore to agree upon a "plan for the regulation of medical practice." A society was organized, dedicated to the realization of this reform in the medical profession, with Wiesenthal as its first president. "We are just about procuring a Medical Regulation in a little more earnest than before," he states in a letter to his son, written on the day following the meeting. A petition to the legislature was circulated in the state and city with a request for signatures. The few good doctors to be found in Baltimore knew very well that "they were surrounded by swarms of quacks," and these fellows did their utmost to stir up opposition to the Wiesenthal plan. Since Wiesenthal died a few months after the Baltimore meeting, this first step toward the reform of the medical profession was the only immediate result. Before it could be put into actual practice, Wiesenthal's plan, so far in advance of the time, remained for many years an unrealized dream. The most he could do was to fight quackery with sound medical practice; and during his life he put forth every effort to build up a new generation of responsible doctors in Baltimore. He founded the first medical school in Maryland, a private undertaking that carried on until the medical faculty of the University of Maryland was created in 1807.[45] Of especial importance was his school of dissection. It was Wiesenthal's Institute that was stormed by the first Baltimore "dissection mob," which insisted upon the delivery of the corpse of an executed criminal.[46]

Wiesenthal was doubtless one of the most attractive personalities among the earliest Germans in Baltimore. Certainly he was the most cultured of them all, and the one with the highest social standing in the flourishing town. The following extract is from the report of a German traveler who spent some time in Baltimore in 1783: "At Baltimore I had the pleasure of knowing Dr. Wiesenthal, a worthy fellow countryman, and old German physician. He has been here since almost the first beginning of the town, and for his private character as well as his attainments is generally esteemed."[47] His portrait, preserved in a sketch by his son, shows the finely molded head of the scholar and reveals a courtly correctness in all external features: high brow, clear eyes, a large, straight nose and a sharply defined mouth. A formally powdered wig surmounts a noble forehead. His letters to his son betray a warm paternal interest as well as an unusually keen realization of his professional responsibilities.

[45] The school was located on Gay and Frederick Streets. Among its students were William Augustus Dashiel, George Buchanan, Ezekiel John Dorsey, Andrew Wiesenthal, Frederick Dalcho.

[46] Patrick Cassidy, who had murdered Captain John de Corse.

[47] Johann David Schoepf, *Travels in the Confederation, 1783-1784.* Translated and edited by Alfred J. Morrison (Philadelphia, 1911), 340.

The manuscript that recounts the first steps of the Lutheran congregation was probably composed by Wiesenthal, and gives evidence not only of his religious zeal, but also of a sense of humor and a friendly, tolerant understanding of the weaknesses and foibles of his fellow men. We find in this manuscript, in its diction and in its underlying wisdom and sympathy, clear evidence of the deep culture and sound human understanding of the physician. On the day following Wiesenthal's death the *Maryland Journal and Baltimore Advertiser* (June 2, 1789) said: "If the strictest attention in his profession which humanity could excite & that success which might be expected from superior medical abilities improved in an uncommon measure by reason and observation deserve to be remembered, the tears of gratitude must flow in sorrowful profusion."

Of the few noteworthy Germans whom Baltimore produced in pre-revolutionary times, Nicholas Hasselbach deserves special mention.[48] Hasselbach had emigrated to Philadelphia from Germany in 1749. He worked for a while in a paper mill in Wissahickon, Pennsylvania; is supposed to have learned the printing trade at Christopher Sower's, and to have set up a printing press in Philadelphia in 1762 with Anthony Armbruster and another German. Two Philadelphia imprints of 1762 and 1763 with Hasselbach's name are still extant. In 1764 he was still in Philadelphia, but that was his last year there; for we learn that he acquired a lot in Baltimore in 1765 and established a printing business there—the first in the city.[49]

No specimens of the work of the Baltimore press are preserved,

---

[48] Lawrence C. Wroth, *A History of Printing in Colonial Maryland* (Baltimore, 1922), 112 ff. *First Records*, 49. Until now we did not know from what part of Germany Nicholas Hasselbach came. In a letter of Christian Mayer, dated December 16, 1830 (Mayer letter, Md. Hist. Soc., 195-96), we read: "that the Hasselbach who died here was the sole surviving brother of the one who died in Batavia (a certain Friedrich Hasselbach, who died in the Netherlands East Indies in 1816) can be proved by the church records in Runkel." This hint led us to a search in the church records in and near Runkel. The church records of Münster near Runkel yielded the following information: a Niklas Hasselbach was born in Weyer on September 3, 1736. He was the son of Johann Heinrich Hasselbach and Anna Catherine, nee Holtig. The church records do not list anything about Niklas Hasselbach except the entry of his birth. It may be assumed that he emigrated, probably together with an uncle Joh. Wilh. Hasselbach. (Runkel is a town in Nassau, on the banks of the Lahn; Weyer, a little village east of Limburg, belongs to the deanery of Runkel.)

[49] The business was located on the northwest corner of Gay and Baltimore Streets.

except a booklet that was undoubtedly printed in Hasselbach's time.[50] It is the first bit of printing that the history of Baltimore has to show.

In 1768, when the inhabitants of Baltimore got up a petition to have the county seat transferred from Joppa to Baltimore, the petition was printed in English and German and put into circulation. These handbills lack an imprint, but it may certainly be assumed that the English as well as the German version was printed by Hasselbach.[51] It has been stated that the principal output of the Hasselbach press were schoolbooks, and some other minor works in German and English. Apparently Hasselbach had also planned to print a German Bible.[52]

Hasselbach lost his life while on a trip to Europe in 1769 or early 1770. His widow sold the printing establishment to the famous Baltimore printer, William Goddard, who began his activities in Baltimore a few years after Hasselbach's death. Hasselbach's business must have prospered, for in 1775 the widow's estate after all debts had been paid ran to 2000 pounds sterling—a considerable sum for that time.

The physician, Charles Frederick Wiesenthal; the printer, Nicholas Hasselbach; the Reformed preacher, William Otterbein; and the Lutheran pastor, Johann Siegfried Gerock—these rank as the foremost German citizens of Baltimore in colonial times. That there were even these few is characteristic of Baltimore. In Western Maryland the German element consisted of the great anonymous

[50] *A Detection of the Conduct and Proceedings of Messrs. Annan and Henderson . . . at Oxford, Pa., Meeting House, April 18 . . . 1764.* By John Redick. It is the story of an unimportant controversy among the members of the Presbyterian Church in Pennsylvania. The only copy of this 47-page booklet is in the possession of Mr. Robert Garrett, Baltimore. It is reprinted in George W. McCreary's *The First Book Printed in Baltimore-Town* (Baltimore, 1903). McCreary also gives a brief sketch of Hasselbach's life and work.

[51] L. C. Wroth has pretty well established this (Wroth, 114). Copies of the bill are in the possession of the Maryland Historical Society.

[52] A story is told which undoubtedly refers to Hasselbach—if it is true. The story is that a Maryland missionary, while addressing a congregation of Indians, held out his Bible and proclaimed that it was "the gospel—the truth—the word of God." "What!" said one of the audience. "Did the great all-powerful spirit make this book?" "Yes," replied the missionary, "it is His work." The literary-minded Indian answered indignantly, "I believe it to be a great lie! I go to Baltimore last month where I see a Dutchman make him. Great spirit want no Dutchman to help him." (Wroth, 113.)

mass of farmers and artisans, all of them fine, honest fellows whose names, however, would be quite forgotten had not the church register preserved them. In Baltimore there are a few names that rise above the average. In the first chapter of the history of two professions that are outstanding in importance for the cultural development of any city we find two German names: Wiesenthal, the physician, and Hasselbach, the printer.

IV. EVERYDAY LIFE

ET US glance briefly now at the daily life of the Germans who immigrated to America in the decades preceding the Revolutionary War. At the outset, life was generally so laborious for them that many a homesteader must have said to himself, "If only I had stayed at home." Most of them arrived in America under most discouraging circumstances. Either they had disposed of all their property abroad to raise the necessary passage money, or else they had come as "redemptioners." The latter meant that a ship's captain had brought them across the ocean without charge, and then sold them into a limited servitude in return for payment of the fare. If someone in America had need of a laborer or a maid servant, he had only to go to the nearest port and wait for the first ship in from Europe, with the assurance that a large percentage of the passengers would be redemptioners. He would select one of them whose sturdy frame gave best promise of good work, pay the passage money to the captain and then be free to take his charge home with him as a servant. The average term of service was five years.

We touch upon the question of redemptioners lightly at this point in our story, as we shall have occasion to discuss it in greater detail later on in connection with the founding of the German Society. Suffice it to say that in Maryland the greater part of the redemptioners were German. Many of them had to put in five or even more unproductive years before they could begin to live their own lives.

Financially, even those who retained their freedom on arrival were in very poor circumstances. Most of them rented their land and paid for it in annual installments. Whenever they could they settled along the border, because that was where the land was cheapest. If they finally managed to attain a degree of prosperity and security, it was only by overcoming great obstacles and in spite of innumerable odds which were against them.

Whether they came from Pennsylvania or directly from Germany, they appeared largely in groups, and as such pressed on into the wilderness. At first they settled, not in established communities, but in scattered settlements; not, however, so far apart—if that could be avoided—that they lost all contact with their neighbors. First a log house was built, to be replaced later, though usually not until the second generation, by a stone dwelling. By preference they settled on the banks of a river; and in the years before the cities provided a concentration of their own, it was the rivers, the Monocacy and the Conococheague, which provided the bond that united the far-flung settlements and held them together.

The first task was to clear the land of trees. The Germans never accepted the usual easy custom of "girdling" the trees and then allowing them to dry out: they felled the trees, carefully removed the undergrowth and thus converted the land into genuine arable acreage in the course of a year or two.[1]

The various lots were often given the most remarkable names— an indication that the men from the Palatinate, despite their many difficulties, still retained their sense of humor: "I Have Waited Long Enough"; "Bachelor's Delight"; "Bird in the Cage"; "More Stones"; "All I Can Get"; "Adam's Fall"; "Abraham's Intrigue"; "Bone Him, Secure Him"; "Better than None"; "Double Trouble"; "Frosty Morning"; "I Wish There Was More"; "Drunkards not Mistaken"; etc.[2] The average size of the lots can be approximated from the debt books of the counties. In Frederick at the middle of the eighteenth century the average size of a farm was 370 acres.[3]

Water and woodland were the two things the Germans sought when they chose their land—water, because it promised good pasturage for their cattle; woodland, because it was considered especially productive. The Germans started a new chapter in the agricultural history of Maryland. With cool disdain of the allurements of tobacco culture, they began at once with the cultivation of grain, which became, as Eddis tells us, an important article of export to Europe as early as the close of the colonial period.[4] Apple and peach

---

[1] Benjamin Rush, "An Account of the Manners of the German Inhabitants of Pennsylvania," *Proceedings of the Pennsylvania German Society* (Lancaster, Pa., 1910), XIX, 58.

[2] General Index of Deeds, 1748-1778, Frederick County Court House, Frederick, Md. Also J. Thomas Scharf, *History of Western Maryland* (Philadelphia, 1882), I, 374 ff.

[3] Gould, *Land System*, 77.

[4] Eddis, 102. Newton D. Mereness, *Maryland as a Proprietary Province* (New York, 1901), 120 ff. Avery O. Craven, *Soil Exhaustion as a Factor in the Agricultural History of Virginia and Maryland, 1606-1860* (Urbana, Ill., 1925), 30 ff.

orchards were planted as soon as the first rough work of clearance was over.[5] To provide water for pasture and garden, they contrived a simple system of irrigation—one of the first of its kind anywhere in America.[6]

The planting of flax was undertaken early, because it was needed for the manufacture of linen. The wearing apparel of the settlers soon began to look more American—or at least more Indian—than German, as we learn from a number of sources.[7] With astonishing rapidity the farmer adapted himself to the requirements of country and climate.

For all the necessary articles of everyday life—tools, household necessities, clothing, etc.—the settlers were thrown upon their own inventive resources, as is of course the case in any exclusively rural community. But gradually the situation changed, as a few individuals here and there turned away from farming to learn a trade. Moreover, among the new arrivals from Germany there was a large number of artisans, weavers, smiths, cobblers, bakers, butchers, clockmakers, saddlers and the like.[8] Their importance became increasingly greater as the settlements grew larger and more concentrated.

In the first decade, communication between the newly settled districts and the outer world was very difficult. Goods could be transported only by boat along the waterways, or in the unwieldy Conestoga wagons by the old Indian trails. But this condition was soon improved. The government of Maryland was concerned to connect the hinterland, where German settlers had numerous connections with Pennsylvania, with tidewater Maryland. Therefore, as early as 1740 a road was built from Annapolis to the back counties on the Monocacy and the Conococheague. This means of communication soon assumed great importance in the export trade of grain. "A considerable quantity of grain is sent from hence, by

[5] Peter Kalm's Travels in North America, edited by A. B. Benson (New York, 1937), 41.
[6] Kalm, 162. Frederick Schrader, The Germans in the Making of America (Boston, 1924), 92.
[7] "Moravian Diary," Virginia Magazine of History and Biography, XI, 117. "We came to a German house (near the Potomac, 1749), where we found the whole family clothed in Indian fashion." Williams, Frederick County, I, 17.
[8] Scharf, Western Maryland, I, 63. Williams, Frederick, I, 9.

Court house and public square in Hagerstown about 1776

Otterbein Church in Baltimore, the oldest church building still standing, erected by the German Reformed congregation shortly after the Revolutionary War

HEINRICH SCHEIB (1808-1897)
Pastor at Zion Church in Baltimore for sixty-two years, outstanding educator and preacher, known for his liberal theological views

land carriage, to Baltimore, for exportation to the European markets," so writes Eddis from Frederick in 1771.[9]

As soon as the settlers had provided a roof for their heads, they proceeded to build a log church, and attempted to get the services of a preacher. We have already referred to the difficulties connected with that attempt. When there was no preacher available, the schoolmaster assumed the spiritual leadership of the community. Furthermore, in his capacity as a sort of town clerk, he performed all necessary clerical tasks, and in general was the man to whom recourse was had when counsel was needed. Several of these schoolmasters, such as Thomas Schley in Frederick, Benjamin Spyker in Sharpsburg and Moritz Wörschler in Baltimore, undoubtedly rendered invaluable services to these early German settlements.[10]

Church and school tried to be mutually helpful. As has been said, the schoolmaster was often called upon to assume the office of preacher. On the other hand, the churches took an active interest in matters of education. In 1753 the Reformed Coetus in Philadelphia decided to subsidize seven schoolmasters, among them the one on the Monocacy. Moreover, to quote the *Minutes*, "The Rev. President has been instructed to have a small catechism printed, for the benefit and education of the youth, on the same principle that last winter already, at his own expense, he had a thousand ABC books printed, most of which he had distributed for nothing and sold the remainder for half price, in order that the youth might not be neglected because of the lack of these books."[11] Frederick too had received its proper quota of these books. In the old manuscript of the Lutheran congregation in Baltimore reference is also made to education. "Already at this stage (at about 1770) we had a desire to increase, if possible, the efficiency of our school. It is an incontestable fact that a good school education lays the foundation to our future happiness. Through it the minds of the children are led to virtue and learning, which enables them to be useful to themselves and to the world. . . . It takes men of intelligence to realize

[9] Eddis, 101.

[10] Benjamin Spyker, the son of Judge Peter Spyker in Berks County, Pa., was born in 1747, and had enjoyed an unusually good education for his time. He became schoolmaster of the German Reformed church in Sharpsburg, Md., where, with the aid of a lottery, he had built a schoolhouse in 1769. Nead, 115.

[11] *Minutes*, 89.

the importance of such an undertaking (to organize a school), men that are fully convinced that money spent for that purpose is very usefully spent indeed."[12] The necessity for thorough schooling is repeatedly stressed by the early churches of America, and wherever it was possible to do so, they carried their good resolutions into effect.

Most Germans were affiliated with a Lutheran or a Reformed congregation; a few belonged to various other sects—Moravians, Methodists, Mennonites, Dunkers; and occasionally a few Catholics would crop up.[13] The influence of the sects was obviously stronger in Western Maryland than in Baltimore, especially so in the westernmost part of the state, in the Conococheague district. The minutes of the Reformed Church (1770) comment on the fact that there were many disputes in that district, and that two delegates were sent there to iron out these differences. "Do. Weymer has been called to that place, and when there is peace in the congregation he will accept the call with the approval of the Coetus. The sects make strong efforts there, and the district is populous."[14]

Only very few Germans were members of the Anglican Church. Officially they were rated as "dissenters." "Frederick contains . . . several chapels for the accommodation of the Germans and other dissenters," says the Englishman Eddis (1771).[15] From 1692 on a law was in force in Maryland which raised the Anglican or Episcopal Church to the status of state church, and required every inhabitant of the province to pay an annual tax of forty pounds of tobacco for its support.[16] The Anglicans were a minority in Maryland, and the law of 1692 was therefore much resented by all other congregations. Of course, the Germans had also to submit to it. In the early years of the settlement of the Monocacy Valley the government had not enforced the law, because of its wish to make conditions as attractive as possible to German settlers; but later on the German Lutherans and Reformed, like all other congregations, were made subject to the church tax. It was a heavy burden on them. Only with great difficulty had they succeeded in raising sufficient funds to build their own church and support their own pastor; and now they had, in addition, to pay an annual tribute to the Episcopal

[12] *Early Accounts*, 16.
[13] Lucy F. Bittinger, *German Religious Life in Colonial Times* (Philadelphia, 1906).
[14] *Minutes*, 296.   [15] *Eddis*, 101.   [16] MA, xiii, 425 ff.

Church, with which they had no connection whatever. Practically no Germans were members of the Episcopal Church, as appears from the fact that a petition of that church in Frederick, dated 1756, can show only two German names in a membership of some two hundred.[17] Generally speaking, the Germans had no connection at all with the official church and derived no benefit from it. Quite naturally, therefore, they paid the tax only unwillingly. We know that in 1758 the Frederick Lutherans made an energetic effort to rid themselves of the burden.[18] So anxious were they to bring this about that they even called upon Muehlenberg to help them attain their purpose. Muehlenberg reports as follows regarding the matter: "They [the Lutherans in Frederick] stated the case in this way: 1. We, the German residents of Maryland are required by law to pay an annual tax for the support of the English minister of the High Church in the Province. We derive no benefit from it as we have no need of English if we wish to hold fast to our language and religion, establish churches and schools out of our own means, and support ministers and schoolmasters out of our scanty earnings. It is also very difficult to find good ministers and stewards, and to control a congregation consisting of voluntary members, for here all are equals. When, in addition, disputes arise one runs here, another there, and falls into disbelief and superstition. Our children are ashamed of the religion of their parents, and unite, when it turns out best, with the High Church. 2. The English minister of the province has recently died; would it not be possible to petition the high authorities, that either a) the tax should be remitted in the case of the German Lutherans, or, b) that a German minister should be supported by their part of the tax, or, c) that a minister should be appointed who should serve both the English and the Germans." But none of these suggestions bore fruit; not even Muehlenberg could shake the solid foundation of the government church tax. And there the matter rested.

The suggestion that a bilingual pastor be appointed was clearly absurd, as Muehlenberg had pointed out to the people of Frederick. In the Episcopal Church there were, as has been said, practically no Germans; and among the Lutherans there was only one who could qualify for admission, and that was Muehlenberg himself, who had for various reasons declined such an offer in the past. The

[17] MA, LII, 670 ff. [18] Wentz, Frederick, 106.

language problem was at that time not as difficult as it was to become in the following century; however, even then, in 1758, there was an indication of what was to come, for the Memorandum of the Lutherans in Frederick adverts to the fact that children were already occasionally transferring their allegiance to the Anglican Church. In general, however, there was at the time unanimous agreement that preaching should be in German, or that entries in the church records should be in that language. It was at first only those Germans who were personally anxious to establish closer relations with the English portion of the inhabitants who introduced the use of English in the church services. The Moravian congregation in Graceham passed a resolution on July 18, 1762, "that there should occasionally be English preaching here for the sake of our English neighbors, and it was held once in four weeks for some time."[19]

Quite characteristic, and interesting as a foreshadowing of the language problem that was to arise in the next century, is an event that took place in the Lutheran congregation in Baltimore in 1771. After the congregation had acquired a building lot for their new church, Dr. Wiesenthal said in a circular letter: "Daily experience taught us that our children almost entirely learned and understood the English language quicker and better than our German tongue." Wiesenthal feared two possible outcomes from this situation: first— and this was to become the persistent fear of all German congregations in the next century—"that the language would be lost entirely and the religion with it"; meaning, of course, that the younger generation, faced with the language barrier, would drift into the English churches of various denominations. Moreover, it might easily happen that the children and grandchildren of present members, if they lost their ability to understand German, would also lose their interest in the church. Wiesenthal thought it best to make no direct reference to language in his letter, thereby leaving the matter in abeyance and providing for the possibility of the eventual introduction of English into the service. "He thought it safest and most prudent not to mention any language at all in the deed, but only the religion, considering that in case a German church were expressly mentioned therein, there might be some who without any special love for religion and inclined to quarrel, might deny the right of using the English language to those who needed it for

[19] Oertel, 26.

their edification under the pretext that it had been stipulated that it was to be a German church, even if there were only ten Germans."[20]

Wiesenthal's suggestion met with violent opposition on the part of schoolmaster Wörschler, who moved heaven and earth to break up the plan. "He had a hundred things to say against it. But one thing was sufficient and created a complete uproar: that it was a German church and should remain such. . . . If this happens now for the mere sake of a deed, what will happen in case it should actually be necessary?" queries the manuscript in gloomy premonition of the coming language controversy. The Baltimore debate soon extended far beyond the city. In all German settlements along the Atlantic seaboard the general opinion was that Wiesenthal had planned to suppress the German language and to supplant it secretly by English. Severe disciplinary measures had to be taken to free Wiesenthal and Lindenberger—another vestryman who had cooperated with him—from the widespread condemnation to which they were subjected. The whole business led to an interesting conclusion which, we believe, found frequent corroboration in future years, namely, that the higher social strata of the immigrant population more easily and quickly accommodated themselves to the cultural conditions of their new home, and therefore offered less resistance than the middle and lower strata to the spread of the English language among them. Wiesenthal stood without question at the top of the social ladder among the Germans in Baltimore, and was one of the few in the group who had access to the upper class of society; the same applies to Lindenberger. Wörschler, the schoolmaster, represents the middle stratum, which clung much more tenaciously to the cultural tradition of the homeland and to the German language. As far as we have observed, this is the first time in the history of the Germans in Maryland that such a division arose.

The first generation very naturally had protracted difficulty with the English language. This is made very clear in a petition of forty-three German citizens of Baltimore, dated 1767.[21] "The Principal Inhabitants of Baltimore Town" complained to the governor that various officials of the city, taking unfair advantage of the Germans'

[20] *Early Accounts*, 18 f.
[21] MA, xxxii, 194-204. German names often appear in more or less anglicized form in the Petition: Steiger as Stigar; Wörschler as Wersler; Hartweg as Hartway, etc.

unfamiliarity with the English language, taxed them unduly for their activities. They therefore requested that one or more officials be appointed who were familiar with both languages. What happened to this petition we do not know. We only know that it stirred up a good deal of official dust and produced numerous counter petitions on the part of the officials concerned. The importance of the whole affair lies merely in the fact that it throws a little light on the language problem as it existed in that early period.

A real concession as regards language was made to the immigrants during the French and Indian War: companies were organized in which commands were given in German. In a letter from Henry Fox, Secretary of State of the King, to the governor of Maryland (March 13, 1756) we read: "It having been Represented that a Considerable Number of foreign Settlers in America might be now willing to enter into the Kings Service if they were Commanded by Officers of their own Country, An Act of Parliament has been passed of which I send you inclosed a printed Copy, enabling his Majesty to grant Commissions to a Certain Number of German Swiss and Dutch Protestants, who have served as Officers . . . in Order to assist in Raising and commanding Such of the foreign Protestants in North America, as shall be able and willing to serve with the rest of the forces."[22] Lord Calvert, too, in a letter to Governor Sharpe, recommended that a foreign legion be organized, "raising 1500 to consist of Swiss and Germans."[23] Calvert stated that considerable opposition arose against the plan in London, but admitted that a "Force composed of Foreigners who have always been true to hired Trust, their Service most likely will be best Effected by Command received in Language from Native Officers." Not only in London, but also in Annapolis, the plan for a foreign legion met violent opposition. Governor Sharpe wrote to his brother William (1756): "I am sorry to find the Scheme for raising so many Regiments here under Swiss Officers approved of, because no Step could have been taken that would have been more disagreeable to his Majesty's American Subjects and because I look upon it as

---

[22] MA, LII, 591. The regiment was known on organization as the 62nd or Royal American Regiment of Foot, and consisted almost entirely of Germans from Pennsylvania and Maryland. The First Battalion of the regiment was commanded by Henry Bouquet, a Swiss who had settled in Pennsylvania. Nead, 156.

[23] MA, VI, 327.

absolutely impracticable. . . . Can it be supposed that 4000 of our Inhabitants will hasten to enlist and serve under Foreigners for I shall be much deceived if these Swiss are not esteemed as such by the Germans who have for any considerable time resided among us as well as by the English. . . . I think I could soon convince the Switzers that they are not the proper persons to be sent to raise Men in these parts."[24] The governor made an unwarranted distinction here between Germans and Swiss. Swiss and Palatinates immigrated together in complete harmony, made joint settlements and considered themselves a common national group in respect to British settlers. If the governor had asked the people of Frederick for their opinion, they would undoubtedly have said that they preferred to receive their commands in German rather than in English, even if the German had a Swiss accent.

Governor Sharpe was always somewhat pessimistic in regard to the military reliability of the Germans in Western Maryland. Shortly after the outbreak of war on November 3, 1754, he wrote: "It is expected . . . that the Germans who have imported themselves into these Provinces will be found as ready as they are capable of bearing Arms on the Occasion, but I can assure you that whatever Character they may deserve for Courage or military skill I despair of seeing any of them so forward as to offer themselves Voluntiers under my Command unless the Enemy was to approach so far as actually to deprive them of their Habitations & Possessions of which alone they are found tenacious."[25] And in a letter to Lord Baltimore, in which he spoke of the flight of the Conococheague settlers, he stated: "What an opinion will this give you of our hardy & resolute Germans, Experience teaches us that they are possessed with much the same spirit as the Natives & that Bravery is by no means their distinguished Characteristic."[26] And a little later on: "The people who dwelt at conecochieg are again for the most part returned to their plantations under cover of the Militia that I ordered to their Relief but as they appear to be a Dastardly People I am afraid the first Indian that shall be discovered on the Frontiers will throw them again into Confusion & entirely break up that Settlement."[27] The Palatinates in Western Maryland had left their old homes because they

[24] MA, VI, 398. The Swiss were considered exceptionally good soldiers in Europe up to the close of the eighteenth century; which is probably why the king of England wished to entrust them with the organization of the regiment.
[25] MA, VI, 110 f.   [26] MA, VI, 484.   [27] MA, VI, 492.

hoped to find a place somewhere in the world where they could live their lives in peace. It may well be that they did not join the colors with as much speed and enthusiasm as the governor had hoped; but in this respect they were no different from the other inhabitants of Maryland, or from the members of the legislature in Annapolis, all of whom manifested considerable reluctance to go to war. Yet, there is no doubt that the settlers on the Conococheague and the Monocacy later on did their full share in the defense of the province.[28] And it was Western Maryland which suffered earliest and most severely from enemy attack.

Generally speaking, it took the Germans a long time to develop an interest in politics. Lack of political experience and training, a tendency to keep out of public affairs and the difficulties with a foreign language—all these contributed to their political inactivity. There were no German language newspapers in Maryland at that time. In Pennsylvania the famous Christopher Sower did his best to arouse an interest in public affairs among the Germans, and to that end printed the Charter of Pennsylvania in German (1743); some years later he did the same service for the most important state laws.[29] All these Sower publications were widely read by the Germans in Maryland; but whether they succeeded in arousing an interest in politics among them remains a question. Decades had to pass before the erstwhile subjects of German princes could accustom themselves to the English forms of self-government. Nor did they receive much encouragement to do so. The English inhabitants of the province did not relinquish their political sovereignty without a struggle;[30] and if the immigrants wanted to get into politics they had to fight their way in. A case like Jonathan Hager's, who had to conquer his seat in the legislature despite violent opposition, is symptomatic for the situation. The Germans were completely lacking in the aggressiveness through which the

[28] During the course of the war various references were made, even by Governor Sharpe himself, to the "Laudable Spirit which many of the Gentlemen of Frederick County in Particular showed." MA, LVI, 8 f.

[29] James Owen Knauss, Social Conditions Among the Pennsylvania-Germans in the Eighteenth Century as Revealed in the German Newspapers Published in America (Lancaster, Pa., 1922), 144.

[30] Even in a section as thoroughly German as Frederick County there were —as far as can be gathered from the published Acts of the Maryland Assembly (from the beginning of the county, 1748-1761)—no German names whatever among the county representatives.

other great immigrant group, the Irish, succeeded from the very beginning in gaining recognition in the political life of America. It took a world-shaking event like the American Revolution to stir up a little activity along political lines among the Germans.

It must not be forgotten that there was another reason, aside from the language difficulty, why the Germans were at a disadvantage in comparison with the English, Irish and Scotch immigrants, and that was the right of citizenship. When the inhabitants of the British Isles came to America, they at once automatically and fully enjoyed that right as subjects of the Crown. On the other hand, the Germans had to pass through a lengthy process before they could attain it. And only after attaining it could they enter politics. The English Parliament had passed a Naturalization Act in 1740 for Protestant immigrants to the American colonies; but it was a difficult and involved law, and we do not know how many Germans availed themselves of it at this time.

In their own defense, however, the Germans were diligent enough. In 1748, for instance, a strong protest was lodged with the Council by the Monacacy settlers against the county sheriff, regarding his inconsiderate methods of collecting back rents.[31] Most of the names signed to the protest are familiar to us from the German church records in Frederick. This time the Germans showed unwonted energy. They declared "that a Great Number of the Germans and some others were so much alarmed by the Sherriffs Proceedings, that several of them have already Left the Province, and others have declared, that as soon as they could Sell what they were Possessed off, they would go away, many of the Germans declaring, that they being Oppressed in their Native Country, Induced them to Leave it, and that they were Apprehensive of being Equally oppressed here, and that therefore they would go away to avoid it." Since the government under no circumstances wished to lose settlers, we may assume that it took steps to alleviate the "great Uneasiness at the Rigorous Treatment."

The government and the large landowners in Western Maryland took all possible steps to keep the stream of German settlers from drying up. We still have a curious document, a copy of a letter which twenty-five German settlers sent to their people in Germany,

[31] MA, xxviii, 422 ff. St. George L. Sioussat, *Economics and Politics in Maryland, 1720-1750* (Baltimore, 1903), 81.

in which they portray in glowing colors the splendors of Maryland and the promising future of the country.

"We whose names are hereunto Subscribed all Natives of Germany by this do acquaint our Country men with our Settlement in the Province of Maryland, into which Province we came from Pensilvania for the sake of Better Land, and Easier terms, & we assure you, that the Land in this Province is very fertile, and produces everything in Great Abundance, we here Enjoy full Liberty of Conscience, the Law of the Land in this Province is so Constituted, that every man is secure in the Enjoyment of his Property, the meanest person is out of the reach of Oppression, from the most Powerfull nor Can anything be taken from him without his receiving Satisfaction for it, all such of our Countrymen who have an inclination to Settle in this province, & will be industrious, Cannot fail of a Comfortable Subsistance, we take this Opportunity to Acquaint you that the Ship in which we agreed to go to Pensilvania is not Arrived but in the province of Maryland, where we found many of our Countrymen, that have Estates and Live very Comfortably, they received us with great Kindness, Giving us all Possible Assistance, the Land seems to be good, & we have observed that an industrious man may Live with great Comfort. One of the Principal Gentlemen of this Country [Mr. Dulaney] who lives at Annapolis, the Capital of the Province, was so Kind as to Assist us with 306 Pistoles & to free us from the Captain's power, we are perswaded that this Gentleman will be serviceable to Aid & Assist all Germans that will Settle in this Province."[32]

It may safely be assumed that this letter was prompted by Daniel Dulaney. Some parts of it sound like extracts from a travel folder. Every statement has been so carefully weighed, and so painstakingly selected with a view to appealing to the politically and religiously oppressed inhabitants of the Palatinate, that it is more likely to have sprung from the highly trained legal and political mind of Dulaney than from the heavy hand of German settlers. Conclusions from the letter regarding the Eden-like nature of the life of the Monocacy settlers should be drawn with caution; but no doubt the letter reflects the real relationship of the official and unofficial office

[32] MA, xxxxiv, 697. The letter is not dated, but was probably written toward the end of the forties. The German original has been lost; but the English copy which Daniel Dulaney sent to Lord Baltimore is still extant.

holders to the immigrant situation. The fact that Dulaney sent a copy of the letter to the Proprietor indicates that he was in accord with the official viewpoint. This document is undoubtedly one of the first of those innumerable *Amerikabriefe* which were sent across the ocean by the dozens to lure the people of Europe into emigrating to America.

Along the same line is a pass and letter of recommendation issued by Governor Samuel Ogle to four Germans from Frederick County in 1748. Stephen Ramsperger, Nicholas Benedick, Jacob Bruner and Henry Thomas, "all natives of Germany," desire to go home on a visit; and the governor requests in his pass that all "Princes States Magistrates & others whom it may concern" should treat the four Germans as proper British subjects and render them all necessary assistance.[33] It may be assumed that these four Germans were also expected to act to some extent as immigration agents.

Daniel Dulaney's son was, like his father, especially interested in the progress of the German settlers. To be sure, he owed them much, as they had largely increased the value of his land. But quite aside from that, he took a warm personal interest in them—a fact revealed, for instance, in the fight that he had with the legislature in 1758 to simplify the naturalization procedures, and above all to clarify for the benefit of the immigrants the question of legal title to land purchases and sales.[34] The law which he sponsored, "An Act for the Security of Purchases & other Claiming by or from Protestant Aliens," generally known as the Naturalization Bill, was not passed; the text is not preserved, and we can only gather from several proposed amendments what it was all about. Dulaney Jr., one of the most capable of Maryland lawyers, declared that many Germans had come to the province attracted by the promise that full security of property was assured them. Many, through ignorance of the law, had failed to become citizens, and for that reason frequently found themselves in difficulties in the matter of land transactions. The first section of Dulaney's memorandum, read before the Upper House, is as follows: "Because aliens who have settled in this Province, and by their Labour Industry & Frugality improved a Wilderness into regular Fruitfull and well Stocked Plantations, were invited hither by Proclamations Trans-

[33] MA, xxxxiv, 698.
[34] MA, LVI, lxiv, 59, 90, 115, 209, 212, 220, 309 ff.

lated into the German Language and Carefully Dispersed in Germany and the Faith of this Government which ought to be religiously observed, hath been in the most solemn and explicet Terms engaged to them that they should be secure and protected in the enjoyment of their property."[35] The Maryland law, continues Dulaney, was in this respect much less liberal than the laws of neighboring states; and this, if it became common knowledge, might lead the settlers to emigrate out of the state. He therefore attempted to improve the status of the settlers in this regard; but without success, as the proposed law failed of passage.

In a preceding chapter we have referred to the case of Jonathan Hager and his eligibility. At this time, shortly before the Revolution, it was realized that greater political rights would have to be accorded to the settlers than they had hitherto enjoyed. Governor Robert Eden reported the Hager case to Lord Dartmouth, and strongly supported the political eligibility of the foreign-born, if only to bring it in line with that of other colonies. He drew attention to the fact that the immigrants in Pennsylvania, for example, had the right to vote: "If they should not have the same privilege in Maryland it would be a great disadvantage to this Colony, especially as they are taxed with others to support the established clergy."[36] Hager's success in this matter established a precedent which became of far-reaching significance to the Maryland settlers in general.

The problem of fitting the immigrants into the political framework of the state, and of making them participants in the rights, and hence the duties, of citizenship, had been given considerable attention at this time. The Germans brought the first great wave of immigration to Maryland. This made it necessary that definite steps be taken to establish the legal and political status of the immigrants. In the Naturalization Bill which Daniel Dulaney proposed for his German settlers in Frederick County, one of the first steps was taken toward the wide citizenship measures of a later period— toward the "American Way of Life." The elder Dulaney had brought the Germans into the Maryland hinterland and settled them there; the younger Dulaney now attempted to build up their status as citizens of the state. It has been stated, and quite accu-

[35] MA, LVI, 56.
[36] "Correspondence of Governor Eden," *Maryland Hist. Mag.*, II (1907), 302 f.

rately,[37] that the Germans in Western Maryland set in motion new forces that caused the old conservative system to totter to its fall —forces that led to the Revolution and through it to the new American form of government.

[37] St. George L. Sioussat in *Maryland Hist. Mag.*, xxxvi (1941), 76.

V. REVOLUTIONARY WAR PERIOD

BUNDANT proof has been brought to light in recent years to show that the idea of a revolution did not suddenly and unexpectedly spring into being, but rather that it was preceded by decades of preparation before crystallizing in the great outburst of 1776.[1] It has been shown that in the State of Maryland, in addition to the general desire for emancipation from the English mother country, there was an internal political motivation which encouraged the idea of a revolution, here briefly reviewed as the "Anti-Proprietor Movement." All sorts of movements, political and economic, spiritual and material, decentralizing and democratic, generally American and specifically Maryland, united forces from various directions toward the common goal, July 4, 1776.

What caused the Germans in Maryland to take up the idea of a revolution?

The preparatory, broadening influence of enlightened thought is hardly to be noted among the Germans. The heritage of Enlightenment was surprisingly widespread in Maryland, not only among the upper classes but also among the middle classes and even the lower levels of society.[2] Questions of inherent rights and similar problems were discussed in clubs and societies of all classes, smoothing the way for liberal political ideas and even for the Revolution itself. But this phenomenon did not occur among the Germans. The religious element played too great a part in the lives of most of them to allow them to open their minds to rationalistic trends of thought. Of course, there were, especially in Baltimore, some exceptions, notably Wiesenthal, who was undoubtedly familiar with enlightened thought. But on the whole, the Church built a watertight barrier around the souls of the average Germans, keeping out the floods of rationalistic ideas as far as possible.

But, on the other hand, the Church served the Germans as a

[1] Charles A. Barker, *The Background of the Revolution in Maryland* (Yale Historical Publications, 38; New Haven, 1940). This is one of the best books in the literature of the history of Maryland and cannot be too highly recommended.

[2] Charles A. Barker, "The Revolutionary Impulse in Maryland," in *Maryland Hist. Mag.*, xxxvi (1940), 128 ff.

focal point for the gathering of explosive, revolutionary sentiment of a different kind. The idea of religious unity, the bond formed by the Anglican Church between the Anglo-Saxon population of Maryland and the English mother country, unquestionably acted as a sobering element for the members of the official Church in their conscientious struggle to decide for or against revolution. The Germans were spared this problem. On the contrary, the thought of the Episcopal Church and the unjust church taxes which they had had to pay for years served to hasten the Germans toward revolution. The Germans comprised the largest group of immigrants who remained outside the official Church. They had introduced a new feature into religious affairs in Maryland—a strong, active, relatively closed group of dissenters who had long demanded equal rights with the dominating official Church.[3] Thus explosive materials had gathered whose force among the church-conscious Germans should not be underestimated. It is significant that in all the colonies the German clergy almost unanimously and without delay supported the Revolution.

What was true of the religious situation was also true to some extent of the political. Among the Anglo-Saxon settlers certain sentimental ties to their old homes in England served at times to stem the tide of revolution. For the Germans these conflicting emotions did not exist. The Germans, with their tendency to stress the individual rights of various regions as demonstrated again and again in German particularism, were no doubt in their hearts unsympathetic with the centralization of the English colonial system and its laws necessarily suppressing political and economic independence. Artisans and merchants, among whom were many Germans, suffered particularly under the English Trade Acts. This anti-English feeling provided the Germans with much more powerful revolutionary impetus than they gained from the domestic political issues that were important for the rest of Maryland. Since the Germans had in the past hardly taken any active part in politics, the tyranny of the Calvert Proprietor Laws hardly claimed their attention. The battle cry, "No taxation without representation," could hardly have been expected to be re-echoed by the Germans, for they had no more representation in Annapolis than in the

[3] On the eve of the Revolution there were fifteen Lutheran and fourteen German-Reformed churches in Maryland.

Parliament in London.[4] Social grounds for the Revolution were far
less important in the "German counties" of the west than in the
English lower counties; in the tidewater counties the class differences between rich and poor were much greater than in the
western hinterland, where a relatively equal state of middle-class
well-being prevailed among the farmers and artisans. Economic
motives resulting in general in Maryland from the unbalanced
conditions of tobacco-raising did not affect the Germans, for, as we
have seen, they had nothing to do with raising tobacco.

One more point should not be overlooked: the psychological
side of the matter. The Germans, most of them "have-nots" unfamiliar with the language and customs of the country, had in the
past never been fully recognized. The fact that they were not
English and did not belong to the Anglo-Saxon part of the population had occasioned them various disadvantages and humiliations.
Now it seemed as if what had been a handicap in their lives might
even turn into an asset. What wonder that the dissatisfaction that
had been gathering in the hearts of the constantly slighted Germans
now broke out in an elementary hatred of England? Now, in a
sense, they could repay her for the fact that they had never belonged
to the English cultural and language group and therefore had felt
repressed from all sides. And then, too, they could finally prove to
their Anglo-Saxon fellow American countrymen that it had been
unfair of them always to look somewhat askance at the Germans.
Now was the time for the Germans to show that they did not lack
patriotism. In a negative way, this political and social inferiority
complex of the Germans had much to do with hastening the outbreak against England, and in a positive manner it did much to
whet their enthusiasm for the young American cause.

These prevailing conditions explain why the idea of a revolution
encountered such ready support and surprisingly fertile ground
among the Germans in Maryland. The very fact that the largest
and newest group of recent immigrants had settled in Western
Maryland and that this group by its very existence demanded the
changing and reconstituting of the old conservative, political system, was reason enough always to keep the western counties one
step ahead in the march toward the Revolution.

[4] Andreas Dorpalen, "Political Influence of the German Element in Colonial America," *Pennsylvania History*, VI (1939), 223.

It was in Frederick that for the first time a Maryland court rebelled openly against the law.[5] In 1765 the Stamp Act was proclaimed, stating that all official transactions were to be drawn up on paper supplied with certain stamps by the government. In August 1765 the new stamp collector for Maryland was burned in effigy by the population of Frederick; in November of the same year the court of Frederick in its capacity as highest court in Maryland declared the act to be unconstitutional. In spite of violent opposition, the court clerk was forced to register the decision.[6] True, among the judges of the courts at this time we find hardly any German names. Thanks to their political lethargy, the Germans had not yet worked themselves up to being judges. However, the court would certainly not have dared to reach such a decision if it had not known that it expressed the general opinion of the settlers in Frederick. This became clear when the decision of the court was celebrated by a public parade by the citizens of Frederick.[7]

With punctual regularity during the following decade Frederick County replied with protests and defiance to every new taxation act of the English government. Now for the first time German names begin to appear—names that we have already encountered in church registers but which up to this time have not appeared in connection with any political action. Among those attending a protest meeting in 1770 we find a great many of our old friends from the church records: Weller, Koontz, Hoover, Westfall, Nead, etc. In 1773, Jonathan Hager was elected deputy for Frederick County; in 1774 a great many German names appear on a political committee in Frederick (Schley, Groth, Hoffmann); and to an even greater extent than in the older section of the county the Germans were

[5] Barker, 308.

[6] Esther M. Dole, *Maryland During the American Revolution* (Baltimore, 1941), 25 ff.

[7] See description of this procession in the *Maryland Gazette* for December 16, 1765. Reprinted in Scharf, *Western Maryland*, 1, 122 f. A coffin was carried through the streets with the inscription, "The Stamp Act expired of a mortal stab received from the genius of liberty in Frederick County Court, 23rd November 1765, aged 22 days." The tea incident, which occurred in August 1774 in Frederick County deserves special mention as a forerunner of the Peggy Stewart affair in Annapolis and the Boston Tea Party. A tea ship (*Mary and Jane*) that was to have landed in Georgetown was prevented from landing by the Frederick County Committee and was forced to sail back to England with its full cargo. (*Maryland Gazette*, August 11 and 18, 1774.)

taking part in the political development of the western territory around Hagerstown.[8]

Besides Jonathan Hager, other German names appear in the political life of Western Maryland. In 1775, Jacob Funk, the founder of Funkstown, went as deputy for Frederick County to the state convention in Annapolis.[9] In Hagerstown the number of Germans sitting on political committees at the time of the outbreak of the Revolution is really striking. The most important organization, The Committee of Observation, was in 1775 and 1776 nearly half German—John Stull, Andrew Rench, Christian Ohrendorff, Conrad Hogmire, Jonathan Hager, John Sellars, George Zwingley, David Schnebley, John Rench, Michael Falkner, John Kerschner and Christian Lantz.[10] This sudden entrance of Germans into political affairs may be observed along the whole geographical line between Hagerstown and Baltimore. John Stull and Henry Schnebely take office as Justices of the Peace for Washington County and they are soon appointed members of the Orphan's Court.[11] John Kleinhoff is appointed Justice of the Peace for Frederick County;[12] Barnet Eichelberger and George Lindenberger sit on political committees in the city of Baltimore and later Lindenberger was for years Justice of the Peace for Baltimore.[13] Later in the course of the Revolution, two more Germans, Andrew Rench and Henry Shryock, join Stull and Schnebely in the position of Justice of the Peace for Washington County.[14] All this is not a passing phenomenon of revolutionary times; after this time we find German names again and again among the politicians of the western counties and of the city of Baltimore. The revolutionary cause was the vehicle upon which the Germans rode into the previously forbidden territory of local and state politics. The German immigrants who had formerly been entirely non-political became political-minded through the Revolution.

In farthest western Frederick County, the part around Hagers-

---

[8] *American Archives* (Washington, 1837), Series IV, I, 433, 986, 1009, 1173 f. Nead, 180 ff. Scharf, *Western Maryland*, I, 126 ff. Williams, *Frederick*, I, 75 ff.

[9] MA, XI, 4.

[10] Steiner, 32. The record book of the committee is now in the possession of the Maryland Historical Society; it was published in part in Scharf, *Western Maryland*, I, 132 ff.

[11] MA, XVI, 275; XXI, 141.   [12] MA, XXI, 248.

[13] Griffith, 58. MA, XXI, 287, 310.   [14] MA, XXXV, 293; XLVIII, 331.

town which established itself as a separate county at the outbreak of the Revolution, we find the strongest revolutionary impulse. When in 1776 the Convention of the Province in Annapolis handed Governor Robert Eden a laudatory resolution of appreciation, the district around Hagerstown was the first to express its dissatisfaction with this action. It stated that the "adultory address presented to the Governor Eden, supplicating his interposition with a people that has hitherto treated our just petitions with the greatest contempt . . . has very much alarmed the good people of this district," and followed with the summons to declare independence without further delay.[15]

Yet, the people in Annapolis were not nearly so much in a hurry to take such radical steps, much to the annoyance of the local politicians in Hagerstown, who tried again and again to hasten the revolutionary developments. In political matters it was necessary to conform to the tempo set by the state convention in Annapolis and the Continental Congress in Philadelphia. But in another field, the military, it was possible to give one's revolutionary enthusiasm free rein. In no aspect of public life during the Revolution did the German-settled counties of Maryland in general and the German inhabitants in particular contribute more to the advancement of the American cause than in the military.

In the summer of 1775, during the weeks between the battles of Lexington and Bunker Hill, the Continental Congress decided to call up a battalion of riflemen for which Pennsylvania was to contribute six companies and Virginia and Maryland each two. The two Maryland companies were assigned to Frederick County and they were raised there without any great difficulty in the shortest possible time.[16] The musters have not been preserved, but it is certain that a large percentage of those joining were Germans.[17] In the farthest western portion of the state (now called Garrett County) the names of two German settlers from the Allegheny Mountains appeared on the lists—George Reinhart and David Seibert.[18] We have the lists of officers of four companies in Frederick

[15] Bernhard Steiner, *Western Maryland in the Revolution* (Baltimore, 1902), 21.
[16] John A. Silver, *The Provisional Government of Maryland* (1774-1777), (Baltimore, 1895), 18.
[17] Dole, 69. Steiner, 14. Nead, 198.
[18] *The Glades Star* (Oakland, Md., 1942), 5, 39.

and they show that about a third of the officers had German names.[19] In June 1776 Congress decided "that a flying camp be established in the middle colonies," for which Maryland was required to secure 3400 men. This request was complied with just as willingly as the first one. We still possess the musters for the flying camp and they indicate again that the Germans of Western Maryland were very well represented.[20]

But this did not suffice. Immediately at the beginning of the Revolution an organization was created which shows clearly that the Germans were regarded as an unbeatable *pièce de résistance*. Since the spring of 1776 Congress had debated the question as to whether a regiment should be made up composed entirely of Germans. On June 27, 1776, the following decision was reached: "That four companies of Germans be raised in Pennsylvania and four companies in Maryland, to compose the said regiments." The Maryland Convention decided that two of these companies should be raised in Baltimore County and two in Frederick County.[21] These German regiments were specifically set up only for Germans; they were closed to citizens of other descent, as we may see clearly from the wording of the act itself.[22] The rolls of the German regiments have been preserved and, like the church records, they make an almost complete membership list of the German families who lived in Maryland around 1776.[23] Some names appeared that had not been heard before that time. War, in which anyone whether rich or poor can make his mark, brings to light for the first time in the historical records the large, previously anonymous masses. Of course, the

[19] Nead, 205 ff.

[20] MA, xviii, 42 ff. Nead, 208 ff. Cf. also the German names in the pension claims and bounty land applications of the Maryland veterans gathered together by Harry W. Newman in *Maryland Revolutionary Records* (Washington, 1938).

[21] MA, xviii, 181. Beverly W. Bond, *State Government in Maryland, 1777-1781* (Baltimore 1905), 40. Dole, 74.

[22] The case is cited of one James Fox, who was enrolled by George Keeports but who then had to be transferred to another regiment "not being a German or the son of a German could not serve in that Regiment." MA, xliii, 174.

[23] The enlistments of the Germans are to be found piecemeal in MA, xviii, on the following pages: 184, 190, 198, 203, 204, 212, 217, 220, 222, 225, 234, 235, 236, 239, 243, 250, 253, 254, 258, 260, 262, 267. Of the Baltimore Germans the names of Mackenheimer, Keeports, Gerock, Myers, Lindenberger, Cole and Ritter deserve special mention. (Griffith, 72.) In a letter to Governor Lee, George Washington stated that the number of enlistments in the German Regiment was 1074. MA, xliii, 430.

rolls that we have mentioned so far did not contain the names of all the Germans in Maryland who took part in the Revolutionary War. Many of the Germans were scattered in the various regiments of the Maryland line, and they were scattered so far and their names so often unrecognizably changed that it is impossible to make up a complete and accurate list.[24]

The names of members of a few of the German companies have been preserved. We know, for instance, that Benjamin Spyker, the previously mentioned schoolmaster in Sharpsburg, organized a company.[25] The names of many other German commanders, mostly in Western Maryland, also appear: George Scybert (Scheibert), Christian Ohrendorff, John Damwitz, John Rench, Daniel Stull, Adam Ott, Christopher Burkheart, Henry Shryock, Valentine Creager, Ludwig Weltner, William Keyser, George Stricker, Peter Mantz, Caspar Keller, Richard Baltsell and various others.[26] In Baltimore a Captain Philip Graybill undertook to raise two companies of Germans.[27]

One of the best-known German commanders was George Stricker. Again and again we find his name in the laws of the Maryland Council, in connection with payments for the soldiers, marching orders, opinions and recommendations. In January 1776 he reported that he had raised twenty-one men for his German company in two days, and therefore T. Johnson recommends to the Council at Annapolis that it assist Colonel Stricker for "he has had and will have good success in inlisting."[28] The Council soon passed this

[24] In Daniel McCurtin's "Journal of the Times at the Siege of Boston" (*Papers Relating to the Maryland Line During the Revolution*, ed. by Thomas Balch, Philadelphia, 1857), are to be found some indications regarding Germans in the Maryland line. At one point it is mentioned that Daniel Stull was made a sergeant (p. 27) and elsewhere is the statement: "Adam Ott and Company came into this Island. I see him and all the boys from HagersTown" (p. 37). McCurtin, the author of the Journal, probably came from Hagerstown himself.

[25] Nead, 210.

[26] MA, xviii, 43, 44, 50, 55; xi, 356, 497, 545; xii, 187, 215; xvi, 325.

[27] MA, xvii, 27, 29, 32, 165. The names of the officers of the two Graybill companies are: Keeports, Lhora, Gerock, Myers, Ritter, Lindenberger and Shugart. The name "Graybill," which sometimes appears as Graybell or Grable, was originally Krähenbühl. The family came from the Emmenthal in Switzerland and had to emigrate from there because of religious persecution, remaining for a time in the Palatinate and then coming to America (Maryland and Pennsylvania).

[28] MA, xi, 102, 108, 120.

recommendation on to the Maryland delegate at the Continental Congress and could hardly say enough in praise of Stricker as a good officer. "We think the service will be bennefitted by his Appointment. If he should be commissioned the sooner 'tis done the better as it will probably be a great inducement to his Countrymen to enlist."[29]

The name of John Stull of Hagerstown appears not only in political offices but also as an officer. He, too, raised a company, the names of whose officers were Heyser, Ott, Conrad, Shryock and Fackler, and the Council gave him full recognition for his military accomplishments. "The spirited behaviour of your Battalion has done the officers & men a great honour."[30] It may be seen from the acts of the Council at Annapolis that it considered John Stull a kind of confidential agent in the western part of the state. When, in 1777, the Council sent a detachment of prisoners of war to Hagerstown it requested John Stull to take care of the matter: "We are sorry to be obliged to trouble any Gentleman with this Business, without consulting him, but we know of no Body who will more likely than yourself, take the necessary Trouble or conduct the Matter to more general Satisfaction."[31]

The name Lawrence Everheart was alive in Western Maryland up to the middle of the nineteenth century. He was born in 1755 in Middletown Valley, Frederick County. In 1776 he joined the "Flying Camp" as a volunteer and, except for brief interruptions, remained in the army until 1781. It is reported that during a battle of the Southern Campaign, 1781, he saved the life of George Washington and that for a great many years thereafter he and Washington were friends.[32]

The name of a German baron, Felix Louis Massenbach, appears at the beginning of the war. We learn that he became a lieutenant in Captain Fulford's Artillery Company in February 1776.[33] Only a few weeks later he handed in his resignation, and the records tell us why his stay in Maryland was ended so suddenly. Apparently Massenbach was a particularly capable military man, for in a letter

[29] MA, XII, 12, 35.   [30] MA, XVI, 42, 50.

[31] MA, XVI, 246. Cf. also XLIII, 208.

[32] James McSherry, History of Maryland (Baltimore, 1904), (edited by B. B. James), 233. "Sketch of the Life of Lawrence Everheart," in Balch-Papers, 42 ff.

[33] MA, XI, 148, 173, 175.

to the Council is the statement: "General Lee has taken Mr. Massenbaugh with him to Virginia & says he understands his business & that he can't do without him. . . . Mr. Massenbach would have waited on you to thank you for your favors, but the Gen.l was in so great a hurry and said he must go with him."[34] Unfortunately this is all we know about the Maryland sojourn of the lieutenant, a man whom General Lee felt he could not do without.

A great many German names are to be found among the people in Maryland who had to do with the organization and the feeding of the army. The most important purchasing agent for the army in Maryland was a German whose name has already been found among the first German immigrants in Baltimore—Captain George Keeports. It is impossible to describe adequately the manifold, ceaseless activities of this man during the decade of the Revolution. No matter what the army needed—arms, powder, tents, horses, clothing, shoes, flour, meat, paper—Keeports concerned himself with everything. He was certainly one of the busiest people in Baltimore and that he discharged the duties of his office most excellently is proved not only by his long tenure in office but also from time to time by official recognition by the Council. "From every Thing that has past," reads a report of the Council in 1779, "we believe, he is not only very capable of conducting that Business, but that . . . he would cheerfully do every Thing in his Power to promote it."[35]

In addition to Keeports, a number of other German names are mentioned in the records that report on the feeding of the army. In Western Maryland Henry Schnebely, a physician of German-Swiss descent whom we have already mentioned in another connection, was particularly active.[36] He was named medical purveyor of Frederick County in 1780, was active in obtaining horses, food and clothing for the army, supervised prisoners of war and the production of war materials, making himself useful to the cause of the Revolution far beyond the limits of his medical profession.

In Baltimore Engelhard Yeiser supplied the militia with meat,

[34] MA, XI, 274, 279, 286.
[35] MA, XXI, 404. It is impossible to list all the places where Keeports' activities are mentioned. Suffice it to say that in the six volumes of the Maryland Archives, the Journal and Correspondence of the State Council of Maryland between 1777 and 1784, the name Keeports appears about 300 times.
[36] MA, XVI, 301, 423, and other places in MA, XXI, XLIII, XLV, XLVIII.

and he must have been a very loyal patriot, for the Council came to his defense most energetically when officers marching through the city illegally requisitioned his herd of cattle.[37] In Washington County two Germans, Henry Shryock and Henry Ackheart (Eckhardt), were named purchasing agents.[38]

Wherever possible the skill of the German artisan immigrants was used in the cause of the Revolution. Michael Cochinderfer in Frederick County received a loan of three hundred pounds from the Council of Safety "to enable him to carry on a Stocking manufacturing"; Jacob Myers in Baltimore received the same amount for his wire factory.[39] John Leypold, apparently a flour expert, was ordered by the Council to examine all the flour that the Council considered buying.[40] The Council ordered shoes for the soldiers to be made by two German artisans in the western part of the state, Jacob Shalman and Michael Boyer.[41] In a paper mill in Baltimore County William Hoffman produced paper for the cartridges of the American army.[42] In the payment memoranda which the Council addressed to the state treasurer we find German names again and again. For example, in a single memorandum in 1778 there are nine German names: Keeports, Rine, Kemp, Heldibrand, Brodbeck, Keeplinger, Yost, Grim and Schaup.[43]

There is one more point that requires special emphasis—the part which the Germans played in the manufacture of munitions in Maryland. There were in Maryland about a dozen arms factories in those sections of the state settled by the Germans—Baltimore, Georgetown, Frederick, Hagerstown.[44] Other than these, a great many Germans made weapons privately or on a smaller scale than

[37] MA, XVI, 347, 438.   [38] MA, XXI, 332.   [39] MA, XII, 134, 404.

[40] MA, XI, 505; XII, 187. Leypold's name also is mentioned frequently in the payment instructions that the Council addressed to the treasurer. Cf. MA, XXII, 119, 158, 194, 214, 232, 275.

[41] MA, XLV, 617, 620.   [42] MA, XI, 435.

[43] MA, XXI, 124. It is appropriate to recall here that it was a German who housed the Continental Congress in Baltimore from December 1776 to March 1777. When in the winter of 1776 the situation in New Jersey became acute and the Congress no longer felt safe in Philadelphia, it moved to Baltimore for a few months and met there in the house of a German, Henry Fite (Veit), located where Sharpe and Baltimore Streets cross. At that time it was one of the largest houses in the city and for a long time thereafter it was called "Congress Hall." (Griffith, 73. Hall, 31. Edith R. Bevan, "The Continental Congress in Baltimore," Maryland Hist. Mag., XLII, i [1947], 23.)

[44] MA, XI, 65. Steiner, Revolution, 45. Bond, 53.

the factories. Also, the most important saltpeter mines lay in the middle and lower districts of Frederick County. It is clear that the prospects for munition and weapon manufacturing were more favorable in the western part of the province, where the Germans had settled, than in the tidewater section. The farmers and pioneers who traveled westward to the open borderland supplied themselves with weapons and ammunition in the last large settlement, Frederick or Hagerstown. For these reasons the manufacture of weapons and powder was concentrated exclusively along the Potomac, Patapsco and Monocacy Rivers.

One of the largest gun factories was that of a German family named Yost in Georgetown. During the years 1775-1776 the name "Yost" appears numberless times in the Journal and Correspondence of the Maryland Council, and always in connection with supplying weapons. We hear of a Henry Yost, who, together with another German, John Unselt, received a weapons contract in 1776, and further that the Council impatiently and angrily cancelled the contract because they did not deliver the order fast enough.[45] John Yost is mentioned much more frequently.[46] He seems to have delivered his orders quite regularly; we hear that the Council paid him the sum of "two pounds eleven shilling seven pence for repairing guns," that the muskets which he manufactured were tested, or that he requested ten pounds of powder from the Council to season the muskets. Apparently he too could not deliver his goods as fast as the Council expected, for in March 1776 the Council warned him "to be as expeditious as possible." But it does not seem to have been Yost's fault that the deliveries were not made as promptly as was desired. In a report to the Council Yost declared that the lack of materials, especially the scarcity of steel, was enormously hampering his production.[47]

[45] MA, xi, 400 f.

[46] MA, xi, 99, 100, 169, 214, 293, 439, 464, 500. Christian Strack (Berichte der Deutschen Historischen Gesellschaft für den Distrikt Columbia, 1, 32 ff.) attempts to prove that the two arms manufacturers, Yost and Hughes, who are mentioned so frequently, are identical and that Hughes is only the anglicized form of the German name "Yost." It is a very incomplete and untenable hypothesis, and it is completely disproved by a document in MA, xi, 439, "The Minutes of the Council of Safety of May 23, 1776." The Council directs certain payments for shipments of arms, and in the same document mentions both the arms manufacturers, John Yost and Dan. & Sam. Hughes. Thus it is clear that there was both a Yost and a Hughes.

[47] MA, xii, 271.

Besides the Yosts, there were a great many smaller German gunmakers. In Baltimore George Lindenberger, who has already been mentioned, together with a Scotch business partner received a contract for powder and was granted a financial advance by the Council in order to complete the work.[48] Jacob Schley in Frederick County was commissioned by the Council to make guns and received fifty pounds upon completing the contract.[49] John Unselt, Henry Yost's partner, has already been mentioned.[50] Erasmus Uhler, a German artisan in Baltimore, was paid fifty-nine pounds by the Council for making gear; he had delivered cartouche boxes, bayonet belts, gun slings, etc.[51]

It is not necessary to set up a complete list here, but the examples given will serve to show clearly that the Germans cooperated actively in this field, probably because the percentage of Germans was particularly high among the artisans. The Anglo-Saxon settlers remained to a much greater extent in the tobacco industry; the Germans were farmers or artisans. This artisan element among them was increased after the middle of the eighteenth century since they very often settled in or near the urban centers of the state—Baltimore, Frederick or Hagerstown. The Anglo-Saxon immigrants settled the Eastern Shore and southern Maryland, where tobacco grew; since there were no cities, there were also fewer artisans.

In the city of Baltimore the most prominent German was one of the most zealous advocates of the revolutionary cause, Dr. Charles Frederick Wiesenthal. In January 1775 he was elected to the Committee of Observation of Baltimore County and in December of the same year he was appointed superintendent of the manufacture of saltpeter for Maryland.[52] A few months later he was commissioned by the Continental Congress to journey to Virginia in order to inspect the saltpeter works along the south branch of the Potomac.[53] In March 1776 the Council of Safety appointed him surgeon-

[48] MA, XI, 135, 137.

[49] MA, XI, 353, 356, 526. Later on, Schley also received frequent contracts from the state, especially for gunlocks. Cf. MA, XII, 140, 356.

[50] MA, XI, 308.   [51] MA, XI, 499.

[52] Cordell, Wiesenthal, 171 f. The Maryland Gazette of January 2, 1776, contains an article by him on methods of treating saltpeter.

[53] The Maryland Council voted him thirty-five pounds as his salary for this journey. MA, XII, 10. Wiesenthal's official report on the saltpeter works in Virginia is in MA, XII, 314. Cf. also Johann David Schoepf's travel account, op.cit., 342 ff.

major in the 1st Maryland Battalion under Colonel Smallwood.[54] Wiesenthal took his position very seriously. Furthermore, he eagerly plunged into what might be called an early form of Red Cross activity, for he addressed an appeal to the public (March 12, 1776) for "linen rags & old sheeting for bandages."[55] He was keenly aware of the dangers to public health resulting from war; he pointed out the danger to the army of the smallpox raging in Baltimore and urged inoculation.[56] The public offices that he held during the first years of the Revolution increased from month to month. Apparently he was in charge of the general supervision of medical affairs in Baltimore. We find him as examiner of candidates for medical positions in the service, as surgeon-general of the Maryland troops (for which he received a salary of "35 shillings a day and no rations") and as medical purveyor for the Maryland troops, in which position he gave advice on drugs that the Council contemplated buying. In this latter capacity he supervised the medical equipment for the army for years.[57] He concerned himself with everything that had to do with the hygiene of the army, examining the health conditions of the Flying Camp and suggesting changes in the organization of the care of wounded soldiers.[58] We find him helpfully assisting a soldier, who was blinded in the war, to obtain a pension from the state,[59] and we see him elsewhere consumed with indignation, complaining to the governor about a major who interfered in an amateurish way with the management of hospitals and needlessly endangered the lives of the wounded.[60] The importance of his school for physicians, where he trained young doctors, was perhaps even greater in wartime than in peace.

One of the most interesting documents that we have from his pen is a memorandum which he handed to the Council of Safety on April 10, 1776, entitled, "Remarks concerning the future treatment of the Sick in our Troops."[61] He suggests measures that to us today seem indispensable but that in Wiesenthal's day were not

---

[54] MA, XI, 197, 421. For the first three months he received a salary of forty-five pounds.

[55] Scharf, *Chronicles*, 138. Appeal in Dunlap's *Maryland Gazette or the Baltimore General Advertiser*, Baltimore, March 12, 1776.

[56] MA, XI, 399.

[57] Quinan, 15, 178. Cordell, 171. MA, XI, 137, 150, 222, 294; XVI, 378, 409; XLV, 487; XLVII, 368; XLVIII, 448.

[58] MA, XII, 13, 172.   [59] MA, XII, 513.   [60] MA, XXI, 243 ff.

[61] MA, XI, 321.

common practice at all. He suggested that even in peacetime the health of the troops must be more carefully cared for and that "Garrison or Regimental Hospitals" be created. However in war it was even more important to take certain hygienic precautions. He suggested that as soon as the troops were on the march a "moving or flying hospital" should follow them, equipped with beds and medicine. For the sick or wounded whose convalescence would require some time, another hospital "called the fix't Hospital" should be set up in some safe location. Wiesenthal then goes on to give very detailed practical suggestions for the supply of medicines, the physicians and the whole organization which his system would require. All this proves once more what we said earlier about Wiesenthal's character—a combination of warm, sympathetic humanity and a cool, practical feeling for reality. A century before the founding of the Red Cross, he anticipated, if only fragmentarily and in broad outlines, the great plan promulgated by Henri Dunant. And in his case, enthusiasm for the American cause was added to his general humanitarian attitude. In a letter to a member of the Council in the year 1776, he wrote, "I am as ready and willing to assist to the utmost of my power strength and abilities as the cause may require."[62]

We know the names of a few other German doctors besides Wiesenthal who distinguished themselves in Maryland during the Revolution.[63] John Peter Ahl (1748-1827), who came from Germany in 1772 and settled in Baltimore, served as surgeon's mate in Colonel Armand's Maryland Legion and was wounded at White Plains; after his recovery he returned to the army for the remainder of the war, serving finally under General Muehlenberg.[64] Alexander Smith is repeatedly mentioned as the surgeon of the German Regiment.[65] Henry Schnebely, the physician in Frederick County, appears again and again in letters of the State Council; his manifold activities have already been described.

However, relations between the Council and the German inhabitants of the state were not always so constructive and smooth as in the cases of Stricker, Keeports and Wiesenthal. For example, we

[62] MA, XI, 144.
[63] Henry J. Berkley, "Maryland Physicians at the Period of the Revolutionary War," in Maryland Hist. Mag., XXIV (1929), 3 ff.
[64] Cordell, Annals, 298.
[65] MA, XLIII, 23, 295; XLV, 332, 555, 612.

hear repeatedly of the affair of Samuel Gerock, the son of the pastor of the German-Lutheran congregation in Baltimore. He seems to have volunteered at the beginning of the war, for in a later letter to the governor is the statement, "He [Sam. Gerock] is a person that has fought Bravely in our Service in the Beginning of the War."[66] In November 1777 he was appointed quartermaster to the state hospital; it may certainly be assumed that this was done upon Wiesenthal's recommendation, since he was in charge of the hospital authority and also a prominent member of the Lutheran congregation.[67] Samuel Gerock was in office no longer than a year, for in November 1778 Lieutenant Samuel Sadler (because of his name, probably a German) was appointed as his successor. At about this time the hospital was moved from Baltimore Town to the fort at Whetstone Point and the personnel change was justified by the Council on the grounds that "Lieut. Sadler is much more conveniently situated than Mr. Gerock and therefore we have appointed him."[68] Obviously, however, there was more to the matter than just a question of geographic inconvenience, for a few weeks previously Lieutenant Samuel Gerock had received the Council's acceptance of his resignation as a matross officer.[69]

A short time later a minor scandal was brought to light. Captain Keeports reported to the Council that Samuel Gerock had stolen eleven barrels of the public powder. The Council commissioned the attorney general to start suit against Samuel Gerock in case he did not immediately return the powder. In this connection Samuel Gerock was given a discharge which included the statement, "that he has behaved with very great Impropriety."[70]

Samuel Gerock's situation became even more unpleasant when, two years later, the Council expressed its suspicion that he was in contact with the enemy and that he was trading with the other side.[71] Gerock was thereupon arrested and put in jail in Frederick.[72]

[66] MA, xlv, 337.

[67] MA, xvi, 409. In this document the name is John Gerock instead of Samuel. However, in later papers it is clear that Samuel was meant, for John Gerock, the pastor, would hardly have accepted the post of Quartermaster.

[68] MA, xxi, 230 f.

[69] MA, xxi, 207. A matross was one of the soldiers in a train of artillery who assisted the gunners in loading, firing and sponging the guns.

[70] MA, xxi, 235.   [71] MA, xlv, 507.

[72] We possess a long letter which old Reverend John Gerock sent to his son Samuel in prison. He tells him about family affairs and consoles him, attempt-

He was detained here for a quarter of a year, until his father succeeded in helping him. The Reverend Mr. Gerock guaranteed his son's conduct and the Council thereupon ordered Samuel Gerock to be set free.[73] It is further mentioned that the case was to be acted upon at the next meeting of the General Court, but we find nothing of the results. Whether or not the suspicion was justified cannot be determined. The fact that the Council gradually relaxed all the personal restraints that it had placed upon the accused would indicate that the accusation could not be corroborated. However, no certain conclusion may be drawn.

As in all feverish times, suspicions were all too easily aroused. This is shown by the case of a certain John Schley. John Schley belonged to a branch of the large German Schley family which had migrated to the south. He had lived for years in Charleston, South Carolina, and as a loyal American joined a German company of the town militia at the beginning of the war. John Schley had a hobby: mineralogy. Apparently he was considered an expert in this field in South Carolina, for in 1780 the governor commissioned him to search for mineral deposits in the interior of the Carolinas. For two months John Schley wandered about in the mountains looking for deposits that might be useful to the state at war. When he wanted to return in order to make a report to the governor, he learned that the enemy had entered South Carolina and that the governor had gone northward toward Philadelphia. Schley, who had sworn the Oath of Allegiance and Fidelity in 1778, would have nothing to do with the enemy, and so he started north also, in order to see the governor in Philadelphia. Still looking for mines, he gradually worked his way north along the Allegheny Mountains into Maryland until in the region between Cumberland and Hagerstown his fate overtook him: he was arrested as a spy. In his notebook he had written down the names of various people who had given him information about the location of mineral deposits on his tours of discovery and whose help he later expected to request should the state care to exploit any of these locations. Without further

---

ing to give him courage. The letter made such a strong impression on the commandant that he later sent it to the governor, "As it seems to be An Essay on a Religious Kind of Trade carrying on." The letter is reprinted in MA, XLVII, 415 ff.

[73] MA, XLVII, 429; XLV, 635, 648.

investigation the people in Hagerstown declared that this was a list of Tory traitors and angrily knocked out a few of Schley's teeth, further promising to hang him immediately if he refused to enter the army and fight against the English. Schley, fifty-seven years old, very nearsighted and a little shaky on his legs—as he himself explained in an appeal to the Maryland Council—wanted neither to hang nor to go to war, and so he appealed to Annapolis for help.[74] The answer to his petition has not been preserved, but it may be assumed that the Council granted freedom to the innocent mineralogist who wandered through the mountains pounding stones with his little hammer, though it could not make up for the personal assault.

Tories whether real or imagined, were not treated very gently in Western Maryland. An English Royalist, John Smyth, who was detained in Western Maryland and who escaped only to be caught once more, has left us a vivid report of his experiences. According to what he says it was especially the Germans in Frederick and Hagerstown who wanted to root out the Tories. He therefore describes them in blackest terms. Smyth describes the guards who caught him as "unfeeling German scoundrels, upon whose brows are written assassination, murder and death." In Frederick he was hauled before a committee "which consisted of a tailor, a leather breeches maker, a shoemaker, a gingerbread maker, a butcher, and two tavern keepers. The majority were Germans and I was subjected to a very remarkable hearing as follows: One said 'You infernal rascal, how darsht you make exshkape from this honorable committee?' 'Sacrament,' yelled another, 'dis committee will let Shorsh know how to behave himself,' and the butcher exclaimed, 'I would kill all the English tieves, as soon as ich would kill an ox or a cow!' "[75] In spite of the caricature treatment of the German artisans in Frederick, the angry Englishman's report unquestionably draws a valid characterization of the political attitude among the Germans in the western portion of the state.

But all of this notwithstanding, it may not be said that all the Germans in Maryland sided with the Revolution. Of course, there

---

[74] MA, xlv, 168 ff.

[75] Steiner, 44. Der Deutsche Pionier, ix (1877), 157. SHGM, iv, 35 f. John Smyth published his travel diary in London in 1784, entitled A Tour Through the United States of America.

were Tories among them. We read about one John Shriver from Arundel County who restrained someone from swearing the Oath of Allegiance "which conduct appears to be inimical to the cause of America" and for which reason he was made to appear before the Council and the governor to answer for his conduct.[76] A certain John Wayland had even worse things on his conscience and was arrested in North Carolina in 1782. The Maryland Council requested the governor of North Carolina to turn Wayland over to them, for he had served the enemy and while he lived in Maryland had committed "the most horrid and wanton depradations."[77] It was said of two brothers of German descent, the Gainsbergers of Frederick County, that they had been so careless in their utterances against the revolutionary cause that they had finally been arrested and forced to enlist.[78]

Even more dramatic was the course of a Tory conspiracy around 1780 in which various German settlers in Western Maryland were involved. Seven of the leaders were sentenced to death in Frederick for treason; four of them, Henry Shell, Yost Placker, Caspar Fritchie and Peter Sueman, were of German descent. A few of the condemned men were pardoned, but three of them (among them Caspar Fritchie, the father-in-law of the famous Barbara Fritchie) were executed in a horrible manner reminiscent of the Middle Ages.[79]

It is a well-known fact that in the War of Independence German soldiers fought on both sides. On the American side were the German immigrants and their sons, while on the British side were the Hessian and South German troops whose services had been sold to the English by their princes. Much has been written about the difficult and pathetic position of the Hessian soldiers who were forced to fight for a cause that did not in the least concern them. It is not surprising that they were not among the most dependable troops in the English army and that their enthusiasm for battle was slight or that they often deserted and joined the enemy. The American commanders rightfully took advantage of the psychological situation of the German mercenaries time and again. We hear of such a case in Maryland. A German officer, Colonel Beyerfalk, in

[76] MA, xxi, 29.   [77] MA, xlviii, 263.   [78] Steiner, 26.
[79] MA, xlv, 467, 469; xlvii, 328. Nead, 268 ff. Williams, *Frederick County*, i, 96. Dorothy M. Quynn, "The Loyalist Plot in Frederick," *Maryland Hist. Mag.*, xl (1945), 201-210.

the army of Chevalier de la Luzerne requested permission from the governor of Maryland to take into his company of Germans any German soldiers who had deserted the English. His request was granted.[80]

For various reasons Western Maryland was considered an especially safe region, secure from the enemy. Therefore, many munitions dumps and provisions warehouses were located here; also, many prisoners of war were sent to Frederick. This practice created the curious situation that whole regiments of German prisoners of war from the British army were suddenly sent to this German-settled region in order to be guarded by their former countrymen. After the battle of Saratoga and especially after Cornwallis' surrender at Yorktown, whole regiments of Hessian mercenaries were sent to the prison camp at Frederick.[81] The soldiers who, though they had been fighting for the English king, actually came from Kassel, Ansbach, Stuttgart or Darmstadt, suddenly heard familiar sounds—their own Suabian or Hessian or Frankish dialects.[82] True, they were still at war and had to forego personal freedom, but they made themselves as comfortable as possible in the barracks and soon forgot His British Majesty and even His Very Serene Highness, the count, duke or prince of their own country, who had unscrupulously sold them to England. In the interim they tried to make themselves useful; many of the prisoners worked for the German farmers, helping in the cultivation of the fields and gradually working themselves into the life of the countryside. In March 1783 news came to Frederick of the end of the war. A great celebration was arranged, and the harmonious atmosphere in Frederick may be illustrated by the fact that it was a prisoner of war, an officer from Bayreuth, who with his men prepared the fireworks and later had his band play at the ball which celebrated the American victory. Shortly after, the German prisoners were released and it has been reported that their departure was not nearly so lighthearted as is usually the case when prisoners are freed. One of the

[80] MA, xlv, 187, 227, 231. In an American corps stationed in Frederick in 1782 were forty Ansbach-Bayreuth soldiers who had formerly been in the British service and were now on the American side. (Steiner, 51.)

[81] Steiner, 50. Lucy L. Bowie, The Ancient Barracks at Fredericktown (Frederick, Md., 1939). Cf. The Pennsylvania German, xi (1910), 573.

[82] Max von Eelking, The German Allied Troops in the North American War of Independence (Albany, N.Y., 1893), 215 ff.

Germans wrote in his diary "that the people, and especially the women, were very sorry to bid them good bye."[83]

But not all of them said "good-by." Many of them actually never returned to their homes. An appreciable number of them bought farms, married the daughters of German settlers and established permanent homes. This pattern was not at all unusual; it happened so frequently that the Congress had to pass a law in order to legalize the entry of these "immigrants." Those who settled in Frederick County could buy their freedom for eighty Spanish dollars and those who could not raise this money were often assisted with loans by their neighbors.[84] These involuntary immigrants, whose passage King George had paid, quickly mixed with the remaining population in Western Maryland and just as successfully acclimated themselves as their civilian immigrant countrymen.

The name of General Johann DeKalb belongs in this description, in spite of the fact that he never lived in Maryland.[85] Despite this, one of the two memorials erected to DeKalb in America stands in Annapolis. The reason is that DeKalb's name is closely associated with the Maryland troops, with the "Maryland Line."

George Washington planned to use DeKalb as the successor to General Lincoln, who in 1780 was established in Fort Sumter, South Carolina, as the commander of the entire Southern Division. However, Congress ignored Washington's suggestion and named General Gates as commander of the Southern Division—a vain,

---

[83] Steiner, 57. Lucy L. Bowie, "German Prisoners in the American Revolution," *Maryland Hist. Mag.*, XL (1945), 185-200.

[84] Williams, *Frederick County*, I, 100. It has been estimated that of the 30,000 Hessian soldiers who were sent to America 12,000 never returned; about 5000 of these remained to settle in America.

[85] DeKalb was born in 1721 in Hüttendorf, Franken, Germany, the son of a simple peasant. His aristocratic title is false; he acquired it in France in order to advance his military career. His gifts for languages, mathematics, army organization and strategy are the basis for his speedy rise. He joined the army in France, fought in the war of the Austrian Succession and in the Seven Years' War and was sent to America in 1768 on a diplomatic mission, though he returned to France very soon. When he left France in 1777 to go to America for the second time he was a brigadier-general in the French army. The American Congress appointed him a major-general. DeKalb served in New England, Philadelphia and Valley Forge. He was not really commissioned until 1780. *DAB*, x, 253 f. Friedrich Kapp, *The Life of John Kalb* (New York, 1884, German edition 1862 in Stuttgart). "Men of Maryland specially honored by the State or the United States," in *Maryland Hist. Mag.*, XII (1917), 223 f. Faust, I, 328 ff.

stubborn and incompetent man not nearly so gifted in matters of strategy as DeKalb.[86] DeKalb was given the command of the "Maryland Division" composed of troops from Maryland and Delaware, and commissioned to free Charleston, South Carolina, from the English forces that were occupying it.

Under the command of DeKalb the Maryland Line marched south in the summer of 1780 in one of the major disasters in the whole history of the American Revolution. DeKalb knew perfectly well that the whole expedition was hopeless. He did not have enough men, he lacked food and munitions and he knew that Gates was a poor general.[87] He strongly urged Gates not to make a surprise attack on the English at Camden, but Gates would not listen and DeKalb had to obey. Thus began the fateful battle at Camden. The Americans were decimated; Gates fled and left DeKalb behind in an impossible situation. In the tumult of the battle he was seriously wounded and taken prisoner by the English, dying three days later on August 19, 1780, in Camden.

During the entire following century DeKalb's name appeared from time to time in the history of Maryland. First, DeKalb's adjutant, Chevalier Du Baisson, made an effort to help the widow and two sons, and asked Governor Lee to proclaim the survivors citizens of Maryland and to provide the sons, though they were only fourteen and sixteen years old, with commissions in the Maryland Line.[88] Whether the state did anything about the family or how much was done cannot now be determined from the papers that we have.[89]

On October 14, 1780, the Continental Congress in Philadelphia passed a resolution "that a monument be erected to the memory of the late Major General the Baron DeKalb, in the City of Annap-

[86] J. G. Keys, "Baron de Kalb," in *The Patriotic Marylander*, 1 (1915), 30 ff.

[87] Edward G. Daves, "Maryland and North Carolina in the Campaign of 1780-1781," in *Fund Publications* (Baltimore, 1893), xxxiii, 30 ff. DeKalb asked the Maryland Council for provisions for the troops, who were in a miserable condition. But the Council refused, saying that the distance was too great and that North Carolina and Virginia should take care of the troops since Maryland had often enough provided for troops from distant places just because they happened to be in Maryland. MA, xliii, 235.

[88] MA, xlvii, 131, 234.

[89] For an account of the involved and lengthy matter of the demands of the DeKalb heirs which spread out over the years from 1819 to 1855, see Kapp, *John Kalb*, 246 ff.

olis, in the State of Maryland."[90] For various reasons the execution of this act was postponed again and again, although during all of the nineteenth century repeated petitions were sent to Congress —from the Maryland legislature or the Maryland Historical Society —insisting on the fulfillment of the resolution of 1780.[91] Not until 1886 could the official monument to the memory of the fallen general be erected in Annapolis, though the Congress had ordered it during the time of the Revolution. It stands in State House Circle in Annapolis, dedicated to the German general who led the Maryland Line and who risked and lost his life for the cause of the American Revolution like many of his countrymen who had found a new home in Maryland.

As we said, DeKalb is only an incidental figure in our description. His is the most prominent name in this chapter, and yet for us the anonymous mass of Germans in Maryland in whose memory no monuments were erected are more important. We have attempted to describe their attitude and their activities in the Revolution and we shall cast one more backward glance upon this restless decade between 1774 and 1783 and attempt to evaluate its importance in the history of the German settlers in the Province—or, as we must now call it—the State of Maryland.

The decisive fact is that for the first time the Germans took an active part in a basic event in the history of their new country. We have seen that not all the Germans were on the side of the Revolution and that there were some indifferent ones as well as some Tories among them. However, the large majority of them joined the camp of the revolutionists as a matter of course and without mental conflicts. Not only did they give revolutionary speeches, but they turned their convictions into action—some as soldiers on the battlefield, others as citizens on the home front. Many German settlers were forbidden by their religious principles to take up weapons; Quakers, Mennonites, Dunkers and other sects were conscientious objectors, but most of them were more sympathetic with the Patriots than with the English and frequently, though they could not bear arms, they supported the American

[90] *Journal of the Continental Congress, 1774-1789*, XVIII, 1780 (Washington, 1910), 923.
[91] For the history of the memorial, see Dieter Cunz, "DeKalb and Maryland," *SHGM*, xxv, 18 ff.

cause with money.[92] In the revolutionary history of Maryland one hears again and again of Tory uprisings on the Eastern Shore; Tory conspiracies in the Western or German-settled portion of the state appeared only sporadically and awakened no interest in the bulk of the population. For a long time there was a loyalist majority on the Eastern Shore; in Western Maryland public opinion was for the Revolution and there was never any doubt about it. The famous letter that a nine-year-old German boy, William Keyser, in Western Maryland wrote to his father who was a captain in the revolutionary army will serve to illustrate the feeling: ". . . that God may prosper you and your united Brethren, in your laudable undertaking and in the end crown you with the laurels of a complete victory over the Enemies of the inestimable Rights, Liberties, and Privileges of distressed America and hand them down inviolate to the last posterity."[93] The diction and style of the letter certainly lead us to conclude that the mother of the young letter writer guided his hand, but undoubtedly these lines characterize the attitude of the German settlers of the state.

The fact that the government of the State of Maryland was very anxious to win the Germans for the revolutionary cause and to keep them in line is seen in the decision of the Assembly to have the most important laws translated into German.[94] When, in 1789, the problem of the ratification of the federal constitution appeared, a printer in Frederick (probably Matthias Bartgis) was commissioned to print two hundred copies of the constitution in German; the copies were then distributed in Baltimore and in Frederick and Washington Counties among the German population.[95] That the Germans completely fulfilled these hopes has been frequently acknowledged.[96]

The Oath of Allegiance since the end of 1777, required of every-

[92] Dole, 219. Steiner, 23. A list of names of the citizens of Frederick who subscribed to the government loan in 1780 clearly shows the large percentage of German names. MA, XLIII, 519 f.

[93] Steiner, 7.

[94] *Maryland Senate Proceedings*, March 25 and August 15, 1779.

[95] Order of the House of Delegates, Annapolis, December 1, 1787. Cf. Philip A. Crowl, *Maryland During and After the Revolution* (Baltimore, 1943), 118.

[96] Beverly W. Bond, *State Government in Maryland, 1777-1781*, 78. "These Germans, who were among the most prosperous and patriotic citizens of the State, afforded much aid to the Revolution."

one who wanted to make use of his rights of citizenship, was sworn by the Germans without hesitation and wherever it might have been omitted the lapses occurred through ignorance of the law.[97] The lists of people who had sworn the Oath of Allegiance are not completely preserved, but those which we still have show a great many German names.[98]

The revolutionary impulse certainly did not originate among the Germans in the state. However, their existence helped to turn the wheels of history. The settlement of the hinterland was necessary in order to transform the dependent coastal colony into an independent state. "Western settlement," says Barker, "was a great part of the general growth of population and economic life of Maryland. Without it some of the dynamics of the eighteenth-century history of the province—the accumulation of wealth, the growth of confidence—could hardly have been possible."[99] The Revolution of 1776 was not only a revolution of the American colonies against the English motherland; it was also a revolution of the western frontier territory against the overwhelming eastern oligarchy within the individual states. From this point of view, the opening of the western part of Maryland by the Germans gains particular importance.

Starting at the time of the Revolution, the Germans in Maryland began to take an interest in public affairs and to take part in them. For the first time, the idea of the state had gotten hold of them; for the first time, they were getting hold of the idea of the state.

[97] Bond, 95, 98. A few Germans complained that they had seen no German translation of the law in question and that therefore they had neglected to swear the Oath in the prescribed time, that is, before March 1, 1778. Apparently there were a great many German settlers who could neither read nor write English. We know of the case of a German in Frederick, Martin Everhart, who was burdened with triple taxes because he had not sworn the Oath of Allegiance. He asked the authorities for help and apologized for his delay "because he did not understand the nature of the oath." MA, XLIII, 500. This certainly was not an isolated case. The government of Maryland handled such lapses with great leniency.

[98] The lists for most of the counties are now in the Hall of Records in Annapolis. The names of the Germans living in Baltimore who swore the oath were published in "The Baltimore Germans and the Oath of Allegiance in 1778," edited by Dieter Cunz, SHGM, xxv, 32 f.

[99] Barker, 375.

PART TWO

THE MIDDLE AGES OF

IMMIGRATION

1790-1865

VI. CONSOLIDATION OF THE OLD STOCK

HE year 1789, the year of the official ratification of the Constitution and the year George Washington took office as President, marks the conclusion of the American revolutionary period. The same year, 1789, saw in Europe the beginning of a revolutionary epoch which was to last for a generation and to involve the entire continent. Emigration to America declined during these years, ceased entirely for a time and did not resume in full force again until after the Congress of Vienna, that is, after 1815. Thus for the United States the year 1789 marked the beginning of a certain rest period. It provided an opportunity for the new country to make use of its hard-won independence, to secure a foundation and build up an economic structure. At the same time, the French Revolution and the Napoleonic Wars cut Europe off from the rest of the world. As a result of the European disorders, America had no new masses of immigrants to assimilate. During these years the older stock of immigrants received no new additions.

The history of the Germans in Maryland continued to progress in line with this state of affairs. It was now not a matter of pushing on into new and unknown territory, as the first Monocacy settlers had done; it was not a matter, as in 1776, of helping to fight for the birth of a new country. Now it was a question of securing a place for oneself in the newly won, free, democratic community—to be an active, responsible citizen in it.

The most striking event in the history of Maryland at the turn of the century was the rapid rise of one city: Baltimore. The Germans had a vital part in its surprising development, though in a much more subtle manner than the local German-American patriots assert.

During the whole colonial period Maryland had been an agrarian state without an important urban center. But a change was wrought in the entire economic structure of the state, chiefly as a result of the German settlement of Western Maryland. As long as tobacco-growing comprised the economic basis of the state, ships came into the bay and loaded tobacco directly from the wharves of the growers located in the tidewater section. With the settlement of Western Maryland the growing of grain was introduced. But farmers on the frontier could not undertake the fifty-mile journey to the coast on the chance that a ship might happen to be at hand to take their grain. The grain farmers of the west needed a middleman, the merchant whom the tobacco planters of the coast could do without because they could transact their business themselves. The grain farms of the west demanded an intermediary, a port of deposit, an urban center. Hand in hand with this change went the fact that after the middle of the eighteenth century the emphasis in world trade shifted more and more away from tobacco and toward grain. Tobacco prices sank continuously; the tobacco trade suffered one crisis after another, while the demand for grain in Europe continually rose. Out of this situation arose Baltimore's great opportunity; the tremendous development of the city became a certainty at the moment when the battle between tobacco and grain for world trade was decided in favor of grain.[1]

Therefore, without the hinterland in Western Maryland there would have been absolutely no need for an urban settlement. At first Baltimore was no different from many other settlements and of about the same importance as Annapolis, Chestertown or Oxford. Until 1773 there was not even a newspaper in Baltimore. Yet, when the first newspaper, the *Maryland Journal and Baltimore Advertiser*, appeared it was evident that Baltimore had turned its attention toward the hinterland and not toward the bay. All the Baltimore advertisements that had up to this time appeared in the Annapolis paper, the *Maryland Gazette*, now shifted immediately to the Baltimore newspaper. The Baltimore merchants did not cater any more to people living in the tidewater section; they concentrated entirely on the *Journal and Advertiser*, the paper which circulated in the country back of Baltimore.[2] The impetus that singled out Baltimore from the other towns in Maryland originated in the border-

---

[1] We refer the reader here to the unusually keen article by Clarence P. Gould, "The Economic Causes of the Rise of Baltimore," in *Essays in Colonial History* (New Haven, 1931). P. A. Crowl, *op.cit.*, 66, has shown that the raising of grain in the western territory of Maryland was responsible for the fact that even in the decade before the Revolution Maryland had succeeded in emancipating herself from British credit control to a far greater degree than her neighboring states.

[2] Gould, *op.cit.*, 244 ff.

lands. The settlement of Western Maryland and the rise of Balti-more go hand in hand. The Germans took a lively part in both.

"Directly after the peace (1783) several merchants from other states . . . settled here" is written in the old annals.[3] Among the names of merchants listed, several of undeniable German origin are to be found: Zollicker, Stouffer, Starck, Seekamp, Schroeder, Konecke, Kimmel.[4] Von Kapff and Anspach was one of the leading shipping companies of Baltimore. Frederick W. Brune came to Baltimore from Bremen in 1799, and soon became one of the most successful merchants in the city.[5] He started the trade relations between the two cities of Bremen and Baltimore which drew them ever closer together during the nineteenth century. The flourishing mercantile business of Baltimore created a demand for other trades and occupations; an insurance office was founded where the mer-chants could insure their goods against marine risks, and this office was run by one of the best-known Germans in the city, a man whom we already know from the revolutionary period—George Keeports.[6] Engelhard Yeiser, also a well-known Baltimorean of German descent, was among the founders of the Bank of Maryland in 1790.[7]

Among the German businessmen of Baltimore after 1785 two names appear which became more and more prominent in the next fifty years: Christian Mayer and Lewis Brantz.[8] In 1802 these two

---

[3] Griffith, 103 f.

[4] *Biographical Cyclopedia of Representative Men of Maryland and District of Columbia* (Baltimore, 1879), 462. The Kimmels came from Mannheim in the Palatinate, Germany.

[5] *Ibid.*, 10.

[6] Hall, 45. Griffith, 114, 121. Keeports later on also became a notary public.

[7] Griffith, 129.

[8] Christian Mayer, a nephew of Christopher Bartholomäus Mayer who came to Frederick in 1752, was born in Ulm in 1763. He came of a prominent, well-to-do family, learned the linen business in Ulm, worked three years in a firm in Zurich and then emigrated to Baltimore in 1784. Here he worked until 1800 with Valck and Co. In 1785 he married Anna Katarina Baum of Kutztown, Pa.; one of the wedding guests was a poor young German immi-grant who had just landed in Baltimore, Johann Jacob Astor. Despite occa-sional setbacks, Mayer always belonged to the wealthy upper class of German merchants. He was the first president of the German Society after the re-vival of that organization in 1817. In 1825 he became the first consul for Wuerttemberg in America.

Lewis Brantz was born in Ludwigsburg near Stuttgart in 1776. He grew up in Aarau in Switzerland, where he went to school with Ferdinand Rudolf Hassler, the astronomer, and later founder of the Coast and Geodetic Survey

men founded a business concern. In the circular in which they announced their firm we find the statement: "They trust that having been engaged for eighteen years past, in extensive mercantile concerns in Baltimore, their experience, and the punctuality and attention which they mean to devote to the interest of their friends, will entitle them to their confidence." They started in the tobacco trade and in export and import trade with Holland, Denmark, Italy and India. Later on, Christian Mayer was president of two large Baltimore insurance companies for many years (Patapsco Marine Insurance Company, and Neptune Marine Insurance Company). Lewis Brantz made a name for himself in other fields besides the commercial. In 1816-1817, he undertook the first scientific survey of the Patapsco River and a part of Chesapeake Bay. His map was published and used by all mariners until it was supplanted by the official map of the United States Coastal Survey.

A physician, Dr. Christian Börstler, also deserves special mention among the Germans in Maryland at the close of the century. Born in the Palatinate, he emigrated to Maryland in 1784, and settled in Funkstown, near Hagerstown. He kept a diary which has since given us detailed information about his journey over here and his medical practice in Western Maryland. It is unquestionably one of the most interesting documents of the early history of Western Maryland. Toward the end of his life (1817) Börstler sums up his medical achievements: "Here in this country I have vaccinated over twelve hundred persons against smallpox and three hundred against cowpox. I have cured several insane people, have healed many broken arms and legs and have assisted many women in labor pains; and for twelve years I have written for calendars and newspapers

---

of the United States. In 1784, Brantz came to Baltimore in order to lead a colony of German immigrants to the Middle West. He took his group to Pittsburgh, and from here by boats, which they had built themselves, he led them down the Ohio to their destination in western Tennessee. (The account of his experiences was translated and published by Brantz Mayer in School-craft's History, Condition, and Prospects of the Indian Tribes, III, 335.) After 1802 he worked together with Christian Mayer. Between 1824 and 1828 he took long business trips to Peru, China and Sumatra. In 1830-1834 he represented a Philadelphia trading concern in Mexico City. After this he was president of the Philadelphia-Wilmington-Baltimore Railroad. He died in Baltimore in 1838. For further information on Christian Mayer and Lewis Brantz, see Brantz Mayer, Genealogy and Memoir of the Mayer Family (Baltimore, 1878), (rare item). Cf. also Dieter Cunz, "Christian Mayer—Baltimore Merchant," American German Review, x (1944), iii, 11 ff.

under the name of 'Volksfreund' without anyone's suspecting my identity. Now, however, I am old and stupid." It is not necessary to explain how important Börstler's medical work was in the remote parts of Maryland. The diary speaks for itself.[9]

As in the revolutionary period, so in the following decades we find German names especially among those men plying handicrafts. We hear of a saddler named Philip Uhler, who came from Pennsylvania to Baltimore at the beginning of the nineteenth century; of Michael Conrad, who in 1800 established himself at Baltimore as a bookbinder and bookseller; of Joseph Anton Heuisler, a Bavarian, who came over at the end of the eighteenth century and made a good reputation for himself as a horticulturist; and Thomas Bollmann, a baker, who moved from Bremen to Baltimore in 1779.[10] A German by the name of Georg Rohrbach was a prominent architect in Baltimore in 1800.[11] Engelhard Yeiser must have been a very versatile worker because we find him again as the man who built a canal to straighten the course of Jones Falls in the city.[12] At the beginning of the nineteenth century William Birely was one of the early manufacturers of writing paper in Western Maryland (Middletown Valley).[13]

A general idea of the percentage of Germans in the population of Baltimore may be gained by scanning the first Directory of the City of Baltimore, which was compiled in 1796.[14] Of course, many of the names had been anglicized or mangled so that their German origin may not always be recognized. About ten per cent of the three thousand names in the Directory, however, are undoubtedly German. Among the Germans are to be found representatives of almost all the vocations then in existence: laborer, tanner, carpenter, cordwainer, bricklayer, waggoner, weaver, locksmith, harnessmaker, innkeeper, merchant, musician, notary public, clergyman, to name only a few of the most common ones. Particular emphasis is found among the Germans on the industrial trades. On the basis of Hamilton's federalistic principles, a Manufacturing Society was founded in Baltimore in 1789; half of the tradesmen and workers

[9] The diary has been published only once, in the German original in *Deutsch-Amerikanische Geschichtsblätter*, I (Chicago, 1901), 17 ff; II, 29 ff. It contains a list of names of people vaccinated by Christian Börstler from 1787 to 1802. *Ibid.*, III, 40.

[10] *Cyclopedia*, 576, 525, 599.   [11] Griffith, 148, 189.
[12] Hall, 49. Griffith, 127.   [13] *Cyclopedia*, 87.
[14] Photostat copy in Pratt Library.

who joined together to form the organization "desirous to promote the internal manufactures of this country" were German.[15]

German names are to be found frequently among those trades which cater directly to the daily needs of the population: baking, butchering, saddling, brewing and similar lines. Among the somewhat finer handicrafts, the French immigrants in general took the lead, although, of course, even in this more artistic work we find a few Germans. This fact may be observed in the silversmith's trade, which has been the subject of a thorough study in Maryland.[16] Among the first-class silversmiths active in the city at the end of the eighteenth and beginning of the nineteenth centuries three German names are especially important: Charles Louis Böhme, Lewis Buichle and Philip Benjamin Sadtler.[17] At the same time there were others in this profession, which usually included also "clock and watch making." The names of Georg Dowig, John G. Gering, Jacob Mohler, Andrew Osthoff, John William Pfaltz and Jacob Walter have come down to us as silversmiths of German descent in Baltimore.[18] In Western Maryland about half of all the men who called themselves silversmiths were German; here, in the smaller towns, the silversmith was always the watchmaker also. A few names of silversmiths of German origin in Western Maryland at the turn of the century may be mentioned: Frederick Heisley, Jacob Holtzbaum, Henry Koontz, Frederick Nusz, Valentin Steckel, Henry Biershing, John Steikleader, Georg Woltz.[19]

German immigrants took part in the founding of some of the most important industries. Two Germans, Charles Gartz and John Leypold, built a sugar factory in Baltimore in 1784.[20]

Still more important was the paper industry, which owed its beginning to William Hoffman. He was born near Frankfurt a.M. in 1740, his name originally being Friedrich Wilhelm Hoffmann. He learned paper-making in Germany, came to America in 1768, worked for a few years in a paper mill belonging to a German in Pennsylvania and then moved to Maryland in 1775. He built his first paper mill, the Clipper Mill, on the shore of Great Gunpowder

[15] *Maryland Journal and Baltimore Advertiser*, May 15, 1789.
[16] J. Hall Pleasants and Howard Sill, *Maryland Silversmiths 1715-1830* (Baltimore, 1930).
[17] *Ibid.*, 80, 101, 107, 178.   [18] *Ibid.*, 115, 124, 162, 166, 179, 191.
[19] *Ibid.*, 234, 235, 236, 242.
[20] Griffith, 111. *Maryland Journal*, March 14, 1784.

Falls, about thirty miles north of Baltimore. This was either at the end of 1775 or the beginning of 1776, and the mill was either the first or one of the first two paper mills in Maryland.[21] In 1781, Hoffman built his second paper mill, the Gunpowder Mill. From that time on the Clipper Mill produced simple kinds of wrapping paper, while the Gunpowder Mill concentrated on paper for fine books and writing paper. Since Hoffman was very outspokenly on the side of the American Revolution, it is not surprising that the Continental Congress placed with him an order for a large part of the paper on which the first paper money of the Continental Congress was printed.[22] William Hoffman's paper industry flourished to a greater and greater extent. He founded an entire settlement of about two hundred workmen who were employed in his mills and called it Paper Mills. His sons worked in the mills and later on made new developments in the field of paper manufacturing which their father had begun. For more than a century the paper mills were the most important industry in the "Upper end of Baltimore County."[23]

One of the most interesting chapters in the history of early American industry is the attempt of a German to start an extensive glass industry in Maryland. That is the undertaking of John Frederick Amelung.[24] Amelung came from Bremen. He had received his

---

[21] In the *Genealogy and Biography of Leading Families of the City of Baltimore and Baltimore County* (New York, 1897), 248, it is stated that, "William Hoffmann . . . made the first paper manufactured in this State." In the *Maryland Archives*, xi, 435, a government order for May 27, 1776, mentions, ". . . ordered the said Treasurer pay to William Lux, for use of William Hoffman, Five pounds Fourteen Shillings, for nineteen reams of Cartridge paper." If Hoffman received a government order as early as May 1776, it may be assumed that he began to build his mill in 1775. This fact has been overlooked by Lawrence C. Wroth in his book, *The Colonial Printer* (Portland, Me., 1938), 132 f.

[22] George W. Howard, *The Monumental City, Its Past History and Present Resources* (Baltimore, 1876), 818, gives the most favorable evaluation of William Hoffman's accomplishments.

[23] Dieter Cunz, "Maryland's First Papermaker," *American-German Review*, xii, i (1945), 21 ff. May A. Seitz, *The History of the Hoffman Paper Mills in Maryland* (Towson, Md., 1946).

[24] Amelung bibliography:
Rhea M. Knittle, *Early American Glass* (New York, 1927), 172-80.
Vernon S. Vavrina, Manufacturing of Glass in Baltimore and Maryland (Johns Hopkins University Thesis, Typewritten Manuscript, 1936), 1-7. Only copy in E. Pratt Library, Baltimore, Maryland Room.
Dieter Cunz, "Amelung's Old Frederick Glass," *American German Re-*

training as a glass blower in Bohemia just at the time when Bohemian glass was beginning to present serious rivalry to the old Venetian glass trade. Then he returned to Bremen and there came in contact with a merchant from Baltimore, Benjamin Crocket, who happened to be in Bremen on a visit. Crocket told Amelung so many favorable things about Maryland that he decided to go there and start a glass factory. We are well informed about these facts, for Amelung himself later wrote them down in a long advertisement and a special pamphlet.[25] Amelung was more than just a small artisan; he planned a venture on a large scale. First he secured a substantial sum of money from several investors, 10,000 pounds in Germany and 15,000 pounds in America, in order to buy land and to build a glass-blower's town on it. Benjamin Crocket of Baltimore had assured him that he would find the most essential raw materials, wood and potash, in Maryland "in abundance." "I had letters of recommendation from those great men, Franklin and Adams, and the American Consul at Paris, to the first men in this country, viz. to his excellency General Mifflin, President of Congress Thomas Johnson Esq. William Paca Esq. and Charles Carroll of Carrollton Esq. All these letters prove that I had the Character of a worthy and honest man in Germany."

With sixty-eight trained glass workers, their families, a pastor

---

view, XII, v (1946), 16 ff.
Williams, Frederick County, I, 268 f.
Scharf, Western Maryland, I, 596.
Griffith, 111.
Schultz, Early German Settlements, 16 f.
Faust, I, 172; II, 94.
Alfred C. Prime, The Arts and Crafts in Philadelphia, Maryland and South Carolina, 1721-1785 (Philadelphia, 1929), I, 134; II, 152.
F. P. Stone, "The First Glass Factory in America," in The Patriotic Marylander, III (1916), 89-93. (The title is misleading; Amelung's undertaking was not the first of its kind in America.)
Edward T. Schultz, History of Freemasonry in Maryland (Baltimore, 1884), I, 72 ff. Amelung was one of the first German Masons in Maryland.
Baltimore Sun, March 17, 1929, and March 19, 1933.
George S. and Helen McKearin, American Glass (New York, 1941), 100 ff. This is the most recent and best investigation of Amelung's undertaking. It gives a description and pictures of authentic examples of Amelung glass, treats possible types of Amelung commercial tablewares and possible Amelung influence in the Baltimore and Philadelphia area.
[25] Remarks on Manufacture, Principally on the Established Glass House near Frederick-Town in the State of Maryland (1787).

and two teachers, as well as a few other tradesmen, Amelung sailed from Bremen the beginning of June 1784. At the end of August the group arrived in Baltimore only to proceed directly to Frederick County. Near Frederick, on the Monocacy and Tuscarora Creek Amelung bought land, more than 2000 acres, which was later augmented by another thousand acres. Here the projected glass-blower's town was erected, including living quarters and factories with glass furnaces. It was called New Bremen, and was a purely German settlement. Amelung not only looked after the glass factory; he also supervised the organization of the community life itself. "On this land I have erected all the necessary buildings for the manufactory as glass ovens for bottles, window and flint glass, and dwelling houses for one hundred and thirty-five now living souls. . . . I have established a German School. . . . I am now establishing an English School . . . that children may get a complete education in the same, as in the English, German and French languages, writing, ciphering, music, to play on the harp, harpsichord, flute and violin."

In spite of its promising beginnings, the project lasted for only a few years, from 1784 to 1790. After 1790 its production was greatly reduced and at last the work stopped completely. Amelung had evidently miscalculated. He started with a sum of 25,000 pounds and within two years he had paid out 32,000 pounds. There were difficulties of all kinds. He sent for additional glass blowers from Bohemia and Thuringia, though few of them ever actually arrived in America. England, wanting to prevent the establishment of a competing glass industry in America, did everything to hinder the emigration of German glass blowers, and is even said to have had plans to intercept the ships in which the artisans traveled in case they did eventually get started. Even worse were the financial calamities that soon confronted Amelung, and that even caused him to address a petition to the House of Representatives in May 1790. He received help from various sources. Charles Carroll, for instance, sponsored a tariff on foreign glass products. Congress, however, after a spirited debate refused to provide a loan. This sealed the fate of the undertaking; after 1790 little glass was produced in New Bremen. In 1795 Amelung tried unsuccessfully to put his entire project up for sale.

The real reason for Amelung's failure was probably the fact that he could not adjust himself to the demands of the new country. He had high-flown, artistic notions; he apparently wanted to produce artistic glass products in the style of the Venetian and Bohemian glass blowers and realized too late that the time for this sort of thing had not yet arrived in America. The country needed window-panes and medicine bottles, not delicate wine glasses and flower vases. Amelung was apparently unable to change over to the pro-duction of practical products. This was perhaps not the only reason for his failure, but certainly one of the most important.

Later on Amelung moved to Baltimore, where he died on No-vember 20, 1798. In 1804, the installation and the land in New Bremen were sold in bankruptcy. The glass blowers left the town and scattered all over the country; a few of them settled in other states and carried on their trade on a smaller but more successful scale.[26]

In the history of the American glass industry Amelung's glass is usually called "Old Frederick Glass." A few examples of it still exist and they confirm the statement which Representative Boudi-not made during the Congressional debate about Amelung's glass in 1790. He said that it was "superior to any ever produced in America."[27]

Perhaps the most important contribution that the German ele-ment in Maryland made toward the building up of the democratic community in the decades following the Revolution was in the field of printing. Connected with this are the beginnings of the news press in Maryland.

[26] A few names of the New Bremen glass-blower families: Kramer, Kimber, Eberhart, Reitz, Gabler, Shunk, Duval, Carl, Weltzer, Reppert, Swearer. The fate of these glass blowers is described further in an article by Rhea M. Knit-tle, "Rex Absolutus of the Monongahela," in *Antiques*, XIII (1928), 290-92. Besides Amelung's there were in Frederick County probably a few other glass factories, among them another run by a German, A. Kohlenberg. But their products could not be compared with those of Amelung, either in quantity or quality. See Charles M. Stow, "Amelung and Contemporary Maryland Glass-blowers," *Antiquarian* (December 1930), XV, 58-60. Amelung's son, Fred-erick M. Amelung, founded a glass factory in 1799 in Baltimore at the foot of Federal Hill at the Patapsco River basin. (McKearnin, 116 f.)

[27] Amelung glass is to be found in the Metropolitan Museum, New York; in the Museum of Art, Baltimore; in the Masonic Lodge at Alexandria, Vir-ginia; and in the Holland Masonic Lodge (VIII) in New York. A few years ago another piece of Amelung glass came to light in Waltham, Massachusetts, a drinking glass which Amelung had sent to the city of Boston with the in-scription, "Our best wishes for every Glassmanufactory in the United States, God bless the City of Boston," followed by Amelung's name. *Antiques*, XXVI (1934), 88-91; XXVII (1935), 7-8.

We know of numerous attempts to establish a German newspaper in Maryland. It was more difficult, however, than most anticipated, for in the half-century after the Revolution not one German paper lasted even a generation. The beginnings of the German press in Maryland constitute a history of failures which can hardly be reconstructed for we have almost no evidence of these early papers. The expression, "quickly read, quickly lost," applied to the newspapers of the eighteenth century as well as to those of a later period, before there were libraries which collected them systematically, as at present. We must work with very meager sources, with second-hand information and indirect clues and we are aware that we can produce only a very sketchy picture.

The oldest newspaper in Maryland of which we have heard anything is the *Baltimore Post*, which allegedly was published in the latter part of the eighteenth century by Samuel Sower in Baltimore. There is no copy of this paper extant and indeed there are various reasons for believing that it may never have existed.[28]

The first German newspaper whose existence is definitely proved is Henry Dulheuer's weekly in 1786. Though by indirect means, its existence may positively be determined by the following advertisement appearing on June 16, 1786, in the *Maryland Journal and Baltimore Advertiser*: "The Subscriber respectfully informs his Friends in particular, and the Public in general, that he commenced the Publication of his German Newspaper Yesterday, and intends to continue it Weekly. Subscriptions for the same, are taken in by him at his Printing-Office in Market Street, nearly opposite the Green Tree, at the small Price of Ten Shillings pro Annum; Five Shillings of which is paid at the Time of Subscribing, the better to enable him to prosecute his Undertaking. All kinds of Printing in

[28] Eduard F. Leyh, in *Baltimore, Seine Vergangenheit und Gegenwart* (Baltimore, 1887), is the only source for the existence of this mysterious *Baltimore Post*. Leyh speaks of a copy of the paper which is preserved as an heirloom in a Baltimore family, but so far no one has seen it. George C. Keidel, in his essay, *The Earliest German Newspapers of Baltimore* (Washington, 1927), repeated Leyh's assertion. He mentions 1780 as the year of its first appearance, a date which we believe is not tenable. The supposed printer, Samuel Sower, was born in 1767; he could not have published a newspaper in 1780. Samuel Sower was active in the end of the eighties and beginning of the nineties as a printer in Chestnut Hill and Philadelphia. He did not come to Baltimore until 1795. If there was a *Baltimore Post* in the eighties, we do not know in which year it appeared and we do not know anything about the printer; certainly it was not Samuel Sower.

the German, performed by Henry Dulheuer. Baltimore June 15, 1786."[29] We know nothing of the name or the life of Dulheuer's weekly paper. It can hardly have been in existence very long because in the oldest Baltimore Directory, of 1796, Henry Dulheuer's name is not mentioned.

Only toward the end of the century do we hear of a German newspaper again in Baltimore, this time actually in connection with the Samuel Sower who was mentioned above. Again we must rely on indirect evidence: Samuel Sower mentions the newspaper in his own almanac of 1800.[30] "The publisher of this calendar takes this opportunity to inform the valued public that for some time he has again been publishing a German newspaper; it appears three times a week on a large half-sheet, and costs two and a half dollars a year. . . ." Again we do not know how long the paper lasted, but we do know its exact title from the single copy of the year 1796 which has been preserved. At the head of the first page is the statement: "*Der Neue Unpartheyische Baltimore Bote und Märyländer Staats-Register, Mittwoch, den 4 May 1796. Num. 59. Diese Zeitung wird erstlich alle Mittwochen heraus gegeben von Samuel Sower, Buch-drucker in der Fayettestrasse zu Baltimore für zehn Schilling des Jahrs, wovon die Hälfte beym Einschreiben bezahlt wird.* (This newspaper will appear every Wednesday, published by Samuel Sower, printer in Fayette Street, Baltimore, for ten shillings a year, of which half is payable upon subscription.)"[31]

[29] Keidel (p. 6) has determined that this advertisement was repeated twice, on June 20 and 23, 1786.

[30] It is the *Neue Hoch-Deutsch Americanische Calender auf das Jahr Christi 1800* (Baltimore), a copy of which is in the possession of the Historical Society of Pennsylvania. See Oswald Seidensticker, *The First Century of German Printing in America, 1728-1830* (Philadelphia, 1893), 151. Keidel, op.cit., 7 ff. Seidensticker (p. 140) sets 1795 as the first year of publication for Sower's Baltimore newspaper. The reason for this is probably the fact that the one remaining copy is for May 4, 1796, and carries the number 59; if we figure back from this date, the first copy must have appeared on March 25, 1795. For a detailed description of this number of the *Baltimore Bote*, see Keidel, op.cit.

[31] Again by indirect means the name of a German paper in Baltimore in 1809 has come down to us: *Baltimore Correspondent*. No copy of the paper has ever been found; we know of its existence through the *Readinger Adler* of February 21, 1809, where a poem was reprinted with the note "From the Baltimore Correspondent." (Brigham 25:143.) It is not known whether the newspaper was published by Samuel Sower or another German printer, Christian Geist, who was in Baltimore that year.

Aside from Nicholas Hasselbach's short career, Samuel Sower was the first important German printer in Baltimore. He was born in Germantown, Pennsylvania, on March 30, 1767, the youngest son of Christopher Sower II, the greatest German printer in the eighteenth century in America. Samuel Sower first practiced the trade of printer in Chestnut Hill, Pennsylvania, and later in Philadelphia.[32] In 1795 he moved to Baltimore, where he lived for the rest of his life; he died on October 12, 1820.[33] He ran his Baltimore print shop with a partner, William Gwinn.[34] Apparently business was excellent; in later years the partner gradually retired and left Sower to run the shop. A letter which Samuel Sower addressed in 1808 to his brother in Philadelphia gives a little information about the progress of the business: "I am chained down to business closer than ever. . . . My partner will not bother himself with business, having invested between $7000 and $8000 in the business and built for me a home costing at least $3000. I see him not more than once a month and he leaves everything in my hands to manage, saying if he had not the utmost confidence in me, he would not have gone into it. The business of type founding is making great strides. Orders are pouring in from everywhere so we can not fill half of them. We have undertaken to cast the smallest types that have been used in the world. . . . We have eleven boys and six journeymen at work and orders for 5000 pounds of type. I am working night and day."[35]

Samuel Sower was the only printer in Baltimore toward the end of the eighteenth century who printed German books.[36] They cer-

[32] In Chestnut Hill and Philadelphia he published an almanac and a weekly paper as well as a number of smaller pamphlets. (Seidensticker, 125, 127, 131, 136.) The Chestnut Hill weekly had a decided moral-religious character; it printed articles in favor of nonresistance, and strongly attacked higher education, in line with the teachings of the Dunker sect to which Sower belonged to the end of his life. James Owen Knauss, *Social Conditions Among the Pennsylvania Germans in the Eighteenth Century, as Revealed in the German Newspapers Published in America* (Lancaster, Pa., 1922), 88.

[33] Griffith, 183. J. M. Henry, *History of the Church of the Brethren* (Elgin, Ill., 1936), 80 ff. In 1813 the Baltimore Church of the Brethren elected him minister, but because of ill health he was not very active in this capacity.

[34] According to other reports, his partner's name was Hewes.

[35] Henry, op.cit., 83. SHGM, III (1889), 15 f.

[36] While this book goes to the printer Dr. Felix Reichmann of Cornell University is preparing a "Bibliography of Maryland German Imprints" which will soon be ready for publication. For a list of Sower imprints see Dr. Reichmann's monograph.

tainly had no literary value, for they were schoolbooks and account books, or books with moral, religious or patriotic content. However, Samuel Sower's modest attempt to turn the attention of his fellow citizens to things beyond their daily lives must not be underestimated.[37]

The discussion of Samuel Sower and his first German newspapers in Baltimore has led us to the nineteenth century. We must go back, however, to the revolutionary period, because two decades before Sower came to Baltimore another German started a long, varied career as a printer in the German settlements of the western part of the state: Matthias Bartgis, of Frederick.

We do not know much about Matthias Bartgis. He was born in 1750, the son of an immigrant from the Palatinate, in Lancaster, Pennsylvania.[38] He learned the printing trade from William Bradford in Philadelphia, fought in the first battles of the Revolution and then moved to Frederick. We do not know the exact date of his arrival, but it was most probably some time in the fall of 1776.[39] He must have opened a print shop immediately, and by the end of the year published his first German almanac for the year 1777. No copy remains of this first issue, but we do still have one for 1780 which says "published for the fourth time," from which we deduce the beginning of his printing career.[40]

[37] Samuel Sower seems also to have had another partner named Cole, with whom he had a bookstore. In the almanac of 1804 (copy in Pratt Library in Baltimore) Sower and Cole advertise that they have a large assortment of English books and that they constantly import German ones.

[38] Views differ about the origin of the Bartgis family. A. Stapleton, "Researches in the First Century of German Printing in America" (*The Pennsylvania German*, v [1904], 88 ff.) calls Matthias Bartgis the son "of a Palatine immigrant, the first German printer south of the Mason and Dixon Line." In Williams, *Frederick County*, II, 858, it is stated that his ancestors came from France. The name certainly sounds more German than French and the fact that Bartgis spent his whole life printing German books and newspapers makes the version of his German origin more convincing than the other. Perhaps he came from the German-French borderland country. Bartgis' full name was Matthias Echternach Bartgis; Echternach was the maiden name of his mother. The town of Echternach is one of the most famous places of pilgrimage in Europe, on the German-French frontier in Luxemburg. Perhaps the name gives a general indication of the geographical territory from which the Bartgis family came.

[39] We follow here the short essay on Bartgis in Joseph T. Wheeler, *The Maryland Press 1777-1790* (Baltimore, 1938), 57 f.

[40] *Der Allerneuste, Verbesserte und Zuverlässige Americanische Reichs-Staats-Kriegs-Siegs- und Geschichts-Calender Auf das Jahr, nach der Gna-*

The earliest imprint which we have from Bartgis' print shop is his English almanac for 1778.[41] In the following year he published simultaneously a German and an English version of his almanac. How long he did this we do not know, but it must have been until the middle of the eighties and perhaps even to the end of the century. On January 4, 1786, the first number of his English newspaper appeared, *The Maryland Chronicle or the Universal Advertiser*. Shortly after, he announced the publication of a German paper which was to be delivered along with the English edition. We have no copy of this German paper, but there is no doubt that it was in existence for at least a year.[42] Various indications show that the Bartgis newspapers were distributed mainly along the line of the old Monocacy Road and its northern and southern extensions, that is, between York, Pennsylvania, and Winchester, Virginia. Bartgis suggested to his subscribers that they get together in groups of fifty-two, each person traveling to Frederick once a year in order to get the newspapers for all. Aside from this he developed a plan for a postal system from Frederick to the Shenandoah Valley "for the purpose of conveying my English and German News-papers to Funk's-Town, Hager's-Town, Sharpsburg, Sheperd's-Town, Martinsburgh, and Winchester."[43] He did not rely entirely on the postal system but soon went about founding his newspapers in the German-settled sections of neighboring states. It was he who published the first newspapers in the most important towns of the hinterland —York, Pennsylvania, and Winchester, Virginia. At the end of the eighties he was the publisher of four newspapers, the German paper and the *Maryland Chronicle* in Frederick, the *Virginia Gazette* in Winchester and the *Pennsylvania Chronicle* in York. Thus he was

---

denreichen Geburt unsers HErrn und HEylands JEsu Christi, 1780. . . . Copy in the American Antiquarian Society in Worcester, Massachusetts. Wheeler 60, 98. Seidensticker, 104.

[41] *The Maryland Almanac for the Year of our Lord 1778.* Copy in American Antiquarian Society. Reproduction in Wheeler, 58.

[42] The German paper is mentioned in a notice in *The Maryland Chronicle* for February 28, 1787. Cf. Brigham 25:187.

[43] Wheeler, 173. One copy, a complete one-year volume of an eighteenth-century Bartgis paper in German, is in the possession of one of his descendants, Mrs. D. O. Griffin of Frederick, Md. Until now the paper was believed to be lost; it is not listed in any newspaper list or bibliography. Unfortunately, the owner of the paper is not willing to make it available to research.

at this time something like a newspaper king in the old Piedmont district. The last number of the *Maryland Chronicle* of which we know anything is that of May 28, 1788. For the next few years we know nothing of a Bartgis newspaper in Maryland. On May 22, 1792, he started a weekly paper which was continued under various titles until the year after his death.[44] In the decade between 1803 and 1813, he published a paper in German and English, *The Hornet*, whose motto proclaimed, "To true Republicans I will sing, But aristocrats shall feel my sting."[45] In the years 1807 and 1808, he had an interest in the English-German newspaper in Frederick called *The Independent American Volunteer.*[46]

Along with the publication of newspapers the daily business of the print shop had to be carried on. We can understand that things sometimes were too hectic for Bartgis and that he soon tried to find a partner. But there were not many good printers in America at this time and so we read repeated advertisements in Bartgis' papers stating that the publisher was looking around for helpers and co-workers. His requirements were not too high; he was even willing to take in a boy and teach him the business. "Wanted immediately, By the Printer hereof, A Young Lad, about 14 or 15 years of age, who can read well, and write tolerably, in the English and German languages, as an apprentice to the Printing-business," reads an advertisement in the *Maryland Chronicle* for February 1, 1786, but we do not know whether these appeals for help were answered. In later years (1811) Bartgis was able to make his son, Matthias E. Bartgis, his partner.[47]

The business grew and grew; he began a bindery and a paper mill, and besides this he ran a print shop in Lancaster, Pennsylvania, for a couple of years. The list of books published by him is long;

[44] In 1792, it was the *Maryland Gazette, or Frederick County*; in 1794, *Federal Gazette*; in 1801, *Republican Gazette*. In 1820 Bartgis sold the paper and retired from business. He died on April 6, 1825, in Frederick. Scharf, *Western Maryland*, 1, 528.

[45] *Ibid.*

[46] Only the last page of this newspaper appeared in German, "Gedruckt: bey M. Bartgis." The last issue located is that of December 28, 1808. Copies at Maryland Historical Society, Harvard University, American Antiquarian Society. Cf. Brigham 25:187.

[47] Scharf, *Western Maryland*, 1, 528.

it contained leisure reading, historical works, Lutheran hymn and prayer books and small pamphlets of all kinds.[48]

At the turn of the eighteenth to the nineteenth century certainly no man made so great a contribution to the spiritual development of the German settlers in Western Maryland as Matthias Bartgis. No doubt it was on a very modest intellectual level, but actually Bartgis' strength and the secret of his success was the fact that he knew what was needed and how to find a point of contact with his public. He did not make the mistake that Amelung did in his glass factory of starting on much too high a plane to appeal to the people whom he needed for his business. Unquestionably, Matthias Bartgis sensed the level and the quality of the spiritual needs of the people of Western Maryland and this assured him of lasting effect upon them.

Aside from the Bartgis newspapers we know of only one other paper in Frederick at the beginning of the nineteenth century, the *Freiheitsbote*, appearing from 1810 to 1813. Since only one number of it is in existence not much can be said about the paper.[49]

Washington County in farthest Western Maryland developed its own printing center toward the end of the eighteenth century: John Gruber's print shop in Hagerstown. The town had developed more rapidly after the end of the Revolutionary War. "The number of inhabitants in Hagerstown is about two thousand. . . . The inhabitants are chiefly Germans," writes a traveler in the year 1794.[50] Here was a good opportunity for a German printer.

John Gruber came from an old west-German family. An Eberhard Ludwig Gruber (1665-1728) was a well-known German clergyman who had had to give up his parish because of his tendency toward mysticism, and then became a leader of the mystics in South Germany. His son, Johann Adam Gruber, who belonged to the same religious movement, emigrated in 1726 to Pennsylvania and settled in Germantown. Eberhard Gruber, Johann Adam's son, was born in 1736; he lived for the greater part of his life in Lancaster County,

[48] Index of Imprints, see Reichmann; cf. footnote 36.

[49] The *Freiheitsbote* appeared weekly starting April 7, 1810, and was published by C. T. Melsheimer. It is mentioned in an advertisement in Bartgis' *Republican Gazette* of February 13, 1819. The only existing copy of the *Freiheitsbote* (April 14, 1810, vol. 1, no. 2) is in the American Antiquarian Society. Brigham, 25:184.

[50] Henry Wansey, *An Excursion to the United States of North America in the Summer of 1794* (Salisbury, 1798), 167.

Pennsylvania, and made a name for himself as a physician and in a few political offices. His son was John Gruber, the printer.[51]

John Gruber was born on October 31, 1768, in Strasburg, Lancaster County, Pennsylvania. At fifteen he became an apprentice to Carl Cist, a printer in Philadelphia. Six years later Gruber left Philadelphia and spent some time in the West Indies, where he barely escaped the notorious uprising of 1793 in San Domingo; then he lived for a while in Reading, Pennsylvania, where he assisted in the publication of a German newspaper.[52] In the year 1795 he moved to Hagerstown, where he was active for many years.

A Maryland politician, General Samuel Ringgold (1770-1829), induced John Gruber to settle in the county seat of Washington County and to found here a German language newspaper with the purpose of supporting Thomas Jefferson's Republican-Democratic Party. This was the *Westliche Correspondenz*, which was published by Gruber for a few years in Hagerstown. A later attempt of Gru-

1796.]   Die   [Num. 68.

Westliche Correspondenz,
und
Hägerstauner Wochenschrift.

Mitwochs, den 28sten September.

Diese Zeitung wird alle Mitwoch Morgens herausgegeben von Johann Gruber, in der Deutsch- und Englischen Buchdruckerey zu Hägerstaun, für Einen Thaler des Jahres: Ein Halber Thaler wird beym Einschreiben bezahlet.

Newspaper masthead of *Die Westliche Correspondenz*, published in Hagerstown in 1796, one of the earliest German papers in Maryland

[51] Gruber bibliography:
Scharf, *Western Maryland*, II, 1141 ff.
Williams, *Washington County*, I, 129, 245, 435.
Seidensticker, op.cit., 13, 141.
Stapleton, op.cit., 89.
Knauss, op.cit., 27 f.
Oliver L. Fassig, "A Sketch of the Progress of Meteorology in Maryland and Delaware," in *Maryland Weather Service* (Baltimore, 1899), I, 344 ff.
Cyrus H. Eshleman, "John Gruber and the Hagerstown Almanac," in *The Morning Call*, Allentown, Pa., December 3, 1938.
Augustus J. Prahl, "The Hagerstown Almanac," in *American German Review*, VIII, v (1942), 7 ff.
[52] It was the *Neue unpartheyische Readinger Zeitung und Anzeigs-Nachrichten*, which was published by Gottlob Jungmann and a few other men. Gruber was a partner in the business in 1793-1794.

ber's to start another Jefferson party newspaper in English, *Sentinel of Liberty*, was unsuccessful because a competitor was already publishing a similar one.

John Gruber's fame rests not so much on his daily papers as on his yearly almanac, *The Hagerstown Town and County Almanack*. It was first published in 1797, and has since appeared in an unbroken series to the present day.[53] Today it appears in editions averaging 150,000 copies and has subscribers in every state in the Union as well as in Canada. In the first twenty-five years it appeared only in German. After 1822 there were simultaneous German and English editions; in 1918 the German edition was discontinued and since then the almanac has appeared only in English.

Almanacs abounded in Maryland, as elsewhere at that time. But not one of them was so popular as the *Hagerstown Almanack*, which has been read regularly in thousands of families over the generations, not only in Maryland but in Pennsylvania, Delaware, Virginia, Indiana and Ohio. Besides the actual calendar, it contains the weather prophecies so eagerly sought by farmers. These are based on a principle that has long since been declared unscientific and highly misleading by meteorologists and that has been proved to be correct only sixty per cent of the time at most. But the rural population of Western Maryland and the neighboring states has sworn for decades by them and in spite of countless errors has continued to be guided by the almanac in agricultural matters. It has even been said that a Maryland governor in the nineteenth century, William T. Hamilton, consulted the *Hagerstown Almanack* before setting the date for a public hanging—so that the popular event would not be marred by rain.[54]

The almanac is directed definitely and mainly to the rural population, as its emphasis on the weather indicates. It is also full of practical hints: medical and veterinary advice, recipes, methods of exterminating vermin, etc. A moral-religious character is to be noted at first glance. In the short literary contributions such subjects as "Womanly Virtues," or "On the Inclination to Unfaithfulness

[53] Seidensticker (p. 147) lists 1798 as the first year of publication; this is unquestionably an error because we have a reproduction of the first edition of 1797. The title of the German edition was at first *Der neue Nord-Amerikanische Stadt und Land Calender*, which was later changed to *Der Volksfreund und Hägerstauner Calender*.

[54] *Maryland, A Guide to the Old Line State*, WPA Project (New York, 1940), 284 f.

among Married Men," are to be found. Stories of virtue rewarded and faithlessness punished alternate with appeals for the Christian life and exhortations urging tolerance. Occasionally a belated off-spring of the Age of Reason is to be found among these gems at the beginning of the nineteenth century. The story of the self-sacrificing love of a heathen Chinese girl for her father contains the searching question: "Christian child, how do you feel when you hear of the love of this non-Christian child?"[55] Also, a moral-pedagogical trend is commonly found in all almanacs. Along with it is entertaining and educational material, such as popular travel descriptions and short historic, patriotic treatises.[56] In the course of their more than a century of activity there is no question that the almanacs have had a wide, if not very deep, pedagogical influence on their tremendous number of readers.

John Gruber did not limit his printing to the publishing of the almanac. We have already mentioned the *Westliche Correspondenz*. At the beginning of the nineteenth century he seems to have published a weekly paper for a few years; however, we know nothing of the title or life of the paper since we have only two indirect and very brief references to it.[57] Further, a large number of books were printed on the Gruber press, most of them works of religious content—hymns and prayer books, and volumes of sermons. For instance, in the year 1831 he published the first edition of the psalms and hymns of the German-Reformed Church under the direction of the synod of the church.[58] For the first few years Gruber worked alone; later he took in his son-in-law, Daniel May, as a partner.[59]

[55] This last example is from the *Dietrich Almanac*, Hagerstown, 1807 (copy in the Pratt Library, Baltimore) not from the Gruber. However, the almanacs are of the same general character throughout; there are only minor differences between them.

[56] For details of the history, make-up and content of Gruber's almanac, see the above-mentioned article by A. J. Prahl.

[57] Seidensticker, 170, 181. Perhaps this paper is identical with the *Westliche Correspondenz*. We do not know how long the *Westliche Correspondenz* appeared. Williams (*Washington County*, I, 129) mentions that it appeared until about 1830 and then was discontinued because the use of the German language had greatly declined at this time. However, it is impossible to determine anything definite about the length of publication of the *Westliche Correspondenz*.

[58] Scharf, *Western Maryland*, II, 1142. Index of Gruber imprints, see Reichmann; cf. footnote 36.

[59] Complete genealogical information about Gruber's ancestors and descendants may be found in the above-mentioned article by C. H. Eshleman,

Gruber died in Hagerstown on December 30, 1857. However, on the old-fashioned cover decoration and under Gruber's old motto, "By Industry We Thrive," is still to be found the traditional statement, "Printed by John Gruber," when the *Hagers-Town Town and Country Almanack* appears for sale on the streets of Baltimore, Frederick and Hagerstown toward the end of each year.

The histories of the three most important printers, Samuel Sower (1767-1820), Matthias Bartgis (1750-1825) and John Gruber (1768-1857) show us that after the Revolutionary War the Germans in Maryland did not sink back into the political lethargy that characterized them in colonial times. At the beginning of the nineteenth century we find especially in Western Maryland more and more Germans in political offices. Jacob Schnebley, Henry Shryock, William Heyser, Adam Ott, Matthias Shaffner, Henry Sweitzer, Daniel Schnebley are all names that appear in the offices of sheriff and justice for Washington County. Jacob D. Dietrich, who had a bookstore and a lending library in Hagerstown, was postmaster for a time. Adam Ott and William Heyser were managers of a lottery held to provide money for street improvements. Daniel Heister, George Baer, W. E. Strudwick were Maryland Congressmen of German descent. Jacob Zeller's and William Heyser's names are to be found in accounts of the organization of the Hagerstown Bank. In Baltimore in 1797, one year after the incorporation of the city, we find several German names among the members of the City Council: Adam Fonerden, Baltzer Schaeffer, Peter Frick and Frederick Schaeffer. Engelhard Yeiser was Elector for the Mayor, and Adam Fonerden later became a delegate to the Maryland legislature. In the eight years between 1806 and 1814, we find twenty Germans in the City Council: George Decker, Peter Diffenderfer, Adam Fonerden, Samuel Frey, Peter Frick, Ludwig Hering, Peter Hoffman, George P. Keeports, William Lorman, John Makkenheimer, John Miller, Christopher Raborg, Baltzer Schaeffer, Frederick Schaeffer, John Schirm, Jacob Small, John Snyder, Henry Stauffer, William Warner and George Woelper.[60] In Baltimore, as

---

as well as in an unpublished manuscript by Eshleman in the Pratt Library, Baltimore. The Pratt Library owns a complete set of the Gruber almanacs, starting from 1836.

[60] Williams, *Washington County*, I, 127, 130, 131, 134, 135. The Whiskey Rebellion of 1794 failed to interest most of the Germans of Western Pennsylvania and Maryland; the majority of them were indifferent to the whole

well as in the west, an intense interest in public affairs is to be seen among the German settlers.

Little definite comment may be made on the political affiliations of the Germans during these decades. In Western Maryland we find German names on both sides of the tickets, the Federalist as well as the Republican-Democratic.[61] It is true, however, that apparently the Republican-Democratic Party was especially popular among the German as well as among all other immigrant groups. John Gruber's German newspaper, the *Westliche Correspondenz*, was founded in order to draw the German followers of Jefferson more closely together, as we have already mentioned. John Gruber himself was on the Republican-Democratic side all his life. The opponents of Jefferson in Washington County knew perfectly well how strong Gruber's influence was. Secretly they got in touch with him and made him attractive financial propositions to swing his paper to their side. But John Gruber refused. He was convinced that Jefferson was right and he remained true to his conviction.[62]

In general, the political line of the Germans in Maryland did not differ greatly from that of the Germans in Pennsylvania during these decades.[63] Until about 1796 we find strong adherents to the Federalist Party among the Germans, but then the majority shifted within a comparatively short time to the Republican-Democratic Party. The election of Thomas Jefferson showed this very plainly and John Adams later realized that the defection of the Germans had a great deal to do with his defeat. It is characteristic of the Germans that one of the reasons for their desertion of the Federalist Party was the rumor that the Federalists wanted to change the government to a monarchy. The bare rumor was enough to send them in droves to the Jeffersonians.[64] It need hardly be said that the infamous Alien and Sedition Acts did much to make the Adams administration unpopular with all immigrant groups.

---

affair, as has been convincingly shown by Andreas Dorpalen, "The German Element in Early Pennsylvania Politics, 1789-1800," in *Pennsylvania History*, IX, iii (1942), 187 ff. See also L. Baldwin, *Whiskey Rebels* (Pittsburgh, 1939), 106 f. Griffith, 281. Hennighausen, *German Society*, 48 f.

[61] Williams, *Frederick County*, I, 128-32.

[62] Williams, *Washington County*, I, 129.

[63] This question has been very thoroughly examined in the previously mentioned article by Andreas Dorpalen, *Pennsylvania History*, IX, iii (1942), 176 ff.

[64] Andreas Dorpalen, *Pennsylvania History*, IX, iii (1942), 190.

In the presidential election of 1808 the majorities in the German-settled counties were again for the Republican-Democratic candidate, Jefferson's political heir, James Madison. The lists of committees, meetings, resolutions, etc., for Madison in Frederick and Hagerstown were crowded with German names.[65] John Brengle's Company in Frederick, which placed itself at the disposal of the governor of Maryland and the President in 1808, consisted in large part of citizens of German origin.[66]

The newly awakened interest in public affairs probably also explains the fact that shortly after the Revolution the Germans banded together for the first time to form an organization of non-religious character and entirely outside the German churches, which had up to this time taken care of all necessary collective activities. The new organization was the German Society of Maryland.

We do not know the exact year of the founding of the society. Probably it was in the beginning of the eighties. The first documentary evidence we have is for the year 1783, and this date is accepted by the society today as the beginning of its long history. "A Society for the aid of the Germans, not speaking the language of the country, was founded," so we read in the *Annals of Baltimore* for 1783.[67] Again in the following year the society is mentioned in a notice in the *Maryland Journal* in which a little is told of the basis and aims of the society. "The brutal advantage which has been taken by some Masters of Vessels, of their power over their passengers has induced a number of inhabitants of this place (in imitation of their brethren in Philadelphia) to form themselves into a Society, for the protection of such of their countrymen as may be induced to come to this State, and guard them from the oppression and barbarity of unfeeling men. . . ."[68] Thus the main purpose of the society was the protection of the redemptioners, destitute immigrants who sold themselves into voluntary slavery for the first few years after their arrival in this country in order to pay the cost of their trip across the ocean. In the same number of the *Maryland Journal* which mentions the founding of the German Society is to be found an advertisement in which a shipload of German immigrants is offered for sale as follows: "German Redemptioners. Just

[65] Williams, *Frederick County*, 1, 132 f. *Washington County*, 1, 143 f.
[66] Williams, *Frederick County*, 1, 163.   [67] Griffith, 104.
[68] *Maryland Journal*, August 10, 1784.

arrived in the Brig Lavater, Captain Kulkens from Bremen. A number of healthy German Redemptioners, Men and Women; among whom are a Number of valuable Tradesmen, viz. Ropemakers, Gardeners, Weavers, Shoemakers, Blacksmiths, Bricklayers, Carpenters, Butchers, Hostlers, Tailors, Papermakers, Tilers etc. etc. For Terms apply to the Subscribers or Purviance Wharf. Valck, Burger and Schouten. Baltimore, August 7, 1784."

After the middle of the eighteenth century such advertisements appeared in the newspapers of all American coastal cities. The term "slavery" is rightly used in this connection. This does not mean that all the redemptioners were badly treated. Many of the captains who organized the sales and many of the buyers who had the redemptioners in their employ for a time behaved humanely. For example, the Captain Kulkens mentioned above was publicly commended by the German Society of Maryland, which stated that he "has rendered their situation as easy and comfortable as circumstances permit."

In spite of this, the nature of the redemption system brought about incredible hardships. If one member of a family died en route, the rest of the family had to work so much the longer; and if a deceased passenger left no family, the extra years of service were divided among the rest of the immigrants. Couples, parents and children were torn asunder upon arrival, often never to be reunited in the vast, strange country. These hardships resulting from the conditions of the system itself were not even the worst that had to be endured. Many captains exploited their helpless passengers in the most barbaric manner, making them work like slaves, withholding from them even the most primitive necessities of life, so that countless numbers of them succumbed to overwork, hunger and sickness on the voyages. Their possessions then reverted to the captain, a condition which led many a captain to hasten the death of a sick passenger. The worst aspect of this system was that it gave free rein to all the brutality, cruelty and low instincts of utterly unscrupulous captains. In order to mitigate wherever possible the hardships attendant upon this inhuman system, charitable societies were formed by Germans in the cities along the Atlantic coast during the second half of the eighteenth century. There were such societies in Pennsylvania, South Carolina, New York and Maryland.

Again we shall mention the name of our old friend, Charles

Frederick Wiesenthal. We who know his character will not be surprised to hear that he was one of the fathers and the first president of the German Society. Along with his name, those of John Conrad Zollikofer as secretary and Dr. William Zollikofer as physician of the society have come down to us. Other than this there is, unfortunately, no other information about the beginnings of the German Society for all of its records of the first decades were lost. In the following chapter we shall have more to say about the society since its period of greatest activity began after the reorganization of 1817.[69]

The life of the German church parishes continued in a "normal" way during these decades after the Revolution. Pastors came and went; matters of contention arose, were fought for a time in the bitterest manner and finally laid aside; we read of splits and separations, of newly organized and expanded churches, in short, the "ordinary affairs" which occur in the life of a church community. Decisive innovations are not to be found in this generation between 1785 and 1815.

The Lutheran congregation in Baltimore had to enlarge its church edifice in 1785. This happy event, however, was the signal for a two-year period of inner quarrels and misunderstandings. A young pastor from the outside, Johann Daniel Kurtz, spoke at the dedication of the enlarged church. The account in the church record is very brief but full of intimations of unchristian disputes. Apparently part of the congregation was dissatisfied with the old incumbent, Pastor Gerock, and these people aligned themselves behind the young preacher Kurtz and threatened to break away. After two years, in April 1787, peace was finally restored with the understanding that the Reverend Mr. Kurtz was to serve as a second preacher along with Pastor Gerock. "Both preachers are expected to behave in sincere brotherly respect and honor to which they are entitled by their high office by carefully avoiding every offense," reads the peace contract, which gives us a general picture of the feuds in a very discreet manner.[70] From now on the two preachers were expected to attend jointly to the duties of the office. Shortly after,

[69] The history of the society has been presented in a comprehensive manner in a book by Louis P. Hennighausen, *History of the German Society of Maryland* (Baltimore, 1909), and in an article by Karl A. M. Scholtz, "German Pilgrim Fathers," which appeared in the publication issued for the 150th anniversary of the society (Baltimore, 1933). Cf. also three poems, "The Redemptioner," by Ernst Feise, in the same publication.

[70] Julius Hofmann, *History*, 24 ff.

elderly Reverend Siegfried Gerock died and in the fall of 1787 young Pastor John Daniel Kurtz became the sole head of the Lutheran community.

J. Daniel Kurtz is considered by Lutheran Church historians to be one of the patriarchs of the church in America. He was the first president of the Lutheran Synod of Maryland and held this office for four consecutive terms. Besides, he became the first president of the General Synod and was re-elected twice to this office. For half a century he was pastor of "Old Zion" in Baltimore; although he retired in 1833 his influence was felt among the Lutherans of Baltimore until his death in 1856 at the Biblical age of ninety-three years.[71]

The church records show that the congregation increased every year.[72] In 1806 the building of a new church was begun and in 1808 it was dedicated. In this year we find for the first time the name "Zionskirche," used for the congregation, a name which became more and more generally used and today is still the official name of the church.[73]

The Reformed church of Baltimore lost its preachers in the Revolution. Reverend Georg Wallauer, who had come to Baltimore in 1772, exchanged the church for a military camp. He entered the army, yet surprisingly not the American but the British army. This is one of the few cases where a prominent German in Maryland joined the English.[74] His position was taken over in 1779 by the Reverend Karl L. Böhme who remained only a short time. In 1783, he was replaced by Pastor Nikolaus Pomp. His tenure of office was marked by the decision to build a new church in 1784; the work began in 1785. Michael Diffenderffer seems to have been

[71] Wentz, Synod, 75 ff. J. D. Kurtz was born in 1763 in Germantown, Pennsylvania, the son of Reverend Johann Nicholas Kurtz. Of all the pastors whom the German-Lutheran church of Baltimore has had to the present day, he is the only one who was born in America.

[72] The church register of the "Evangelisch-Lutherischen Gemeinde in Baltimore im Staate Maryland" begun in 1786 gives us the first accurate figures on church activities. In the following tabulation, the first figure is for the year 1787, and the number in parenthesis is for the year 1800; births 45 (102), marriages 18 (64), communicants 98 (183), deaths 23 (101).

[73] In 1806, when the call to build the church was issued, the plain designation "Lutheran church" was used. However, the Order of Ceremonies for the dedication, found by a lucky accident by Pastor Julius Hofmann, used the name "Zionskirche" for the first time. (J. Hofmann, Festschrift 1905, 7.)

[74] Scharf, Chronicles, 42.

the most prominent and active member of the congregation at this time. He was the moving force behind the building project. Along with his name there are a few others of outstanding persons in the old church records: Heinrich Lorch, Andreas Grenzet, Philipp Crusius, Jakob Coberts, Andreas Steiger, Konrad Schmidt, Nikolas Tschudy, Johann Hull, Peter Herr, Johann Dorgenberg, Friedrich and Jakob Meyer, and Daniel and Peter Diffenderffer. About a hundred members helped to build the church. However, the undertaking seems to have been ill-starred. In 1786 the church had hardly been roofed over when half of it was torn away by the flood waters of Jones Falls. Under the leadership of the Diffenderffer family, the undaunted congregation set about rebuilding what had been lost. It speaks well for the Christian spirit of the rest of the Baltimore church organizations that the Lutheran, Episcopalian and Presbyterian churches assisted the unlucky Reformed group with financial aid. The church had hardly been completed when dissatisfaction with the pastor arose. In November 1789 Nikolas Pomp preached his farewell sermon; his successor, Reverend Georg Trodelnier, a native German in spite of his name, was called from York, Pennsylvania.

The location of the new church was obviously ill-chosen. Aside from the frequent danger of flood from Jones Falls the close proximity of a bridge caused constant traffic noise which disturbed the church services. And so in 1795 a new church was begun, this one dedicated in 1797; the old edifice was sold to St. Paul's Episcopal church. At the close of 1800 Pastor Trodelnier died. A new pastor, Johann H. Dreyer, was called from Germany. He served for only four years; when he resigned in 1806 he was replaced by the Reverend Dr. Christian L. Becker of Lancaster, Pennsylvania.[75]

Of course, there was also the Separatist Reformed congregation which became stronger and stronger during these decades and twice had to move into larger churches. This congregation had an advantage over the old Reformed in that it had a very capable, dynamic pastor who guided the fortunes of the church for an uninterrupted span of forty years from 1774 to 1813. He was Philip

[75] Eduard F. Leyh, *Baltimore, Seine Vergangenheit und Gegenwart* (Baltimore, 1887), (hereafter abbreviated *BVG*), 263 f. Scharf, *Chronicles*, 44 ff. A poetic necrology written in 1808 after Becker's death by a friend and published in a newspaper is to be found (it is the only copy) in the Enoch Pratt Library.

William Otterbein. In 1786 the congregation moved into the church, known as "Otterbein church," today the oldest church building in Baltimore.[76]

Till the end of his days Otterbein belonged officially to the German-Reformed Church, but in matters of dogma and church affairs he went his own way. He came in contact with some of the leading Methodists and one of the most radical Mennonites, Martin Boehm. At Otterbein's suggestion these people met in conference in Baltimore in 1789, and set up a faith upon the basis of which the Church of the United Brethren in Christ was founded, with which Otterbein's name was now associated. The group called itself The Evangelical Reformed Church. William Otterbein and Martin Boehm were elected bishops in 1800; this bishopric had no sacerdotal significance; it was purely an administrative office.[77] The churches had few but very devout followers. More than all the other German churches in Maryland, this one was pervaded with evangelistic-spiritualistic-mystic ideas which are so often found among the pioneers of the American frontier.

Toward the end of the eighteenth century we notice for the first time traces of the existence of German Catholics in Baltimore. In the *Maryland Journal*, February 17, 1792, we find the following announcement: "Notice is hereby given, that the German Roman Catholicks have concluded to open, next Sunday, for the first Time, their Divine Service, in their own Language, at the House of John Brown, near the Centre-Market. On Wednesdays and Fridays, in Lent, will be sung the Psalm Miserere, accompanied with a Sermon in the German Language, delivered by the Reverend John Baptist Clouse." We know nothing of the development of the congregation during the next few years. Apparently the demand for a German service grew stronger, for in 1799, exactly a decade after the Catholic diocese was founded in Baltimore, a group of German Catholics assembled under the leadership of Father F. Caesar Reuter. Father Reuter tried to organize a German-Catholic congregation, but he was strongly opposed by his superior, Archbishop John Carroll. Reuter laid his plans before the Pope and asked for a German church, a German catechism and even a German bishop.

[76] C. C. Hall, *Baltimore, Its History and Its People* (Baltimore, 1912), 683 f. The Otterbein church is on Conway Street, near Sharpe Street.

[77] Paul E. Holdcraft, *History of the Pennsylvania Conference of the Church of the United Brethren in Christo* (Fayetteville, Pa., 1938), 38 f.

The answer from Rome was entirely negative. The Pope gave Bishop Carroll a free hand to manage the affairs of a possible German congregation according to his discretion. Upon hearing this, Reuter formed his own church on October 11, 1799, with a few other German Catholics.[78] However, the separation lasted only a short time; in 1805 the Separatists returned to the jurisdiction of Bishop Carroll and in 1806 Father Reuter was succeeded by Reverend F. X. Brosius.[79] The number of German Catholics was still small at this time; it was another forty years before they came to Maryland in great numbers. Father Reuter's attempt showed that it was apparently a difficult thing to weld a national group into a separate congregation in the Catholic Church. The looser organization of the Protestant Church was more adaptable to the formation of special groups, while the centralized, strict structure of the Catholic Church demanded uniformity in language as well as in other matters. Therefore, Father Reuter's attempt failed after a few years.

During the decades after the Revolution the old Lutheran congregation in Frederick was under the leadership of Reverend John Andrew Krug.[80] Here also things were not always peaceful and harmonious. The Reverend Mr. Krug was an outspoken antimilitarist. His sympathies were certainly on the side of American freedom, but he hated every sort of force, even when it was used for a good cause. And so, although most of the enthusiastic members of the flock expected their pastor to respond, the call of the Revolution was not re-echoed by him. Added to this was the fact that for many years Krug was in poor health and not equal to the demands of his position. His gloomy strictness in questions of morals and church discipline was often in conflict with the lusty good humor and love of gaiety that was in the blood of these sons of the Palatinate. Their discontent finally found expression in a petition to the Lutheran synod; they asked for another pastor. At first the synod laid aside this unpleasant complaint; then it tried to pacify

[78] The church was St. John's church on Park Avenue and Saratoga Street, the first Catholic German church in Baltimore. For further information see the article by Charles R. Gellner, "Ecclesiastical History of the Catholic Germans in Maryland," SHGM, xxvi (1945), 37-48, and Peter Guilday, The Life and Times of John Carroll (New York, 1922), ii, 723 ff.

[79] F. X. Brosius, 1806-1820. His successors were: J. Beschter S.J., 1820-1828; L. Barth, 1828-1838; B. Bayer, 1838-1840.

[80] Wentz, Frederick, 140 ff.

the group. Finally, the apparently hopeless situation was settled in 1796 when the Reverend Mr. Krug died of old age.

The next three pastors did not work out much better. It was twelve years before the group obtained a pastor who stayed and who could work on long-range plans. Krug's successor, Reverend Charles Frederick Wildbahn, came from Saxony. He arrived in America in 1755 as a soldier in the British army. Brought up in the pietist tradition of Halle, a well-educated, versatile man, he had been active for three decades in America as a printer, teacher and preacher before coming to Frederick. However, he stayed hardly two years; in 1798 he retired and went first to Virginia and later to Pennsylvania. We do not know of any definite reason for his early resignation, but it seems as though the extensive outside demands of the position of pastor in Frederick were too strenuous for him.

A younger man followed him who came from northeast Germany and had studied at the University of Königsberg—John Frederick Moeller. The congregation in Frederick engaged him at first for a half year. But apparently young Moeller was such an attractive person in every respect that he was soon asked to stay permanently. However, in 1802, he gave up his position in order to accept a call to Chambersburg, Pennsylvania, where he stayed for the next twenty-seven years.

The third man in this series of short-term pastors in Frederick was the Reverend Frederick William Jasinsky. He was probably originally of Polish descent, but he had served as a soldier under Frederick the Great. Most likely he had come to America with the British during the Revolution. For many years he had petitioned the Lutheran synod in vain to ordain him officially. He had been refused numerous times, but Jasinsky was stubborn, and finally he wore down the opposition of the synod, which duly ordained him. He had already been active among various congregations in the region of the old Monocacy Track, and it can hardly be said that he spread peace and harmony wherever he went. In 1802 he appeared in Frederick. At first he was well liked, for he was a good preacher, and he impressed people by his massive figure. However, he became so tyrannical, so overbearing and so coarse in his manners that the church members soon wished they still had friendly, well-bred young Moeller. Tradition has it in Frederick that in spiritual and church quarrels Jasinsky occasionally soundly beat up the members of his flock, and since he was so enormous, as strong as an ox and in every way "domineering and overbearing," there was soon an atmosphere of fear and terror in the group. A report on him which one of his successors made, merits repetition: "He was already beyond the zenith of life; yet neither his physical nor mental energies gave any symptoms of decay. He was a man of muscle and sinew; of nerve and spirit; of boldness and military strictness. . . . He was endowed with a full, round and strong voice. His manner in the pulpit was not bland but rather stern. No insults were offered to him, nor outrage perpetrated upon his premises. The rebellious spirits of the congregation doubted whether it would be safe to do so. They feared his early warlike spirit might be aroused; and in personal courage they knew him to be immensely their superior. He boldly rebuked the vestry and held them up to ridicule before the whole congregation for their inefficiency. Yet they endured it. The same individuals who had insulted the kind-hearted Dr. Krug in his old age, and who had found fault with the young Dr. Moeller, because his step was too elastic, and his manners too polished, and his attire too fashionable said nothing openly against the plain-spoken, harsh and denunciatory Jasinsky. . . . There was something in the man, his eye and countenance and bearing, that told them plainly that he who had once commanded the conquering battalions of the great Frederick had not come here to be their football. . . . You may imagine that although no flaw could be found in his Christian character, nor want of pastoral fidelity, he was not a popular man."[81] Of course, it was quite a while before a few people in the thoroughly terrorized community mustered enough courage to lay a complaint before the synod against this stormy Prussian bully. In 1807 they were at last rid of him, for he transferred the scene of his pastoral violence to Pennsylvania.

His successor, David Frederick Schaeffer, ushered in a period of quiet and composure. His very important tenure of office will be further discussed in the next chapter.

The other German church in Frederick, the Reformed church, was not free of rebellion and dissension during this time either. The Reverend Frederick L. Henop, who led the flock during the whole revolutionary period, was a peaceful soul; everything that we know about his pastorate (1770-1784) is favorable. The group

[81] Wentz, *Frederick*, 168.

must have been well-established for it bought the first organ and church bells, and laid out a large cemetery.[82] However, more dramatic things happened under Henop's successor, John William Runkel, who was pastor from 1784 to 1801. In 1787 a certain Reverend Mr. Schneider came down from Albany, New York, to preach in Frederick and to raise money to build a church. He did this at first with the consent of the Reformed Church organization in Frederick, but he repaid their friendliness badly, for he seized the opportunity to form his own party in the congregation, and stirred it up against the rightful Pastor Runkel. His followers tried in vain to depose the Reverend Mr. Runkel in order to set up Schneider in his place. Since they could not accomplish this by legal means, they tried force. They occupied the church and let no one in, "a portion of them literally encamping in the church for days and nights, armed with various kinds of unevangelical weapons," wrote a chronicler with heavy heart. The loyalists in the congregation were forced to hold their services in the schoolhouse. The synod stood firmly behind Runkel, since Schneider was an independent preacher it did not recognize. But what good was this, for Schneider still held the church edifice with the aid of powder and shot? There was nothing to do but to beg for the aid of the secular authorities, who in 1800 decided in favor of the rightful party headed by the Reverend Mr. Runkel. A citizen of Frederick, Valentine Brunner, was ordered by the Civil Court "to lead Reverend Runkel into the Church and surrender it to him," an order which, gun in hand, Brunner obediently carried out. This happened just in time, exactly a week before February 22, 1800, when a large service was to be held in honor of George Washington, who had died shortly before. Ex-Governor Thomas Johnson delivered the address in the church and the Reverend Mr. Runkel presided at the altar. In the following year (1801), Runkel paved the way for a reconciliation of the hostile factions by his resignation. He was followed by the Reverend Daniel Wagner, who came from the Duchy of Nassau in Germany, and had been brought to America in 1750 as a small child. In order to establish peace and order, a new constitution for the congregation was drawn up in 1803 under Wagner's leadership.[83] Wagner stayed in Frederick until sickness and old age forced him to give up his position in 1812.

[82] Eschbach, op.cit., 20 ff.
[83] The constitution bears the signatures of the most important members of

Compared to all this, the German churches in Hagerstown did comparatively little worthy of special mention during these decades. From 1773-1793 the Lutheran church in Hagerstown was under the leadership of the Reverend John G. Young; and from 1793-1810 under the Reverend John George Schmucker. There is hardly anything noteworthy about Young; Schmucker, an important figure in the history of the Lutheran Church of America, was born in 1771 in Michelstadt in the Odenwald, Germany. He came to America in 1785, settling first in Pennsylvania, then in Virginia and finally in Maryland. When he accepted the position in Hagerstown, he was only twenty-two years old, and was called "the boy preacher." He was well known to the end of his days (1854) for his work in the synod and through various publications.[84] However, for the Hagerstown Lutheran community his pastorate was of no more than average significance.

The Reformed church of Hagerstown had the advantage of long, continuous pastorates. In the first half-century of its existence it had no more than two pastors: Jacob Weymer (1770-1790) and Jonathan Rahauser (1792-1817). They had an extensive parish to administer, including Funkstown, Boonesboro, Troxels, Greencastle, Mercersburg, Besore's, Millerstown, Emmitsburg and Appel's, as well as Hagerstown. It was certainly no small task to travel this large circuit on horseback in all kinds of weather. On one of these journeys the Reverend Mr. Rahauser was nearly drowned in the swollen flood waters of the Conococheague; he was saved, but he died shortly after, probably from the effects of the accident.

It will be necessary for us to enlarge our geographical scope at this time. Before the Revolution we stopped along the Conococheague about in line with Hagerstown. However, in the last two decades of the eighteenth century German settlers pushed farther west into territory—the present Allegany County—which around 1750 was gradually and cautiously being settled by English and

---

the congregation: Jacob Steiner, Henry Kuntz, John Brunner, Joseph Doll, John Gebhart, Jacob Rohr, Christian Webber, Peter Wolff, Philip Rohr, George Baer, Daniel Hauer, Conrad Doll, George Kessler, Michael Baltzell, John Baer, Mathias Buckey, Michael Houser, John Schley, George Jacob Steiner.

[84] Cf. P. Anstadt, *Life and Times of Reverend S. S. Schmucker* (York, Pa., 1896), 14 ff. Samuel Schmucker was certainly more important than his father, J. George Schmucker.

Irish immigrants. In 1787 the Maryland legislature officially permitted the establishment of the city of Cumberland at a place previously called Will's Creek. At this time there were but few houses there, and we find only a few German names among the approximately thirty-five families which comprised the population of Cumberland at that time. These were: Michael Kerschner, George Hoffman, David Hoffman and George Blocker. Aside from these, nevertheless, there were a great many Germans living in the general vicinity of the new town. "A list of the settlers then located upon the lands lying in Maryland west of Fort Cumberland" gives us the following names: Adam Eckhart, George Eckhart, John Eckhart, John Keyser, Christopher Myers, John Steyer, Garrett Snedeger, Adam Hicksenbaugh, William Korntz, Henry Kemp, Henry Myers, John Metz, John Neff, Nicholas Pittinger, Henry Pittinger, Peter Stuck, John Sayler, Jacob Krager, Leonard Kimble, John Liptz, Samuel Postlewait, Benjamin Rush, Adam Seigler, Jacob Seigler, Charles Uhl, Jacob Trullinger, Alexander Wilhelm, George Wilhelm, John Strickler.[85] Among the names of families which settled in Cumberland between 1790 and 1800 are to be found the following which are undoubtedly of German origin: Bridenhart, Deetz, Erb, Gephart, Lichlider, Rizer, Shuck, Stonesifer. In a Court Meeting in 1797, a few Irish immigrants "and Christian Deetz, tailor, a native of Germany, were naturalized and fully invested with all the rights of American citizenship."[86]

The German settlers here emulated their brothers elsewhere on the frontier and built a church as soon as they had gained a foothold in the wilderness. The Lutherans were the first; in May 1794 they organized themselves into a congregation, bought a piece of land and built a simple log building upon it.[87] This church was used at first by the Episcopalians and Presbyterians as well for their services. The first constitution of the Lutheran church was written in German and signed by twelve members. The first pastor was Friedrich Wilhelm Lange, about whom the church records have given us no information. The first church records which we have of

[85] Will H. Lowdermilk, *History of Cumberland* (Washington, D.C., 1878), 264 ff.

[86] *Ibid.*, 277.

[87] They bought one acre of land for the church at a price of 15 pounds, about $75. The Lutheran church in Cumberland still stands on this property, which now lies in the center of the city, and is valued at about $125,000.

the congregation are those of the second pastor, John George Böttler, who held the position in Cumberland from 1805 to 1816, and who also preached in Frostburg, New Germany, Williamsburg, Will's Creek and Hartz's Station. His records were written partly in German, partly in English and partly in Latin. The organization and consolidation of a church community seems to have taken much longer in Cumberland than in Frederick and Hagerstown. No doubt the percentage of German settlers in farthest Western Maryland, in the Alleghenies, was much smaller than in "middle-western" Maryland, the territory between the Conococheague and Monocacy.

Toward the end of the eighteenth century a few German settlers pushed out to the farthest boundary of the state, the section now called Garrett County. In 1788, a small group of German pioneers, John Stauch, Jacob Wagner and Jacob Deidrick, started out from Hagerstown bound for the west. They had really planned to go to the Mississippi Valley, but when they got to the "Green Glades," about 160 miles west of Hagerstown, they liked the country so well that they decided to stay. Other German families, such as the Rhinehards, Hauers and Ridenauers, followed them during the next few years. They had no ordained pastor, but John Stauch acted as lay preacher. In religious as well as in worldly matters he was the undisputed leader of the group. The settlement developed quickly and later became known by the names "Aurora" and "Red House." After 1806 a German-Lutheran pastor, John Georg Butler (formerly Böttler), came out regularly from Cumberland to preach.

At this time in almost all parts of what was later Garrett County there were German settlers. Ebenezer Kitzmiller and Henry Bittinger, of whom the names of two modern towns remind us, were among the first German immigrants. George Fazenbaker, a Hessian prisoner of war, refused return transportation to Hesse and settled in Allegany County about 1787. Emanuel Custer (originally Küster) settled in Sandy Creek about 1795; John and Frederick Weimer are mentioned around 1780; John Rodeheaver and Solomon Sterner came shortly after 1800. Henry Sines began to farm at Sang Run about 1820. In a list of taxpayers for 1798 the following names appear from the region of the present Garrett County district: Philip Fierbach, David Melinger, George Rinehart, Emanuel Custard, Aron Brandenburg. It would be easy to mention more names, but we shall confine ourselves to these best-known ones.[88]

With the War of 1812, the period which has been discussed in this chapter comes to a close. It will be mentioned only briefly here, for it did not have nearly the importance for the history of the Germans in Maryland that it had for the general history of the United States. The Revolutionary War stirred up the Germans; the Civil War caused them to support passionately one side or the other; the War of 1812 did neither.

Patently, the majority of the western counties settled by the Germans were against the declaration of war.[89] We read of various meetings of antiwar factions, though these were not confined to Western Maryland; they were held in all the other states of the nation. It is well known that a large part of the American people embarked on "Mr. Madison's War" with misgivings and lack of enthusiasm. However, after they were finally in the war, the farmers of Western Maryland did their part to help win it. Washington County raised its quota of soldiers through volunteers. Among the officers appeared such well-known German names as: Christian Hager, Ezra Mantz, George Shryock, Samuel Rohrer, David Schnebly, Matthias E. Bartgis, Thomas B. Pottinger, William Kolb, Frederick Schley, Henry and Stephen Steiner. We also find on the muster of enlisted men a great many Germans, in keeping with their percentage of the population of Western Maryland.[90] The longer the war lasted, the more people forgot their original scruples about its necessity. When the Englishmen appeared in Chesapeake Bay, and as the direct danger grew, the enthusiasm and military spirit grew also. Captain John Brengle, the son of a German immigrant in Frederick, recruited a whole company of volunteers in four hours on August 25, 1814, in Frederick. The pastor of the German-Lutheran church in Frederick, the Reverend David F. Schäfer, marched at the head of a procession through the city and urged the men to join the army and defend their country. Lieutenant Colonel Charles G. Börstler, the son of the German physician, Dr. Christian Börstler of Funkstown, who has already

[88] Thanks are due Mr. Charles E. Hoye of Sang Run, Maryland, for the material for Garrett County. See his series of articles on "Garrett County History of Pioneer Families," *Mountain Democrat* (Oakland, Md.) from 1934 to 1938. Also *The Glades Star* (Oakland), June 18, 1945.

[89] Scharf, *Western Maryland*, I, 183.

[90] Williams, *Washington County*, I, 144 ff. Frederick County, I, 166 ff. Scharf, *Western Maryland*, I, 183 ff., 192 ff.

been discussed, is mentioned again and again. His heroic though unsuccessful defense of his position at Beaver Dam, Canada (1813), is known to us in every detail through contemporary accounts.[91]

In Baltimore as in Western Maryland we find Germans on both sides of the domestic political camps, among the Federalists as well as among the Republican Democrats. Right at the beginning of the war, a German, Jacob Wagner, was talked about a great deal as one of the bitterest political enemies of the Madison administration. Jacob Wagner was editor-in-chief of the *Federal Republican*, and he attacked Madison in the most vehement manner two days after the declaration of war against England. Weeks before the outbreak of the war it had been prophesied that the offices of the *Federal Republican* would be stormed and mobbed by the Baltimore crowds; this happened now. For a time the publication of the paper was moved to Georgetown, but hardly had it returned to Baltimore when the attacks began again. About thirty persons, along with the two editors (Wagner and Hanson), barricaded themselves inside the offices in order to protect the freedom of the press at all costs. There were other Germans in this group besides Jacob Wagner—William Schroeder, David Hoffman, Mark Pringle and Jacob Schley.[92] They were all put in jail by the police in order to protect them from the mob, but the mob stormed the prison the very first night and raged among the prisoners in such a manner that afterwards Baltimore was given the not very honorable name of "Mobtown."

Jacob Wagner is not typical of the attitude of the Germans in general. A great many German names, such as Peter Diffenderffer, Charles Bohn, George Warner, Christian Baum,[93] are to be found among the signers of a resolution drawn up by the Republican Democrats in May 1812, to set forth their agreement with Madison's war program. The German part of the population had no special preference for one side or the other; the Germans were probably about equally divided between the two parties, with perhaps a slight majority on the side of the Republican Democrats.

[91] Reprinted in Scharf, *Western Maryland*, I, 184-86. All four sons of Dr. Börstler fought in the War of 1812; one of them fell in the battle of Brownstown near Detroit (Börstler's *Diary*, 21).
[92] William M. Marine, *The British Invasion of Maryland, 1812-1815* (Baltimore, 1913), 9.
[93] Scharf, *Chronicles*, 309.

The Maryland Roster of the War of 1812, a list of about 25,000 names, has a great many German names that we have already met in earlier chapters. To give in detail the part played by the various individuals lies outside the scope of this history.[94]

The Germans were particularly active in the defense of Baltimore in September 1814. On the Committee of Vigilance and Safety, which was organized by the mayor of Baltimore, eight of the thirty members were of German birth or descent. There were also many Germans on the other committees which were charged with the arming and defense of Baltimore.[95]

It is not certain whether George Armistead (1780-1818), who defended Fort McHenry near Baltimore in the famous bombardment of September 1814, was of German or English descent; the story that his ancestors emigrated from Hesse to Virginia may be only cited here, not proved.[96]

Unquestionably of German descent, however, was another prominent soldier who made a name for himself in the defense of Baltimore in 1814—General John Stricker. To be exact, he was of German-Swiss descent. The son of Colonel George Stricker, who became known in the Revolutionary War, John Stricker was born on February 15, 1759, in Frederick, Maryland.[97] He had fought in his father's regiment in the War of Independence as a seventeen-year-old cadet; when the war was over John Stricker had the rank of captain. In Baltimore, where Stricker settled after the war, he

[94] The above-mentioned roster was set up by Louis Henry Dielman; cf. Appendix of the book by W. M. Marine, 199-495, mentioned previously. There is as yet no article on the part played by the Germans of Maryland in the War of 1812. The article by Julius Hofmann, *The Germans of Maryland 1812-1814* (Baltimore, 1914), does not include the information which the title promises. A few details are to be found in BVG, 292.

[95] Hennighausen, *German Society*, 54 f. L. P. Hennighausen, "The Germans in the Defense of Baltimore in the War of 1812 to 1814," SHGM, XVI (1907), 55 ff. Griffith, op.cit., 209, mentions that George Keyser had a commission in the army.

[96] DAB, I, 346.
Faust, op.cit., I, 514.
Hermann Schuricht, op.cit., II, 21 f.
William S. Appleton, *The Family of Armistead of Virginia* (Boston, 1899).
Virginia A. Garber, *The Armistead Family 1635-1910* (Richmond, 1910).
Charles P. Keith, *The Ancestry of Benjamin Harrison* (Philadelphia, 1893), 13.

[97] John Stricker Jr., "General John Stricker," in *Maryland Hist. Mag.*, IX (1914), 209 ff.

was soon active in the founding of a militia unit and then promoted to command a brigade of the town militia. In 1794 he was put under the command of General Smith in order to suppress the so-called "Whiskey Rebellion" in the vicinity of Pittsburgh.[98] In 1801, Colonel Stricker was given a position with the naval agency in the port of Baltimore, which he kept for nearly ten years. Politically, Stricker was in the camp of the Jeffersonian Democrats, and this explains various attacks directed against him by the Federalists in 1812. In particular, he was accused of not having exercised the obligations of his office vigorously enough to suppress the outbreak of the mob that besieged the Federalists. When the English appeared in Chesapeake Bay in August 1814, Stricker was given the mission to stop the attack on Baltimore.[99] His troops met the English at North Point, and it was due to Stricker's clever retreat maneuvers that the English could proceed only very slowly and with heavy losses. An Order of the Day reported that "every praise was due him."

We mentioned that Stricker was a Republican Democrat. At this time the Federalists ruled Maryland. After the war, when some of the higher military ranks had to be filled, Stricker was ignored; he did not receive the promotion that his services and his age merited. Therefore Stricker retired from his command at the end of 1814. In the official report exaggerated gratitude was expressed for his services, but it is doubtful whether this helped Stricker to overcome the disappointment of his resignation.[100]

Various attempts were made later to bring Stricker back into public affairs. He accepted one position, that of President of the

[98] In a part of Pennsylvania, resistance to internal taxes rose to the extent of a real rebellion, but it collapsed before force had to be brought to bear. Andrews, Tercentenary History, I, 667.

[99] Hamilton Owens, Baltimore on the Chesapeake (Garden City, N.Y., 1941), 194 ff.
Frederick M. Colston, The Battle of North Point (Baltimore, 1907).
Marine, op.cit., 161 ff.
Niles Register, VII, 23-30.

[100] In an official announcement of Major General Scott, the following statement about Stricker is made: "Baltimore will long recollect what is due to her gallant defender and in him the Nation will recognize a public Benefactor." (Maryland Hist. Mag., I, 215.) Niles Register (VII, 170) mentions Stricker's forced resignation because of party politics as follows: "Where this business will stop we know not; but fear it may end in the full disorganisation of one of the finest corps of militia in the world."

Bank of Baltimore, but remained cool to all other lures of public life. He was elected to the Maryland Senate; he was asked to run for mayor of Baltimore, but he refused everything. In 1824 he belonged to the group of prominent men of Baltimore who greeted and entertained Lafayette in Maryland on his visit as a guest of the Republic.[101] The next year he was at last offered the major-generalship that he had been refused ten years before. However, now he had to refuse it on account of his health. Shortly after, on June 23, 1825, he died.[102]

John Stricker represents the type of citizen-general in the best sense of the word. At the beginning of the nineteenth century he was certainly the most prominent Marylander of German descent. On a smaller scale his case is symptomatic of the Germans in Maryland as a whole. He illustrates how firmly the Germans were now anchored in the democratic community. Stricker was a member of the second generation; he was born in America and did not need to overcome the difficulty of a foreign language. The defeats and setbacks that occurred in his life were the result not of his German descent but of his party loyalty. The fact that he was so much at home in the American party system shows that he had become entirely acclimated.

Stricker is only one of many who went through the same course of development. He was one of the first members of that generation which was of German descent but spent its whole life in America. He proves how firmly this generation was established in the new country and how completely it had adjusted itself to the needs and demands of the state. "To a country without men came men without a country. The country was stronger than the men, and the men became part of the country thus contributing their share to its wealth and strength."[103]

[101] It seems appropriate to mention that in Lafayette's party was the great German economist, Friedrich List. He had arrived in America a short time before, and Lafayette invited him to accompany him on the journey.

[102] "He was one of the most amiable and best men." Niles Register, XXVIII, 272. He was one of the charter members of "The Protection Society of Maryland," an organization of prominent citizens (1816) for the protection of the rights of the Negroes. Maryland Hist. Mag., I (1906), 358-62.

[103] Andreas Dorpalen, in Pennsylvania History, VI (1939), 239.

VII. NEW WAVES OF IMMIGRANTS

URING the years following the end of the War of 1812 and after the termination of the disorder created by the Napoleonic Wars in Europe, a new wave of immigration set in. The economic conditions in war-devastated Europe, a scarcity of goods, crop failures and hunger all combined to cause thousands of people to study maps of the world to find a country that offered a decent living in exchange for honest work. In Germany the reactionary trend of politics served only as a supplementary evil to the economic ills; the number of liberal political refugees, like Charles Follen and Francis Lieber, must not be overestimated. Be that as it may, and for whatever reason, during the years following the Congress of Vienna (1815) thousands of people arrived at the decision to emigrate. Traditionally as well as for economic and political reasons, America was the country that first came to mind when a man cast about for a place to which to emigrate. Far more intensively than in the eighteenth century America had now worked its way into the minds of the people of weary Europe who were tying up bag and baggage and starting off. It is an extremely significant symptom that in the year 1817 the word "immigrant" may be observed for the first time in connection with the migration across the Atlantic.[1] Up until this time only "emigrant" was used, for the emphasis had been on going out from Germany, Ireland, Sweden, etc. Now the emphasis had changed to the common goal of all these journeys: America, a goal which promised liberally to repay all the difficulties of such a move. From the point of view of the history of the trans-Atlantic migration, the year 1817—when this interesting psychological change took place—marks the transition of America from a colony to an autonomous country.

Among the Germans in Maryland we can also find indications that the years following 1815 ushered in a new immigration period. It will be remembered that in 1783 a German Society was founded in Baltimore whose purpose was to try to help newly arrived Germans. In the following decades we hear almost nothing of this society; the slackening of immigration in general naturally reduced

[1] Marcus Lee Hansen, *The Immigrant in American History* (Cambridge, 1940), 11.

the necessity for it. Now, after 1815, when the stream of new arrivals suddenly swelled again, people remembered the old German Society. It is interesting to notice that in 1817, the year in which the word "immigration" was first observed, the German Society of Maryland came back into existence and soon engaged in very lively activity. The curves of activity of the society rose and fell according to the immigration curves.

Again it was the problem of the redemptioners which caused the revival of the old organization. Since the first steps of the society were of great importance not only to the Germans but to all immigrants in the State of Maryland, we shall go into the events in detail here.[2]

In November 1816 a Dutch ship, the *Juffrow Johanna* sailed from the harbor of Amsterdam. There were over three hundred passengers on board whom the captain of the ship, H. H. Bleeker, had promised to carry to Baltimore. The winter was one of the coldest in many years. The voyage, an unusually stormy and strenuous one, lasted fifteen weeks before the ship finally sailed into Chesapeake Bay in February 1817. It anchored off Annapolis in the half-frozen bay and the captain offered his passengers for sale in the usual manner.

The following notice appeared in the *Baltimore American* of February 7, 1817: "To the citizens generally and to the benevolent Societies. A ship with upward of 300 German men, women and children has arrived off Annapolis, where she is detained by ice. These people have been fifteen weeks on board and are short of provision. Upon making the Capes, their bedding having become filthy, was thrown overboard. They are now actually perishing from the cold and want of provision." On the following day appeared an advertisement about the passengers: "Principally farmers and mechanics of all sorts, and several fine young boys and girls, whose time will be disposed of." For six weeks the *Juffrow Johanna* lay in the ice outside Annapolis before it finally arrived at its destination, Baltimore. Again advertisements appeared in the *Baltimore Ameri-*

<hr>

[2] L. P. Hennighausen, *German Society*, 57 ff. The minutes of the German Society for its first period from 1783 to 1817 were lost sometime during the first half of the nineteenth century. The records from 1817 on were preserved. In the great fire of 1904, however, the minutes of the society for 1817 to 1861 were destroyed. Only the minutes of the meetings of the officers of the society are in existence for the whole period from 1817; they are the chief source material for Hennighausen's book.

can, the first on March 21, the last on April 7. Presumably by that time the captain had sold all his passengers. Five months had elapsed between the departure from Amsterdam and the sale of the last passenger in Baltimore—five months of drudgery and fatigue, humiliation and degradation, hunger and sickness.

The case of the *Juffrow Johanna* was certainly not unusual. What Captain Bleeker did to his passengers had been done by hundreds of others before him. The *Juffrow Johanna* incident differs from countless other occurrences only in that it provided the stimulus for the revival of the German Society and through it for a wholesome reorganization of the immigration laws of the State of Maryland.

While the ship was still lying in the ice before Annapolis, a number of Baltimoreans of German origin joined together to find means to regulate the redemption system and to protect its victims from abuse. At the head of the movement was a man of high reputation throughout the state, General John Stricker. Along with his name appeared those of a few well-known Baltimore attorneys: William Frick, Charles F. Mayer and David Hoffman. Most of the men taking part, however, were merchants: Christian Mayer, B. J. von Kapff, Heinrich Schroeder, Lewis Brantz, Frederick Leypold, Johann Hoffman, Frederick W. Brune, Michael Kimmel, F. L. E. Amelung, William Krebs, John Frick, Samuel Keerl, John F. Fries, Peter Sauerwein, Frederick Waesche, Jesse Eichelberger, Justus Hoppe, Lewis Mayer, Philip Sadtler, J. J. Cohen, Samuel Etting, Conrad Schultz, A. J. Schwartz, Benjamin J. Cohen, Charles W. Karthaus, Michael Diffenderffer and Lawrence Thomson.

These people, who met on February 13, 1817, decided to revive the old German Society of Maryland. They set up a constitution, elected officers and stated the aim of the society as follows: "The protection and assistance of poor emigrants from Germany and Switzerland and of their descendants who may reside in the State of Maryland or be temporarily sojourning therein." No less than 149 citizens—all immigrants from Germany and Switzerland, or descendants of such—signed the constitution of the society.[3]

The goal of the society was to improve the condition of immi-

[3] Christian Mayer was the first president from 1817 to 1821. A list of officers and members in 1817 is published in Hennighausen, op.cit., 171 ff. Members were recruited in Frederick and Hagerstown also.

grants in general. The case of the *Juffrow Johanna* was taken as an example and used to prove the necessity for legal regulation of the redemption system. The prominent lawyers in the society supplied the necessary legal knowledge; there was the moral authority surrounding the name of John Stricker; there were financial means, for many of the members were wealthy merchants, and with all this backing it was possible to exert powerful influence on public opinion in behalf of the aims of the society. In February 1818—shortly after the society was officially incorporated—the first important step was accomplished. The Maryland legislature passed a law that had been drawn up by the officers of the German Society which decreed the first state supervision of the redemption system.[4] The state engaged a man whose business it was to oversee all details of redemptioning. All redemption contracts had to be submitted to this commissioner and deposited in his office; without his consent they were not valid. It was ruled that everyone who secured a redemptioner under twenty-one years of age was required to send him to school at least two months in every year. No immigrant was to serve longer than four years; no one could be held on board ship longer than thirty days. Further regulations protected children, sick persons and the families of redemptioners who died on the journey.

Anyone who knows the terrible hardships which accompanied the unregulated, unchecked and unsupervised system realizes what a blessing this law was. The German Society took it upon itself to see that the law was adequately enforced. It recommended to the governor the man most suitable for the newly created position of registrar—the secretary of the German Society, Lawrence Thomson. Thomson was duly appointed by the governor; unfortunately he died in 1819. The German Society recommended Lewis Mayer as his successor; he was accepted by the governor and he held the position until 1823.[5]

The German Society protected the rights of immigrants with vigor and marked success. The Bodenweber case and the affair of the Breuning boys became famous during the first few years. Johann Bodenweber, a German redemptioner, was mistreated by his master;

[4] An Act Relative to German and Swiss Redemptioners. The law seems important enough to merit complete reproduction. See Appendix II.

[5] This position, which was so important for the welfare of immigrants, was held during the following decades by Henry G. Jacobsen, Charles Starke and Justus Höppe.

he called on the society for help and it succeeded in obtaining a conviction in the Criminal Court of Baltimore for the defendant. The Breuning boys, two minor youngsters, were forcibly kidnaped from their ship. The kidnaper, W. Denny, a farmer in Queen Anne's County, refused to set up or sign any sort of contract. It was a flagrant defiance of the law. The society brought this case to court also, and fought it to a successful conclusion: the two boys were set free. These are only two cases taken from the first few years; we could easily cite others, but these two will suffice to illustrate the good work done by the German Society.

The charitable activities of the society received universal praise. This is shown particularly clearly in a law that was passed in December 1832 by the Maryland legislature. The purpose of this law was to relieve the society of its financial burden and to supply it with more means to carry on its work. From then on, the captain of each ship arriving in Maryland was required to state the number of immigrants he had brought over. Then each immigrant had to pay a sum of $1.50 to the state. This money was to be used for the support of poor immigrants. Three-fifths of the money was allocated to the "Trustees for the Poor of Baltimore City," and two-fifths to the German and Hibernian Societies in Baltimore who were to use it for charitable purposes.[6]

Henceforth the German Society received sixty cents for every German or Swiss immigrant who landed in Maryland.[7] It is obvious that under this law the society was able enormously to increase the effectiveness of its activity on behalf of the poor and helpless new-

[6] This law was introduced into the legislature by Charles F. Mayer, the counselor for the society and a member of the state legislature; the wording of the law was set up by Mayer's brother, Brantz Mayer, a well-known Baltimore lawyer. The Hibernian Society did the same kind of work among the Irish immigrants as did the German Society among the Germans. Originally the law of 1832 stipulated that two-fifths of the tax be divided equally between the two societies, an unfortunate arrangement, for more Germans immigrated to Baltimore than Irish. Therefore, in 1833, an amendment was passed providing that the money be divided proportionally between the two groups according to the number of Irish or German and Swiss arrivals. In 1842 an attempt was made to repeal the law, but it did not succeed and the societies kept their two-fifths of the tax. Hennighausen, op.cit., 107.

[7] Between 1833 and 1876 the number of German immigrants who landed in Maryland was 272,218. These people paid the city the sum of $408,327, probably more than actually was paid out for the support of indigent immigrants. Hennighausen, 105.

comers. We also now have the first official figures for the number of immigrants as listed in the government books:

1833-1840 . . .	44,584	persons
1840-1850 . . .	50,660	persons
1851-1860 . . .	73,722	persons

In the three decades before the outbreak of the Civil War, therefore, about 200,000 German immigrants landed in Maryland. This does not mean, of course, that they all remained there; most of them went on to the Middle West. Baltimore was the favorite port for Europeans and especially for Germans during these decades, partly because of the tobacco trade, partly because of the close relations that existed between Baltimore and Bremen. From year to year the number of ships carrying tobacco from Baltimore to Bremen grew larger. For the return journey the captains loaded them with human cargo. This went on for many years; the ship that sailed down Chesapeake Bay loaded with bales of tobacco sailed a few weeks later down the mouth of the Weser packed full of German emigrants.

Constantly the German Society sought to mitigate the lot of the immigrants or to help them to avoid difficulties. It printed circulars and gave them to the captains of the immigrant ships to distribute among the new arrivals, informing them about exploitation and possible impositions. At the suggestion of the society a state law was passed in 1841, providing that a German interpreter be made available at all the courts in Baltimore in order to be of service to people ignorant of the language.[8] It soon was obvious that many immigrants had an entirely wrong conception of America, and so thousands of copies of circulars were sent by the society to Germany and distributed there. Prospective immigrants were given many useful hints and were warned against exaggerated expectations.[9] In order to keep too many poverty-stricken tramps and vagabonds from coming over, the society got in touch with the embarkation authorities in various European ports and, thanks to its good connections with Bremen, succeeded in 1838 in having a law passed by the senate of that city "preventing the exportation of paupers and vagrants."[10]

Most of the immigrants traveled on the national turnpike to Frederick, Hagerstown, Cumberland and from there to Wheeling,

[8] Hennighausen, 106.   [9] *Ibid.*, 99 f.   [10] *Ibid.*, 104.

Virginia, Pittsburgh, Pennsylvania and into the valley of the Ohio or the Mississippi. So long as they were within the boundaries of Maryland, the German Society looked after them. In the forties, when it was found that a transportation firm in Cumberland consistently cheated the immigrants, steps were taken immediately by the society to stop this practice.[11]

Naturally it happened that many immigrants, whether or not they had originally planned it, remained in Baltimore. The development of the German element in Baltimore in the first half of the nineteenth century is the result partly of the fact that many immigrants decided to make Baltimore the destination of their journeys, although they had originally planned that it should be only a way station. Of course, the German Society took these people under its wing and established in 1845 a so-called "Intelligence Bureau." This was a free employment agency for German immigrants. In the first year (1846) it found positions for 3500 applicants. The bureau became known far and wide outside of Baltimore and in the next few years thousands of German laborers were sent to Cumberland, York, Washington and Pittsburgh. Many factory owners, railroad companies, etc., used the Baltimore bureau in order to secure workmen from among the German newcomers.[12]

The Germans in Baltimore were certainly not free of social prejudices, of cliques or of consciousness of rank; the wealthy German merchants of the city often emphasized the social hierarchy in the most unpleasant manner. But it must be said in their favor that hardly ever did one of them refuse an appeal of the German Society. Many of them contributed time and money for years in order to preserve this oldest and largest German organization in the state and to enable it to continue its useful work.[13] The old stock of German settlers in Western Maryland did not need this help any more, but for the new group which started to arrive in 1817 the society was invaluable. Thousands of inexperienced German immigrants were able through the society to find places for themselves

[11] *Ibid.*, 109.　　　　　　　　[12] *Ibid.*

[13] The following are only a few of the names of citizens of Baltimore who were particularly generous toward the society: William Frick, Charles F. Mayer, Justus Hoppe, Charles Karthaus, Solomon Etting, Frederick Brune, Albert Schumacher, Claas Vocke, Frederick Schepeler. Benjamin and Israel Cohen succeeded one another as treasurers of the society from 1825 to 1875. The records are full of praise for the conscientious, self-effacing work of the two Cohens. Hennighausen, 98.

in the shortest possible time and to make their own contributions to the economic structure and development of their new homeland.

If we take a general view of this period of our history, between about 1815 and 1860, there is one phenomenon that appears above all others and merits careful attention. This is the speedy, surprisingly evident Americanization of the German element in Western Maryland. Of course, this development was actually spread out over many decades, but it did not always leave concrete evidence for the historian to cite. A few indications, however, show plainly that in the second and third decades of the nineteenth century a decided change occurred among the descendants of the German settlers on the Monocacy and the Conococheague.

It will be remembered that all church registers of the Lutheran and Reformed congregations of Western Maryland were written in German during the eighteenth century; we mentioned the Muehlenberg constitution of the Lutheran congregation in Frederick (1747) as a notable exception because it was written in English. During the decades before and immediately after the Revolution, German was the daily language of the German settlers in Frederick and Hagerstown; German was spoken at home; in the evenings German papers were read and on Sunday German services were attended.

In 1808, the Lutheran church in Frederick received a new pastor, Reverend David Frederick Schaeffer.[14] One of the first projects undertaken was a reorganization of the congregation and the adoption of a new church constitution. This constitution was written in German; an English translation was made because it was to be registered in the county office. The Reverend Mr. Schaeffer had hardly been in Frederick for two years when he began to conduct an occasional service in English. At first these services were only irregular occurrences, but they apparently were liked by the younger members of the church, for in 1816 regular English services were introduced for the first time. This innovation met with some opposition; many of the older members of the church objected. But in Frederick, as elsewhere, the new development continued in spite of opposition.

We find similar symptoms in Hagerstown during this time. The fact that since the beginning of the century English had been used

[14] Wentz, Frederick, 177 ff.

in conversations with government authorities and that even in 1806 the incorporation plan of the Lutheran church in Hagerstown was written in English means little. Pastor Goering, who dedicated the new church in 1806, gave his sermon in German as a matter of course, and he spoke of the ". . . Teutsche Sanct Johannis Kirche. . . ." But in Hagerstown as in Frederick the beginning of a new era became apparent within the next few years. In 1812 a meeting of the Lutheran congregation in Hagerstown was called in order to discuss whether "henceforth all services should continue to be held in German, or whether an English sermon should be preached every four weeks, excepting on Sunday mornings."

The pastor and the council of the Lutheran church in Frederick wrote all church records in German until 1822; thereafter they were written in English. The change took place in Hagerstown at almost the same time. In 1819 we find the last German entries, and in 1820 appear the first English ones. Names were anglicized: Krueger became Creeger, Heim became Hime, Bäuerle became Birely, and instead of Johann, Heinrich, Friedrich, we now read John, Henry, Frederick, etc.

We have made a thorough study of the Lutheran church in Hagerstown in regard to the language issue.[15] A review of the figures pertaining to the number of communicants who attended communion during these critical decades shows clearly the inevitable shift to English. In 1820 there were 214 members of the congregation who came to the German service, 48 to the English communion service. This relation of 214 to 48 had changed markedly four years later: 203 to 118. After another four years, the figures were 181 to 189. In 1835 the register listed 122 German and 167 English communion goers; five years later (1840) the relation was 90 to 206. Statistics are dry evidence, but here they speak plainly.

The German communities in Western Maryland experienced the same difficulties that beset all immigrant churches after two generations. Either the language of the fathers was lost, or the loyalty of the sons was lost. Let us take a young man (we shall name him Jakob Schenkel) who was born of German parents about 1800 in Western Maryland. His grandfather, who had emigrated from Germany around 1750, had never really learned English. His parents had no difficulty with the new language, but at home they generally

[15] The material was taken from the church registers of Hagerstown.

spoke German for the sake of the grandfather. The boy who was born in 1800 understood German, but went to school where English was used and played with children who spoke English. More and more Jakob Schenkel used English for his daily language and he became more and more accustomed to answering his parents in English even when they spoke to him in German. Now, year after year his German becomes more rusty, and it is difficult for him to follow the German sermon on Sunday. How will it be on Sundays at church, Jakob Schenkel wonders, after he is married to Ann McCracken, who belongs to the Presbyterian church and does not know a word of German? Anyhow, the Presbyterians and the Episcopalians are much more influential than the Lutherans, and their pastors speak a language that is spoken every day, and that he can follow without any difficulty.

Many young people think things out in this way, so that finally, instead of a Lutheran Jakob Schenkel, we have an Episcopalian Jimmy Shankle. The Lutheran and Reformed German pastors had their choice: either to remain adamant and use only German and watch the younger generation flock to other churches; or give the young people what they wanted—English in the church—and thus save the new generation for the congregation. The pastors had enough of the healthy instinct of self-preservation to choose the second course.

The older generation watched this development with antipathy and anger, indeed often with violent opposition. Dr. Christian Börstler, the German physician in Funkstown, Western Maryland, of whom we have already spoken, provides a typical example of the attitude of the older generation. In about 1820 he wrote in his diary: "It is too bad that the German language and customs are declining so rapidly among us, for on account of the law the young people are learning English and neglecting German. I have grand-children who do not know my mother tongue, and this has happened frequently; in many families the parents can speak German but the children know nothing but English and if it were not for the many German emigrants it would be only a few years before the German language were forgotten entirely, while our pastors, in many cases, are already beginning to preach and to teach in English."[16]

[16] Deutsch-Amerikanische Geschichtsblätter, I:1 (1901), 22.

The annoyance of the older, conservative generation at the introduction of English into the church often led to separation and the founding of their own German congregations. But wherever the history of these separatist congregations is studied in Western Maryland, it will be seen over and over again that the inevitable progress of the English language triumphed. Take, for example, the Lutheran community in Hagerstown, which is typical for the general development. We will remember that in 1812 there was a discussion on the question of occasional English services; that in 1820 English began to be used for entries in the church registry; that between 1820 and 1840 the number of English communicants grew at the cost of the number of Germans. In 1844, under date of July 4, we find an entry that is most interesting because it clearly illustrates in a few sentences the vital language issue and reveals to us an unsuccessful attempt to found a German congregation: "Whereas a number of Germans connected with the Evangelical Lutheran Congregation of Hagerstown, under the plea of being aggrieved and unkindly dealt with, absented themselves from the ordinary worship of said Congregation, as well as from its communions, and whereas said Germans organized themselves into another congregation . . . and whereas said congregation is now dissolved and said Germans seem to manifest their penitence for such conduct by attending the regular worship and expressing a wish to attend the communion of said Hagerstown Congregation again, . . . Therefore resolved that we disapprove of the conduct of said Germans in their withdrawing and organizing, and that they might justly have been excommunicated therefore, . . . Resolved that . . . as they now appear desirous of returning and penitent as afore said, they be hereby pardoned, and all whose conduct has not been inconsistent with their professions since their withdrawment, be permitted again to enjoy the free privilege of said Congregation."

This long ukase speaks for itself. It is the typical story of an unsuccessful attempt to found a congregation whose purpose it was to save German as the language of the church. The manner in which the penitent sinners were summarily handled here shows very clearly what had happened during the preceding thirty years. In 1812 there was a debate as to whether English-speaking members might occasionally have an afternoon sermon in English; now, in

1844, the returning German language members are graciously conceded the privilege of using the church every second Sunday afternoon for a German service, and twice a year they may hold a German communion in the morning. Within one generation this striking change took place.

In Frederick we can see a very similar development. The pastor of the Lutheran congregation was a man of broad vision, the Reverend D. F. Schaeffer, and probably thanks to him the change from German to English in the Lutheran congregation of Frederick went fairly smoothly. One of Schaeffer's especially noteworthy acts was the founding of a Sunday School; it was set up in Frederick in the year 1820, one of the first of its kind in the whole country, four years before the American Sunday School Union (1824) was founded.[17] Aside from its pedagogical and religious influence, this school did much to hold the younger generation of Frederick to the old Lutheran church. With its help, the change from German to English was accomplished without great loss.

When Schaeffer's successor, the Reverend Simeon W. Harkey, gave the congregation a new constitution in 1840, it was a matter of course that it be written in English.[18] Apparently these men were not so harsh toward the German-speaking members as the group in Hagerstown had been; the German-speaking members were always courteously taken into consideration. This is seen particularly clearly in 1850 when the congregation had to find a successor for Harkey and in every case the invitation to a candidate had the added sentence: "We desire to have English and German preaching as there are a good number of Germans connected with the church here."[19] This condition made it very much more difficult to find a pastor; several candidates had to be excluded because of it. Harkey's successor, the Reverend George Diehl, spoke both languages; for nearly thirty years he held a German service on the afternoon of every second Sunday and prayer meeting every Friday evening.

In the Reformed congregations a similar development took place. In the Reformed churches of Western Maryland the church language and the entries in the church register were likewise German at the beginning. But here again, and at the same time (during the third decade of the nineteenth century), the shift to English took

[17] Wentz, *Frederick*, 180 ff.   [18] *Ibid.*, 213.   [19] *Ibid.*, 247.

place. We chose the Lutheran congregation of Hagerstown as a typical example of the development of the language problem, and now we shall list a few dates in the history of the Reformed church of Frederick for comparison. Pastor Jonathan Helfenstein, who became pastor of the Reformed church in Frederick in 1811, preached in German; there was no question about language in Frederick in 1811. But in 1825, things had progressed so far that the introduction of English services was energetically demanded. A nephew of the pastor, the Reverend Samuel Helfenstein, was called from Virginia to assist his uncle and especially to take charge of the English-speaking members of the congregation. It is clear that it was high time this change was made, for according to the arrangement of 1825 three English services were held to one in German.[20]

The Reverend John H. Smaltz became the successor of Pastor Jonathan Helfenstein in 1829. He was the first pastor of the Reformed congregation who could not preach in German; when he took office the German services were abandoned entirely. This was a premature, hasty decision, for at this time there were still a great number of members who expressly desired a German service. The only pastor in Frederick who preached in German was the Lutheran Pastor Schaeffer. So it happened that because of the German language many of the Reformed flock left it and joined the Lutheran congregation. The Reformed church had misjudged the times and made the change too abruptly. If a congregation was backward about introducing English, the young people changed over to the Episcopalian church; if the change was made prematurely, the church lost the older generation. It was certainly not always easy to seize the right moment and to gauge the right speed for the change. Probably no congregation achieved the transition from German to English without some setbacks, quarrels and schism.

The Reverend Smaltz's pastorate came to a premature end after only four years; "dissatisfaction arose as the result of some pastoral indiscretions," and so he resigned more or less voluntarily. His successor, Charles Reighley, had an even shorter incumbency. We hear of "scandal, misdeeds, irregular habits, gross immorality," and so he left the scene of his unchurchly activity after two years (1835) and disappeared as an adventurer in the West. He was followed in

[20] Eschbach, 30.

the position by the Reverend Daniel Zacharias, who started in 1832 and who loyally served his pastorate for four decades.[21] Even as early as the election of the pastor in 1833, a part of the congregation had voted for Zacharias for the express reason that he was the only candidate who could preach in both English and German. At this election it was very clear that many members were very much dissatisfied because it was impossible to hear any German services in the Reformed church. The election of the Reverend Mr. Zacharias in 1833 failed because of a few technicalities and formal details. After the unfortunate intermezzo of Reighley's pastorate, Zacharias was elected by a great majority and it was soon obvious that the choice of this man had been a very wise one.

When Zacharias took up his duties, the majority of the older Germans who had gone to the Lutheran church because of the German language returned to the Reformed congregation and were taken back into the fold. Zacharias conducted German services regularly until after about ten years, when a new arrangement was introduced. The German-speaking members joined together in a separate group which at first was ministered to by the Reverend Mr. Zacharias, but later (1844) engaged its own pastor. This occurred in an atmosphere of greatest harmony; the consistory itself helped the new group to get established. The Reverend Isaac Gerhart was engaged as the German preacher. Relations between the English and the German sections of the congregation remained entirely peaceful and harmonious. The German group was obligated to pay the salary of the German pastor, but the English group provided, free of charge, the building in which to hold their services. When the German group lost its pastor in 1850, the Reverend Mr. Zacharias took over the added duties for the interim. Thus the relations between the two were entirely friendly.

During this time an incident occurred which could have happened only during the uncertain period of the language conflict. In the summer of 1851, a Reverend P. A. Meister appeared, who called himself an "Evangelical Minister." He made contact with the German-speaking members of both the Lutheran and Reformed

---

[21] *Ibid.*, 34 ff. Daniel Zacharias was born on January 14, 1805, in Clearspring, Washington County, Maryland. He went to school in Pennsylvania, was ordained in 1828, was pastor in Creutz Creek, Pennsylvania, until 1830, and in Harrisburg, Pennsylvania, until 1835. From here he was called to Frederick, where he remained until his death on March 31, 1873.

churches and made the surprising proposition of bridging the confessional differences of the two by means of the common language and establishing a German congregation independent of synodal authority, built up on "Evangelical bases" and on the common German language. The plan was opposed by the pastors and the church elders of both congregations. However, in spite of them Reverend Mr. Meister went to work and founded St. John's German congregation of Frederick in November 1851.[22] This congregation, made up of Lutherans and Reformed but leaning in its organization more toward the Reformed Church, existed for two years under the leadership of the Reverend Mr. Meister. It was never determined whether he was actually an ordained pastor; he always promised to send for his ordination papers from Germany, but since they never appeared the Reformed synod dismissed him in 1853. The congregation which he had founded remained in existence; it affiliated itself officially with the Reformed Church and existed henceforth as an exclusively German congregation which used for its services a chapel belonging to the Reformed congregation.[23]

The language problem during the first half of the nineteenth century betrays more clearly than all other aspects of its daily life the pulse-beat of the German element in Maryland. In the farthest western portion of the state the same difficulties are to be found everywhere. In Cumberland, where a German-Lutheran congregation (St. Paul) was founded toward the end of the eighteenth century, the language of the church was changed to English between 1820 and 1830. However, within the congregation remained a small group of people who continued to speak German and regularly heard German sermons. The pastors of the church were required to preach in both German and English. Gradually, however, it became more difficult to secure preachers who knew both languages. In the middle of the forties, St. Paul's congregation engaged a pastor who could preach only in English; immediately the German group felt itself confronted with the necessity of creating a separate organization. Quarrels arose between the two factions which eventually led to a break. In February 1848 the Germans founded a "Deutsch-Evangelisch-Lutherische Gemeinde," and immediately began to build a church. A German pastor from Pennsylvania, the Reverend

[22] Eschbach, 41 ff. Bready, 78.
[23] The successors of the "Reverend" Mr. Meister were Pastors E. W. Reinecke, John Külling, Peter A. Schwartz and George W. Glessner.

Martin Reizer, took care of the group during its first year. In 1849, when he retired, it happened that a German pastor, Konrad Schwandowsky, who had just come from Germany passed through Cumberland on his way to the Middle West. He was persuaded to stay and henceforth led the group, which persevered in trying to save German as the church language.[24] Thus there were two congregations in Cumberland. One was a large English-Lutheran congregation, most of whose members were of German extraction but who spoke English, demanded English sermons making possible the acquisition of non-German members and were also able to hold the younger generation. The other was a small German-Lutheran congregation which insisted upon German and because of the language barrier was in constant conflict with its American environment.

Farther west of Cumberland, in the later Garrett County, German settlers were scattered throughout the whole western tip of the state. The Aurora settlement, of which we have already spoken, continued to grow. Its nucleus was St. John's church in Red House, not far from Oakland. From 1817 to 1823 the congregation was under the direction of an energetic pastor, the Reverend Christian Frederick Heyer (born in 1793 in Helmstädt, Germany) who was really stationed in Cumberland but who journeyed over vast regions of the Allegheny Mountains as a traveling preacher. After Aurora and Red House, the town of Accident developed into one of the most important German settlements in Garrett County. We still have the names of the early German settlers in Accident, all of whom came directly from Germany and established themselves here in the decades before the Civil War. They were Conrad Spoerlein, Georg Alt, Michael and Frederick Engelhart, Georg and Adam Goehringer, Gottfried and Andreas Fuchs, Michael Mennhorn, Peter Kahl, John Eckhardt, Edward Margraf, Leonard Burkhard, Friedrich Kolb, Karl Schlossnagel, John Ries, Michael Hobach, Christian Heinrich Richter, Leonard Fischer, Andreas Dietrich, Leonard Fratz and Georg Stark. Also in other parts of Garrett County German farmers were found, like the Beeghlys (Büchli) and Hinebaughs, old "Pennsylvania Dutch" stock but most of them, like Peter Gortner or Christian Schwartzentruber, directly from Germany. The influx of these immigrants directly from Germany

[24] The material for Cumberland was taken from the church registers and various anniversary pamphlets of the congregations.

was so great around 1850 that the three Lutheran congregations in Accident, Cove and Frostburg in 1854 engaged their own German pastor, the Reverend Charles A. Schlögel. Three years later Accident and Cove alone supported a preacher, the young theologian, Johann Ulrich Hoffmann. The two westernmost counties (Allegany and Garrett) were not so thickly populated as Frederick and Washington Counties, but even today, scattered through Garrett and Allegany, may be seen clear traces of German settlement on any modern map. The names of towns betray the origin of their early settlers—Boetcherville, Kreigbaum, Keifer, Schaidt, Eckhardt, Finzel, Bittinger, Keyser's Ridge, Sines, Gortner, Strecker, Steyer, Weber, Kitzmiller, New Germany, all names of communities in Allegany and Garrett Counties.[25] Most of these settlements were established by immigrants fresh from Germany. Around 1850 in a town like Accident more German was spoken than English. Historically these settlements were far behind the old German communities like Hagerstown, Frederick and Baltimore. From the standpoint of the history of immigration these new German settlements in Garrett County belong to the new wave of German immigration to the Middle West rather than to the old Maryland immigration group. Many of the men were actually on their way to the west, but simply stayed here. And now we must turn back from the border of the Middle West to the center of the German element in the state, the city of Baltimore.

In Baltimore, too, the history of the German churches in the twenties and thirties of the nineteenth century is marked by the language issue. Pastor Daniel Kurtz was the only preacher in the Church of Zion, the old Lutheran congregation, up to the year 1823, but in that year a second pastor, the Reverend Johann Uhlhorn, was engaged. Apparently Uhlhorn was such a cultured and talented man and such an excellent preacher that he soon outshone old Pastor Kurtz. He was quiet and learned by nature and certainly not the person to engage in intrigue and argument; however, whether or not he wished it, he was soon drawn into the vortex of a violent congregational battle. The two pastors had always had their own followings in the congregation, but things finally went so far that two vestries were elected and ruled the congregation side

[25] The above-mentioned series of articles by Charles E. Hoye in the *Mountain Democrat* is recommended for further genealogical information.

by side. An agreement was finally reached. Shortly after, old Pastor Daniel Kurtz resigned. Johann Uhlhorn was the sole pastor in the Zion church in 1833 and 1834, when he died suddenly while paying a visit to his native city of Bremen. According to all descriptions of him, he must have been one of the most attractive persons among the Germans of Baltimore. Marvelous tales were told of his preaching ability and of his wide culture. His name also appears in the early history of the University of Maryland, where he taught Greek and German.[26]

The Kurtz-Uhlhorn quarrel was one of hundreds of church quarrels which occurred when an old doddering pastor and an attractive young one worked side by side in the same congregation; it had nothing to do with the language question, for both men preached in German. But in the same year that Uhlhorn came to Baltimore (1823) it happened for the first time that a group of Lutherans joined together and founded their own English-Lutheran congregation, where English was the language of the sermon. The majority of these people were of German descent, as may be seen by glancing at the names of the people who attended the first meeting of the group: David Bixler, John Reese, Thomas Henning, Michael Klinefelter, George Stonebraker, Joshua Medtart, Jacob Deems and Frederick Seyler.[27] Probably all of them came originally from Zion church, but since that organization was firmly attached to the German language some of the members decided to arrange for English services to be held outside of the old congregation without having to give up their own Lutheran beliefs. Money was raised, the Lutheran synod was approached, the Reverend C. P. Krauth of Martinsburg, Virginia, was asked to preach several times and in 1825-1826 a church was built. After its completion, the first regular pastor was called, the Reverend John G. Morris.

We will see his name frequently in the following chapters. Here we shall include only such information about him as has to do with the founding of the first English-Lutheran church. John Morris was a Pennsylvania Dutchman. His father emigrated from Rinteln on the Weser in Germany in 1776; upon his arrival in America he

[26] Incidents in the quarrel that occasionally flared up even in public during the church service are described in Hofmann, Zion Church, 44 ff. See also p. 70. Cordell, University I, 470.

[27] List of names of the communicants at the first communion of the congregation (1827) will be found in Wentz, Synod, 191.

immediately joined the army. His original name of Moritz he changed to Morris upon the advice of American officers, so that in case he was made prisoner the English would not suspect him of being a Hessian deserter and shoot him. John Morris was born on November 14, 1803, in York, Pennsylvania, studied theology at Princeton and Dickinson and was called to Baltimore in 1827.

The preachers of the German-Lutheran congregation found themselves in a difficult situation. Since they were committed to retaining German in the church, they had to disapprove the founding of an English-Lutheran congregation although they knew that a large part of the younger generation would be lost to them. As Lutherans, however, they had to approve of the organization, for if the young people of their congregation wanted to hear English services they did not need now to turn Episcopalian or Presbyterian; they could attend English services and remain Lutheran. The German Zion church lost members, but they remained true to the Lutheran cause. In his autobiography the Reverend Mr. Morris described the attitude of Pastors Kurtz and Uhlhorn: "These men received me with polite coldness, but did nothing to encourage my project, for the fact was that most of the persons engaged in our enterprise had been members of their congregation. Dr. Kurtz was aware of the necessity for an English church, but it was not his interest to show any decided approbation of ours. He was well aware that many young German Lutherans, and even whole families of the more respectable portion of his church had left, and joined other English churches, and he was too honest to put any obstacles in our way. Whilst he would perhaps not directly advise any one to leave his church and join ours, yet I am sure he would not have thrown obstructions in the way of their going. Some of their influential members opposed us directly, but I had the satisfaction, not many years after, of receiving some of these very men and their large families into my church, where some of their descendants remain to this day as most efficient members."[28]

Morris had realized more clearly than most of his colleagues that the Lutheran Church had to break out of its German-American isolation if it were to take part in American life as an active institution. "Every English name in our churches is a gain." More farsighted than the majority of the orthodox Lutheran pastors, he

[28] John G. Morris, *Life Reminiscences of an Old Lutheran Minister* (Philadelphia, 1896), 99.

had foreseen the development. The difficulties that he encountered in Baltimore were typical for the situation in the whole country. "The German pastors generally oppose the founding of English churches, and by their influence many of their young people are kept away. . . . Severe church discipline is threatened, if not exercised. Unless the Missourians form English churches, the third generation of their members will be lost to them, and I fear to the Church entirely."[29]

The English-Lutheran congregation in Baltimore grew year by year. The fact that the Reverend Daniel Kurtz, after having led the German Zion church for decades, dissolved his connection with the German church after resigning his position and entered the English-Lutheran congregation can hardly be interpreted as a demonstration in favor of the English language. Kurtz remained so bitter and angry even after the quarrel in the Zion church had been settled that he turned his back on the congregation for purely personal reasons; objective reasons probably played no part in this spectacular step. But there are other indications that show that the founding of an English-Lutheran congregation was in line with the future trend of the church. Four additional English-Lutheran congregations were founded in Baltimore, all of which flourished and grew steadily before the outbreak of the Civil War. In most of them the Americanized descendants of German immigrants formed the basic stock, but more and more Americans of non-German descent were drawn into them.

The situation of the old Lutheran Zion church, which did not care to give up the German language, might have become very critical if just at this time it had not obtained the services of a pastor who had all the qualifications necessary to lead a congregation through the difficult times confronting this one. He was Pastor Heinrich Scheib. After the death of the Reverend Mr. Uhlhorn the congregation was run temporarily by Pastors Domeier and Haesbaert, but neither of them seemed suitable for the position. In 1835 the long, fruitful incumbency of Pastor Scheib began.

Heinrich Scheib was born on July 8, 1808, in Bacharach, a small town on the Rhine. He went to school in Kreuznach, studied theology in Bonn and then attended the University of Utrecht for a year. All that we know about him indicates that he was a whole-hearted liberal. He was the son of a Rhenish wine grower; the free, tolerant disposition of the typical son of the Rhineland who hated force and regimentation of every sort was deeply ingrained in him. He hated the reactionary, conservative element which set the pace in Germany—that mixture of Prussian militarism and the Metternich constabulary-state, and so he burned all his bridges behind him and went to America. In April 1835 he landed in New York and on October 18 of the same year he was elected minister of the Zion church in Baltimore.[30]

We stated that Scheib was a liberal, a fact that very soon became evident in his church politics: he was too progressive for the orthodox Lutheran synod of America. His liberal theological views caused people at first to shake their heads, then withdraw and finally become angry. After a few years the differences of opinion became so violent that Scheib decided to withdraw from the Lutheran synod with his congregation. That occurred in 1840. Since that year Zion church has remained a free congregation, having no connection with the synod. It took the synod a long time to recover from the incident. Sixty years later the official cyclopedia of the Lutheran synod could not resist making the following testy comment in connection with the breaking away of the Zion church: "The mother church was alienated from the Lutheran Church and from synodical connections through a rationalist pastor."[31]

As for the language problem, there was no question about the fact that in Scheib's church German was to be used. The language separation of 1823, which saw the founding of the English-Lutheran congregation, turned out to be a very wholesome development. Zion church became the focal point for all the Lutherans of Baltimore who wanted to attend German services; all the English Lutherans, whether of German or non-German extraction, were divided among the various English-Lutheran churches. Such a clean break made it possible for the Lutheran congregations to develop as they liked, free of the language problem.

The German congregations sought to solve the language problem in a variety of ways. Finally, if we study the Reformed congregation of Baltimore we shall see how the transition was made unusually swiftly, even abruptly. For the first time on September 27,

[30] Hofmann, *History of Zion Church*, 73. Evers, 19.
[31] *Lutheran Cyclopedia* (New York, 1899), 38.

1818, services in the Reformed church in Baltimore were conducted in German and in English.[32] Just at this time the congregation was faced with electing a new pastor. The Reverend Christian L. Becker, who had stubbornly opposed the introduction of English, had died in July 1818. The new pastor, Albert Helfenstein, arrived in February 1819; although at first he conducted both German and English services, in 1827 he abandoned German entirely.[33] The German part of the congregation was urged to find its own German minister and continue to use the old church building, but apparently it did not take advantage of this offer. These members either made the transition to English within the Reformed congregation, or joined the German-Lutheran Zion church. Not until 1845 was a German-Reformed congregation founded, but in the following decades it justified its existence by a very active congregation.[34] However, most of the Reformed in Baltimore as well as in Western Maryland made the transition from German to English with little delay and without much difficulty.

Again we are reminded of the sentence that the Lutheran church in Frederick attached to the invitations which it sent in 1850 to a few ministers for trial sermons: "We desire to have English and German preaching as there are a good number of Germans connected with the church here." This sentence illustrates in a few words how the situation had changed. Around 1800 these words would have been pointless; at that time it was assumed that all members of the Lutheran Church were German. With the introduction of English the Lutheran Church broke away from its German isolation, opened its doors to the whole varied mixture of nationalities in the American nation and the Americans entered the Lutheran Church in such great numbers that as early as 1850 the Germans were spoken of as a respected but very small minority. Many of the old people complained of the loss of the German language. But the example of the German-Protestant congregations in Maryland shows a positive gain which may not be overlooked.

[32] See the memoirs of Reverend Dr. Elias Heiner, BVG, 264.

[33] Henry E. Shepherd, *History of Baltimore* (1898), 335. Scharf, *Chronicles*, 44. In February 1818 thirty-six members of the congregation handed a petition to the consistory asking that English services be introduced.

[34] This was the Fourth German Reformed St. John's church. The first pastor, Christian Hacke, came from Hagerstown. The names of early members and the various pastors are to be found in BVG, 265.

True, the Germans and their descendants had abandoned the language of their fathers, but they had succeeded in making a cultural institution such as the church, which they had brought over from Germany, into such an integral part of the structure of the new country that it was open not only to the German immigration group, but also to every American citizen. The history of their churches provides convincing proof of the acclimatization and Americanization of the German settlers in Maryland.

The transition from German to English occurred in a relatively short period of time. This shift to English appeared almost simultaneously in all of the German-settled sections of Maryland. In the Lutheran church in Hagerstown in 1812, the question was first raised as to whether English services should be allowed. In 1816 the Lutheran congregation in Frederick introduced English services; in 1818 the same thing happened in the Reformed church in Baltimore, in 1825 in the Reformed church in Frederick. In 1822 the Reformed church in Taneytown erected its own building for English services. In 1823, the first English-Lutheran church was founded in Baltimore. Around 1820 almost all the church registers changed from German to English. In 1822, John Gruber in Hagerstown decided to supplement his German almanac with an English edition. The first indications of the encroachment of English appeared in the second decade of the nineteenth century; in the twenties the battle raged back and forth; in the thirties the predominance of English among the German settlers was finally established. When the Reverend Dr. Lewis Mayer preached the first English sermon in the Reformed church in Baltimore in 1818, he was literally threatened with violence by a few of the embittered members of the congregation.[35] "As late as 1826, at the Reformed Synod of Frederick, Maryland, when a young minister attempted to deliver an English address, the president promptly reproved him, at the same time expressing his horror that the abominable English language had found its way into that solemn place."[36] With the be-

[35] "The excitement was intense. Some of the members, regarding English preaching as an innovation that ought not to be tolerated, threatened violence to the minister, and said and did many things which they afterwards regretted." Scharf, Chronicles, 45.

[36] Joseph Henry Dubbs, History of the Reformed Church, German (New York, 1895), 342. This language problem was found in almost all the German churches of America around 1830. See Raymond W. Albright, A History of the Evangelical Church (Harrisburg, Pa., 1942), 237.

ginning of the thirties, indications that the German language was in decline increased. Hymnbooks appeared in English; the number of English-speaking communicants grew from year to year at the expense of the German-speaking; some of the old German churches abandoned German services entirely; John Gruber's German weekly newspaper, which had been read for decades in Western Maryland, was discontinued about 1830 because the German language was disappearing so rapidly. Many more occurrences could be cited, all of which point to the important fact that the descendants of the old German settlers in Western Maryland and Baltimore had accomplished an important step in the process of their Americanization.

The history of the founding of German congregations within the Catholic Church differs radically from that of the Protestant denominations. The Protestant congregations, whether Lutheran, Reformed or some special sect, started with the founding of purely German groups. Then, as we have observed, in the third or fourth generation they shifted to the English language, which, in turn, brought about the development of an American institution from what had originally been an immigrant church. In the failure of Father Reuter's attempt in Baltimore (1799-1806) to found a German Catholic congregation we observed that the Catholic Church was cool to the idea. However, gradually the number of German immigrants increased, and with it the number of German Catholics. Many of the new immigrants understood nothing but German. The situation which developed for the Catholics was the reverse of that which confronted the old German-Protestant congregations; they were faced with the choice of clinging to the English language and eventually losing the German immigrants to the German-Protestant congregations, or of creating an official organization in which to take care of these people. The Protestants were clever enough not to cling stubbornly to the German language, and the Catholic Church was clever enough not to exclude German and to create German congregations for the German immigrants.

This trend started in about 1840, and was closely connected with the Redemptorists.[37] The Reverend Benedict Bayer, who was in

[37] Congregatio Sanctissimi Redemptoris, called briefly Redemptorists, was a society of missionary priests "consecrating themselves especially to the preaching of the word of God to the poor." It was founded in 1732 by an Italian aristocrat, St. Alphonsus de Liguori in Scala, Italy. The members

charge of the Baltimore German-Catholic congregation, was no longer able to fulfill the task; he had a congregation of 4000 members scattered all over the city. While a student in Switzerland he had come in contact with the work of the Redemptorists. In 1840 an agreement was reached between Archbishop Samuel Eccleston and the Redemptorists "that they (the Redemptorists) assume charge of the German Catholics of our archiepiscopal city and of the whole diocese, employing for this purpose a sufficient number of German priests who are qualified and competent missionaries."[38]

In pursuance of this agreement, the one German-Catholic church in Baltimore, St. John's church, was turned over to the Redemptorists that same year, 1840. The church edifice had long been outgrown. It was now torn down and a new and larger church begun on the same location; it was consecrated in 1845 and named for the founder of the Redemptorist congregation, St. Alphonsus.[39]

While its new church was being built, the congregation used a church in East Baltimore, St. James.[40] Up to this time it had housed an Irish-Catholic congregation, but the group had built a new church that same year. Since the number of German Catholics grew so rapidly, it was decided to retain St. James's church, which the Irish no longer needed; it continued in existence as a second German-Catholic church. After the consecration of St. Alphonsus'

---

swore to poverty, celibacy and obedience; they were not allowed to accept any church honors outside of the congregation. They concentrated their efforts at first in Italy, but later spread out—though temporarily—to Austria, Poland, Germany and Switzerland. After 1832 a new field opened up for them in America. They began an energetic, though not very successful, program of preaching in the northern part of Ohio and in Michigan. They soon concentrated their efforts on the German Catholics in America, organizing German-Catholic congregations and founding parochial schools. In 1839 they were called to Pittsburgh, where the German-Catholic congregation was in an extremely disorganized condition. Their astonishing success in Pittsburgh soon brought them calls to other cities: Baltimore in 1840, New York in 1842, Philadelphia in 1843, Buffalo in 1845, Detroit in 1847, New Orleans in 1849 and Cumberland, Maryland, in 1849. *Catholic Cyclopedia* (1911), xii, 683 ff.

[38] Documents in the Redemptorist Archives at Esopus, New York. See Charles R. Gellner, "Ecclesiastical History of the Catholic Germans in Maryland," SHGM, xxvi (1945), 38 ff.

[39] The cost of building was raised partly by the congregation and partly by gifts from missionary societies in Germany, Austria and France. King Ludwig I of Bavaria is said to have personally donated $4000. The church still stands; since 1917 it has been in the possession of the Lithuanian congregation.

[40] At Aisquith and Eager Streets.

church it was decided that the German Catholics living to the east of Jones Falls should attend St. James's, and those living to the west of Jones Falls, St. Alphonsus.

The fact that before the Civil War two additional churches had to be built, St. Michael's (1852) and Holy Cross (1860), testifies to the speed with which the number of German Catholics in Baltimore increased during these years. All of these German-Catholic churches grew from year to year and engaged in energetic activity.[41]

The development of German schools is closely connected with the life of the German church congregations. All the old German churches, whether Lutheran, Reformed or Catholic, very early built church schools. During the nineteenth century their importance increased in regard to the churches. In the beginning the schools had been founded for general educational purposes. But when the German-English language problem arose, the schools acquired a double purpose. It was the younger generation that was gradually outgrowing the German language and demanding the use of English in the churches. In order to make the young people at least partially acquainted with the German language it was necessary to make it either a required course in their education, or else to make it possible to give them their entire education in German. This explains the enormous enthusiasm which all the church congregations expended upon their schools. If they wanted to retain German as the language of the church, their existence depended to a great extent upon the success of their schools.

It would require too lengthy a discussion to go into detail in connection with each of the schools, especially since most of their histories run parallel. Most of them were founded simultaneously with the founding of the congregations, and ceased to function at about the same time—during the last third of the nineteenth century, when they were defeated in the competition with public German-English schools.

The German-Catholic St. Alphonsus congregation started its

[41] For particulars, see Gellner, op.cit., and BVG, 245 ff. In 1846 a German priest who wrote to a friend in Germany, describing the conditions among the German Catholics in Baltimore, mentioned St. James and St. Alphonsus parishes with the following comment: "The two parishes are intended to care for about 6000 Catholic Germans." Der Katholische Hausfreund, Regensburg (1847), Nr. 4, Col. 55 ff.; Social Justice Review, St. Louis, XXXVII, i (1944), 23.

school at the beginning of the forties when the new church was built and the congregation was taken over by the Redemptorists. The other German-Catholic congregations—St. James, St. Michael, Holy Cross—also had their own schools where classes were carried on in both German and English. Members of religious orders, such as the Christian Brothers, or the Sisters of Notre Dame, were the teachers.[42]

As early as in the period of the Revolution, the Reformed congregation had its own school. We do not know exactly when the school was first started, but in the church register of the old Reformed congregation the following notice is to be found: "Since for some time the congregation has needed a competent school master who could sing at divine services on Sundays and teach school in German during the week the elders and council have, with the consent and express desire of many members of the congregation, engaged Mr. Johann Weber for this position for they have found him competent to fill it." Johann Weber took over his position on October 1, 1784. But there must have been a school in existence before this date, for when Weber started to teach there was already a school building. Probably the school was taught by the preacher himself until 1784. The minutes of the congregation indicate that the school was active and successful for many years.

We shall remember that it was this same German-Reformed congregation which in 1827 abruptly abandoned the German divine services and changed over to English with surprising speed. For some decades, therefore, there was no German school for the Reformed congregation of Baltimore. Not until 1846 (a year after the founding of the St. Johannes congregation of the German Reformed church) was a school started again. It flourished for some time, having as many as three hundred pupils at a time. Best-known among the teachers who taught there were Valentin Scheer and Friedrich Knapp. The school was in existence until 1879 and then lost its pupils to the German-English schools.[43] The other German-Reformed congregations sponsored schools whose fate was similar to that of the St. Johannes Church School.

We need only add that the Lutheran congregations also supported their own schools, the three belonging to the Missouri

[42] BVG, 245 ff. The number of pupils in these congregations in 1887 were: St. James, 933; St. Michael, 1300; Holy Cross, 357.
[43] BVG, 265.

synod—St. Paul, St. Martini and St. Emmanuel—as well as those within the Maryland synod.[44] Many of them had day schools; others, the smaller congregations, had only Sunday Schools, but all of them tried more or less intensively to keep alive the German language in the younger generation.

Of all these schools, the most important and the most influential one will be discussed last, and at greatest length. It was the school belonging to the oldest Lutheran congregation, the Zion church and was known best as Scheib's School.

Zion church had also started a school very early. "We considered it necessary at this time," reads an entry made by the Reverend Mr. Kirchner in 1769, "to create a firm foundation for our school system. It is an undeniable truth that a good education lays the basis for future happiness, leads children in the paths of virtue and wisdom, and teaches them to be useful in the world." We will remember that the first schoolmaster for the congregation, Moritz Wörschler, had made his mark in the early history of the Germans in Baltimore. In the next few decades we hear little of any importance about the school.[45] It was run in much the same manner as the many other church schools in the city and there is no reason to suppose that it was in any way superior to the average; on the contrary, its standing seems to have been lower than the average at the beginning of the thirties.

This state of affairs was suddenly changed in 1835 when Pastor Heinrich Scheib took up his duties at Zion church. Scheib, a progressive liberal with unbounded faith in the possibilities of educating people, was from his first day in his ministry as much interested in the school as in his preaching.[46]

[44] Ibid., 253 ff.

[45] Once mention is made of an Adam Gottlieb Rabb, who was the organist of Zion church and a teacher in the school about 1800. Cyclopedia, 600.

[46] There is a great deal of material available on the history of the Zion school. We still have (in the archives of Zion church) the minutes of the meetings of the school board, Verhandlungen, Beschlüsse und Gesetze des Schul-Vereins der bei der deutschen Zions-Gemeinde zu Baltimore bestehenden Bürgerschule ("Discussions, motions and laws of the school board in charge of the elementary school of the German Zion congregation of Baltimore") which give us a colorful picture of the life of the school. Further sources: the yearly reports of the school (published in both German and English); a speech by H. Scheib for the fiftieth anniversary of the school (published in Baltimore, 1887); an article by Charles Miegel, "The Passing of Scheib's School," Baltimore Sun, July 10, 1932; Faust, II, 241 f. Also a very

Pastor Scheib has described the conditions that he found when he started his work in Baltimore as follows: "The first time I walked across the dirty, unpaved yard of this institution of culture in order to pay a visit to it I was painfully touched by what I saw all around me. In the unclean, desolate school room whose floor was unswept and whose walls and windows were festooned with spiderwebs I found seventeen unhappy children of various ages and both sexes ranged on shaky benches around a long broken-down table. Physical and mental poverty cried aloud to me from all sides. The school had existed in this condition for decades, neglected, uncared for, unloved even by those whose sacred duty it was to look after its growth and increased activity. Deserted by the preacher, forgotten by the vestry, it had been turned over to an entirely incompetent man who, besides beating the catechism into the heads of the poor youngsters for the benefit of the preacher, along with a little reading, writing and arithmetic, left everything else up to the powers above, in other words, his own laziness and irresponsibility. . . . I took the vestry with me to visit the school, showed them the misery in the place and told them to rid the congregation of this disgrace and not allow such a dreadful place to be called a school any longer."[47] Scheib gave a series of lectures on schools and education; for a while conditions were improved, but before long the old state of affairs reasserted itself and Scheib was convinced that it was necessary to start entirely anew.

Scheib introduced two fundamental changes through which the new school differed radically from the old one. First, he was against having a sectarian school. According to his view, a child should be equipped by the school for his future role as a citizen quite independently of his religious affiliation. The second change was that the new school be carried on in two languages; that is, that the classes should be conducted equally in English and in German for all pupils. This plan at first gave rise to strong misgivings among the older generation, for many of them had the mistaken impression that Scheib was moving in the direction of anglicizing the church.

Scheib overcame all the early difficulties; on November 21, 1836,

---

positive, contemporary appreciation dating from the early period of the Zion school in *Didaskalia* (Baltimore, 1849), 293 f.

[47] Annual report of Zion school in 1886 for the fiftieth anniversary of the school reprinted in BVG, 173 f.

he opened the first German-English school in Baltimore with seventy-one pupils. He wrote a school charter which remained essentially the same during the entire sixty years of the school's existence. The aim of the school was "to educate its pupils to be morally good people, and to make them into well-informed and useful citizens of the state." It will be noted that the religious emphasis ordinarily an integral part of parochial schools is entirely absent. But after 1836, the new Zion school was no ordinary, old-fashioned parochial school; it was a secular school which was only loosely connected with the Zion church. The pastor was always the principal of the school, and the board of directors was made up of members of the Zion congregation. Any citizen could send his children to the school; soon the Catholic, Jewish and Anglo-American children, as well as the children of parents who did not belong to Zion church, outnumbered the "real" Zion church pupils. Religious instruction was not allowed in the school; the school was to remain entirely free of church dogma.[48] The use of the two languages was one of the unshakable principles of the school. "An exclusively German school would be only half a school for the Germans in America; but a wholly English school would also be only half a school for us."[49]

There was no question in the Zion church about the wisdom of German instruction. But Scheib considered it a mistake to confine the instruction entirely to German; the children would need English later in their daily life and, since the school aimed to equip them for the struggle for existence, English was imperative. Again and again Scheib emphasized the fact that one of the main purposes of the school was to make the children good American citizens; this goal could not be accomplished without English "the language of the citizens of the state."

The school quickly made progress. On January 3, 1837, the first large school celebration was held, attended by the directors, teachers, pupils and parents. The number of pupils rose to ninety-four during the first year; at the end of the school year the first public exercises were held.[50] The school building was destroyed

---

[48] See the *Allgemeine Deutsche Schulzeitung*, Baltimore, August 24, 1839.
[49] *Ibid.*, November 30, 1839.
[50] This first "graduation and commencement" ceremony of the school took place in the old assembly rooms on the corner of Holliday and Fayette

by fire in the spring of 1839, but this setback was overcome, a new school was built and the number of teachers and pupils began to increase steadily. Just before the Civil War the school had seven grades (four of which had two sections) outside the kindergarten, and a total enrollment of 418 pupils.

The minutes of the meetings of the board of directors of the school during all these decades are still in existence. They give us a real picture of the life of the school—its difficulties and reverses, as well as its progress and growth. Above all, they show the progressive spirit which breathed through the school and for which Heinrich Scheib, the founder of the whole undertaking, was responsible. Scheib consistently stood for the principles of modern, liberal pedagogy. He employed pedagogical theories which were not generally recognized until the next or a later generation. His methods of punishment were highly humane. He rejected the proposal that pupils be locked up in a dark cell as a form of punishment. Corporal punishment of the children by the teachers was firmly prohibited.[51] Scheib held monthly faculty meetings in order to discuss school matters with them, and in order to increase their education in their profession he gave lectures on pedagogical problems.

Perhaps the most interesting document which survives from this early period of Zion school is the *Allgemeine Deutsche Schulzeitung*. It was published by H. Scheib and P. M. Wolsiefer, a German teacher in the school, and it ran for a year, from June 15, 1839, to May 30, 1840.[52]

The paper was not a pupil publication. It was written for the teachers, for the parents of the pupils and for anyone who was interested in educational matters. The audience to whom the paper

---

Streets, where later the "High School" (then called Baltimore City College) was opened.

[51] This point appears again and again in the minutes. Two teachers were dismissed because they had punished children too violently; instructor A. May had to resign for this reason (1844) and instructor Jacob Schmidt was strongly warned in 1862 "not to let his temper get out of hand" and he too resigned shortly thereafter. Not until 1862 was corporal punishment allowed for very severe infractions and then the teachers were strongly warned to use it only very rarely and "with caution" "never injuring any vital parts," and "never punishing girls."

[52] The newspaper appeared biweekly, on alternate Saturdays. All twenty-six numbers of the *Allgemeine Deutsche Schulzeitung* are preserved in only three complete volumes: Library of Congress, Library of the Society for the History of the Germans in Maryland, Archives of Zion church, Baltimore.

was directed was thus a kind of early "Parent-Teachers Association." Aside from purely literary pieces in prose and verse, the newspaper featured especially pedagogical articles written in a popular scientific manner. Just which contributions were written by Pastor Scheib himself cannot be determined definitely, for most of the articles appeared anonymously. However, we may be sure that the majority of the unsigned articles came from Scheib's pen. A long series of articles dealt with "Education in General"; another with the "Schools of our Country." The pro and con of confessional schools was discussed and the newspaper finally took a stand against them. The necessity of physical education was emphasized; sexual problems were discussed with great frankness; mothers were given practical hints on the care of babies; general questions of hygiene were approached, and a few articles were written on Montaigne's ideas on education. All these problems were debated on the basis of a free, liberal, rationalistic point of view.[53]

Of the articles dealing with practical questions of education, those dealing with a plan for a German teaching seminar in America deserve special mention. We have already mentioned that Scheib advocated schools using both German and English; this teaching was not to be done by men imported from Germany, but by men who had grown up in America and were perfectly familiar with the country.[54] Therefore, Scheib was enthusiastic about the plans for a teaching seminar. This idea had been conceived at the German Convention in Pittsburgh in 1837.[55] Two years later the idea was carried out; a seminar for the training of German teachers was founded in Philipsburg, Pennsylvania. The Germans in Baltimore had met previously and had elected a Dr. Freytag as their delegate to the third German Convention in Philipsburg.[56] But this did not suffice; on December 13, 1839, the German citizens of Baltimore, under the direction of Scheib, founded a "Bildungsverein" (Cultural Association).[57] This organization was created expressly for the purpose of providing spiritual and material support for the Philipsburg Seminar.

[53] Fritz O. Evers, "Allgemeine Deutsche Schulzeitung," in SHGM, XXIV, 38 ff.
[54] Allgemeine Deutsche Schulzeitung, November 30, 1839.
[55] Faust, II, 239 f.
[56] Allgemeine Deutsche Schulzeitung, July 13, 1839.
[57] Ibid., January 11, 1840.

We also know of an action taken by the Bildungsverein in order to aid the cause of general education in the State of Maryland; it directed a letter to the governor of Maryland asking for a report on the condition of the public-school system in the state and demanding improvement of the existing system. The answer sent by Governor William Grason to the association was published in the *Allgemeine Deutsche Schulzeitung* and sharply criticized. The governor admitted that he was not in a position to give a detailed report, but that he knew perfectly well that the existing school system in the state was extremely inadequate. The newspaper editorial was highly critical of this statement. "There is no question about the fact that Governor W. Grason pays much more attention to bank, railroad, canal building and such affairs than to our forgotten and often wholly untutored and wild youth. It is bad enough that the average citizen usually pays little attention to educational matters, but it is inexcusable that the highest official of the state is not better informed on the condition of the schools and that he is not interested in opportunities for their improvement."[58]

The Bildungsverein existed for a few more years, even after the Philipsburg Seminar was long forgotten; for a time it acted as an auxiliary organization for the Zion school and came to its assistance when the school needed expensive equipment, such as scientific apparatus and instruments for instruction in physics. We do not know exactly when the organization was dissolved.

The *Allgemeine Deutsche Schulzeitung* did not awaken the response that its sponsors had anticipated. After one year the paper had to be discontinued.[59] In the last number the editors once more emphasized their goal, namely, to pave the way for general public education in America. A last article on "Freedom of Thought, Speech, Expression and the Press" breathes once more the progressive, enlightened spirit which characterized this modest and yet so noteworthy undertaking.[60] "God gave us our reasoning power so that we would think; whoever hinders us from using it desecrates the deed of the Giver who intended that our spirits should roam freely in the realm of thought. . . . Thought must be free and inde-

[58] *Ibid.*, January 25, 1840.

[59] In the second last number (May 16, 1840) Scheib published a financial statement for the single year of publication as follows: income, $252; expenditures, $597, making a deficit of $345.

[60] May 30, 1840.

pendent of the jurisdiction of any ruler because only under such conditions is the development and exaltation of the spirit possible. . . . A government which suppresses the freedom of the press proves by this action that its purposes are contrary to the eternal interests of the human spirit. . . . Liberal, wise and good governments which are more interested in the welfare of the people than in themselves need not worry about differences of opinion; the freer and more unhampered is the spirit of a people, the less possible is it that a system remains in existence which is fundamentally wrong and which achieves disadvantagous results. . . . The State should never take sides in the realm of opinion, and it should be especially careful not to take steps to suppress opinions which it does not like. The human spirit cannot be conquered through physical force; it can only be conquered by itself."

Another private school flourished in Baltimore at the same time as Scheib's Zion school and increased in size and importance so greatly that for a few decades it was considered the best and most fashionable school in the city. This school was called Knapp's Institute.

Its founder and master was also a German. Friedrich Knapp was born on April 26, 1821, in Degerschlacht in Wuerttemberg.[61] He went to school in Reutlingen and attended the teachers' seminar in Esslingen. His pedagogical abilities were recognized early, for in 1840 the government of Wuerttemberg sent him (after a short period of teaching in the country) as a teacher in the schools of Reutlingen, which he had left as a scholar only a few years before. He became familiar with the liberal ideas of his time during the nine years that he spent in Reutlingen and he was soon an enthusiastic member of the German republicans. But this was not the right cause for a government official who wanted to make a career for himself in Germany. The year 1848 came. Knapp was decidedly on the side of the revolutionaries and was soon haled before court by the government on charges of treason. The outcome was that Knapp was stripped of his professorship in Reutlingen and sent as schoolteacher to a remote village where his republican ideas could do no harm. At this time he was persuaded by a friend to go to America, and he left Reutlingen in May 1850. In order to avoid arousing the suspicion of the government, he pretended that he was about to go

[61] *Cyclopedia*, 353 f. BVG, 176 f.

out to his forsaken village, but actually he went to Bremen, where he took ship for America. In August 1850 he arrived in Baltimore. At first he took a position as private tutor and bookkeeper in the household of William A. Marburg. A few months later he became the principal of the parochial school of the German-Reformed congregation, where he remained from February 1851 to February 1853. On March 1, 1853, he opened his own school with sixty pupils.

We shall quote a few sentences from the statement of principles of the Knapp school in order to show the spirit that pervaded it: "Everyone, the state as well as the church, the communities as well as the government, tries to control and influence schools and teachers. The Knapp school emphatically refuses any such influence; freely and independently it will strive to realize its aims and bid farewell to the dead, memory-stuffing procedure of the past while holding with Pestalozzi that teaching and training must be suited to the nature of the child and that the school must be revamped into a training institution. It must always be the main purpose of the school to develop naturally the abilities and talents present in each person."

Built up on these principles, the school grew from year to year. In 1859 it was legally incorporated; "F. Knapp's German and English Institute," was the official name. The constant growth of the school was the reason why it was forced to change its location several times during its first few years until it finally found its permanent home opposite City Hall. It need hardly be stated that the school was open to followers of any faith and to members of all nationalities. Aside from the good reputation of the school, the reason why the well-to-do Germans of the city were glad to send their children to Knapp's school was that here they could receive German instruction if they so desired. The school became famous outside of Baltimore and pupils arrived from all the states of the Union. At the time of the Civil War the number of pupils had grown to seven hundred.

In the same year, 1853, another German, Philipp Wacker,[62] founded a similar school in the southern section of the city. He came from the vicinity of Heilbronn in Wuerttemberg (he was born on February 18, 1827, in Bonfeld), studied at the teaching seminar in Heilbronn, went to America and taught for a few years in a Lutheran parochial school in Baltimore. He was a good friend

[62] *Cyclopedia*, 178.

of Knapp's, built up his school on similar principles and was successful in his project for about two decades. At the beginning of the
seventies the school gradually declined and finally in 1875 it was
taken over by the city as a public English-German school. It cannot
be compared in importance to Scheib's and Knapp's schools.

During the 1850's and 1860's there were a number of smaller
German private schools. We shall simply mention the names of
some of the masters of such schools: Gustav Facius, Valentin Scheer,
Albert von Degen, J. H. H. Männer, G. G. Koch, Philip Knobloch,
Karl Hessler, W. Grünewald, W. H. Daiger, Georg A. Lang, L. B.
Schäfer. There were probably more of them, but it is superfluous
to go into further detail. Many of them existed for only a few years;
some of them taught only one class and not all of them were in good
hands. They did not have any great importance, and so they may
be mentioned only briefly here.[63] Usually the competition of the
two large institutes run by Scheib and Knapp was too strong, and
in the seventies, when the public-school system began to expand
rapidly, these ephemeral private schools disappeared.

The speedy development of German schools which may be observed in Baltimore after 1840 provides a measuring rod for the
great increase in the number of Germans in the city. Furthermore,
it indicates that now a higher social group had grown up among
them—people who were not satisfied automatically to accept the
existing schools with all their defects but who cared a great deal
about providing a good education for their children. Sociologically,
the German element which arrived during the first few decades
after the Revolution were from the lower middle classes; there were
bakers, butchers, wagoners and men of similar trades. But after
1825 German names appeared in the upper middle classes; we find
Germans as physicians, lawyers and teachers.

Brantz Mayer, a lawyer and historian, took a prominent part in
the public life of the city; for several years he was the president of
the Maryland Historical Society in whose founding he had been
very influential.[64] His brother, Charles F. Mayer, also a well-known
lawyer, was very active politically. Lewis Henry Steiner of Frederick

[63] The ever-growing demand for teachers at that time led many unqualified
men to find their way into the schools. A former policeman from Darmstadt
came to this country in 1863 and immediately opened his own school. Luckily,
it failed in a few months. (BVG, 180.)

[64] Cyclopedia, 679.

became well known after 1850 for his medical, scientific and literary works.[65] Philip R. Uhler made a name for himself through his natural history and zoological works.[66] William Baer, a farmer and chemist in Frederick County, was one of the first to attempt to put agriculture on a scientific basis. Starting in 1839, he gave popular lectures in Hagerstown in this field and he gained such a high reputation that he was appointed head of the newly established Department of Agricultural Chemistry in the County Academy in Frederick. Here he presented the results of the experiments of the great German agricultural chemist, Justus von Liebig, in popular form for the farmers of Western Maryland.[67] In the forties and later, William Schley and Frederick Brune were among the foremost lawyers in Baltimore.[68] We have discussed Friedrich Knapp in detail; another teacher who was of German descent and who was known beyond the limits of the city was Gustav Facius.[69]

In the early history of the University of Maryland, which was founded in 1807, several Germans or descendants of German immigrants played important parts. In the twenties and thirties the Bakers were one of the most important medical families in the city.[70] Samuel Baker (1785-1835) was Professor of Materia Medica at the University of Maryland from 1809 to 1833; one of his sons, Samuel George Baker, later became his successor and a second son, William Nelson Baker, occupied the chair of anatomy. George W. Miltenberger became Dean of the Faculty of Medicine in 1855; he made a name for himself in the field of obstetrics through his numerous publications.[71]

Charles Frick (1823-1860), who was also a professor of medicine

[65] *Ibid.*, 616.   [66] *Ibid.*, 576 f.

[67] Leland G. Worthington, "Forces Leading to the Establishment of the Maryland Agricultural College" (University of Maryland M.A. Thesis), College Park, 1933. Typewritten Manuscript, pp. 110 ff. See also *The American Farmer* (Baltimore), December 1839, July 1845, August 1845.

[68] *Cyclopedia*, 10. SHGM, vi, 48. William Wirt (1772-1834), the famous Virginia lawyer and author, of German and Swiss descent, lived in Maryland at the beginning and end of his life. He was born in Bladensburg and grew up in Georgetown; the last five years before his death he lived in Baltimore. But since the most important part of his life was spent outside Maryland, his name is mentioned only briefly here. DAB, xx, 418 ff. Nat. Cycl. of Amer. Biogr., vi, 86. Faust, ii, 181.

[69] *Cyclopedia*, 141.

[70] Eugene F. Cordell, *The University of Maryland, Its History 1807-1907* (New York, 1907), i, 193, 205, 206, 209, 210.

[71] *Ibid.*, 218, 224, 270.

at the University, was considered an authority on renal diseases.[72] A member of one of the oldest Baltimore German families became the father of the University of Maryland Law School—David Hoffman (1784-1854). He began to lecture in law in 1823 and soon acquired the reputation of an outstanding, stimulating teacher. His legal works and his zealous efforts to raise the ethical standards of the legal profession earned for him honorary doctors degrees from Oxford and Göttingen.[73] Mention must be made of the efforts of William Frick, a Baltimore judge of German descent, to create a department of humanities in the University at the beginning of the thirties. The great speech that he wrote in 1831 for this purpose is one of the most brilliant documents in the history of American civilization. His vehement defense of the liberal arts, the so-called "impractical things of life," is as impressive today as it was a hundred years ago.[74]

An especially large number of German names appear during the first half of the nineteenth century among the lists of Maryland physicians. It happened very seldom that an immigrant succeeded in the legal profession; the language obstacle was too great a disadvantage. On the other hand, a physician could start to practice soon after his arrival in the country, even though he had only the most rudimentary knowledge of the language. In addition to the immigrant German physicians, we find a good many who were members of old Maryland-German families, men whose parents had begun as poor farmers in Western Maryland and who now, in the second or third generation, had reached a higher social class. It seems that after 1830 in no other academic profession was the number of Germans as great as in that of medicine.[75]

[72] Ibid., 224, 227, 233, 234.

[73] Ibid., 54, 337, 338, 344. DAB, IX, 111 f.

[74] Cordell, University, 341, 460. William Frick, An Address Preparatory to Opening the Department of the Arts and Sciences in the University of Maryland (Baltimore, 1831).

[75] We cannot provide here a series of biographies. We must be content merely to list the names of the German physicians whose names have come down to us from the half century preceding the Civil War: John Frederick Hüttner, Carl Gotthilf Hintze, George Miltenberger, Morris Wiener, Jacob Honck, Gustav Liebmann, Augustus Erich, Abraham Arnold, George Frick, Charles Frick, Charles Baer, Jacob Baer, Michael Baer, John A. Bencke, Michael Diffenderffer, William Diffenderffer, Robert Duerr, John Fonerden, Thomas Littig, Leopold Franz Morawetz, Charles Henry Ohr, Augustus Schwartze, Edward Schwartze, Lewis Henry Steiner, Henry Stinnecke, Au-

Business and industry was another field in which the Germans were firmly established after the 1830's. In 1839, William Knabe began to manufacture the pianos that keep his name alive today.[76] August Hoen opened his lithographic shop in 1835, and it soon developed into a flourishing business.[77] Gustav Christian Dohme, who came to Baltimore with the great migration of 1848, later was to found the chemical factory that still operates under the name of Sharp and Dohme.[78] After 1837, Wendel Bollman was one of the most famous bridge-builders in America. His fame was so widespread that he was called to all parts of the United States and later even to Mexico, Cuba and Chile to construct bridges.[79] William Julian Albert, Justus Hoppe, Claas Vocke, Albert Schumacher, William Wilkins are all names closely associated with the industrial and commercial development of the city.[80] We could give an account of such merchants as Ludolph Wilhelm Gunther, Joel Gutman, Daniel Hoffman, Marcus Wolf, Otto Eichelberger, or of such printers as Johann T. Hanzsche, Lorenz B. Schwarz, Theodor Kroh and Carl William Schneidereith and of the brewers Georg Rost, Thomas Beck, Jacob Seeger, J. Neissendörffer. There were also the two Stein brothers, Eduard and Leopold, who started a fur-dyeing plant; and Philip R. J. Friese, who manufactured window glass; William Numsen, who preserved food; John William Birely, the banker, and Charles M. Stieff, the piano manufacturer.[81] But these few names will suffice to indicate the wide variety of activities in which the German immigrants were now engaged.

During the decades between 1850 and 1870 the tobacco trade— the tobacco industry and tobacco export—was dominated almost

---

gustus W. Wegner, Samuel Weisel, Henry Zeller, William Zollikoffer. For further information see *Cyclopedia*, 80, 193, 268, 366, 406, 574; Cordell, *Medical Annals*, 309, 320, 327, 356, 377, 383, 398, 401, 402, 439, 448, 478, 505, 510, 522, 561, 579, 583, 615, 636, 637, 795, 807. *Maryländische Teutsche Zeitung*, July 4, 1821; February 13, 1822.

[76] *Cyclopedia*, 403. BVG, 276.

[77] *Cyclopedia*, 495. BVG, 278. Faust, II, 110. SHGM, VII, 74.

[78] *Cyclopedia*, 186. Faust, II, 89.

[79] *Cyclopedia*, 599-603. B. H. Latrobe, chief engineer of the Baltimore and Ohio Railroad, called him, "The first successful iron bridge-builder in this country."

[80] *Ibid.*, 47, 620. BVG, 271, 292.

[81] *Cyclopedia*, 83, 116, 351, 243, 404, 229, 87, 686. Cf. also Charles F. Stein, "Pioneer Days in America," in SHGM, XXIV, 24 ff.; V, 93 ff. Faust, II, 66.

completely by Germans. Georg Wilhelm Gail, the son of a German tobacco manufacturer, had come to America numerous times after 1840 in order to buy tobacco. He became well-acquainted with the country and realized that he would be successful here when he opened his tobacco factory in Baltimore in 1850. The factory soon developed into a million-dollar concern, and in later years the firm of Gail and Ax became one of the largest tobacco firms on the continent.

Tobacco did not play nearly the dominant role in Maryland economics that it had during colonial times. But, still, it was one of the most important items on the list of exports from the Union. During the forties and fifties, Baltimore was the largest tobacco export harbor in America; simultaneously Bremen developed into the largest tobacco import center in Europe.[82] The close relations between Baltimore and Bremen were first established through the tobacco trade and they became more and more cordial as the years went by, through personal and commercial contacts, lasting even into the twentieth century. We have already shown the close connection between the exportation of tobacco and the importation of immigrants between Baltimore and Bremen.

The steadily increasing stream of German immigrants called forth new social forms and leisure activities among the Germans. The founding of German clubs and associations began in the early forties and grew from year to year to such an extent that it finally achieved the proportions of an obsession among the Germans.[83]

To some extent this "club mania" characterizes the German element in the entire United States during the last two thirds of the nineteenth century. In the history of the Germans in Maryland, however, this characteristic was evident chiefly in the city of Baltimore; it does not apply to the western part of the state, which was for a while the center of our attention. This point may help us to make clear the difference in the characteristics of the two important regions of German settlement in Maryland and to sharpen the contrast between them.

Most of the German settlers in Western Maryland had left the

[82] Hermann Wätjen, *Aus der Frühzeit des Nordatlantikverkehrs* (Leipzig, 1932), 17, 19.
[83] At the Steuben Festival, which occurred at the end of the period here discussed (1858), the program lists about sixty German clubs, societies, groups, lodges, circles, etc.

old country chiefly because of a combination of economic and religious reasons. Without doubt, for many of them, whether they came from Pennsylvania or directly from Germany, the religious motive was dominant. They were all "church conscious"; those few who might not have been at first, soon became so. Those who belonged to no church, congregation or sect were soon isolated and felt both economic and social disadvantages which were psychologically much more oppressive in the thinly populated rural sections than in the cities. There were certainly very few people in Western Maryland who did not belong to some sort of religious institution.

But the conditions were different among the Germans who landed in Baltimore after 1830. The large majority of them came for purely economic motives. Some of them, it is true, fled from the era of German reaction and restoration into a land of freedom; the abortive revolution of 1848 soon increased their number. But their influence should not be overestimated; we wish to emphasize the fact that the greatest number of Germans who settled in Baltimore between 1820 and 1860 came chiefly because America was a country of economic freedom. The religious motives that dominated the immigrants one hundred years before were not the main ones now. On the contrary, many of these men had had to leave their German homes because they had criticized religion and the church very much more sharply than the reactionary German governments were inclined to permit.

The Germans who came to Baltimore after 1830 also differed sociologically in a marked degree from those Western Maryland Germans who came after 1730. The people who lived along the Monocacy and the Conococheague were mainly farmers. The people in the city on Chesapeake Bay were merchants, tradesmen, professional men—an urban, middle-class group.

Why did German clubs appear like mushrooms during the decades after 1840 in Baltimore, and not in Frederick and Hagerstown? In Western Maryland there was no need for such clubs. The German farmers who settled on the frontier of the wilderness around 1750 would have thought it absurd to found clubs. They lived the hard, laborious lives of pioneers, full of misfortune, defeat, the daily battle against nature and the weather, threatened for years by the Indians. In the lives of such people there was not much time for the activities of societies; and the small amount of energy that was left them when they were finished with their daily toil was utilized for the church—the center of their spiritual and social lives.

Later the picture changed. With every piece of land wrung from the wilderness, life became easier. After the Revolution no one in Maryland was annoyed by the Indians. Frederick and Hagerstown became urban centers. A degree of middle-class well-being appeared; there was enough leisure for the founding and support of social organizations, but by this time Western Maryland had passed that period when the founding of such clubs on the basis of a common German ancestry might have occurred. We have attempted to make clear the fact that after 1815 a very strong tendency toward Americanization had set in. Around 1750 it would have been absurd to found a German *club*, because among these church-conscious pioneers there was no desire for a "profane" organization. Around 1820 it would have been absurd to found a *German* club; the generation that was now growing up spoke English better than German, had already mingled with other nationalities and had no desire to retard the process of acclimatization through a German organization.

The situation was entirely different in Baltimore around 1840. The Germans who came there could satisfy their social desires either in the German-speaking churches or among the American clubs. The former did not appeal to them because, although the church was one field of interest, it was not the center of their spiritual lives. The latter choice was unsatisfying in the long run because the Germans were often received with coolness or outright unfriendliness in the American organizations. So they used a third method and founded their own clubs. In Hagerstown around 1820, it would probably have been possible only with great difficulty to round up a few people for German clubs; they would have been attended by the older generation and would have disappeared after about ten years. In Baltimore these clubs existed for decades (a few for a century) because of the large reservoir of newcomers which was constantly being refilled with the arrival of every new shipload of immigrants. Such clubs require a constantly renewed stream of immigration. This was the case in Baltimore during the entire nineteenth century.

In Western Maryland, on the other hand, immigration had been almost entirely cut off after the Revolutionary War. The main mass of German settlers in Frederick and Washington Counties was forced out to the western part of the state before 1790. Then, as we saw, there was a pause of more than two decades. The Napoleonic Era acted as a kind of immigration blockade. No large numbers of people arrived in Western Maryland between 1790 and 1820 to interrupt or deter the process of acclimatization. When immigration was resumed around 1820, the Germans in Western Maryland had become Americans. The new immigrants who crossed the Atlantic from Germany had other destinations in view than the Monocacy or the Conococheague. They drove through the Western Maryland counties on their way to the Ohio, the Missouri or the Mississippi, or else they remained stationary in the place of their first arrival, Baltimore.

For this reason there was an ever-growing desire for social organizations through whose very existence the German element in Baltimore was characterized, and differed from that in Western Maryland.

The oldest purely social German organization in Baltimore is the Germania Club. For decades it was one of the richest and most influential clubs in the city and therefore it deserves special consideration. Of all the German clubs which still exist in Baltimore, it has the longest and most brilliant history.[84]

The club was founded by a dozen young German businessmen. They met in the summer of 1840 and started "a German society for literary and social purposes." The founders of the club were all poor young men, and they alone could not have kept it alive. But it was soon obvious that they had a good idea. There were, around 1840, a good many well-to-do German businessmen to whom such an organization was very welcome. Four years after its founding, the club counted over a hundred members—people who did not have to count their pennies and who were willing to give the club financial support. At first two club rooms were rented, but as early as 1846 a four-story club house was secured in which lively social intercourse was soon to develop.

In the first constitution of the club is the statement, "The undersigned, born in Germany or descendants of Germans, unite themselves in a Club with the name of Germania with the intention of

[84] The records of the Germania Club have been preserved complete through the more than one hundred years of the club's existence. Cf. Dieter Cunz, A History of the Germania Club of Baltimore City, Maryland (Baltimore, 1940). Here (p. 26) is a list of the founding members and a list of all the club presidents from 1840 to 1940.

establishing a library and reading room for English and German books, newspapers and other literary productions." At first, then, there were literary ambitions. A library was furnished and the editor of a newspaper in Germany was requested from time to time to buy books for the club and send them over.[85] The works of the German classical poets, Goethe, Schiller, Lessing, Klopstock, Herder and Wieland, were acquired; we also find, on the list of books works of the Romanticists and the exponents of young Germany, such as Hauff, Heine, Börne and Laube, as well as popular scientific works on history, geography and natural history. About a dozen German newspapers, several English newspapers from London and Liverpool and a few satiric political periodicals complete the list.

Actually, the literary purpose was only an excuse. The real purpose of the club was social. Most of the German societies, whether they began as literary, choral or gymnastic clubs, showed a habitual tendency to transform themselves into purely social organizations. This was also the fate of the Germania Club. We read occasionally of lectures, and musicals, but there is no doubt that billiards, chess, dominoes, banquets and picnics were much more popular than literary and musical soirees. The Germania Club was unique as a social organization. At the outbreak of the Civil War it had grown to a membership of 150. It could hardly have become larger, for membership was open only to a carefully selected group of people. The Germans who were gathered here comprised a very uniform group; almost all of them were businessmen, most of them from Bremen, and all of them very wealthy. The Germania Club was the organization of the highest social group of Germans. The tobacco importers in Bremen would send one of their sons to Baltimore to supervise the buying of tobacco. Many of these young men remained permanently in Baltimore, founded their own firms, married, became wealthy—and then joined the Germania Club. During the period before the Civil War, probably half of the members of the club were somehow connected with the tobacco trade. It need hardly be mentioned that such an organization of wealthy upper-class citizens was highly exclusive. The people who secluded themselves in the Germania Club were not very popular with the middle- and lower-class Germans in Baltimore. Stories of the social arro-

[85] The editor was a Dr. Arend of the Weser Zeitung, an indication again of the close relations with Bremen.

gance of the Bremen merchants in the Germania Club have been handed down for a century.

The most prominent figure in the club during the time before the outbreak of the Civil War was Albert Schumacher (1802-1871). In this account we must refrain from describing the life histories of individuals in detail, for that is the work of the genealogist. However, if we devote a few lines here to Albert Schumacher it is not because we are especially interested in him, but because he was typical of the wealthy, upper-class Germans in the first half of the nineteenth century.

Albert Schumacher was born in Bremen, the son of a Bremen city counselor.[86] He received an excellent education and at the age of seventeen entered a large firm (H. H. Meier & Co.) as an apprentice. He advanced very quickly, and six years later was made confidential clerk of the firm. His predecessor in this position, C. A. Heinecke, had gone to America at the beginning of the twenties and had founded an exporting company in Baltimore. Following Heinecke's advice, Schumacher decided to try his luck in America; he landed in 1826 and immediately became a member of Heinecke's firm. For a long time he traveled on business for the firm in South and Central America and in Europe, making contacts that soon spread over half the world. Everything he attempted seemed to be successful. In 1839 Heinecke left the firm, and from that time on Schumacher ran the business alone. He became more and more prominent in the city, was made consul general for Hamburg and Bremen[87] and held numerous offices on the boards of directors of industrial companies and other organizations (Baltimore and Ohio Railroad, Baltimore Chamber of Commerce, and various banks). He was president of the German Society, the Germania Club, the Zion school and was made honorary citizen of the City of Bremen—to name only a few of the offices and honors heaped upon him.

Here we see no poor immigrant standing on a pier with his wife and children and a bundle of household necessities, not knowing what to do next. Schumacher was a young man, coming from a

[86] *Der deutsche Pionier*, III (1871), 137 ff. BVG, 271.

[87] For his book, *Aus der Frühzeit des Nordatlantikverkehrs* (1932), Hermann Wätjen used the reports which Albert Schumacher sent to Germany as Hanseatic Consul General. However, Wätjen was very much disappointed at the colorlessness and brevity of the reports (p. xi).

wealthy, prominent Bremen family who went to America in order to make business connections. If he had not been successful he could always have returned home. But he was successful; he liked the new country; and so he stayed and was content merely to visit his old home occasionally on business or pleasure trips. Schumacher's case is typical of that of a large percentage of the Baltimore Germans in the middle of the nineteenth century. Only a few of them became as wealthy as he, but the general outlines of his case apply in a greater or less degree to many other people. The pioneers who settled along the Monocacy in 1740 had burned all their bridges behind them when they decided to go out to the nameless, unknown wilderness. The young Bremen merchants in 1840 made their business contacts and moved to another country. Of course, around 1840 the pioneer type was still to be seen; indeed, these pioneers came on the same ships as the Bremen patricians, but in a different class, and they usually stayed only one day in Baltimore, for it was only a way station on their journey to the Middle West. Their situation was fundamentally different from that of the commercial emissaries of the Bremen exporting firms who became independent in Baltimore and from the beginning were at home in the urban, middle-class world of banking, export, import, trade and commerce.

The Germania Club represented only a small part of the German element in Baltimore. It was consciously exclusive and through its unreasonable financial demands on its members made certain that its rooms were available only to the highest social class. Another society, which was somewhat less demanding, ruled the social life of the Germans in the city for some decades. This was the Concordia.

The Concordia was founded in 1847, at which time a German liberal, Georg Fein, lived in the city.[88] He stayed only a few months,

---

[88] The minutes of the Concordia have not been preserved. They were burned at the time of the great fire of the Concordia Hall. Some meager information on the Concordia is to be found in BVG, 228 f. The names of the officers for the first twenty years are listed there. In the constitution of the Concordia, the purpose of the society is described as follows: "It shall be the purpose of the Concordia to further the education of its members through scientific lectures, to raise their ethical feelings through social gatherings and an exchange of ideas, and to ennoble their spirits and to encourage the fine and the good through dramatic performances."

Georg Fein (1803-1869), a well-known German liberal, had to leave his country after the famous Hambacher Fest (1832). He spent some time in Oslo, Strassburg, Paris and Zürich, where he was for a while one of the editors of the Neue Zürcher Zeitung. He lived in the United States from 1845 to

for his real goal was the West. He must have had a genius for organization, for in the short time that he was there he gathered a number of cultured Germans together who founded the Concordia on June 16, 1847. Their main task was to be the founding of a library in the city for the Germans, to organize lectures on literary, scientific and civic questions—in short, the Concordia was to be a social society on an intellectual level. The society rented rooms and for years fulfilled its purpose in a really astonishing degree. Its members came from a much broader social group than those of the Germania Club. However, the literary and musical ambitions of the Concordia made it appeal especially to people from the upper middle class. The membership was not so exclusively mercantile as was that of the Germania Club. Among the names of the presidents during this time, not one of the many tobacco men who formed the backbone of the Germania Club is to be found. In the course of years the Concordia developed more and more into *the* entertainment organization of the Germans. The music and dramatic divisions became famous; we shall have occasion to speak of them again when we present the beginnings of the German theater in Baltimore.

Of course, neither the Germania nor the Concordia was a social organization for the great masses. Hundreds and thousands of German immigrants who came over during the decades before the Civil War and settled in Baltimore organized themselves into another form of society—the singing and gymnastic clubs. Here we find the middle and lower level of the German element. These clubs were, of course, much more numerous than the exclusive clubs of the wealthy merchants. It is doubtful whether the activity of the

---

1848, returned to Europe during the German revolution and lived thereafter in Liestal in the Canton Basel-Land. He became known in Switzerland as an organizer of German workers' associations. Particularly noteworthy are his efforts to stimulate cultural interests among the working classes. For additional information on Fein, cf. *Allgemeine Deutsche Bibliographie* (1877), VI, 606 f. *Historisch-Biographisches Lexikon der Schweiz* (1926), III, 132. Otto Oppermann, "Georg Fein, ein Politiker der burschenschaftlichen Linken" in *Quellen und Darstellungen zur Geschichte der Burschenschaft und der deutschen Einheitsbewegung*, ed. by Hermann Haupt (Heidelberg, 1910), I, 240-79. Wilhelm Marr, *Das Junge Deutschland in der Schweiz* (Leipzig, 1846), 224-64. Veit Valentin, *Geschichte der deutschen Revolution 1848/49* (Berlin 1931), II, 334 f. Ricarda Huch, 1848, *Die Revolution des 19. Jahrhunderts in Deutschland* (Zürich, 1944), 51 f. Otto Brugger, *Geschichte der deutschen Handwerkervereine in der Schweiz 1836-1843* (Bern, 1932), 18, 22, 201 f., 208.

choral and gymnastic societies went very deep. However, there is no doubt that the club spirit was very widespread and included practically every member of the great masses of the Germans.

The oldest German society in Baltimore (aside from the half German, half English "Wilhelm Tell Loge" of the Odd Fellows of the year 1827) was the Baltimore "Liederkranz." It was the second singing society which was formed in the United States, following by only one year the oldest society of the kind, the Philadelphia Männerchor.

The founding of the Liederkranz is associated with the history of the Zion church. In the middle of the thirties there was a small church choir there which, it must be noted, was not especially important. This "Singe Verein" was given new impetus in 1835 when Pastor Heinrich Scheib came to Baltimore. As a Rhinelander, he was well acquainted with the spirit and achievements of choral societies. The first singing society, the Liederkranz, was constituted in the rooms of the Zion church on December 30, 1836. A teacher from the Zion school, Friedrich Lüdeking, took over the office of director. When he left Baltimore the next year, Philipp Matthias Wolsiefer came to Baltimore from Philadelphia at Scheib's instigation to be director of the society.[89]

In March 1837 the Liederkranz gave its first public concert. We do not know what the program was for the evening, but we do know that, before the actual choral program began, a symphony by Beethoven was played. Therefore, the society must have had a division for instrumental music. It is assumed that this was the first time that a Beethoven symphony was performed in Baltimore. Which symphony it was and the quality of the performance are not known.[90]

Wolsiefer must have been a gifted and stirring director. Under

[89] H. A. Rattermann, "Anfänge und Entwicklung der Musik und des Gesanges in den Vereinigten Staaten während der ersten Hälfte des 19. Jahrhunderts," in *Deutsch-Amerikanische Geschichtsblätter*, XII (1912), 340 ff. For biographical material on Ph. M. Wolsiefer (1808-1872), cf. H. A. Rattermann, *Gesammelte Werke*, XII, 431 ff.

[90] The minutes of the Liederkranz are not preserved. The Society for the History of the Germans in Maryland, however, owns an old, hand-written history of the society which was composed in 1869 by its president, Dr. Heinrich Windwart, and which was obviously based on the minutes that were still available at that time. Cf. also *BVG*, 144 ff., and *Deutsche Musik-Zeitung* (Philadelphia), January 1857, 69.

his direction the society soon attempted larger projects. At the first performance (on April 14, 1840) at which Weber's "Freischütz" was heard, the Liederkranz sang the choruses. At the rededication of the Zion church after the fire of 1839, Schiller's "Lied von der Glocke," with music by Andreas Romberg, was produced. The high points in the early history of the society were the performances of the great Haydn oratorios "Die Jahreszeiten" and "Die Schöpfung." Toward the end of the forties, a slack period set in, and for a few years the society declined. In 1850 a new director was engaged, one Charles Lenschow, who had come to America in 1848 with an orchestra that had been founded in Germany. Lenschow brought new life into the society and he was soon one of the mainstays of Baltimore's musical life. Under his direction even an opera was attempted. A few years before, the society had presented a concert arrangement of Mozart's "Don Juan"; now, under Lenschow's experienced direction, Mozart's "Zauberflöte" was rehearsed and produced in 1852 with great success. Donizetti's "Regimentstochter," Flotow's "Martha" and Kreutzer's "Nachtlager von Granada" were performed in succeeding years.

Just as the Liederkranz developed from the Singe Verein of the Zion church, so a similar society developed from a similar church choir of the German-Samaritan church.[91] This choir was led by Philipp Wacker, whose name has already been mentioned in connection with the German schools of the city. There were constant disputes between the choir and the pastor of the congregation. At an outing which the congregation held on Independence Day, July 4, 1853, the underlying tension burst out into a vehement, unchristian quarrel. The choir decided to desert the church and establish itself independently as a secular singing society, adopting the name "Harmonie" (a very appropriate choice, in the face of the dramatic birth of the society). The first directors were Philipp Wacker and Karl Mahr. The Harmonie's ambitions were more modest than those of the Liederkranz; in place of operas and oratorios, simple German folk songs were to be found on the program. The first folk song which was rehearsed was "Aennchen von Tharau."

For fifteen years the Liederkranz was the only choral society in

[91] The Samaritan congregation, which was founded by a German minister, Carl Meister, joined the German St. Stephanus church in 1850.

the city. The Liederkranz and Harmonie, both formed from church choirs, had a definite middle-class character. The choral society which comprised the lower social group was the "Arion," founded in 1851. Shortly after this, a special "Arbeiter Gesangverein" (Laborer's Singing Society) was founded, but the two joined in 1855 under the common name "Arion." The first public appearance of the Arion was characterized by the liberal-revolutionary spirit of this group; it serenaded the Hungarian liberator, Kossuth, when he visited Baltimore in 1852. Naturally, Arion, like Harmonie, attempted only the simpler folk music, not the more difficult and demanding art that was practiced by the Liederkranz.

The musical clubs as social institutions became more and more integrated into the life of the Germans. Originally, as we said, they were organizations of the lower social levels. But the upper levels also began to enjoy them, and in order to fulfill a growing desire the Germania Männerchor was organized in 1856. Here were men even from the wealthy German merchant families. Higher artistic ambitions appeared alongside the social ones; and, in addition to folk songs, oratorios and operas are to be found on the programs of the various festivals.[92]

Liederkranz, 1836; Arion, 1851; Harmonie, 1853 and Germania Männerchor 1856—these were the four large German choral societies in Baltimore during the pre-Civil War period. During this decade similar organizations were founded in all the American cities where there were Germans. Once a year they gathered together in a so-called National Sängerfest, the meeting place rotating in the 1850's among Philadelphia, New York and Baltimore. The second, fifth and eighth National Sängerfest (1851, 1854 and 1859) took place in Baltimore. The choral society as an institution was the exclusive monopoly of the Germans during this time, and the idea of a Sängerfest was universally identified with the Germans.

In our account of the history of the German choral societies we have automatically touched on the beginnings of the German theater in Baltimore. We do not know exactly when German was first spoken on a stage in Baltimore. Legendary sources report that a German play, *Lola Montez*, was performed in the 1840's. This would be the earliest report of a German performance, but we are

[92] The *Geschichte des Germania Männerchor*, by Carl Laegeler (1906), contains information concerning the members, the life of the society and other activities of the chorus.

not certain that we can credit this report.[93] More plausible are the reports of the unfortunate and unsuccessful efforts of a theater director named Hermann, who tried his fortunes in Baltimore in the middle of the forties. A producer named W. Rullmann was more successful than Hermann a few years later and with a few interruptions his company played until the Civil War. We know little about what he did before 1853, but from this time on the available issues of the *Wecker* contain an occasional review of Rullmann's productions. Ordinarily the performances represented only the first part of a social evening, the audience remaining to drink and dance. This combination of theater and beer garden grew more and more to be a characteristic kind of German-American entertainment.

At the beginning of 1856 a competitive undertaking appeared for Rullmann, J. Dardennes' "Deutsches Nationaltheater." We do not know how long it existed. Furthermore, in the late 1850's we hear of various other theatrical producers who came to Baltimore with German troupes for a season (or more). We know of a Carl Düringer and a C. Thielemann who played in Washington Hall as well as in the Baltimore Museum; we hear of W. Böttner, whose Philadelphia Nationaltheater appeared successfully in Baltimore's Front Street Theater. A Carl Burgthal was associated with the above-mentioned Mr. Thielemann, first in competition with him and then as his partner, and finally he disappeared with the entire proceeds of both their endeavors.

Of the actors themselves we know little. A Wilhelm Dietz, who stopped in Baltimore on his way to New York (1853), appeared in several great roles as a guest artist and was apparently a great attraction. A Mme. Pelosi and a Mr. Waldmann seem to have enjoyed special popularity. The "star family" among the German actors of Baltimore for many years was the Mojean family, about whom we frequently read enthusiastic reports.[94]

The dramatic fare of the various German stages does not indicate a very high level of art. In general the companies attempted to

[93] For further information, see the article by A. E. Zucker, "The History of the German Theater in Baltimore," *Germanic Review*, XVIII (1943), ii, 123-35. All that we shall have to say here on the development of the German theater in Baltimore is based on the material which Dr. Zucker gathered for his article. Cf. also *BVG*, 137 ff. and *Deutsche Musik-Zeitung* (1857), I, 58, 76.

[94] The Mojeans, despite their French name, were German. Before her marriage, Mrs. Mojean had enjoyed great triumphs as Miss Dietrich.

produce only entertaining wares, seldom daring to produce a tragedy which would dampen the spirits of the gay crowd of drinkers afterwards. We shall not trouble to list the titles of these literary May flies. Kotzebue was the *pièce de résistance* of every producer, but in this respect the German theater in America differed little from the German theater in Germany during the fifties. A few titles will be listed which rose above the beer-garden level: Schiller, *Die Räuber, Kabale und Liebe, Maria Stuart, Jungfrau von Orleans, Wallenstein;* Goethe, *Faust;* Kleist, *Kätchen von Heilbronn;* Laube, *Die Karlsschüler;* Körner, *Der Nachtwächter;* Nestroy, *Einen Jux will er sich machen* and *Lumpacivagabundus;* Hugo, *Glöckner von Notre Dame;* Grillparzer, *Die Ahnfrau;* Gutzkow, *Uriel Acosta.* Twice we hear that dramatic products of two Germans living in Baltimore were produced, Moritz Wiener's *Die Waise von Lucca* and Carl Heinrich Schnauffer's *Christ und Jude.* However, only the titles of these plays have been handed down to us.[95]

As we have seen, a visit to the theater for the Germans in Baltimore was a half-artistic, half-social affair. Toward the end of the 1850's the German theatrical companies could count on a fixed group of patrons in Baltimore, and when they succeeded in interesting a few German societies en bloc in their performances, they could count on full houses. The two kinds of organizations that were especially interested in the theater were the choral and gymnastic societies.

Of all the German societies, the Turnvereine had the strongest appeal for the broad mass of German immigrants.[96] They deserve special mention not only because of their educational purpose, but also especially because of their political influence.

Only two Turnvereine were really important in the history of the Germans in Baltimore—the Turnverein Vorwärts (Forward) and the Sozialdemokratische Turnverein. The history of Vorwärts does not begin until after the Civil War, and so in this period we shall deal only with the Sozialdemokratische Turnverein.

The society was founded in 1849, a year after the unsuccessful revolution in Germany, and this is not accidental. It is well known

[95] For further information on the repertory, see the previously mentioned article by A. E. Zucker.

[96] The German verb *turnen,* i.e., "to perform gymnastic exercises," is of French origin: *tourner.* From it derive: *der Turner*—gymnast; *Turnfest*—gymnastic festival; *Turnverein*—gymnastic society.

that the whole Turner movement was closely connected with the liberal German movement. It had begun during Napoleonic times, when Friedrich Ludwig Jahn in Germany attempted to form an organization of German youth through his Turner movement. Jahn was not a clear, systematic thinker; his book *Deutsches Volkstum*, in which he developed his program, is a very much confused, romantic book. He dreamed of the ideal person, the ancient Greek type who was equally well-developed physically and mentally. He did not believe in letting the mental education of a man lag behind his physical education; he desired a well-balanced combination of both lines. But since in Germany there was an old and well-tried system of education for mental development, the Turner movement necessarily laid overemphasis on physical development. This overemphasis occurred because of existing circumstances, not as one of the principles of the program of the Turner movement. Its program emphasized again and again the close association of physical and mental development. *Mens sana in corpore sano* was its constantly quoted motto and at the heading of every number of the German *Turnzeitung* published in Baltimore one read, "Only culture makes nations, like individuals, free!"

As long as the battle against Napoleon was on the agenda of the Turner movement in Germany, it was pervaded by a national, liberal tone. The fight was against the foreign tyrant. But after 1815 this was changed: the foreign tyrant was no longer a menace. The head of the dragon had been slashed off, but in its place a hundred other heads had grown—domestic tyrants, the German reactionary princes à la Metternich. The Turnvereine, which had formerly been national-liberal, became liberal-revolutionary after 1815. After 1819 the Turnvereine were banned by all the German governments, but they continued to be active as an underground movement. The young, liberal generation which had been betrayed by the reaction organized itself into student fraternities and Turnvereine. They founded secret societies, committed political disturbances, were sentenced and imprisoned and had to flee, but there were always others to take their places until the last great, yet unsuccessful, attempt: the revolution of 1848. History decided against the free German movement. Along with the persecuted, revolutionary "'48ers" who sought asylum across the Atlantic and finally adopted America as their permanent home, the Turner movement was brought over to the New World.[97] It belongs to the progressive-liberal cargo of ideas and human beings which German governments to their own detriment have been sending to America for centuries.

Around 1850 Turnvereine were founded in all the American cities that had a German population, and these societies banded together into the North-American Gymnastic Association. Every year a joint Turnfest was held; a newspaper, the *Turnzeitung*, was created as the official organ of information. It was published in various cities, appearing in Baltimore from 1859-1861 and edited by Dr. Adolph Wiesner, Wilhelm Rapp and Dr. Georg Edward Wiss.[98]

The Baltimore chapter of the North-American Gymnastic Association was the Sozialdemokratische Turnverein, whose name (Social Democratic) indicates clearly its political program.[99] After only a year (1850) the society had 278 members. At this time it was the most active of the seventeen Turnvereine which were then in existence in America. It secured a hall, organized groups of gymnasts and thus provided an outlet for the interest in physical education which most of the Germans had brought with them from abroad. However, the society did not overlook the mental training that was to supplement the physical, and it organized lecture series on literary, political and national questions. It even built its own hall for play production. The society was not on good terms with the church; most of the Turners were free thinkers and of all the pastors in Baltimore they were on friendly terms with only Pastor Scheib, whom the orthodox Christians called "a rationalistic heathen."

[97] The beginnings of the Turner movement in America are to be found as early as the twenties and thirties in the early efforts of Charles Follen and Francis Lieber. But it did not become popular on a large scale until after 1848. For a description of the intellectual climate from which the Turner movement grew, see Augustus J. Prahl, "The Ideological Background of the American Turner," *Comparative Literature News-Letter*, III (1944), 11-13.

[98] There is only one copy in existence of the volumes of the *Turnzeitung* published in Baltimore; this is in the Boston Public Library.

[99] The minutes of the Sozialdemokratische Turnverein were burned in the great fire of 1904. Some meager information is to be found in BVG, 288 f. A few of the founders were Carl Giller, Conrad H. Becker, Louis Binderwald and Adam Geyer. Conrad Becker became the first manager of the "Baltimore Gymnasium," founded in 1858, which had two hundred pupils two years later. In 1860 gymnastic classes were introduced in Knapp's school. Cf. *Turnzeitung*, April 10, 1860.

The lower social groups among the Germans joined the Turn-verein. In addition to its gymnastic activities, the purpose of the Turnverein was to add to its members' education, to organize their social needs and desires, to explain to them the political forces in the country and to assist them to take part in these political activities. And it may well be said that the Turnverein fulfilled its mission to an astonishing degree during the two decades before and after the Civil War.

In connection with the Turner movement we have mentioned the *Turnzeitung,* which was published in Baltimore the year before the outbreak of the Civil War. We must go back a few decades to follow the development of the German press in Maryland during the first half of the nineteenth century. We said, "in Maryland," but "in Baltimore" would be better, for the activities of the German element became more and more concentrated in Baltimore. In connection with the language problem we have tried to show how completely Americanized the German settlers in the western counties had become. German church services gradually died out, and it is no wonder that the demand for German newspapers in the older settlements decreased from year to year. From 1822 the *Hagerstown Almanack* appeared in both German and English, although we do not know what was the percentage of each. In any case, such figures would not allow us to draw conclusions for Maryland, for the *Hagerstown Almanack* was not a German or even a Maryland institution; it was an American institution, read by German and non-German farmers in every state in the Union.

John Gruber's Hagerstown weekly seems to have disappeared about 1830, after having appeared for probably two decades in German. While at this time the demand for a German newspaper quickly declined in Western Maryland, the fresh wave of German immigrants after 1817 gave a Baltimore publisher the courage to try a German paper again.

On March 7, 1821, the first number of the *Maryländische Teutsche Zeitung* appeared, published by Johann T. Hanzsche, who was owner, printer and publisher. It was apparently read outside of Baltimore as well as within, for many of the advertisements refer, not to Western Maryland, but to Philadelphia. A comparison of the few numbers of the *Maryländische Teutsche Zeitung* that are still in existence with what was printed in German in Western Maryland shows that Hanzsche displayed a much greater interest in Europe than did Gruber and Bartgis. For instance, the May 2, 1821, number devotes nearly three pages to European affairs and the fourth page is almost entirely taken up with advertisements, so that there is hardly any space left for local events. It may be assumed that this was a mistake on the part of the publisher, for in later numbers American news is covered at the expense of the European. The newspaper was not very colorful. Much of the material consisted of reprints from other papers (for instance, Bremen newspapers); there were dry articles on early Germanic history and other subjects that would not interest many readers. Politically, the newspaper stood without reservation for the liberal German movement; it stormed against the reactionary, conservative governments of the German states, urged the emancipation of Jews in Germany, pleaded for complete religious tolerance, made poisonous jabs at the newly established Ancien Régime in France and applauded the revolutionary movements in all European countries. "All Italy is in flames," we read on May 9, 1821. "God grant that they will hunt down and destroy so completely that no pillar of despotism remains, and that the rights of nations to be free and independent will arise bright and shining from the ashes like a Phoenix."

We do not know how long the newspaper appeared. It must have been in existence as late as 1828, but it may be assumed that it was discontinued shortly after, perhaps in 1830.[100]

In addition to the newspapers, there were a considerable number of German almanacs in Baltimore. The William Warner, Schaeffer & Maund, Johann T. Hanzsche print shops produced them almost continuously and they apparently sold well. The style of these almanacs does not differ in any way from that of John Gruber, which we have adequately described above.[101] These same print

[100] Seidensticker, op. cit., 215, mentions the Maryländische Teutsche Zeitung the first time in 1822, yet he knew about it only indirectly. Apparently when Seidensticker compiled his bibliography there was only one number of the newspaper, that of January 30, 1828, at hand and it was owned by the son of the editor. (Seidensticker, p. 236.) In the meantime, various other copies have appeared which have been preserved in Goucher College, Yale University and the Society for the History of the Germans in Maryland. Cf. Union List of Newspapers.

[101] The Enoch Pratt Library owns a whole series of German almanacs which appeared in Baltimore during the second and third decades of the nineteenth century. They are listed individually in Seidensticker's bibliography. Schaeffer

shops also usually bought and sold German books imported from Germany. Occasionally they printed German books themselves. A very courageous effort was made by a German printer, Lorenz Schwarz. Between 1839 and 1841 he published in Baltimore a twelve-volume German edition of Friedrich Schiller's complete works. The Baltimore edition is identical with the Cotta edition of 1838. However, various orthographic differences indicate that Schwarz did not use the same plates. He must have prepared and printed his own edition.[102]

We know nothing about any German newspapers at the beginning of the thirties. There were no signs of life in German print shops in Baltimore until toward the end of the decade. Then a family came to Baltimore whose name from this time until the beginning of the twentieth century has been connected with the history of the German press in Baltimore—the Raine family, Wilhelm Raine the father, and his three sons, Wilhelm, Friedrich and Eduard.

On the father's side, the Raines came from England. In the middle of the eighteenth century one of their ancestors went to Germany as a soldier under the Prince of Wales, and when the war was over he stayed there. He married a lady in the court of Brunswick and lived in Hannover. His grandson was Wilhelm Raine, who was born toward the end of the eighteenth century in Minden in Westphalia and who emigrated to America in the third decade of the following century. He had married a daughter of one of the prominent, old Westphalian families (Wundermann)—a family of book dealers, writers and composers, all people of intellectual

---

& Maund's almanac was somewhat more conservative than most of the others. It has a few friendly remarks to make about some of the German princes and has a faintly anti-Semitic tone such as we would certainly not find in Hanzsche's newspaper. Now and again it has a few caustic remarks against the Irish. Schaeffer & Maund had a prosperous bookstore. The new common hymnal which had just appeared in the Protestant churches of the city was advertised in their almanac of 1818; in 1820 Nürnberg folio Bibles were offered for sale, as well as the German edition of Weems's *Life of Washington*, which was much read by the Germans.

[102] A complete set of the Lorenz Schwarz Schiller edition of 1839-1841 is still preserved at the Library of Franklin and Marshall College, Lancaster, Pennsylvania. For a discussion of Lorenz Schwarz's printing, see Elwood C. Parry, "Friedrich Schiller in America," *German American Annals* (Philadelphia, 1905), III, 46 f. Cf. also *Das Neue Baltimore* (Baltimore, 1905), 69 (hereafter abbreviated *DNB*).

interests. The literary talent that all three of Raine's sons, especially
Friedrich Raine, displayed was probably inherited from their mother's side.[103]

When old Wilhelm Raine arrived in Baltimore in the middle of
the thirties, there was apparently no German newspaper. Wilhelm
Raine was not without journalistic experience. In his native city of
Minden he had run a bookstore and a bindery and also had published a small county paper. A few years after his arrival in Baltimore in 1838, he and his oldest son, Wilhelm, began the publication of a religious weekly called Die geschäftige Martha (Industrious Martha). Again, we do not know how long the paper appeared
—probably about three or four years.[104] At the end of 1839
or the beginning of 1840 Raine shifted his interests from ecclesiastical to political affairs; he started with the publication of
a political weekly, Der demokratische Whig, which took an active
part in the election campaign of 1840, on the side of Harrison and
Tyler. The political opinions of the Demokratische Whig were
somewhat vague; it was more Whig than Democrat. We do not
know the exact length of life of this paper, but it must have finally
been withdrawn in 1845.[105]

[103] The church records of the Otterbein church say that Wilhelm Raine
left the mother of his sons in Germany and contracted a new marriage in
America. It seems that he did not have his first marriage officially dissolved,
for in 1842 the Otterbein church, of which at that time he was secretary,
accused him of polygamy. For details on Wilhelm Raine, cf. Dieter Cunz,
"The Otterbein Church Incident," American German Review, xiv (1947),
15 ff.

[104] BVG, 300. Deutsche Pionier, x (1878), 442 f. No collector has as yet
succeeded in finding a copy of Geschäftige Martha. We know of the existence
of the paper only through indirect sources. In the church records of the Otterbein church we discover that one of the publishers of the Geschäftige Martha,
Jacob Erb, was the preacher of the Otterbein congregation. The Reverend
Mr. Erb was in Baltimore from 1841 to 1848. From this information, it
must be assumed that the Geschäftige Martha appeared at least until 1841.

[105] In the older literature (Cyclopedia, 27; BVG, 300; Scharf, Baltimore,
626) whenever the work of the Raines is spoken of, the statement is made
that the Demokratische Whig appeared for only about a year and that in 1841 it
was abandoned. Scharf makes it look as though the Correspondent, which was
founded in 1841, was in a sense a continuation of the Demokratische Whig.
This is not correct. We have no copies of the paper, it is true, but we have
some information about it in its democratic opponent, the recently discovered Demokrat. According to this it seems that the Demokratische Whig was
chiefly a presidential campaign paper. It appeared for about a year in the campaign of 1840, which ended in the first great Whig victory. Then the publication of the paper seems to have been interrupted for about three years, only

The political enemy of the *Demokratische Whig* was *Der Demokrat*, which we shall discuss here in somewhat greater detail because no one knew of its existence before now. The name of its editor was known, Samuel Maclea, but only in connection with a different paper. Nothing was known about Maclea except his name. Through the fortunate rediscovery of the *Demokrat* we are now in a position to say a little more about Maclea.

In spite of his Scottish-sounding name, Samuel Maclea must have been German, or at least have grown up and been educated in Germany. A great many of the literary contributions appearing in the *Demokrat* came from his pen, and an analysis of this work shows unquestionably that German was his mother tongue. He came from Frankfurt am Main, and his name is possibly an anglicized form of "Mäckel" or "Meckle." He must have engaged in literary activities in Germany before coming to this country and have worked for various newspapers. Why he left Germany we do not know; perhaps, since he was a decided and very radical liberal, he left for political reasons. He was in Greece for a time, but for what purpose we do not know. In the summer of 1843 he arrived in New York as a penniless young man of about thirty years, moved to Baltimore a short time later and in the winter of 1843 became editor of the *Demokrat*. In March 1844 he married Elisa Riddel; the marriage was performed in the Zion church. In later years we hear of him again as the publisher of a literary magazine in Baltimore. Rather belatedly he discovered that there was no money to be made in

---

to be resumed in 1844, again an election year. On April 20, 1844, the *Demokrat* wrote: "Der Demokratische Whig. The first number of a German newspaper bearing the above Title, under the ostensible editorship of Mr. Wme. Raine, has made its appearance in Baltimore, and is to be continued weekly from the 1st of May until the next Presidential Election. It is to support the Whig principles, and the claims of Mr. Henry Clay as the candidate of that party, for the Presidency of the United States. Its title indicates sufficiently of what manner of spirits its editor is. . . . It will make but few proselytes to Whigism among the Germans." The *Demokrat* which followed and commented enviously on every step taken by the *Demokratische Whig* would have been overjoyed to report that its opposing paper had been discontinued. Therefore, it must have existed until January 1845, because we read nothing of the death of the *Demokratische Whig* in the *Demokrat*, which we have up until January 1845. Through an indirect indication (*Didaskalia*, 1849, 473), we have been able to determine that Wilhelm Raine, together with F. T. Zanders in Chillicothe, Ohio, started the publication of the *Ohio Correspondent* in April 1849.

literature, and so he decided to change to the more lucrative occupation of innkeeper. He died in the middle of the fifties in Baltimore, the owner of the hotel "European House."[106]

No doubt Samuel Maclea was the driving force back of the Demokrat.[107] That was one of the reasons why the quarrel between the two competing German papers was so violent and personal. The insults that the two editors heaped on one another's heads are beyond all conception. In the first number of the Demokratische Whig, Raine unceremoniously picked Maclea to pieces and the latter answered him, in one of the few English articles appearing in the paper, as follows: Raine had called him "an alien who has but lately arrived in America, and who must of course be ignorant of the political institutions and true interest of the country." "We believe willingly that Mr. Raine knew nothing of the institutions and the interest of the United States when he emigrated to America; but what right has he to suppose such ignorance, in such a calumnious manner, in other and better informed Germans."[108] The unfortunate, tactless remark that Raine made is a well-known tendency in the whole history of immigration; the earlier immigrants feel superior toward the later ones and often display more chauvinistic arrogance than the most radical nativists.

On the whole, the Demokrat was a well-made-up, lively paper. The literary contributions were supplied mostly by Maclea himself. There were also contributions by Hans Christian Andersen, Hoffman von Fallersleben, Georg Herwegh and Heinrich Heine. Politically, in regard to Germany, the paper was unequivocally on the side of the liberal movement and in regard to America it was a

[106] Most of these dates have been gathered from the columns of the Demokrat in connection with his reports of a personal feud which Maclea had with a German singer in Baltimore named Boucher, who objected bitterly to Maclea's sharply critical reviews. The fact that the quarrel was vehement and did not stop at dragging forth personal details is responsible for our acquiring biographical information that was formerly unknown. Through Ludvigh's Fackel (v, 250) we know that Maclea undertook a long journey to California shortly after gold was discovered there, but he returned in 1851 just as poor as he was when he left. In various numbers of the Wecker in 1853, we find Maclea's advertisements as owner of the "European House."

[107] At first the Demokrat appeared twice a week, then once a week and later changed several times from once to twice a week and back again. The publisher was at first J. Stimpson, but after three months the paper changed hands and Johann T. Hanzsche owned it. The only remaining set of the newspaper is in the Enoch Pratt Library.

[108] Demokrat, April 20, 1844.

hundred per cent democratic. It warmly defended old Andrew Jackson, attacked Henry Clay whenever possible, advocated the election of James K. Polk and came to grips whenever the occasion arose with the American nativists. However, it urged the Germans not to accentuate their German background too strongly, not to hinder artificially the natural process of Americanization and in this way to take the wind out of the sails of the nativists.[109] In the middle of the forties, the *Demokrat* provided the most important center for the crystallization of the ideas of those Germans who believed in the Democratic Party. It is to be hoped that at some future time more volumes of the newspaper will be found. But at present we do not even know how long the paper was published.[110]

During the years when the *Demokrat* and the *Demokratische Whig* were appearing in Baltimore, there was a third German newspaper, one which outlived all other German newspapers in Maryland and the only one still in existence today, more than a hundred years later. Today it is the second oldest German newspaper in the United States, the *Correspondent*.

The publisher of the *Democratische Whig* had a son, Friedrich Raine.[111] He was born on May 13, 1822, in Minden, Westphalia, learned the printing trade and at seventeen became assistant editor of the *Westfälische Zeitung*. In 1840 he followed his father and brother to Baltimore and worked for a time on the *Demokratische Whig*, but then, in the spring of 1841, he founded his own paper, which he called *Der Deutsche Correspondent*.[112] It started on a modest scale. Nineteen-year-old Friedrich Raine was simultaneously owner, editor, typesetter, printer and newsboy. He had eight subscribers for the first number. The *Correspondent* started as a weekly paper, but when the number of subscribers increased with surprising rapidity, it was changed in 1843 to biweekly and later in the same year to triweekly appearance. In 1844 Raine even attempted daily

[109] Article "Deutschtum in Amerika" in the first number, December 20, 1843.

[110] In the *Didaskalia* appearing in 1848-1849 Maclea lists the *Demokrat*. It appeared twice a week at that time, but was edited by W. E. Miller, not by Maclea.

[111] *Cyclopedia*, 27 f. BVG, 281 ff., 300 ff. Scharf, *Baltimore*, 625 ff. Hall, *Baltimore*, 706 f. John H. Hewitt, *Shadows on the Wall* (Baltimore, 1877), 36.

[112] Edmund E. Miller, *The Hundred Year History of the German Correspondent, Baltimore, Maryland* (Baltimore, 1941).

publication, but that was a somewhat premature step and he was soon forced to return to the triweekly status. Not until 1848 did the *Correspondent* finally appear daily.[113]

Friedrich Raine was not only a gifted journalist but also an unusually clever businessman and politician. He was one of the first German journalists in America to abandon the clumsy German system of newspaper publishing and to adapt himself to his American environment. Although his paper appeared in German, its make-up was entirely that of an American paper; that is, the reader's eye was focused on the news column, which presented a quick, short, pregnant account of the news. Now and again Friedrich Raine startled people by a journalistic tour de force, as when he published a German translation of John Tyler's presidential address simultaneously with the publication of the English original. But it was not only in the technical aspect of journalism that he adapted himself quickly. He also had a special gift of quickly acclimating himself mentally and he soon made a place for himself in the political and social structure of the city, the state and the country. He began as a Whig politically, only to change to the Democratic Party at the beginning of the fifties when the Whig party began to break up. Thus he was seldom in opposition to the main current of public opinion. He remained true to the Democrats to the end of his life. He knew how to make contacts and how to use them and so it is no wonder that he gradually established a public reputation in the state such as few other Germans ever attained.

His newspaper, the *Correspondent*, was the paper with the greatest influence on the Germans in Baltimore; it lasted longer than any of the other German newspapers in Maryland. It is difficult to determine the actual political stand of the paper because the *Correspondent* confined itself mainly to the printing of short, objective reports and in the decades before the Civil War seldom printed editorials colored by personal opinions. The *Correspondent* avoided ticklish, controversial subjects and wherever it did have to mention

[113] Only a few numbers of the *Correspondent* from the time before the Civil War are in existence. The earliest available number is that of September 7, 1842. The Society for the History of the Germans in Maryland owns eight numbers for the years 1842-1843, and two of the weekly editions of the *Correspondent* for 1851. (The weekly edition was introduced in 1848.) The Maryland Historical Society has one number from 1846, the Enoch Pratt Library has some odd numbers from the years 1856 to 1859 and the Maryland Historical Society has a complete set from January to June of 1858.

them did so with such a degree of tact and reserve that the result bordered on boredom. The early Whig relationship was soon forgotten; soon the *Correspondent* allied itself to the Democratic Party and remained in its camp until the first World War. Only against the nativist Know-nothings did the *Correspondent* lash out energetically. After 1856 it was in definite opposition to the young Republican Party. In the gathering storm of the great conflict it stood on the side of the South, although it admonished its southern friends to be moderate and prudent. It almost never indulged in press feuds such as those which its competitive papers, the *Demokrat* and *Wecker*, carried on with such glee. The *Correspondent* was much less interested in Europe than was the *Wecker*, but when an occasion arose it took an antireactionary stand, though even this was done with the customary genteel reserve.[114] Indeed, one may certainly not identify him with the opponents of the European reaction. Raine was clever enough to see immediately that the loud anticlericalism of the '48ers would shock a great many of the puritanic, churchly people in America. For that reason he withdrew his paper from the influence of the new liberal immigration.[115]

The very fact that the '48ers were denied the columns of the *Correspondent* led to the founding of their own German paper in Maryland—a paper that was run for decades as the constant opponent and competitor of the *Correspondent*; it was named the *Baltimore Wecker*.[116] The *Wecker* was the product and mouthpiece of the liberal immigrants. Later in this chapter we shall deal more thoroughly with its founder, Carl Heinrich Schnauffer; here we shall say only a few words about the newspaper. Carl Heinrich Schnauffer started the publication in October 1851. From the very beginning the newspaper appeared daily and was read by most of the Turners as well as by all the Germans in Baltimore who definitely supported the ideals for which the '48ers stood. After the death of the founder (1854), his widow took over, and then his brother, Wilhelm Schnauffer, became the editor.

[114] On the occasion of the death of Metternich, the *Correspondent* wrote on June 28, 1858, "In the course of this century no greater sinner has died than Metternich, the evil genius of the Austrian monarchy. . . . He dies unmourned and unwept by those who knew him; he cast unspeakable misery upon millions. . . . Thus dies a statesman who used the unusual abilities which Providence gave him for the ruin of nations."

[115] Miller, op.cit., 8.   [116] Scharf, *Baltimore*, 630. BVG, 303.

The *Wecker* differed fundamentally from its opponent, the *Correspondent*. Politically it was on the side of the Republican Party. During the turbulent 1850's and 1860's it was the only Republican paper in the State of Maryland, and the only paper which expressed radical opinions against slavery, a fact which is even more amazing when one realizes how much courage it required in "Mobtown Baltimore" to swim against the prevailing current of public opinion. The Schnauffers were born fighters. Unlike the Raines, they did not want to report cold, objective facts; they preferred to take a stand in regard to what occurred. For this reason the editorials in the *Wecker* were much more important than in the *Correspondent*, and for this reason also the *Wecker* had much more color and life than its competitor, the Democratic paper. True, the *Wecker* was often too extreme; it was inexorable in its hatred and unbounded in its attacks. When it took the field against the reaction in Germany, the slaveholders of the South or the political influence of the Church, sparks flew and there were no compromises, no conciliation. But in every line one feels that there were people of character behind these ideas, people with convictions that they were ready to proclaim and defend, even if such action brought on the greatest personal and business sacrifices. Of all the German newspapers that appeared in Maryland, the *Wecker* was the most youthful, lively, courageous and freedom-loving.

Only about half of the issues of the *Wecker* which appeared in the decade before the outbreak of the Civil War have been preserved, and only one volume dates from the time when Carl Heinrich Schnauffer himself was still publisher of the paper.[117] One senses the free and vital spirit of the '48ers in every line, whether the subject be political, social or literary. In the earlier volumes one frequently finds poems by C. H. Schnauffer. The literary section is on a fairly high plane; in addition to contributions from the ever-present Louise Mühlbach, who held forth in all the German-American papers in the second half of the nineteenth century, stories are to be found by people of greater reputation, such as Heinrich Zschokke and Berthold Auerbach. A long article on David Friedrich Strauss shows that the *Wecker* informed its countrymen not only about the political, but also about the intellectual heritage

[117] From the pre-Civil War period, the Enoch Pratt Library has the following volumes: July-December 1853; January-June 1856; January-June 1859; January-December 1860.

ALBERT SCHUMACHER (1802-1871)
Baltimore merchant, particularly well-known in the tobacco trade and the shipping business

FRIEDRICH RAINE (1821-1893)
Founder and editor of the biggest Baltimore German newspaper, active in politics, leader of the German-Americans in the latter part of the nine-teenth century

of the German liberal movement. No expression was strong enough to convey their thoughts against the German reactionary governments. If anywhere, it was on this matter that the *Wecker* was uncompromising and ruthless. It even summarily dropped its former hero, Kossuth, when it had reason to believe (1858) that Kossuth through his "narrow-minded Hungarian nationalism had forgotten the great cause of freedom."

In American politics the *Wecker* backed the Republican Party, though it did not hesitate to criticize the party when the occasion arose. The resolutions of the Republican convention in Pittsburgh in 1856, for instance, did not seem to it to be radical enough; the paper would have desired sharper language used against the institution of slavery and against the Know-nothings. Of course the *Wecker* supported Fremont in the presidential campaign of 1856; and during his whole term it heaped ridicule and contempt upon Buchanan.[118] It need hardly be mentioned that the Know-nothings received a few thrusts in almost every number of the paper, and that in the process expressions were coined whose nastiness could be compared only to those of the nativists themselves.[119] The close relations between the *Wecker* and the Turners has already been pointed out.

Overshadowed by the two most widely read daily papers (*Correspondent* and *Wecker*) the remaining German newspapers in existence during the decades before the Civil War played a minor role. There were a great number of them—political, religious and literary periodicals—but they never survived more than a short time. Of most of them we know nothing more than their titles and the year of their appearance; hardly any trace has survived of these journalistic attempts.[120]

Dr. Samuel Ludvigh, who hatched numberless German periodicals and usually was forced to bury them very soon, started several in Baltimore.[121] In 1839 he founded a weekly paper called *Der*

[118] *Wecker*, February 28, 1856. The *Wecker* and the *New Era* in Washington, D.C., were the only newspapers in the South which, in 1856, supported the first Republican presidential candidate.

[119] The *Wecker* compared the position of the Germans in America with that of the Jews in Europe; legally, they had the same rights, but actually there was a prejudice against them everywhere (August 2, 1853).

[120] BVG, 301 ff.

[121] Samuel Ludvigh was born in Günz, Austria, on February 13, 1801. He studied law, traveled extensively in the Orient, was secretary to a German prince who lived in Constantinople and then returned to Austria in 1836. In

Wahrheitsverbreiter (The Truth Spreader), of which we know
nothing but the title. During the following year he spent some time
in the city in order to publish a campaign newspaper for Van Buren,
called *Der Herold*. When Ludvigh returned to America after the
unsuccessful revolution of 1848, he started a periodical which made
his name famous; it was called *Die Fackel* and appeared in Baltimore during the 1850's.[122]

An undertaking similar to the *Fackel* was Samuel Maclea's quarterly periodical published in 1848-1849, *Didaskalia—Vierteljahr-
schrift für Geist, Gemüt und Publizität* (Quarterly for the Mind,
Soul and Public Affairs).[123] In the first article of the first number,

---

various articles he criticized the Austro-Hungarian government, which now
demanded of him that he cease all further criticism in the future. This embittered him so much that he emigrated to America in 1837. In Philadelphia
he was co-editor of *Die alte und die neue Welt* (The Old and the New World),
and then followed his short-lived paper *Der Wahrheitsverbreiter* (Truth
Spreader) and Van Buren's campaign paper in Baltimore. After its early
demise, the print-shop equipment was bought up by Friedrich Raine. *Die
Fackel* (The Torch) appeared in Baltimore until the year 1859; then Ludvigh moved to Cincinnati, where he died in 1869. Ludvigh's main aggressiveness was aimed against the Catholic Church and against slavery. After his return from Europe he founded in 1850 in Baltimore a *Bund für Aufklärung
und sociale Reform* (Society for Enlightenment and Social Reform), but it
apparently was limited to a small circle of radical men—C. Frey, W. Müller,
G. Facius, C. H. Schnauffer. He was undoubtedly a great idealist, though a
little romantic and eccentric. Alex. J. Schem, *Deutsch-amerikanisches Kon-
versationslexikon* (New York, 1874), VI, 657.

L. P. Hennighausen, "Reminiscences of the Political Life of the German-
Americans in Baltimore During 1850-1860," in SHGM, VII, 55 ff. See also
H. A. Rattermann, *Gesammelte Werke*, XII, 220.

[122] The subtitle of the *Fackel* was *Literaturblatt zur Förderung geistiger
Freiheit* (Literary Periodical for the Advancement of Intellectual Freedom).
It was very radical on all social questions and was on a high intellectual plane.
It probably had only a small, select group of readers. Most of the contribu-
tions were by Ludvigh himself. Volume 1852 is in the Wisconsin Historical
Society and Volume 1854 in the Society for the History of the Germans in
Maryland. Cf. *Der Deutsche Pionier*, 1 (1869), 358.

[123] Friedrich Raine was the printer of the periodical, and this leads us to believe that Maclea had come to an understanding with the Raines following
the violent political battles they engaged in during 1843-1845. Franz Löher
is the only one of the contributors to the *Didaskalia* whom we know, other
than the editor himself. There are in existence only four copies of the first
(and probably only) volume of the periodical: Library of Congress, New
York Public Library, Carl Schurz Memorial Foundation Library, and University of Illinois. The four numbers comprise 634 pages. The most important
literary piece of the *Didaskalia*, Samuel Maclea's "Todtentanz," was reprinted
in *Monatshefte*, XXXIX (1947), i, 25-53.

Maclea outlined one of the main purposes of the publication as being to present to the public in its right light the part which the Germans had played in building up the United States. Actually, the scope of the periodical went far beyond this field. Maclea wrote about three-quarters of the text himself, partly literary contributions, such as a story called "Die ersten Kentuckier" (The First Kentuckians), which described the life of a German family among the early pioneers of the wilderness, as well as historical articles such as a description of the war between the United States and Mexico in 1846-1848. Maclea's articles are peppered with quotations from Confucius, Shakespeare, Schiller, Jean Paul, Thomas Moore, Pope, Goethe, Byron, Rückert, Freiligrath, Körner and others, a fact which reveals the high cultural level and wide reading of most of the German liberal refugees of this time. A "Gallery of Famous Men" contains portraits of Steuben, DeKalb, Johann Jacob Astor and Zachary Taylor. The periodical took a lively interest in the revolutionary events in Europe which will be discussed in detail later. Along with the historical articles we also find a few geographical descriptions of the Middle West and discussions of the possibilities for settling in the Mississippi Valley. An essay by Maclea on "Baltimore" (history, population, economics) gives us some otherwise unknown information on the German element in the city. The most valuable literary piece in the magazine is Maclea's dramatic poem "Todtentanz" (Dance of Death), which, along with the poems of C. H. Schnauffer, is among the few commendable literary pieces which the Germans in Maryland produced. Of all that Maclea wrote, "Todtentanz" is by far the best.

We shall mention briefly the titles of the magazines whose names at least we know. Between 1837 and 1840 the German printer Lorenz Schwarz published a newspaper called *Der Freisinnige Beobachter* (The Liberal Observer). According to the meager information that is available, the paper changed its name to *Der Bürgerfreund* (Friend of the Citizen), but we know nothing about the span of its life. According to some sources there was a *Maryland Staatszeitung* in the middle thirties and a *Täglicher Maryland Demokrat* from 1847-1849, but all reports on these journalistic undertakings are very vague.[124] Then there were the *Hirtenstimmen*

---

[124] No one has succeeded in finding even one copy of either of these newspapers. Cf. H. A. Rattermann, *Gesammelte Werke*, XII, 345, 347. Ratter-

(Shepherd's Voices), which were published by a Dr. Kurz from 1842 to 1845. Starting in 1842 there seems to have been a magazine called *Der Lichtfreund* (The Friend of Light).[125] Through indirect indications we know that in Baltimore in the 1840's there must have been a paper appearing weekly and edited by Maximilian Oertel called *Katholische Kirchenzeitung* (Catholic Church Newspaper), and a bimonthly periodical under the direction of Pastor H. Weyl called *Lutherische Kirchenbote* (Lutheran Church Messenger).[126] We know only the title and publisher of a political weekly appearing in the middle of the forties and associated with the Democratic Party; it was the *Maryland Demokrat*, published by J. C. Koch.[127] After a time the publisher changed the newspaper into a scientific and literary weekly called *Minerva*. A small paper, *Das neue Vaterland* (The New Fatherland), founded in 1852 by a Dr. F. Dieffenbach, does not seem to have survived even to its first birthday. In 1853 the *Correspondent* attempted a literary weekly, *Novellen Zeitung* (Story Magazine), and in 1856 a person named L. Wundermann tried an illustrated newspaper, *Der Leitstern* (The Guiding Star), but both undertakings lasted only a short time.[128]

mann reports that the *Täglicher Maryland Demokrat* was owned by Wilhelm Raine Jr., and that the *Bürgerfreund* and later the *Maryland Staatszeitung* were edited by Johann T. Hanzsche and Gustav Adolf Neumann, who later was connected with the beginnings of the *New Yorker Staats-Zeitung*. Cf. *Deutsche Pionier*, xv, 454 f. Sources on these early German papers in Baltimore are so conflicting that it is impossible to establish a clear chronology.

[125] It is mentioned in the *Correspondent* of September 7, 1842. The first number must have just appeared at that time. The magazine is mentioned again in 1850 in Ludvigh's *Fackel*; though it was not orthodox, it still had a religious tone, and for that reason the anticlerical Ludvigh bestowed a few unfriendly adjectives upon it. F. Mühls is mentioned as the publisher of the *Lichtfreund* in 1850.

[126] Maclea mentions both periodicals in his article on Baltimore in *Didaskalia*. He calls the *Katholische Kirchenzeitung* an organ of "crassest Jesuit nature." Maximilian Oertel (born in 1811 in Ansbach, Germany; died 1882 in Jamaica, New York) was at first co-publisher of the first German-Catholic magazine in the United States, the *Wahrheitsfreund* (Friend of the Truth) founded by Archbishop J. M. Henni in 1837. Oertel left the *Wahrheitsfreund* in 1846 and immediately afterwards started the publication of his own paper, the *Katholische Kirchenzeitung*, which appeared in Baltimore from 1846 to 1851. After this Oertel moved the place of publication to New York; the paper was discontinued after Oertel's death. Georg Timpe, *Katholisches Deutschtum in den Vereinigten Staaten von Amerika* (Freiburg, i.B., 1937), 5 f.

[127] Cf. Maclea's essay in *Didaskalia*.

[128] Scharf, *Baltimore*, 629. Chronicles, 107.

Longer life was granted to the *Monatsschrift der Neuen Kirche* (Monthly Paper of the New Church), which Pastor Arthur O. Brickmann published from 1856 until his death in 1883. This same Pastor Brickmann, who belonged to the Swedenborgian New Church, published a *Kinderzeitung* (Children's Newspaper) from 1859 to 1862 in Baltimore.[129] A German-Jewish monthly magazine, *Sinai*, was edited by Dr. David Einhorn from 1856 to 1863.[130] It has already been stated that the *Turner Zeitung* appeared in Baltimore in 1859-1860.

All in all, we know the titles of twenty-five German newspapers that appeared in Baltimore during the four decades between 1820 and 1860; of all of these, only the *Correspondent* and the *Wecker* enjoyed a deep or lasting influence.

The fact that the Germans were able to support in the forties one, and at the beginning of the fifties two, daily German newspapers indicates that their interest in public affairs was constantly growing. From the end of the 1820's on, Germans held more offices in the political life of the city and of the state. Between 1820 and 1860 various German names appeared in the House of Delegates in Annapolis: John Stricker, Mendes Cohen, John Seidenstricker, C. D. Barnitz, Charles Kraft. As Electors of the President, William Frick functioned in 1833 and David Hoffman in 1837 and 1841.[131] In 1836 William Frick became Collector of the Port; later he became a state senator, then chief judge of Baltimore County (1848), and in 1851 first judge of the Superior Court of Baltimore City.[132] Charles F. Mayer was a state senator from 1830 to 1835.[133] From 1826 to 1831 the city of Baltimore had a mayor who was of German descent, Jacob Small.[134] He was particularly interested (he was an

---

[129] Schem, op.cit., note 121, VII, 762.

[130] *Sinai*—"An organ for the recognition and ennobling of Jewry." Einhorn was born in 1809 in Dispeck, Bavaria. In 1855 he was made rabbi of the Har Sinai congregation in Baltimore. His monthly magazine was the voice of radical reform Judaism.

[131] Scharf, *Baltimore*, 194 f.

[132] Hennighausen, *German Society*, 89.

[133] *Cyclopedia*, 711. Charles F. Mayer was an active member of the Whig party. He was president of the Whig convention in 1838.

[134] *Niles Register*, XXXI, 84, 170; XXXV, 129. Griffith, *Annals*, 169, 209, 215, 262, 276. *Municipal Journal*, VII (Baltimore, 1919), 5. (With picture of J. Small.) Schultz, *Freemasonry*, II, 758. Hennighausen, *German Society*, 90. W. F. Coyle, *The Mayors of Baltimore* (Baltimore, 1919), 33 ff. Jacob Small was manager and vice-president of the German Society for several years.

architect by profession) in the construction of public buildings and his regime was politically so clean that at his third reelection the *Niles Register* wrote: "We are glad that a majority of the people . . . reelected a zealous and efficient officer by so handsome a vote. Many changes have taken place in the City Council—a large majority of them for the better."[135] In 1826 two German Jews were elected to the city council of Baltimore—Solomon Etting and Jakob Cohn.[136] In 1831 we find Josua Medtart and Charles F. Mayer as members of the National Committee of the Whig party.[137] Henry Snyder took a prominent part in political affairs from the end of the 1830's.[138] A great many German names are to be found in the history of the early railroad companies which were so important for opening the country. Justus Hoppe was a director of the Baltimore & Susquehanna Railroad from 1829, while Solomon Etting had an important position with the Baltimore and Ohio Railroad, and Benjamin Cohn was connected with the Chesapeake and Ohio Canal.[139] Albert Schumacher's connection with the Baltimore and Ohio Railroad Company has already been mentioned. When the Hungarian patriot, Kossuth, arrived in America in 1851, the mayor of Baltimore sent the publisher of the *Correspondent*, Friedrich Raine, to New York as the official representative of the city to greet Kossuth and invite him to visit Baltimore.[140] Joseph Hecker, a German, was nominated by the Democratic Party in Cecil County for the Maryland Senate, and he was elected by popular vote.[141] In the United States House of Representatives we find Francis

[135] *Niles Register*, xxxix, 138.

[136] This event is remarkable, for it was the first time that Jews were elected to public office in Maryland. A law granting political equality to Jews was passed by the Maryland Legislature in February 1825. *Tercentenary History*, I, 767. Solomon Etting (1764-1847) was a member of a very old Frankfurt Jewish family. Cf. Aaron Baroway, "Solomon Etting," *Maryland Hist. Mag.*, xv (1920), 1-20.

[137] *BVG*, 292.

[138] *Cyclopedia*, 176. Snyder (born in 1802) came of a Pennsylvania-German family; in 1835 he had come to Baltimore, where he bought a hotel. In 1839-1845 he was a member of the city council, in 1845-1849 city collector, 1850-1854 deputy postmaster. Later he was a member of the Maryland Senate for six years and was finally elected president of the senate. He was a member of the Democratic Party.

[139] *BVG*, 292.   [140] *Ibid.*, 282.

[141] *Correspondent*, October 26, 1859, November 7, 1859. The *Correspondent* makes use of this opportunity to prove that the Democratic Party is not unfriendly to foreigners.

Brengle (1843-1845) and Henry W. Hoffman (1855-1857). Grason Eichelberger was Maryland Secretary of State in 1861-1862. Thus, the Germans were showing more courage than in earlier times and were daring to enter the public and political life of the city and the state.

It is not possible to associate the Germans with one political party. We find German names on the side of the Whigs as well as of the Democrats, although perhaps there was in general a stronger tendency toward the Democrats. So vehement and polemic a newspaper as the *Demokrat*, which took a strong interest in the politics of the day, gives us some insight into the political party activities among the Germans. In the beginning of 1844 a German Democratic committee was formed in Baltimore; a few months later we read of a Democratic-Antinativist association.[142] However, the *Demokrat* complained that the meetings were not well-attended and sharply scolded the Germans for their indifference to politics. Through the tirades of the *Demokrat* we also hear of the founding of a German Whig Club which was strongly for Henry Clay and against James K. Polk.[143] Wilhelm Raine, Charles F. Mayer and Gustav Lürmann were apparently very active workers for the Whigs at the beginning of the forties. Raine seems to have considered himself somewhat in the position of representative of the Germans in Baltimore, and for this the *Demokrat*, which was in the other political camp, roundly denounced him.[144]

[142] Samuel Maclea was the secretary of both societies; the presidents were L. Hammer and G. Ott. *Demokrat*, January 6, 13, 20, 1844, and June 15, 1844.

[143] The main leaders of the German Whig club were Wilhelm Raine, Charles F. Mayer and a Mr. Kaylor (Köhler). The club received its chief financial aid from one of the wealthiest German merchants of Baltimore, Gustav W. Lürmann. *Demokrat*, June 8 and 22, 1844. A wealthy German Whig who worked very hard for Henry Clay is said to have remarked (*Demokrat*, October 2, 1844): and if it cost him a fortune he would force every German to vote Whig. Actually, the Whig sympathizers were confined to a numerically small but very influential group of the socially higher-class Germans.

[144] *Demokrat*, January 10, 1844. Raine and the Prussian consul, Brauns, had called a meeting of the Germans for the purpose of endorsing two recommendations to the legislature: (1) that the laws of the state be printed in German, and (2) that the Negro workmen in the state warehouses be discharged and German workmen be hired in their places. The *Demokrat* violently repudiated the undertaking with such expressions as "infamy, arrogance, insolence, selfishness," and was gratified that the resolutions were not signed by

It is unfortunate that with the exception of the nonpolitical *Didaskalia* none of the German newspapers or magazines published between 1844 and 1853 have been preserved, for it was during these years that certain changes in party affiliations took place. The Whig sympathizers among the Germans declined steadily. The Raines, who at the beginning of the forties had made an effort to maintain cordial relations with both sides, gradually noticed that the Whigs were almost exhausted and so this politic family found itself inclining more and more toward the Democratic Party. Around 1850 they must have thrown overboard the last of their Whig sympathy, for from that time on they were consistently Democratic without wavering. The majority of the Germans who had emigrated to Baltimore before 1848 were probably Democratic; and the old German element in Western Maryland was, of course, also Democratic. On the other hand, the newer immigrants who had come after 1848 had at first joined the Democratic Party because for them it was still the most acceptable party, but were now, after 1854, gradually shifting over to the new Republican Party. Here the *Wecker* stepped in as the most enthusiastic advocate of the Republican Party in Maryland. It happened at this same time—in the middle of the 1850's— that the Germans acquired highly intellectual political leaders from among the '48ers, and that American nativism rose to an unexpected degree of aggressiveness against the Germans. This attack stimulated greater political activity and greater unity among the Germans. Unification was encouraged from within and from without; it was desired both by the Germans and by the local party politicians. For the latter, it was simpler to align the whole organization of the Germans on one side or the other through the efforts of a few influential leaders than to deal with hundreds of individuals. The new feeling of the political possibilities, fostered from within and without, hastened the process of joining organizations. In the summer of 1853 the Germans in Baltimore held various meetings in order to discuss the merits of the several candidates. Finally a German-American Convention was constituted whose purpose it was

---

anybody. The matter of the printing was a very transparent business proposal of the Raines, for they owned the largest print shop. The *Demokrat* exclaimed that the Prussian consul was an ardent Whig and "a conceited fool" who had not yet learned that conditions were different in America from what they were in Prussia.

to create more interest among the Germans of the state for political affairs, to give them directives for the elections and in general to wield a certain amount of political influence in the state in favor of the Germans.[145] How long this organization existed and how much it accomplished we do not know. But we may be sure that it aroused to the utmost the ire of the Know-nothings, who were especially strong in Maryland.

We mentioned briefly the importance of the new '48er immigration group for the reorientation of the Germans in the whole country as well as in Maryland along political party lines. In the original plan of this book a break was to be made at the year 1848, and the liberal '48ers were to begin a new chapter. However, it later appeared that such a break would follow the personal inclination of the author, not the actual course of historical development; and the plan was therefore abandoned. The year 1848 does not have the great importance in the history of the Germans in Maryland that it does in the history of the Germans in America. The lines of historical development run in a wide arc here beyond the year 1848, and it would have created an artificial caesura if we had interrupted our account in 1848. However, at the end of this long chapter, which traces the development from the end of the English-American war to the beginning of the Civil War, a few words must be said about the '48ers. They did not usher in a new era in the history of the Germans in Maryland, but without doubt they did bring new elements into the picture.

During the years after 1815, the new tide of immigration was predominantly of a nonpolitical character. The people who came over from Germany came chiefly for economic reasons. Whether they were sons of wealthy Bremen merchant families, such as Albert Schumacher and C. A. Heinecke, or whether they were anonymous poor people from Swabia or Nassau who knew that they would make more money as butchers and bakers in Baltimore than in Heilbronn or Wiesbaden, the majority of them were moved by economic

[145] Wecker, July 16, 20, 21, 1853. Laurence Fr. Schmeckebier, History of the Know Nothing Party in Maryland (Johns Hopkins University Studies, XVII, 4, 5. Baltimore, 1899), 51 f. The German-American Convention finally even sent questionnaires to all candidates for Congress, asking "1. If he is convinced of the justice and necessity of our organization? 2. If he openly pledges himself to represent us in Congress according to the laws of equity and justice without any reference to native-born American citizens?" (Sun, July 4, 1853. American, July 9, 1853.)

motives. Then, beginning in the thirties, people began to appear in Baltimore who had left Germany for ideological reasons, hatred against the reaction, militarism and Prussianism. Christopher Pagels, a manufacturer from Hesse-Kassel who had been guilty of revolutionary activity, left his home and came to Baltimore in 1833, his departure occurring not a day too soon, for almost simultaneously came the news that the Hessian electorate government had sent out a warrant for his arrest.[146] Heinrich Scheib, the pastor, as well as Samuel Ludvigh and Samuel Maclea, the journalists, belong to the very small group of "Grauen," (Grays), pre-'48 liberals, in Baltimore.

The year 1848 arrived. The Germans in Baltimore followed with intense interest the course of the revolutionary events in France and Germany. At the end of March 1848, when the first news of the French February Revolution arrived, a "German Patriotic Meeting" was held; they desired to celebrate properly the event which they rightly interpreted as a precursor of the German revolution. The members decided to send a congratulatory address to the French nation and also to found a permanent association for the furthering of liberal ideas.[147] Shortly after, news of the revolution in Germany came across the sea. By the end of April the liberal elements within the German and French population in the city decided to arrange a large, joint, public announcement and demonstration in honor of the victorious revolution. This tremendous mass meeting, held on the evening of May 3, 1848, in Monument Square, Baltimore, was the high point in the revolution celebrations of that year. The blue-white-red flag of the French and the black-red-gold flag of the

[146] Christopher Pagels later moved to Chevy Chase, Maryland. His son, George H. Pagels, a well-known businessman in Baltimore, became a member of the city council. *Cyclopedia*, 121.

[147] *Sun*, March 31, 1848. Dieter Cunz, "The Baltimore Germans and the Year 1848," *American German Review*, x, i (1943), 30 ff. The resolution which was adopted by the meeting read: "First, to congratulate the French people on the success of their efforts in the cause of liberty; second, commiserating the inhabitants of the Germanic European States and inviting them to throw off the yoke of despotism; third, that the Germans in Baltimore should be active in promoting the spread of republican principles, and should do what they could by subscribing money, and issuing encouraging addresses to their friends in the fatherland." The permanent committee which was created that evening was made up of the following names: William Eyer, Dr. Freitag, Dr. Otto, Dr. Hess, Samuel Maclea, T. Draege, L. Lauer and M. Seeger.

Germans waved beside the Star-Spangled Banner above the heads of the meeting. All of the German societies were represented and among the "vice-presidents" of the meeting are to be found many important German names.[148] On behalf of the Germans Charles F. Mayer spoke in English and Dr. Georg Fein in German. "The doctor who is a political refugee having been banished from Germany on account of his opinions," wrote the *Baltimore American* the next day, "spoke in an animated style, which drew from the Germans present frequent bursts of applause, in which they were joined by the mass of the meeting." And the *Baltimore Sun* states: ". . . his remarks were received with that thorough hearted approbation expressive of the genuine sympathy of the German people with their countrymen in their struggle for liberty."[149] For days the mass meeting was discussed in the Baltimore papers with many friendly comments.

However, it was very soon apparent that the revolution in Germany had been a failure, and not long after the first beaten and pursued German liberals began to arrive as refugees from across the ocean in order to find a temporary haven in America or to seek a permanent home. The year 1848 rang in a new epoch in the history of German immigration in America. Most of these liberal refugees went to the North or the Middle West; because of the political, social and economic structure of the South, they stayed, on the whole, north of the Mason and Dixon Line. Thus, this new liberal immigration was not so important for Maryland as for other states, such as New York, Ohio or Wisconsin. However, quite a number of '48ers came to Maryland; in fact, Baltimore became the farthest southern city with an appreciable number of German '48ers.

The new group of immigrants was characterized by an astonishingly high percentage of distinguished individuals. In this group

[148] Charles F. Mayer, William Frick, Dr. A. Freitag, Philip R. J. Friese, J. P. Eyer, Jacob Hiss, S. Maclea, William Schley, Aaron Hoffman, Charles M. Keyser, Gustav W. Lürmann, Lewis Lauer, S. O. Hoffman, Dr. Friedrich Hess, Henry R. Landermann, Otto Berg, John W. Pentz, J. I. Cohen, Marcus Wolf, John B. Seidenstricker, Charles Myers, Jacob Pappler, John C. Rau, A. Schumacher, Thomas O. Sollers, F. Bredemayer, Ch. W. Lentz, Henry Snyder, Dr. G. C. A. Otto, A. Fischer, F. Raine, Adam Fresch. Besides Charles F. Mayer and Georg Fein, other speakers of the evening included Jacob G. Davies, the mayor of Baltimore, Reverdy Johnson, a Maryland senator, General Sam Houston and Judge LeGrand.

[149] *American*, May 4, 1848. *Sun*, May 4, 1848. Scharf, *Chronicles*, 527.

more than in any other were to be found intellectuals of all the various branches of learning—writers, journalists, professors, physicians and lawyers. Unfortunately, we shall never be able to compile a complete list of the "ideologic immigrants" of the middle of the century, but we do know the names of many of them who, in one way or another, earned respect and esteem.

Upon earlier occasions we have already mentioned a few '48ers, such as Dr. Georg Fein, who founded the Concordia Society; Friedrich Knapp, the principal of the famous school; Gustav Christian Dohme, the chemist, all of whom came over here as political refugees. Dr. Peter Unger, a '48er, was considered one of the best educated and most highly cultivated Germans in Baltimore; he taught German for two years (1855-1857) at City College and later became a journalist.[150] Dr. Adolph Wiesner, one of the most radical German liberals, at the beginning of the 1850's came to Baltimore, where he soon became one of the leaders of the Republican Party.[151] Adalbert J. Volck, who took part in the revolution in Berlin, was forced to flee in 1849; he settled in Baltimore in 1851 and soon acquired prominence even among non-Germans.[152] E. F. M. Fähtz had taken part in the revolution in Austria; he too was forced to flee and after a temporary stay in Baden, Switzerland, and in France and England came to America in 1850, where he started as a teacher in Elkton, Maryland.[153] Johann Straubenmüller had been arrested various times during the turbulent days of 1848; in

[150] *BVG*, 191.

[151] Wiesner was born in Prag in 1815. He took part in the revolution and sat as a delegate from Vienna in the left wing of the St. Paul's church parliament in Frankfurt.

[152] A. J. Volck (1828-1912) was born in Augsburg, Germany. After his participation in the revolution, he came to the United States in 1849. Following a two years' stay in the Middle West, he was called in 1851 as instructor to the Baltimore College of Dental Surgery. He was a charter member of the Maryland State Dental Association and a founder of the Association of Dental Surgeons. *DAB*, xix, 288. *Encyclopedia Americana* (1939), xxviii, 172 f. A full account of his life is given by George C. Keidel in *Catonsville Biographies* published in *Argus* (Catonsville, Md.), October 2 to November 20, 1915.

[153] *Der Deutsche Pionier*, xiv (1882), 115. Fähtz, born in 1823 in Linz, Austria, studied law in Salzburg and Vienna. During the 1850's he was the director of a school in Elkton, Maryland. In the Union army he advanced to the rank of lieutenant-colonel during the Civil War. Later he became an interpreter in the criminal court in Baltimore and was also active in various public offices and private undertakings. He died in Washington, D.C., in 1882.

1852 he came to Baltimore, where for ten years he was a teacher.[154] Georg Geiwitz had fought in the streets of Dresden as a revolutionary and, like the composer Richard Wagner, a fellow enthusiast, had to flee. Geiwitz finally found refuge in Baltimore, where he earned his living as an artist for church and stage painting.[155] Wilhelm Müller also found refuge in Baltimore from political persecution and became a teacher in the school of the Sozialdemokratische Turnverein. One volume of his works has been preserved under the appropriate title, *Radikale Schriften* (Radical Writings).[156] Many former street-barricade fighters from abroad gathered together again in the Turnvereine; of these, Wilhelm Rapp, August Becker and Georg Edward Wiss may be mentioned, each of whom enjoyed renown among the Germans of Baltimore as editors of the *Wecker* and the *Turnzeitung*.[157] The Turnverein was the central

[154] Straubenmüller was born in Schwäbisch-Gmünd in 1814. He taught in various towns in Wuerttemberg before his career as a citizen in Germany was cut short through his political activities. From Baltimore he moved to New York, where he became the director of the Freie Deutsche Schule (Free German School) in 1863. He became very well known in German-American circles through his literary works, especially his Turner poems. His works are listed in G. A. Zimmermann, *Deutsch in Amerika* (Chicago, 1894), 75. Cf. also M. D. Learned, "The German-American Turner Lyric," SHGM, x (1896), 109 ff. W. F. Kamman, *Socialism in German American Literature* (Philadelphia, 1917), 84.

[155] A. E. Zucker, "German Theater in Baltimore," op.cit., 130 f.

[156] The single remaining copy of the volume is in the Library of the Society for the History of the Germans in Maryland: Wilhelm Müller, *Radikale Schriften*, Zweite Auflage, Baltimore, 1852. In both poetry and prose, it preaches materialism and atheism in a manner as radical as it is primitive.

[157] Wilhelm Rapp (1828-1907) had been very active in the revolution of 1848 in Wuerttemberg. For a time he was held prisoner in a fortress, and after a short stay in Switzerland he came to America in 1852. From 1857-1861 and 1866-1872 he was editor of the *Wecker*; later he was for thirty-five years editor of the *Illinois Staatszeitung*. His German translation of the autobiography of Thomas Jefferson appeared in Philadelphia in 1853; in 1857 appeared *An Illustrated Geography of North and South America*, and in 1890 his own autobiography, entitled *Erinnerungen eines Deutsch-Amerikaners* (Memoirs of a German-American), Chicago. DAB, xv, 384. *Deutsch-amerikanische Geschichtsblätter*, vii (1907), 57-61. One of his many addresses, "Abraham Lincoln and Immigrants," is to be found in *Deutsch-amerikanische Geschichtsblätter*, i, 7 ff.

August Becker was born in Biedenkopf, Hesse, 1813, the son of a minister. He was a friend of the Hessian pastor Weidig, whose name became famous in the "Demagogenverfolgung." Becker was in prison for three years and then lived in Switzerland a few years, returning to Germany at the outbreak of the revolution in 1848. However, he had to leave Germany after

organization of this group of people. Many prominent '48ers paid visits to Baltimore during the 1850's and the gala receptions for them were usually held in the Turner Hall. Such men included Friedrich Hecker, Gottfried Kinkel, August Willig, Alexander Schimmelpfennig, Joseph Gerhardt.[158]

We do not mean to imply that the Turnverein was composed only of such decided liberals as Becker, Rapp, Lohmann and Schnauffer. But in the social sphere of the Turners—the small artisans and skilled laborers—the '48ers met with the strongest sup-

---

the fiasco of the liberal revolution. In 1853 he came to Baltimore, where for a few years he was editor of the *Wecker* and energetically disseminated Republican and antislavery propaganda. For three years he took part in the war against the South as a chaplain of the New York Steuben Regiment. Afterwards he worked again for a time on the *Wecker*, but later went to Cincinnati, where he published the *Courrier* and died in 1872. *Berühmte Deutsche Vorkämpfer für Fortschritt, Freiheit und Friede* (Cleveland, 1888), 343. *Deutsche Pionier*, 1 (1869), 283 ff.

Dr. Georg Edward Wiss was born in Bavaria (probably in 1822) but became a naturalized citizen of Prussia. He immigrated to the United States in 1848, with the full consent of the Prussian government. Around 1852 he settled down in Baltimore as a practicing physician. He was a prominent member of the Turnverein, from 1859-1861 one of the editors of the *Turnzeitung*, but in 1861 he resigned this post after a number of violent quarrels. He was a member of the executive committee appointed to look after the choice of the electoral ticket in 1860. In 1861 he applied for a consular post in Germany and was recommended by the Republican candidates for the presidential electors of the City of Baltimore and the State of Maryland. According to the appointment records in the Department of State, he was appointed American consul at Rotterdam, Netherlands, on June 5, 1861, and on July 26, 1861, and served from November 28, 1861, to August 29, 1866. (*Deutsch Amerikanische Turnerei*, 1 [1890], 91, and *New York Herald*, April 27, 1860, p. 10, col. 1.) In 1866 he applied for the position of minister resident in the Hague, but was not appointed. His official dispatches to the Department of State while consul at Rotterdam comprise about four hundred manuscript pages. There are also on file in the National Archives his letters of application and others recommending him. In E. F. Cordell's *Medical Annals of Maryland*, 628 f., he receives only brief mention: "He was a regular graduate of a European medical school and sustained a satisfactory examination before your Board." (*Report of the Board of Examiners of the Western Shore*, June 1, 1850.) In the *Index Catalogue of the Library of the Surgeon-General's Office of the United States Army*, XVI (1895), 514, two of his works are mentioned: *De tenotomia in universum*, 32 pp., Berolini, 1845 (obviously his doctoral dissertation written in Latin) and *The Healing and Preventing of Diphtheria* (Berlin, 1879), 37 pp. One of his essays, "Der Einfluss der Naturwissenschaften auf die Moral." (The Influence of the Natural Sciences on Moral Philosophy) appeared from March 2 to 6, 1858, in the *Wecker*.

[158] L. P. Hennighausen, *Reminiscences, op.cit.*, 55 ff.

port. The wealthy Germans, the Democrats with a Whig past, the rich tobacco dealers of the Germania Club, had little sympathy for the radicalism of the '48ers. The newly arrived intellectual revolutionists and the numbers of the lowest social element in the German population extended to each other the hand of fellowship, ignoring the wealthy, satisfied, upper-class citizenry. Their newspaper was the *Wecker*, their social organization was the Turnverein. We also occasionally hear of another organization, founded in 1853 and betraying clearly the intellectual stamp of the '48ers. It was called the "Bund freier Menschen" (Society of Free Men), whose aims were chiefly anti-clerical and anti-religious.[159]

It would be wrong to assume that the new liberal ideology was confined to the Turners. In a body the Turners were entirely on the side of the '48ers, but of course the liberals also found sympathizers among other German circles in the city. Even in the aristocratic premises of the Germania Club zealous exponents of liberal thought were to be found. The minutes of the club tell little, but we do read that during the eventful year of 1848 discussions in the club house were carried on with such verve and energy that the neighbors raised justifiable complaints; no doubt about it, the liberal side had its defenders in the club. In 1848 the Germania Club, along with the Concordia Society, organized an official reception with honors for the South German revolutionary, Friedrich Hecker.[160] When the Hungarian patriot, Kossuth, came to Baltimore in 1851, he was wildly acclaimed and feted after having been welcomed in New York by Friedrich Raine; almost all of the German societies contributed to the Kossuth fund. The *Didaskalia*, the sole remaining German magazine for the years 1848-1849, indicates how strong was the interest of the Baltimore Germans in the German revolution. Although *Didaskalia* was at first meant to be a literary journal,

[159] *Wecker*, November 15 and 30, 1853. The names of the founders have been preserved as follows: Th. Hielscher, F. Fürst and C. H. Schnauffer. At the end of 1853 the society had about sixty members. It held public meetings every Sunday morning, the choice of day and hour indicating clearly enough its anticlerical stand. At the beginning it agitated strongly against the visit of the Papal Legate Bedini, whose journey was followed with misgivings by many people throughout the country. We do not know how long the "Bund freier Menschen" existed in Baltimore. This society was a nationwide association of German radicals, with local chapters in many cities.

[160] Cf. *Friedrich Hecker und sein Anteil an der Geschichte Deutschlands und Amerikas* (published by the Deutsch-Amerikanische Hecker Denkmal Verein, Cincinnati, 1881).

it dealt even in the second number in detail with the political events in the Old World, and (as we learn from an Editor's Note) it did this upon the express desire of many of its subscribers. Thus, a long article, probably written by Samuel Maclea, describes "Europe, Its Movements and Revolutions." The article embodies the point of view of the most radical group of '48ers, attacking most vehemently the cult of compromise and partial results. A picture of the great German revolutionary, Robert Blum, appears at the beginning of the number and sets the tone of the article which ends with the words: "May every drop of his spilled blood awaken a new fighter for freedom; then Germany can count on having a better future."[161]

The most important figure among the '48ers in Baltimore was Carl Heinrich Schnauffer.[162] He was born on July 4, 1823, in Heimsheim near Stuttgart and because of his father's early death received only inadequate schooling, becoming an apprentice in a trading firm in Mannheim in 1842. Here he met two people who had a decisive influence upon his life—Friedrich Hecker and Gustav von Struve, two of the most important liberals in the Grand-Duchy of Baden. In 1846, probably with the assistance of his magnanimous and understanding employer, J. M. Tunna, he managed to spend some time studying at the University of Heidelberg. His first poetic attempts fall in the Mannheim and Heidelberg period; they aroused the unwelcome attention of the state censor. From 1847 Schnauffer belonged to the regular contributors to the liberal *Mannheimer Abendzeitung*. In 1848 he re-echoed Hecker's call to arms. With the revolutionists he took part in an unsuccessful battle near Freiburg, was afterwards forced to flee and spent some time in Alsace and in Switzerland. He worked for a few months on Hecker's news-

---

[161] *Didaskalia* (1849), 251. The following quatrain printed at the end of the article is characteristic for the magazine as a whole:

> Nur die sind des Jahrhunderts Glanz,
> Die Menschenglück erwerben.
> Nur diese schmückt ein Lorbeerkranz,
> Die für die Freiheit sterben.

[162] *DAB*, xvi, 444. The best biographical sketch of him is the article "Carl Heinrich Schnauffer," by A. E. Zucker, *SHGM*, xxiv, 17 ff. See also the *Jahrbücher der deutsch-amerikanischen Turnerei*, published by Heinrich Metzner (New York, 1892), I, 130 ff. G. A. Zimmermann, op.cit., 42. Clement Eaton, *Freedom of Thought in the Old South* (Durham, N.C., 1940), 228. Martin Drescher, "Carl Heinrich Schnauffer," *Die Glocke* (Chicago, June 1907), II, 164-66. W. F. Kamman, *Socialism in German-American Literature* (Philadelphia, 1917), 87.

CARL HEINRICH SCHNAUFFER (1823-1854)
Liberal Forty-eighter, writer, poet, and journalist, who fled Germany after
the collapse of the revolutionary movement

OTTMAR MERGENTHALER (1854-1899)
Engineer, who won fame through his revolutionary invention in the printing field—the Mergenthaler linotype machine

paper, *Volksfreund* (Friend of the People). After another engagement between the revolutionists and the state troops he was taken prisoner and transported to Prussia. He succeeded in escaping and again traveled by way of Strassburg to Switzerland. The Swiss government was under pressure of the Holy Alliance. What happened a generation before to Charles Follen happened now to Schnauffer; in April 1850 the Swiss government was forced to take action against Schnauffer. He was forcibly deported to France. A short time later we find him in England; in 1851 he left Europe. He followed Elise Moos, a girl whom he had loved in Mannheim in his youth and who had emigrated to Maryland with her family. The marriage took place shortly after his arrival in Baltimore. Baltimore remained his home to the end of his life, September 4, 1854. Here he founded his famous newspaper, the *Baltimore Wecker*, which outlived its founder for many decades. We have already indicated Schnauffer's connection with the Turners and described his journalistic efforts. A few words will be devoted to his literary works.

In Schnauffer poet and pamphleteer are hardly to be separated. Even when he writes poetry Schnauffer is still interested in politics. Whether he writes an editorial for a newspaper or a historical drama, we always hear the accents of the freedom-loving '48er. His first poetic attempts draw their inspiration directly from the revolutionary events of the year 1848. Of his earliest works we know only the titles through indirect mention of them: *Gedichte* (Poems), *Studentenbriefe* (Letters of a Student), *Schilderungen des Flüchtlingslebens* (Life of an Exile), *Neue Lieder für das deutsche Volk* (New Songs for the German People), *Alexander VI* (a tragedy), *Veronica* (a play). At the beginning of his exile, he started a cycle of poems which were later published under the title of *Totenkränze* (Funeral Wreaths). *Totenkränze* is a collection of memorial poems, short, poetic orations at the graves of the martyrs of the German revolution.[163] It was this collection which gave the

[163] The first volume *Gedichte* (Mannheim, 1846) was dedicated to his friend, Gustav von Struve. The *Neue Lieder*, with an introduction by Friedrich Hecker, were published by F. Hollinger in Rheinfelden (Switzerland), 1848. The only copies of these volumes still extant are in the Zentralbibliothek Zürich. The first editions of the *Totenkränze* were published in Rheinfelden and Bern; the fourth edition, of which three copies are extant, appeared in

author the flattering by-name of "Tyrtæus of the Baden Revolution."

During the three short years which were granted him to live in America a series of additional poems came from Schnauffer's pen. They appeared in the literary section of the *Wecker*, and not until twenty-five years after Schnauffer's death were they published in a collection entitled *Lieder und Gedichte* (Songs and Poems).[164] The range of subject matter is enlarged in this collection; here we find nonpolitical poems as well as those of political nature. Many of the purely lyrical stanzas express the emotion of homesickness, the longing for Germany. Among the German-Americans, Schnauffer became known especially for his Turner songs. They are consciously placed on a simple folk level and for a long time they had the effect of true folk songs among the Germans in America.[165] The political poems make up a large part of the collection and are undoubtedly the most valuable part of it. The basic theme of the German revolution—the great dream of an internally and externally free German republic and of the liberation of all peoples—appears in ever new variations. Schnauffer's literary force appears most impressively in the political songs. Here he is most successful in his word pictures and here are to be found the most pregnant verbal formulations. Perhaps his greatest strength lies in short political epigrams. Only rarely either before or since his time has the essence of freedom been expressed in such vivid, precise and convincing form as in Schnauffer's concise, steely, optimistic epigram:

> *Die Freiheit ist ein Diamant,*
> *Der nie wie Glas zerschellt,*
> *Wie oft er auch der zagen Hand*
> *Des armen Volks entfällt.*

Baltimore in 1851, printed by Theodor Kroh in the printshop of the *Baltimore Herold*.

For additional information on Schnauffer's early years, cf. Werner Näf, *Die Schweiz in der deutschen Revolution* (Frauenfeld 1929), 109, and Hans Gustav Keller, *Die politischen Verlagsanstalten und Druckereien in der Schweiz 1840-1848* (Bern, 1935), 115 f.

[164] The volume appeared in 1879 in Baltimore, published by the printers of the *Wecker* and edited by the poet's brother, Wilhelm Schnauffer. Various poems from the *Totenkränze* were reprinted and the collection also includes some of the unpublished poems which the author had left. Only a few copies of *Lieder und Gedichte* are still in existence.

[165] Marion D. Learned, "The German American Turner Lyric," in *SHGM*, x, 109 ff. Some of the Turner poems were set to music by Charles Lenschow.

In addition to the poems we also have a drama by Schnauffer, *König Carl I. oder Cromwell und die englische Revolution.*[166] After his arrival in England, Schnauffer had found refuge for a while at the estate of an English aristocrat whom he had known during his student days at Heidelberg—Lord Thomas A. Fothergill. His friend had turned Schnauffer's attention to the history of the English revolution, "the mother of all the later revolutions," as Fothergill called it. During his stay at the estate in the county of York, Schnauffer had begun to gather material for his historical drama, and before immigrating to America he sent the first act to his friend. After his arrival in Baltimore he was forced to abandon his plan for a time because of the pressure of everyday affairs, but in the beginning of 1854 he sent the completed drama with a dedication to "Thomas Fothergill, Esq." to England.

No matter what Schnauffer attempted, he always came back to the German revolution. Even *Cromwell* was written with an eye to German events. Schnauffer's preface to the drama leaves no doubt about this: "While doing justice to by-gone times I wanted to be useful to the present. 'Thus it should be done!' is the theme of my play." He sends his call out to the Germans, showing them the English people who sent their tyrants to the scaffold. If the Englishmen once beheaded a despotic king, why can you not do it?

We do not know whether Schnauffer's *Cromwell* was ever produced on the stage. We know that in the last months of his short life he started a second historical drama, *Washington,* but we know nothing of it except the title.[167] Through a newspaper notice we have learned that he also wrote a short play, apparently of one act, entitled *Christ und Jude* (Christian and Jew). From the brief article it appears that the play followed the Lessing ideal of tolerance; not a line of it has survived.[168]

It would be interesting to discover whether and to what degree America introduced a new note in Schnauffer's poems. Not much may be said on the matter, for we have no chronological list that would indicate when the various poems were written. Apparently,

[166] *Cromwell,* as the play is usually called, appeared on January 1, 1854, in Baltimore, published by the author and printed in the print shop of the *Wecker.* Only three copies of the drama have survived.

[167] L. P. Hennighausen, *Reminiscences, op.cit.,* 56.

[168] In the *Wecker* of February 5, 1856, a production of the play in Baltimore is mentioned.

most of his homesick poems were written after his arrival in America. As with most immigrants, so it happened to him that in the new surroundings the picture of that which was left behind suddenly becomes greatly intensified and constantly occupies the soul. In the last year before his death may be found a few small indications that the surroundings of his new home were beginning to supply inspiration and material for his writings.[169] It seems that for Schnauffer the more firmly his newspaper became established, the more he was drawn into the life of the new country through his journalistic activities, and the more definitely was he able to shake off his early mood of resignation and nostalgia. The fight for the abolition of slavery was beginning to appear on the political horizon. Here were problems whose dignity could well be compared to those of the '48ers. If Schnauffer had lived longer, he would undoubtedly have fought under Lincoln's banner, for the Union. Hecker's call to the battle against slavery in America would have been taken up by him just as enthusiastically as he had once taken up Hecker's battle cry against the reaction in Germany in 1848. We can be sure that Schnauffer, like most of the '48ers and especially the Turners among them, would have known how to incorporate his liberal impetus into the realities of American life. Not Schnauffer's poems but his editorials indicate that his eyes had turned away from the past and were contemplating the future, and that his place of exile had become a home. The mere fact that he had contemplated writing a play about Washington indicates that his American environment seemed to him worthy of poetic effort.

If we attempt once more to characterize Schnauffer's literary works, we shall discover as its most important characteristic that poetry was for him almost always a means to an end.[170] For him the stage was chiefly a pulpit from which to preach the gospel of the liberal revolution. There are to be found only a few verses of

[169] There is a poem in the *Wecker* for December 3, 1853, which sings of the heroic life of the American pioneers on the border. In the *Wecker* of October 22, 1853, there is a poem glorifying the famous Koszta affair, a diplomatic incident in which the American government intervened with the reactionary Austrian officials on behalf of a liberal refugee. Cf. *Dictionary of American History*, III, 217.

[170] For a more extensive evaluation of Schnauffer's literary efforts and for samples of his poetry, see Dieter Cunz, "Carl Heinrich Schnauffers literarische Versuche," in *Publications of the Modern Language Association of America*, LIX, ii (1944), 524-39.

purely poetic nature, relaxed and relieved of the daily strain of politics. His poems move in the literary tradition of Ernst Moritz Arndt, Theodor Körner, Georg Herwegh and Ferdinand Freiligrath; his drama shows the influence of Schiller. *Cromwell* is more than the work of a mere dilettante; its style and meter show that Schnauffer had mastered the tools of the literary trade. The drama is interesting because of its political teaching and because of its revolutionary theme. Really poetic material will not be found in it. One thing is evidenced by the drama as well as by the poems, by the editorials and every line that came from Schnauffer's pen or comment we have on him: he was one of the purest and most upright of characters and one of the bravest and most convincing fighters for the cause of freedom on either side of the ocean. What Carl Schurz is for the Americans of German descent on the whole, Carl Heinrich Schnauffer is for the German element in Maryland; he is the personification and symbol of the great and eternal spirit of 1848. In the history of liberalism in Germany and in America the mention of his name always commands respect.

Glancing back over this long chapter, we shall see what a motley, variegated throng the group of people represent whom we gather together under the designation "the German element in Maryland." At the end of this epoch, around 1860, the old stock in Western Maryland had become almost entirely Americanized. In Baltimore the constantly renewed stream of immigrants had markedly retarded the process of Americanization. Though they willingly adapted themselves to American ways, they were still consciously and preferably German, an attitude strengthened by the hatred of foreigners spread by the Know-nothings. But even this new group of immigrants that appeared in Baltimore was by no means unified or homogeneous. It comprised the most extreme types with violent political feuds and the widest social differences.

Only seldom was it possible to unite all these divergent groups so that they could appear together as "the Germans in Baltimore." The Steuben celebration of 1858 was such an occasion.[171] It was

---

[171] BVG, 26 ff. In connection with the Steuben celebration, the Baltimore Germans began raising money for a Steuben monument. However, since they were not able to collect more than $2000 and since the Civil War interfered with the project, they decided in 1867 to spend the money for a Steuben portrait. The order was carried out by a German painter in Baltimore, Ludwig

hoped that by forcefully drawing the attention of the public to General Steuben, who immediately after his arrival in America re-organized the American army and then rendered valuable assistance at the birth of the young nation, the nativists and Know-nothings who were trying to hinder immigration and naturalization could be made ridiculous. All the Germans were united in the battle against the Know-nothings. But more impressive than this common defense demonstration against the nativists was a purely German and thus less constrained jubilee—the celebration in honor of the one hundredth birthday of the German poet, Friedrich von Schiller.[172] Schiller was one of the few common denominators on which all the divergent German groups could unite. He appealed to the conservative, upper-class people for sentimental, national, German reasons, and to the liberal '48ers, Turners and lower social classes because of his revolutionary fervor. In 1859, when it was decided to honor Schiller, the quarrels between the *Correspondent* and the *Wecker*, between Democrats and Republicans, between the elegant merchant's club and the plebeian Turnverein, between churchgoers and atheists, between Protestants and Catholics, all were forgotten. Since the days of Charles Follen, Schiller had always been especially beloved and admired by the Germans in America.[173] Schiller was perhaps the only subject upon which all the Germans in Baltimore and elsewhere could agree. Thus the Schiller jubilee of 1859 fittingly stands at the end of this chapter as the most impressive concerted

---

Enke. When the portrait was finished, it was placed in the German Orphan Home, where it remained until the 1930's. Thereafter the portrait was preserved in the exhibition hall in the foot of the Washington Monument in Baltimore. Cf. Ernst C. Linden, *Gen.-Major von Steuben, Das Steuben Fest und das Steuben-Denkmal in Baltimore, Md.* (Baltimore, 1878).

[172] Reports on the Schiller celebration in *Correspondent*, November 10 and 11, and in the *Sun*, November 11, 1859. Schiller's "Lied von der Glocke" and "Wallensteins Lager" were performed. A literary contest was held for the best poem about Schiller; the first prize winner was Johann Straubenmüller, who was mentioned previously and who was very helpful in the Turner movement in Baltimore. The Turners in Washington performed Schiller's "Die Räuber" for the Schiller celebration. A few of the poems which were submitted for the contest in Baltimore were published in a pamphlet of which the Society for the History of the Germans in Maryland owns one copy, called *Erinnerung an die Feier des hundertjährigen Schiller-Jubiläums in Baltimore* (Baltimore, 1859).

[173] Elwood C. Parry, *Friedrich Schiller in America* (Philadelphia, 1905).

effort in the history of the Germans in Maryland. It was one of those rare events which united the representatives of all the many colorful and varied German groups in a single endeavor.

Into the midst of the preparations for the Schiller jubilee burst the news of John Brown's raid on Harper's Ferry, the first indication of the approaching great storm.

VIII. THE CIVIL WAR YEARS

N PREVIOUS chapters we have pointed out that the Germans figured not only as voters but also as active politicians in the political parties of the United States in general and of the State of Maryland in particular. Germans and people of German descent were to be found among the Federalists as well as among the Democrats and Whigs. Since the end of the 1820's, however, one political organization had become increasingly attractive to all immigrants and especially to the Germans: the Democratic Party. More and more the struggle between the Democratic Party and the Whig Party was identified with the struggle of the little man against wealth. The broad masses, aroused by the ideals of "liberty and equality," flocked to the camp of the Democrats. More than any of the other political groups, the Democratic Party had avoided nativistic tendencies and had thereby attracted the immigrants, for they were faced with the same problems as the "common man," who comprised the basic voting stock of the party.

For a long time the majority of the Germans were faithfully devoted to the Democratic Party, and they had good reason to be. All they had obtained in their struggle against the nativists and Know-nothings had been achieved with the help of the Democratic Party, which through all the years had shown a special interest in the immigrants.[1]

In the beginning, the German "Forty-eighters" were on the side of the Democrats too; the principles of Jefferson and Jackson were their own. Their attitude changed, however, as the slavery issue was pushed more and more into the foreground of political discussion. The liberal German refugees were not willing to make the slightest compromise on this question; they were abolitionists to the core.

In regions with old German settlements, most of the conservative German farmers remained faithful to the old Democratic Party, with the mental reservation that they themselves neither theoretically nor practically wanted to have anything to do with slavery. They did not own any slaves; they avoided making an issue of the problem and thereby maintained their connection with the Demo-

[1] Ernest Bruncken, *German Political Refugees in the United States During the Period from 1815-1860* (Milwaukee, 1904), 47.

cratic Party to which they had been attached through generations. This point of view developed in a quiet, unobtrusive manner, in keeping with the mentality and slow temper of the German farmers. It was different in the cities, where the Forty-eighters stepped into the picture—active, intellectual, politically trained orators and journalists, who for ideological reasons would rather give up traditional party connections than yield an inch in their basic political convictions. This group could hardly be overlooked. Although comparatively small numerically, they very soon pushed themselves into the limelight of the political stage. The passionate fire with which these new political leaders of the Germans adopted and propagated the program and platforms of the newly founded Republican Party was completely new in the history of German immigration. Never before had German newcomers become involved so quickly and taken sides so vehemently in the rough and shrewd game of politics.

Some writers considered the conflict between the North and the South which led to the Civil War to be the result of the divergence of a democratic and an aristocratic republic. Taken from this point of view, for the majority of the new German immigrants there could be no doubt whatever as to which side they should join. The liberal German immigrants, after having undergone all the difficulties and hardships of emigration, would scarcely have felt inclined, now that they were on this side of the Atlantic, to fight for the preservation of the aristocratic landowners of the South. The concept of slavery stood in sharpest contrast to their liberal and progressive ideas. Naturally they knew nothing of the specifically American background—the economic conditions that for a certain period had made slavery understandable and pardonable. What they did observe was the horror of slavery as judged from the standpoint of their ideals and theories.

The constitutional aspects of this struggle left these Germans cold. Older Americans were influenced—frequently in favor of the South—by the fact that the conflict hinged, among other things, on the question as to whether the individual state could act as it pleased or whether it must surrender important rights to the federal government. German immigrants of the nineteenth century cared little about "states' rights"; in fact, they tended to oppose the principle because it appeared to be tantamount to splitting the nation into numerous petty states, a phenomenon that had had a pernicious effect on the course of German history. For them the United States was an entity; it made no difference to them whether they lived in Pennsylvania, Wisconsin or Texas, as long as they could live according to the ideals for whose preservation they had undertaken the long journey to a foreign land.

In addition to the idealistic motives, there were purely economic reasons to win the Germans to the side of the North. In general, the Southern plantation owners were opposed to immigration. They had no conception of the high cultural value of European immigration. The economic system of the South did not require new blood, for it was based on mass production by unskilled labor. The social structure in the South supported a relatively small top class; there were only about 2300 large plantations whose slave populations numbered between 100 and 1000.[2] The middle class was very small and quite insignificant. Hence there was no social sphere, except in the cities, where a German immigrant might win a position for himself. Especially for the small farmer of German stock, who contributed so much to the winning of the West, there was no room in the economic system of the South. This applied also to the new territory of the southwestern states just opening up at this time. Every sensible farmer knew that his laboriously conquered farm land would lose enormously in value if a plantation worked by Negroes could be established on the land adjoining it.

These idealistic, practical and emotional considerations constituted the main reasons (although, of course, there were various minor ones) why the majority of the Germans in America joined the side of the North in the Civil War.

This attitude not only brought new allies to the cause of the Union, but also ultimately proved extremely useful to the newcomers among the Germans.[3] Most of the Forty-eighters who had fled because of the German Revolution at first considered their stay in America strictly temporary. Only reluctantly did they learn English, and they did little or nothing to acquaint themselves with American conditions; there seemed no reason to do so, since many of them hoped shortly to return to the Republic of Germany. Carl Schurz was one of the very few to follow a different course. Most

[2] A. E. Parkins, *The South, Its Economic-Geographic Development* (New York, 1938), 206.

[3] Cf. Wilhelm Kaufmann, *Die Deutschen im amerikanischen Bürgerkrieg* (München, 1911), 101 ff.

of the German radicals maintained in their relationship to the new country a tone of carping criticism toward everything. This sterile, negative attitude was the reason why many of them, far from progressing materially and intellectually, found themselves in a sort of blind alley. When, after a few years, they became aware that they would have to establish themselves permanently in this country because there was not the slightest chance for the revival of liberal ideas in Germany, their despair and gloom was great. They considered the fight for their ideals a total loss. Furthermore, most of them had by this time exhausted their financial reserves without having gained any footing in the social or economic structure of America.

At this very time, around the year 1854, when the danger of moral and intellectual decay was greatest for the Forty-eighters, the antislavery struggle entered its final and decisive phase. An entirely new and welcome field of activity for liberal German hotheads thus opened up. The old humanitarian ideals they had vainly fought to realize in their fatherland could now be fitted into the scheme of current American politics. They arose from the rut of emigrant cliques; through their agitation against slavery they got into touch for the first time with the American people and with American conditions, and learned to know, to love and to struggle for their adopted country. The significance of the antislavery movement for the Forty-eighters lies in the fact that a burning question of current American politics touched the very core of their natures, and enabled them to find a bridge leading from the dry ideas and theories of their past to a responsible, useful activity in the present.

This explanation refers particularly, of course, to the North and the northern part of the Middle West. The only Atlantic state south of the Mason and Dixon Line in which the ideals of the Forty-eighters were carried over into American politics and in which they played a part in the decision of the Civil War was Maryland.[4]

Since Maryland lies on the borderline between North and South, the attitude toward the issues of 1860 was far from unanimous there. This state reflected in a microcosm the situation as it existed in the entire country. The tobacco plantation owners in the southern part of the state stood opposed to the independent farmers of the

---

[4] For the special situation of the Germans in Texas, see Ella Lonn, *Foreigners in the Confederacy* (Chapel Hill, N.C., 1940), 417 ff.

northern and northwestern counties who raised grain and cattle. Between these two sections lay the only metropolis of the state, Baltimore, which belonged economically to the North through its great industrial development, but socially and intellectually was very closely linked with the South.[5]

In the South it was taken for granted that Maryland was Democratic and favorably inclined toward secession. Everyone in the South believed that the state would join the Confederacy as soon as Confederate troops entered its territory. This proved to be true only in part. It was undoubtedly the case as far as the southern counties and the Eastern Shore were concerned. However, on their first visit to Western Maryland in 1862, the Confederates were annoyed and surprised to find that feeling was definitely divided, with a considerable majority favoring allegiance to the Union. The two counties which most energetically opposed secession were Frederick and Washington, the very counties that contained the oldest and largest settlements of German stock.

To be sure, from the point of view of party politics, this region was Democratic; in the election of 1860 there was but a small scattering of votes for Lincoln.[6] Breckinridge was particularly popular among the Germans; leaflets printed in German hailing Breckinridge "as the enemy of Know Nothingism" were distributed in Frederick. The press of this region expressed frank regret concerning Lincoln's election, but was far from considering this a cause for secession. A large Union meeting was held in the town of Frederick on December 15, 1860, and was followed a few days later by a big, county-wide meeting "for the preservation of the Union."[7] The names of the leading men at these meetings show that they were of good old Maryland-German stock: Haller, Eberts, Baer,

---

[5] Cf. Dieter Cunz, "The Maryland Germans in the Civil War," *Maryland Hist. Mag.*, xxxvi (1941), 394-419. The author is indebted to an unpublished study by Henrietta Louise Krone, "The Germans in Maryland During the Civil War," special honor work, Goucher College (1942).

[6] The results of the voting in Washington County were: Bell, 2567; Breckinridge, 2475; Douglas, 283; Lincoln, 95. Williams, *Washington County,* 304. In Frederick County: Bell, 3617; Breckinridge and Douglas, 3609; Lincoln, 103. T. J. C. Williams, *Frederick County,* 364. The Frederick *Examiner* (October 10, November 7, 1860) described a German election meeting for Breckinridge as follows: "It was a queer sight; the spectacle of a political meeting, where nothing but a foreign tongue was spoken, was an unusual one here."

[7] Williams, *Frederick County,* 364 ff.

Biser, Cramer, Eichelberger, Brengle, Snyder. Similar meetings were organized in Hagerstown after the election and after the outbreak of the war, and we find among the most ardent fighters for the Union men called Daniel Weisel, Daniel Startzmann, and Henry Dellinger—all purely German names.[8] Indeed, it was a descendant of an old German family who after Lincoln's call for troops in 1861 organized the first regiment of soldiers from Frederick County: Captain B. H. Schley, who was later advanced to the rank of major.[9] Thomas E. Mittag, of German descent, was the owner of the Western Maryland newspaper which stood most emphatically for the preservation of the Union, The Herald and Torchlight of Hagerstown. It invariably referred to the Confederacy as "the hellish rebellion" and frequently expressed the view that the steps undertaken by Lincoln's government against the Secessionists were far too feeble.[10]

Of course, there were also German names among the minority sympathetic toward the South in these two "German counties." In Hagerstown a Colonel George Schley belonged to the leaders of the Peace Party, a group consisting almost exclusively of camouflaged Secessionists.[11] The organ of this Peace Party, The Hagerstown Mail, was edited by Daniel Dechert, a man of pure Pennsylvania-German stock. His articles, no less violent than those of the Herald, led to his arrest and a jail sentence of six weeks. After this experience his tone became somewhat milder, but not sufficiently conciliatory for the Unionists, for in the course of an anti-Secessionist riot the office of the Mail was attacked and plundered.[12] It is interesting to note that the Germans in Western Maryland had by this time become so completely acclimated that some of them even engaged in nativistic excesses. The New Citizen, a small Secessionist paper in Frederick published by John W. Baughman, a man of German

---

[8] Williams, Washington County, 306. J. Thomas Scharf, History of Western Maryland (Philadelphia, 1882), 216. Other German names appearing at Union meetings in Hagerstown, Keedysville, Middletown (all in Western Maryland) were: Spigler, Sprecker, Kitzmiller, Rohner, Christmann, Lantz, Ecker, Christ, Hoppe. Cf. Scharf, 197 ff.

[9] This Frederick regiment fought throughout the entire course of the war.

[10] Williams, Washington County, 307. The following is a striking sentence characterizing the attitude of this paper during the year 1860: "It is our duty as Southern men to hold back secession until the sober thought of the North can be put into operation for the preservation of the Union."

[11] Williams, Washington County, 304.

[12] Ibid., 317.

descent, commented on the government of the Confederacy: "This new Government . . . has been duly and formally established by free, brave, intelligent, native born Americans—sons of the Sirs of 1776."[13] From Middletown, Maryland, came the report of an enduring enmity between two German families, the Riddlemosers and the Crouses, the one in sympathy with the North and the other with the South.[14] The Reverend P. B. Schwartz of the Frederick old German-Reformed church was warned by a church member, Christian Eckstein, that he would be forced to leave town if he continued to pray for Lincoln—another incident that proves there were Germans on both sides of the political fence.[15]

In general, however, the attitude of Western Maryland was pro-Union.[16] The story of Barbara Fritchie, who, according to Whittier, fearlessly hung out the Union flag in the face of the Confederate troops, is certainly more legendary than historical, yet it characterizes in a striking way the prevailing mood of Frederick.[17] Significantly, in the previously mentioned German-Reformed church were to be found the most active followers of the Union cause; in August 1861 fifty women members formed a "Ladies' Relief Association," to

[13] Quoted from *The Maryland Union*, April 4, 1861. *The Maryland Union* adds: "The above quotation shows that the *Citizen* has turned Native American, and we invite the special attention of the hundreds of honest and worthy naturalized citizens of this vicinity, upon whom the *Citizen* has turned its back, to this additional manifestation of ingratitude towards its old political companions." John W. Baughman was arrested in July 1861.

[14] J. H. Apple, "The Border Woman," in *The Pennsylvania German*, xi (1910), 300 ff.

[15] *Examiner*, August 7, 1861.

[16] Wentz, *Lutheran Church of Frederick*, 233 ff. The municipal election in Cumberland shows clearly the steady increase of the Union Party in Allegany County. The same trend is illustrated by the election to the Maryland legislature of the Unionist delegate, Fiery, from Washington County. George L. P. Radcliffe, *Governor Thomas H. Hicks of Maryland and the Civil War* (Johns Hopkins Studies, Baltimore, 1901), 94.

[17] Barbara Fritchie (1766-1862) was the daughter of Germans, Nicholas Hauer and his wife, nee Catherine Zeiler. Hauer immigrated to Pennsylvania in 1754 and in 1770 settled in Frederick. *National Cyclopedia of American Biography*, 113; Williams, *Frederick County*, 378; *The Pennsylvania German*, iv (1903), 339 ff.; J. H. Apple, "Barbara Fritchie," *Pennsylvania German*, viii (1907), 336 ff.; *New York Times*, December 4, 1927; *Baltimore Sun*, January 17, 1937. For the case of Barbara Fritchie, see Dorothy M. and William R. Quynn, "Barbara Fritchie," *Maryland Hist. Mag.*, xxxvii (1942), 227-54, and 400-13. It is the most extensive and the first sober, critical investigation of the Maryland heroine, telling the story of the growth of the legend and sharply discriminating between truth and fiction.

take care of sick and wounded soldiers.[18] When, on September 7, 1862, the Confederate general, Stonewall Jackson, attended the Sunday service of the German-Reformed church in Frederick, his presence did not deter the preacher, the Reverend Mr. Zacharias, from saying a prayer for the President of the United States "in a firm voice."[19] Henry Lewis Steiner, one of the most prominent citizens in Frederick, worked incessantly for the cause of the Union.[20] He took charge of the enlistments of troops and served later as chief inspector of the Sanitary Commission in the Army of the Potomac. After the abolition of slavery he was especially interested in the organizing of schools for colored people in all parts of the state. Peter Lugenbeel, a merchant from Unionville in Frederick County, was elected to the Maryland House of Delegates on the Republican ticket; when the Confederates pushed up towards Gettysburg he had to endure many inconveniences because of his pro-Northern sympathies.[21] In 1864, Hagerstown sent a Republican delegate to the Maryland Constitutional Convention—Peter Negley, a banker of German and Swiss descent.[22] A quotation from the memoirs of the most famous German soldier on the Southern side, Colonel Heros von Borcke, is very illuminating. He relates that during the days when Confederate troops were in Western Maryland he once observed some Germans sitting in an inn, smoking and drinking. "I am quite sure that most of them were decided Yankee sympathizers, but as a gray uniform was right among them, and many others not far off they talked the hottest secession."[23] Though this testimonial is not altogther flattering to the Germans in Frederick, it shows clearly that even the Confederates no longer had the slightest doubt regarding the Union sympathies of the Germans in Western Maryland.

Some quotations from an unpublished diary of Jacob Engelbrecht (1797-1878), a citizen of Frederick, may illustrate the feelings of the German element in the western counties. On November

[18] *Examiner*, August 28, 1861; October 2, 1861.
[19] Frank Moore, *The Rebellion Record* (New York, 1861-1868), v, 607 (Document 202).
[20] *Cyclopedia*, 617. Steiner became a Senator (Republican) in 1871.
[21] *Cyclopedia*, 136.
[22] *Ibid.*, 379. Negley, an ardent Union man, later became assistant treasurer of Baltimore City.
[23] Heros von Borcke, *Memoirs of the Confederate War of Independence* (New York, 1938), I, 190.

17, 1860, Engelbrecht wrote: "As soon as the election of Abraham Lincoln to the Presidency was known, the South Carolineans, & Allabamaens were ready to seceed from the Union of the U. States and at this time they are making wonderful preparation to leave this glorious Union. For my own part I say go as quick as you please . . . the sooner they go the better for the piece & quiet of our Country." On December 21, 1860, after the secession of South Carolina, we read: "Thank you, Gentlemen, you have been domineering long enough, and I hope you will stay out of the Union"; on January 21, 1861: "I do think old Maryland will never leave our glorious Union, at any rate not by my Consent." On April 11, 1861, we find the remark: "I hope Uncle Sam (or rather now Uncle Abe) will give the seceding boys a good sound drubbing. The Constitution and the laws must be sustained."[24]

Further proof of the fidelity of the Western counties to the Union cause may be derived by examining the exciting history of the Maryland legislature at the beginning of the war. George L. Radcliffe has described in detail the policy of the governor, Thomas H. Hicks; through "masterly inactivity" Hicks prolonged the delay in summoning the legislature, because he wished to prevent all hasty or anti-Union resolutions. When he finally did call the legislators together, he summoned them to Frederick, as he himself explained at the time, because of the well-known pro-Union attitude of this town.[25] The legislature, meeting on April 26, 1861, held its first session in the Frederick County Court House, but then moved to the German-Reformed church at the corner of Church and Market Streets for all subsequent meetings.[26] Even before the legislature convened in Frederick, the Home Guard of Frederick had been founded; it was often called the "Brengle Home Guard" after its organizer, Captain Alfred F. Brengle. The name "Brengle" leaves no doubt concerning the German descent of its bearer, and the list of members contains so many German names—about half

[24] Jacob Engelbrecht was the son of a German immigrant; the family originally came from Eichig, near Bayreuth. From 1865-1868 Engelbrecht was mayor of Frederick. His diaries are still in the possession of his descendants in Frederick. In our quotations the original orthography of Engelbrecht has been reproduced.

[25] Radcliffe, op.cit., 69. Frederick and Baltimore were designated by Lincoln in his call for troops in April 1861 as the two places in Maryland where troops were to be mustered into service.

[26] Ibid., 71.

of the four hundred—that lack of space prevents us from listing them. This Brengle Guard had been founded to espouse the cause of the Union in Western Maryland and was supported by the citizens of Frederick.[27]

In Baltimore the situation was slightly different. While at the beginning of the war the Germans in Western Maryland, being loyal Democrats, had no love whatever for Lincoln, for the most part they favored the preservation of the Union. In Baltimore, party politics were further complicated by a new factor. Here was published the only Republican newspaper in the State of Maryland —the only one in Maryland to advocate openly and energetically the election of Lincoln—the German daily, *Der Wecker*. Its founder, Carl Heinrich Schnauffer, had died seven years before the outbreak of the Civil War, but his family had continued the spirit of his publication and the *Wecker* maintained the attitude of its founder, a liberal '48er. In its papers we see clearly that the younger generation of German immigrants in the fifties conceived of the Civil War as a continuation of the struggle of 1848.[28]

As a Republican paper the *Wecker* advocated the unconditional freeing of slaves. It returned to the slavery question again and again. It was well aware how difficult this problem was and that the abolition of slavery would by no means establish Negro equality before the law. After emancipation there should come education for the colored people. "The Negroes ought to become whatever they can make of themselves,"[29] but they must be given the opportunity to make something of themselves. True emancipation cannot be attained by law; it must grow historically, and must be followed by

[27] *Maryland Hist. Mag.*, vi (1912), 196 ff. The Brengle Guard was later transformed into the Sixteenth Regiment of the Maryland Militia. After Brengle's resignation, Captain William D. Reese commanded. *Examiner*, May 1; July 3, 1861. Bernard C. Steiner, "The Brengle Family of Frederick," *Maryland Hist. Mag.*, vi (1912), 91 ff.

[28] An appeal by Leonard Streiff to his German fellow citizens (*Wecker*, June 18, 1861) showed this plainly; he stated that the same principles were involved in the Europe of 1848 and in the America of 1861. An address delivered at a Turner festival in Berlin in 1861 harks back to an even earlier point in German history. In welcoming representatives of American Turner Societies, the orator assured them of his sympathy in their fight against barbarism and went on to state that the year 1861 represented for German-American Turners the same crucial test in the fight for freedom that 1813 had meant for German Turners. (*Ibid.*, July 18, 1861.)

[29] "More Schools for the Negroes," *Wecker*, June 22, 1865.

legal, political and social emancipation. It would not be right, said the *Wecker*, to tax the Negroes without giving them the vote, for taxation without representation was the injustice that drove the Colonies to revolution in 1776.[30]

To be sure, when compared to the radical abolitionist New England sheets, the *Wecker* appears decidedly moderate. In reply to some complaints from readers that the *Wecker* did not attack the slavery question with sufficient energy, the editor wrote that he must perforce impose moderation on himself since the paper was being published in a slave state and that he could not wilfully endanger the only progressive organ in Maryland. He would prefer, he said, to win over to his side fellow citizens who were still undecided in their attitude, rather than rebuff them by violent fanaticism.[31] Shortly afterward he took sharp issue with some bigoted abolitionists when he argued that their plan to send the Negroes back to Africa after their liberation did not spring from a feeling of humanity but from arrogance and intolerance. These people were eager to free the slaves, but after that they wished never to see them again. Such a course would prove impossible, argued the *Wecker*. It was nonsense to call the Negroes "Africans," for they were no more Africans than Lincoln was a European. The Negroes were Americans; they formed the lowest class of agricultural laborers, and as such they had as much right as anyone else to their position in the American economic system, regardless of color or race.[32]

Though the *Wecker* at times showed a conciliatory attitude regarding the question of slavery, in regard to Lincoln it proved all the more absolute and adamant. It never felt the slightest doubt that Old Abe was the best man in the country. This conviction was all the more noteworthy since the *Wecker* and the Turner paper were the only ones in Maryland at the time taking this point of view. Originally the *Wecker*, like most German papers, had been more inclined to favor Seward. When on May 16, 1860, the paper presented to its readers the ten men who might be candidates for the Republican nomination, Lincoln—in contrast to Seward and

[30] *Ibid.* The fact that Professor W. C. F. Walther in the *Lutheraner*, published in St. Louis, defended slavery on the basis of his interpretation of some Biblical passages as well as citations from the works of some Reformation leaders was eagerly seized upon and castigated by the *Wecker*. This is part and parcel of the anticlerical attitude of this paper as well as of most papers conducted by Forty-eighters. *Ibid.*, January 14, 1864.

[31] *Ibid.*, July 4, 1860.   [32] *Ibid.*, December 7, 1861.

Wade—was mentioned only briefly and not very hopefully. He was characterized briefly as "America's greatest debater, witty and original." But two days later, after Lincoln had been nominated, the *Wecker* did all it could to strengthen Lincoln's position in Baltimore, and on the day of Lincoln's visit to Baltimore it extended a cordial greeting to him.[33] The paper printed in full every one of Lincoln's messages; in 1864 it came out as one of the first to advocate his reelection, and on the day after his assassination it appeared in mourning with a wide black margin.[34] When some German Republicans attacked Lincoln because his administration did not seem sufficiently energetic, the *Wecker* defended the President's deliberate hesitation.[35] When the same group complained regarding a rebuff Carl Schurz had received, the *Wecker* came forward with conciliatory explanations. It reported with evident pleasure how Lincoln had expressed himself in an interview regarding the Germans, stating that he appreciated them as "straight-forward honest people," that he regretted he could not talk with them in German, but that one of his secretaries regularly translated for him clippings from German papers, for he was very much interested in knowing what the Germans in America thought about him.[36]

The *Wecker* was in full accord with Governor Hicks because it realized very quickly that the hesitant policy of the governor was quite favorable to the Union cause.[37] In view of this the *Wecker* even forgave Governor Hicks his old association with the Knownothings, even though at regular intervals it continued to attack in the sharpest terms this as well as other nativistic groups. "It is wrong to say that adopted citizens should keep aloof from the quarrel. They are citizens and as such they must take their place— for the preservation of the Union."[38]

"Preservation of the Union" was the chief slogan of the *Wecker*

[33] *Ibid.*, November 1, 1860 and February 23, 1861.
[34] *Ibid.*, June 13, 1864 and April 15, 1865.
[35] *Ibid.*, April 5, 1861.   [36] *Ibid.*, January 31, 1861.
[37] *Ibid.*, January 2 and 8, 1861. Similarly, the *Turnzeitung* called Governor Hicks a "white raven" and defended his policy (January 10, 1860). The Democratic *Deutsche Correspondent*, however, was against Hicks, "the Know-Nothing man," all the more since it lumped together the Know-nothings and the New England Puritans, identifying both with Governor Hicks. His inaugural address was commented upon as a "web of historical lies, clumsy deceits and open distortions." *Correspondent*, January 14, 1858.
[38] *Wecker*, June 2, 1861.

throughout the years of the Civil War. It warned the Germans in Virginia, "Within the Union happy, outside the Union unhappy."[39] For this very reason, the Wecker showed such great interest in the events in West Virginia and did everything to strengthen the anti-Secessionist position of this state.[40] Once the war had gotten under way, the paper demanded that it be fought to the end for the sake of the Union. "No talk of peace now," it exclaimed in August 1861; "that would be too soon. A peace concluded now would not serve the Union cause."[41]

These quotations characterize sufficiently the attitude of Baltimore's German-Republican paper. What about its Democratic counterpart, the Deutsche Correspondent? Friedrich Raine, its founder, had been moving in the Democratic atmosphere of the State of Maryland for fully twenty years before the Civil War broke out; he had become rooted in the Democratic Party, and he never left it. Thus he and his Correspondent took their attitude toward current events on the basis of the Democratic Party position.[42]

The volumes of the Correspondent from the Civil War years unfortunately were not preserved. We must attempt to fill in this gap from a secondary source and from items in the later volumes of the paper. On the occasion of its fiftieth anniversary, the attitude of the Correspondent toward the Civil War was retrospectively outlined and explained.[43] The Correspondent did not openly advocate secession; among a hundred German papers in America in 1860, only three favored secession.[44] Regarding the slavery question the Correspondent took an essentially different position from that of the Wecker. To be sure, the Correspondent did not go so far as to praise and defend slavery as a divine institution. "In our state there was probably not one adopted citizen who was a slave-owner, not one who did not consider negro slavery a regrettable institution within a free republic, but"—there was the Constitution, and the Correspondent always took refuge in that sacred document. Maryland happened to be a slave state and "one must never forget that the Constitution of the United States in support of which every

---

[39] Ibid., January 28, 1861.　　　　[40] Ibid., April 12, 1861.
[41] Ibid., August 31, 1861.　　　　[42] Cf. Edmund E. Miller, op.cit., 9 ff.
[43] Correspondent, May 13, 1891.
[44] Lonn, op.cit., 46. The Correspondent was opposed to all tendencies that favored a centralization of the government. Yet it did not concede the South the right of secession, because it held that a state can leave the Union only with the consent of all.

adopted citizen of the Republic has sworn an oath of loyalty sanctions and protects the institution of slavery." According to the *Correspondent*, it was not the stubbornness of the Southern slave barons that had caused the trouble, but the greed of the northern Yankees.[45] "If the humanitarianism of the North could have persuaded itself in the interest of human kindness to purchase the freedom of the three million slaves in the South at only $600 a head, an arrangement with which the southern states would probably have been satisfied in 1857, then a financial sacrifice of 1800 million dollars could have prevented the Civil War, which cost far more than 2500 million dollars plus vast numbers of human lives and tears! The *Correspondent* can point with pride to the fact that it has recommended this possible compromise very urgently in a number of editorials." The Republican notions concerning the emancipation of the Negroes were treated with irony and mockery, at times even with cheap demagogic arguments. In the New Year's issue, 1866, the *Correspondent* demanded suffrage for white women who should, it claimed, really be considered much more important than Negroes. "Heaven and earth are set in motion to get the vote for four million freed Negro slaves and they forget the white women. Why should these fifteen million paragons of creation be less favored politically than the four million bowlegged and flat-nosed kinky heads?" On another occasion, after a discussion of the vast loss of human life and property in the war, the paper commented: "For this triumph, we are eternally indebted to the British Abolitionists, without whose efforts we should still find ourselves in the condition of barbarism which existed here before 1861."[46]

During these years, therefore, the *Correspondent* was none too fond of the great German-American, Carl Schurz. It quoted Schurz as demanding that no state be re-admitted to the Union before it had granted the vote to the Negroes, and commented that this demand was prompted by "pure party-politics." It held this demand to be on the same plane as the remark of the Maryland politician, Henry Winter Davis, "What we need is votes, not intelligence." All these Republican maneuvers, the *Correspondent* stated, had the sole aim of getting votes for the Republican Party, since without the

[45] *Correspondent*, January 1, 1866: The Puritan clergy of the North were to blame for the miserable Civil War. "What good can come from Massachusetts?" was a question the paper repeated again and again.

[46] *Correspondent*, January 3, 1866.

Negro votes of the South the Republican Party of Mr. Carl Schurz would be lost. The *Correspondent* then asked menacingly: "How soon will the nation take a stand and expose these traitors in their true colors?"[47]

While the *Wecker* always spoke with contempt and disgust of the "rebels" and the "slave barons of the South," the *Correspondent* had profound understanding for the difficult situation of the former "insurgents" and "Southern landowners" after the war.[48] Their money had been swallowed up by the war; their soil was ruined; their property—the slaves—was now lost; in fact, the South could be saved only by means of generous loans on the part of the Northern financiers. But the *Correspondent* had grave doubts as to whether "Yankee patriotism" would go so far. It held that Southern prosperity was essential to the welfare of the entire nation. The government in Washington had not yet grasped the fact, for the unfortunate Freedmen's Bureau,[49] instead of helping to solve the problem, was making it worse. It encouraged the Negroes,[50] and thus was turned into a purely political tool, the strategic center of the Republican Party for the domination of the South.

Since the volumes of the *Correspondent* from the early sixties are no longer extant, we are not in a position to learn anything about its attitude toward Lincoln. We find some discussion, however, of President Buchanan. As late as 1891, the paper said of him that history had not yet accorded him justice, that writers still continued to minimize his merits and that he had never neglected his duty in defending the Constitution.[51] Such praise sounds quite different from the peppery articles of the *Wecker* on, or rather, against, Buchanan, "that old sinner."[52] In the election campaign of 1860, the *Correspondent* automatically supported Breckinridge, the candidate of the Southern Democrats.

[47] *Ibid.*, January 6, 1866. [48] *Ibid.*

[49] The purpose of this organization of the federal government was to aid Negroes in setting themselves up on small farms or in various trades.

[50] Naturally enough, the *Correspondent* mentioned every Negro uprising in the country, designating each as one more failure of the Republican Party.

[51] *Correspondent*, May 13, 1891.

[52] On one occasion when a Cincinnati paper spoke of Buchanan's poor health, the *Wecker* remarked savagely, "Buchanan, the old billy goat, won't die so soon, as he is an extremely tough fellow for his age" (August 11, 1860). Naturally enough, the *Turnzeitung* also viewed Buchanan extremely critically. "His course vacillated between love of peace and incitement to rebellion, truth and illusion, honesty and hypocrisy" (December 11, 1860).

In one respect the *Correspondent* deviated from its usual line—whenever it turned to a discussion of European politics. In a retrospective New Year's Day article, the events of 1865, that unhappy year for the Democratic Party, suddenly took on a new, constructive aspect. The editor called on his readers to be proud of this victory of a republic, for it would serve to strengthen republican tendencies in Europe.[53] Thus when there was a question of evaluating the Republic of the United States against monarchistic Europe, the *Correspondent* showed a sort of "feeling of American solidarity" and, face to face with the thrones of European princes, the old party fights between Republicans and Democrats were forgotten.[54]

The presidential election of 1860 was the first great political event in the history of the United States in which German Turners played an effective role. Five weeks before the Republican convention, the associated Turner societies issued an appeal in the Baltimore *Turnzeitung* for the formation of local organizations for the purpose of exerting some influence on the course of the convention in Chicago.[55] In Baltimore, too, one of the leading Turners, Dr. Georg Edward Wiss, was closely associated with the early beginnings of the Republican Party. The first steps of the young Republican groups in Baltimore were not particularly fortunate. They stood completely under the influence of the Blair family, which was vigorously working in the three border states, Maryland, Missouri and Kentucky, for the nomination of Edward Bates. Under the leadership of Dr. Wiss, the German Republicans of Baltimore had joined the American Republican Association with the understanding that they be permitted to vote for Seward or some other equally prominent Republican. At the Maryland State Republican Convention, which met in Baltimore April 26, 1860, with only about thirty delegates

[53] *Correspondent,* January 3, 1866. The article was reprinted from the New York *Staatszeitung* without comment, hence with the editor's approval.

[54] Polemics between the two German papers occurred rather rarely during these years. Occasionally one finds in the *Wecker* a few digs at its Democratic rival: "It is not at all ashamed of its incredible lies," *Wecker,* October 17, 1860. On November 15, 1860, the *Wecker* felt it its "painful duty" to report that the Baltimore *Correspondent* remained the only German paper still attacking the Republicans.

[55] *Turnzeitung,* April 10, 1860. "We must have our own representatives on the spot lest we be treated as on former occasions when before the election we were called 'our German friends' and afterward 'the voting cattle' and then treated accordingly."

present, there were some extremely turbulent scenes.[56] The adherents of Bates—according to the *Turnzeitung*, almost all of them former Know-nothings—under the leadership of Montgomery Blair pushed through a vote to the effect that the eleven Maryland delegates to the Chicago convention were to vote as a group for Bates. This candidate, a judge from Missouri, was anathema to the Germans because in 1856 he had identified himself completely with the Whig platform, one plank of which aimed to increase the probationary period for immigrants from five to twenty-one years. Dr. Wiss, the representative of the German Republicans of Baltimore, declared that he could not accept his appointment as alternate delegate to the convention because an obligatory vote for Bates would be contrary to his convictions and very poor representation of the German Republicans in Baltimore. He said he would not go to the convention as a delegate, but that he hoped to find ways and means of informing the convention regarding the position of the German Republicans.[57]

For a while the Germans planned to agitate violently against Bates, but then his chances began to grow more and more hopeless anyway. Wiss was present at the Chicago convention, though not as an official delegate. He was the only representative from Maryland at a meeting held at the Deutsches Haus in Chicago, May 15, 1860, at which the German Republicans agreed on the position they would take. Some historians believe their united stand on the convention floor brought about the nomination of the "dark horse" candidate, Abraham Lincoln.[58] Even without the presence of Dr. Wiss on the floor, the Maryland delegates protested immediately against the instructions of the Blair clan to vote en bloc and insisted on voting individually.[59] James F. Wagner was the only German Republican who took part in the convention; he became chairman of the executive committee of the Maryland Republican Party, and

[56] *Wecker*, April 27, 1860.   [57] *Turnzeitung*, May 1, 1860.

[58] Frank I. Herriott, *The Conference of the German Republicans at the Deutsches Haus, Chicago, May 14-15, 1860* (Transactions of the Illinois Historical Society, 1928).

[59] *Report of the Proceedings of the Republican Convention in Chicago, 1860.* One of the delegates, Charles L. Armour, declared, "We were recommended, not instructed." On the second ballot, eight of the eleven Maryland votes were given to Bates and three to Seward; on the third vote, two to Seward and nine to Lincoln.

was appointed to the National Committee for 1860 to 1864.[60] His name does not appear in any other record. Dr. Wiss, however, deserves considerable credit for helping to make the candidacy of the reactionary Judge Bates impossible and thus to clear the road for Lincoln's nomination.

We know of some other prominent Germans who openly and actively supported the Union side. At the next Republican convention, held in Baltimore in 1864, William H. Hoffman played an important part. Grandson of William Hoffman, whom we have mentioned as the founder of the first paper mill in the state,[61] Hoffman had distinguished himself in the political life of Maryland during the years before the Civil War; among other things, he had served for some years as a member of the legislature. As chairman of the Maryland delegation to the convention of 1864 Hoffman seconded the renomination of Lincoln.[62] At the close of the convention he was elected the Maryland representative on the National Committee of the Republican Party.[63] A member of the Maryland Constitutional Convention in 1864, Hoffman advocated the insertion of a clause stating that slavery should no longer exist in Maryland. In the autumn of the same year his name once more became prominent. When the state was to vote on the adoption of the new constitution abolishing slavery, Hoffman turned to Lincoln for an expression of his opinion. Two days before the voting, October 10, 1864, the President sent an open letter to W. H. Hoffman which, as the latter had hoped, aided in winning over the public in favor of the new constitution.[64]

Jacob Tome's share in the activities of the newly founded Republican Party in Maryland must not be overlooked. Tome (1810-1898), one of the wealthiest merchants in Maryland during the latter part of the nineteenth century, was a descendant of Pennsylvania-German forebears. The original form of the name was Thom. Tome's memory was preserved in the name of the school he founded—Tome School, at Port Deposit, Maryland. He was elected state senator in

[60] *Report of the Republican Convention*, 1860, 144. *Ibid.*, 1864, 1. The only other information we were able to find regarding Wagner was a brief mention in John Tweedy, *A History of the Republican Conventions* (Danbury, Conn., 1910), 42.

[61] *Cyclopedia*, 316.

[62] *Report of the Republican Convention in Baltimore in 1864*, 31 and 74.

[63] *Ibid.*, 76.

[64] Nicolay and Hay, *Abraham Lincoln* (New York, 1890), VII, 467.

1863 by the Union Party in Cecil County, and retained his seat until 1867, taking an active part in questions of finance.[65]

Another enthusiastic follower of Lincoln was William Julian Albert, the director of a large mining company in Baltimore.[66] Albert presided over the first meeting of members of the Union Party held in Maryland, at Catonsville, to denounce the proceedings of South Carolina and to pledge Maryland to the support of the government. In 1861, Albert was delegated to go to Washington to explain to President Lincoln Baltimore's difficult situation and to ask for help; his attempt to bring new life to the commerce of the city, which had been injured by the war, was as successful as it could be under the circumstances. Albert's house was the gathering place of the Unionists in Baltimore. He cooperated most ardently in organizing the Republican Party and in founding the Union Club, of which he later became president. In 1864 he was president of the electoral college of Maryland for the approaching presidential election.

John L. Thomas, a lawyer whose paternal ancestors were German, was one of the staunchest fighters for the Union in the days when Baltimore suffered most under mob rule. From the very beginning he had spoken against secession. On the evening of April 18, 1861, one day before the great riot, when he met with Governor Thomas Hicks, H. W. Davis and some other prominent Unionists in the Old Fountain Inn in Baltimore, the mob had gathered to attack the governor. John L. Thomas at that time made a speech in front of the hotel to give the governor a chance to escape to safety. When the mob discovered what had happened, Thomas found himself in a very unpleasant situation. The next day, when violence broke out, Thomas was present wherever help was needed; he took many wounded to the hospital. Although he was threatened repeatedly by the Secessionists, he remained in town. It was he who made the first public Union speech after the days of the riots. During the Civil War he went into politics, became counselor for the City of Baltimore, state's attorney for Baltimore, and, in 1864, a member of the state constitutional convention, where he took a very active part. He energetically advocated the emancipation of the Negroes. In

[65] *Cyclopedia*, 5 f.

[66] *Baltimore Past and Present* (Baltimore, 1871), 169 ff. Hamilton Owens, *Baltimore on the Chesapeake* (Garden City, N.Y., 1941), 281. *Cyclopedia*, 47, His great-grandfather, Lawrence Albert, had emigrated from Würzburg, Bavaria, to America in 1752, and had settled in York County, Pennsylvania.

1865 he was elected for the first post-war Congress, and held numerous public offices in later years.[67]

A wild outbreak of mob violence took place against Leopold Blumenberg (1827-1876), a merchant with strong Union sympathies. Blumenberg, of German-Jewish descent, was born in Brandenburg, Germany, and came to Baltimore in 1854, where he soon attained considerable prosperity. He was one of the first to follow Lincoln's appeal in 1861. In 1863, together with other Germans, he founded a special German *Unionsverein*. He retired from business for the purpose of devoting himself to the Union cause, and spent a good deal of his own money in helping to raise the Fifth Regiment of Maryland Volunteers.[68] This action earned him the bitterest enmity of Baltimore Secessionists, who openly threatened his life and made it necessary for Blumenberg's house to be guarded by the police for several nights because of an attack, luckily unsuccessful. Blumenberg became a major in the Fifth Regiment and fought for some time under McClellan. He led his troops against Lee's army in the Battle of Antietam and was wounded so severely that for more than a year he was bedridden.[69] Lincoln then appointed him provost-marshal of the Third Maryland District, a post he held until the close of the draft, and, for his valiant services in battle, President Johnson appointed him a brigadier-general.

When such an influential and prominent Baltimore citizen as Brantz Mayer, president of the Union State Central Committee and Colonel of the U.S. Army, declared himself for the Union cause, he drew many of his fellow citizens to his side.[70] David Creamer's uncompromising attitude deserves special mention also; he was foreman of the jury of inquest after the riots of April 19, 1861. Along with H. L. Steiner, he was one of the most ardent protagonists for the organization of schools for colored people. He worked for this cause in several public positions.[71] Two Baltimore German physicians were doctors in the Union army: Dr. Philip Adolphus and

[67] Cyclopedia, 317 ff.

[68] Cyclopedia, 477. Wecker, April 30, 1861. Jewish Encyclopaedia, III, 272.

[69] History and Roster of Maryland Volunteers, War of 1861-1865 (Baltimore, 1898), I, 179, 181. Scharf, Western Maryland, I, 249. Some of the German names among members of the Fifth Regiment killed or wounded at Antietam were: (Officers) Magnus Moltke, Leopold Blumenberg, William Bamberger; (Privates) Warmboldt, Preiss, Stahl, Harockkamp, Bruder, Kohler, Merling, Kohlmann, Braun, Bremermann.

[70] Cyclopedia, 680.   [71] Cyclopedia, 410.

Dr. Mathias Ad. Edw. Borck.[72] The Reverend Arthur O. Brickmann, pastor of the Swedenborgian New church and editor of various German church periodicals, entered the Union army in 1862 and served as a chaplain. In a private memorandum of the highest official in the State of Maryland, "Governor Bradford's Private List of Union Men in 1861," we find the names of eight prominent Germans who obviously were considered especially reliable; the two lawyers, William Schley and Brantz Mayer; the merchants, W. J. Albert, Albert Schumacher and Peter G. Sauerwein; two businessmen, Philipp Littig and John B. Seidenstricker; and one manufacturer, Eduard S. Myers.[73]

The Turners were the first group in Baltimore to support energetically the nominee of the Chicago convention, Abraham Lincoln. The headquarters of the Turner Societies of America were located in Baltimore at the time and here its organ, the weekly *Turnzeitung*, was published. Consequently the history of the *Turnzeitung* of these years forms part of the history of the Germans in Baltimore.[74] One should not underestimate the political influence of the *Turnzeitung*, since it spoke for 20,000 members of the "German Socialist Turner Society." When, therefore, the Baltimore *Turnzeitung* first raised its voice in favor of Lincoln, there was great joy in the Lincoln camp because of these new adherents.[75] Needless to state, the Baltimore editors of the paper—Wilhelm Rapp, Dr. G. E. Wiss and Dr. Adolph Wiesner—were all thorough Republicans. From Baltimore the Turner headquarters sent an appeal to all Turner societies on October 16, 1860, to campaign for Lincoln. "We Turners fight against slavery, Nativism, or any other kind of restriction based on color, religion, or place of birth, since all this is incompatible with a cosmopolitan view-point."[76] Since the attitude of the *Turnzeitung* was identical with that of the *Wecker*, it is unnecessary to repeat details, except to mention its reaction to the events at Harper's Ferry. Both papers showed no sympathy for John Brown; his actions were described as "a mad Putsch of a fanatic driven to despair by an

[72] Official War Records, ser. 1, xii, pt. 1, pp. 552, 603. Cordell, *Medical Annals*, 327.

[73] *Maryland Hist. Mag.*, VII (1912), 85 ff.

[74] Cf. the volumes of the *Turnzeitung* published in Baltimore 1859-1861, preserved in the Boston Public Library.

[75] William Baringer, *Lincoln's Rise to Power* (Boston, 1937), 190. R. H. Luthin, *The First Lincoln Campaign* (Cambridge, Mass., 1944), 84

[76] BVG, 234.

unkind fate."[77] The *Turnzeitung* blamed the South for making a mountain out of a molehill by demanding a search for "wire-pullers," of which there were none at all. It went on to say that one could almost believe that Southerners had been the stage managers of the affair—for the mad raid certainly served to inflame public opinion in Dixie—were it not that John Brown was as honest as he was fanatical. The calm, measured judgment here expressed concerning John Brown was angrily criticized by more violent Turner groups from the Northern states; the Boston Turners in particular protested against the location of the editorial office in a slave state where it was subject to a certain amount of local pressure.[78] The riots of April 19 and 20, 1861, caused the precipitate removal of the editorial offices of the Turner Societies from Baltimore.

It seems appropriate to say a little more about these riots. The Turners had never made a secret of their enthusiasm for Lincoln. The first large mass meeting in Baltimore in support of Lincoln was held in the Turnhalle on October 30, 1860.[79] Among the thirty-two Germans who, in the middle of April, on the very day after Lincoln's appeal went to Washington to enlist as volunteers, fully one-half were Turners.[80] Regiments of German Turners, among them many from Baltimore, held Washington until troops from the North arrived.[81] Thus everyone in Baltimore knew what was to be expected of the Turners, and a tragicomical incident followed the turbulent Baltimore street battles of April 19, 1861.[82] On this very day a violent mob appeared before the Turnhalle on West Pratt Street to demand from the Turners that they lower the Union banner and hoist the Maryland flag. The demand was to no avail, for the Turners had declared that they would rather blow up their hall than lower the Union flag.[83] On the following Saturday, April 20, a violent riot occurred when news spread throughout the city that the German company of Turner Rifles had sent arms to Washington two days before and had offered the services of the company to the

[77] *Turnzeitung*, October 18, 1859.   [78] *Ibid.*, November 1, 1859.

[79] *Ibid.*, October 30 and November 6, 1860. *Wecker*, November 1, 1860. Among the speakers were Wilhelm Rapp, Christian Bartell, Adolph Wiesner, G. E. Wiss, Dr. Riesler.

[80] *Wecker*, April 19, 1861.   [81] *Ibid.*, May 20, 1861.

[82] *The Pennsylvania German*, VIII (1907), 19, 62, 117.

[83] Heinrich Metzner, *Geschichte des Turnerbundes* (Indianapolis, 1874), 77. Franz Hubert Cortan, *Geschichte des Turnvereins Vorwärts 1867-1892* (Baltimore, 1892).

government. A mob collected before the Turnhalle containing the armory of the Turners, invaded the building and smashed everything to bits, from heavy furniture and gymnastic apparatus to the dishes in the kitchen and the bottles in the bar. The only weapons that the mob discovered were four old muskets, which they carried off. Then the police appeared—after everything had been smashed and the mob had disbanded—and Captain Gardener with his fifteen policemen solemnly locked the building. The majority of the Turners had to flee, most of them joining the Union army.[84]

On the same day a similar fate overtook the office of the Wecker on Frederick Street. Here, too, a boisterous mob appeared and made preparations to storm the building. Windows were smashed and some of the machinery employed in printing the only two Republican papers in Maryland—the Wecker and the Turnzeitung—was destroyed. However, the rioters had to withdraw before they could complete their vandalism. Whether this was because the wife of the founder, courageous Mrs. Schnauffer, faced down the mob or whether the police arrived more promptly this time, is a matter regarding which reports differ.[85] The Wecker building was evidently not destroyed completely. The editors had to flee and the paper could not be published in its full format for several weeks. Only after the city had been occupied by troops could Wilhelm Schnauffer, the editor of the paper, return to resume publication.

Dr. David Einhorn, editor of the German-Jewish monthly Sinai, suffered the same fate as the editors of the Wecker. Einhorn advocated the abolition of slavery so intrepidly that on the same fatal day, April 20, 1861, the mob destroyed the press and two days later

---

[84] Baltimore Sun, April 22, 1861. Cortan, op.cit., 1. Scharf, Chronicles of Baltimore, 600. Cortan reports that the mob "was led by a German," but investigation has yielded no information on this point. Scharf, who on account of his sympathies with the South did not wish to represent the outbreak as a violent act of the mob, says that "this act was committed by a number of indignant Southern men."

[85] Zucker, op.cit., 22. Scharf, History of Baltimore, 630. Sun, April 22, 1861, reported: "The crowd soon dispersed, not, however, until the Southern flag had been thrown out. No violence was done, and all good citizens regretted that any such demonstration was made." However, the Sun stands alone in reporting no violence. Cortan as well as Scharf speaks of destruction: "Office completely wrecked, building seriously injured" (Scharf). Probably the machinery was destroyed in part, for the Wecker could not be published from April 20 to 29; and after that it appeared for a considerable period as a so-called "extra," a single sheet.

forced the editor to leave town.[86] Later his congregation asked him to return, on the condition that he refrain from all political discussions; Einhorn, however, refused and did not return to Baltimore.

We have mentioned several Union meetings and Union clubs composed of Germans, and more need be said on this point. The first German Union Meeting took place on May 9, 1861. "The German Union men of East Baltimore held a large and enthusiastic meeting at Logan Hall, and passed some strong Union resolutions well worthy of our German fellow-citizens."[87] Two weeks later Dr. Adolph Wiesner appeared at an American Union Meeting at Bellevue Gardens, and "was quite animated in an address in the German language."[88] Again, in the fall of the following year we find Dr. A. Wiesner and Dr. A. Schwartz as the German speakers at a great Union Meeting.[89]

At the same time, several Union organizations were founded. In 1862, a Sigel League was formed in East Baltimore (named after the Union General, Franz Sigel), and in 1863 the Germans in West Baltimore joined in the Germania Union League.[90] Even more important was the *Deutsche Unionsverein von Maryland*, which likewise was founded in 1863; Christian Bartell, Leopold Blumenberg, Hugo Kühne and Johann Straubenmüller were the driving forces of the organization.[91] Another political instrument of

[86] Because of the slavery issue, Einhorn had a violent press feud with a Dr. Raphael in New York, who had declared that slavery was sanctioned by the Bible. In *Sinai* (February 1861) this position was sharply refuted. Einhorn was one of the staunchest Republicans in Baltimore, so it is not surprising that the *Wecker* mentioned Einhorn always with the greatest respect. The quarrel between Einhorn and Raphael was discussed extensively in the columns of the *Wecker* (February 5, 6, 7, 1861). From Baltimore, Einhorn moved to Philadelphia, where he became rabbi of the Congregation Keneseth Israel. His *Ausgewählte Predigten und Reden* were edited after his death by K. Kohler (New York, 1880). Cf. *Jewish Encyclopaedia*, v, 78 f.

[87] *Baltimore American*, May 11, 1861. *Wecker*, May 11, 1861. A few days later, an American Union Meeting was held in East Baltimore, where one of the best-known Germans of the city, Justus Brühl, acted as vice-president. *American*, May 15, 1861.

[88] *American*, May 28, 1861. *Wecker*, May 28, 1861.

[89] *American*, October 7, 1862. *Wecker*, October 7, 1862.

[90] *Wecker*, February 18, 1863; July 3, 1863.

[91] *Wecker*, September 23, 1863. This *Unionsverein* was formed as the local branch of a great nationwide political organization of the Germans which was to be inaugurated in Cleveland in the fall of that year. The liberal elements among the Germans tried to come together in a far-reaching organization which pursued a decided policy against the South, for Lincoln's administra-

the Germans was the *Deutsche Reform-Central Verein*, organized in 1864, originally planned as a weapon against the Blue Laws and later also used as a sponsor organization for Republican rallies.[92]

From the fall of 1864, political activity increased daily because of the plebiscite on the new Maryland constitution and the presidential election. It need hardly be mentioned that the German Republicans favored Lincoln's re-election. A German mass meeting which took place in the Turnhalle on October 11, 1864, ended with a resolution for a positive vote for the new constitution, the re-election of Abraham Lincoln, emancipation throughout the Union and denunciation of the rebellion.[93] On the eve of the election, the Unionsverein called a similar meeting in the Turnhalle, where for the last time August Becker stumped for the Republican ticket.[94] As a result of the election of 1864, one of the most active German Republicans, Christian Bartell, was sent to the House of Representatives of Maryland.[95]

Besides these purely political organizations of German Republicans, there was also a benevolent society of Union men; in July 1863 the *Deutsche Union-Volksverein* was founded to support sick and wounded Union soldiers; after a few months thousands of Baltimoreans of German descent had joined this organization.[96] From the columns of the *Wecker* we also know that during the Civil War the German theater in the Turnhalle gave several benefit performances for wounded Union soldiers.[97]

But the most far-reaching activity for the cause of the Union

tion and for the emancipation of the Negroes. The Baltimore Germans appointed August Becker and Christian Bartell as delegates to the Cleveland convention; however, since they disagreed with the platform of the convention, they did not join the organization. *Wecker,* September 4, 29; October 12, 15, 26; November 18, 1863.

[92] A big meeting was recorded in April 1864, where Blue Laws and slavery were attacked. August Becker was the main speaker. *American,* April 6, 1864. *Wecker,* April 6, 1864. *Sun,* April 6, 1864.

[93] *Wecker,* October 12, 13, 1864. Leopold Blumenberg was president of the meeting; Montgomery Blair the main speaker.

[94] *Ibid.,* November 8, 1864.   [95] *Ibid.,* November 10, 1864.

[96] *Wecker,* July 17, 21, 1863. Adolph Wiesner and George Rost were the most active members of the association. At a celebration in the following year, General Franz Sigel delivered the address. *Wecker,* July 21, 28, 1864. *American,* July 21, 28, 1864. The *American* wrote: "It was pleasing to see so many adopted citizens . . . uniting upon such a praiseworthy occasion."

[97] Zucker, *German Theater,* 131.

was displayed by the Germans in the military field.[98] In a statistical survey of the year 1869, B. A. Gould of the United States Sanitary Commission gives 27,900 as the total number of all white men enlisted in the State of Maryland.[99] Of these, 22,435 were native Americans, 403 English, 1400 Irish and 3107 German, a surprisingly high percentage. We mentioned previously that in April 1861 the German Turners of Baltimore joined the Union Army practically en bloc. This time there were not, as in 1776, purely German regiments. However, there were companies with a majority of Germans.[100] It is impossible to enumerate here the names of all Maryland Germans who fought in the Civil War for the Union cause. Of those who advanced to higher military ranks, we may mention Brigadier General Leopold Blumenberg, Colonel Ernest F. M. Faehtz,[101] Colonel Joseph M. Sudsburg, Colonel Brantz Mayer, Lieutenant Colonel Charles Wetschky, Colonel Eugene von Keilmannsegge, Lieutenant Colonel William H. Bamberger and Lieutenant Colonel Vincent E. von Körber.[102]

If, on the other hand, one examines the troop lists of the Maryland regiments that fought on the side of the South, the absence of German names is most striking. Of course, here and there a few German names are to be found, but the percentage is extremely small, especially among the officers. Only one German, or rather German-Swiss, name occurs among the officers of the Maryland Infantry—a Lieutenant William P. Zollinger, who distinguished himself particularly in reorganizing the Second Maryland Infantry

[98] Cf. *History and Roster of Maryland Volunteers, War of 1861-1865* (Baltimore, 1898).

[99] Faust, I, 523.

[100] Comp. A and B of the Eighth Battalion, Comp. E and H of the Third Maryland Infantry. Comp. C and K of the Fifth Maryland Infantry. Comp. H and I of the Tenth Maryland Infantry.

[101] The *Official War Records* (ser. 1, xlvi, pt. 3, p. 924) report of Colonel Faehtz that his "distinguished behavior as commander of his regiment, his cool, even cheerful bravery and martial bearing when most exposed to danger, splendidly exemplified in the charge on the enemy's works at Five Forks, April 1, 1865."

[102] Among the lower ranks of officers are the following names: Henry Kunitz, Conrad Boettger, John Schwab, F. W. Heck, Louis Fleckenstein, John H. Suter, Martin Suter, Henry Wilhelm, John Schley, Fritz Schleunig, John E. Ramsburg, Francis Shamburg, Charles M. Schad, Gottlieb Schmidt, Joseph M. Roeser, Ernest Osswald, John R. Fellman, Michael Schmidt, Louis Beyer, Louis Scherzer, Nicholas Gauster. Space does not permit enumeration of the great number of privates.

Regiment in Richmond.[103] In addition, there are just a few more in the lists of the Maryland Infantry: W. H. Slingluff, William Ritter, Alfred Riddlemoser, Joseph Wagner, William Ackler, Charles Hitzelberger, William Heimiller, Frederick Hendorf, Jacob Kneller, Henry Wegner, F. Fillmer.[104] In the First Maryland Cavalry we find only two German names among the twenty officers: A. F. Schwartz and F. C. Slingluff. In the Second Maryland Cavalry, Herman F. Keidel is mentioned among the staff officers.[105] In the Maryland Artillery the only Germans named are Corporal W. F. Bollinger and Captain W. L. Ritter.[106] There were thus some Germans among the Maryland Confederate troops, but they were a mere handful and their percentage, as compared with the great participation of Germans in the Northern cause, is strikingly small. It might be noted that the Maryland Line in the Confederate Army was recruited particularly from southern Maryland, where there had been the least German immigration.

Up to this point mention has been made only of riots against German groups faithful to the Union. Naturally enough, in the later years of the war we find that the opposite took place, namely, that Southern sympathizers—among these also some Germans— were pelted with rocks. In the course of such a demonstration on May 25, 1862, the building of the *Deutsche Correspondent* was visited by an excited mob. Scharf reports on this as follows: "The office of the German *Correspondent* was then visited, but the proprietors stated that they were about to display their flag, when the crowd proceeded. . . . On returning, the crowd went again to the *Correspondent's* office, where a portion of the flag, showing the stripes, was hanging from an upper window, but this was not satisfactory to the crowd, who demanded that the entire flag, with the stars, should be exposed to view."[107]

It has been stated that the *Correspondent* was Democratic but not Secessionist. Among the Germans of Baltimore, particularly among those of the upper classes, there were quite a number of adherents to the Confederacy. The Turner Societies which sympathized with the Union were composed mostly of members of the middle and lower classes. The social center of the elite was the

---

[103] W. W. Goldsborough, *The Maryland Line in the Confederate Army, 1861-1865* (Baltimore, 1900), 85, 86, 152.

[104] *Ibid.*, 76, 155 ff.   [105] *Ibid.*, 166, 246.

[106] *Ibid.*, 270, 315.   [107] *Chronicles*, 624.

Germania Club, and this club was considered a hotbed of Secession-ism.[108] Hence, when the city was placed under martial law, the club was very quickly closed on the command of General Butler. The Germania Club in these years was an organization of merchants, particularly tobacco traders. This fact explains why the members sympathized with the tobacco-raising South; their economic inter-ests and friendly social relations with Southern planters had naturally produced this result. The events of the war years were felt by this club when, in 1862, the president, Frederick Schepeler, a tobacco merchant, had to withdraw because he had been too free in his expressions of sympathy for the South and thereby had endangered the existence of the club during the period of martial law under General Butler.[109] In the guest books of the club, one finds during the early years of the war innumerable entries of the names of merchants from Southern states, all the way from Virginia to Louisiana. At times a guest entered as his place of residence "Con-federate States" or "Confederacy," which in those days was meant to convey a declaration of political principles. From 1863 on, the Union sympathizers came more and more to the fore. The Seces-sionist president, Schepeler, was succeeded by his business partner, Albert Schumacher, a thorough Unionist. When the club issued a declaration to the effect that in political matters it was absolutely neutral, General Butler gave permission to have it reopened. There-upon the members foregathered again—to be sure, under a Union flag suspended in the club house, whether they liked it or not.[110]

There was also to be found a fairly large Secessionist group in the Concordia Society. August Becker, for some time editor of the *Wecker*, related an occurrence that was probably fairly typical of the general attitude in the Concordia Society. One evening in 1861, Becker was chatting in the club rooms with his friend, Justus Brühl, about the probable outcome of the war, and giving frank expression to his Union sympathies. Thereupon all other members left the room by way of a demonstration of their feelings, finally leaving Becker and Brühl quite alone. "You spoke too vigorously," said

---

[108] From an unpublished speech by Henry G. Hilken on the occasion of the seventieth anniversary of the club, 1910. (In the possession of the Society for the History of the Germans in Maryland in the Enoch Pratt Library, Balti-more.)

[109] Unpublished speech by Henry G. Hilken.

[110] Dieter Cunz, *Germania Club*, 13.

Brühl. "These gentlemen are all devoted to the Confederate cause."[111]

We know of more than one case where members of old Baltimore-German families joined the Confederate side. Sometimes a family split, as did the Mayers, where Brantz Mayer favored the North while his brother, Charles F. Mayer, supported the South. Charles F. Mayer, one of the best-known lawyers and politicians of the city, was a Douglas-Democrat; he was decidedly against Lincoln. The longer the war lasted, the more stubborn he grew in his anti-Lincoln, pro-Southern attitude.[112] William Kimmel, likewise a Maryland politician descending from an early German immigrant family, followed the same line.[113] Pro-Southern was Herman Stump, who was a radical member of the Democratic Party all through his life.[114] In the Confederate Army we also find the name of a Maryland-German physician: Dr. William C. Kloman.[115] Strongly pro-Southern, too, was Gustav Wilhelm Lurman, a wealthy Baltimore merchant who had come from Bremen before 1835.[116] In April 1861 the lithographic company of A. Hoen offered to print the postal stamps of the Confederacy, a fact from which we may safely conclude that old Mr. Hoen was not quite free of Southern sympathies.[117]

A very strong anti-Republican feeling characterizes the editors of a German-Catholic weekly published in Baltimore, the *Katholische Volkszeitung*. Joseph and Christopher Kreuzer, founders, owners and editors of the paper, opposed Abraham Lincoln in such vehement terms that in May 1863 Joseph Kreuzer was imprisoned. To be sure, he was released after a few days, having sworn an oath of loyalty, but the paper continued to criticize the Lincoln administration. It did not hesitate to draw parallels between Lincoln in 1863 and the English king in 1776; it took Lincoln to task for his alleged

---

[111] *Der Deutsche Pionier* (Cincinnati, 1869), I, 286.

[112] *Cyclopedia*, 711.   [113] *Ibid.*, 462.   [114] *Ibid.*, 548.

[115] Cordell, *Annals*, 469. DNB, 56. Kloman was born in Eschwege, Hesse, in 1835.

[116] Elinor S. Heiser, his granddaughter, characterizes him in her reminiscences, *Days Gone By* (Baltimore, 1940), 90: "His sympathies were strongly with the South in the Civil War, and in its behalf he gave and lost largely his fortune."

[117] August Dietz, *The Postal Service of the Confederate States of America* (Richmond, Va., 1929), 5 f. Hoen did not get the order; it was given to the firm of Hoyer and Ludwig in Richmond, Virginia, likewise a German company.

lack of deep religious convictions; it castigated the "nigger-nonsense" of Republican newspapers and defended the institution of slavery, justifying it on the basis of the Bible. In 1864 it advocated the election of General McClellan and favored a quick, negotiated peace.[118]

Even one well-known '48er was among the adherents of the Southern cause: Dr. Adalbert John Volck.[119] His house in Baltimore became a rendezvous for Southern sympathizers in the earlier years of the war, and at times he offered Confederate soldiers a hiding place there. Further than that, Volck actively assisted in smuggling medical supplies into the South. Suspicion fell on him so definitely that in 1861, at the instance of General Butler, he was incarcerated for some time in Fort McHenry.[120] It was as a caricaturist that Volck gained his chief importance during the Civil War. Quite consciously he attempted to counteract the influence of the famous cartoonist on the Northern side, Thomas Nast, who also happened to be a German '48er. Under the pseudonym, "V. Blada," he published a series of cartoons in which he attempted to heap ridicule on the Union, especially on President Lincoln and General Butler.[121] His *Confederate War Etchings* and his *Sketches from the Civil War*, in which he shows markedly artistic gifts, were of considerable aid to the cause of the South. It was either he or his brother, the well-known sculptor, Frederick Volck, who made the famous bust of Jefferson Davis which was engraved on the ten-cent stamps of the Confederacy.[122] Adalbert Volck's sketch of Stonewall Jackson was very popular in the South; his portrait of Robert E. Lee hangs in the Valentine Museum in Richmond. Volck continued in his love for the South to the very end of his days, dis-

---

[118] *Wecker*, May 8, 1863. *Katholische Volkszeitung*, June 6, August 15, December 12, 1863; February 27, September 3, 10, 1864. Although the paper was very much disappointed at Lincoln's re-election, it was visibly moved and impressed by the President's Second Inaugural Address, and it condemned strongly Lincoln's assassination. *Ibid.*, November 19, 1864; March 11, April 22, 1865.

[119] *DAB*, xix, 288.

[120] When, after the conclusion of the war, General Butler was a candidate for the governorship of Massachusetts, Volck's caricatures helped considerably to bring about his defeat.

[121] Albert Shaw, *Abraham Lincoln, A Cartoon History* (New York, 1929), I, 12, 63; II, 236, 253. Gardner P. H. Foley, "Adalbert Volck, Dentist and Artist," *Maryland*, xix (March, 1948), 4 ff.

[122] August Dietz, *op.cit.*, 22.

playing it also in another art at which he later tried his hand—the work of the silversmith. The last significant work he undertook in this field was a memorial shield, completed in 1909, three years before his death: "To the Women of the South—as a continual reminder . . . of the splendid example of self-sacrifice, endurance and womanly virtues displayed during the War between the States." Volck is particularly interesting because he was an exception to the vast majority of the liberal '48ers who favored the side of the North.

From all this it becomes evident that the picture presented by the Maryland Germans during the Civil War was by no means a homogeneous one and that their attitude cannot be set down in a simple statement. Still, one might generalize from the evidence as follows: in the western part of the state, where the German element had largely become amalgamated with other groups of settlers, the exceptionally vigorous pro-Union attitude of Frederick and Washington Counties can probably be justly attributed to the strong German element in the population. It is in the rural districts, in the western counties, that we find the large number of Marylanders of Pennsylvania-German stock who clung conservatively to their traditional membership in the Democratic Party and yet remained adherents to the Union. In Baltimore, where there were Germans who had recently arrived, the German language and German social life still flourished, and therefore one can speak of a more definitely German attitude here than in the western settlements dating back to colonial times. The Germans in Baltimore represented the most southerly outpost of the Republican Party. Hence the most fiery Lincoln adherents south of the Mason and Dixon Line were to be found here. In Western Maryland the Union sympathizers remained within the Democratic Party organization, whereas in Baltimore they were Republicans as a matter of course. This keen party feeling in turn drove the Democratic Germans of Baltimore into the radical Secessionist wing of the party, in contrast to the conservative Democrats of Western Maryland. The urban section of the German element in Maryland separated itself, politically speaking, approximately along the lines of sociological stratification. Among the wealthy Germans, bound to the South by the ties of the tobacco trade, there were many Secessionists or at least Southern sympathizers.[123] Just as there was in Baltimore the south-

[123] Cf. Robert T. Clark, Jr., "The New Orleans German Colony in the Civil

ernmost group of Lincoln enthusiasts, so here also was the northern-most group of German adherents to the Confederate cause. The latter were mostly men who had been in the country for a consider-able time, generally more than ten years, and had become quite thoroughly acclimatized. The middle and lower social strata of German immigrants, men who were in general associated with the Turner movements, stood as a group behind the Union cause. Their intellectual leaders were liberal refugees from the Revolution of 1848, who without the least hesitation flocked to the Republican banner. We have mentioned above how important it was for this group, perhaps the most valuable to America of all German immi-grants, that they found it possible to unite themselves spiritually with their new country by joining in the fight for a great cause. On the other hand, it is unnecessary to dwell at length on the advantages accruing to the Union cause through the fact that the strong and enterprising young men of this generation of German immigrants placed their strength at the disposal of the North. This allegiance was of decisive importance especially in the border states, where public opinion was divided and where a few brave individuals counted for much more than in the homogeneous and safe atmos-phere of Northern states. How important it was to preserve Mary-land in particular for the Union can be seen by a glance at the map, noting its relation to the capital of the nation.

A quotation from a speech by President Theodore Roosevelt, delivered in 1903, may close this chapter: "The other day I went out to the battle-field of Antietam, here in Maryland. There the Memorial Church is the German Lutheran Church, which was founded in 1768, the settlement in the neighborhood of Antietam being originally exclusively a German settlement. There is a list of its pastors, and curiously enough, a series of memorial windows of men with German names—men who belonged to the Maryland regiment recruited largely from that region for the Civil War, which Maryland regiment was mainly composed of men of German extraction. In the Civil War it would be difficult to paint in too strong colors what I may well-nigh call the all-importance of the

---

War," *Louisiana Historical Quarterly*, xx (1937), 990-1015. Clark shows that in New Orleans also, the wealthy members of the German colony were ardent adherents to the Confederacy, "because their income was derived in one way or another from the proceeds of slave labor."

attitude of the American citizens of German birth and extraction toward the cause of the Union and liberty, especially in what were then known as the border states. It would have been out of question to have kept Missouri loyal had it not been for the German element therein. So it was in Kentucky—and but little less important was the part played by the Germans in Maryland."[124]

[124] Quoted in *The Pennsylvania German*, v (1904), 44.

PART THREE

THE LAST GENERATIONS

1865-1940

IX. THE GERMAN-AMERICANS

N the history of American immigration a distinction has been made between "Colonial, Old and New Immigration."[1] Chronologically and geographically, the two latter chapters in the history of immigration are very distinct. The old immigration is that of the late eighteenth and the first half of the nineteenth century, from the Revolution to the Civil War. The mass of immigrants was drawn mostly from western, middle and northern Europe—England, Ireland, Germany and Scandinavia. After the Civil War, the new immigration was recruited from the seemingly inexhaustible surplus population of southern and eastern Europe. Of course these two groups were not mutually exclusive. The southeastern European immigration became noticeable during the decades before the Civil War, and the German-Irish immigration certainly did not cease with the advent of the Civil War—indeed, it continued into the twentieth century. Despite this, the representatives of the "old" emigration countries were soon outnumbered by those from the "new" emigration countries toward the end of the nineteenth century.

These generalizations must be kept in mind if one is to understand the history of the Germans in Maryland. The western counties, which occupied such a dominant part in the first third of our presentation, now disappear almost entirely from the stage. From about 1830 the number of new immigrants in the western counties had been steadily declining; and from 1820 on the early German settlers in Frederick and Washington Counties had been advancing so rapidly in the process of complete acclimatization that at the turn of the century many of them were hardly aware of their German origin. It was different in Baltimore; there the stream of fresh German immigrants increased steadily till the Civil War. It continued at its height even during the decade after the Civil War, only to decline rapidly toward the end of the century.

We have already pointed out that the German immigrants in Western Maryland and those in Baltimore developed quite differently both psychologically and sociologically. The pioneers along the Monocacy and Conococheague came over as Germans and

[1] Carl Wittke, We Who Built America (New York, 1939).

remained German until their death. However, their grandchildren were completely Americanized. The transition—as we saw in the case of the language conflict in the churches—did not always occur without friction; but the process of Americanization advanced irresistibly and in a relatively short period of time.

In Baltimore, however, there emerged a type which never appeared in Hagerstown and Frederick: the German-American. Modern historical research has attempted to analyze and explain the German-Americans as a sociological-psychological phenomenon.[2] According to these investigations, the German-American type existed only during the period between the Civil War and the first World War. At about the same time, the 1850's, two elements arose which clashed violently with one another, namely, the American nativists, called Know-nothings, and the liberal German refugees, the '48ers. In the tense political atmosphere of the decade before the Civil War the attacks of the Know-nothings were concentrated more and more on the Germans. At this same time, through the recently arrived '48ers, the Germans received their first active, politically experienced leaders. They joined together consciously in German or German-American groups and made their influence felt in the young Republican Party and in the presidential elections of the fifties and sixties. Whereas they had always been slower than most of the other immigrants to join in the process of assimilation, now they were directly deterred by the heated attacks of the nativists. They cut themselves off, founded their own societies, churches, schools, newspapers and built a wall around their German-American individualism that was to hinder the acclimatization of even the next generation. One of the conditions necessary to the existence of the German-American group was the continuation of German immigration. When, toward the end of the century, German immigration began to fall behind the influx from southern and eastern Europe the German-American structure began to crack, and during the first World War it collapsed completely. The era of the "Hyphen-Americans" lasted in round numbers from 1860 to 1920.

All the conditions necessary for the growth of German-Americanism were present in Baltimore. Around the middle of the nineteenth

[2] We refer here particularly to the excellent book by the English historian, John A. Hawgood, *The Tragedy of German-America* (New York, 1941). See also Dieter Cunz, "Die Deutsch-Amerikaner," *Monatshefte für Deutschen Unterricht*, XXXIII (1941), 343-48.

century the Germans in Baltimore were in close touch sentimentally, materially, commercially and through family connections with those in their old fatherland. The steady stream of German immigrants to the end of the century helped to keep alive their consciousness of their German origin. The old German families in Baltimore had achieved public esteem and wealth. They had no intention of yielding ground to the radical mob of Know-nothings. In order to overcome the stealthily gnawing feeling of inferiority which all immigrants consciously or unconsciously feel toward those who have come before them, there seemed to be only one method—that of emphasizing loudly and clearly their German origin. The oftener the Know-nothings broke into a German Turnfest or attacked and beat a German, the more stubbornly the Germans stuck together in order to show that they were not ashamed of being German. Thus German-Americanism arose everywhere. Thus it arose in Baltimore.

The existence of German-Americanism was soon accepted by public opinion; more than that, it was even acknowledged by the Maryland legislature. On March 30, 1868, a bill became law: "Every public general law . . . shall immediately after its passage be published, at the expense of the state, daily for one week in two daily newspapers of the city of Baltimore, one of which shall be printed in the German language. . . ." This law remained in existence for more than seventy years; it was abolished only during the second World War.

During the last third of the nineteenth century the founding of societies among the Germans of Baltimore reached a height never before or since experienced. The expression, "When three Germans meet they found a society," arose at this time. It is not necessary to include even an incomplete list of the German clubs here, for life in most of these societies was uneventful and uniform. We can limit ourselves to a few of the largest and most typical of these organizations.[3]

Most of these organizations tended more and more to become purely social. Even those societies which started out to be choral or gymnastic clubs yielded to the social element. We have previously

---

[3] For anyone interested in details of the societies, reference may be made to the two books which stem from the height of the activity of the societies, *Baltimore, Seine Vergangenheit und Gegenwart* (1887) and *Das Neue Baltimore* (1905).

shown that the Germans in Baltimore are not in any sense to be considered as having formed a closed sociological group. They were divided according to the social scale into various groups, and this division along sociological lines increased in intensity toward the end of the century, especially during the time when the lower classes were augmented through fresh immigration.

It is clear that the most definitely social organizations observed the sharpest social discrimination. As in the time before the Civil War, so in the following decades until the World War the Germania Club was the social organization of the German upper class. The Germania Club did not survive the Civil War scatheless. In the Turner and choral societies of the lower classes where all the members stood en bloc on the side of the Union, the life of the organizations resumed full blast immediately after the war. In the Germania Club, however—the club of the successful, wealthy merchants and especially tobacco dealers—there was a large percentage of Confederates. Political tension and quarrels had not exactly stimulated the club spirit. Added to this was the inadequacy of the club rooms, a condition which was particularly noticeable during these years when so many organizations shot up like weeds. Not until 1874, when the club secured its own club house, was this "Post Civil War Crisis" overcome. From that time on, things began to go better. The succeeding decades, until about 1910, were the happiest and most brilliant in the history of the club. The Germania Club retained its exclusiveness, a circumstance which did not make it well liked by the Germans of the middle and lower classes.[4] Up to the time of the first World War, the club remained chiefly a merchant's club. A list of the names of some of the most active members of the Germania Club—Henry Schürmann, Claas Vocke, Henry Lauts, Ernst Schmeisser—is simultaneously a list of the leading Germans in Baltimore business circles.[5]

[4] A very characteristic occurrence is the following: The German Society held its meetings in the rooms of the Germania Club. When an attempt was made in 1888 to increase the membership of the German Society, it was decided not to accept the hospitality of the Germania Club any longer because many members of the society remained away from meetings rather than set foot in the Germania Club. Subsequently the German Society held its meetings in other rooms, but returned to the Germania Club house in 1893. Cf. Hennighausen, op.cit., 136.

[5] For further particulars on the history of the Germania Club, see Cunz, Germania Club, 14 ff.

During the decades after the Civil War, the most important gathering place for German social functions was Concordia Hall, the club house of the Concordia Society, which was opened on September 11, 1865. In the Concordia Hall the Germans of the city had a social center in which their theatrical productions, concerts, celebrations and meetings could be held. The Concordia Hall was used not only by the Concordia Society; it was frequently rented by other German societies for their own purposes.[6]

Many Germans were members of the various Free Mason lodges. Even in this field the strong tendency of the Germans of that time to create separate German-American groups may be seen; in 1872 and in 1886 two exclusively German lodges—Germania Lodge and Sincerity Lodge—were founded within the Masonic Order.[7]

These clubs constituted the most important social organizations. There were also an increasingly large number of singing and Turner societies which satisfied the social needs of the middle and lower strata of society. Space does not permit mentioning all of them individually here. Suffice it to say that at the turn of the century there were fifteen German choral societies and five German gymnastic societies in Baltimore.[8]

Of these, the Turnverein Vorwärts deserves special mention. Founded on June 17, 1867, it soon became the largest and most popular society among the Germans in Baltimore. We have quoted the saying that "When three Germans meet they found a society." We might have added, "And when a fourth German joins them he wins over one of the three original members and together they found a competitive organization." We will remember that since 1849 there existed in Baltimore the Sozialdemokratische Turnverein. Since the beginning of the sixties, the old Sozialdemokratische Turnverein had been developing further and further into a purely social and drinking club and had drifted away from its original ideal, "Mens sana in corpore sano." How far the decline had gone is indicated by the fact that in 1865 among 130 members only ten were mentioned in the lists as active Turners; all the others

[6] A few dates in the early history of Concordia Hall will be found in BVG, 229.

[7] DNB, 112, 113.

[8] See the list of societies in DNB, 114 ff. During the years after the Civil War, twenty new German choral societies were founded in Baltimore, some of them very short-lived. Cf. Baltimore Correspondent, May 13, 1891.

were "passive members" so far as gymnastics were concerned. In 1867 there was a large Turnfest in Baltimore at which General Franz Sigel presided as honorary president. It was probably at this celebration that the idea of founding a new Turnverein was conceived; 1867 was the year of the founding of the Turnverein Vorwärts, an organization showing vigorous activity throughout the following generations down to the present time and one which was especially popular among the younger Germans.[9]

We shall quote a section of the charter of the society in order to indicate its character. "The object of the Turnverein Vorwärts is educational, ethical, and social. It has for its purpose the physical, mental, moral and social improvement of its members and scholars by the maintenance of educational classes, lectures, a library and reading room, a gymnasium, social meetings, and such other means as will promote the harmonious development of mind and body." There was to be a lecture and discussion once a week. Musical and dramatic offerings were to supplement the gymnastic activities. By the end of June 1867 the constitution of the society was drawn up and July 4 (Independence Day) was designated officially as Founders' Day for the future.[10] A gymnasium was rented; furthermore, a gym school for boys between ten and eighteen years of age was attached to the society. Attempts to establish a library and a drawing school for boys failed. On the other hand, the organization was very successful in the presentation of popular lectures which were well attended and which undoubtedly helped to raise the cultural level of the members. Among those who lectured we find

[9] The history of the Turnverein Vorwärts has been dealt with in various monographs: Franz Hubert Cortan, *Geschichte des Turnverein Vorwärts 1867-1892* (Baltimore, 1892). Karl A. M. Scholtz, *The Turnverein Vorwärts* (Baltimore, 1937). The best and most complete description of the Turner movement in Baltimore is the article by Augustus J. Prahl, "History of the German Gymnastic Movement of Baltimore," SHGM, xxvi (1945), 16-29.

[10] Among the founders of the society may be mentioned: Emil Dapprich, who later became head of the German-American Teacher's Seminary in Milwaukee; Louis Tiemann and Edward Hunsicker, two well-known businessmen; Gustav W. Lehmann, one of the most famous chemists in the state, and Charles Trowe, head of a lithographic firm in Baltimore. One of the early members was Arnold Siegfried Jahn, the son of the founder of the so-called Turner Movement in Germany, Friedrich Ludwig Jahn. One of the most active members was Heinrich Lohmann (born in 1820 in Bremen; died in 1889 in Baltimore). Lohmann came to America in 1848 as a liberal refugee; he volunteered immediately after Lincoln's call to arms for service in the Civil War. Later he taught in Knapp's Institute.

such well-known names as Robert Reitzel, Karl Heinzen, Adolph Douai, Carl Otto Schönrich, Christian Strack, Gustav Facius, Richard Ortmann, Heinrich Scheib, Henry Wood, Marion D. Learned, Konrad Nies, Otto Fuchs, Ernst Henrici, Julius Hofmann and others.[11] These lecture series were continued until 1917, though apparently since the beginning of the century the enthusiasm for the lectures had been declining. At the beginning of the nineties the society decided to build its own hall. A Vorwärts Hall Building Association was founded and on December 31, 1895, the new hall was dedicated officially.

Like most of the German-American societies, the Turnverein Vorwärts reached its height in the last decade of the nineteenth century. Nearly five hundred people were directly associated with the society during these years (active and passive members, pupils, ladies' classes, etc.); the large circle of friends and interested spectators was at least four times as great.

The many German choral societies of Baltimore joined together in a federated organization in 1885 called The United Singers. At first the group consisted only of five organizations, but later almost all of the singing societies of the city joined. It is significant for the general development of the people that in the eighties two German "Laborer's Choral Societies" were founded, the Arbeiter Männerchor, 1882, and the Arbeiter Liedertafel, 1883. The choral societies, too, reached their best periods around the turn of the century; in 1903 Baltimore was the site of the National Sängerfest of the northeastern states, at which President Theodore Roosevelt gave the main address.[12]

Along with the choral and Turner societies, there was another typical German-American organization, the Baltimore Schützengesellschaft, or shooting club, which was founded in the middle of the century but did not achieve its greatest development until after the Civil War.[13] It was a kind of country club for the lower classes. It owned a park on Belair Avenue with target ranges, dance floors, bowling alleys, banquet rooms, etc. When the organization was at its height in the eighties, it had a membership of approximately

[11] For the full list of these lectures, see Prahl, *Gymnastic*, 23.
[12] Cf. *Baltimore and the Saengerfest* (Baltimore, 1903); *Baltimore Sun*, June 15 and 16, 1903.
[13] The society was organized in 1851 by Heinrich Wittig, Karl Frey and a few others, but it was not important during the first decade of its existence.

1500 families. For the large affairs there were often no less than 20,000 people in the club's park.

During this period the Germans also began to gather in occupational groups; that is, they tended to select those occupations in which Germans were especially numerous. The existence of such occupational societies gives us the percentage of Germans in certain professions; therefore, it is interesting to know that in Baltimore there were brewer, butcher and engineering societies. These societies were certainly only loose organizations, having nothing to do with modern unions. But, besides these occupational societies, there was one closely organized union patterned after the German ones. In a report for the year 1885 the German Central Labor Union is mentioned for the first time under the name "Vereinigte Deutsche Gewerkschaften."[14] Germany was one of the first countries in which labor unions were formed. Therefore it is not surprising that the German immigrants in Baltimore built up an organization similar to those which they had joined in Berlin or Hamburg for the sake of the rights of labor. It was the third city-wide labor organization in Baltimore.

The Germans who had emigrated during the time of Bismarck's social security legislation were familiar with the idea of social insurance organizations. At the turn of the century there were more than twenty such sick benefit and assistance societies in Baltimore. Above all, in the lower social stratum among the laborers the need for such organizations was most obvious.

It is also characteristic of the Germans that at this time a series of German regional clubs were established. Those from Hesse, Swabia and Baden formed separate clubs. The Bavarians were not satisfied with one organization; they established a "Bayern Verein" and a "Wittelsbach Verein," and the North Germans gathered together in the "Uncle Bräsig Vereen" and in the "Plattdeutscher Verein."

A "Gesellschaft für Deutsche Literatur und Kunst" appears on the list of societies in 1903; this is the only time during the period that we hear of such an undertaking. Such an aesthetic venture

[14] *Biennial Report* of the Bureau of Industrial Statistics and Information of Maryland (Baltimore, 1884-1885), 13. Charles Hirschfeld, *Baltimore 1870-1900: Studies in Social History* (Baltimore, 1941), 67. For the vanguard activities of the German union, cf. also *Maryland*, WPA Guide (New York, 1940), 80.

could not possibly compete in popularity with the Turner, singing and shooting clubs.

The only German society with intellectual ambitions that maintained an almost constant number of members for six decades was the Society for the History of the Germans in Maryland. It was founded in 1886, rose to a membership of about seventy during the first few years and in the next fifteen years developed so much activity that it was able to publish an annual report each year containing articles on the history of the German element in Maryland. The Reverend John G. Morris, previously mentioned, and Attorney Louis P. Hennighausen were the most zealous promoters of the society in the early years. It was the first German historical society of its kind in America and it has outlived all other similar organizations in other states. Its part in the historical research of the State of Maryland and German immigration has frequently been acknowledged.[15]

The most fruitful task was accomplished by the oldest and wealthiest organization of Germans in Baltimore, the German Society of Maryland. Much of the work that the society had set out to accomplish during its long years of existence was gradually taken over by the government. For example, after the United States government in the eighties took over the control of immigration and supervised the landing and expediting of the immigrants to the West, the German Society was able to discontinue this aspect of its work; the agent who had handled this project was discharged in 1889.[16] But the very fact that this task was brought under the jurisdiction of the federal government shows how necessary and important this work of the society had been. From this time on,

[15] Besides the historical publications, the *Reports* of the society contain all the important information on the history of the society itself. At first the *Reports* were published annually; the last of these "Annual Reports" (No. 15) appeared in 1901. After this, they appeared at irregular intervals, the last (No. 26) appearing in 1945. A complete bibliography of the publications of the society appears at the end of the 24th report (1939). Cf. *DNB*, 66 ff. Apparently the interest of the Germans in their own history was especially lively in the eighties. In the year in which the Historical Society was founded, a "Deutsches Literarisches Bureau" was established, which published a collected volume, a kind of chronicle of the Baltimore Germans: *Baltimore, Seine Vergangenheit und Gegenwart* (1887). The editors were not historians, but dilettantes. The book is put together in an amateurish way, but it contains a large amount of material and is therefore not entirely worthless.

[16] Hennighausen, *op.cit.*, 136.

the society concentrated its attention upon charitable works, i.e., the support of indigent Germans in Maryland.

However, there was one more occasion when the German Society appeared before the public. It will be remembered that the society started its praiseworthy fight against the misuse of the redemption system in 1817, and carried it to a successful conclusion a few years later. Now, in the 1880's, an appeal was made again to aid a class of people who were being mistreated in a barbaric manner and badly exploited—the oyster dredgers.

Oyster dredging was one of the main sources of income for the inhabitants of the Chesapeake Bay region. It was difficult, poorly paid work, being done in the coldest months of the year, October to April. The captains in charge of the oyster fisheries always had difficulties getting workers; therefore, they usually tried to hire new arrivals who were unfamiliar with the country and to put them under contract in New York, Philadelphia or Baltimore before they knew what lay in store for them. Once an oyster ship was out on the bay, the men were sometimes without contact with the outer world for months at a time. From time to time a ship came out to remove a load of oysters. The laborers were entirely at the mercy of the captains; they often had to work for sixteen to eighteen hours at hard labor. The cold and dampness often caused illness, which the captains ignored. Maltreatment was the order of the day. It often happened that an oyster boat landed in the spring with a reduced crew and no one ever knew what had happened to the missing persons. There was no legal means to control the oyster fisheries. Every winter in the hospitals of Baltimore there were dozens of poor devils, sick and broken, who had fled from the oyster boats. And then there were those who never returned.

In December 1884 the murder of a young German immigrant by an oyster boat captain became known.[17] Otto Mayher and two other Germans who were recent immigrants, still ignorant of the language, had signed up for service on an oyster boat. For a few weeks things went well. Then Mayher became sick. The captain, beside himself with anger at the prospect of losing the help of a man for a few days, mistreated the young man in the most brutal manner. Mayher became daily more ill, and was daily subjected to inhuman beating by the captain. One night, when the boat landed at a lonely spot,

[17] Hennighausen, op.cit., 128 ff.

Mayher was killed by the captain in a violent fit of anger. The county authorities investigated the case the next day, but they accepted the testimony of the captain that Mayher had fallen down a hatch and broken his neck. The two other Germans who were still on board were not heard; the captain prevented them from getting in contact with anyone. But finally they were discharged, went to Baltimore and informed the German consul of the crime. The consul turned the matter over to the authorities. Mayher's body was exhumed and examined; the captain was arrested and indicted. The German Society supported the two witnesses until the end of the trial. The captain was finally sentenced to eighteen years in the penitentiary for murder—a sentence that was upheld by the Court of Appeals.

The court's action did not bring the unfortunate Otto Mayher back to life, but it served to help prevent the recurrence of such crimes in the future. At the beginning of 1886 the German Society decided to appeal to the legislature in Annapolis for the necessary laws to protect the oyster workers. The oyster industry of the lower counties thwarted their attempts. During the next winter renewed reports of brutality and mistreatment on the oyster boats came in. In order to investigate a particular case, the German Society sent a boat out into the bay at its own expense with a United States marshal on board; the captain they were seeking fled, but was later arrested on land and punished. In January 1888 the German Society sent a commission to the legislature in Annapolis for the second time, this time consisting of twenty-five people who fought the matter through with such vigor that the legislature finally accepted the laws suggested by the society.[18] These laws, which went into effect on January 1, 1890, provided for sharp control over the oyster industry, establishing contracts and salaries, registering captains and their crews and requiring exact reports by the captains on any men who did not return with the crew. Disregard of the law was severely punished. Of course, this legal regulation benefited not only the Germans but all new immigrants who had to resort to oyster fishing.

During the succeeding years the German Society learned many times of dreadful maltreatment on the oyster boats. Each time it lent its assistance. Together with similar organizations of Irish,

[18] The following men distinguished themselves at the decisive meetings: L. P. Hennighausen, F. W. Brune, H. C. Tieck and O. Wolff.

Scotch, Welsh and French immigrants, it finally established a "Bureau for the Protection of the Oyster Dredgers." Numerous attempts of the oyster industry to have the protective laws revoked were quashed. In 1894 the politically influential oyster industry succeeded in undermining the protective laws with amendments to such an extent that the labors of the German Society were nullified for a time. Years of work on the part of the German Society and similar charitable organizations were required to secure the help of the United States Congress, which finally put the protective laws back in power and thus closed one of the darkest chapters in the history of immigration into Maryland.

One of the results of the segregation of the German-Americans from the rest of the Americans was the founding of various charitable institutions for the exclusive use of German-Americans after the Civil War. The oldest institution of this kind in Baltimore was the orphanage. It was started on a religious basis and given impetus by the rigors of the Civil War. In 1863, Martin Kratt, pastor of the German-Lutheran Trinity church, sent out an urgent appeal for the founding of an orphanage for German children who were victims of the ravages of war. His appeal was successful, but it soon became obvious that there was not much future for the organization if it remained in the precincts of the church. It was just at this time that the free, antireligious spirit was rife among the German-Americans. Many people hesitated or declined to support even so charitable an institution as long as it remained in the hands of the church. Therefore, in 1866 the orphanage was reorganized and the "German-Protestant Orphanage" became the "General German Orphan Home." As soon as the religious element had been dispensed with, the institution experienced an unexpected upsurge. It received endowments from all sides, from private Germans and from German organizations. Two of the best-known German pedagogues in the city, Friedrich Knapp and Gustav Facius, were especially interested in the orphanage and were very active in its organization and management. It has led a very useful existence, without interruption from the Civil War to the present.[19]

As a kind of supplement to the orphanage, the "General German

[19] Twenty years after the reorganization (1887) there were 160 pupils in the home. Reports on the orphanage have been published at irregular intervals to the present. A chronicle of the home from 1863 to 1903 is to be found in DNB, 74-80. Cf. also BVG, 218 ff.

Aged People's Home" was established in 1881. The impetus for this came from one of the laborers' aid societies and, like the orphanage, was supported by all the German-Americans of the city without regard to religion. After 1885 the Aged People's Home had its own building. It was aided particularly by the wealthy upper class of merchants, who supported it throughout the last decades.[20]

A few charitable institutions were run on a definite religious basis. To this group belong the German-Catholic St. Joseph's Hospital and the German-Jewish orphanage endowed in 1872 by William S. Rayner.[21]

We shall take this opportunity to say a few words about the German Jews. There were in 1840 no more than about a hundred German-Jewish families in Baltimore. But after 1860 the immigration of German Jews increased greatly; toward the end of the century there were about 10,000. A few of them rose to great prominence, such as the physician Aaron Friedenwald,[22] one of the greatest ophthalmologists of his time, or the banker W. S. Rayner, Senator Isidor Rayner and the merchant Leopold Blumenberg. In the world of business, especially textiles and department stores, German Jews were among the leaders; the Hutzler, Hochschild-Kohn, Guttman and Hamburger families may be mentioned in this connection. Among the German-Jewish rabbis there were quite a number during these decades who distinguished themselves in the fields of Semitic language and literature. We have already mentioned Rabbi David Einhorn, and to his name we shall add those of Benjamin Szold, William Rosenau and Alois Kaiser.[23] Benjamin Szold's daughter,

[20] DNB, 81 f. A few of the names of the people who were especially active in the founding of the Aged People's Home: Christoph Bartell, Charles Weber, Gustav Facius, Ernst Knabe, L. P. Hennighausen, Ernst Hoen, H. H. Graue.

[21] BVG, 223. SHGM, VIII, 17.

[22] Aaron Friedenwald (1836-1906) was the son of a German Jew who had emigrated from Hesse. Cf. Harry Friedenwald, Life, Letters and Addresses of Aaron Friedenwald (Baltimore, 1906). DAB, VII, 31.

[23] Benjamin Szold (1829-1902) had fought in Vienna for the revolution of 1848 and subsequently emigrated to America. In Baltimore, after the Civil War, he advocated the education of the freed Negroes, and for this was dubbed "The Rabbi of Timbuktu" by his opponents. Among his publications was a memorial essay, Moses Mendelssohn (Baltimore, 1879) written in German in honor of the 150th anniversary of the birth of the great philosopher. Jewish Encyclopaedia, XI, 652. William Rosenau (born 1865 in Wollstein, Germany) taught for several years in the Department of Semitics at Johns Hopkins University; he published a book, Semitic Studies. Jewish Encyclo-

Henrietta Szold (1860-1945), deserves mention. In 1889 in Baltimore she opened a night school for immigrants in order to make these people acquainted with America; later she was one of the early advocates of Zionism.[24]

The first generation of these German Jews belonged to the German-American group. There are very few indications of anti-Semitism among the German-Americans of this period. Apparently as long as the German Jew spoke German and allied himself with the German-American group, he was welcomed as an addition to the German-American ranks.[25] On the whole, however, this connection was restricted to the first generation. The second and third generations of these German-Jewish immigrants became either Jewish or American. If they were orthodox, the Jewish element outweighed their German background; if they were liberal, the process of Americanization overcame the German-American isolation.

It will be readily understood that with the beginning of the "German-American" epoch the German churches received new life. The new immigrants, especially those from the middle and lower social strata, desired to attend services in German. During the first three decades after 1860 twelve new congregations of the various faiths were organized in Baltimore. The life of the religious congregations runs parallel to the development of German-Americanism as a whole. It rises rapidly until the end of the nineteenth century only to decline gradually after this and to drop to a minimum during the World War. At the turn of the century there were more than thirty congregations in Baltimore which had Sunday services in German. Today there is but one church where the sermon is preached in German every Sunday morning—Zion church. It is strange to see how this one church in the course of nearly two centuries, through the pseudo-flowering of German-Americanism, through good and bad times, was able to endure almost unchanged. In the eighteenth century it was the religious center for the Ger-

---

paedia, x, 473. Alois Kaiser, who grew up in Prague and Vienna, was an authority in the field of synagogue music.

[24] Marvin Lowenthal, *Henrietta Szold, Life and Letters* (New York, 1942).

[25] When in 1905 a collected volume on the German element in Baltimore was made up, one chapter on "The German Jews" was included. Cf. *DNB*, 61-65. Information may be found here on the various German-Jewish congregations. Cf. also Isidor Blum, *The Jews of Baltimore* (Baltimore, 1910).

mans in Baltimore; during the latter part of the nineteenth century it was overshadowed by dozens of similar German congregations and in the twentieth century it again became the sole institution in the city where German was spoken unchanged and undiminished, and is still spoken to the present day.

The congregation was undeniably fortunate in its choice of ministers. They stayed a long time (since 1835 there have been only three different ministers) and they were all men—a few of them stubborn but all of them strong—whose personalities were above the average. Heinrich Scheib remained in office until 1896. We mentioned previously his liberalism in political and religious questions. He lost none of his radicalism with the years and aroused some antipathy among the more conservative elements in his church.[26] Toward the end of the nineteenth century there was considerable tension in the congregation as a result of Scheib's stubborn liberalism, and it was certainly of great advantage to the congregation that in 1889 it engaged a second preacher, Julius K. Hofmann, who was able to counteract with great tact some of old Scheib's headstrong ideas.

Julius Hofmann was born in Friedberg, Hesse, in 1865 and studied theology at the University of Giessen. At the beginning of 1890 he took up his position at the Zion church in Baltimore. Less prone to quarreling than was Pastor Scheib, he very soon became, even to a greater degree than his predecessor, a focal point for German-American activity in almost all fields. His name appears

[26] For more information on Pastor Scheib, cf. H. A. Rattermann, *Gesammelte Werke* (Cincinnati, 1911), XII, 435-39. These dogmatic controversies about Scheib were often conducted with a zeal reminiscent of the religious quarrels of the sixteenth century. Cf. a little pamphlet *Die Zions-Gemeinde von Baltimore und ihre jüngsten Verketzer, die Baltimore-Pastoral Konferenz und die St. Louiser Fakultät* (Baltimore, 1881). It was written and published by a group of German Lutherans in Baltimore refuting some vitriolic attacks on Reverend H. Scheib from the orthodox wing of the powerful Missouri Synod. Reinhold Niebuhr has pointed out that the old dogmatic orthodoxy, which the German Church was first to overcome, has been nowhere more obstinately maintained than in the German-American Church, particularly the Missouri Synod. The German-American churches adhered to tradition with a pertinacy that presents a strange contrast to the readiness of the German Church to abandon it. Niebuhr showed that in their theological positions "German liberalism and German-American conservatism" were in a striking divergence. Scheib was decidedly a liberal, but the lifelong difficulties he encountered prove Niebuhr's point. Cf. Reinhold Niebuhr, "The Failure of German-Americanism," *Atlantic Monthly*, CXVIII (1916), 13-18.

so often in the history of the German societies that it is impossible to give a detailed account of his work.[27]

At the beginning of the twentieth century most of the congregations which had started as German organizations began to lose their German character. This change holds true for all Lutheran, Reformed and Catholic congregations, with the exception of the Zion church. The development of all these congregations ran so parallel that it is unnecessary to describe them individually.[28]

We mentioned previously that some of the German schools were connected with the congregations, and in this connection we described in detail Scheib's school. This German school reached its height in the decade after the Civil War.[29] Knapp's Institute and Scheib's school were still the leading private schools in the city. Around the year 1870 there were more than eight hundred pupils in Scheib's school; since the number was increasing, the old schoolhouse was torn down in 1871 and a new, three-story school building built next to Zion church. Knapp's school was also still growing during the seventies.[30] At the same time (1884) Eduard Deichmann opened his "Englisch-deutsche Klassische Schule," whose nine grades were patterned exactly after the German "Gymnasium" and which worked on a dual language basis.[31]

After the mid-eighties all these German private schools declined and disappeared entirely within a decade—a very remarkable phenomenon. At a time when German-Americanism was still developing vigorously and was increasing in scope and strength each year, at such a time the German schools died out. How was such a thing possible?

Actually this phenomenon is only seemingly a failure of German-Americanism. The German schools died out not because the German element was too weak but because it was too strong. It became

[27] SHGM, xxiii, 38 ff.

[28] Particulars of the history of the congregations will be found in BVG, 241 ff. DNB, 132 ff. Julius Hofmann, A History of Zion Church in the City of Baltimore, 1755-1897 (Baltimore, 1905). Fritz O. Evers, Zion in Baltimore (Baltimore, 1930). Gellner, op.cit., 37 ff. E. F. Engelbert, "Martini Lutheran Church in Baltimore," SHGM, xxvi, 30-32. George Prechtel, "Saint Paul's Lutheran Church of Arcadia," SHGM, xxii, 23-28.

[29] For information on the German schools in Baltimore, see Faust, ii, 241-45.

[30] A detailed and amusing description of life in Knapp's Institute is to be found in H. L. Mencken, Happy Days (New York, 1940), 20 ff.

[31] BVG, 198.

so strong that in the year 1873 it succeeded in having German-English schools erected within the Baltimore public school system.

In 1873 the Board of School Commissioners of the City Council of Baltimore was instructed "to consider the propriety of introducing the study of the German language in the public schools of the city."[32] After long consideration the school authorities decided to start an experimental school in which parallel instruction was to be given in German and in English. When this plan was announced hundreds of pupils immediately applied for admission. In 1874 the first school was opened under the direction of Valentin Scheer and Karl Hessler; a few weeks later there were 1500 requests for admission. Of course the first school was not adequate; within two years five new German-English schools had to be opened. In 1876 the number of pupils was about 3000.

"Instruction is given to pupils in both languages every day. The benefit . . . is twofold: First, to the children of English parents who wish to obtain a knowledge of German; and secondly of German parents who wish to receive instruction in the English language as well as their own. The great advantages of a knowledge of the German language for business purposes are apparent to everyone; and if we can furnish the foundation for this knowledge in the lower department of our schools, it will be much easier for the pupils to acquire greater efficiency as they are advanced. . . . The success [of these schools] will depend very much upon public sentiment with reference to the subject. Our purpose is to furnish the best teachers, and every possible facility which will assist them in their work. . . . In other cities they have grown rapidly in public favor, and a large proportion of pupils in attendance at the public schools are availing themselves of the opportunity thus offered. . . . If a like success follows in this city, it will indicate that we are not mistaken in supposing that the people earnestly wish the establishment of such schools for the public benefit."[33] "These schools have thus far been eminently successful, and have met with

[32] For the following paragraphs, compare BVG, 182 ff., and especially the detailed article by Ernest J. Becker, "History of the English-German Schools in Baltimore," SHGM, xxv, 13 ff., from which the material for this section was taken. Cf. also Heinz Kloss, Das Volksgruppenrecht in den Vereinigten Staaten von Amerika (Essen, 1940), I, 494 f.

[33] Report of the Board of School Commissioners, Baltimore, 1875.

public favor to such an extent that we find it difficult to meet the large demand for admission."[34]

These two quotations from the official reports of two successive years present a clear picture of the success of the experiment. We hear that at first there was some opposition against the schools from certain quarters, but since they were unquestionably a pedagogical success and since the press, school board and city council were warmly in favor of them, their early opponents were silenced.[35]

In 1897 the seven English-German schools of Baltimore had an attendance of 6780 pupils, more than ten per cent of the total enrollment of pupils in the city schools. At the turn of the century there were about 7000 pupils in the schools. This figure was the maximum; in succeeding years the number declined. After 1904 the schools were no longer mentioned in the reports of the school board and the superintendent. At the beginning of the century the Baltimore school system was reorganized. The English-German schools disappeared just as rapidly as they had risen. They existed in reduced and altered form until the World War, and in 1917 they disappeared completely.

The fact that for decades seven public schools in the city had operated as half-German schools was perhaps the most far-reaching recognition of the German-American bloc that it ever achieved. Of course, there was a negative factor in the establishment of the public English-German schools; it spelled the end of the old German private schools. If the German-Americans could receive free German instruction for their children in the public schools, why should they spend money for private schools? The members of the higher social strata who, as we have already seen, were more willing and able to acclimate themselves, had given scant patronage to the German schools, sending their children to American schools instead. The financially weaker groups were unable to support the private schools. Therefore, simultaneous with the increasing popularity of the English-German schools in the 1880's and 1890's was the steady decline of the old German private schools, notably the Scheib and

[34] *Ibid.*, 1876.
[35] The most enthusiastic public advocates and defenders of the German-English schools were: John B. Wentz, Friedrich Raine, Christian Emmrich and H. B. Römer. Among the teachers in the schools were: Carl Otto Schönrich, K. A. Miller, Philipp Wacker, J. H. Männer, Ludwig C. Heuser and L. B. Schäfer.

Knapp institutes. Heinrich Scheib had turned over the management of Zion school to Richard Ortmann and August Schmidt at the end of the eighties, but he continued to regard the school as his own beloved hobby. It was a bitter day for him in 1895 when Scheib's school finally closed its doors permanently. The private schools connected with German-Catholic congregations functioned a little longer; in 1887 the five German-Catholic parochial schools in the city still showed an enrollment of 3193 pupils.[36] However, at the beginning of the twentieth century not a single German parochial school remained.

Strangely enough, even at the height of the German-American era no one ever succeeded in establishing a German kindergarten in Baltimore, in spite of the fact that the idea of the kindergarten originated in Germany and was brought to America by Germans. In 1876 Ernst Christof Hiehle attempted to start a German kindergarten in the city but failed miserably. He found support only among the German Jews, who alone were responsible for the fact that he did not go completely bankrupt when he had to close his institution after barely a year of existence.[37]

One phase of public-school education remains to be discussed, one in which the influence of the Germans toward the end of the century was decisive and in which it achieved an innovation that became a permanent part of the schools, surviving all political storms: the introduction of physical education into the curriculum of the city schools.

We have already spoken of the strong position that the Turner movement occupied among German-Americans. For decades the Turners had sponsored the idea that the physical education of young people should be given greater prominence in the general plans for their upbringing. Toward the end of the nineteenth century this goal was achieved in Baltimore. At that time one of the most prominent German-American Turners, Louis Hoffmann, was a member of the city council. At his suggestion the city council passed an ordinance in 1895 "to introduce physical training as a regular course of study in the public schools of the city."[38] Funds were voted; gym teachers employed and one of the best-known

[36] BVG, 196.   [37] BVG, 198.
[38] Journal of the Proceedings of the First Branch City Council of Baltimore at the Session of 1894-1895, 351, 650, 940.

German Turners, C. F. Emil Schulz, a member of the Turnverein Vorwärts, was made director of physical culture of the Baltimore Schools.[39]

In a sense it was well that the German-American private schools and the English-German public schools disappeared at the turn of the century. The Germans were forced to attend the broad, American public-school system. Whatever good and useful ideas or valuable teachers they had had no longer remained in the isolated circle of German-Americans; they worked for the good of the whole. Thus, toward the end of the nineteenth century and to an even greater extent in the twentieth century we find good German trained teachers in the public-school system of Baltimore. Here, as in so many other instances, it is impossible to give a complete list of them; only a few of the most prominent will be mentioned.

Charles F. Raddatz (1838-1914), a German immigrant, was professor of German at Baltimore City College; for many years he was head of the German Department, and for eight years was vice-president of the school. He was a highly cultured man, who had a good reputation as a philologist, and who enjoyed the friendship of such men as Basil Gildersleeve and Sidney Lanier.[40] William F. Wardenburg, who was principal of Eastern High School from 1877 to 1906, deserves mention in this connection; he was in favor of modern educational methods and initiated reforms aimed at dispensing with the senseless practice of memorizing in schools.[41] The name of John B. Wentz has come down to us, a man who taught languages at City College during the fifties and sixties and then served for twenty years on the Board of Commissioners of Public Schools.[42] Glancing through the history of Western High School, we meet again and again the names of Pamela A. Hartman (vice-principal, 1870-1902) and David E. Weglein (principal, 1906-1921); both of these are among the first ranks of the people who

[39] Schulz's first report on his work is in the *Report of the Public School Commissions* (Baltimore, January 17, 1899), 61. Cf. also Prahl, *Gymnastic, SHGM*, xxvi, 26.

[40] Raddatz was born in Rostock. He came to America in 1858, lived for a time in Texas and then from 1870 until his death in Baltimore. *SHGM*, xxiii, 40 f.

[41] *Through the Years of Eastern High School* (Baltimore, 1944), 48 ff.

[42] James C. Leonhart, *One Hundred Years of the Baltimore City Colleges* (Baltimore, 1939), 24.

assisted in the development of the school.[43] An honorable place in the history of the Baltimore school system belongs to Ernest J. Becker (born in Baltimore, 1875); he was at first head of the Modern Language Department at City College, then principal of Eastern High School from 1909-1921, and from 1921 to 1937 principal of Western High School. As head of the two most important Baltimore high schools he deserves a great deal of credit.

A German who taught German and French at Baltimore City College for many years, Carl Otto Schönrich (1847-1932), also deserves mention. He emigrated from Germany in 1867 in order to avoid Prussian military service, and settled in Baltimore. His greatest service was the establishment of night schools for foreign-born people. In 1876 he began this task under great difficulties. At first the courses were given only for German and French immigrants, but by the turn of the century the idea had become so popular that the immigrants of all nationalities took advantage of the opportunity to learn the language and customs of the new country. For decades Schönrich was the moving spirit behind this useful institution.[44]

In the histories of the various colleges and universities in Maryland one will also find the names of a great many men of German descent, particularly at Johns Hopkins University, Goucher College and the University of Maryland. The fact that Johns Hopkins University was patterned after the German universities (1876) and that many of its early professors studied in Germany has often been pointed out and need not occupy us here.[45] In addition to the spiritual influence of German educational ideas, there were also

[43] E. J. Becker (ed.), Western High School, Past and Present, 1844-1944 (Baltimore, 1944), 34, 36, 113, 117.

[44] See "Making Good Americans of Polyglot Europeans," Baltimore Sun, March 31, 1907.

[45] DNB, 58 ff. SHGM, xxiii, 10. Faust, ii, 228. John A. Walz, German Influence in American Education and Culture (Philadelphia, 1936), 54 f. Ira Remsen, the second president of Johns Hopkins University, said in an article in 1903, "If I were asked what American scholarship owes to Germany I should unhesitatingly answer that it is more than anything else this quality of thoroughness. . . . For more than a quarter of a century the Johns Hopkins University has been upholding the ideals of German scholarship." (Baltimore and the Saengerfest, 91, 93.) ". . . a university permeated by the spirit of the universities of Germany, with research as the center, the heart, of the whole organism." Cf. Fabian Franklin, The Life of Daniel Coit Gilman (New York, 1910), 227.

various Germans who did a great deal through their years of teaching at Johns Hopkins to assist in the speedy rise of the university.

The most prominent scholar in the early history of Johns Hopkins was Paul Haupt (1858-1926).[46] He was born in Görlitz, Silesia, studied at the University of Leipzig, specializing in Assyriology, and was made Professor of Semitic Languages at Johns Hopkins University in 1883. He remained in this position until his death. He soon became one of the most prominent orientalogists in the country. The list of his publications comprises 522 titles. The value of his work in the field of Biblical criticism has been contested among scholars. His contributions to Assyriology and to Sumerian philology, however, have received widespread acclaim and are the basis on which his reputation as one of the greatest scholars in his field is founded.

Starting in 1907, another great German philologist worked at Johns Hopkins University: Hermann Collitz (1855-1935).[47] He came from the province of Hannover. His philological training he received at the universities of Göttingen and Berlin, and in 1886 he came to America. At first he taught at Bryn Mawr College, later at Johns Hopkins. During these decades he became an authority in the field of comparative linguistics and comparative philology; his work in the phonology and morphology of Indo-European languages became internationally famous. He held the chair of Germanic Philology at Johns Hopkins for two decades (1907-1927).

The very fact that Johns Hopkins University in its beginnings so strongly stressed its indebtedness to the German ideals of education led many wealthy and cultured Germans in Baltimore to become its staunch friends and patrons. When the great German teacher of political science, J. K. Bluntschli, died in 1881 the German-Americans in Baltimore raised the funds to secure the valuable Bluntschli library in Heidelberg for Johns Hopkins University. And in later years German businessmen in the city repeatedly came to the assistance of the university in financial crises.[48]

[46] DAB, VIII, 401 f. SHGM, XXIII, 34 f. *Oriental Studies in Commemoration of . . . Paul Haupt* (1926).

[47] SHGM, XIV, 55 f. *Studies in Honor of Hermann Collitz* (Baltimore, 1930).

[48] Daniel C. Gilman, *The Launching of a University* (New York, 1906), 98. President Ira Remsen paid great tribute to the Germans of Baltimore in his address at the Schiller Festival in 1905. Cf. Albert Pfister, *Nach Amerika im Dienste Friedrich Schillers* (Stuttgart, 1906), 44.

In the development of Goucher College in Baltimore a man of German descent, or more exactly of German-Swiss descent, played an important role: Hans Froehlicher. Froehlicher taught modern languages and also founded a new department, Art Criticism. For many years he was a member of the city school board and for a time was acting president of Goucher College. He was a zealous exponent of progressive educational methods and was one of the founders of the progressive Park School in Baltimore, where his son later became principal.[49] William W. Guth, who was president of Goucher College from 1913 to 1929, was also of German descent, as was Herman L. Ebeling (1857-1945), who was in charge of the Department of Classical Languages for more than twenty years.[50]

In Frederick, Maryland, Henry Joseph Apple was president of Hood College from 1893 to 1934; Apple, who came from a Pennsylvania-German family, was one of the leading educators in the state. The Reverend Benjamin Sadtler (1832-1901) was also well known among educators as the president of two colleges before he became a minister in a Baltimore church in 1886.[51]

We shall confine ourselves to only three names in the history of the Medical School of the University of Maryland—Jacob Edwin Michael, Harry Friedenwald and John C. Hemmeter. Jacob E. Michael (1848-1905) was associated with the university from 1874 on as professor of anatomy and obstetrics and as dean of the faculty. He was surrounded by a large circle of friends and admirers gathered through his publications as well as by his teaching.[52] Friedenwald and Hemmeter were sons of German immigrants. For many years Harry Friedenwald, one of the most outstanding American ophthalmologists, was a professor at the university and a member of the board of trustees.[53] John C. Hemmeter (1863-1931) was associated with the university from 1884 to the end of his life. A list of his medical publications covers many pages; especially noteworthy was his interest in the history of medicine, a new field which Hemmeter

[49] Hans Froehlicher was born in 1865 in Solothurn, Switzerland. He studied philology in Zürich and came to Baltimore in 1888; he died there in 1930. Anna H. Knipp and Thaddeus P. Thomas, *The History of Goucher College* (Baltimore, 1938), 301 ff.

[50] *Ibid.*, 216 ff.   [51] *SHGM*, XII, 43.

[52] Eugene F. Cordell, *History of the University of Maryland 1807-1907* (New York, 1907), I, 281 f.

[53] Dieter Cunz, "Contributions of the German Element to the Growth of the University of Maryland," *SHGM*, XXVI, 7-15.

helped to explore in various publications.[54] There was an especially large percentage of Germans who were active in the development of the School of Pharmacy connected with the University of Maryland. Lewis H. Steiner, a member of one of the oldest German families in Western Maryland, and William Simon, a German immigrant, attained good reputations in the second half of the nineteenth century as chemists.[55] At the same time the Dohme family achieved a leading position in pharmacology; both Louis Dohme and Charles E. Dohme were presidents of the College of Pharmacy.[56] Toward the end of the century Charles Caspari, whose father had emigrated from Germany in 1841, became increasingly important in the Department of Pharmacology. For many years he was professor of Theory and Practice of Pharmacy and he finally became dean of the faculty of pharmacy.[57] In connection with the College Park Branch of the University of Maryland, it is interesting to note that this institution, which was founded in 1856 as Maryland Agricultural College, was consciously based on the work of the greatest German chemist of the time, Justus von Liebig. Liebig is considered the father of agricultural chemistry; he believed that agriculture should be carried on as a science and to this end the school in College Park was opened. Among the professors who taught agriculture here in the course of years there were a great many people of German descent or of German birth.[58]

A field in which Germans were particularly prominent in Baltimore was library science. The organizer of the Enoch Pratt Library, Lewis H. Steiner (1827-1892) and his son and successor, Bernard C. Steiner (1867-1926), did a great deal for the education of the common man and for the development of the public library

[54] DAB, VIII, 519. SHGM, XXIV, 56. Cordell, op.cit., I, 301, 329. *Medical Life*, XXXIV, No. 4, Hemmeter Festschrift Number (New York, April 1927). *Die Medizin der Gegenwart in Selbstdarstellungen*, edit. by L. R. Grote (Leipzig, 1924), contains Hemmeter's autobiography, 1-62. Lists of Hemmeter's publications may be found in the two latter works.

[55] Cordell, op.cit., I, 417, 420, 425, 435 ff. Steiner exerted a great influence through his numerous lectures, articles, books, etc.; he did much for the scientific education of the masses. Simon, who taught at the university from 1892 to 1902, was the first man to install a modern chemical laboratory in Baltimore. Cyclopedia, 466, 616.

[56] *Ibid.*, 443.   [57] *Ibid.*, 444.

[58] For particulars, see Dieter Cunz, op.cit., 13 f.

system of Baltimore.[59] John G. Morris merits mention a second time as librarian of the Maryland Historical Society and the Peabody Institute. The biographies of two men, Philip R. Uhler and Louis H. Dielman, are almost identical with the history of the library of the Peabody Institute from 1870. "Dielman's Morgue," a broad collection of dates concerning Maryland families, is today an invaluable aid to local historians and genealogists.[60]

An institution in the artistic life of Baltimore whose development was aided by a particularly large percentage of representatives of the German element is the Maryland Institute of Art. We shall discuss William Henry Rinehart, the greatest sculptor in Maryland, in greater detail below. Next to him in importance was Otto Fuchs (1828-1906). From 1883 to his death he was director of the institute; his accomplishments in reorganizing the institute after the great fire of 1904 were widely recognized.[61]

Two additional German names are closely connected with the history of the Maryland Institute—Ephraim Keyser and Hans Schuler, both sculptors and both for many years teachers in the Rinehart School of Sculpture in the institute. Ephraim Keyser (1850-1937) was born in Baltimore, the son of a German immigrant who had left the old country in 1832. He started his studies at the Maryland Institute, continued in Munich, Berlin and Rome and then worked for thirty years at the Maryland Institute. Toward the end of the nineteenth century his was one of the best-known names among American sculptors. Among his works were the DeKalb monument in Annapolis, the tomb of President Chester A. Arthur in Albany, busts of Cardinal Gibbon, Sidney Lanier and Daniel Gilman, the "Toying Page" and "Psyche."

When Ephraim Keyser retired to private life in 1923, one of his students took charge of the Maryland Institute—Hans Schuler, who had been associated with the institute since 1890 at first as a student and then as a teacher. Schuler, who was born in 1874 in Morange, Alsace-Lorraine, came to America as a six-year-old boy. The Rinehart scholarship made it possible for him to study for a few years in Europe, and then he settled permanently in Baltimore. The Johns

[59] DAB, xvii, 561 ff. SHGM, vi, 87 ff. L. H. and B. C. Steiner, *The Genealogy of the Steiner Family* (1896).
[60] *Maryland Spectator*, ii (1936), 23; *Biogr. Cyclopedia*, 576.
[61] SHGM, xxi, 87; xxiii, 11. Faust, ii, 303 f. *Men of Mark in Maryland*, i, 131 ff.

Hopkins Memorial and the Luther monument in Baltimore, the Buchanan monument in Washington and a few statues such as "Young David," "Narcissus" and "Ariadne," established his fame.

Among the painters in Maryland during this period there is only one who rose above the average—Carl Bersch (1834-1914). Bersch was born in the Palatinate; he had lived in Baltimore since the seventies and became known particularly as a portrait painter there and in Washington.[62] Some other noted Maryland painters of German descent were Louis P. Dietrich, August Weidenbach, Frank B. Mayer and Charles Volkmar.

In the realm of music, the Germans were of more than average importance. It is difficult to evaluate the extent of the musical education which the singing societies gave to the common people. But the Germans were also active in the higher realms of the musical life of the city. They took an active part in the development of the Peabody Conservatory. When Tchaikovsky came to Baltimore for a concert in 1891 he was the guest of Edward Knabe, the famous piano manufacturer, who was given this honor as the leading representative of Baltimore. Richard Burmeister's activities as head of the Piano Department of the Peabody Institute, Otto Sutro's performances of oratorios and Richard Ortmann's music criticism belong to the musical life of Baltimore during this period; these men did their share in raising the musical taste of the city. Numberless German music teachers plied their crafts in the city during this time. They created no immortal works, but their influence quietly spread abroad and helped to create an appreciation of music among the broad masses of the population. Through a coincidence, one of them was raised from anonymity to the light of history, for he adapted the text of the song "Maryland, My Maryland," today the official state hymn, to the melody of an old German Christmas carol. Charles Ellerbrock is responsible for the fact that the melody of "O Tannenbaum, O Tannenbaum" is sung at every official state function in Maryland today.[63]

[62] Albert B. Faust, "Carl Bersch—Artist and Portrait Painter," *American German Review*, x, vi (1944), 4-7.

[63] Charles W. A. Ellerbrock, a German music teacher, was employed by a Baltimore publishing house (Miller & Beacham) during the Civil War. He took the text of "Maryland, My Maryland," which until then had been sung to the melody of a Yale song (Lauriger Horatius) and adapted it to the Tannenbaum melody. Like James Randall, the author of the text, Ellerbrock was a Southern sympathizer. In 1935 the song was elevated to the official state

Outside of Baltimore as well, a few German names became known to the musical world. Heinrich Dielmann built up the Music Department of St. Mary's College in Emmitsburg.[64] A German, Charles A. Zimmermann, was professor of music and band master at the United States Naval Academy in Annapolis for twenty-nine years; his best-known composition, the song "Anchors Aweigh," is familiar to every American today.[65]

The members of what might be called the academic professions— the university professors, physicians, lawyers, artists and musicians among the German-Americans—showed the greatest inclination to break out of the German-American isolation. Wider possibilities were open to these professional groups through speedy acclimatization. Therefore, they lost their pronounced German-American characteristics and made more rapid progress in their American surroundings. On the other hand, the artisans and businessmen held fast to their German individuality and it was from their ranks that the German-American type was built up—a group which built its own world with its own social forms and institutions. The businessmen and industrialists supplied the financial backbone of German Americanism.

Money was needed in order to support all the German-American churches, schools, societies, philanthropies, newspapers, etc. The necessary sociological subsoil for the flourishing of this Ger-

---

hymn. Cf. *The Poems of James R. Randall*, introduction by M. P. Andrews (New York, 1910), 15. L. C. Elson, *History of American Music* (New York, 1925), 156. Lelia Carey, "Maryland, My Maryland," *The Southern Magazine*, 1 (1934), 6 ff. *Century Magazine*, May 1887. Baltimore *Sun*, June 21, 1925.

[64] Heinrich Dielmann (1811-1882) came from Frankfurt a.M. He went in 1827 to Baltimore, where he founded a music school. From 1843 to his death he was at Emmitsburg. Further information about him may be found in H. A. Rattermann, *Gesammelte Ausgewählte Werke*, x (1911), 337-40. *Deutsch-amerikanische Geschichtsblätter*, xii, 339. *Der Deutsche Pionier*, xiv (1882), 444.

[65] Charles A. Zimmermann, born in Newport, R.I., 1861, spent most of his life in Maryland. He studied music at Peabody Institute in Baltimore and from 1887 to his death in 1916 he was connected with the Naval Academy in Annapolis. He composed a march for each graduation. "Anchors Aweigh" was the song which he composed for and dedicated to the Naval Academy Class of 1907. From the very beginning it was one of the most popular Navy songs. Additional information about him may be found in the Annapolis *Evening Capital*, January 17, 1916. Cf. also *The Book of Navy Songs* (New York, 1926).

man-American self-sufficiency was made up of a large, well-to-do middle class. During the decades after the Civil War, the financial strength of the German-Americans began to be consolidated chiefly because the Germans were able to secure a place for themselves in the commercial and industrial life of the city, where the most money was to be made. Hundreds of Germans who immigrated after 1840 became wealthy people; thousands of them achieved at least moderate well-being.

One of the most important dates in the business life of Baltimore is March 23, 1868. On this date the steamship *Baltimore* docked at the wharf of the Baltimore and Ohio Railroad. The *Baltimore* was the first ship which the Baltimore-Bremen Line of the North German Lloyd sent over, the first ship of the regular service between Baltimore and Bremen which was inaugurated that day. We have already had occasion to mention the commercial connections between the two cities. Their interests had long since branched out beyond the tobacco trade; they included the whole gamut of export and import trade. From the beginning the North German Lloyd worked in close co-operation with the Baltimore and Ohio Railroad. For both passenger traffic and freight, Baltimore became the most important transit port to the Middle and Far West in the exchange business between the North German Lloyd and the Baltimore and Ohio Company. Albert Schumacher was the connecting link between the two and after his death his firm continued to represent the North German Lloyd in Baltimore (until 1930). Twenty years after the first Lloyd steamer docked, there was regular weekly service between Baltimore and Bremen.

It is impossible to make an even partially complete list of the Germans who became established in the business life of Baltimore during the second half of the nineteenth century. A visit to the business section of the city today and a glance at the numberless German names to be found in firms even now will afford convincing proof of the activity of the Germans. They remained firmly entrenched in the tobacco trade and allied industries: Christian Ax, George W. Gail, Ernst Schmeisser, Henry Lauts, William A. Marburg, F. W. Felgner, Gieske & Niemann, August Mencken and others. To an even greater extent than tobacco, the brewing industry was almost entirely a German monopoly: Georg Gunther, John Wiesner, J. H. Vonderhorst, Gottlieb-Bauernschmidt-Strauss,

Georg Brehm, Sebastian Helldörfer, Frank Steil, Christian Heurich, etc. In addition to these two fields, the Germans entered all branches of industrial and commercial life; there were such men as F. X. Ganter, H. G. von Heine, William Knabe, Charles M. Stieff, Christopher Lipps, Kummer & Becker, Nicholas Rittenhouse, Henry Smith, William Heinekamp, Johann Faust, Edward A. Prior, Charles and August Vogeler, William H. Hoffman and many others. These names are taken from the various branches of business: chemical and lithographic industries; piano, iron, textile, lumber, paper and shoe manufacture; building firms; department stores; shipping offices and other lines. In 1885 a German-American, Robert Rennert, built the famous Rennert Hotel, which became the gathering place for the social and political life of the city for two generations.[66]

It is characteristic of the German-Americans that during this time they attempted to isolate themselves in financial affairs, too. No less than four German-American banks were founded in Baltimore after the Civil War, the "Deutsche Bank von Baltimore" (1868), "Deutsch-Amerikanische Bank" (1871), "Deutsche Central Bank" (1874) and "Deutsche Sparbank von Baltimore" (1876).[67] Of course these banks were purely local; their activity was confined to the German-American sector of the population and especially the lower classes in it.

That the Germans were able to establish themselves securely in the various industries was partly due to the fact that at this time technical sciences began to develop rapidly in Germany and that among the immigrants were many German engineers whose skill was utilized by the older German-Americans. Proof that the city

[66] Faust, II, 66, 75, 89, 90, 100, 117. BVG, 93 ff., 309 ff. DNB, 42 ff., 161 ff. Biogr. Cycl., 316, 395, 419, 621. Baltimore, Its History and Its People (New York, 1912), II, 376 ff. Alfred Dolge, Pianos and Their Makers (Covina, Calif., 1911), I, 282 ff., 291 f.; II, 120 ff. Edward F. Leyh, "Baltimores Deutsch-Amerikaner in Handel und Industrie," SHGM, VI, 77 ff. For additional information on German-American business, see Appendix III.

[67] BVG, 107; DNB, 40. The German influence was also very strong in the Hopkins Place Savings Bank and in the St. James Savings Bank, both of which for many years had almost exclusively German directors. The leading German-American banker during these years was Robert M. Rother. There were also a few entirely German insurance companies in Baltimore. Cf. SHGM, VIII, 19.

was particularly rich in German engineers is the fact that a German Engineering Society was founded in 1895 in Baltimore.[68]

Next to the German engineers, the German chemists were particularly important in the city, also because of the rise of chemical science in Germany. Otto Dieffenbach and William Simon were two chemists who were employed at the Baltimore Chrom Works. Toward the end of the century, Charles Glaser, a student of the famous Carl Remigius Fresenius, won a reputation as an outstanding analytical chemist. Gustav Liebig worked in the field of agricultural chemistry; he was partly responsible for the fact that a vast industry producing artificial fertilizer sprang up in Baltimore. G. W. Lehmann, also a student of Fresenius, made a name for himself in the field of metallurgy. Victor Bloede ran a laboratory for the improvement of dyeing processes.[69]

The German-American of these years was well aware of his individuality. He was aware of it when he read his German newspaper in the morning or during the day when he worked in his office or shop. This consciously German-American atmosphere did not cease with his professional life. His leisure time and relaxation also fit into this picture. We have already discussed the many German-American societies. Along with them, there was a whole series of opportunities for entertainment outside the organizations; among these was the German theater.

The German theater in Baltimore reached the high point of its brief history during the decade following the Civil War.[70] The opening of the Concordia Opera House in 1865 marked the beginning of a period of excellent German performances. The names of a few German theater directors who were particularly popular among the Germans in the city have come down to us: Georg Geiwitz, Adolph Meaubert, Oscar Mojean and Heinrich Maret. According to all reports, never before or since were there such good German performances to be seen as between 1865 and 1875. Financially, it is true, the stock companies had to struggle hard during this time. A few wealthy German businessmen provided the funds

---

[68] The names of a few well-known German engineers at the end of the nineteenth century: Rudolf Stueler, John Adt, John Maiberg, Fritz Mayer, Theodor Zwermann, Richard Sandlass, Gustav Lehmann and William Simon. DNB, 46 ff.

[69] Cyclopedia, 168. DNB, 311.

[70] A. E. Zucker, "Theater," 132 ff. BVG, 140 ff.

and engaged a good manager (Gustav Scherenberg) for the 1874-1875 season. The result was a good season but a financial disaster. After this the German theater sank to the level of occasional club performances. Thus the circle was complete, for it had started with amateur performances, risen for a time to professional heights and then fallen back again to the amateur level. At each level the choice of programs offered could only be called mediocre. There were occasional presentations of the great German classic writers like Schiller and Grillparzer (*Wilhelm Tell, Maria Stuart, Die Ahnfrau*), but the usual repertoire consisted of sentimental melodramas and stupid farces like Birch-Pfeiffer's *Die Waise von Lowwood*, Kotzebue's *Die beiden Klingsbergs*, Blumenthal's *Ein Tropfen Gift*, Sardou's *Divorçons*, etc. On the whole, the German theater in Baltimore was definitely inferior to that of other American cities with a German population, such as New York, Philadelphia or Milwaukee.

The German concerts were in less danger (artistically and financially) than the drama; performances of music required less money and in addition were usually in the hands of the great singing societies. Now and again German operas were staged. But the choral concerts of the various societies were even more popular. One characteristic feature of Baltimore's musical life was the prominence of oratorio music. In 1880 a special Oratorio Society was founded, which lasted for many years and performed a great many famous oratorios, such as Händel's *Messiah*, Bach's *Passions*, Haydn's *Schöpfung*, Mendelssohn's *Twenty-fourth Psalm* and many more. The leading spirit of the Oratorio Society was one of the most prominent German musicians in the city, Otto Sutro.[71] A Philharmonic orchestra and the Haydn Society were devoted exclusively to the performance of classical orchestral music.[72]

[71] Otto Sutro was born in Aachen in 1833. He studied music at the conservatory in Brussels and gained a good reputation as a pianist. In 1858 he came to Baltimore, where he was an organist and music teacher. Later he opened a music store. He was the founder of the well-known "Wednesday Club," a musical-literary club. Sutro's oratorio concerts were famous far beyond the limits of Baltimore. He died in 1896. BVG, 164. Baltimore *Sun*, January 20, 1896. Ottilie Sutro, "The Wednesday Club," *Maryland Hist. Mag.*, xxxviii (1943), 60 ff. In addition to Otto Sutro, Joseph Pache and F. Finke were the most active promoters of the Oratorio Society.

[72] BVG, 154 ff. The Haydn Society was founded in 1860, and the Philharmonic orchestra in 1880 (by William E. Heimendahl).

All these social events, these clubs, these community dramatic performances and concerts naturally exerted an enormous solidifying pressure upon the German-Americans. The barrier set up by the German language excluded all strangers and compressed those who belonged to the group into an almost solid block.

The most effective means of drawing together the Germans in the city and setting them apart from their surroundings as a minority group of one nationality was the German newspapers. After the Civil War they developed and throve as never before and flourished with undiminished vigor until the end of the century. After that time a slow decline set in until the first World War caused the complete collapse of the German press.

As in the years before the Civil War, so in the seventies and eighties, the *Deutsche Correspondent* was the most widely read German paper in the state. None of the newspapers founded later could ever compete in importance with the *Correspondent*. Despite various attempts at competition it retained the greatest influence upon the German element throughout the entire German-American period. The various editors of the paper were the spokesmen for the Germans in the city, particularly in local questions where the party differences between Republicans and Democrats were obliterated. Friedrich Raine, the founder, was the decisive personality on the staff until 1893. But Friedrich Raine had political ambitions and in order to gain more time for public offices he arranged to have his brother, Eduard Raine, take over the management of the newspaper at the beginning of the seventies.[73] Eduard accepted and, following his brother's wishes, took over a great part of the task of editing; after Friedrich Raine's death (1893), Eduard ran the paper independently. He was particularly interested in improving the methods of presentation and he did much to increase the circulation of the paper. It was he who, in 1898, introduced the *Sonntags-Correspondent*. Among the members of the staff Eduard F. Leyh was particularly important; during the first decade after the Civil War he was one of the leading figures among the Germans in Baltimore. He was one of the best-loved newspaper people in

[73] Eduard Raine (1834-1911) was born in Minden, Germany; he came to America in 1842 and in the fifties founded a print shop in Baltimore with his brother-in-law, W. Polmyer. After this he was associated with various German newspapers in North Carolina and Ohio until his brother asked him to come back to Baltimore, where he stayed for the rest of his life. DNB, 250.

the city and was considered the best German-American journalist in the history of the Germans in Maryland.[74] Besides Leyh, Richard Ortmann, August F. Trappe and John F. Pruess played an important part in the history of the newspaper since the end of the nineties.[75] After Eduard Raine's death in 1911 his daughter, Annie V. Raine, and Evan A. Heinz took over the management of the *Correspondent*.

Because of the political affiliations of the Raine brothers, the *Correspondent* remained consistently and emphatically in the service of the Democratic Party, which means that during most of the time covered in this chapter it was an opposition paper. At election time the Democratic candidate was always endorsed. The administration of Ulysses S. Grant was sharply criticized during all of its eight years. However, in spite of this, the *Correspondent* was not so fanatically Democratic that it could not distinguish between two Republican administrations of different quality. The *Correspondent* always had words of praise for the Hayes cabinet; it disapproved of the election maneuver with which the Republicans got Hayes into the White House, but it conceded that Hayes was more to be trusted than Grant.[76] In very stormy and aggressive words the *Cor-*

[74] Eduard F. Leyh (1840-1901) came from Meiners in Thüringen. In Germany he studied to become a teacher and in 1861 went to Baltimore, where he taught for a few years in German schools. In 1864 he became a reporter on the Baltimore *Wecker*, in 1867 editor of the *Maryland Staatszeitung*, in 1871 assistant editor of the *Correspondent*. In 1881 his friend, Carl Schurz, offered him a position on the *Westliche Post* in St. Louis, but Leyh remained in Missouri only two years, for Friedrich Raine made every effort to get him back to Baltimore. Leyh remained on the staff of the *Correspondent* until his death. Raine always had great respect for him; in his will he even made a stipulation that Leyh could never be discharged. Leyh made various attempts in the field of literature, especially in translations of American poetry. His best-known translations are Francis Scott Key's *Star Spangled Banner*, Joaquin Miller's *Golddigger of Arizona* and William Motherwell's *Hannah Morrison*. He was an ardent admirer of the Hohenzollern empire. Occasionally he espoused theories of the superiority of the blond, Nordic race, which, in a most unfortunate manner, anticipated later racial delusions. He possessed great influence among the Germans in the city, especially among the younger people. For a long time a group of young Germans met in his house every Saturday evening for gatherings which started out with literary lectures and ended with alcoholic beverages. Cf. Albert B. Faust, "Die Sonntagsschule des Herrn Eduard F. Leyh," *Die Glocke* (Chicago, 1908), III, 19 ff. *SHGM*, xv, 45-51.

[75] *SHGM*, xxiv, 61, 65.

[76] *Correspondent*, March 7, April 27, 1877. Carl Schurz was repeatedly attacked by the *Correspondent* because in 1872 he was against the Repub-

respondent demanded an end to the long Republican period at the election of 1880. The temperamental bases of the parties were said to have changed completely; the Democrats who for years had called themselves conservative were now desirous of change.[77] It need hardly be mentioned with what joy the election of Grover Cleveland was greeted. At the election of 1888 the prohibition question came up. Since the majority of Germans were anti-Prohibitionists, the *Correspondent* pointed out again and again that one of the most ardent feminine Prohibitionists (J. Ellen Foster) had declared herself in favor of the Republican candidate, Benjamin Harrison. This hint was intended to drive the Germans into the Democratic Party.[78] After the election of Harrison, when the *Correspondent* was analyzing the causes for the defeat of the Democrats, it blamed particularly the fact that the Democrats had brought up the tariff issue in the campaign.[79]

When Cleveland was elected the second time, the *Correspondent* stated that in many states his election was accomplished because of the German vote. Most of the Germans had voted Democratic in 1892.[80] When William Jennings Bryan was nominated by the Democrats in the summer of 1896, the *Correspondent* was cool and noncommittal. It was soon evident why—the *Correspondent* was against monetary experiments. When the Gold Democrats set up

---

licans and in 1876 for them. (*Correspondent*, October 27, 1876.) But then when Schurz was appointed Secretary of the Interior the paper called him one of the best and most highly acceptable Republicans. In later years Schurz was always treated in a friendly manner by the *Correspondent*. When in 1904 Schurz was attacked by a few German-Americans he was warmly defended by the *Correspondent* (November 5, 1904); it was said that Schurz did not follow party lines but principles and that he was honest and true to his convictions.

[77] In the campaign of 1880 there is an interesting reference in the *Correspondent* to the German revolution of 1848. The slogans of the Democrats and the Republicans were compared to those of the Revolutionists and Reactionaries of 1848. The Democrats say, "Es muss annerscht werre!" (It's time for a change!); while the Republicans say, "A Ruh' wolln mer hab'n" (We want quiet). *Correspondent*, July 29, 1880.

[78] *Ibid.*, August 27, October 6, 1888.

[79] *Correspondent*, November 9, 1888.

[80] *Ibid.*, November 11, 1892. The votes for Cleveland were said to have increased in Baltimore from 5000 (1888) to 12,000 (1892); these, if we may believe the *Correspondent*, were the German voters. "The Republican Party tried prohibition, and lost half of the German votes. It tried nativism and lost the other half. Trusts and monopolies—and it lost the farmers and labourers."

a separate ticket in the fall the newspaper supported it fully even though it was obvious that the ticket could not win. The *Correspondent* left no doubts about the "Silver Heresy." One can almost find a trace of relief between the lines when the paper's own party was defeated in November 1896. The Democratic Party had merited defeat because it had deserted its tried and true leaders in favor of a standard bearer from the ranks of the Populists. William J. Bryan was a man to be respected, but not one to be supported.[81]

When in 1900 Bryan was a candidate for the second time, the *Correspondent* indulged in even more pointed criticism. It said that he was to blame for the weakness of the Democratic Party; that the Republican Party had made one mistake after another and that its imperialistic policy, with the consequent burdens of a senseless foreign war, had netted it many enemies. If the Democratic Party was unable to make the most of this favorable position, the fault lay entirely with Bryan. He had forced himself upon the party, behaved like a dictator and again dragged the unfortunate monetary platform of 1896 into the campaign. The Democratic Party needed rejuvenation—less Bryan and more Jefferson.[82]

When Alton Parker, a Gold Democrat, was nominated in the summer of 1904 there was great joy in the columns of the newspaper.[83] For the first time since Cleveland's campaigns the *Correspondent* plunged eagerly into the election campaign. It demanded reduction of the high protective tariff, which only served to increase the cost of living for the little man and allowed only a small clique to become wealthy. It bitterly condemned Theodore Roosevelt's foreign policy, pointing out that the imperialist policy in regard to the Philippines was bound to frighten and antagonize the South American countries. Not imperialism but the improvement and development of our home country was the problem of the day. "The domestic problems of the country will give Mr. Roosevelt more headaches during the next four years than any defense against attacks of one of the great powers."[84] Despite the fact that the *Correspondent* was very much disappointed at Alton Parker's defeat, it was only mildly critical of Theodore Roosevelt and in the inauguration editorial it went so far as to state that the President had improved.

[81] *Ibid.*, July 11, September 4, November 4, 5, 1896.
[82] *Correspondent*, November 7, 1900.   [83] *Ibid.*, July 10, 11, 1904.
[84] *Ibid.*, November 1, 5, 7, 1904. March 4, 1905.

With diabolical glee the *Correspondent* observed the split in the Republican camp in 1912. At this time Theodore Roosevelt had reached the height of his popularity among the German-Americans. In regard to the Roosevelt-Taft family quarrel, the *Correspondent* aligned itself clearly on the side of Roosevelt. All the anti-Republican leanings of the newspaper were concentrated against Taft.[85] It stated that the Taft steam roller was the instrument of reaction, while Roosevelt represented progress and reform. However, the party political machine was so powerful that even a Roosevelt could not reform it. Result: Elect Woodrow Wilson!

Wilson's nomination, which the *Correspondent* witnessed in Baltimore, was joyfully proclaimed.[86] He was said to be progressive enough to take the wind out of Theodore Roosevelt's sails. And it was pointed out that the very fact of his not having the support of Wall Street and of his receiving only the lukewarm support of the Democratic Party machine could only be of advantage to him with the great masses of the people. On the other hand, the *Correspondent* showed that Wilson was not against trusts as such but that he believed they must be made to serve the people, which, in the long run, could only be in the interests of the trusts and big business. The readers of the *Correspondent* belonged to the well-to-do socially upper-class German-Americans. This latter comment was clearly aimed to make the Democratic candidate palatable to the upper classes, who tended more to the support of the Republican Party. The *Correspondent* was not at all sure of its German-American readers. It knew that they would not vote for Taft. But it also knew what an attraction Theodore Roosevelt had for them and it feared that many Germans would succumb to his fascination. It clearly remained aloof from all attacks on Theodore Roosevelt. It conceded that he had a right to try for a third term and did not feel that this endangered the nation's liberties. It made friendly comments on Roosevelt's attempt to reform the GOP. But it hoped that he would not be elected.[87] When Wilson's victory was won and consequently there was no longer any danger of Roosevelt's success, the *Correspondent* found time in the midst of its joy about the start of the long-hoped-for Democratic era to write a few appreciative words for the defeated Bull Moose candidate.[88]

[85] *Ibid.*, June 22, 1912.
[86] *Ibid.*, July 3, 1912.
[87] *Ibid.*, October 10, 16, 1912.
[88] *Ibid.*, November 7, 1912.

In the ten years before the Civil War, the *Correspondent* had a rival in Baltimore in its Republican counterpart, the *Wecker*. After the Civil War the *Wecker* existed for more than ten years as a daily paper. It provided strong competition for the *Correspondent* and was more consistently Republican than the *Correspondent* was Democratic. The *Wecker* continued to appeal to the Turners. It endorsed each Republican presidential candidate. It found Ulysses S. Grant beyond criticism; his first term was volubly defended. At the end of the first term the *Wecker* was bound to admit that the country was badly in need of reform, but it was convinced that Grant was more capable of achieving it than that "Hanswurst" (Clown) Horace Greeley.[89]

Unlike the *Correspondent*, the *Wecker* used vehement and sometimes almost vulgar language. Its views were remarkably consistent; even a novel which was printed in installments mirrored the anti-Catholic, radical views of the political editorials.[90] One cannot escape the impression that the newspaper, founded in the fifties by an idealist like Carl Heinrich Schnauffer and kept on a high journalistic level during its first decade, was now gradually falling into decay in the seventies. This deterioration must be partly blamed on the fact that it no longer had uniform, purposeful leadership and that the owners and editors frequently changed. In 1865 General Franz Sigel secured an interest in the business, but he sold it the next year to Wilhelm Rapp.[91] In 1871 Rapp sold his share to a Dr. Morwitz in Philadelphia and later the business went to a prominent Turner, J. R. Fellmann.[92] But the decline was not to be checked. After an existence of twenty-five years the *Wecker* ceased to appear

---

[89] *Wecker*, May 22, June 1, 10, November 4, 1868. October 26, 1872.

[90] This was the Reformation novel by A. E. Brachvogel called *Der Deutsche Michel*, which appeared in the *Wecker* in 1868. Upon this occasion the newspaper stated that it felt much greater sympathy for a German-Protestant revolutionary like Thomas Münzer than for the more conservative Martin Luther.

[91] *BVG*, 304. W. Rapp had edited the *Wecker* once before; after this he edited the *Illinois Staatszeitung* for a while.

[92] Johann Rudolf Fellmann was a German-Swiss. He was born in Staffelbach, Aargau, in 1825. A teacher by profession, he came to America in the fifties, fought in the Civil War as a captain in the Union Army and was closely associated with the German Turners. In 1875 he founded a Swiss Society in Baltimore. Until his death (1886) he held a position in the U.S. Customs Office in the Port of Baltimore. Adelrich Steinach, *Geschichte und Leben der Schweizer Kolonien in den Vereinigten Staaten von Nord-Amerika* (New York, 1889), 117 f.

as a daily paper in 1878. Wilhelm Schnauffer (1835-1889), the brother of the founder, and after him Charles H. Milter used the title for another thirty years for a literary weekly.

In the chapter on the Civil War we mentioned briefly the German-Catholic weekly newspaper appearing in Baltimore called the *Katholische Volkszeitung*, which we must now treat a little more fully, for in the last third of the century it expanded in an unexpected manner. Two brothers, Joseph and Christoph Kreuzer, who came from the Bavarian Upper Palatinate, founded the paper in 1860. It was a Maryland newspaper only during its first few years. Even during the Civil War its circulation began to spread out beyond the border of the state so that soon there were subscribers in the neighboring states and the circulation spread to all parts of the Union and Canada, finally including regular readers as far away as Germany and Austria. We know that as early as 1876 it had a circulation of 22,000, and later this figure increased somewhat.[93] There were few secular German newspapers in America which could boast such a large number of readers. Though the paper particularly emphasized German-Catholic affairs in Maryland (as in Baltimore and Cumberland) it was not a local German newspaper in the narrower sense. For the Catholic Germans it achieved national importance.

The Kreuzer brothers were pillars of conservative Catholicism in America. They were interested in politics only to the extent that seemed advisable from the religious point of view. "We are not politicians. We challenge the political party leaders only when we see that they are treading on religious or political rights. . . . Only a comparatively small amount of space is devoted to politics in the

[93] A. W. Baumgartner, *Catholic Journalism, A Study of Its Development in the United States, 1789-1930* (New York, 1931), 17. Charles G. Fehrenbach, "German Literary Activities of the Redemptories in the United States," unpublished M.A. thesis, Catholic University, Washington, D.C., 1937. The newspaper had regular agents in all the states in which there were sizable German-Catholic congregations: Maryland, Virginia, Kentucky, Tennessee, Louisiana, Missouri, Iowa, Indiana, Illinois, Minnesota, Wisconsin, Michigan, Ohio, Pennsylvania, New Jersey, New York, Massachusetts. The *Katholische Volkszeitung* was as much a Baltimore paper as the *Christian Science Monitor* is today a Boston paper. At that time Baltimore was the center of American Catholicism; it was the established meeting place for large Catholic gatherings, the Plenary Council, Catholic Lay Congress, Catholic editors' meetings, etc.

paper because our main task is to battle against error and unbelief and to counteract the godless revolution."[94]

Christian meekness was not by any means the outstanding characteristic of the newspaper; on the contrary, it was a very quarrelsome paper. Its two archenemies which it fought for half a century with remarkable consistency and undying hatred were Liberalism and Protestantism. Its hatred of Liberalism included Catholic Liberalism as well. The liberal Catholics were said to be the worst and most dangerous enemies of true Catholicism.[95] It warned its readers against all kinds of nonsectarian Christianity; even so innocent an organization as the YMCA aroused the abhorrence of the paper because it represented a form of "washed-out Christianity."[96] The subtitle and motto which appeared at the heading of each number were highly indicative of the general attitude: "A Weekly Paper in the Interests of the Church," "United—Holy—Catholic—Apostolic." The last word merits particular emphasis. A very literal rendering of the German proverb "More Catholic than the Pope" may be used to describe the paper. At a time when numberless Catholic editors were receiving reprimands or warnings from the Apostolic See for deviating from the official church line, the *Katholische Volkszeitung* could boast of the fact that it always instinctively followed exactly the course prescribed by Rome and that it never received anything but praise and appreciation from the Pope. It is well known that during the second half of the nineteenth century there were great tensions on matters of dogma within the Catholic Church. If in the course of such discussions decisions had to be made, the Kreuzer brothers always made them in favor of the conservative, apostolic side. Their newspaper was one of the most zealous advocates of the theory of the infallibility of the Pope and entered into argument with anyone, whether Catholic or not, who doubted this dogma. At the beginning the paper published many articles on Catholicism in Europe, but gradually its interests became fixed upon the Catholic congregations in the United States. "First Catholic, then German," was a slogan often repeated; that is, the Catholic faith was more important as a binding heritage than German descent. Actually, this newspaper exhibited far less feeling

[94] *Katholische Volkszeitung*, April 28, 1866.
[95] *Ibid.*, February 27, 1864.
[96] *Ibid.*, November 14, 1908. The reader is advised to avoid the YMCA "like the plague."

for the German background than was the case among other German-Americans. But the adjective "German" was not entirely forgotten. This is clearly seen in numerous articles expressing sharp resentment against the dominating position of the Irish element within the Catholic Church.

The antiliberal attitude of the paper determined its reaction to all political and religious events of the epoch. The German liberal '48ers and the Italian liberator Garibaldi were deluged with contempt and ridicule. When Lincoln's assassination became known the Katholische Volkszeitung saw in this event the fruit of political liberalism; and it went on to say that since for years the liberals had been preaching the assassination of the reigning princes one need not be surprised at the complete demoralization of political life. The treatment of the Pope in 1870-1871 was reported with profound indignation. The founding of the German Reich in 1871 was discussed in a friendly but cool manner; the paper had little affection for Protestant Prussia, but it felt it could not ignore the advantages of the Bismarck state. This state fulfilled the first obligation of government to uphold order and justice and since this was also to the advantage of the Catholic Church, the paper saw no objections to the Bismarck Reich.[97] This attitude changed radically, however, as soon as Bismarck came in conflict with the Catholic Church. After 1873 hardly a week passed when the newspaper did not report on Bismarck's Kulturkampf. From that time on Bismarck's name was mentioned only with loathing and bitterness. Following a Papal encyclical against the Masonic Order in 1884, the paper published a long series of articles on the hidden and dangerous activities of the Free Masons and Freethinkers. When in 1883 the Protestant Church celebrated the 400th anniversary of Luther's birth, the newspaper greeted this event in the life of its sister Christian Church with a series of no less than sixty-two poisonous articles, tearing the whole structure of Protestantism to bits. There are also many articles on educational problems in which the advantages of parochial schools are set forth again and again. Articles on "Evils of the Theater," "Indecent Publications," "The Moral Decay of the Times" and "Growing Criminality" alternate with others on "Hollowness of Protestant Sermons," "Religious Persecution in Germany" and "Jewry." If there happened to be

[97] Katholische Volkszeitung, January 28, 1871.

nothing to be said about Protestants or liberals, then there was always an opportunity for anti-Semitic utterances. In 1876 the newspaper reprinted a long anti-Semitic novel *Der Talmudjude* by August Rohling, which advocated in literary form the anti-Semitism otherwise zealously preached only in editorials. The German-Jewish press was said to have started the anti-Catholic *Kulturkampf*; in literary essays the paper always spoke of the "Jew" Heinrich Heine; wherever there was anything wrong in the world it professed to see the sinister machinations of a "Gold International"; and in a review of Constantin Frantz's book on Federalism, the author's anti-Semitic doctrine is joyfully seconded, namely, that the Jews are "the ruination of the body and soul of the German nation."[98] Many of these articles betray such an uncivilized, primitive anti-Semitism as would have made them eligible to be published unabridged and unchanged in a Nazi paper such as the *Stürmer* in 1933.

The Kreuzer brothers gathered a small group of German-Catholic authors about their newspaper who submitted more or less regular contributions. At St. Michael's church in Baltimore there was a Reverend Peter Frischbier who contributed a great many articles and poems.[99] Another regular member of the writing staff was the Jesuit, F. X. Wenniger. The main standby among the free-lancing volunteers was a teacher named Damian J. Litz, who sent in contributions over a period of several decades, and used various pseudonyms.[100] Between 1880 and 1903 there was hardly a number in which there was not at least one article by Damian Litz, and often there were two. The founders of the newspaper, the Kreuzer

[98] *Ibid.*, July 19, 1879. September 11, 1880.
[99] Peter Frischbier was born in Prussia in 1827. He came to America in 1865 and died in Baltimore in 1900.
[100] Damian J. Litz was born in 1822 in Eschbach, Baden. He came to America in 1849 and taught in Catholic parochial schools in various states (Ohio, Wisconsin, New York, New Jersey, Maryland, Louisiana and Texas). In 1870-1873 and 1883-1886 he taught at St. Michael's church school in Baltimore. He wrote for various Catholic papers, though chiefly for the *Katholische Volkszeitung*. For years he ran regular columns ("Unter Uns," "Schnittwaren und Gedankenspäne," etc.). A collection was made of the first series and published in book form by the *Volkszeitung*, entitled *Unter uns, oder kleine Scharmützel mit dem Zeitgeist* (Baltimore, 1884). With his homespun, folksy, jovial manner, he seems to have catered exactly to his readers' taste, for his articles were admittedly the main attraction of each number. Litz died in 1903 in San Antonio, Texas. Anthony L. Saletel, "Damian Litz and the Catholic German-American Press, 1870-1903," M.A. thesis, Catholic University, Washington, D.C., 1939.

brothers, died within a few years of each other, Joseph in 1874 and Christopher in 1878. Christopher's widow, Barbara Kreuzer, continued to publish the paper, and from that time on she was even more dependent upon the assistance and contributions of Damian Litz. Without him the periodical would certainly not have been able to keep its unusually large and far-reaching circulation.

As far as domestic politics were concerned, the *Katholische Volkszeitung* supported the Democratic Party fairly consistently. It was against Abraham Lincoln in the Civil War, and later it was against Ulysses Grant. In 1868 it earnestly supported the Democratic candidate, Horatio Seymour.[101] Four years later, in the race between Grant and Horace Greeley, the paper remained neutral. Since the one candidate was a Republican and the other a liberal, the whole problem of the presidency revolved, as far as the *Katholische Volkszeitung* was concerned, around the question as to which one was the lesser evil, a question which the Kreuzer brothers could not decide.[102] In 1876 they were definitely for Samuel Tilden, though Rutherford B. Hayes was also honored with a few friendly words because he promised civil reform.[103] In the race between W. S. Hancock and James A. Garfield in 1880, Hancock was supported, though with not much enthusiasm. In the next three campaigns, 1884, 1888 and 1892, the paper supported Grover Cleveland with increasing enthusiasm.[104] It was certain that Divine Providence had sent the country a man like Cleveland, a true successor to Jefferson and Jackson, whose political views were far beyond his time. Once the editors had so firmly backed Cleveland the gold and silver issue in the Democratic Party in 1896 caused them some difficulties. Several months after the Democratic convention had named William Jennings Bryan to carry its banner in the election of 1896 the paper barricaded itself behind colorless, neutral reports on the

[101] *Katholische Volkszeitung*, July 18, 1868. The Republicans were called "radical Jacobins."

[102] *Ibid.*, July 20, 27, 1872.

[103] *Ibid.*, July 22, 1876. An article entitled "Der Purzelbaum des Herrn Schurz" (Mr. Schurz's Somersault) contained strong criticism of Carl Schurz, who was now returning to the Republican camp after having criticized Grant's administration for years. (In 1904, when Schurz issued a warning against the election of Theodore Roosevelt, he was again roundly censured by the *Volkszeitung. Ibid.*, October 22, 1904.)

[104] *Ibid.*, November 15, 1884. November 10, 1888. December 8, 1888. January 5, 1889. July 2, 1892.

campaign. After long consideration a decision was finally reached: For Silver Money, For Bryan![105] From this time forward articles appeared not only against the Republicans but also against the Gold Democrats. The gold standard was said to be only a gigantic speculation of the Jewish banking kings, an enormous, international plot of the Jews—as the paper explained it, using its own peculiar kind of insight into the racial background of world history. With righteous indignation it declared Bryan free of the taint of being anti-Catholic.[106] The paper supported Bryan in all three of his attempts to gain the presidency—1896, 1900 and 1908. William McKinley was said to be a spineless weathercock, an anti-Catholic Mason and a puppet of international Jewry.[107] Heavy salvos were fired at McKinley's successor, Theodore Roosevelt, in 1904; he was said to exemplify imperialism, lust for money, trusts, delusions of great power—all errors that would bear bitter fruits.[108] And again at the next election campaign between Taft and Bryan, the Democratic ticket was endorsed while the paper pointed out with approval that Bryan had modified many of his earlier radical views. The election of Taft was said not to do honor to the political insight of the people, though Taft was better than Roosevelt because he was better balanced than his predecessor.[109] Woodrow Wilson's nomination in 1912 was greeted with marked coolness, the newspaper taking no part in the campaign at all. Apparently the publishers had little interest in Wilson, for they treated him in a very reserved manner, and only at the time of his inauguration did they warm up to the subject somewhat, by admitting that in his speech he had spoken "golden words," and that he "seemed to possess the makings of a good president."[110]

A little more than a year later, in October 1914, the *Katholische Volkszeitung* ceased publication. The ominous date, 1914, might lead to the assumption that there was a connection with the outbreak of the war, but this was not the case. Neither political nor

[105] *Ibid.*, September 5, 1896.   [106] *Ibid.*, September 5, 1896.
[107] *Ibid.*, May 19, 1900. An article on March 9, 1901, reported on the inauguration of the "uncrowned emperor of America." True to the anti-Semitic attitude of the newspaper, it was stated with reference to the vice-president, Theodore Roosevelt, that forty people bearing the significant name of Rosenfeld had been present at the coronation celebration.
[108] *Ibid.*, October 22, November 19, 1904.
[109] *Ibid.*, July 18; October 3, 24; November 14, 1908.
[110] *Ibid.*, November 16, 1912; March 8, 15, 1913.

financial reasons were responsible. The only reason was that Barbara Kreuzer, the owner and official publisher, had grown too old and wanted to retire. The impending demise of the newspaper was kept secret until the very last. The readers were very cleverly shifted over to another German-Catholic paper in Philadelphia, called *Nord-Amerika*. This sudden but gentle transfer was accomplished so smoothly that hardly one of the old subscribers bolted. The history of the *Katholische Volkszeitung* reaches from 1860 to 1914, corresponding exactly to what is known as the "German-American" period.[111]

It is characteristic of the strength and intensity of German-Americanism during this time that during the height of this "hyphen-epoch" in the eighties a successful attempt was made to found a second German daily paper to compete with the other daily, the *Correspondent*, and with the many German weekly periodicals. The external stimulus was provided by a typesetters' strike at the *Correspondent*. When it was found that the quarreling parties could not reach an agreement, the striking typesetters organized the "Journal Publications Gesellschaft," in February 1882, starting the publication of the *Baltimore Journal* on February 13. Of course the paper would not have survived if there had not been a real demand for it. Apparently this demand existed, for the *Journal* grew from year to year and soon surpassed all other German newspapers. In 1896 it had reached the point where it could state that it now enjoyed "a larger circulation than any other German paper in Baltimore."[112]

First and foremost, the *Journal* was an advertising paper. It gave special notice to the activities of the German societies and paid special attention to happenings in the families and business firms of its readers and advertisers. Very frequently it lifted whole articles from other German papers, using the "scissors and paste method," a practice employed by so many German-American papers. Politically it confined itself to short, informative reports, and at the beginning it made an effort to report domestic and foreign politics in

---

[111] The only complete file of the *Katholische Volkszeitung* is in the library of Catholic University, Washington, D.C.

[112] *Baltimore Journal*, September 26, 1896. This statement appeared in English in the otherwise entirely German paper. The *Sonntags Post* was connected with the *Journal* and was the Sunday edition of the paper. See BVG, 305.

as colorless a manner as possible so as not to offend any one of its long list of subscribers. It prided itself upon being the mouthpiece of the independent voter who was not attached to a certain party but could arrive at his own choice in each individual case.[113] A careful study, however, will reveal that the *Journal's* decisions were never in favor of the Democratic Party. In the first election campaigns it remained cool and reserved, but its coolness was subtly employed in such a manner as to induce its readers to vote Republican. Grover Cleveland was not attacked, but was treated with indifference.[114] W. J. Bryan's monetary experiments were definitely rejected; the *Journal* was for stable currency. The paper took a definite stand for the Republican Party during the election in 1896. It considered the Republican Party to be the exponent of "healthy and progressive principles."[115] It pointed out that this gradual shift from benevolent neutrality to active support of the Republicans could only be construed as being helpful to business. German-American votes fluctuated greatly during the last third of the nineteenth century. But at the beginning of the twentieth century something like a Republican bloc consolidated itself among the German-Americans behind the magic personality of Theodore Roosevelt. However, in Baltimore the most influential German paper, the *Correspondent*, was Democratic. Thus the *Journal* stepped into the void left by the *Wecker* when it ceased publication in 1878. As long as Cleveland, who was very popular among the German-Americans, represented the Democratic Party, it was not advisable for a large advertising paper to hold to a decidedly Republican line. But when Theodore Roosevelt appeared upon the national scene, there was no holding the *Journal*. It entered the 1900 and 1904 election campaigns with great enthusiasm. It stated with great pride that the German-Americans were behind Roosevelt and that their votes would turn the tide. The *Journal* compiled a series of quotations from Roosevelt's early writings in order to win over those people who were still uncertain. These quotations showed that Roosevelt had a friendly attitude toward immigrants, that he believed in equal rights for naturalized citizens and that every discrimination between

---

[113] This attitude is evidenced in an article (October 1, 1892) describing the special mission of the *Journal*: to crystallize the opinion of the independent voter.

[114] *Journal*, November 16, 1888; September 28, November 10, 1892.

[115] *Ibid.*, October 13, November 4, 5, 1896.

naturalized and native citizens should be done away with. It reported proudly that a number of former German Democrats had declared themselves in favor of Roosevelt in Baltimore.[116] There is an interesting brief reference to Theodore Roosevelt's foreign policy: it was said that the German-Americans would always remember the fact that through his wise policy he had strengthened the friendship between the United States and the German Empire.[117]

The *Journal* observed the split in the Republican Party with profound regret. From the very beginning it realized clearly that Roosevelt's third party would cost the Republicans the victory, and it was very much annoyed that Roosevelt had split the Republican vote. Aside from this, the paper seemed to become a little fearful of Roosevelt's constantly increasing progressiveness, and when the presidency went to the Democrats in 1912 it resumed the reserved, distant manner that had characterized it at the beginning of its history. The *Journal* said nothing against Taft or against Roosevelt but on election day it merely expressed the hope that Wilson would run the country in an "intelligent, conservative, cautious manner."[118] "Conservative" and "cautious" were the adjectives that accurately characterized the whole history of the *Baltimore Journal*.

A year later there was a sudden and very radical change. On December 19, 1913, the *Journal* appeared in English carrying the subtitle, "A progressive Democratic daily newspaper." An editorial notice explained the new policy as follows: "The Baltimore Journal which for several years has been a Republican paper, published in German, today goes before the public as a Democratic organ to be published seven days in the week." A detailed article on William Jennings Bryan, the leader of the progressive Democrats, shows clearly the new direction that the paper took. But the paper did not last very long after its political and language change; the *Journal* folded up at the beginning of 1914, never to appear again either in German or in English.[119]

In addition to the large German newspapers mentioned thus far,

[116] *Ibid.*, October 31, November 8, 1900; September 19, October 10, 18, 1904. Among the Germans in Baltimore in 1904 there were a great many Roosevelt Democrats just as in 1892 there had been a large number of Cleveland Republicans.

[117] *Ibid.*, November 3, 1904.

[118] *Ibid.*, November 7, 1912.

[119] The *Journal* is not mentioned in either the 1914 or the 1915 Baltimore Directory.

there were a great many attempts to start newspapers in Baltimore in the half century following the Civil War. Often these lasted for only a short time and we know nothing about them but their titles and their publishers.[120] In 1869 a small group of newspapermen who had heretofore been working for the *Correspondent* tried to start a competitive paper which they called *Der Neue Correspondent*. The names of the founders have come down to us; they were E. H. Makk, Rudolf Worch, G. Faul, Paul Scholvien. Their undertaking met with little success; only a few weeks after the founding Makk resigned and Eduard Leyh took over the position of editor. Leyh persuaded a wealthy businessman, August Douglas, to invest money in the business and after a reorganization the paper appeared in November 1869 as the *Maryland Staatszeitung*. A little later Douglas encountered financial difficulties, and therefore the paper was sold to Friedrich Polmyer, a nephew of Friedrich Raine, to whom the *Correspondent* belonged. Polmyer published the paper for about a year (1870/71) as a daily afternoon paper; then it went out of circulation.

Siegmund Jünger attempted to start a daily paper, the *Baltimore Volksfreund*, in 1879. He was well known to the public because he had been publishing a weekly periodical, *Die Biene von Baltimore*, since 1873. The daily paper proved to be an unsuccessful speculation. Jünger soon had to content himself again with a weekly periodical, which he then published until well into the twentieth century under the name *Volksfreund und Biene*.

The *Bayrische Wochenblatt*, founded in 1881, was read by Bavarians in all states of the Union.[121]

Unsuccessful and short-lived were most of the literary periodicals, such as *Belletristische Blätter*, started in 1867 by the author, Willibald Winkler; the *Leuchtturm* edited in the sixties by Dr. Philipp Munder; and *Bunte Blätter*, founded by Albert von Degen in 1878.[122]

A large number of family papers suffered similar fates: *Glocke am Sonntag* (1863, C. W. Schneidereith), *Deutsche Fami-*

---

[120] BVG, 304 f.

[121] The paper had been started in Philadelphia by August Walther, but during its first year its place of publication was changed to Baltimore. Louis Heise and August Strauff were the two editors who saw the paper through thirty years of its life. DNB, 220.

[122] *Bunte Blätter* ceased publication in its third year; *Belletristische Blätter* in its second year; and the *Leuchtturm* ran only three numbers.

lienblatt (published in 1878 by C. A. Schlögel), *Protestantische Volkszeitung* (1873, F. Donner), *Aus beiden Welten* (1873, R. Wehrhahn), *Baltimore Argus* (1882, Otto Stutzbach). Twice during this epoch periodicals appeared entitled *Der Deutsch-Amerikaner* (1878 and 1901), both times apparently without success. The *Jewish Chronicle* (since 1875) and *Fortschritt* (1881, founded by J. Rosenfeld) appeared half in German and half in English. For two years (1893 to 1895) the Turnverein published a monthly magazine called *Vorwärts*. Untouched by any historical events, the *Monatsblatt der Zionsgemeinde*, a periodical for the Protestant Zion church, appeared regularly through the decades.

From our review of the German newspapers we have come to the conclusion that the Germans in Baltimore could not be classified as belonging to one political party. One cannot say that the German vote was either Democratic or Republican. Throughout the century the German vote was divided between the two main parties. There was a "German-American Jefferson Club," as well as a "German-American Republican Lincoln Club" and a "German-American Roosevelt League."[123] From time to time an outstanding personality, like Cleveland or Roosevelt, rallied the majority of German voters to his side despite previous party loyalties. But on the whole the German vote fluctuated until toward the end of the century when a gradual consolidation in the Republican Party became apparent.

In one way, however, this period differed from those which preceded and succeeded it. The Germans were a political factor with which the politicians reckoned. In a city like Baltimore, where there were more than 80,000 Germans around 1900, it was not advisable for a man seeking public office to offend them. A party that had a German on its ticket and put emphasis on this fact could count on receiving an appreciable increase of votes. Neither before nor after this time were the Germans so conscious of their origin. They were not only aware of it themselves, but their fellow citizens were also aware of it and took it into consideration in all their calculations. This awareness was one of the characteristics of the "German-American Epoch"; no such thing existed before the Civil War or after the first World War. There were frequent complaints during this period in the German newspapers about the fact

[123] *Correspondent*, October 7, 1900. *Journal*, September 19, 1904.

that the Germans were not sufficiently organized and that they were unable to exert enough political pressure. But even without a political organization they wielded enough political power so that they often decided whether the ship of state should lean toward the Republican or the Democratic side. They constituted a political power, and the knowledge of this fact sometimes went to their heads.

Enthusiastically they entered into local, state and national politics. It is surprising that during this period there was never a mayor of Baltimore or a Governor of Maryland of German descent. But in the Baltimore City Council and in the Maryland Legislature there were a great many people of German origin. Many of them were judges or held other offices in cities, counties or the state.[124] Frederick Th. Dorton (b. 1872), the son of a German immigrant, became famous in the Maryland legislature through his interest in regulating child labor; the "Dorton Child Labor Law" has perpetuated his name.[125] Friedrich Raine, publisher of the *Correspondent*, and for decades the spokesman of the German element in Baltimore, held a great many public offices; he was a member of many public committees, was a presidential elector in 1872 and 1876 and American consul in Berlin from 1885 to 1889.[126] It is interesting to note that for the German newspapers and the German voters the bond of their common German origin was often stronger than the severing element of differing party affiliations. The Democratic *Correspondent* reported with satisfaction that there were two Germans on the Republican ticket for Congress (House of Representatives) and strongly urged its readers to vote

---

[124] The following are a few German names (not a complete list) of men in the Baltimore City Council in the years following the Civil War: Otis Keilholz, Heinrich Seim, Georg Pagels, August Berkemeyer, Friedrich Raine, Heinrich Kaschmeyer, Nicholas Togges, Louis Beck, Heinrich Hellbach, Samuel Harman, Emil Budnitz, Ch. J. Wiener, Johann Weyler, J. B. Wentz, Johann Long, Louis Reitz, H. G. Fleddermann, J. A. Kampe, D. Heffner, P. Ch. Hennighausen, Louis Hoffmann. Otis Keilholz was president of the City Council and later speaker of the House of Representatives in the State Legislature at Annapolis; J. B. Wentz was a state senator. For additional names see BVG, 293 f. As a matter of curiosity we mention the fact that in 1896 a Baltimorean of Pennsylvania-German descent, Joshua Levering, was the Prohibition Party candidate for the Presidency. Cf. Faust, II, 147; SHGM, VI, 47.
[125] Cordell, *University of Maryland*, II, 112.
[126] SHGM, VII (1893), 71 ff.

for them: Frank C. Wachter and Charles R. Schirm. Both were elected, to the great joy of the *Correspondent*.[127] Four years later the Democratic Party cast its nets for the German vote and nominated a German named Lee S. Meyer for Congressman from Wachter's district; but Frank Wachter, who had often won elections and belonged to the victorious Theodore Roosevelt Party, retained his seat.[128]

One state agency in which the Germans had a great deal of influence at the beginning of the twentieth century was the Bureau of Immigration, established in 1896 and charged with promoting immigration to the State of Maryland. Since Germany was the primary source of immigration to Maryland during the entire second half of the nineteenth century, it is not surprising that for many years the most important office in this agency was occupied by a German. Herman J. Badenhoop was Secretary of the Bureau of Immigration from 1900 to 1906, and August F. Trappe held the office from 1906 to 1912.[129] A German, Percy Ch. Hennighausen (b. 1866), was U.S. Commissioner of Immigration of the Port of Baltimore from 1897 to 1901. Isaac L. Straus (1871-1946) was Attorney General for Maryland from 1907 to 1911.[130] Theodore Marburg (1862-1946), one of the most outstanding promoters of international peace organizations, was Minister to Belgium from 1912-1914.

Of all the Americans of German descent, the man who achieved the most prominent place in public life during this period and who

---

[127] *Correspondent*, November 8, 1900. *Journal*, October 31, 1900. The *Correspondent* states that up to this time nominations for Congressmen in Baltimore had been reserved only for members of the "English-American original aristocracy," but that things had begun to change. This statement is one of those exaggerations so frequently found in the German-American press at this time. Between the Civil War and the first World War there were a great many German-American representatives from Maryland: William J. Albert (in Congress 1873-1875); Eli J. Henkle (1875-1881); William Kimmel (1877-1881); Milton Urner (1879-1883); F. S. Hoblitzell (1881-1885); Isidor Rayner (1887-1889, 1891-1895); Herman Stump (1889-1893); G. L. Wellington (1895-1897); Frank C. Wachter (1899-1907); Ch. R. Schirm (1901-1903); John Kronmiller (1909-1911); George König (1911-1913). George L. Wellington was United States Senator for Maryland from 1897 to 1903, and Isidor Rayner held the same office from 1905 to 1912.

[128] *Journal*, November 3, 1904.

[129] *DNB*, 162; *SHGM*, xxiv, 65. Badenhoop was born in Verden, Germany, in 1863. Trappe (1857-1935) came from Stockhausen, Thüringen.

[130] *Tercentenary History*, ii, 44 ff.

reached the highest rung on the political ladder was a German Jew named Isidor Rayner (1850-1912).[131] After his first election as a delegate to the Maryland Assembly in 1878, he never disappeared from the political scene until the end of his life. In 1885 he was elected to the State Senate, but he resigned from this office in order to run for Congressman on the Democratic ticket; he represented his district for three terms. In 1899 he became Attorney General of Maryland. Two years later his name became known throughout the country when he defended the famous Admiral W. S. Schley before a Naval Court of Inquiry when his conduct at the battle of Santiago was assailed. Rayner crowned his career in 1905 when he went to the capital as a United States Senator. He was very critical of Roosevelt's policies, attacking the imperialism and tariff protection advocated by the administration. He remained in the Senate until his death. The reader will find his writings and addresses dry and colorless, but those who heard him speak claim that he was a brilliant and dynamic orator and that he possessed an unusual understanding for both domestic and foreign political questions.

One symptom of the political ambitions of the German-Americans was the founding of a society that called itself the "Unabhängige Bürgerverein" (Independent Citizens' Union). The guiding spirit of this society was a German, John G. Tjarks (1865-1943), who worked for thirty years to bring about the political activation of the German-Americans.[132] In a newspaper article in February 1900 he called upon his German-American compatriots to form a strong German central organization to guard the personal freedom of citizens of German extraction and to counteract any affront made against the German element in Baltimore.[133] At the founders' meeting on May 9, 1900, the representatives of more than fifty German societies appeared. The constitution stated that: "The league will strive to awaken a feeling of solidarity among the population of German descent, and to encourage the useful, healthy

---

[131] DAB, xv, 415 f. Baltimore Sun, November 26, 28, 1912. J. F. Essary, Maryland in National Politics (Baltimore, 1915), 264-86. Isidor Blum, The Jews of Baltimore (Baltimore, 1910), 153. Addresses of Isidor Rayner (1914), Essays of Isidor Rayner (1914). Rayner's father was a schoolteacher in Bavaria who emigrated to America in 1840 because of his liberal convictions. He changed his name from Röhner to Rayner. Isidor Rayner was educated at Knapp's Institute; later he studied law at the University of Maryland and at the University of Virginia. In 1871 he started to practice law in Baltimore.
[132] SHGM, xxvi, 52 f. DNB, 224.   [133] DNB, 110.

development of the power existing in such centralization; . . . to ward off nativist encroachments, to cultivate and assure good, friendly relations between America and the old country. . . . It has no intention of founding a state within the state, but considers that a central organization of the population of German extraction provides the shortest way and the best assurance of achieving its aims." At the same time the hope was expressed that similar leagues would be established in every state in the Union and that together they could be formed into a large, powerful organization.

This society, then, was intended to be an all-inclusive organization of the German societies existing in Baltimore. The energy formerly dispersed among dozens of small groups was to be gathered here into the channel of the Independent Citizens Association and directed into the great stream of a German-American central organization. This in turn would speak for the interests of the Germans in America in all questions pertaining to public affairs—especially politics. The year 1900 and the founding of this organization certainly constitutes the height of the German-American period in its development in Maryland. At first glance it would seem that the German-Americans were on the defensive, and the term "nativist encroachments" reminds one of the years previous to the Civil War. At that time, between 1850 and 1860, such an organization would have been a reaction against the vulgar nativism of the times —a kind of defense precaution. But in 1900 German-Americanism was not on the defensive; it was advancing and the constitution of the Independent Citizen's Union was a signal for attack.

No American citizen could raise any objection to the program of the Union: "clean, good government," liberating the schools from politics, eliminating obsolete laws, encouraging immigration, urging all immigrants to become citizens as soon as possible and to exercise regularly the right to vote, etc. Their program included: "Exercising the beneficial supervision over public affairs and to secure an honest, efficient and economic government of municipality and state; ascertaining the fitness and character of candidates for office; and, when elected, keeping a record of their official action; to safeguard the principles of representative government and protect the civil and political rights of its members; to effect the repeal of obsolete and pernicious laws; and generally to promote the welfare of the people by all honorable and legitimate means."[134]

However, one point was clear from the beginning: this society made no attempt to hasten the Americanization of citizens of German descent. On the contrary, through energetic emphasis on the German background, through the continuation of the German language, by making people conscious of their German descent and by cultivating German customs and manners, the process of acclimatization was retarded. Whether the people who founded this organization were conscious of this or not is difficult to decide. But it is certain that in this "league" we can most clearly feel the pulse of German-Americanism, the most public manifestation of the "Tragedy of German-America."

The significance of the Independent Citizen's Union becomes clear when it is seen in relation to the large, national organization. At the instigation of Charles J. Hexamer a similar overall organization was founded in Pennsylvania in 1899, including all the German societies. Other states soon followed the lead. In 1901 the representatives of all these organizations met in Philadelphia and founded the "National German-American Alliance," which stood for about the same kind of thing on a national basis as the Independent Citizen's Union did on the local level. In Baltimore, the Independent Citizen's Union was the strongest, most representative organization of the Germans; but in the national organization it was only one cog in the large, powerful machinery of the "Alliance," which soon developed into the largest organization of a racial, national group in American history. On paper the objectives looked harmless, rational and constructive, and probably very few of the people who signed them had any idea that they might lead to conflicts. Actually they developed an explosive power which did not become apparent until the World War.

People who read pan-German propaganda in every Bismarck herring and beer mug often attempted to prove that the founding of the National German-American Alliance was one of the political machinations of the Imperial German government. It has been proved that this is an error.[135] The Alliance received no directives from Germany; it was the product of specifically American condi-

---

[134] SHGM, XXIII, 48.

[135] The most complete presentation of the history of the Alliance is to be found in a book by an English historian, Clifton James Child, *The German-Americans in Politics 1914-1917* (Madison, Wis., 1939).

tions. It received more benevolent attention from the American brewers than from the German imperialists. It is, of course, surprising that these countless German groups and societies allowed themselves to be joined into one organization. This would not have been possible if they had not all had a common enemy: the threat of Prohibition. The common platform upon which all of them could unite was the anti-Prohibition battle.

The fight against the puritanical Blue Laws, which curtailed Sunday entertainments, and the fight against Prohibition were the points on the program that the Baltimore Independent Citizen's Union pursued most actively at its inception. By means of pamphlets, newspaper articles, lectures, etc., German-American public opinion was made audible. But it also entered into other questions that had arisen in municipal politics; it stood for better school administration, for the building of public parks and playgrounds, for a topographical survey of the city, for the reorganization of taxes and other "recommendations of reform and improvement, all for the benefit of the taxpayer."[136] On the whole, the Independent Citizen's Union appeared until the World War to be an organization for good government, civil liberties and constitutional rights, and as such it won respect and a good reputation in the city.

The occasion upon which the Independent Citizen's Union made its most impressive appearance each year was German Day. As early as 1890 a similar attempt was made by the Society for the History of the Germans in Maryland. At that time the sixth of October was chosen in memory of the arrival of the Concord on October 6, 1683, with the first group of German immigrants for America. October 6, 1890, was a very impressive celebration in Baltimore.[137] But the idea did not take root; it did not become a standing institution until the Independent Citizen's Union took up

[136] This is the subtitle of a pamphlet entitled For the Public Good, published by the Independent Citizen's Union, Baltimore, 1904. Publications which dealt only with the situation in Maryland were written and published in Baltimore. Since the anti-Prohibition campaign was carried out on a national scale the publications dealing with it were published by the central committee of the National German-American Alliance and sent to the affiliated local associations to be distributed. The right to decide when, where, what and how much to drink was set up as a "civil liberty." "Prohibition signifies the annihilation of the principle for which the War of Independence was waged and carried through victoriously."

[137] L. P. Hennighausen, "The German Day in Baltimore," SHGM, v, 43-72, presents a detailed description of the celebration in 1890.

the idea in 1901. From this time on it became the traditional holiday of the Germans in Baltimore. A day was chosen which was already a holiday in Maryland—Flag Day, September 12—and in 1901 this day was turned into a gigantic demonstration of the German-Americans in Baltimore. 25,000 of them met in Darley's Park, and year after year German Day was celebrated there under the auspices of the Independent Citizen's Union. The celebrations did much to popularize the Union among the Germans (and not only among them); they also became an important source of revenue for the organization. Usually the family groups appeared complete from great-grandmother to the youngest infant. Of course, the singing and Turner societies took advantage of the opportunity to display their talents. Animated speeches were held; people marched, sang, danced, drank—in short, the proverbial German *Gemütlichkeit* was poured out by the bucketful and everyone, whether he was German, Irish, English, Swedish, Lithuanian or Spanish, was happy and satisfied.

The German-Americans of this period appeared to be insatiable celebrators. They allowed no opportunity to pass, no memorial day or birthday, without celebrating it in the proper manner. They were not always joyous festivals. The deaths of historical personages were also marked, but the celebration of happy events was much more popular among the gaily singing and drinking Germans. It is impossible here to list all the large parades staged by the German-Americans. Only a few of the more important dates on the calendar of celebrations will be listed: For Friedrich Ludwig Jahn, founder of the Turner movement (1878); for the 150th anniversary of the founding of the City of Baltimore (1880); for General DeKalb (1886); for the German poet, Ludwig Uhland (1887); for Kaiser Wilhelm I (1888); for Columbus (1892); for the twenty-fifth anniversary of the Battle of Sedan (1895); for the death of Bismarck (1898); for Richard Wagner (1901); for Friedrich Schiller (1905); and for Carl Schurz (1906). Often enough, unimportant occasions became the excuse for large festivals. If the occasion was no more than the arrival of a German training ship or the visit of the German Prince Heinrich, they were happy to have a reason for a celebration. From time to time it happened that one of the large, national German-American organizations, such as the singing societies, Turners, Schützen or the National German-American Alliance held their annual meetings in Baltimore. When this occurred, Singers, Turners and Schützen from every part of the Union gathered in the city which, often for days at a time, witnessed all sorts of parades. One of the best-loved festivals was the so-called "Cannstadter Volksfest," held in the fall of each year. Though it was actually a Swabian holiday, it became more and more popular with all the Germans and became such a firm tradition that a "Cannstadter Volksfestverein" was founded in order to assure the continuation of the festival.[138]

An unusual festival held only once was the Flower Game of 1904. It was a kind of poetry contest for which all German-American writers were urged to send in literary works to be read aloud at a tournament, and judged. The prize poems were later printed.[139] With few exceptions they were of such poor literary quality that the world quickly and rightfully forgot them even though a few well-known German-American writers, such as Konrad Nies and Edna Fern, were among the prize winners. It was one of those pleasant German-American festivals that was important for the day but left no mark in the history of German poetry.

Without doubt, the many festivals and the general joyousness of the Germans left certain lasting impressions in the city of Baltimore and gradually helped to rid it of the Blue Laws. This buoyancy of the German element was perhaps not a very deep influence, but certainly a very wide one in Maryland.[140]

On the basis of the festivals that the German-Americans in Baltimore celebrated, certain deductions may be made about their relationship to the old country. It is striking to see how closely the curve of their celebrations fits into the course of joyous or depressing events bearing upon the history of the German Reich. The found-

---

[138] King Wilhelm I of Württemberg decreed in 1818 that his birthday was to be celebrated every September in Cannstadt. The Swabians brought this ceremony to America and changed it here into a harvest thanksgiving festival which lasted for three or four days. It was first celebrated by the Swabians in New York, but it was quickly taken up in all American cities where there were Germans. In Baltimore it was started in 1904.

[139] *Das Baltimore Blumenspiel* (Baltimore, 1904). DNB, 97. SHGM, xvi/xxii, 61 ff. The Flower Game was sponsored by the Germania Club. The people directly responsible for the contest were: Ernst Henrici, Fritz Mayer, Julius Hofmann, Henry Wood, Richard Ortmann, John Hinrichs, Henry G. Hilken and W. Simon.

[140] Albert B. Faust, "Undercurrents of German Influence in Maryland," SHGM, xxiii, 5 ff.

ing of the German Empire in 1871 is not without its connection with the appearance of the German-American in history. The long desired and newly won feeling of national consciousness among the Germans in the Empire spread out to the Germans in America. They were proud of the powerfully established political structure of their old country, and that pride gave them renewed reason to cling to their German heritage and customs even in foreign countries. Frequently and loudly proclaiming their German background and pointing out their German origin meant to them that they took part in the glory of the distant Bismarck Empire.

From the very beginning, the German immigrants after 1848 took a much greater interest in the political development of Germany than the earlier immigrants. Naturally, those who had to leave for political reasons were bitter enemies of the political powers that had sent them into exile. Prussianism, the military and reactionary powers, were flailed in all the newspapers of the political emigration. In the course of the years, however, most of the people forgot the old grudge against the house of Hohenzollern. The more clearly it became apparent that the Hohenzollerns were taking over the political hegemony and that sooner or later they would found, not a liberal, but at least a unified nation, the more the former '48ers allowed their national feelings to outweigh their liberalism. True, there was always a small group of definite radicals not ready to make any compromises; Karl Heinzen, Robert Reitzel and Friedrich Hecker belong to this group and their followers often came in conflict with the more conciliatory majority. For example, when in 1860 Dr. Wiss, a former '48er, published in the *Turnzeitung* in Baltimore an evaluation of the political acts of the Prussian King Wilhelm the First which was not wholly uncritical but in the main quite favorable, there were stormy protests. A Boston radical, Adolph Douai, was horrified that Wiss had set up that perfidious "Kartätschenprinz" as the "representative of German justice and German honesty." The quarrel involved many people and finally led to the resignation of Wiss from the staff of the *Turnzeitung*.[141]

In the course of the 1860's identification with Prussian-German politics became more and more intense. When the Franco-Prussian War broke out, the Germans in Baltimore gathered in a powerful demonstration in Monument Square.[142]

[141] *Turnzeitung*, August 14, 21, 28, 1860.
[142] *Correspondent*, July 20, 1870.

Among the instigators of the demonstration are to be found the names of many German '48ers: Wilhelm Schnauffer, Peter Unger, Wilhelm Rapp, Gustav Facius. The main speaker of the evening was Wilhelm Rapp, the man who had been worlds apart from Crown Prince Wilhelm in 1848. Apparently he did not feel quite at ease during his speech, for more than once there is a feeling that he is defending himself against unspoken remonstrances. He asked whether they should fail to acclaim the aged marshal of the German people simply because he wore a crown. "Once we fought gladly for the German Republic. But if we cannot have it, let us at least have a powerful, constitutional German Empire, and grant a German crown to the Hohenzoller who flings the crown from the French usurper's head." Rapp presented the assembly with an address thundering with "Sieg" and "Heil"; his talk was acclaimed and a copy sent to the North German Parliament.

A few weeks later the Germans in Baltimore staged a similar demonstration, this time "to show in a concrete and practical manner their loyalty to Germany's just cause."[143] It was hoped that in this manner more substantial sums of money than before could be raised and sent to Germany. Wilhelm Rapp and Peter Unger made speeches whose hypernationalistic chauvinism can hardly be surpassed.

In January 1871, when the first news of the proclamation of the emperor was announced, the *Correspondent* could not suppress a slight feeling of disappointment in the fact that the nation had been created from above and not by the people. It regretted openly that the proclamation did not mention the German people "the most powerful factor for the re-establishment of a united Germany."[144] But this mood of disappointment proved to be only a passing one. It was soon replaced by nationalistic jubilation, and everyone was united in resounding "Hoch's" and "Hurrah's." For most of the people, the "united, strong Empire" was more important than a "free, liberal Republic." In April 1871 a great peace celebration was arranged which crowned this epoch of hectic nationalism.[145] Robert Reitzel, the famous German radical, came to

---

[143] *Ibid.*, September 16, 1870.   [144] *Ibid.*, January 27, 1871.

[145] Detailed information on the festival will be found in the *Correspondent*, April 11, 1871. The German Catholics who were loyal to their church did not take part in this celebration. The *Katholische Volkszeitung* (March 18, 1871) stated that although the Catholics were glad that peace had been declared,

Baltimore just at this time as a poor vagabond, hoping to obtain help from his German compatriots. He wrote bitterly: "If we were given something to eat, it was certainly by people who were poor themselves; the rich people had to contribute their money for victory celebrations and congratulatory addresses to the German Emperor."[146]

In trying to find an explanation for the political about-face of many of the former radical street fighters of 1848, one should not forget that the Bismarck of 1870 was more acceptable to liberal eyes than the Bismarck of the late seventies and the eighties. For the liberals of 1870, the aura about the nation's founder had not yet been dimmed by such events as the *Kulturkampf* or the anti-Socialist laws. The founding of a German Empire was an aim of the St. Paul's Church Parliament of 1848; this dream was now at last fulfilled, though in somewhat different form. Besides, the Germans in America, with their enthusiasm for Bismarck, were swimming in the great stream of general public opinion of the times. During the years before 1870, Napoleon III was looked upon as the potential menace to peace, the dictator who was trying to upset Europe and who was stirring up quarrels everywhere. When Bismarck outsmarted Napoleon, he did it to the grateful applause of the entire public opinion in America. Small wonder that the German-Americans shouted as loud or louder than the rest! The fact that the more unsophisticated spirits among them slipped into the narrowest and blindest form of nationalism is not a racial phenomenon but a sociological one. In all countries and at all times it may be seen that a certain stratum of lower middle-class people slips into this attitude when arrogance and ignorance join into a repul-

---

still they were not interested in these celebrations of "the German Indians, Masons, singers, Schützen, etc.," which always ended in beer halls. The Catholic paper was noncommittal about the founding of the German nation. Its attitude was summarized in an article published January 28, 1871, approximately as follows: "Blood and iron are not the best cement with which to build a nation. We are not friendly to Protestant Prussia, but we are not blind to its good qualities. It entirely fulfills the first duty of the State to uphold order and justice and since the Catholic Church benefits by this we are for Prussian Germany." We have already shown how this attitude of the paper changed after Bismarck's *Kulturkampf* (1873).

[146] Robert Reitzel, *Des Armen Teufel Gesammelte Schriften* (Detroit, 1913), I, 75.

sive and dangerous combination. Among the Germans in Baltimore there were innumerable illustrations of this sort of perversion.[147]

The numerous celebrations in honor of various Germans are symptoms of the increasingly strong devotion to the old country. Congratulatory telegrams for Moltke's birthday, mourning parades for the death of Kaiser Wilhelm I and memorial celebrations for the Battle of Sedan are all characteristic of the German-American period. As long as the old fatherland remained on terms of perfect peace with their adopted country, there were no conflicts. But when finally the historical development of the two countries ceased to run parallel, the typical German-American was faced with a painful decision.

It would be an oversimplification to say that all the Germans in Maryland accepted the German-American isolation as their way of life. Many of them took up American ways entirely and ignored the cramping barriers of German-Americanism. They were aware of their German descent, but they saw no reason for stressing it or for preserving their German individuality in any artificial manner. Among them, of course, the process of Americanization proceeded much more rapidly than among the German-Americans.

Among the people in Maryland who belonged to the German element but not to the German-Americans (in the restricted sense of the word) were three men whose names were known far beyond the boundaries of their state, three men whose fame spread over the whole country and even into far corners of the rest of the world. These three men of German descent or German birth were an admiral, an inventor and a sculptor: Winfield Scott Schley, Ottmar Mergenthaler and William Henry Rinehart.

Winfield Scott Schley (1839-1909) was a descendant of Thomas Schley, one of the first German settlers in Western Maryland, the first schoolteacher in Frederick who emigrated from Bavaria in 1739 and settled on the Monocacy River.[148] He was born on a farm near Frederick, grew up in Frederick and graduated from the Naval

---

[147] Besides numerous speeches and essays in German newspapers in Baltimore, a small pamphlet that appeared in 1870 belongs in this category. It was *Das rechte Verhältnis zwischen Deutschland und Frankreich*, by Georg A. Witte, a teacher at Baltimore City College. It is a crassly distorted history of German-French relations through the centuries, a primitive black-and-white sketch in which all the light falls on Germany.

[148] DAB, xvi, 437 ff.
Richard S. West, Jr., *Admirals of American Empire* (Indianapolis, 1948).

Academy in Annapolis. He was in the service during the Civil War, took part in a very dangerous arctic expedition in 1884 and achieved great fame in the Spanish-American War for his part in the Battle of Santiago (1898). Later there was a great quarrel over his conduct and Schley finally requested that a Court of Inquiry be set up. The decision of the Court (1901) was against Schley (Admiral Dewey rendered a minority opinion in his favor). But despite the decision, Schley lost none of his great popularity; on the contrary, the great mass of people believed that he had been treated unjustly and they adored him even more than before.

Ottmar Mergenthaler (1854-1899) was born in Hachtel, Germany.[149] He came of a family of teachers and was expected to follow in the family tradition, but at an early age he displayed such an extraordinary talent for mechanical things that he was allowed to continue in this field and was sent to a relative in Württemberg as an apprentice watch maker. After receiving his training as a mechanic, he went to America in 1872, worked four years in an instrument factory in Washington, D.C., and then settled in Baltimore in 1876. During these years he started his work on typewriters and printing machinery. For a long time he had been trying to invent a printing machine that would make the lengthy process of type-setting obsolete; after many reverses and disappointments he arrived at his first great success in July 1884, and a few weeks later he was able to take out his first patent on a type-setting machine. This was the invention that is known all over the world today as the linotype and which entirely revolutionized printing in the eighties. Above all, it was important in the history of the newspaper, where speed is an essential factor. A new era in printing was begun on July 3, 1886, when the first Mergenthaler machine was set in motion for the publication of the *New York Tribune*. Mergenthaler continued to work on improvements for his machine with unabated energy, and recognition of his achievement poured in from all parts of the world. His name is well known even to laymen today. The engineering building at Johns Hopkins University is named Mergenthaler Hall in his honor.

William Henry Rinehart (1825-1874) came from a family that emigrated from the Palatinate in 1733 and settled in Pennsylvania

---

[149] *DAB*, xii, 549 f. Otto Schoenrich, *Biography of Ottmar Mergenthaler* (Baltimore, 1898).

and Western Maryland. They were mostly ministers and farmers.[150] W. H. Rinehart was born on a farm near Union Bridge, Maryland. After completing the usual schooling without any special success, he worked for a time on his father's farm without much pleasure, coming in contact with the art of sculpture in a roundabout way by working in a marble quarry. He educated himself in evening courses at the Maryland Institute, and one of the first examples of his talent is a bust of the well-known Reverend John G. Morris. Supported by W. T. Walters, the Baltimore connoisseur, and other protectors, he journeyed to Europe to study, his most important experience being his stay in Florence. Later he returned to Baltimore and considered the city as his home in America, but he spent most of his life in Italy, where the majority of his great works were created. A few figures in Baltimore cemeteries; the bronze doors on the Capitol in Washington; the memorial to Chief Justice Roger B. Taney before the State House in Annapolis; the bust of Severn T. Wallis; the figure of Clytie; and one of his last and perhaps most beautiful pieces of sculpture, Endymion, a replica of which is on his grave in Baltimore—these are permanent records of his great and mature art. Lorado Taft, the greatest authority on the history of American sculpture, stated: "Beauty first entered into American sculpture with Rinehart."

In this chapter we have concerned ourselves almost exclusively with the Germans in Baltimore, for here the main part of our story took place. We have already pointed out that the German settlers in the western part of the state had become so entirely Americanized by the end of the Civil War that they were hardly conscious of their German descent. In Frederick the mixture with other national groups had been so complete that at the end of the century there was not one German society, not one German church, not one German newspaper and no German language to be heard. In Hagerstown, a little farther west, most of the German population belonged to the old stock of German settlers of the eighteenth century, but along with them here was a small group of Germans who made one

[150] DAB, xv, 615 ff. Lorado Taft, *History of American Sculpture* (New York, 1930), 171 ff. L. P. Hennighausen, "Der Bildhauer William Henry Rinehart," SHGM, xxii, 67. The most complete work on Rinehart is the book by William S. Rusk, *William Henry Rinehart, Sculptor* (Baltimore, 1939). Besides a biography and an appreciation of his art, it contains a series of pictures, a list of his works and of his pupils, a bibliography, etc.

last attempt to retain the German language, at least in church. And still farther west, in Cumberland, there was a German element toward the end of the nineteenth century more akin to the Germans in Baltimore than to the German settlers in Western Maryland. We must study in somewhat greater detail these different German groups in the western part of the state.

There were a few signs at the beginning of the fifties which indicated that there was a group of people in Hagerstown who were not content with the complete disappearance of the German language from the old German churches. There were only a few in each congregation, but if they were willing to forget their specifically Reformed or Lutheran characteristics they could meet on the common ground of the German church language and found a small congregation. From 1852 on there was a small group which met in the Old Chapel of Zion Reformed church and held German services. This group was the nucleus of the congregation that organized itself in 1853 into Christ's Evangelical and Reformed church; the first minister was a Reverend C. Cost, who preached in German. The congregation was mixed; it consisted of both Reformed and Lutherans, and it did not continue long before there were quarrels between the two factions. The confessional differences were dormant for a time, but not for long. For fifteen years the pastors were Reformed ministers, though the majority of the members were Lutherans. In 1871 when for the first time a Lutheran, the Reverend Theobald Heischmann was engaged as the common pastor, there were protests among the Reformed, who decided that no Lutheran might preach in their church. This made a split unavoidable. The Lutherans separated and left a small handful of German Reformed, whose congregation soon proved itself unable to survive. A few years later, the Reformed Christ's church abandoned the custom to which it owed its existence—the use of the German language. In 1877 they changed from German to English. In this manner the crisis in the life of the congregation was overcome; it opened its doors to everyone and became an English-speaking congregation, as it is to this day.

The fate of the German Lutherans is more interesting. They had already made an attempt, in 1850, to establish themselves as a German congregation within the old St. John's Lutheran church. The attempt failed. The connection with the Reformed group was only a temporary solution. Then, in 1871, the prospects looked more favorable. After the Civil War there was a new wave of German immigration. Though it was bound chiefly for the Middle West, some of these Germans remained in Maryland instead. Small as their number was, it was enough to give new impetus to the persevering Germans in Hagerstown. Therefore, in 1871, their attempts met with greater success than they had enjoyed twenty years before.

As an organization, the new congregation, the "Deutsche Evangelische Lutherische St. Matthäus Gemeinde," remained a part of the English-Lutheran St. John's church. The constitution of the St. Matthew congregation, written in German and English, stated categorically that all divine services were to be held in German. All transactions in the meetings were to be in German. All ministers had to have studied at German or American universities. Any German of good reputation or anyone who spoke German might become a member of the congregation.[151]

But the little German community could not sail against the prevailing wind. Twenty years later it had to change its course somewhat. A decision of the elders taken in 1890 shows that it could not continue without making some compromises. "Since it is necessary for the continuation of our work as a congregation, it has been decided to allow the use of the English language along with German in our divine services as needed, but only so long and to such an extent as it works to the general advantage of the congregation and the Kingdom of God."

The next few years were to show that the Kingdom of God in Hagerstown could better be served in English than in German. The first arrangement was that the main service on Sunday morning was to be held in German and the evening service in English. In 1895 the arrangement was reversed. The minister who came to the congregation in 1895 was required to preach a test sermon in German and also one in English. These symptoms indicated the direction in which things were moving. In 1905 the "Deutsche Evangelische

---

[151] All material was taken from the church records in Hagerstown. The first pastors, from 1871 to 1875 (Heischmann, Dietrich, Steinhauer and Reitz) did not keep records. After their time the records to the end of the congregation have been preserved. The German pastors of the congregation were: G. H. Brandau (1875), Richard Schmidt (1889), George W. Streib (1892), Max F. Schulz (1895), F. T. Heinicke (1896), Wme. Hoffmann (1904), F. B. Cunz (1905).

Lutherische St. Matthäus Gemeinde" was dissolved and newly organized as "St. Matthew's German-English Evangelical Lutheran Church." The constitution written in English in 1905 begins with the words: "Whereas, prevailing conditions demand, that we employ the English language in our divine service and other proceedings . . . ." The congregation was still a half German, half English church. Sermons and communion were held in both languages, but everyone knew that the end of the era of German as the church language was in sight.

The very certainty of their defeat made the old champions of the German language especially bitter. There were violent quarrels about the language issues among the members of the congregation as well as among the ministers. The entry made in the records upon the occasion of a change in pastors in 1905 is characteristic of the tense feeling that prevailed. The last entry by the Reverend Wme. Hoffmann before he left Hagerstown reads: "In view of the fact that there was a great deal of hostility to the English language before I came, most of the young people left and joined English speaking congregations, and so the outlook for the future was such, as to discourage me." For this reason it is apparent that the Reverend Mr. Hoffmann helped to hasten the reorganization of the congregation into a bilingual church, but his successor, the Reverend F. B. Cunz, was not at all of the same opinion. To the Reverend Mr. Hoffmann's last entry the Reverend Mr. Cunz added the following: "This is all rot! Mr. Hoffmann, one of that hybrid class, neither German nor American, did his utmost to humiliate, misrepresent and vilify the men and women loyal to the German and Lutheran traditions upon which this Church was founded." After administering this unchristian kick to his predecessor, the Reverend F. B. Cunz revealed his own program for the coming activity of the Hagerstown congregation. "His principal efforts will be directed towards nursing, cultivating and deepening the love and loyalty for the noble, matchless, estimable German heritage of the Fathers: the German language—German honesty—German sincere piety—the German-American personal liberty and opposition to deception in church matters . . . and to try to keep the young people true to their own church by continuance of English services which will not debase and defame as many hireling preachers do their tradition and their ancestry."

In spite of these earnest principles, the German congregation did not last much longer. A year later (1906) it had shrunk so much that it could no longer support its own minister and the Reverend F. B. Cunz resigned. His last entries complain of the fact that no help was received from the English-Lutheran mother congregation, even though this group had become so greatly enriched by the addition of the young people. Of course, this did not justify the situation; if the young people preferred the English church, then the German congregation had lost its reason for existence. The last German minister in Hagerstown departed with the melancholy Biblical text: "He must increase, but I must decrease." The congregation vegetated for another ten years. A German minister from Woodstock, Pennsylvania, came at irregular intervals to preach a German sermon. But gradually the old German members died. There were no additions from the ranks of the young people, and in 1917 the congregation consisting now of only seventeen members was dissolved. The year 1917 is of no great importance in this case. The war between Germany and the United States may have hastened the end of the German congregation, but it did not cause it. It had been an historic anomaly from the beginning.

We mentioned previously that from the end of the eighteenth century on there were German settlers in both of the western counties of the state, Allegany and Garrett, and that in Cumberland, especially, the largest city in this region, there were a great many Germans. The early German settlers in this region had become Americanized in the course of the nineteenth century, just as had the old German settlers in Frederick and Hagerstown. But in Cumberland after the middle of the nineteenth century the Americanization process had been markedly retarded by the arrival of fresh German immigrants. There were absolutely no new immigrants in Frederick, while in Hagerstown they came in in very small numbers, as shown by the German congregations. Frederick and Hagerstown had hardly any industry and so they were not considered by the new arrivals. In Cumberland the situation was different. There and in a few neighboring towns, like Lonaconing, Frostburg, Eckhart Mines and Grantsville, the coal-mining industry had been prospering since 1840; also, Cumberland had become more and more important as a railroad center. Only a few of the German immigrants who settled in Allegany County after the Civil War had left Germany with the intention of coming to Cumberland. Most of them had really wanted to go to the Middle West. Because Baltimore lay so far inland, it was one of the favorite landing places. The Baltimore and Ohio Company had good connections with the Middle West, and the great highway from Baltimore via Cumberland and Wheeling to Columbus, Indianapolis, Vandalia, called "The Cumberland Road" or "The National Pike," was the traditional route during the whole nineteenth century to the Missouri and Mississippi Valleys. Most of the German late arrivals in Cumberland were prospective Middle Westerners who never reached their destination. Many of them stayed in Baltimore; others started out, but then a job in Cumberland in one of the mines or factories looked more promising to them than an uncertain future in the Middle West. Thus Allegany and Garrett Counties received an invasion of German immigrants in the second half of the nineteenth century who created certain social forms and establishments that had not been known before in the farthest western part of Maryland.[152]

At first, the few German churches that were in existence received new life. The old German farmers had founded Lutheran and Reformed congregations which, like the churches in Frederick and Hagerstown, had gradually lost their German character. If the new immigrants had not come, the German element would have become entirely Americanized as in Frederick. After 1850 the "stubborn" Germans, there as everywhere, received unexpected support from the new immigrants. No less than five German congregations were established during the last few decades of the century—two German-Lutheran, a German-Reformed, a German-Catholic and a German-Israelite congregation. Combined with these churches were a few German parochial schools. At the end of the century there were two German singing societies (Arion and Germania) which were exactly like the German-American organizations in Baltimore. A German savings bank was founded, similar to the German banks in Balti-

---

[152] The material for Cumberland was taken from the files of the *Cumberland Freie Presse* and the Cumberland church records. Besides, the author received certain information personally from Mr. John F. Pruess. Cf. also *St. Peter and St. Paul*, op.cit., 76 ff. and Thomas J. Stanton, *A Century of Growth, or the History of the Church in Western Maryland* (Baltimore, 1900), 43-78.

more.[153] And after 1891—this is the clearest indication of a fairly cohesive, conscious German-American element—there was a German weekly paper, the *Cumberland Freie Presse*.[154]

The *Freie Presse* was founded by two German immigrants, John F. Pruess and August F. Trappe.[155] After a year it was apparent that the paper could not support two families and so August Trappe resigned. From that time on, the *Freie Presse* was more or less a product of John Pruess's brain. Only two of the eight pages of the paper were written for Cumberland and printed there. It would be more accurate to say for the "Cumberland district," for the paper was read by the Germans in all the mining towns in the vicinity. Written for the German element in Allegany and Garrett Counties, Maryland, and Somerset County, Pennsylvania, it was the only German paper between Washington, Pittsburgh, Wheeling and Memphis.

Like most of these small foreign-language papers, it was colorless politically. In national elections it never took sides, while in local elections it took a lively part and was especially eager to support the Allegany politician, George Louis Wellington. John Pruess, the publisher of the *Freie Presse*, was a Democrat; but in spite of this the paper supported the Republican, George Wellington, whenever he ran for office, since Wellington, despite his name, was the son of a German immigrant.[156] The Germans in Cumberland and

[153] The founders of the bank will be mentioned because they were also the names of the leading families in the German colony in Cumberland. They were: George Schwarzenbach, G. D. Landweber, S. Rosenbaum, J. H. Holzshu and John Schiller.

[154] The only existing set of the *Cumberland Freie Presse* is in the possession of the Enoch Pratt Library, Baltimore (years 1891-1896).

[155] John F. Pruess was born in Bredstedt (Schleswig-Holstein) in 1864. He learned the printing trade in Germany, came to America in 1882, worked in the Middle West (Detroit, Iowa, Kansas) for a few years, was then a printer in Baltimore and Johnstown, Pa., for two years, coming to Cumberland in 1891. In 1896 he returned to Baltimore, where he was connected with the *Correspondent* until 1918; after this he worked in the record office of the Baltimore City Court. August F. Trappe (1857-1935) came from Stockhausen, Germany. He also learned the printing trade in Germany and came to America in 1882 with Pruess, planning at first to go West. However, he lived most of his life in Baltimore; the year in Cumberland was only a brief interruption. In Baltimore he was a reporter for the *Correspondent*. He was very much interested in public and political affairs; from 1906 to 1912 he was secretary of the Bureau of Immigration. SHGM, XIV, 65 f.

[156] *Men of Mark in Maryland*, III (1911), 224-29. The Wellington family emigrated from England to Germany during the reign of Mary Tudor and became thoroughly German. John Adam Wellington, who lived near Worms,

the vicinity followed Wellington through thick and thin, no matter what their party affiliations. For example, at the congressional elections in 1894 there were 8000 voters in Allegany County, of which 1500 were Germans who stood solidly behind Wellington.

This spokesman of the Germans in Cumberland, George L. Wellington (1852-1927), merits further attention because he was a characteristic representative of the German element and its political attitude. Wellington was born into a family in reduced circumstances; the beginning of his life was spent in a constant struggle against poverty. It was this fact that later won him the confidence of the many German miners and German farmers in the western part of the state. He was the typical self-made man of the end of the nineteenth century. His interests revolved entirely around finances and politics. He allied himself with the Republican Party, became county treasurer of Allegany County and later subtreasurer in Baltimore. He was one of the key men in the Republican Party of the state. The German votes and the efforts of the *Freie Presse* were partly responsible for the fact that Wellington was in Washington from 1895 to 1897 as a member of the House of Representatives, and from 1897 to 1903 as a United States Senator. His adherence to the Republican Party did not hinder him from bitterly opposing the Republican administration's Spanish-American War. He violently attacked President McKinley for his imperialist policies and refused to support McKinley for re-election. In the fall of 1900 he traveled to the western states, urging people to vote for the Democratic candidate, William Jennings Bryan. There was a great tumult at a meeting in Baltimore where the old-line Republicans accused him of treason. Wellington answered as follows: "I do not believe in making a fetish of a party. If it leaves the old lines, it is time for candid and sincere men to leave it, if they can find anything better. I have kept my self-respect and that is something." Like his great compatriot, Carl Schurz, Wellington did not hesitate to change his party when the old party no longer represented his views. This fluctuation between parties is characteristic of the German-American element during the four decades after the Civil War. Later, Wellington supported Theodore Roosevelt, and in 1912 brought him a great majority in Western Maryland.[157]

---

became involved in the German revolution of 1848 and then came to America. George L. Wellington was his son.

[157] SHGM, XXIII, 44.

The strong influence of the Catholic Church is characteristic of the Germans in Cumberland. The majority of the new German immigrants came from Catholic South Germany; most of them joined the very active St. Peter and St. Paul congregation which offered broad fields of endeavor through its monastery and its school. The congregation was run by the Carmelite Order from 1866 to 1875, and when the Carmelites moved away the Capuchins took their place. Their arrival had some connection with Bismarck's *Kulturkampf*. Because of the harsh "May Laws" in Germany (1873) the Capuchin monasteries in Münster, Werne, Cleve and Ehrenbreitstein were discontinued. In 1875 the order sent two representatives, Anthony M. Schuermann and Francis Wolf, to obtain information as to possible fields of action in America. The two brothers bought the Cumberland monastery for the Capuchin Order and that same year a large number of German Capuchins came to Cumberland. It is not surprising that the group of people associated with the St. Peter and St. Paul church retained an anti-Bismarck feeling. The German chancellor and all the European statesmen who opposed the Holy See were the objects of the undiminished antipathy of the Capuchin brothers for decades.[158]

The German-American colony in Cumberland cannot be compared in intensity of feeling and variety with that of Baltimore. The intensity of German-American life increased at a far greater rate than the increase in the number of participants would indicate. The reverse was also true, for when the numbers were reduced and new blood ceased to enliven the group it shrank with inordinate speed. The majority of Germans in the Cumberland district immigrated between 1850 and 1890. After 1900 there were hardly any new arrivals in this region and so the wall that had been formed around the German-American group crumbled at the turn of the century. Soon its isolation was broken down. It is a characteristic symptom for Cumberland that a number of attempts to form a German Turner Society failed. At the end of the century the German churches introduced English services. The *Freie Presse* always had to struggle for its existence. It never obtained more than five

[158] On September 20, 1895, when the Italian government celebrated the twenty-fifth anniversary of the occupation of Rome, which event had made the Pope a "prisoner," the church of St. Peter and St. Paul held a special high mass at which prayers were said for the freedom and independence of the Holy See.

hundred subscribers and ceased to exist some years after John Pruess left Cumberland. When a German theatrical troupe came to Cumberland in 1892, it had to play before an almost empty house. No more than a hundred people came to enjoy the rare experience of attending a German performance.[159] All this is indicative of the fact that here where the German-Americans were a relatively small group they presented fewer obstacles to the Americanization process than did the groups in the larger cities.

In Garrett County, the last Maryland County west of Cumberland, there were a good many German settlers but they were scattered far apart. Only in a few places, such as in Cove and Accident, did the German element crystallize so far as to form German church congregations. But even here the consciousness of German individuality lessened from year to year. Shortly after the Civil War there were two flourishing German Lutheran congregations in Cove and Accident. All the sermons were held in German. The Reverend Fr. Dreyer, who served in Accident from 1870 to 1877, was asked to hold an English service only once during these seven years. Shortly after 1900 English services were held every fourth Sunday; a few years later the point had been reached where English and German sermons alternated. During the first World War the German services disappeared entirely. Here as elsewhere this was the natural course of events. A sociological type like the German-American of Baltimore could not have developed in these sparsely settled rural communities. The German as an isolated individual was always drawn into the great American melting pot.

In addition to the complicated German-American colony in Baltimore and the various types of German settlements in the western part of the state, there was another unusual kind of German immigrant in Maryland toward the end of the nineteenth century along the Eastern Shore, a section avoided by the Germans for centuries with surprising consistency. Since the early days of Augustin Herrman and the unsuccessful Labadist settlements (the end of

---

[159] *Cumberland Freie Presse*, April 7, 1892. Karl Königstein's Theatrical Company of New York played Hermann Sudermann's *König Ludwig II von Bayern*. The dramatic critic of the *Freie Presse* who came from Schleswig complained that the play was more Bavarian than German and that it was difficult to understand the lines. However, he deplored the fact that of the few people who did attend, the majority left the hall in the most inconsiderate manner before the end of the performance.

the 17th century) the eastern counties had been entirely ignored by the German immigrants. Modern place names on the Eastern Shore, like Berlin and Vienna, are misleading; these were not German settlements.[160] But after 1890 there were German immigrants on the Eastern Shore.

In the eighties a group of German farmers emigrated from Germany to America, partly to avoid German military service and partly because the cheap farm land of the Middle West had been highly recommended. They settled on government tracts in Iowa and Nebraska, but in spite of hard work they were unsuccessful. The soil and climate were not as they had expected. The Eastern Shore of Maryland was brought to their attention through the German-American newspapers. So they moved East again and settled in a small town, Cordova, Maryland, where they lived from that time on as successful farmers. Such settlements are to be found today scattered over Talbot, Caroline, Dorchester, Kent, Salisbury and Wicomico Counties. The farmers were all Lutherans and soon organized small Lutheran congregations which joined the Missouri Synod and exist today as German congregations with German services. Cordova and Preston received the largest of these German colonies. In Preston there was even a German parochial school after the beginning of the century, but it succumbed in the war year, 1917. The German services in these congregations, however, have survived both world wars. Most of these German families came from North Germany, many from Pomerania, some from Saxony and there are even a few Volga German families among them. Aside from those who had first tried their luck in the Middle West there were later other families who came directly from Germany. As soon as they arrived many of them were directed to the Eastern Shore by the Maryland Bureau of Immigration which was established in 1896 and was strongly influenced by the Germans. But the majority of the Eastern Shore Germans were the rare type of former Middle Westerners and unsuccessful returnees. As excellent farmers they soon won the respect of the usually anti-foreign population of the Eastern Shore.[161]

[160] Berlin is a contraction of Burleigh's Inn; Vienna, according to tradition, is the mutilation of an Indian name, Vinnacokasimmon.

[161] For further information, we recommend the article by Arthur L. Davis, "German Settlements on the Eastern Shore of Maryland," SHGM, xxv, 23 ff.

In the last few paragraphs we have been dealing with the history of the periphery of the German element in Maryland. In conclusion let us return to the center of the circle. The focal point of the description of this epoch lies not in a few great names like Mergenthaler and Rinehart, nor in the rapidly decreasing German congregations in the rural western counties, but rather in the "little Germany" of the city of Baltimore. The typical German-American with all his strength and weaknesses is the characteristic product of this epoch. To develop he requires the background of city life. He must be in the minority, for a certain amount of pressure from the outside is necessary in order to weld together the not always homogeneous group. However, if, as in the rural counties, the non-German majority is too great, the small German minority is stifled and it becomes Americanized, relinquishing its existence as an individual national group. Baltimore was the only city in Maryland in which German-Americanism was able to flourish throughout the allotted time. It was a broad, middle-class group. None of its leading personalities achieved the level of "nationwide fame," but almost all of them enjoyed good reputations within their communities; they were esteemed and respected for their dependability and honesty, their capability and energy, and for their conservative civic virtues and dislike of political radicalism. They were what in obituaries are usually called "substantial citizens."

Let us review once more the names of the most important ones: Heinrich Scheib, John G. Morris, Julius Hofmann, Eduard Huber, pastors; Louis P. Hennighausen, Karl A. M. Scholtz, lawyers; Friedrich Raine, Richard Ortmann, Eduard Leyh, journalists; C. O. Schönrich, Charles Raddatz, teachers; Otto Fuchs, William Heimendahl, Otto Sutro, artists; John Hemmeter, physician; Louis Dohme, chemist; Christian Ax, Wilhelm Knabe, Frederick Bauernschmidt, Louis Schneidereith, Henry Hilken, Ferdinand A. J. Meyer, a few of the businessmen. Our purpose in repeating these names is not to present a very incomplete list but rather to indicate the wide range of occupations from which the leading German-Americans were drawn.

In the course of this presentation we have avoided the use of numbers to indicate the extent of the German immigration or the size of the German colonies. Most of the figures which we have are incomplete and cannot be checked. For the first time we can present a few figures for the period treated in this chapter, that is, for the fifty years following the Civil War. They must be regarded with care—as is the case with all statistics—but they will give an approximate idea of the extent of German immigration into Maryland. These figures were taken from the official United States census between 1850 and 1910 and they indicate in general the curve of German immigration.[162]

Number of Maryland residents who were born in Germany:

1850	26,936
1860	43,884
1870	47,045
1880	45,481
1890	52,436
1900	44,990
1910	36,657

We can see that the curve rises rather steeply between 1850 and 1890 and then recedes quickly. It is interesting to add the numbers of all foreign-born residents in Maryland and then to determine the percentage of Germans in the entire group. We present the figures here, with the approximate percentage of German born.

Year	Total of Foreign Born	Percentage of German Born
1850	53,288	50%
1860	77,536	56%
1870	83,412	56%
1880	82,806	55%
1890	94,296	55%
1900	93,934	48%
1910	104,944	35%

Thus we see that since 1880 the total number of foreign born increased consistently, but that within twenty years the percentage of Germans dropped from 55 per cent to 35 per cent.

The census figures also give us some information on the geographical distribution of the Germans in Maryland. During the

[162] Census of 1850, p. xxxvi. Census of 1860, Vol. I, p. xxix. Census of 1870, Vol. I, pp. 312, 339, 758. Census of 1880, Vol. I, pp. 435, 493, 513. Census of 1890, Vol. I, 1, pp. cxxxix, 632. Census of 1900, Vol. I, pp. cv, 732, 758. Census of 1910, Vol. I, p. 809; Vol. II, p. 842.

last decades of the nineteenth century about 85 per cent of all those residents of Maryland who had been born in Germany lived in Baltimore City and Baltimore County. In 1900 more than half of all the foreign-born residents in Baltimore were German immigrants; in Allegany County, where the city of Cumberland is located, a quarter of all the foreigners were German. (1270 German born in Allegany County.) On the other hand, the two old German counties, Frederick and Washington, which had received the main stream of German immigrants in the middle of the eighteenth century showed no more than 516 German-born in 1900, a little more than one per cent of the total of Maryland Germans. We can see how the weight shifted from the western counties to Baltimore.

An unofficial estimate in 1887 placed the number of German-Americans in Baltimore at a round 100,000.[163] This cannot be proved. However, when one takes into consideration the fact that according to the census of 1890 there were more than 52,000 German-born people in Maryland, most of whom undoubtedly resided in Baltimore, and that this number may be easily more than doubled by the inclusion of first- and second-generation German-Americans born here but still speaking German, as well as a few thousand German-speaking Austrians and Swiss, the estimated 100,000 does not seem to be too high a figure for the peak of the German-American period around 1890. There were sections of the city where more German than English was spoken. These German-American sectors of Baltimore's population lived in their own world, cut off from their American surroundings by the language barrier. The conditions of 1850 no longer prevailed when the mob of radical nativists made life miserable for the Germans. Now they lived peacefully with the rest of the city. They were recognized and respected as an isolated group. Never before nor after the two decades before the first World War did they experience such coherence and strength as a homogeneous group.[164] This does not imply that they ceased to complain about the lack of recognition. The speeches that they made at their festivals often went to extremes, showing a dangerous lack of balance and political tact. But since this querulousness was

[163] BVG, 85. At that time the city had a population of 425,000 (360,000 white, 65,000 colored).

[164] Dieter Cunz, "Rise and Fall of the German-Americans in Baltimore," *Common Ground*, VII (Spring 1947), iii, 61-71.

always expressed in German it seldom penetrated to the outside world and seldom disturbed the friendly relations with the rest of the city. Certainly the happiest period in the long history of German immigration into Maryland lay in the five decades between the Civil War and the first World War.

X. BETWEEN TWO WORLD WARS

O N THE occasion of the celebration of German Day, October 6, 1904, Carl Schurz delivered an address in St. Louis in which he said: "The German Day in the United States is the celebration of the friendship of the German and American peoples. We German-Americans are the hyphen between Germany and America; we present the living demonstration of the fact that a large population may be transplanted from one to another country and may be devoted to the new fatherland for life and death, and yet preserve a reverend love for the old. We are the embodiment of the necessity of peace and friendship between the two nations."

The address was delivered at a time when German-Americanism was at the height of its flowering and in a decade when diplomatic relations between America and Germany were especially cordial. Hardly a single one of Schurz's audience noticed the undertone of warning contained in the last sentence. However, ten years later it was evident how clearly so wise and far-seeing a man as Carl Schurz had recognized the problematic character of the German-American. Peace and friendship between the two nations was an absolutely necessary condition for the existence of the German-American type. Should this condition ever be removed, his fate was sealed.

The German-Americans in Baltimore reacted to the European events of 1914 exactly as did the Germans in the rest of the nation. They passionately aligned themselves on one side. They declared their sympathies for the Central Powers in newspaper articles, speeches and demonstrations. They watched the course of the European war from 1914 to 1917 with undiminished confidence.

In Baltimore as well as in all the other large American cities the local chapter of the National German-American Alliance became the most important organization for the political activity of the German-Americans. Up to this time the Independent Citizen's Union, of which we have already spoken, had functioned chiefly as a political instrument to be used in favor of good government and civil reform, and against Prohibition and Blue Laws. Now these domestic issues sank into the background. The Independent Citizen's Union now considered its most important task the counteracting of English propaganda in the country, and the influencing of public opinion in America in favor of the Central Powers. "Blood is thicker than water," was the cry of Charles Hexamer, president of the National German-American Alliance, when he set in motion the entire propaganda machine of his enormous organization on August 4, 1914.[1] Only three days later the Baltimore chapter of the Alliance called a protest meeting against the anti-German attitude of the Anglo-American press.[2]

Along with these attempts to influence public opinion, the local group of the National German-American Alliance undertook to organize a far-reaching project for the support of the widows and children of the war dead in Germany. Every week the Baltimore *Correspondent* published the names of individuals and societies that had contributed to the fund.[3]

The Baltimore *Correspondent* displayed the same aggressiveness and confidence in victory as did almost all the other German-American newspapers in the country.[4] In the beginning its chief interest was concentrated on the Eastern European front, where it saw the war as a conflict between "Asiatic-Balkan semi-barbarians" and the representatives of civilization. But very soon England appeared on the scene more often. Because it feared that the greatest danger to American neutrality came from England, the *Correspondent* concentrated its attacks ever more strongly in John Bull's direction.

The English question very soon began to influence the domestic

[1] We have two excellent monographs for the general background of the history of the German-Americans during the World War: Carl Wittke, *The German-Americans and the World War* (Columbus, Ohio, 1936), and Clifton James Child, *The German-Americans in Politics 1914-1917* (Madison, Wis., 1939).

[2] *Mitteilungen des Deutsch-Amerikanischen Nationalbundes,* vi, 9 (1914), 18. A similar meeting was organized again at the end of the year (December 27, 1914) "for the purpose of more effectively preserving and demanding American neutrality." It was a public meeting attended chiefly by Germans and Irish. *Ibid.,* vii, 1 (1915), 18 f.

[3] The National Relief Fund of the National German-American Alliance received the following sums of money from the Germans in Maryland: 1914, $15,000; 1915, $22,500; 1916, $6,088. The total amount collected during these years was $43,588. Cf. *National German-American Alliance: Hearings Before the Subcommittee of the Committee on the Judiciary,* 265. *Mitteilungen des Deutsch-Amerikanischen Nationalbundes,* vi, 12 (1914), 14; vii, 9 (1915), 32.

[4] A very sharp article on the necessity of being aggressive appeared in the August 19, 1914, issue.

political line of the *Correspondent*. True to its long Democratic past, the paper had campaigned for the election of Woodrow Wilson in 1912. From spring of 1915 on, especially after the Lusitania affair, the paper rapidly turned away from Wilson. Since it was certain, on the one hand, that the Democratic Party would renominate Wilson, and on the other that the *Correspondent* would not endorse him, it began early in 1916 to follow developments in the Republican camp with a new interest. In May 1916, the name of Charles E. Hughes began to appear in editorials in the *Correspondent*. The paper stated that one could have confidence in him because he was first and foremost an American. "The people want to put a real American in the White House, a man who does not subordinate the interests of his country to those of another."[5] A short time later the editorials were even more pointed when they declared that Wilson had lost the confidence of the people because he had worked more in the interests of the "mother country, England" than for America.[6]

The election campaign of 1916 placed the *Correspondent* in a very difficult position, of course. It regarded both the Republicans and the Democrats with mixed feelings. On the Republican side there were two people who had become anathema to the German-Americans: Theodore Roosevelt and Elihu Root. Like all the other German-American newspapers,. the *Correspondent* very early raised objections against the possibility of nominating Root or Roosevelt.[7] Hughes's nomination was received with great relief, though the newspaper took violent issue with the administration press for calling him the candidate of the "Hyphen-Americans."[8] There was only one point that the German-Americans objected to in connection with Hughes, and that was his association with Theodore Roosevelt; each one of Roosevelt's speeches cost Hughes 10,000 German-American votes.[9]

On the other hand, the *Correspondent* could not quite make up its mind to desert the Democratic Party entirely. It carefully differentiated between Wilson's domestic and foreign policies. It was still full of praise for the President's domestic policy. It said that he had freed the businessman and the farmer from the rule of Wall

[5] *Correspondent*, May 30, 1916. [6] *Ibid.*, June 1, 1916.
[7] *Ibid.*, June 7, 1916. [8] *Ibid.*, June 13, 1916.
[9] *Ibid.*, October 6, 7; November 6, 1916.

Street. "If the European war had not broken out during Woodrow Wilson's administration one could say of him that he served his country well. . . . Wilson's foreign policy, however, ruins the good impression made by his domestic policy."[10] Wilson was now a dangerous person who had to be removed.[11]

On election night the *Correspondent*, like most voters, was under the false impression that Hughes had been elected. Its premature funeral oration for the Wilson administration was designed to make clear the fact that although the paper was glad of Wilson's defeat, it still continued very definitely to be a Democratic sheet. "Wilson's defeat is not a defeat of the Democratic Party. This year's presidential election campaign was not a battle of party against party; it was a battle between true Americans and un-Americans. The Democratic Party emerges from this campaign not defeated but rather purged, freed from the false leaders who attempted to place the stamp of un-Americanism on it and make it the vehicle of ideas inimical to the country. In four years when a real American of the type of Cleveland and Jefferson is its standard bearer it will appear in all its old strength and then we shall see a battle again between one party and the other."[12] When the true result of the election became known, the *Correspondent* tried to interpret it as the country's dismissal of Theodore Roosevelt. It said that Wilson could thank Roosevelt for his reelection. The election was a protest against Theodore Roosevelt's warmongering. Wilson was reelected as the "Peace President." "We hope that in four years he will still be able to say, 'I kept the country out of war.' "[13]

Only a few months later, the *Correspondent's* hopes for peace were markedly reduced, when in the course of the U-boat war the tension between Germany and the United States became increasingly great. After the breaking off of diplomatic relations between the two countries, the paper felt it necessary to warn its readers to be careful. "It is not yet a crime to defend Germany's position, but it is unpatriotic and, above all, unwise. . . . In this case one's sense of duty must triumph over one's heart."[14] A short time later, rules of conduct appeared frequently in the columns of the *Correspondent*, printed both in English and in German, as follows: "Be calm! Keep your tongue! Keep wisely silent! Remember your oath of

[10] *Ibid.*, June 17, 1916. [11] *Ibid.*, October 9, 1916.
[12] *Ibid.*, November 8, 1916. [13] *Ibid.*, November 11, 1916.
[14] *Ibid.*, February 4, 1917.

allegiance! Keep in mind that while Germany is the land of our fathers, this is the land of our children and children's children. Yonder the past—here the future!"[15]

In April 1917, the *Correspondent*, like most German-American newspapers, was faced with the necessity of a complete reorientation.[16] Until just a short time before, the various papers had openly sympathized with the Central Powers. After the United States declared war on Germany, what had been a right guaranteed by the Constitution had suddenly become high treason. The *Correspondent* did its best to assist its confused German-American readers to understand the sudden change and to show them how to steer their course through the dangerous pitfalls of April 1917 without losing their self-respect. An editorial on April 5, 1917, was entitled, "Our Duty—Our Choice." It stated: "It may seem incomprehensible to immigrant Germans that they must consider the country of their origin as an enemy country. But we became citizens of the United States of our free will, and we swore to be loyal to the land of our choice. This is the most solemn oath a man can take; anyone who breaks it brings only shame, not honor, to the country where his heart lies. . . . No matter what opinion we had and may still have about the cause of the war, if the Congress of the United States has declared war then it is as binding upon us as upon the native citizens. . . . We must do our duty toward the land to which we swore fealty."

During the succeeding weeks and months the entire German-American press was regarded with suspicion by the government and by the public. A week after the declaration of war, the *Correspondent* found it necessary to make clear its position and purpose by means of an English statement printed above the masthead as follows: "This is an American newspaper published in the German language. Its function is to acquaint the immigrated Germans with the social and political conditions in the United States, and to familiarize them with their duties toward their adopted country and with the rights conferred upon them by the Constitution."[17]

[15] *Ibid.*, February 6, 1917.
[16] See Wittke, *op.cit.*, 128 ff. F. P. Olds, "Disloyalty of the German-American Press," *Atlantic Monthly*, cxx (1917), 136-40. C. W. Park, "The Strategic Retreat of the German Language Press," *North American Review*, ccvii (1918), 706-19.
[17] *Correspondent*, April 12, 1917.

In the course of the next year, the *Correspondent* succeeded in a tactful way in integrating itself in the war effort of the country. The readers were informed of various government instructions; appeals for the Red Cross and the various Liberty Loan drives were printed and emphatically supported; all Germans were urgently requested to fulfill the draft regulations, and patriotic meetings of German-Americans for the promotion of Liberty Loans were loudly advertised. There were, finally, even a few friendly words for Woodrow Wilson. The President's message to Congress at the beginning of December 1917 was reported with warm appreciation. An editorial praised Wilson for wanting to have the war waged for a good cause and for desiring a just peace free of all injustice or revenge.[18] The *Correspondent* expressed the hope that this message would strengthen the Peace Party in Germany. The paper drew a distinction that Wilson himself had often mentioned in earlier years, namely, the difference between the warlike German government and the peace-loving majority of the German people. After the *Correspondent* had celebrated Emperor William II's birthday in January 1917 with articles, poems and pictures, this discrimination between people and government such a short time later looked a little peculiar.

Whether the war spirit that entered the columns of the *Correspondent* after April 6, 1917, was genuine or not is difficult to decide. However, there is no doubt that after America's entry into the war the *Correspondent* did its best to support the war effort of the country as effectively as possible. Not another word was written that might have been construed as disloyal or against the interest of the country. The government appreciated these efforts, for the Baltimore *Correspondent* was one of the first German newspapers in the nation to be freed of the necessity of depositing translations of its articles with the postmaster.

Despite all this, the *Correspondent* did not live to see the end of the war. The anti-German hysteria of 1918 put an end to the *Correspondent* in its 77th year of publication. The year 1916 had been one of the best years in the business history of the paper. But because of public pressure, the number of subscribers fell rapidly; advertising disappeared almost entirely, and the jibes of competing Anglo-American papers daily became worse. When the list of casualties resulting from the spring offensive of 1918 appeared,

[18] *Ibid.*, December 5, 1917.

anti-German sentiment increased in all aspects of daily life. In an issue in the middle of April the Baltimore *Sun* published both the news that the Germans in Baltimore had raised $500,000 for the Third Liberty Loan, and the rumor that the *Correspondent* was soon to cease publication.[19]

On April 28, 1918, the *Correspondent* bid farewell to its readers. An editorial written both in English and in German called, "A Farewell to the Readers of the Correspondent," explained once more the well-known reasons for its disappearance and once more energetically protested against any suspicion that it might have lacked patriotic spirit.[20]

It was a time when, under similar protests, many German-American institutions disappeared from the scene. In this same spring of 1918, the National German-American Alliance was dissolved, an organization to which many Germans in Baltimore had belonged through the Independent Citizen's Union. A Senate hearing was held in Washington from February to April 1918, regarding the contemplated revoking of the Alliance charter. Two of the best-known German-Americans of Baltimore—John G. Tjarks and Karl A. M. Scholtz—played important roles at the hearing.[21] But their efforts were of no avail in changing the unsatisfactory result of the hearing. The Alliance dissolved itself before its charter was revoked.

The year 1918 concluded the history of a great many German-American clubs, organizations, newspapers, and churches. The Germans in Baltimore, like those in the other cities, were surrounded by suspicion and mistrust. As individuals as well as in groups they frequently encountered humiliations and accusations. A symptom of the general feeling was a decision of the City Council of Balti-

[19] *Sun*, April 16, 1918.

[20] After referring again to the confidence that the Federal Government had had in it, the *Correspondent* continued: "But nevertheless our critics at home differed from the Government in Washington. One of the morning contemporaries, printed in the language of the country, thought it had to show its patriotism by assailing the *Correspondent* for certain utterances about some of the Allies, calling it disloyalty towards the United States, and distorting certain phrases to prove its point." (*Correspondent*, April 28, 1918.)

[21] Tjarks was Chairman of the Finance Committee; Scholtz was Counsel for the Alliance. Cf. *Hearings Before the Subcommittee of the Committee on the Judiciary*, United States Senate, Sixty-fifth Congress, Second Session on S. 3529. A Bill to Repeal the Act entitled "An Act to Incorporate the National German-American Alliance," approved February 25, 1907 (Washington, 1918); for mention of Tjarks and Scholtz, see pp. 131-34, 160, 175, 223-26, 245-64, 325, 343-47, 493-97, 546 f., 568, 570 f.

more in September 1918 to change the name of one of the main streets in the older section of the city from German Street to Redwood Street in honor of the first officer from Maryland to die in the World War.[22] Unimportant as this incident may be, it is indicative of the atmosphere of 1918, and the Germans in Baltimore regarded it with great bitterness. After things had quieted down, they pointed out that they had done their part in winning the victory like every other national group. A glance through the honor rolls of Maryland troops shows on every page such names as Eichelberger, Hoffman, Myers, Snyder, Klingelhoefer, Reuter, Fuchs, Brandau—to pick only a few of them at random.[23]

The war-time hysteria disappeared in a few years. Tensions eased, heads became clearer and more sober. But German-Americanism was never to rise again. The era of the hyphen was past. The German-Americans as a group did not survive the year 1918. The old German-American stock was forced to reorient itself. No new additions came from Germany, or, if so, then only in very small numbers. The history of unchecked, large-scale immigration to the United States came to a close with the passing of the quota laws in the twenties. In place of the old free immigration, there was a rigorous allotment system according to which only about 27,000 Germans could immigrate into the United States in any year.

In Maryland, as in all the other states, the number of German born in the population constantly decreased. The three last census figures show this plainly:

	Total Foreign Born in Maryland	Percentage German Born in Maryland
1920	103,179	21.4%
1930	95,093	19.9%
1940	81,715	17.6%

[22] There was a story circulated among the Germans in Baltimore for many years that German Street was named for an old English family whose name was "German," and that "Redwood," on the other hand, was an anglicized form of the German name "Rotholz." There is not the slightest bit of proof for this story. German Street was so named because many German merchants had their stores here. Lt. George B. Redwood came of a Virginia family (probably English) which was always named "Redwood." There are "Redwoods" on an immigrant list for York County, Virginia, 1648, and also in the first census of 1790.

[23] Maryland in the World War 1917-1918 (Baltimore, 1933), I, 210 ff.

Within one decade, from 1930 to 1940, the number of German born in Baltimore dropped from 13,568 to 9,744, or from 18.2 per cent of the total foreign born in the city to 16.0 per cent.[24]

However, after the middle of the twenties there was something like a resurgence of German-Americanism, though in a much modified form. These German-Americans of 1925 were different from those of 1890. They were less noticeable; they had more modest ambitions, and they did not emphasize their German origin upon every occasion. It was now simply a group of Americans, mostly native, who kept alive the folk traditions of their parents in various clubs and societies. For Germany itself they had only a friendly but very distant interest. Only a few of them had ever seen Germany.

The choral societies (Sängervereine) were the first to come to life again after 1918; by the end of the 1930's there were once more a dozen German singing societies in Baltimore. They soon began to appear in public concerts again and were given a friendly reception. At the soft tones of *Ach, wie ist's möglich dann*, or *Du, Du liegst mir im Herzen* many an Anglo-American forgot his old grudge against the Kaiser's U-boats in 1917. A few chorus directors like Eduard Boeckner, Theodore Hemberger and Johann Eltermann held these German singing societies together for decades; most of these directors were connected with a German-American church as organist or choir leader.

Along with the singing societies, the Turnvereine again began to appear—the Turnverein Vorwärts and the Germania Turnverein. Then in 1923 a third gymnastic organization was founded, the German Sport Club. Here gathered all the younger people, who found that they had nothing to say in the older clubs because of their own youth. The old Germania Club was also restored, though it was no longer exclusively a merchant's club as in the nineteenth century. From this time on, German-Americans of all occupations belonged to the Germania Club, which was now much more loosely

[24] *United States Census of 1920*, ii, 698, 822.
    Census of 1930, ii, 276, 354, 520.
    Census of 1940, ii, Part 3, 524, 573.
    Immigration from Germany into Maryland:
        1901-1910—2,197
        1911-1914— 835
        1915-1919— 205
        1920-1924—1,262
        1925-1930—1,488

organized; its main purpose was to provide a setting for entertaining prominent visiting Germans. The Independent Citizen's Union functioned once more, though on a smaller scale; it took part in questions of community politics but lacked the influence that it had exercised before the first World War. The Steuben Society of America founded a local chapter in Baltimore and named it the Schley Unit in honor of the famous Schley family which had been connected with the history of Maryland since 1735.[25] Immediately after the war, the German Society of Maryland resumed its charitable activities once more. The Society for the History of the Germans in Maryland, which had long been inactive, showed signs of new life. In 1929 it issued a publication for the first time in twenty-two years, and since 1939 it has published every three years collections of articles dealing with German immigration into Maryland.

In connection with the centennial of Goethe's death, the Goethe Society of Maryland was organized in 1932. Its first task was to arrange for the Goethe celebration of 1932 in Baltimore, at which the German poet, Gerhart Hauptmann, was the main speaker. After this, the Goethe Society constituted itself as a small but very stable group of people interested in German literature. According to its constitution, its purpose was "to promote the study and appreciation of Goethe and of German literature, art and philosophy in general." The society's monthly lectures have made it possible to keep alive an interest in German literature. No other German-American group in Baltimore was so successful in cultivating the best traditions of the German spirit.[26]

Understandably, the German-Americans did not indulge in public celebrations during the first few years after the war. Gradually, however, their old pleasure in festivals reawoke. In 1927 they celebrated the 150th anniversary of General Steuben's landing in America; as so often before, the figure of Steuben was a very convenient one to use

[25] The Steuben Society stated its purpose to be "to awaken in the hearts and minds of American citizens of German extraction the necessity for taking a more active part and interest in the political affairs of our great country." The Baltimore Chapter of the Steuben Society existed from 1920 to 1944.

[26] The Goethe Society was founded on November 13, 1931, mainly through the initiative of Ernst Feise and William Kurrelmeyer. It was at first a branch of the Goethe Society of America, but it later became an independent group. For a short history of the society and a complete list of its lectures from 1932 to 1946, see Dieter Cunz, "Die Marylander Goethe Gesellschaft," Monatshefte, xxxviii (1946), vi, 367-70.

in proving the long tradition of American patriotism of the German element. 1929 saw the centenary celebration of Carl Schurz's birthday. During the same year the citizens of German descent took a very active part in the festivities marking the 200th anniversary of the City of Baltimore.[27] A year later (1930) there was the reception for Hugo Eckener, the Zeppelin commander, which again brought the German element in the city before the public eye. In 1932 the German societies joined in the celebrations for the 200th anniversary of George Washington's birthday and that same year the 100th anniversary of Goethe's death was appropriately commemorated. Gerhart Hauptmann's speech on "Goethe as an Educator" was the high point of the Baltimore Goethe celebration.[28] In 1936 the Germans joined together at the dedication of a Martin Luther monument.[29] In the year 1937, the Turnverein Vorwärts celebrated its seventieth birthday with great festivities. A National Saengerfest was held in Baltimore in 1938 for the first time in many years; dozens of German singing societies from the East Coast area took part. For one last time the German singing societies dominated the street scene as they had so often done in the past—the last time, for while the German-Americans in Baltimore were singing tender songs, Hitler's columns had already begun their march over Europe. A year later the second World War broke out and quickly put a stop to the reawakening of German-Americanism.

Despite all the difficulties of the post-war period, the German-Americans in Baltimore were never without a German newspaper. The old *Correspondent* had had to cease publication in the spring of 1918. But there was still the *Bayrische Wochenblatt*, which had been published in Baltimore since 1880. It was for Bavarian readers all over the country, but it had to fight hard for its existence. When the *Correspondent* closed its offices, the *Bayrische Wochenblatt* took over part of the employees. Soon the two undertakings were

[27] The official commemoration book, *Baltimore 1729-1929, Two Hundredth Anniversary*, contains an article on pages 253-59 by K. A. M. Scholtz, entitled "The German Citizens in Baltimore." This fact alone shows that the Germans were again accepted as real citizens.

[28] *Correspondent*, March 13, 1932. For the text of the lecture, see Gerhart Hauptmann, *Das gesammelte Werk*, XVII (1942), 207-33.

[29] Arthur Wallenberg, a goldsmith born in Quakenbrück, Germany, left the city of Baltimore the sum of $50,000 for a Luther monument. The monument is the work of the Baltimore sculptor, Hans Schuler; it stands at the entrance of Druid Hill Park.

merged and a German weekly paper appeared once more, called the *Baltimore Correspondent*. It carried on the traditions of the *Deutsche Correspondent* founded in 1841. The *Baltimore Correspondent* still exists as a semiweekly paper.

The publishers of the old *Bayrische Wochenblatt* and the new *Baltimore Correspondent* were Arthur M. Bömmel and Joseph A. Heisch. Of course, they had to fight for a long while against the suspicion aroused by the World War against German newspapers. Even as late as 1928, they found it necessary to publish occasional editorials in English making clear their purposes: "The Baltimore Correspondent, as all papers published in the United States in the German language, are not German papers but American papers printed in the German language. They represent American interests as completely as the papers printed in the English language. They educate the Germans who come to this country to become good and loyal American citizens. It goes without saying that the Germans love their fatherland, but they love the land of their adoption more, and their first and last allegiance is to the country in which they have settled and raised their families, and where forever every interest they and their children have is centered. There can be no question that the German-Americans and Americans of German descent will follow the American flag wherever it leads. We are first and foremost Americans now and forever." It is the typical overcompensated patriotism of the first and second immigrant generations that one sees in all the nationality groups.

In questions of domestic policy the paper remained entirely neutral. At election time it hardly entered the political scene. The only political question in which the publishers took sides was that of prohibition. The *Baltimore Correspondent* was a descendant of a Bavarian weekly written for Bavarians who had emigrated from the most famous beer country in the world. It will surprise no one, then, if we state that the *Correspondent* was definitely and with the profoundest convictions "wet."

The publisher, Joseph Heisch, died in 1928. His partner, Arthur Bömmel, carried the paper along for two years and then he sold the whole undertaking to Valentin J. Peter, in whose hands the paper is today.

Valentin J. Peter had made a name for himself as the owner and publisher of various German newspapers in the Middle West.[30] The *Baltimore Correspondent* was a new link in the chain of German newspapers that he owned. He himself remained in Omaha, Nebraska, but his two sons, Bernard and Theodore, took charge of the Baltimore branch of the business. The actual journalistic part of the work was done by various editors, among whom were Hans Raid and Walter Palme.[31] At first the paper appeared once a week, then semiweekly, and, since 1935, daily. When the second World War broke out it returned to the semiweekly schedule. The chief purpose of the paper today is to make clear to non-English speaking people the problems confronting the public, and to report to the German-Americans of the city the activities of German-American societies and churches.

Of course, the number of German-American churches was reduced from year to year. Several congregations functioned on a dual language basis, but only one church, Zion church, retains its emphatically German character today. The dwindling remainders of the old German-Americanism are now grouped around this church. Pastor Julius Hofmann guided the congregation with a firm hand through the uncertain times of the war and the post-war period. After his death in 1928, Pastor Fritz O. Evers was chosen as his successor, and from the day of his arrival in Baltimore he became not only the pastor of the Zion church but also the center of German-American life as a whole in Baltimore.[32] Today there are about 2500 people within the spiritual radius of Zion church, of whom about 1000 are actual members. It is thanks to its three last pastors— Scheib, Hofmann and Evers—that Zion church remained steadfast during the difficult years.

[30] Valentin Joseph Peter was born in 1875 in Steinbach, Germany, and emigrated to the United States in 1889. Cf. Miller, op.cit., 21 f. Georg Timpe, *Katholisches Deutschtum in den Vereinigten Staaten* (Freiburg i.B., 1937), 136-45.

[31] Hans Raid was born in 1889, in Bregenz, Austria. He came to America in 1923 and worked on the *Cleveland Wächter und Anzeiger* for several years before he came to Baltimore. Walter Palme was born in 1886 in Austria-Hungary. In the United States since 1913, he worked on the staffs of various German papers; he was editor of the *Baltimore Correspondent* from 1938 to 1947, when he accepted a call from the *New York Staatszeitung*.

[32] Fritz Otto Evers was born in Berlin in 1886. In 1908, he landed in New York. For a few years he was minister of a church in Englewood, New Jersey, and then pastor of the Immigrant Mission in New York. From 1914 to 1928 he preached at the old Lutheran Zion church in Philadelphia. At the beginning of 1929 he came to Baltimore as the successor to Pastor Hofmann.

The group of German-Americans has become smaller and smaller. German-Americans are turning into Americans of German descent. Again our earlier observation has been proved: that the process of Americanization occurs rapidly in the higher intellectual levels. At the universities there are a great number of professors of German birth or German descent whom we can call German-Americans only with certain reservations. Johns Hopkins University called a good many men born in Germany to its chairs of learning: William Kurrelmeyer, Ernst Feise and Arno Schirokauer in the German Department; Leo Spitzer for Romance Languages; Ernst Cloos for Geology; Johannes Mattern for Political Science; Ludwig Edelstein for History of Medicine.[33] After the reorganization of the University of Maryland in 1920, a great many professors of German descent joined the faculty. Among others are: A. E. Zucker (German Literature), Wesley M. Gewehr (American History), G. W. Prange (European History), A. J. Prahl (Comparative Literature), Harry R. Warfel (American Literature), R. G. Steinmeyer (Political Science), Charles G. Eichlin (Physics), Henry H. Brechbill (Education), T. O. Heatwole (Dentistry), John C. Krantz (Pharmacology), S. S. Steinberg (Engineering).[34]

The name of a German-American physician, Frank C. Bressler (1855-1935), holds an honorable place in the annals of the University of Maryland. He was the son of a German immigrant from Bavaria.[35] In his will Bressler left the university a fund for the foundation of the Frank Bressler Research Laboratory. His gift gave the university the opportunity to enlarge its departments of Anatomy, Histology, Embryology and Pharmacology. Several wealthy German-Americans earned the grateful appreciation of their fellow-citizens through large gifts. Among these philanthropists, perhaps Frederick Bauernschmidt, Ferdinand Meyer and Theodore Marburg were the foremost. All of them gave millions for charitable purposes, especially for the city's hospitals.[36]

[33] Cf. John C. French, *A History of the University Founded by Johns Hopkins* (Baltimore, 1946).

[34] For further particulars, see Dieter Cunz, "University of Maryland" (previously quoted), SHGM, xxvi, 10 ff.

[35] *Bulletin of the School of Medicine, University of Maryland*, xxiv, 139 ff.; xxv (1940), 1 ff.

[36] SHGM, xxiv, 50, 60. Frederick Bauernschmidt (1864-1933) was one of the largest brewers in the state. Ferdinand A. J. Meyer (1848-1933) came from Oldenburg; at the age of twenty he came to Baltimore and started his

Among the large number of outstanding German-American physicians in Baltimore we shall name only two great medical research men, Harry Friedenwald and Christian Deetjen. Friedenwald is one of the greatest ophthalmologists in the country; Deetjen earned his fame through his achievements in X-ray research.[37]

In the political life of the city and of the state we see again, as in earlier times, a very small percentage of German names. Twice the son of German immigrants became mayor of Baltimore. The first was William F. Broening, a Republican who was in City Hall from 1919 to 1923, and from 1927 to 1931.[38] In 1943, Theodore R. McKeldin, whose mother was German, was elected mayor of the city and served until 1947. Everyone familiar with the political life of Baltimore knows the name of Mrs. Marie Bauernschmidt. Though she never held public office, she did more than any other private person in an indirect manner. Her fight for the improvement of the public-school system first gained her wide reputation. Honored by thousands of anonymous voters, feared by corrupt politicians, "the guardian of the City's political virtue"—that is Baltimore's "Mrs. B."[39]

In the musical life of Baltimore a few German-Americans played roles of more than average importance. Franz C. Bornschein became known as a violinist and composer. Frederick R. Huber is a well-known figure in all the concert halls of the city. Among the many activities in which he engaged in the course of years were his work as Director of Municipal Music, and Director of the Lyric.[40] Otto

---

successful career as a merchant. Theodore Marburg (1862-1946) descended from a German immigrant who had come to Baltimore in the eighteenth century. Cf. *Men of Mark in Maryland*, II, 237 f.

[37] *SHGM*, xxv, 36 ff.

[38] Broening's father came from Hanau, his mother from Frankfurt. He was a member of the city council from 1897 to 1899; a member of the state legislature from 1902 to 1904; and from 1911 to 1919 he was States Attorney. Cf. W. F. Coyle, *The Mayors of Baltimore* (Baltimore, 1919), 229 ff. K. Z. Donellan, *Roads to Success* (Baltimore, 1927), 17-19. Baltimore *Sun*, May 12, 1931.

[39] Cf. the article by Lee McCardell in the Baltimore *Sun*, May 2, 1937. Marie Oehl von Hattersheim Bauernschmidt, born in Baltimore in 1875, was of German descent on both sides. Cf. Marie Bauernschmidt's article "Public Schools" in *Government of a Great American City*, edited by F. P. Stieff (Baltimore, 1935), 214-31.

[40] Huber was born in Baltimore in 1887. His father came from Frankfurt, Germany, but was originally of German-Swiss descent.

Ortmann's name is connected with the musical history of the city as Director of Peabody Institute of Music and as Professor of Music at Goucher College.[41] Far beyond the boundaries of the city and the state, Gustav Strube, a German, is known for his excellent compositions.[42] He was born in Ballenstedt, Harz, in 1867. He studied music at the conservatory in Leipsic and then became violinist in the most famous German orchestra, the Leipziger Gewandhausorchester. Through Arthur Nikisch he was brought to America in 1890 and was connected for over twenty years with the Boston Symphony Orchestra. In 1913 he accepted a call to the Peabody Institute in Baltimore. Since then he has taken a part in the musical development of the city. From 1913 to 1930 he was director of the Baltimore Symphony Orchestra. He soon became known for his compositions, symphonies, cantatas, concertos, choral works and an opera. His symphonic phantasies, "Harz Mountains" and "Americana," as well as his Lanier Symphony, are his most famous and most often performed works.

An important number of German-Americans stand in the foreground of the cultural life of the city, George Bernhard Meyer, born in Germany in 1873, is a well-known portrait painter. There are a great many sculptors, mostly of the school of Hans Schuler, and thus directly in the tradition of William Henry Rinehart: J. Edgar Stouffer, Edward Berge, Benjamin Kurtz, Isabelle Schultz and Alvin Meyer. Frederic Arnold Kummer became known as a writer of novels, plays, short stories and scenarios. Toward the end of his life he was successful in a new field; he wrote a few historical novels for young people, among which his *Torch of Liberty* was very popular.[43]

Without doubt the most prominent figure among living Marylanders of German descent is H. L. Mencken. We are well informed about his family history. Mencken himself was always very much interested in the history of his ancestors, and since he comes from

[41] Ortmann was born in Baltimore in 1889.

[42] Louis C. Elson, *History of American Music* (New York, 1925), 225. The most complete appreciation of the composer will be found in an article by Gustav Klemm, "Gustav Strube, The Man and the Musician," *Musical Quarterly*, xxviii (1942), 288-301. This article also contains a complete list of his compositions, 299 ff.

[43] Frederic Arnold Kummer was the son of a German physician from Bergedorf bei Hamburg. He was born in Catonsville, Maryland, in 1873, and died in Baltimore in 1943.

a family that early separated itself from the shadows of anonymity and appeared in the limelight of history it is not difficult to piece the family history together.[44] It may be traced back to the sixteenth century, where the lines lead to Oldenburg and Leipsic. An early trend toward mercantile interests was later superseded by an intellectual urge and an interest in scholarly research. One of Mencken's ancestors founded the *Acta Eruditorum*, the first scholarly journal in Germany in 1682. Another member of the family, who was a professor at the University of Leipsic, published a biting treatise against the intellectual quackery of learned men, thus anticipating the aversion of his descendant for the academic profession.[45] The Mencken family line makes some unexpected detours—even appearing at the court of Frederick the Great, and later becoming associated with Bismarck's family—only to swing back to the middle-class occupation of tobacco merchant, an occupation leading to the New World. Burkhardt Ludwig Mencken, the grandfather, born in Saxony in 1828, came to America in 1848. Despite the ominous year, 1848, he was not a liberal refugee; he had nothing to do with the German Revolution. He emigrated, filled not with ideological and revolutionary plans, but equipped with $500 and commercial training, and so he soon arrived at a state of moderate wealth. In Baltimore he established himself in the tobacco trade, which at that time was more or less dominated by Germans. In spite of this, he had on the whole little contact with the German sector of the city. He belonged to none of its societies, and in the history of the German-Americans of Baltimore nowhere do we find his name. August Mencken, the father (1854-1899), also remained in the tobacco business, and for many years had a medium-sized cigar factory in Baltimore. His mother was Harriet McClellan, of Scottish descent, but he married a German, Anna Margarete Abhau, whose family, by tradition of French Huguenot origin, had emigrated from Hesse-Kassel to Baltimore in 1848. These were the parents of Henry Louis Mencken, who was born in Baltimore in 1880.[46]

[44] We refer here to two chapters in the book, *The Man Mencken*, by Isaac Goldberg (New York, 1925): Chapter II, "The Menckenii in Europe" (32-49), and Chapter III, "The Menckens in America" (50-61).

[45] Johann Burchard Mencken, *De Charlataneria Eruditorum* (Leipsic, 1715). H. L. Mencken's enjoyment of this book may be measured by the fact that he had an American edition of it prepared which was published in 1937 by A. A. Knopf in New York: *The Charlatanry of the Learned*.

[46] Besides the above-mentioned book by Goldberg, see also the three vol-

Mencken's literary career began in the editorial rooms of the *Baltimore Morning Herald*. For fifteen years (1899-1914) he confined his journalistic work to the Baltimore scene. *De facto* he never did leave his Baltimore background, even during the years of his greatest fame. He has remained there until the present day, and he succeeded in forcing the literary world of America to turn its attention to Baltimore. It is a strange fact that this bitter enemy of American provincialism has fought stubbornly all his days against the centralization of literary life in New York. In spite of his worldly cosmopolitanism, he represents a type of urbane regionalism that is seldom found in America.

As the editor of the *Smart Set* (1914-1923) and of the *American Mercury* (1924-1933), Mencken was in the limelight of the literary life of the nation. He helped to make the works of Ibsen, Shaw and Nietzsche available to the American public. His books gained more and more influence among the younger generation: *A Book of Burlesques, A Book of Prefaces, Treatise on the Gods, Prejudices, In Defense of Women*, to name but a few. His book *The American Language* was the first great, systematic attempt to make Americans conscious of their linguistic individuality. Mencken reached the height of his fame and influence during the decade after the first World War. During this time he worked untiringly to develop America's literary taste, to overcome the literary infantilism of the country and to free American literature from the Puritan strait jacket of the past. "The Sage of Baltimore," "The King of Debunkers," will always occupy a place of honor in American literature for his battle against "that banality of letters." In his intellectual courage and honesty he can look to Lessing and Voltaire as his spiritual forebears. "If Mencken had never lived, it would have taken a whole army of assorted philosophers, monologists, editors, and patrons of the new writing to make up for him. As it was, he not only rallied all the young writers together and imposed his skepticism upon the new generation, but also brought a new and uproarious gift for high comedy into a literature that had never been too quick to laugh. . . . He was an irrepressible force, a stimulant, an introduction to wisdom. . . . In a culture aching for emancipation from the Prohibition mind, from vulgarity and provincialism

---

umes of H. L. Mencken's autobiographical reminiscences, *Happy Days, Newspaper Days, Heathen Days* (New York, 1940, 1941, 1943).

and conventionality, Mencken was a source of light and strength."[47]

Mencken had little contact with the German element in Baltimore.[48] But he shared with many educated German-Americans an admiration for the great achievements of German poets, musicians and philosophers. In the field of politics he was often by chance on the same side as the German-Americans, but he himself was never a "German-American" in the sense in which we characterized the type in the foregoing chapter. In 1917 to 1918, when he was against the entry of America in the war, his reason was not one of sentimental attachment to the country where his grandfather was born, but rather that he was against the alliance with England from a purely American standpoint. When he stormed against the anti-German hysteria of the American public between 1917 and 1920, this was not because he was pro-German but because he became enraged at the narrow-minded provincialism of the American Babbitt. The fact that he was under suspicion of being a German spy only filled him with wrathful scorn and caused him to send elaborate, anonymous denunciations against himself to the authorities.

The German-Americans in Baltimore who are interested in contemporary literature have honored him and (whether rightly or not) considered him one of their own. The great majority of the German-American sector which satisfies its intellectual needs with the daily paper knows his name at least through the columns of the Sun, and all of them found some angle of his literary or journalistic products that appealed to them. The remnants of the old-fashioned, nineteenth-century infidels among them rejoiced at his acid attacks on the churches and kindred "evangelical filling stations"; the non-interventionists found comfort in his warnings against the British orientation of our foreign policy; the Democrats were grateful for his criticism of the Hoover Administration; the Republicans watched with delight his broadsides against the New Deal; they all, no matter of what denominational or political shade, applauded his determined, brave, laudable and finally victorious fight against Prohibition. His Epicurean philosophy, his "art of living," his deep

[47] Quoted from Alfred Kazin, On Native Grounds, An Interpretation of Modern American Prose Literature (Reynal & Hitchcock, New York, 1942), 198 ff. Cf. also Ernest Boyd, H. L. Mencken (New York, 1925) and Isaac Goldberg, op.cit.

[48] Cf. the chapter "Aliens, but no Enemies," in Mencken's Newspaper Days, 249-59.

attachment to German music are all points of contact that kept him in touch with the civilized among the Baltimore Germans. He even belongs to some of the German-American societies. In spite of this, one of the most devastating evaluations of the German-Americans that was ever written came from his pen.[49] This article is obviously based on his observations of the German-Americans in Baltimore—a brilliant essay written, not in ink, but in vinegar. His verdict that the German-Americans were imposed upon America as a severe but just punishment for her sins will give aid and comfort neither to America nor to her citizens of Teutonic origin.

In this article written ten years after the end of the first World War, Mencken points out the political and cultural vacuity of the German-Americans. At that time they had reached the lowest point in their history. Since 1917 their racial consciousness had been constantly diminishing and now at last towards the end of the twenties they were slowly beginning to reorganize their decimated group. But they had hardly begun to recover from the blows of the World War when world politics swung in a direction that made the recovery of German-Americanism impossible.

We have already noted that the rise and fall of the German-American was caused to some extent by the events in Germany. German-Americanism was born with the founding of the German Empire in 1871, and it flourished as long as the Bismarck Reich lived in satisfied peace and as long as diplomatic relations between Washington and Berlin were undisturbed. The outbreak of the war and the defeat of Germany brought about the collapse of German-American racial consciousness. If the Weimar Republic had lasted three or four decades, it might have stimulated something like a quiet reincarnation of German-Americanism. But the rise of National Socialism in Germany quickly put an end to this hesitant reawakening. Anyone with political foresight could have predicted in 1933 that this would really conclude the last chapter of the story.

The influence of the Third Reich on the German element in the United States requires special investigation which does not fit into the framework of this book. The German-Americans reacted to the arrival of the new National Socialistic member of the family of nations as did the other American citizens: there were some for it and

[49] H. L. Mencken, "Die Deutsch-Amerikaner," *Neue Rundschau* (Berlin, 1928), xxxix, 486 ff.

some against. Perhaps the number of pros made up a larger percentage because their emotional ties with the land of their ancestry led them to minimize or even to overlook the latent dangers of the new nationalistic philosophy.

Most of the German-Americans, individually as well as in groups, avoided the issue. They evaded the question if their opinion was asked and hid behind an indifferent neutrality. Of course, in Baltimore as well as elsewhere, there were public followers of Adolf Hitler. The most radical of them formed a group called "Friends of the New Germany." In 1936 the organization dissolved, only to re-form immediately as the "German-American People's League" (Deutschamerikanischer Volksbund). Its opposite was also formed: the decided anti-Nazis in June 1938 formed the "German-American League for Culture." They cited the liberal German-American tradition of Follen, Lieber, Schurz, Sigel, Hecker and Heinzen, and unequivocally separated themselves from all the theoretical and material emanations of the Third Reich.[50] However, neither group found much support from the main mass of German-Americans. Both the pro and the anti organization were limited to small, uninfluential groups.

Individuals seldom took a stand in public toward events in Germany. Only in the "Letters to the Editor" columns in the Baltimore *Sun* may one occasionally see their reaction. There was a considerable stir in the spring of 1933, when Karl A. M. Scholtz, the undisputed leader of the German-Americans in the city, sent a telegram to the Chancellor of the German Reich: "I appeal to you to exercise toward the German Jews a spirit of justice, humanity and mercy." One of the most memorable documents in the history of the German element in Maryland is an open letter written by one of the most highly respected German-Americans in the city, Dr. Ernest J. Becker. In the fall of 1938, he protested vehemently against the barbarity of the German-Jewish pogrom, against the "negation

[50] The "German-American League for Culture" existed in several cities, such as Philadelphia, New York, Chicago, Cincinnati, Columbus, St. Louis and Milwaukee. Among the people who took part in founding the Baltimore Chapter were Otto Sattler, Erich von Schroetter, Ernst Schneider, William Dunau, William Kreuzig, Harry Lamb, Ernst Feise. At various times well-known German exiled writers and journalists, like Oskar Maria Graf, Walter Schoenstedt and Gerhart H. Seger, were invited to speak. Cf. Baltimore *Sun* and *Evening Sun*, June 25, 1938.

of the dignity and liberty of the individual."[51] Professor Ernst Feise of Johns Hopkins University tried to convince the German-American organizations that it was their first duty to take a stand against the politics of the Hitler government. "It is not an easy matter to accuse one's own brother. But it is better that the brother raise his voice before the neighbor steps in." But the organizations and the broad mass of the German-Americans remained cool and reserved.

Hitler's seizure of power sent a new group of immigrants to America and to Maryland—refugees from the Third Reich for political, racial or religious reasons. Similar to the '48ers of the nineteenth century, this group contained a high percentage of intellectuals and professional men. There were some skilled workmen and laborers among them, but most of them were physicians, professors, merchants, writers, engineers, chemists and men of similar occupations. Like all higher intellectual immigrant groups, these became Americanized extraordinarily quickly. These new refugees seldom came in contact with the old German-American stock. Because of the quota law their number was small. It has been estimated that only a few more than 1500 refugees from National Socialism settled in Maryland. Compared to the great waves of immigration of the nineteenth century, it was an extremely small group, with no coherence, and it was quickly absorbed into the general population.

The years before and during the second World War were remarkably free of hectic anti-German-American excesses such as those which characterized the 1917-1920 period. The Anglo-American press of Baltimore, which had ruined the *Correspondent* in 1918, now published several articles on the difficult psychological situation of the German-Americans. It understood "the travail of spirit which must have been the lot of most German-born citizens and of their sons and daughters in these terrible times. Other Americans, we are sure, will sympathize with them and stand ready to help them think their way through their difficulties."[52]

Many of the German-Americans may have had more sympathy for Germany than the average American liked, but no one thought

[51] The full text of the letter is reprinted in Appendix v.
[52] Cf. two very fair editorials in the Baltimore *Sun*, "Tragic Dilemma" (June 26, 1938) and "Travail" (November 18, 1938).

there was any danger in German-Americanism. Their feeling of solidarity dwindled more and more: they were divided in their political views; they had no power or influence as a group. Therefore, no pressure was built up against them. And again, because there was no pressure against them, their group feeling disappeared. When an old paragraph of the Maryland Constitution, providing that each bill be published in a German language paper, was quietly abolished during World War II, there were not even any protests from the German-Americans. The number of German organizations became smaller toward the end of the thirties and during the second World War. In 1938 there were about seventy-five German organizations in Baltimore, but only a third of them outlived World War II. When German Day was celebrated on September 12 between 1928 and 1938, there were about 20,000 persons present; in 1940, there were only 5000 guests and since then German Day has not been celebrated. Zion church, the strongest German-American institution in the city today, is the only one that can say that it weathered World War II in undiminished strength.

In June 1945 the city and the population of Baltimore prepared a triumphal reception for the first Marylander to win the Congressional Medal of Honor in the second World War. The hero of the day was Sgt. Paul J. Wiedorfer, who is of German extraction on both sides of his family.[53] But the German-Americans of the city hardly took notice of this biological fact—an indication of their greatly reduced consciousness as a racial minority. Nor was Wiedorfer's German descent ignored—also an indication that the atmosphere was much less tense than twenty-five years before.

The first group immigration to bring German settlers to Maryland came between 1730 and 1750. Two main motives caused this mass immigration: these people wanted to be hindered by no one in the exercise of their religion, and they sought land. It is a strange coincidence that we must conclude our history with a group of settlers of German descent who immigrated into Maryland two hundred years later, in 1940, for exactly the same reason; they were members of the Amish sect.

Until 1939 there were few people in Maryland who knew of the existence of the Amish. True, there were a few Amish colonies in

[53] The Wiedorfer family came from Alzesberg in Bavaria. The father, Joseph Wiedorfer, emigrated from Germany to Baltimore in 1912. Cf. Baltimore Sun, May 6, June 3, 4, 1945.

the farthest western part of the state, near Grantsville in Garrett County. There was a small Amish colony north of Hagerstown and another in Frederick County. Most of these Amish people had come to Maryland from Pennsylvania in the eighteenth century. At the end of the nineteenth century a few Amish families had emigrated from South Russia, had first tried their luck in Butler County, Kansas, and had then come to Dorchester County, Maryland, where they had settled on the Nanticoke River. All these Amish movements were without any great importance and were hardly noticed by the rest of the population of the state.

Then, in 1939, a group of Amish people came to Maryland to look for what the Amish seek again and again—land. They were silent, reserved people, but they could not avoid suddenly appearing in all the newspapers of Baltimore and Washington. For two or three years hardly a month passed that some paper did not publish a news item, an article or pictures of them and of their life.[54] Hundreds of times one heard the question repeated: Who are the Amish?

Who are the Amish? The Amish belong to the larger group of Mennonites. Several divisions branched off in the course of the centuries, yet they all have certain fundamental things in common: opposition to the State Church, belief in inner inspiration, strictest adherence to the Scriptures, which are interpreted literally and taken as a guide even for the details of everyday life. These people are all spiritual descendants of the radicals in the Reformation movement of the sixteenth century—those who thought that Luther, Zwingli and Calvin had started out on the right way but had not gone far enough. The superradicals in this group even went so far as to establish a "heavenly city on earth" in the German city of Münster. It was a half-political, half-religious experiment, which collapsed in 1535 after a few months of a reign of terror, confusion and intolerance. After this fiasco, Menno Simons led the movement back to its original religious character, and as an unworldly, pacifist

[54] We list here only the more important newspaper and magazine articles: Baltimore *Sun*, November 26, 27, 28, December 5, 6, 1939; September 29, 1940; May 15, August 5, September 14, December 28, 1941. *Evening Sun*, November 27, 28, 1939; August 4, 18, 1940; April 11, August 27, 1941; October 10, 1942; November 15, 1945. *Washington Post*, November 30, 1939, December 1, 1946. *New York Times Magazine*, February 25, 1940. *Saturday Evening Post*, March 30, 1940. *National Geographic Magazine*, LXXIX, iv (April 1941), 434 ff.; LXXX, i (July 1941), 40 ff.

group the Mennonites came to America and here found the refuge and peace that the Old World had denied them. The Amish were organized by Jacob Amman, a Swiss bishop of the Mennonite Church in 1693. A quarrel about church discipline led to the separation. The Amish have practically disappeared in Europe today. In the New World the group still exists, holding fast to the principles of Jacob Amman in their daily lives and their religious practices.[55]

The Amish are a rural group. Farming is intrinsically integrated into their earthly existence. They avoid cities and discourage their people from going to town. The fact that it is easier to keep their people "in line" in the country is only a superficial reason for this emphasis on country life; much deeper is the realization that their rural existence gives them a greater possibility of leading a life based on Biblical principles. They urge their children to stay on farms, and so they are constantly in need of more land. From time to time, some families move out of the old Amish ground in Lancaster Valley, Pennsylvania, in search of new land because they know that the group will dissolve if they loosen their bonds with the soil. That was the main reason why, in 1939, a number of Amish families decided to migrate south, to Maryland. Thus, in St. Mary's County, about fifty miles south of Washington, D.C., a new Amish center has developed in recent years.

A secondary reason for their migration to Maryland was their conflict with the school authorities in Pennsylvania. All Amish have a profound distrust of human learning. They agree to let their children undergo the most elementary schooling, but they consider seven years more than enough to learn all that is worthwhile knowing in the world. After seven years a boy should devote himself exclusively to farming. According to their views, any government that keeps him in a classroom longer than that keeps him away from the true source of life. When, in the late thirties, the State of Pennsylvania erected a new school building in the Amish district and directed the Amish children to attend the school, opposition

[55] The best scholarly treatment of the Amish sect is a book by Calvin G. Bachman, *The Old Order Amish of Lancaster County* (Norristown, Pa., 1942). Special references to the Maryland settlement are on pp. 69, 203, 261, 264, 265. Cf. also Jane C. Getz, "The Economic Organization and Practices of the Old Order Amish of Lancaster County, Pennsylvania," *Mennonite Quarterly Review*, xx (1946), 53-80.

arose in the community. The fact that the new school was built with borrowed money (a violation of another Amish principle) added to their wrath. Just at that time the Amish heard that in Maryland children were not compelled to attend school after the seventh grade. And so, in 1939 and 1940, some families of old Amish stock, whose ancestors had come over from Germany and Switzerland in the eighteenth century, sold their old farms in Lancaster County and bought new land in southern Maryland. Since the Amish are known in all the Middle Atlantic states as the best farmers in the country, their arrival was enthusiastically welcomed by the Maryland authorities.

Nevertheless, the people of St. Mary's County could not help wondering at the strange habits of the newcomers. They were all dressed alike. The men wore black suits and black hats with very broad brims; more striking was the fact that they all, even the young men, had long beards, but never a mustache. None of the women was ever seen without a bonnet, and their long, plain clothes were characterized by the absence of any fancy, colorful ornament. There would not be a single button on the clothes of any Amish man or woman; instead of buttons they use hooks and eyes. All these habits go back to the times of the founders, and in many cases no other explanation can be given but that "it has always been that way." It is said that in seventeenth century Europe the button was the most conspicuous symbol of a military uniform and the mustache an adornment of a soldier's face, and that for these martial associations buttons and mustaches were put on the Amish black list. This may be an explanation, although the Amish are the last to need one.

Most astonishing is the unpredictability and flexibility of their rules. They are against most modern inventions that one finds in any average American home. They have no radios, no musical instruments, no telephones, since they doubt that these things contribute essentially to make mankind happier. No photographs or portraits are to be found in any Amish house, for the Bible says that no likeness shall be made. To put a lightning rod on a house would indicate lack of faith in God. For a long time life and fire insurance was looked upon with suspicion, for, the Amish felt, it does not become us to mitigate a punishment that the Almighty may have chosen to put upon us; recently, however, some of them have taken out insurance. They are very averse to lending and borrowing money, yet here also a change seems to be taking place; they now make occasional loans among themselves, but the interest is kept very low. There are quite a number of modern conveniences on which the Amish rule has not yet committed itself. Gas and electricity, for instance, are still undecided problems. Some people use them; others avoid them, but they all would conscientiously comply with the rule if the Amish sect as a whole ever should arrive at a decision one way or the other.

Their keen interest in farming makes them more susceptible to the allurements of modern farm machinery. Agricultural engines are in common use. Cultivators, self-binders, hay-making and spraying equipment can be seen on any Amish farm. It is all the more baffling that they uphold so stubbornly their one and only restriction—that against the tractor. To be exact, a tractor may be used for stationary work, around the house or in the barn, but it may never be used in the fields. When, in 1946, alarmed by the world food crisis, the government asked the Amish to introduce tractors in order to increase their output, the Amish turned down the demand with a flat "no" and pointed to the indisputable fact that without tractors they produced considerably more food than their neighbors with tractors. This attitude is one of the many inexplicable features of the sect; apparently such a problem once came up and was decided in the negative, and there it stands.

The automobile is also put under a very strict ban. This surely is a great impediment at a time when transportation is a vital problem for a rural group. The Amish have no objection to traveling as such. Trains, streetcars, busses may be used; even automobiles are allowed for traveling so long as no Amish is the driver or owner of the car. But possession of an automobile is absolutely forbidden. The customary way to go places is to use horse-drawn buggies. Married people ride in buggies with a top; unmarried people never use anything but an open carriage. This is not a rule but a custom.

The Amish make every effort to pattern their lives after the principles of the early Apostolic Church. They uphold a community spirit that is probably unparalleled in our time. After the first Amish had settled in Maryland a new barn was needed. One afternoon about one hundred Amish men from Pennsylvania arrived to assist their Maryland brother to erect his new barn. For two days they worked. At the end of the second day the barn stood finished, to the last door hinge, and ready for use. Work done, the hundred men went back to Pennsylvania. Should any of them ever need help for a big job, his call would not sound unheeded among his brethren in Maryland.

The Amish are community-conscious, but utterly aloof where the state is concerned. They are excellent citizens who never cause any trouble and never do harm to anyone, but they do not possess what one might call civic virtues. They do not participate in the political affairs of the town, the state or the country. They do not vote; they do not take office; they do not swear an oath; they do not bear arms. They "render unto Caesar" only what they must and seek nothing of the government except to be left alone.

Their conscientious objection to military service was constitutionally and legally recognized, but it met with suspicion and disapproval in wide circles of their fellow countrymen. Often enough they were attacked for their refusal to fight against dictatorship and tyranny. The most demagogical of their attackers did not even disdain to unearth their German ancestry in search of explanations for the Amish aloofness toward the European conflict. To be sure, one could point out to the Amish that a totalitarian state would never allow them to live as undisturbed as they live here and that therefore it would be to their own interest to defend a democratic system, the requisite to their peculiar mode of life. Yet, we should not forget that what we call "life" is of less value to them than it is to us. Their categories differ from ours. Their deeply religious orientation allows them to look upon their stay on this earth as nothing but a preface to real life. Their laboring here is in the nature of a preliminary. Whether this preparatory stage takes place under totalitarian or democratic auspices matters little, compared to the joys and pleasures awaiting them in the Heavenly City. Indeed, the hardships of an adverse regime might even give them an opportunity to prove the strength of their faith and emulate the lofty example given by the founders of the Christian Church and the Mennonite Congregation, who willingly underwent tribulations and persecutions. The Amish do not have our sense of reality or our concept of history. What happened three hundred years ago to the founders in the Palatinate and Switzerland, or two thousand years ago in Palestine or Egypt, is closer to them than a Joint Session of Congress fifty miles north in Washington, D.C.

Their strict adherence to the letter of the Bible will again and again amaze the outsider. They do not tell their children stories about Santa Claus because such stories would be a deception, and thus a wrong way to start life. In spite of their general piousness they have no Sunday Schools, for they are not mentioned in the Bible. The Maryland Amish belong to the stricter group of Mennonites called "House Amish" who do not use church buildings. They meet every second Sunday in a different house each time, worship there in the morning and later have a common meal and a social gathering. It is the climax of the year for an Amish family when its turn comes to "have church" and to be host to the community.

Everything takes place according to a rigidly observed ritual. Men and women are seated separately at the service, the men in front and the women in the rear. They sing in German. Their hymnbook, the *Ausbund*, first printed in Switzerland in 1564, has been reprinted many times. Its first American edition was printed by the famous Philadelphia printer, Christopher Sower, in 1742. Their quaint, archaic, colorful Pennsylvania-German dialect is also used for their religious ceremonies. Only adults are baptized. Baptism is the actual entrance into the community. Their private life is governed by a very strict church discipline. Taboos and must-nots put them into a rather tight moral strait jacket; divorces are not allowed. The conviction that there was too much laxity in the Mennonite Church caused Jacob Amman to move out of the church two hundred and fifty years ago and found the Amish group as a separate organization. Ever since, strictness in church discipline has been one of the essential traits in their written and unwritten laws. The Amish are perhaps the most conservative group of people in the country. Traditions and customs are cherished with religious zeal, and serve to set off the group from the rest of the population; they build a wall around the people and prevent infiltration of the modern spirit and alien influence. Their habits and their dialect serve the purpose of creating an impenetrable layer of isolation around the community.

One point on which all people who have ever come in contact with the Amish agree is that they are the best farmers anyone has ever seen. Long farming tradition, handed down for generations, has made them agricultural experts with an unshakable reputation.

Their emotional attachment to the land is coupled with a solid knowledge of agricultural science. Their half-intuitive, half-scientific methods of "field examinations" have often enough puzzled soil experts. When the first Amish from Lancaster County came down to Maryland to buy land, they walked around in the fields, each one equipped with a small shovel, and wherever an acre was offered to them for sale they began digging with their shovels. It took them only a few minutes to find out whether the soil was good or bad, or at least in such condition that it could be improved. The soil of southern Maryland has been exploited through centuries of reckless tobacco farming. The Amish introduced crop rotation—corn, wheat, tobacco, hay—and they succeeded admirably in keeping the soil rich and productive. They were the first ones on the section between the Potomac and Patuxent Rivers who did what generations of southern Maryland farmers failed to do: they built up the soil systematically, letting it work in a definite rhythm of rest and production.

The Amish like to call themselves the "Plain People." To lead a plain, simple life in the country, to avoid contacts with the world, not to be bothered by outsiders, neighbors and government—this is all they ask. Here is one reason why they would never accept a public office. Any position in public life might evoke ambitions and lead away from the plainness with which a true Christian should live. They never rise high enough to risk a fall. They know this very well, and it gives them that peculiar poise and well-balanced tranquillity that characterizes their gestures, their speech and their whole behavior.

The Amish colony in Maryland has been growing steadily since 1939, when these strange men with black hats and long beards appeared for the first time, walked over the fields and dug into the soil with their little shovels. At that time only seven families came down—seven "freindschafts," as they call it, from the German word for "friendship." The leader at that time was an old man who was held in high esteem in the Lancaster Valley, Stephen Stolzfus. His authority was undisputed as long as he lived. After his death his three sons, Benjamin, Amos and John, rose to leadership in the settlement. After the Stolzfus-freindschaft, other Amish men with their families moved down from Pennsylvania: Isaac Fisher, Ammon Wenger, Noah Zook and others. We mention a few names because they are typical combinations. They show the German-Swiss ancestry of the people as well as their emphasis on Biblical tradition.

Today the settlement of the "Plain People" in Maryland comprises twenty-five families, with almost two hundred members. They have about 2000 acres under cultivation, where they grow tobacco, vegetables, hay, wheat and other small grain. Some operate dairy farms and others raise beef cattle and hogs. Their neighbors in St. Mary's County, who at first viewed them with reserved suspicion, have long accepted them as good, honest, law-abiding people and respect them for their success on their farms.

The Amish in Maryland are an isolated group; they have no connection whatsoever with the old German stock of Western Maryland farmers or with the citified German-Americans in Baltimore. Viewed as a whole, the German element in Maryland is rapidly disintegrating by being absorbed by the rest of the population. In all likelihood it will not be long before the last remnants of the German-Americans lose their identity as a distinct minority group. Not without reason was the third part of this book entitled "The Last Generations." By this we mean not only the most recent generations, but also the final generations in the falling curve of historical development. The German element in Maryland and the German-Americans in Baltimore are a historical phenomenon of the past. They have become the object of historical research.

HE history of the Germans in Maryland that we have attempted to set down on these pages covers a period of three centuries. The first German names appear in the documents of the Calvert Colony around 1640. They are names that mean nothing to us—obscure, small people who turned up on the shores of the New World through some unknown combination of circumstances. Only a few of them rose above the broad, anonymous masses. For a hundred years thereafter only a small insignificant trickle of German immigrants appeared, isolated individuals who were immediately absorbed into their surroundings and who entirely lost their identity as Germans.

Then, between 1730 and 1740, the first wave of German mass immigration set in. At first the new settlers were only the van of the wave of immigrants that flooded eastern Pennsylvania, but soon there was a direct stream from Germany and Switzerland. In the wake of this wave, which did not cease until the Revolution, came the founding of concentrated German settlements such as Frederick and Hagerstown in Western Maryland. It was characteristic of these immigrants that they were strongly bound to the land and to their church. They were a rural, church-conscious, conservative group. Friedrich Kapp once said: "In the battles which were fought to conquer the New World the Romance peoples provided officers without an army; the English provided an army with officers; while the Germans were an army without officers." This statement strikingly sums up the characteristics of the early German immigrants in Western Maryland. They were excellent farmers and craftsmen who earned the respect and esteem of their communities in their own, individual ways. None of them reached a social level from which he exerted a decisive influence on the history of the country. Each was content with his own small sphere and never sought to dominate a wider one.

These early German immigrants of the eighteenth century fully adapted themselves to the written and unwritten laws of the country. By a slow process they became amalgamated with their English, Irish, Scottish and Scandinavian neighbors. For generations the region in which they settled bore the stamp of their Germanic individuality, though their own grandchildren had already become thoroughly Americanized.

The immigrants in Baltimore soon differentiated themselves from their German compatriots in the western part of the state. Their occupations were urban and their mentality was urban. The historical function of the Western Maryland Germans was to supply the Tidewater Colony of the Calverts with an agrarian hinterland. The task of the Baltimore Germans was to help organize a commercial center. Though the city dwellers were strongly attached to their churches, the church did not occupy such a central, dominating position in their lives as it did in the lives of the western farmers. The German immigrants in the western counties remained a stable social group: farmers and craftsmen. The Germans in Baltimore soon began to split into various social levels. A few became wealthy and rose above the economic level of the others. They soon developed a greater feeling of solidarity with other members of their higher social plane, regardless of nationality, than with the broad masses of their fellow Germans. The German churches often tried to stress the greater importance of a common German heritage over a purely social one, but they seldom succeeded in their attempt at social equality. If the first wave of German immigration in Baltimore had retreated as completely as it did in the western counties, the Germans in the city would have been as completely amalgamated in the melting pot as were those in the country.

After 1815, however, a second wave of German immigrants arrived. It was larger than the first one and it lasted longer. Of the two centers of German settlement in Maryland, only Baltimore profited by this second wave. The western counties had become saturated by this time. No more did German settlers seeking land remain on the banks of the Monocacy and the Potomac. They had heard of the wide open spaces of the Middle West, and so they drove through Maryland without looking about. However, for a long time to come the city of Baltimore still offered many possibilities to German immigrants seeking general commercial and industrial opportunities. Thus, starting in 1820, the city received another wave of German immigrants. A second layer was laid upon the old eighteenth century colony of Baltimore Germans.

In historical research on the German element in the United States the distinction is often made between "Kirchendeutschen" and "Vereinsdeutschen." According to this classification the German settlers in Western Maryland were unquestionably "Kirchendeutsche." The church was the strongest social institution in their lives and it was the organization that upheld the German tradition for the longest time. At first the Baltimore Germans were also "Kirchendeutsche." But then came the great wave of immigration in the nineteenth century, which changed the character and the structure of the old German colony. The majority of the newer German immigrants had become emancipated from the bonds of the church, though only a few of them were actually radical atheists. Most of them belonged to some church congregation, but for them the church was only one of many social institutions, and decidedly not the central one. For them clubs and societies took on an increasing measure of importance for intellectual, occupational, political and especially social purposes.

The old "Kirchendeutschen" had become Americanized with little difficulty in three generations. The process had been completed in Western Maryland just as the second wave of immigration set in. The Germans in Baltimore, on the other hand, who were directly affected by this second wave strongly felt its retarding influence in the progress of their own assimilation. In the city in which there were at last nearly 100,000 inhabitants of German birth or German descent the Germans kept their national identity about a hundred years longer than did those in the western counties. An additional retarding factor in the Americanization of the Germans was the political development of Germany itself. The immigrants who came around 1830 did not actually come from Germany; they came from a particular German state such as Bavaria, Oldenburg, Hesse, Saxony, Bremen. The founding of the German Empire in 1871 resulted in an enormous increase in the long-pent-up and belated national consciousness of the Germans both within and without the boundaries of the Reich. The immigrant of 1830 had merely broken away from a local tradition when he became Americanized. The immigrant of 1880, on the other hand, was forced to break away from a national tradition. The political fascination of the Bismarck Reich, admired and esteemed throughout America, created a much stronger bond than had the emotional attachment of the earlier immigrants for the home of their youth in the Duchy of Nassau or in the Free City of Lübeck. As long as the German

Reich remained strong and respected, the sense of belonging to it remained very high in the racial consciousness of most German-Americans. When the curve of Germany's destiny turned downward, their German identity and their feeling of solidarity vanished rapidly.

After 1848, the "army without officers," of which Friedrich Kapp had spoken, received leaders for the first time—men who became the spokesmen for the previously inarticulate mass of Germans. They possessed the political acumen and the ability to express what so many of their fellows felt. The '48ers who arrived with definite political ideas of freedom were admittedly only a very small percentage, and they were not really typical of the German element as a whole. Certainly most of the German immigrants had come because of the freedom that they had hoped to find in America, but the word "freedom" must not be interpreted in too political a sense. The old German settlers on the Monocacy came because they wished to have freedom to pray to God in the manner to which they were accustomed, instead of having to unlearn their catechisms every time there was a new incumbent on the throne in the ducal palace. They came because they wanted freedom to buy and sell land; to cultivate it or let it lie fallow as they saw fit without having to follow the instructions of a feudal overseer. Similarly, the Germans who came around the middle of the nineteenth century and settled in Baltimore came because they wanted "freedom," freedom to start a business whenever they thought they saw a favorable chance; freedom to take advantage of every opportunity; freedom to take a position today and to leave it for a better one tomorrow; freedom to do as they pleased.

For the pious Amish and for the nineteenth-century agnostic, for the radical city laborer and for the conservative Western Maryland farmer, for the wealthy Bremen merchant and for the poor, steerage-class immigrant—for all these America was the Land of Promise. And the country between the Chesapeake Bay and the Allegheny Mountains where they settled helped to fulfill their hopes and ambitions. Maryland became for them, in a very literal and very symbolic sense, the New World. Only a few of them came with definite ideas of political democracy, but all of them were adaptable enough to fit into the democratic system which they found here and which by their very presence they helped to evolve.

Among those who emigrated from Germany certainly only a few were familiar with Thomas Jefferson's definition of freedom and democracy. The educated among them actually saw the gleaming light; the blind, ignorant masses only felt its warmth. But they all came because they shared the common vision of all immigrants, because they dreamt the dream of all wanderers seeking homes, and because they hoped that the New World would grant them what the Old World had denied: the right to pursue happiness. And thus each of them, whether consciously or not, and each in his own way, understood the essence of America.

APPENDIX

1. *Augustin Herrman, Bohemian*

There can be no doubt that the name "Augustin Herrman" sounds more German than Czech. Whether his mother tongue was German or Czech can no longer be ascertained, for in the documents from his American period he consistently uses either English or Dutch. We do know that he numbered many Germans among his friends and relatives, whereas we hear nothing of Czechs. Bohemia was at that time under the rule of the German emperor—if we want to cite this external political reason for having brought Augustin Herrman unhesitantly into our discussion. It is, however, as has already been said, impossible to approach the epoch of the Thirty Years' War with the concepts of our present-day period. The German-Czech question, so hotly contested in our own times, is not new; but it has moved in waves, becoming stronger or weaker at various intervals. The matter is presented by Eugen Lemberg in his book, *Wege und Wandlungen des Nationalbewusstseins* (Münster, 1934), 131, 133 ff. He shows that as early as the fifteenth century there was something like a sense of Bohemian cultural unity that included Germans and Czechs alike. In the sixteenth and seventeenth centuries the national difference between the two peoples living in Bohemia became less and less important than the religious difference. Germans and Czechs are equally represented among those sacrificed to the Catholic and Hapsburg victory at White Mountain in 1620. This fact alone proves that we cannot infer a Czech background for Herrman on the grounds that he was the son of a Protestant minister. The Bohemian revolution of 1618-1620 was not a purely Czech insurrection against the denationalizing Hapsburgs. The Czech historians themselves, who have turned more and more away from Fr. Palacky's romantic concept of history, have pointed out that German influence in Bohemia and cooperation in the revolution of 1618 was tremendously strong. (Cf. J. Pekar, *K velkému vyroci 1618-1620* [Prag, 1920], 20 ff.) Even if Herrman's family took part in the revolution, then, that is in itself no indication of their nationality. The fact that he again and again called himself a Bohemian in America may be an indication that he was a follower of the "Bohemianism" that was urging the synthesis of Germans and Czechs to a Bohemian racial group. (Cf.

Emanuel Ràdl, *Der Kampf zwischen Deutschen und Tschechen*
[Reichenberg, 1928], 82.)

The date and place of his birth were long in doubt. H. A. Rattermann wrote in an article entitled "Augustin Herrman" (*Deutsch-
Amerikanisches Magazin* [Cincinnati, 1887], 202 ff.) that Herrman
was born in Prag about 1605, where his father was a respected
citizen and town councilor. The mother, Beatrice—so Rattermann
asserts—was the daughter of a respected patrician, Kaspar Redek.
To be sure, Rattermann gives no source for this information; and,
since his authorities are not always the most reliable, his remarks
do not greatly help us. His statements have nevertheless been in-
gurgitated by American historians (cf. *New York Genealogical and
Biographical Record*). In his treatment, *Augustine Herrman of
Bohemia Manor* (State Printing Office, Prague, 1930), Thomas
Capek contested Rattermann's statement. He had the keeper of the
archives of the Prag Central Library examine the city records of
the time in question, where no mention of a Councilor Herrman
could be found. Capek believes that he has substantiated data to
the effect that Herrman was born in 1621 in Mseno, Bohemia, the
son of a Protestant minister, who left Bohemia that same year in
consequence of the current persecution of Protestants, lived for a
while in Zittau, Saxony, and then moved on through Germany to
Holland. According to Capek's sources from Mseno, the mother
died in 1621 shortly before the father took flight to Zittau. Rattermann presents the opposite view; the father died very soon, but the
mother was still living in New Amsterdam in 1648. As a matter of
fact, we possess a document of September 19, 1648, which reads as
follows: "Power of attorney. Jannetje Claes, widow of Urbanus,
mason, to Beatrice Herrmans, to receive money due to her late
husband by the West India Company, at Amsterdam. . . ." (*Calendar of Historical Manuscripts*, 44.) Rattermann's conclusion that
this Beatrice was Augustin's mother is rather hasty and based on
entirely insufficient evidence. The dates given for his birth vary
between 1605 and 1621. Probably the latter is the correct one, for
in 1684 he closes his will with the words "Aetatis 63"—at the age
of sixty-three. In his naturalization papers Herrman himself gives
Prag as his birthplace.

One point, to be sure, cannot be brought into agreement with
these assumptions. In the *Dictionary of American Biography* (VIII,

592), we read: "In 1633 he was a witness to a transaction whereby the Dutch bought from the Indians all the land now occupied by Philadelphia." The source of this is Samuel Hazard's *Annals of Pennsylvania* (1850), 35. This must be an error. Capek rejected it as "hardly credible." In 1633 Augustin Herrman was a boy of twelve, who could scarcely have been used as a witness in a land purchase. There is surely some mistake or misunderstanding present here, although we cannot explain it as long as we do not know the basis of Hazard's statement.

II. *Help for the Redemptioners*

Laws made and passed by the General Assembly of the State of Maryland, Annapolis, printed by Jonas Green, Printer of the State, 1818, pp. 224-26 (condensed form).

An Act Relative to German and Swiss Redemptioners

Whereas, it has been found that German and Swiss emigrants, who for the discharge of the debt contracted for their passage to this country are often obliged to subject themselves to cruel and oppressive imposition by the masters of the vessels in which they arrive, and likewise by those to whom they become servants, BE IT ENACTED:

Section 1. Providing for the appointment by the governor of a trustworthy person, skilled in the German and English languages, as register of all contracts for apprenticeship of German or Swiss emigrants arriving in this State.

Sec. 2. Regulates the manner of making these contracts, and none shall be valid, unless the same be drawn by the register or approved by him.

Sec. 3. Provides for the recording of these contracts, or indentures, in a court of record.

Sec. 4. Provides that no minor be indented except by his parents, next of kins, or the orphans court.

Sec. 5. Provides that the master must give every minor under the age of twenty-one years at least two months' schooling annually during his servitude.

Sec. 6. No emigrant shall in any case be bound to serve longer than four years.

Sec. 7. That no German or Swiss emigrant arriving here shall be detained longer than 30 days on board of the vessel after such arrival, and receive during the detention on board good and sufficient provisions, without increase in the period of their servitude.

Sec. 8. Makes it the duty of the register to remove on shore any sick emigrant or any emigrant having been cruelly or ill-treated by the officers of the ship, at the expense of the vessel. If no purchaser is found for him within sixty days after arrival, the master or owners of the vessel have no further lien on such emigrant.

Sec. 9. That no children shall be answerable for the passage money of their parents, dead or alive, nor parents for their deceased children, nor a husband for his deceased wife, nor a wife for her deceased husband, any pretense of custom in contract, promise or agreement made beyond sea, to the contrary notwithstanding.

Sec. 10. That the masters of the vessels arriving, in case of the death of any German or Swiss emigrant within ten days after arrival, deliver to the register an accurate inventory of all the property of such emigrant on board of such vessel. The register shall then sell such property, pay the master the passage-money, provided that if the passenger died before the expiration of one-half of the voyage no passage-money shall be due, and the heirs of the deceased shall be entitled to the proceeds, and if after advertisement and due search no heirs of the deceased can be found within three years after the arrival of the ship, then the proceeds to go to the German Society of Maryland.

III. German-American Businessmen

German-Americans, well-known in the commercial and industrial life of Baltimore in the period between the Civil War and the first World War:

John B. Adt, born 1835 in Enstein, Palatinate, in Baltimore since 1860, manufacturer of mechanical machinery.

John Albaugh, born 1829, Grand-Duchy Hesse-Darmstadt, in Baltimore since 1842, well-known carriage and wagon builder.

Christian Ax, born near Koblenz in 1823; in Baltimore since 1851, prominent in the tobacco business; Gail and Ax Company.

C. C. and Georg P. Bartgis, printers, descendants of the famous early Maryland printer, Mathias Bartgis, in Frederick.

Henry Becker, emigrated from Frankfurt a.M., partner of the banking house Kummer and Becker.

Charles and Louis Dohme, in Baltimore since 1852, co-founders of the great drug company Sharp and Dohme.

H. R. Eisenbrandt, originated from Göttingen, manufacturer of musical instruments.

Johann Faust, born in Schlitz, Hesse, in 1828, began shoe manufacturing in Baltimore in 1852, factory moved to Havre de Grace, Md. in 1889; father of Professor A. B. Faust of Cornell University.

Frank A. Furst, known along the East Coast as president of the Maryland Dredging and Contracting Company.

J. H. Furst, print-shop. Founded in 1904 by the four Furst brothers, sons of a Bavarian immigrant, the well-known Baltimore contractor Joseph Furst.

George William Gail, born in Hesse-Darmstadt in 1828, came to America in 1847, started a tobacco firm in Baltimore, which after the Civil War became one of the largest in the country; in 1891 his firm was bought by the American Tobacco Company.

F. X. Ganter, born in Freiburg i.Br. in 1849; in Baltimore since 1876, show-case factory.

Georg Gunther (1846-1912), German immigrant, built the Gunther Brewery in Baltimore in 1875.

Henry G. von Heine (1856-1936), started his coal business in Baltimore in 1882.

Henry G. Hilken, born in Bremen in 1847, in Baltimore since 1868, tobacco and shipping business.

Hochschild, Kohn, Department Store. Max Hochschild, born in Gross-Rohrheim, Hesse in 1855, came to Baltimore in 1870, founded the department store in 1897.

August Hoen, born in Höhn, Westerwald, in 1829, immigrated to the United States in the middle of the thirties, settled in Baltimore and developed one of the greatest lithographic establishments in the Eastern states.

Hutzler's Department Store. Founded in 1858. Three Hutzler brothers, David (1843-1915), Abram (1836-1937), Charles (1840-1907).

Georg Kirschenhofer, born in Regensburg in 1842, settled in Baltimore in 1873, wagon builder.

L. Kraus, born in Baja, Hungary, in 1838, since 1863 owner of a fur factory in Baltimore.

Arnold Kummer, born in Bergedorf near Hamburg in 1839, partner of the Baltimore banking house Kummer and Becker.

Georg A. von Lingen, born in Bremen in 1838, came to Baltimore in 1859, chief of the company of A. Schumacher, agent of the Northern German Lloyd, German consul for many years; died in 1907.

Christopher Lipps, great soap factory, established 1850.

C. F. Meislahn, manufacturer of furniture.

A. C. Meyer, manufacturer of pharmaceutical products since 1874.

Ferdinand A. J. Meyer, born in Zwischenhahn, Oldenburg, in 1848, came to Baltimore shortly after the Civil War, successful wine merchant; died in 1933.

Charles N. Oehm, born in Kassel in 1833, in Baltimore since 1850, garment industry.

U. A. Pollack, furniture industry.

Potthast Company, furniture; four brothers Vinzenz, William, John and Theodore Potthast.

Edward A. Prior, born near Osnabrück in 1841, in America since 1859, various branches of business, toys, tobacco, etc.

Ernst Schmeisser, born in Siegen, Westphalia, in 1851; since the eighties leading figure in the Maryland tobacco industry.

Peter Schmidt, baking business.

Carl W., Louis C., C. William Schneidereith—three generations of printers; printing shop founded in 1849.

Heinrich Senft, wine dealer.

Charles M. Stieff, born in Württemberg in 1805, came to America in 1831, first imported pianos, since 1852 manufacturing of pianos.

Otto Sutro, born in Aachen in 1833, 1858 music teacher in Baltimore, in 1868 established the leading music store in Baltimore.

Henry Wienefeld, born near Kassel in 1871, cigar industry.

Charles Willms, born in Cologne in 1848, began in Baltimore manufacturing of surgical instruments.

Carl Zies, born in Sontra, Hesse, in 1840, founded machine factory
in Baltimore (1884).

IV. German-American Newspapers

Some circulation figures of German newspapers in Baltimore during the
decades when German-Americanism was at its peak; figures gathered from
Ayer's Newspaper Directories between 1880 and 1920.

YEAR	CORRESPONDENT	KATHOLISCHE VOLKSZEITUNG	WECKER	VOLKSFREUND UND BIENE	JOURNAL	BAYRISCHE WOCHENBLATT
1880	15,000	22,000	3,000	—	—	—
1883	8,000	24,000	3,500	4,000	—	—
1887	11,500	25,600	3,500	5,300	6,000	—
1890	12,000	22,000	3,800	3,700	5,500	—
1900	11,000	22,000	7,500	3,500	6,500	9,600
1910	9,000	15,000	6,000	—	5,000	10,600
1914	11,000	12,500	—	—	—	11,000
1916	11,000	—	—	—	—	10,000
1918	11,000	—	—	—	—	10,000

The *Sonntags-Post* had a circulation of 10,600 in the year 1900; of 11,000
in 1910. The figures for the *Cumberland Freie Presse* are 973 in 1896; 1000
in 1900; 1200 in 1906; thereafter the paper is not listed.

V. "I Denounce, I Protest . . ."

To the Editor of *The Evening Sun*—Sir:

As a German-American I protest, with all the vehemence I can
muster, against what is going on in Germany today. I can't disclaim
my ancestry, nor do I wish to. I am proud of the Germany that was,
proud of its culture, its high achievement in art and literature,
science and scholarship; proud of its social and domestic virtues, its
gemütlichkeit, its love of the good life. But I denounce and would,
if I could, renounce the Germany that is. I denounce its negation
of the dignity and liberty of the individual. I denounce its ruthless
assassination of spiritual values and its exaltation of brute force as
the guiding principle of government and governed alike. I denounce
its effort to substitute a silly, pompous, sophomoric paganism for
real religion. I denounce its "naked barbarity" in the treatment of

Jews. I denounce its blatant self-adulation, its all but deification of a power-crazed egotist, its sneers at democracy, its ridicule of democracy's leaders. I denounce its political and cultural arrogance, its smug assumption of superiority over everybody else. I protest against the spiritual enslavement of a great people by the hypnotic will of one man; and I protest against having the word *German* made a synonym for medieval intolerance, persecution and might-makes-rightism. Perhaps that's enough to show how one German-American feels about the whole ferocious business. And he's not the only one.

ERNEST J. BECKER

Baltimore, Nov. 12, 1938

BIBLIOGRAPHY

Abbreviations used in the footnotes:

BVG   *Baltimore, Seine Vergangenheit und Gegenwart, mit besonderer Berücksichtigung des deutschen Elements.* Herausgegeben von dem Deutschen Literarischen Bureau (Baltimore, 1887).

DAB   *Dictionary of American Biography.* (Charles Scribner's, New York), 21 volumes, 1928-1944.

DNB   *Das Neue Baltimore.* (Baltimore, 1905); edited by the German Publishing Company, Baltimore.

MA   *Archives of Maryland.* Published by authority of the State, under the direction of the Maryland Historical Society (Baltimore); 62 volumes, 1883-1945.

SHGM *Society for the History of the Germans in Maryland, Reports* (Baltimore). Issued as Annual Reports, 1887-1901; from that date on published at irregular intervals. 26 volumes, 1887-1945.

BOOKS

Anon., *Baltimore 1729-1929, Two Hundredth Anniversary* (Baltimore, 1929).

——, *Baltimore and the Saengerfest* (Baltimore, 1903).

——, *Baltimore, Seine Vergangenheit und Gegenwart* (Baltimore, 1887).

——, *Biographical Cyclopedia of Representative Men of Maryland and the District of Columbia* (Baltimore, 1879).

——, *Das Baltimorer Blumenspiel* (Baltimore, 1904).

——, *Das Neue Baltimore* (Baltimore, 1905).

——, *Erinnerungen an die Feier des hundertjährigen Schillerjubiläums in Baltimore* (Baltimore, 1859).

——, *First Records of Baltimore Town and Jones Town, 1727-1797* (Baltimore, 1905).

——, *Genealogy and Biography of Leading Families of the City of Baltimore and Baltimore County* (New York, 1897).

——, *History and Roster of Maryland Volunteers, War of 1861-1865* (Baltimore, 1898).

——, *Maryland in the World War, 1917-1918* (Baltimore, 1933).

——, *Men of Mark in Maryland* (Washington, D.C., 1907-1911).

——, *Minutes and Letters of the Coetus of the German Reformed Congregations in Pennsylvania, 1742-1792* (Philadelphia, 1903).

——, *Nachrichten von den Vereinigten Deutschen Evangelisch-Lutherischen Gemeinen in Nord Amerika, absonderlich in Pennsylvania* (Halle, 1787).

——, *Through the Years of Eastern High School* (Baltimore, 1944).

Albright, Raymond W., *A History of the Evangelical Church* (Harrisburg, Pa., 1942).

Alvord, Clarence W., and Bidgood, Lee, *The First Explorations of the Trans-Allegheny Region by the Virginians, 1650-1674* (Cleveland, 1912).

Andrews, Matthew P., *Tercentenary History of Maryland* (Chicago and Baltimore, 1925).

Anstadt, P., *Life and Times of Reverend S. S. Schmucker* (York, Pa., 1896).

Bachman, Calvin G., *The Old Order of Amish of Lancaster County* (Norristown, Pa., 1942).

Bailey, Kenneth P., *Thomas Cresap, Maryland Frontiersman* (Boston, 1944).

Balch, Thomas (ed.), *Papers Relating to the Maryland Line During the Revolution* (Philadelphia, 1857).

Barker, Charles A., *The Background of the Revolution in Maryland* (New Haven, 1940).

Baumgartner, A. W., *Catholic Journalism, A Study of Its Development in the United States, 1789-1930* (New York, 1931).

Becker, Ernest J. (ed.), *Western High School, Past and Present* (Baltimore, 1944).

Bittinger, Lucy F., *German Religious Life in Colonial Times* (Philadelphia, 1906).

Bond, Beverly W., *State Government in Maryland, 1777-1781* (Baltimore, 1905).

Borcke, Heros von, *Memoirs of the Confederate War of Independence* (New York, 1938).

Borgmann, Henry, *History of the Redemptorists at Annapolis* (Ilchester, Md., 1904).

Bowers, David F. (ed.), *Foreign Influences in American Life* (Princeton, N.J., 1944).

Bowie, Lucy L., *The Ancient Barracks at Fredericktown* (Frederick, Md., 1939).

Boyd, Ernest, *H. L. Mencken* (New York, 1925).

Bready, Guy P., *History of Maryland Classis of the Reformed Church in the United States* (Taneytown, Md., 1938).

Brodhead, J. R., *History of the State of New York* (New York, 1853).

Bruncken, Ernest, *German Political Refugees in the United States During the Period from 1815-1860* (Milwaukee, 1904).

Capek, Thomas, *Augustine Herrman of Bohemia Manor* (Prague, 1930).

———, *The Czechs in America* (Boston, 1920).

Child, Clifton J., *The German-Americans in Politics 1914-1917* (Madison, Wis., 1939).

Cordell, Eugene F., *The University of Maryland, Its History 1807-1907* (New York, 1907).

Cortan, Franz Hubert, *Geschichte des Turnvereins Vorwärts 1867-1892* (Baltimore, 1892).

Coyle, W. F., *The Mayors of Baltimore* (Baltimore, 1919).

Craven, Avery O., *Soil Exhaustion as a Factor in the Agricultural History of Virginia and Maryland, 1606-1860* (Urbana, Ill., 1925).

Cronau, Rudolf, *Drei Jahrhunderte deutschen Lebens in Amerika* (Berlin, 1909).

Crowl, Philip A., *Maryland During and After the Revolution* (Baltimore, 1943).

Cunz, Dieter, *A History of the Germania Club of Baltimore City, Maryland* (Baltimore, 1940).

Dietz, August, *The Postal Service of the Confederate States of America* (Richmond, Va., 1929).

Dole, Esther M., *Maryland During the American Revolution* (Baltimore, 1941).

BIBLIOGRAPHY

Dolge, Alfred, *Pianos and Their Makers* (Covina, Calif., 1911).
Dubbs, Joseph H., *History of the Reformed Church, German* (New York, 1895).
Eddis, William, *Letters from America, Historical and Descriptive; comprising occurrences from 1769 to 1777 inclusive* (London, 1792).
Eelking, Max von, *The German Allied Troops in the North American War of Independence* (Albany, 1893).
Einhorn, David, *Ausgewählte Predigten und Reden* (New York, 1880).
Elson, L. C., *History of American Music* (New York, 1925).
Eschbach, E. R., *Historic Sketch of the Evangelical Reformed Church of Frederick, Maryland* (Frederick, 1894).
Essary, J. F., *Maryland in National Politics* (Baltimore, 1915).
Evers, Fritz O., *Zion in Baltimore* (Baltimore, 1930).
Faust, Albert Bernhardt, *The German Element in the United States* (New York, 1927).
French, John C., *A History of the University Founded by Johns Hopkins* (Baltimore, 1946).
Frick, William, *An Address, Preparatory to Opening the Department of the Arts and Sciences in the University of Maryland* (Baltimore, 1831).
Friedenwald, Aaron, *Life, Letters and Addresses of Aaron Friedenwald*, edited by Harry Friedenwald (Baltimore, 1906).
Goldberg, Isaac, *The Man Mencken* (New York, 1925).
Goldsborough, W. W., *The Maryland Line in the Confederate Army, 1861-1865* (Baltimore, 1900).
Gould, Clarence P., *Money and Transportation in Maryland, 1720-1765* (Baltimore, 1915).
——, *The Land System in Maryland, 1720-1765* (Baltimore, 1913).
Griffith, Thomas W., *Annals of Baltimore* (Baltimore, 1824).
Grote, L. R. (ed.), *Die Medizin der Gegenwart in Selbstdarstellungen* (Leipzig, 1924).
Guilday, Peter, *The Life and Times of John Carroll* (New York, 1922).
Hall, C. C. (ed.), *Narratives of Early Maryland* (New York, 1910).
Hansen, Marcus Lee, *The Atlantic Migration, 1607-1860* (Cambridge, Mass., 1940).
——, *The Immigrant in American History* (Cambridge, Mass., 1940).
Harbaugh, Henry, *Fathers of the German Reformed Church in Europe and America* (Lancaster, Pa., 1872).
——, *Life of Michael Schlatter* (Philadelphia, 1857).
Hart, Archibald, *Calvert and Hillyer 1897-1947* (Baltimore, 1947).
Hawgood, John A., *The Tragedy of German-America* (New York, 1941).
Heck, Earl L. W., *Augustine Herrman: Beginner of the Virginia Tobacco Trade, Merchant of New Amsterdam and First Lord of Bohemia Manor in Maryland* (Englewood, Ohio, 1941).
Heiser, Elinor S., *Days Gone By* (Baltimore, 1940).
Hennighausen, Louis P., *History of the German Society of Maryland* (Baltimore, 1909).
Henry, J. M., *History of the Church of the Brethren* (Elgin, Ill., 1936).

BIBLIOGRAPHY

Herriott, Frank I., *The Conference of the German Republicans at the Deutsches Haus, Chicago, May 14-15, 1860* (Transactions of the Illinois Historical Society, 1928).

Heurich, Christian, *Aus meinem Leben* (Washington, 1934).

Hirschfeld, Charles, *Baltimore 1870-1900: Studies in Social History* (Baltimore, 1941).

Hofmann, Jule (Julius), *Gedichte* (Marburg a.d.L., 1907).

Hofmann, Julius, *A History of Zion Church in the City of Baltimore, 1755-1897* (Baltimore, 1905).

———, *The Germans of Maryland 1812-1814* (Baltimore, 1914).

Holdcraft, Paul E., *History of the Pennsylvania Conference of the Church of the United Brethren in Christo* (Fayetteville, Pa., 1938).

Howard, George W., *The Monumental City, Its Past History and Present Resources* (Baltimore, 1876).

Humphry, George P. (ed.), *The Discoveries of John Lederer* (Rochester, N.Y., 1902).

James, Bartlett B., *The Labadist Colony in Maryland* (Baltimore, 1899).

———, and Jameson, J. F. (ed.), *Journal of Jasper Danckaerts, 1679-1680* (New York, 1913).

Janeway, Ralph W., *Bibliography of Immigration in the United States, 1900-1930* (Columbus, Ohio, 1934).

Johnson, John H., *Old Maryland Manors* (Baltimore, 1883).

Johnston, George, *History of Cecil County* (Elkton, Md., 1881).

Kamman, W. F., *Socialism in German-American Literature* (Philadelphia, 1917).

Kapp, Friedrich, *The Life of John Kalb* (New York, 1884).

Kaufmann, Wilhelm, *Die Deutschen im amerikanischen Bürgerkrieg* (München, 1911).

Kazin, Alfred, *On Native Grounds, An Interpretation of Modern American Prose Literature* (New York, 1942).

Keidel, George C., *The Earliest German Newspapers of Baltimore* (Washington, 1927).

Knauss, James Owen, *Social Conditions Among the Pennsylvania Germans in the Eighteenth Century as Revealed in the German Newspapers Published in America* (Lancaster, Pa., 1922).

Knipp, Anna H., and Thomas, Thaddeus P., *The History of Goucher College* (Baltimore, 1938).

Knittle, Rhea M., *Early American Glass* (New York, 1927).

Laegeler, Carl, *Geschichte des Germania Männerchor* (Baltimore, 1906).

Leonhart, James C., *One Hundred Years of the Baltimore City College* (Baltimore, 1939).

Lonn, Ella, *Foreigners in the Confederacy* (Chapel Hill, N.C., 1940).

Lowdermilk, Will H., *History of Cumberland* (Washington, D.C., 1878).

Lowenthal, Marvin, *Henrietta Szold, Life and Letters* (New York, 1942).

Mallery, Charles P., *Ancient Families of Bohemia Manor; Their Homes and Their Graves* (Wilmington, Del., 1888).

Marine, William M., *The British Invasion of Maryland, 1812-1815* (Baltimore, 1913).

Mathews, Edward B., *The Maps and Map-Makers of Maryland* (Baltimore, 1898).

Mayer, Brantz, Genealogy and Memoir of the Mayer Family (Baltimore, 1878).

McCreary, George W., The Ancient and Honorable Mechanical Company of Baltimore (Baltimore, 1901).

———, The First Book Printed in Baltimore-Town (Baltimore, 1903).

McKearin, George S., and Helen, American Glass (New York, 1941).

McSherry, James, History of Maryland (Baltimore, 1904).

Mereness, Newton D., Maryland as a Proprietary Province (New York, 1901).

Metzner, Heinrich, Geschichte des Turnerbundes (Indianapolis, 1874).

Meynen, Emil, Bibliographie des Deutschtums der kolonialzeitlichen Einwanderung in Nordamerika, insbesondere der Pennsylvanian-Deutschen und ihrer Nachkommen 1683-1933 (Leipzig, 1937).

Miller, Edmund E., The Hundred Year History of the German Correspondent, Baltimore, Maryland (Baltimore, 1941).

Mish, Mary V., Jonathan Hager, Founder (Hagerstown, Md., 1937).

Morris, John G., Life Reminiscences of an Old Lutheran Minister (Philadelphia, 1896).

Nead, Daniel W., The Pennsylvania German in the Settlement of Maryland (Lancaster, Pa., 1914).

Newman, Harry W. (ed.), Maryland Revolutionary Records (Washington, 1938).

Oerter, A. L., The History of Graceham (Bethlehem, Pa., 1913).

Owens, Hamilton, Baltimore on the Chesapeake (Garden City, N.Y., 1941).

Packard, F. R., History of Medicine in the United States (New York, 1931).

Phillips, P. Lee, The Rare Map of Virginia and Maryland by Augustine Herrman (Washington, 1911).

Pleasants, J. Hall, and Sill, Howard, Maryland Silversmiths 1750-1830 (Baltimore, 1930).

Prime, Alfred C., The Arts and Crafts in Philadelphia, Maryland and South Carolina, 1721-1785 (Philadelphia, 1929).

Quinnan, John R., Medical Annals of Baltimore (Baltimore, 1884).

Radcliffe, George L. P., Governor Thomas H. Hicks of Maryland and the Civil War (Baltimore, 1901).

Rayner, Isidor, Addresses of Isidor Rayner (Baltimore, 1914).

———, Essays of Isidor Rayner (Baltimore, 1914).

Reitzel, Robert, Des Armen Teufel Gesammelte Schriften (Detroit, 1913).

Rusk, William S., William Henry Rinehart, Sculptor (Baltimore, 1939).

Scharf, J. Thomas, Chronicles of Baltimore (Baltimore, 1874).

———, History of Baltimore City and County (Philadelphia, 1881).

———, History of Maryland (Baltimore, 1879).

———, History of Western Maryland (Philadelphia, 1882).

Schmeckebier, Laurence F., History of the Knownothing Party in Maryland (Baltimore, 1899).

Schoenrich, Otto, Biography of Ottmar Mergenthaler (Baltimore, 1898).

Schoepf, Johann David, Travels in the Confederation, 1783-1784 (Philadelphia, 1911).

Scholtz, Karl A. M., The Turnverein Vorwärts (Baltimore, 1937).

Schrader, Frederick F., The Germans in the Making of America (Boston, 1924).

Schrott, Lambert, *Pioneer German Catholics in the American Colonies 1734-1784* (New York, 1933).

Schultz, Edward T., *First Settlements of Germans in Maryland* (Frederick, Md., 1896).

——, *History of Freemasonry in Maryland* (Baltimore, 1884).

Schuricht, Herrmann, *History of the German Element in Virginia* (Baltimore, 1900).

Seidensticker, Oswald, *The First Century of German Printing in America, 1728-1830* (Philadelphia, 1893).

Seitz, May A., *The History of the Hoffman Paper Mills in Maryland* (Towson, Md., 1946).

Shea, John G., *The Catholic Church in Colonial Days* (New York, 1886).

Shepherd, Henry E., *History of Baltimore* (Baltimore, 1898).

Silver, John A., *The Provisional Government of Maryland, 1774-1777.* (Baltimore, 1895).

Sioussat, St. George L., *Economics and Politics in Maryland 1720-1750* (Baltimore, 1903).

Stanton, Thomas J., *A Century of Growth, or the History of the Church in Western Maryland* (Baltimore, 1900).

Steinach, Adelrich, *Geschichte und Leben der Schweizer Kolonien in den Vereinigten Staaten von Nord-Amerika* (New York, 1889).

Steiner, Bernhard, *Western Maryland in the Revolution* (Baltimore, 1902).

Steiner, L. H., and Steiner, B. C., *The Genealogy of the Steiner Family* (Baltimore, 1896).

Stephenson, George M., *A History of American Immigration, 1820-1924* (Boston, 1926).

Strassburger, R. B., and Hinke, W. J., *Pennsylvania German Pioneers, Lists of Arrivals* (Norristown, Pa., 1934).

Stump, H. Arthur, *Augustine Herrman* (Baltimore, 1929).

Taft, Lorado, *History of American Sculpture* (New York, 1930).

Timpe, Georg, *Katholisches Deutschtum in den Vereinigten Staaten von Amerika* (Freiburg, 1937).

Treacy, W. P., *Old Catholic Maryland and Its Early Jesuit Missionaries* (Swedesboro, N.J., 1889).

Tweedy, John, *A History of the Republican Conventions* (Danbury, Conn., 1910).

Walz, John A., *German Influence in American Education and Culture* (Philadelphia, 1936).

Wansey, Henry, *An Excursion to the United States of North America in the Summer of 1794* (Salisbury, 1798).

Wätjen, Hermann, *Aus der Frühzeit des Nordatlantikverkehrs* (Leipzig, 1932).

Wayland, John W., *The German Element in the Shenandoah Valley of Virginia* (Charlottesville, Va., 1907).

Wentz, Abdel R., *The Beginnings of the German Element in York County, Pennsylvania* (Lancaster, Pa., 1916).

——, *History of the Evangelical Lutheran Synod of Maryland* (Harrisburg, Pa., 1920).

——, *The Lutheran Church of Frederick, Maryland, 1738-1938* (Lancaster, Pa., 1939).

Wertenbaker, Thomas J., *The Founding of American Civilization: The Middle Colonies* (New York, 1938).

Wheeler, Joseph T., *The Maryland Press 1777-1790* (Baltimore, 1938).

Williams, T. J. C., *History of Frederick County, Maryland* (Frederick, Md., 1910).

——, *History of Washington County, Maryland* (Hagerstown, Md., 1906).

Wittke, Carl, *The German-Americans and the World War* (Columbus, Ohio, 1936).

——, *We Who Built America* (New York, 1939).

Wood, Ralph (ed.), *The Pennsylvania Germans* (Princeton, N.J., 1942).

Wroth, Lawrence C. (ed.), *Baltimore, Its History and Its People* (New York, 1912).

——, *History of Printing in Colonial Maryland* (Baltimore, 1922).

Wyckhoff, Vertrees J., *Tobacco Regulation in Colonial Maryland* (Baltimore, 1936).

Zimmermann, G. A., *Deutsch in Amerika* (Chicago, 1894).

ARTICLES

Albrecht, Erich, "Heinrich Zschokke's Version of the Founding of Maryland," *American German Review*, VIII, vi (1942), 15-16.

Barker, Charles A., "The Revolutionary Impulse in Maryland," *Maryland Historical Magazine*, XXXVI (1941), 128-38.

Baroway, Aaron, "Solomon Etting," *Maryland Historical Magazine*, XV (1920), 1-20.

Beck, Herbert H., "Augustine Herrman, Lancaster County's First Map Maker," *Papers of the Lancaster County Historical Society* (Lancaster, Pa., 1931), XXXV, xi, 261-66.

Becker, Ernest J., "History of the English-German Schools in Baltimore," *SHGM*, XXV (1942), 13-17.

Berkley, Henry J., "Maryland Physicians at the Period of the Revolutionary War," *Maryland Historical Magazine*, XXIV (1920), 1-17.

Bowie, Lucy L., "German Prisoners in the American Revolution," *Maryland Historical Magazine*, XL (1945), 185-200.

Carrier, Lyman, "The Veracity of John Lederer," *William and Mary Historical Magazine*, Second Series, XIX (1939), 435-45.

Clark, Robert T., "The New Orleans German Colony in the Civil War," *Louisiana Historical Quarterly*, XX (1937), 990-1015.

Cordell, Eugene F., "Charles Frederick Wiesenthal, Medicinae Practicus, the Father of the Medical Profession in Baltimore," *Johns Hopkins Hospital Bulletin*, Nos. 112/113 (1900), 170-74.

Cunz, Dieter, "Amelung's Old Frederick Glass," *American German Review*, XII, v (1946), 16-19.

——, "Augustin Herrman, Origin and Early Events," *Tyler's Quarterly Historical and Genealogical Magazine*, XXIV (1942), 5-11.

——, "Carl Heinrich Schnauffers literarische Versuche," *Publications of the Modern Language Association of America*, LIX, ii (1944), 524-39.

——, "Christian Mayer, Baltimore Merchant," *American German Review*, X, iii (1944), 11-13.

Cunz, Dieter, "Contributions of the German Element to the Growth of the University of Maryland," SHGM, xxvi (1945), 7-15.

———, "DeKalb and Maryland," SHGM, xxv (1942), 18-22.

———, "Die Marylander Goethe Gesellschaft," Monatshefte, xxxviii (1946), 367-70.

———, "German Settlers in Early Colonial Maryland," Maryland Historical Magazine, xlii, ii (1947), 101-8.

———, "God's Plain People in Maryland," American German Review, xiv, iv (1948), 12-17.

———, "John Lederer, Significance and Evaluation," William and Mary Historical Magazine, Second Series, xxii (1942), 175-85.

———, "Maryland's First Papermaker," American German Review, xii, i (1945), 21-23.

———, "Rise and Fall of the German Americans in Baltimore," Common Ground, vii, iii (1947), 61-71.

———, "The Baltimore Germans and the Year 1848," American German Review, x, i (1943), 30-33.

———, "The Maryland Germans in the Civil War," Maryland Historical Magazine, xxxvi (1941), 394-419.

———, "The Otterbein Church Incident in Baltimore," American German Review, xiv, i (1947), 15-17.

———, "Wiesenthal's Pioneer Medical Work," American German Review, ix, i (1942), 13-14.

——— (ed.), "Samuel Macleas Totentanz," Monatshefte, xxxix, i (1947), 25-53.

——— (ed.), "The Baltimore Germans and the Oath of Allegiance in 1778," SHGM, xxv (1942).

Davis, Arthur L., "German Settlements on the Eastern Shore of Maryland," SHGM, xxv (1942), 23-26.

Dohme, Alfred R. L., "Early History of the Drug Business," American German Review, xiii, i (1946), 24-26.

Dorpalen, Andreas, "Political Influence of the German Element in Colonial America," Pennsylvania History, vi (1939), 147-58, 221-39.

———, "The German Element in Early Pennsylvania Politics, 1789-1800," Pennsylvania History, ix, iii (1942), 167-90.

Engelbert, E. F., "Martini Lutheran Church in Baltimore," SHGM, xxvi (1945), 30-32.

Eshleman, Cyrus H., "John Gruber and the Hagerstown Almanac," Allentown Morning Call, December 3, 1938.

———, "The Pennsylvania German Dialect in Maryland," Allentown Morning Call, February 26, 1938.

Evers, Fritz O., "Allgemeine Deutsche Schulzeitung," SHGM, xxiv (1939), 38-41.

Faust, Albert B., "Carl Bersch—Artist and Portrait Painter," American German Review, x, vi (1944), 4-7.

———, "Die Sonntagsschule des Herrn Eduard F. Leyh," Die Glocke, iii (1908), 19-20.

———, "Undercurrents of German Influence in Maryland," SHGM, xxiii (1929), 5-13.

Gellner, Charles R., "Ecclesiastical History of the Catholic Germans in Maryland," SHGM, xxvi (1945), 37-48.

Gleis, Paul G., "German Catholic Missionaries in Maryland During the Eighteenth Century," *SHGM*, xxvi (1945), 33-36.

Hennighausen, Louis P., "Der Bildhauer William Henry Rinehart," *SHGM*, xxii (1907), 67-72.

———, "Die Revolte der Deutschen gegen die Regierung von Maryland," *SHGM*, iii (1889), 43-59.

———, "Early German Settlements in Western Maryland," *SHGM*, vi (1892), 11-25.

———, "John Lederer's Book of Travels," *SHGM*, iii (1889), 19-23.

———, "Reminiscences of the Political Life of the German-Americans in Baltimore During 1850-1860," *SHGM*, vii (1893), 51-59; ix (1898), 1-18.

———, "The German Day in Baltimore," *SHGM*, v (1891), 41-72.

———, "The Germans in the Defense of Baltimore in the War of 1812 to 1814," *SHGM*, xvi (1907), 55-60.

———, "The Redemptioners and the German Society of Maryland," *SHGM*, ii (1888), 31-54.

Hinke, W. J., and Kemper, C. E. (ed.), "Moravian Diaries of Travels," *Virginia Magazine of History and Biography*, xi (1903), 113-31, 225-42, 370-93.

Keach, C. A., "The Hack Family," *Tyler's Quarterly Historical and Genealogical Magazine*, vii, (1925), 253-62.

Kenkel, F. P., "Christian Börstler, Autobiographische Aufzeichnungen eines deutschen Pioniers in Maryland," *Deutsch-Amerikanische Geschichtsblätter*, i (1901), i, 17-22; iii, 50-57; iv, 85-86; ii (1902), i, 56-58; ii, 29-32; iii, 49-51; iv, 49-55; iii (1903), ii, 40-44.

Klemm, Gustav, "Gustav Strube, The Man and the Musician," *Musical Quarterly*, xxviii (1942), 288-301.

Kuethe, J. Louis, "A Gazeteer of Maryland, A.D. 1673," *Maryland Historical Magazine*, xxx (1935), 310-25.

Leaking, G. Armistead, "A Visit to Bohemia Manor," *Maryland Historical Magazine*, ii (1907), 143-46.

———, "The Labadists of Bohemia Manor," *Maryland Historical Magazine*, i (1906), 337-45.

Learned, Marion D., "The German-American Turner Lyric," *SHGM*, x (1896), 77-134.

Leyh, Edward F., "Baltimores Deutsch-Amerikaner in Handel und Industrie," *SHGM*, vi (1892), 75-85.

Mayer, F. B., "Memoranda in Reference to Early German Immigrants to Maryland," *SHGM*, v (1891), 13-19.

Mencken, H. L., "Die Deutsch-Amerikaner," *Neue Rundschau*, xxxix (1928), 486-95.

Miegel, Charles H., "What's in a Street Name?" *SHGM*, xxv (1942), 27-30.

Pary, Elwood C., "Friedrich Schiller in America," *German American Annals*, iii (1905).

Pleasants, J. Hall, "Justus Engelhardt Kühn, an Early Eighteenth Century Portrait Painter," *Proceedings of the American Antiquarian Society*, xlvi (1936), Pt. II, 243-80.

Prahl, Augustus J., "History of the German Gymnastic Movement of Baltimore," SHGM, XXVI (1945), 16-29.

———, "The Hagerstown Almanac," American German Review, VIII, V (1942), 7-10.

———, "The Ideological Background of the American Turner," Comparative Literature News-Letter, III (1944), 11-13.

Prechtel, George, "Saint Paul's Lutheran Church of Arcadia, Baltimore County," SHGM, XXIII (1929), 23-28.

Quynn, Dorothy M., "The Loyalist Plot in Frederick," Maryland Historical Magazine, XL (1945), 201-10.

———, and William R., "Barbara Fritchie," Maryland Historical Magazine, XXXVII (1942), 227-54, 400-13.

Raddatz, C. F., "German-American Families in Maryland," SHGM, VI (1892), 41-50.

Rattermann, H. A., "Anfänge und Entwicklung der Musik und des Gesanges in den Vereinigten Staaten während der ersten Hälfte des 19. Jahrhunderts," Deutsch-Amerikanische Geschichtsblätter, XII (1912), 327-80.

———, "Der erste Erforscher des Alleghany-Gebirges," Der Deutsche Pionier, VIII (1877), 399-407, 456-60, 484-95.

Rush, Benjamin, "An Account of the Manners of the German Inhabitants of Pennsylvania," Proceedings of the Pennsylvania German Society, (Lancaster, Pa., 1910), XIX, 1-121.

Scheib, Henry, "The Zion Church of the City of Baltimore," SHGM, II (1888), 55-75.

Scisco, Louis D., "Notes on Augustine Herrman's Map," Maryland Historical Magazine, XXXIII (1938), 343-51.

Spencer, Richard H., "Hon. Daniel Dulaney," Maryland Historical Magazine, XIII (1918), 20-28.

Stapleton, A., "Researches in the First Century of German Printing in America," The Pennsylvania German, V, (1904), 81-89.

Steiner, Bernard C., "The Brengle Family of Frederick," Maryland Historical Magazine, VI (1912), 91-98.

Stow, Charles M., "Amelung and Contemporary Maryland Glassblowers," Antiquarian, XV (1930), 58-60.

Strack, Christian, "Die ersten Deutschen im nachmaligen Distrikt Columbia," Berichte der Deutschen Historischen Gesellschaft für den Distrikt Columbia, (Washington, 1905), I, i, 17-55; ii, 11-46.

———, "John Lederer," Berichte der Deutschen Historischen Gesellschaft für den Distrikt Columbia (Washington, 1906), II, ii, 25-52.

Stricker, John Jr., "General John Stricker," Maryland Historical Magazine, IX (1914), 209-18.

Sutro, Ottilie, "The Wednesday Club," Maryland Historical Magazine, XXXVIII (1943), 60-68.

Ward, Townsend, "Augustine Herman and John Thompson," Pennsylvania Magazine of History and Biography, VII (1883), 88-93.

Wayland, John W., "The Pennsylvania-German in the Valley of Virginia," The Pennsylvania German, X (1909), 1-73.

Weisberger, Siegfried, "Wurstfabrik—Butcher's Lane, Baltimore," American German Review, XI, iii (1945), 20-22.

Weishaar, J. A., "The German Element in Maryland up to the Year 1700," *SHGM*, xv (1901), 13-34.

Wilson, James G., "Augustine Herrman," *Proceedings of the New Jersey Historical Society*, Second Series, xi, ii (1890), 21-34.

Winters, Roy L., "John Caspar Stoever, Lutheran Pioneer," *Lutheran Church Quarterly*, xviii (1945), 285-96.

Zucker, A. E., "Carl Heinrich Schnauffer," *SHGM*, xxiv (1939), 17-23.

——, "Natural Selection and German-Americans," *SHGM*, xxv (1942), 7-12.

——, "The History of the German Theater in Baltimore," *Germanic Review*, xviii (1943), 123-35.

INDEX

To facilitate identification, abbreviations indicating the person's residence are used in some instances. These abbreviations are: B for Baltimore, C for Conococheague, Cb for Cumberland, Fr for Frederick, GC for Garrett County, Gr for Graceham, Hgt for Hagerstown, and Sh for Sharpsburg.

Abhau, Anna Margarete, see Mencken, A. M.
abolitionists, see slavery issue
Accident, see Maryland towns
Ackheart, Henry, 140
Ackler, William, 310
Adam (Fr), 76
Adams, John, 178
Adolphus, Dr. Phillip, 303
Adt, John, 348, 434
agriculture, commerce, etc.: banking, 159, 177, 235, 347, 385; brewing, 95, 235, 346f., 372; coal mining, 384f.; flax, 116; fur, 13, 31, 36; grain, 47, 115, 158, 288; indigo, 13; insurance, 159, 160; iron, 57; oyster dredging, 328f., 330; railroads, 160, 241, 266, 346; tobacco, 13, 21, 30, 40, 47, 132, 157, 160, 236f., 287, 346
Ahl, John Peter, 144
Albert, William J., 235, 302, 304, 368
Albough, John, 434
Alien & Sedition Act, see laws
Allegany County, see Maryland counties
Alleghenies, see mountains
Allgemeine deutsche Schulzeitung, see newspapers
Alsop Map, see maps
Alt, Georg, 212
Alter (Hgt), 86
Alvord, Clarence W., 33, 36
Amelung, F. L. E., 199
Amelung, Frederick M., 166
Amelung, John Frederick, 163-66, 173
"Amerikabriefe," 127
Amherst, General, 105
Amish, see sects
Ammon, Jacob, 419, 423
Anders (Fr), 76
Andersen, Hans Christian, 256
Ankelberger (Fr), 72

Ann Arundel County, see Maryland counties
Annapolis, see Maryland towns
Anspach (B), 159
Anti-Catholic Law, see laws
Anti-Semitism, 332, 359, 361
Antietam Creek, see battles; churches; rivers
Apfel, John P., 64
Apfel, Peter, 64
Appel (Fr), 72
Apple, Henry Joseph, 341
Apple's Church, see churches
Appomattox, see rivers
Arbeiter Gesangverein, see choral societies
Arbeiter Liedertafel, see choral societies
Arbeiter Männerchor, see choral societies
Arc, see ships
Arion, see choral societies
Arion (Cb), see choral societies
Armbruster, Anthony, 111
Armistead, George, 194
Arndt, Johann, 60
Arnold, Abraham, 234
arts, crafts: glass, 163-66; journalism, 251-65, 350-66; lithography, 235; music, 243-46, 344-45, 349, 403, 409-10; painting, 44, 237, 313f., 344, 410; paper-making, 161, 162-63, 172; piano-making, 235; printing, 45, 111-12, 166-77, 235, 252-53, 379; sculpturing, 313, 343-44, 380, 410; silverwork, 96, 162, 314
Astor, Johann Jacob, 159, 263
Auerbach, Berthold, 260
Augusta, Ga., see towns
Aurora, see Maryland towns
Aus beiden Welten, see newspapers
"Ausbund," 423
Ax, Christian, 346, 391, 434

Bach (Fr), 72

{ 451 }

Herrman, Francina, 17
Herrman, Jannetje, 17, 25
Herrman, Judith, 17
Herrmann (B), 107
Herwegh, Georg, 256, 281
Herzer (Gr), 77
Hess, Dr. Friedrich, 270, 271
"Hessians," 148-50
Hessler, Karl, 232, 335
Heuisler, Joseph A., 161
Heurich, Christian, 347
Heuser, Ludwig C., 336
Hexamer, Charles J., 371, 396
Heyer, Christian Fr., 212
Heyer, Valentine, 49
Heyner (B), 107
Heyser, William, 86, 138, 177
Hibernian Soc., see companies
Hicks, Gov. Thomas H., 292, 295, 302
Hicksenbaugh, Adam, 190
Hiehle, Ernst Ch., 337
Hielscher, Th., 275
Higginbotham, Charles, 51
Hilken, Henry G., 374, 391, 435
Hiltebrant (Fr), 76
Hinebaugh (GC), 212
Hinkel (Fr), 72
Hinrichs, John, 374
Hintze, Carl Gotth., 234
Hirtenstimmen, see newspapers
Hiss, Jacob, 271
Hite, Jost, 58
Hitler, Adolf, 415, 416
Hitzelberger, Charles, 310
Hobach, Michael, 212
Hoblitzell, F. S., 368
Hochschild-Kohn, 331, 435
Hoen, August, 235, 312, 435
Hoen, Ernst, 331
Hoff (Fr), 73
Hoffman, Aaron, 271
Hoffman, Daniel, 235
Hoffman, David, 190, 193, 199, 234, 265
Hoffman, George, 190
Hoffman, Henry W., 267
Hoffman, Johann, 199
Hoffman, Peter, 177
Hoffman, S. O., 271
Hoffman, William, 140, 162-63

Hoffman, William H., 301, 347
Hoffmann (Fr), 73
Hoffmann (Fr), 76, 133
Hoffmann, Johann Ulrich, 213
Hoffmann, Louis, 337, 367
Hoffmann, Wme., 382, 383
Hoffmann v. Fallersleben, 256
Hofmann, Julius K., 325, 333f., 374, 391, 407
Hogmire, Conrad, 134
Holtz (Fr.), 76
Holtzbaum, Jacob, 162
Holy Cross (B), see churches
Holzshu, J. H., 386
Honck, Jacob, 234
Honig, Georg, 64
Hood College, see schools
Hoover, see Huber
Hoover, Herbert, 413
Hoppe, Justus, 199, 200, 203, 235, 266
Horn (Hgt), 86
Hornell, Nikolas, 106f.
Hornet, see newspapers
Hoss (Hgt), 86
House Amish, see Amish
Houser, Michael, 189
Huber (Hgt), 86
Huber, Eduard, 391
Huber, Frederick R., 409
Huber (Hoover) (Fr), 76, 133
Hudson Bay Co., see companies
Hughes, Charles E., 397, 398
Hugo, Victor, 248
Hull, Johann, 183
Hunsicker, Edward, 324
Hüttner, John Frederick, 234
Hutzel, Hans G., 64
Hutzler family, 331, 435
Hyphen-Americans, see German-Americans

Immigration Law, see laws
Independent American Volunteer, see newspapers
Independent Citizens' Union, see companies
Indians: Delaware, 20; Sara, 34; Susquehanna, 17
indigo, see agriculture
insurance, see agriculture